MEDIA & SOCIETY

Buffering...

MEDIA & SOCIETY

Michael O'Shaughnessy
and Jane Stadler
with Sarah Casey

Sixth Edition

OXFORD
UNIVERSITY PRESS
AUSTRALIA & NEW ZEALAND

OXFORD
UNIVERSITY PRESS

Oxford University Press is a department of the University of Oxford. It furthers the University's objective of excellence in research, scholarship, and education by publishing worldwide. Oxford is a registered trademark of Oxford University Press in the UK and in certain other countries.

Published in Australia by
Oxford University Press
253 Normanby Road, South Melbourne, Victoria 3205, Australia

First published 1999
Second edition published 2002
Third edition published 2005
Fourth edition published 2008
Fifth edition published 2012
Sixth edition published 2016
Reprinted 2017

National Library of Australia Cataloguing-in-Publication entry

Creator: O'Shaughnessy, Michael, 1951- author.
Title: Media and society / Michael O'Shaughnessy, Jane Stadler,
        Sarah Casey.

Edition: 6th edition.
ISBN: 9780195597240 (paperback)

Notes: Includes bibliographical references and index.

Subjects: Mass media.
        Mass media and culture.

Other Creators/Contributors: Stadler, Jane Megan, author.
                        Casey, Sarah, author.

Dewey Number: 302.23

Reproduction and communication for educational purposes

Edited by Mary-Jo O'Rourke AE
Typeset by diacriTech, Chennai, India
Proofread by Liz Filleul
Indexed by Nikki Davis
Printed in China by Leo Paper Products Ltd.

CONTENTS

LIST OF FIGURES

LIST OF TABLES

CASE STUDIES

ACKNOWLEDGMENTS

This book is very much indebted to the numerous scholars and teachers of media, cultural, and film studies who have developed the study of the media so fruitfully; we want to acknowledge their significant work. Our ideas and approaches owe much to them. We are also inspired by the wisdom and insights of our students. However, responsibility for the way these ideas have been presented here is ours alone.

In this new edition we welcome Sarah Casey, the new member of the writing team. We would also like to thank those at OUP who have made publication of this book possible, particularly Karen Hildebrandt, Shari Serjeant, and our copyeditor, Mary-Jo O'Rourke.

Michael O'Shaughnessy, Jane Stadler, and Sarah Casey

INTRODUCTION: THE MEDIA-WORLD

This book aims to explore the media and their role in contemporary society. In introducing readers to media studies, a discipline that has developed since the 1970s, we will explain many of the main concepts, approaches, and key critical terms used in this field.

Throughout the book we use the expression 'media-world'. This suggests three different ways we can think about the connections between media and society.

First, 'media-world' invites us to think about the relationship between the media, their institutions, and the world we live in, how these two areas are connected, how the media affect society, and vice versa. We examine this most specifically in Part 1 (Chapters 2 and 3). We are interested in how the media express or challenge society's dominant values and norms—its ideology—so our study and analysis of the media focus on the social role of the media, especially in Part 3 (Making Sense).

Second, 'media-world' points to the idea that the media construct their own particular views and visions of society for us through their representations and their view of the world. We are interested in exploring these media viewpoints by analysing specific media examples and by giving general methods and guidelines for your media analysis; this is the major focus of Part 2 (Pictures), Part 4 (Stories), and Part 5 (Media and Identity). In Part 1 (Chapters 4 and 5), we explore how representing the world, primarily through language and images, is a particular process, a way of constructing reality.

Third, the term suggests that the world we live in and the ways we live are now so heavily influenced and dominated by the media that we can describe this as a 'media-world'. Most people today, particularly young people, live in a media-dominated world and that is a major reason for writing this book: it is important and useful to understand the media that we are all living with. We consider this throughout, but specifically in Chapters 7 and 25.

We explore the media-world primarily by looking at media texts and stories, and media representations—found in films, television programs, advertisements, and news stories, and on the internet—and by doing textual analysis.

We examine how we read, watch, and listen to media texts, give methods for analysing and interpreting them, and explore the complex relationship between these texts and the 'real' world; in other words, the relationship between the media and society. We consider various aspects of the media, but media stories and representations are our main focus. The pleasures of these stories are what draw us to the media, they are the basis of our media consumption, so we think it is important to offer ways of understanding them. Our examples are mostly chosen from Australia, the USA, South Africa, and the United Kingdom as these are our areas of media experience.

THEMES AND INFLUENCES

There are several themes that run through the book. These are partly the result of our own interests as authors and we think it's important to acknowledge how our personal perspectives have influenced our approach to the media, just as your experiences and histories will influence your approach. We do not write from an objective, neutral position. There are three of us writing this book and we sometimes write in the first person using the pronouns 'we', or 'us', or 'our'. Occasionally, when we write from just one of our positions we will use the pronouns 'I', or 'me', or 'my' and will indicate which author's point of view is being expressed.

THE MAIN THEMES OF THE BOOK

The contradictory nature of the media

We see positive and negative aspects in the media and we try to show both of them. We also recognise that there are often contradictory arguments made about the media and how they work. We want to try to show a variety of perspectives so that you can understand the different ideas people have had about the media and then decide what your position is. We are not offering a definitive series of answers about how the media operate and what they mean, but an exploration of different approaches.

Aesthetic and social aspects of the media

We will present a variety of approaches that can be used for analysing and interpreting media texts. These will focus on two aspects: aesthetic and social concerns. 'Aesthetic concerns' means looking at and evaluating the forms of media—for example, understanding how films communicate through processes such as cinematography and editing. 'Social concerns' means looking at the social and political views that the media communicate to us in their content. The methods of analysis presented here can be applied to many other texts, for example, novels, plays, and paintings.

Global and historical contexts

We want to understand how the media operate in the world as a whole. We can do this better if we have some idea of how they have developed historically, and how the media disseminate culture around the globe.

Technological developments

As media technologies change and develop, we investigate the influence this has on the media industry and its production and distribution practices. Technological change also affects the political role of mass communication and the ways in which people engage with the media in everyday life.

Psychological concerns of the media

As well as thinking about the social aspects of the media, we examine how the media relate to people's inner and psychological lives.

Different factors producing the media

We will explore why and how we get the kind of media we do, asking what produces or determines the media. There is no one answer, but we recognise five distinct factors:

- technological developments: the production of new media forms
- economics: the need and desire to make money/profit
- human creativity: the work of all those producing media content and media technologies
- social controls: implemented by people in positions of power, especially governments, who attempt to control what appears in the media and what does not
- audiences: through their consumption of the media, the audience ensures its success or failure.

No one aspect dominates and they are often interconnected. We need to be aware of all of them as significant.

Ideology, discourse, and hegemony

There are three key theoretical concepts running through the book: ideology, discourse, and hegemony. We introduce them gradually, with many examples, so that readers can build up a full sense of what they mean.

Content

Most of the media examples we discuss come from 'popular' or 'mass' culture—the cinema, television, advertisements, photography, newspapers, and the internet. We have not chosen these either to celebrate or denigrate popular culture but because they are accessible, familiar, and, we argue, socially significant: many people learn how to think and feel about the world in which they live through popular culture. We are not saying they are great works of art that people will look back on in fifty or a hundred years as very significant, but that they are important in that they indicate the social values of our culture. That said, we think many of them have significant aesthetic value, which also makes them worth analysing.

Many examples relate to gender, the family, and ethnicity.

Gender and ethnicity are relevant to anyone who wants to understand their own identity. We all grow up and are positioned as gendered and ethnic subjects. Who we are is affected by this social positioning, and the health of society depends on how well we relate to each other from these positions. We invite this analysis of gender and ethnic issues in the media, which can lead to a fascinating exploration and wider understanding of society, other people, and ourselves. (These concerns are addressed throughout the book, but gender and ethnicity are specifically considered in Part 5.)

Ethnicity and cultural identity are important in the way social groups define themselves and each other, and are crucial in many of today's social and political conflicts within and between different countries.

Gender is significant in two ways. First, gender involves issues of social power and equality: it is not simply a question of the social oppression of women by men, but a more complex situation in which men and women are constructed and oppressed by the patriarchal, competitive, and heterosexist values of society. The media and their representations of gender play a key role in this.

Second, gender relates to sexuality, one of the key human drives. While in some ways sexuality is repressed in Western culture, it is often at the centre of media representations. Sex sells, and the popular media return to issues of sexuality time and time again, making it an important area to examine. Issues of social power and sexuality are often linked in complex ways, and we expect that all readers will be able to relate to these through their own experiences. These issues are also relevant in understanding the family, a major institution of society and one that is undergoing significant change. So we look at many examples of media representations of the family, which again will connect with readers' own experiences.

Overall we are concerned with the political and social considerations of the media. Feminists began using the phrase 'the personal is political' when they realised how the everyday domestic lives of many women—staying at home, looking after children, doing poorly paid work—were part of the wider picture of women's political situation. All personal and social behaviour is political: the clothes we wear, the food we eat, how we work, what we do with our money, the media we consume, how we spend our leisure time, and so on. These behaviours are political because, through social and global interconnections, they relate to and affect how we and other people live in the world, which is what makes them worthy of analysis.

Media studies can be either an attempt at neutral and descriptive analysis that tries to explain, from the outside, how the media work, or it can be politically engaged and aim to challenge how the media work. Much of media studies has been idealistic—a part of the search for a more equal society—and this aspect has given it a political slant. Marx coined the aphorism: 'The point is not to understand the world but to change it.' We see media studies operating in this broad political arena of developing and encouraging social change and debate about political issues, but we also think there is a point to understanding the world. We hope that this book can help in your understanding of the media-world you live in.

We are aware that climate change and ethnic tensions are major social issues that are also linked to economic concerns. The media play an important role in how these are represented.

The book includes a model essay, illustrations, and practical exercises. It includes theoretical overviews and detailed case studies. It encourages readers to reflect on their own identities and media usage. Each chapter includes an overview of the main topics for consideration, a glossary of key terms used, and a summary.

GUIDED TOUR

CHAPTER OVERVIEW

Each chapter begins with a short overview that outlines the subjects the chapter will cover.

> ### CHAPTER 1
>
> ### Defining the Media
>
> All of us who professionally use the mass media are the shapers of society. We can vulgarize that society. We can brutalize it. Or we can help lift it onto a higher level.
>
> William Bernbach, founder, Doyle, Dane and Bernbach (DDB)
>
> This chapter will
> - outline the main characteristics of the media
> - give a brief history of the media
> - explore the media's key determining factors
> - give a definition of the media.

MARGIN NOTES

Key terms are highlighted in bold and defined in margin notes. A glossary at the end of the book contains all the key terms.

> **the global village** points to the way that media
> or further discussion of globalisation, see Chapter 25).
> view, looked at the way the print media have changed
> d culture (an oral culture) into a society based on print
> o McLuhan's other famous catch-phrase 'the medium
> at the medium, or the technology, used to transmit
> io, screen, web, wireless, or via mobile phones) is just
> than the content of the message itself.
>
> ◄ GLOBAL VILLAGE
> The phrase 'the global village' suggests that the globalisation of communication media has brought the whole world closer together, like a village in which everyone is interconnected.

CASE STUDIES

Extensive case studies apply the ideas and approaches presented in the book to specific topics, giving you a model for your own media studies assignments.

> **CASE STUDY**
>
> Banksy—street art, anonymity, and culture jamming
>
> Accessible, affordable, interactive media technologies have enabled culture jamming in its different forms to spread across the globe, informing far-flung groups of people about common concerns. Arguably, some stencil art, such as that by French graffiti artist Blek le Rat, by American Shepard Fairey, who created the Barack Obama *HOPE* poster in 2008, and by 'anonymous' British street graffiti artist and political activist Banksy, offers an innovative form of cultural resistance to neoliberal globalisation.

DISCUSSION POINTS

These exercises and discussion questions prompt you to debate issues with your classmates and investigate how the media influences your own life. These points are raised at the end of each chapter. They include exercises to consolidate, apply, and extend understanding of issues raised in the chapter.

> **? DISCUSSION POINTS**
>
> 1 In what ways are new media more democratic than conventional media?
> 2 Who, if anyone, might benefit from, and who might be responsible for, the digital divide and algorithmic culture?
> 3 Consider why fan communities form around particular digital games and game consoles such as Xbox, Wii, and PlayStation. What advantages and pleasures do these games offer in terms of virtuality and interactivity?
> 4 What impact do you think massive mergers, such as Google purchasing YouTube, might have on the production and consumption of online video? Would smartphone technology have developed and dispersed so swiftly if iPhone had merged with Android and Samsung Galaxy?

> **SUMMARY**
>
> You should now be able to
> - give examples of the impact of digitisation on media production, consumption, and distribution
> - list and explain five important characteristics of new media
> - analyse new communication technologies, and assess their relationships to social change and democratisation
> - evaluate how the digital divide and algorithmic culture impact on your community and the communities of others.

CHAPTER SUMMARY

Each chapter ends with a short summary that lists the key skills and ideas that you should have acquired from the chapter.

PART 1
Getting Ready: The Media and Media Studies

Media is the nervous system of a democracy. If it's not functioning well the democracy can't function.

Outfoxed

Overview

Part 1 presents an overview of what the media are and what media studies is trying to do. It first presents initial definitions, approaches, questions, and assumptions. Then it explores issues of representation, language, the social construction of reality, how we as audiences read media texts, and developments of new media technologies.

CHAPTER 1

Defining the Media

All of us who professionally use the mass media are the shapers of society. We can vulgarize that society. We can brutalize it. Or we can help lift it onto a higher level.

William Bernbach, founder, Doyle, Dane and Bernbach (DDB)

This chapter will

- outline the main characteristics of the media
- give a brief history of the media
- explore the media's key determining factors
- give a definition of the media.

WHAT ARE 'THE MEDIA'?

MEDIA ▶

The technologically developed communication industries, normally making money, that can transmit information and entertainment across time and space to individuals and/or large groups of people; they are literally in the middle of this process, the means for communication.

'The media' is a commonly used term, but what exactly does it refer to? The **media** include a whole host of modern communication systems, for example, cinema, television, newspapers, magazines, advertisements, and radio. They also include video games, computers, phones and mobile phones, pagers, MP3 players, interactive multimedia, and, most importantly, the internet. Defining the media is not easy because the media are constantly changing with the development of new forms and technologies (see Chapters 7 and 25), but there are a number of characteristics, historical developments, and determining factors that delineate what the media are, and these can lead towards a definition.

MEDIA CHARACTERISTICS

- The media are human communication systems.
- The media use processes of industrialised technology for producing messages.
- The media generally aim to reach large audiences or to be used by many people, and hence have been referred to as 'mass media' operating through 'mass production' leading to 'mass communication'; their success is often built on popularity.
- The media usually aim to facilitate communication across distance (and/or time) between people, or to enable communication in which the sender does not need to be present because the communication is recorded and then transmitted.
- The media are called 'media' because they are literally in the middle, or are the middle chain, of this communication (*media* means 'middle' in Latin); they are the mechanisms that connect the senders and the receivers of messages.
- The development of the media has been affected by commercial interests that recognise that the media are potentially highly profitable industries.

MEDIA HISTORY

There have been several important historical moments or periods in the development of the media.

1   The first major medium in Western culture was the Gutenberg printing press in the fifteenth century, which led to the reproduction and distribution of information and entertainment through pamphlets, books, and then newspapers. This meant information was made more widely available to many people. The mass production of paper increased media output.

2   During the late eighteenth and nineteenth centuries, the Industrial Revolution in Europe saw new forms of power and manufacturing leading to rapid developments in printing technologies. At the same time, there was a revolution in the road, rail, and water transport communication systems. Major social changes and new forms of industrial production led to massive growth in urban populations, and new patterns of work and leisure. Demand for rapid communication of information and entertainment increased, alongside rising literacy and population growth.

3   The last part of the nineteenth and the first half of the twentieth centuries saw a further explosion of communication systems and technologies that have come to affect our daily lives in numerous ways. The advent of photography, film, sound recording, radio, and then television alongside the development of the telegraph, the telephone, and the rapidly changing systems of travel, particularly the car and aeroplane, all combined to change the map of human culture forever. People living in industrial, developed countries began to accept all of these as basic conditions for human life.

4   Since 1980 we have undergone—and continue to undergo—another major revolution in communications thanks to the development of new technologies, particularly the computer chip and digital media. Satellite and cable communications, digital television, computers, video games, virtual reality, mobile phones, and the internet are once again changing patterns of human behaviour, changing our modes of accessing knowledge, our entertainment, our ways of seeing the world and of interacting with one another.

For most people today, the media are the main source of their knowledge and entertainment, and are part of the very structure of their lives. According to the Nielsen Corporation, Americans watch more than five hours of television on average every day. That's 35 hours each week, almost three months per year, or the equivalent of watching nine years of non-stop television over an average lifespan. Australians aren't far behind: a 2011 survey showed urban Australians watch 3 hours and 9 minutes of television daily; in 2014, this remained almost unchanged at 2 hours and 58 minutes daily despite the range of other available options and devices <www.freetv.com.au>.

We are also in the midst of a shift away from television towards new media and computer-mediated communication (**CMC**). Indeed, a 2014 Nielsen report, 'The Digital Consumer', reveals that American adults spent an average of 34 hours per month accessing the mobile internet on smartphones, and 27 hours per month on the PC internet, most of that time involved in social networking. While users are increasingly diversifying their

◄ CMC

Computer-mediated communication.

social media use, Facebook still dominates according to the 2014 Nielsen report. Sites like Facebook and Twitter now account for 22.7 per cent of time spent on the web; the next closest activity is online games, which make up 10.2 per cent <www.comscoredatamine.com>. People truly live in a media-world. It is important to note, though, that there is still a global split or **digital divide** (see pp. 117 and 428) between those people who have unlimited media access and those who do not.

DIGITAL DIVIDE ▶

The increasing gap between those who have and those who do not have access to technology, access to content, ICT skills, and money to pay for digital services; most often used to refer to the difference between the developed and developing worlds' access to the benefits of digital technology.

This split can be experienced within one society where there is a big division between rich and poor, or between different countries or different global regions. Figures from 2014 indicate that internet penetration in Africa is 26.6 per cent, whereas in North America and Australia it is about 87 per cent <www.internetworldstats.com>. To further illustrate the extent of the inequity, universal access to basic communications services is defined very differently in South Africa and North America. In the USA, universal service is defined as 'access to a personal computer with a world wide web browser, a personal internet email address, and the capacity to make one's own information available via the Web' (Snow 2001, p. 21). The South African Department of Communications defines universal service as 'the provision of a telephone line within a reasonable distance of 30 minutes travelling' (Fourie 2001, p. 610). This is changing: South Africa is installing telecentres with access to phones, faxes, computers, electronic commerce, and government information in post offices and other community sites. In addition, mobile phones are found increasingly throughout Africa as they are in the rest of the world.

It is estimated that globally there are already more than 3 billion internet users—that's over 42 per cent of the world's population <www.internetworldstats.com>. Indeed, more than 3 million new World Wide Web pages go up every 24 hours (Brown 2004). As media analyst Heather Hudson points out, 'Access to information is critical to development; thus information and communication technologies (ICTs) as a means of sharing information are not simply a connection between people, but a link in the chain of the development process itself' (2006, p. 310). It remains to be seen whether the digital divide will continue to grow as developing nations and underprivileged groups in developed nations leapfrog to new technologies (for instance, bypassing landline installation and going straight to mobile and wireless technologies without investing in outmoded infrastructure), but it is clear that information poverty is an inequity that must be overcome.

MEDIA DETERMINANTS

In the Introduction (p. xiii) we mentioned five factors that are crucial in determining how the media develop. It is worth repeating them here and considering their interconnections. They are:

1 technological developments: the production of new media forms
2 economics: the need and desire to make money/profit
3 human creativity: the work of all those producing media content and media technologies
4 social controls: those implemented by people in positions of power, especially governments that attempt to control what appears in the media
5 audiences: through their consumption of the media, they ensure their success or failure.

We do not think any one of these aspects dominates, and they are often interlinked. We suggest that you become aware of all of them as significant.

Technology is central to the media, but technological changes do not just happen magically. Media analysts need to ask: what brings about these technological changes and developments? The answer is that the media develop within specific economic and social frameworks, and from specific economic and social determinants.

Socially there are three significant factors relating to points 3, 4 and 5 above:

1 First is the role of human creativity, which includes inventors of new technologies, such as Thomas Edison, and practitioners of these technologies, for example, photographers, app developers, film directors, and composers.

2 Second is the role of people in positions of social power and control. These people can limit and control the media, and they can also help develop them. Some governments, concerned about the potential power of the media, have sought to retain control either by actually running the media themselves or through strict censorship laws. President Robert Mugabe's government in Zimbabwe has routinely prosecuted journalists who are critical of government policies and has thus sought to control media information. This has not changed in recent years as Mugabe retains power and strict control over state media. Reporters Without Borders, a journalism advocacy group, stated in 2013 that 'Mugabe is still on its list of 39 "Predators of Freedom of Expression"' <http://en.rsf.org/zimbabwe-journalists-still-being-harassed-25-05-2013,44675.html>.

In Western democracies there is a general principle known as 'freedom of the press', which suggests that the media should be independent of government control. Public broadcast systems in Australia and the United Kingdom—the ABC, SBS, and the BBC—are funded by government, yet are meant to be independent bodies that make their own decisions about program production and content. The private media (for example, television Channels 7, 9, and 10, and the Fox cable network) are funded by independent advertising and thus not linked at all to government. All these media are bound to uphold laws of decency and acceptability, which are monitored through government legislation, for example, censorship boards and libel laws, so there is still some overall control. Additionally, socially responsible citizens may set up watchdog committees or organisations to police the morals of the media.

Currently, there are interesting struggles taking place about how governments and societies control the internet, which crosses all national boundaries. These relate not only to issues of sexuality, pornography, and particularly paedophilia, but also to the concerns of governments such as those of Burma and China, which may be worried about the propagation of Western ideas, values, and media products. When Google, the world's leading internet search engine, entered China in 2005, it had to comply with Chinese regulations including government censorship and surveillance initiatives. In effect, when people searched for topics the Chinese government deemed sensitive or seditious, google.cn could not display the search result. China's internet censorship and content regulation are so extensive that the nationwide firewall is commonly referred to as the 'Great Firewall of China'. The protection of 'cyberspace sovereignty' includes prison sentences for online speech. In 2009, Google's YouTube service was banned and Gmail became unavailable when the Chinese government accused Google of spreading obscene content. In October 2010, Google refused to continue to comply with China's content filtering policy, and its subsequent exit from China indicates that democratisation and control of internet content within and across national borders have become significant topics in media studies. Some companies, such as Microsoft's Bing search engine, comply with China's censorship policies in order to try to tap into the world's fastest growing internet market. However, the tables may be turning: in 2015, Google and Mozilla both blacklisted thousands of Chinese websites for which the China Internet Network Information Center had issued false digital security certificates for Google domains, which would have exposed users to security breaches.

In relation to the development of media technologies, it is important to note that media, politics, and economics have always been tightly entangled. In wartime, governments have supported the development of many new technologies for the military: developments in the First and Second World Wars, the Cold War, the Vietnam War, and the Gulf Wars all contributed to innovations in the media. The development of early video-camera technology, for example, was related to its use for American military surveillance; internet, cable, and satellite technologies were all originally developed for the military. Other media technological advances are spinoffs from decisions by US and Soviet governments to invest in space technologies.

3   The third social factor in the development of the media is audiences and consumers. Media success and viability rely on providing satisfaction for audiences; if audiences aren't buying a media product, it is likely to fail. In the history of photography, film, and video, for example, we can see how the (male) audience desire for pornography was a huge driving force in the development of all these technologies, and the way they were distributed and popularised. Many developments in the internet have similarly been driven by the pornography industry.

This last example and the significance of audience demand point us directly to economic factors. The distributors of pornography are not really interested in making their audiences happy and sexually fulfilled; they want to make money. Most media changes have occurred within **capitalist** economies, so their development has been hugely influenced by profit motives, and we must understand that the media have been developed in the interests of making money. Media history shows that technological changes tend to be implemented when they are seen to be profitable. Thomas Edison, who developed the phonograph and the wireless, was at least as much a businessman as he was an inventor.

All this shows how closely the determining factors in media development—technological, social, and economic—are linked. We want to stress the economic because in some ways it is the least visible or obvious factor, yet it is very important in the production of media. The popularity of reality television (see Chapter 18), for example, is obviously based on audience interest, camera technologies that make it possible to effectively

CAPITALISM ▶

The dominant global economic system, organised by workers selling their labour for wages, and investors making profit through interest and economic growth. Capitalism, which gradually replaced the feudal economic system from about 1600, is characterised by private ownership and control of the means of production (capital) by individuals and corporations.

capture the dance routines on *Dancing with the Stars*, and creative minds coming up with the concept. Another example is *Gogglebox*, which is based in people's living rooms and the viewer watches 'ordinary' people watching television to observe their conversations around their television viewing. The 'cast members' do little more than offer (often) scathing and humorous off-the-cuff critique.

But note how the cheapness of the production of these programs, as opposed to fictional dramas, which need writers, actors, costumes, and sets, is crucial in a time of increasing television competition, and also note how audience participation encourages audiences to use and buy the latest mobile phone and SMS technologies. These programs don't just make money for the telephone companies through the phone-ins; more importantly, they get audiences accustomed to using these technologies. As media analyst Bill Hammock has noted, the US telecommunications company AT&T invested in the development of the *American Idol* television series to 'get Americans into the habit of text messaging' (Hammock 2004). We need to remember these economic factors. Because vested interests and power relations influence both the content and the interpretation of media texts, questions about the relationships between media, profit, and ownership are important, and constitute the basis for studying the political economy of the media (see pp. 22–4).

CONCLUSION

While the complexity of the media makes definitions difficult, the following is a useful starting point: the media are technologically developed communication industries, normally making money, that can transmit information and entertainment across time and space to individuals and/or large groups of people; they are, literally, in the middle of this process, the means for communication.

This transmission of information is not one-way. The recipients of media messages are also involved in the process of communication as part of a feedback loop that influences the production of media. While it is true that many media forms, such as television, radio, film, and newspapers, have an asymmetrical flow of communication from one sender to many receivers, the rise of more interactive media forms has changed this dynamic. But even in television, radio, and newspapers, the audience has always contributed something to the communicative exchange (primarily through the process of constructing meaning, but also through ratings, research, SMSs, tweets, talkback, letters to the editor, Facebook comments, and other feedback mechanisms). The one-to-many model of mass communication is also being transformed by technological advances, as the following chapters demonstrate.

This chapter has

- defined the media
- outlined key media characteristics
- outlined media history
- considered significant media determinants.

? | DISCUSSION POINTS

1 In what ways have media developments affected human societies in the last five hundred years? Think of specific examples.
2 How much of your own time is currently engaged in media activities? How do the media impact on your life?
3 Can you find examples of the five media-determining factors in relation to the development of specific media products? Which, if any, do you argue is the most important? Why?

SUMMARY

You should now be able to

- define terms such as 'the media', 'mass communication', and 'the digital divide'
- give a brief historical overview of how the media have developed
- explain the factors and different determinants that are relevant when considering the development of the media in general
- discuss how these determinants can be related to specific media texts.

CHAPTER 2

Media Studies

They criticised me a lot and I appreciated that, because I used the media—even the conservative ones—as a mirror from which I can see the image I'm projecting.

Nelson Mandela, speaking about the South African press, 2002

This chapter will
- consider why it is important to study or teach about the media
- weigh the pros and cons of the media
- put forward two historical views of the media
- explore fears about the media
- look at media studies as an academic discipline and consider different media studies approaches.

WHY STUDY OR TEACH ABOUT THE MEDIA?

As a starting point for this chapter and your study, we pose two basic questions.

? | QUESTION 1

Why are you studying the media and what are you hoping to get out of this study? Take time to think about this and write down your ideas. It's useful for you to record your position so you can compare it with other people's and also so you can look back on it later.

Commentary

Your answer might be about creativity and expressivity (you may want to create interactive computer games or television programs). It might be vocational (you want to be guaranteed a good job as a journalist), or financial (you see the media as an excellent way of making lots of money), or critical (you want to critique the manipulative power of the media and understand its potential as a mechanism for beneficial social change). Or it may simply be curiosity—you may be fascinated by these technological communication systems that take up such a large part of so many people's lives. Your answer may include aspects of all of these positions and it may raise many other points. It will probably change while you are studying the media.

? | QUESTION 2

Do you think the media, in general, are good or bad?

1   Take time to make a list of all the arguments you can think of both for and against the media, that is, arguments that posit the media as a good or a bad thing.

2   Ask yourself: whose interests do the media serve? Who benefits from the production, distribution, and consumption of media texts and messages? When you answer these questions, try to include general statements about the media as well as detailed examples that support these statements.

This question goes straight to the heart of many discussions about the media. You will probably find strong arguments for and against the media that reflect commonly held opinions that are part of our culture's common sense.

Commentary

The question about 'good' or 'bad' media is designed to reveal the contradictory ways people think about the media, and the different ways the media are used. It may also point out the difference between how the media could be used in society (their *potential use*) and how they are used in society (their *actual use*). Potentially, the media could be used in lots of different ways, for example, to increase our understanding of global inequalities or as a means of democratic voting; actual use refers to the current practices of the media. The potential power of the media, and their regulation and control, are of major concern for all contemporary societies.

The points in the table below suggest a number of different general positions for and against the media; they all contain some truth and highlight many of the concerns of **media studies**.

MEDIA STUDIES ▶

Media studies analyses the role of the media in society and studies media technologies, media institutions, and the production, consumption, circulation, and content of media texts.

Table 2.1 Points for and against the media

For	Against
The media's huge range of cultural information and entertainment contributes to the development of popular knowledge. People are more aware and better educated through the media than ever before.	The media offer people a repetitive diet of worthless trivia. They cater to the lowest intellectual abilities.
The media can inspire and develop us, actively encouraging us to do new things in our lives.	The media make us passive observers—couch potatoes—whereby we lose the ability to think or act for ourselves.

For	Against
The media help us explore and develop our understanding of sex and violence by depicting social attitudes and inviting critique of the behaviours that are represented.	The media corrupt and pervert us and young children, desensitising our feelings and emotions, and encouraging immoral sexual behaviour and violent acts. The media need to be censored.
The media are truthful and informative and, as such, make a major contribution to democracy and social accountability by offering us a window on the world.	The media are a series of false constructions serving minority political interests.
The media are democratic in that they allow all people in the world to have a voice.	The media serve commercial interests and are totally controlled by multinational corporations and advertisers.
The media enable free thought and free speech to be disseminated.	The media are in the business of controlling our consciousness, thereby controlling who we are and how we think.
The media are shrinking the globe, uniting us, and bringing us closer together, thereby creating a global village.	The media are making us all the same and destroying marginalised cultures.
The media give space to the voices of different social groups and cultures.	The media exert a form of cultural imperialism, whereby dominant cultures impose their values on less powerful cultures.
The media are agents for social change.	The media maintain the status quo.

Two examples illustrate some of these arguments. Media researcher John Hartley, showing the 'good' side of the media, has noted how Nelson Mandela writes in his autobiography (Mandela 1995) about his visit to Canada, where many Inuit people greeted him and celebrated his arrival. They had witnessed his release from prison in South Africa on television. Mandela's freedom struggle connected with their own struggles in Canada for land and political rights, and it was television that made possible the connection between these different and geographically very distant people. As Mandela says, 'Television had shrunk the world and had, in the process, become a great weapon for eradicating ignorance and promoting democracy' (Mandela 1995, quoted in Hartley & McKee 1996, p. 74).

On the other hand, showing the 'bad' side, the media can be seen as part of a purely self-serving and profit-motivated consumerist culture. Consider the *Terminator* films: *The Terminator* (1984) and its sequels have been heavily promoted and packaged for release to a new generation of filmgoers. An estimated US$50–100 million was spent on marketing *Terminator Genysis* (2015). This, combined with the system of film distribution and release, and other marketing tools, made its release commercially successful, a veritable money-making machine.

Spanning more than thirty years, the *Terminator* franchise comprises five films, a television show, a novel, comic books, video games, and other products. The long-term critical and commercial success of the franchise has seen over US$1.4 billion grossed at the box office. *Terminator* merchandise includes toys such as *Terminator Genysis* action figures and Schwarzenegger statues, T-shirts, products such as endo-skull mugs and lanyards, and tie-ins with a video game, as well as product placement deals with companies such as Pepsi and Windows. The original film's most notable product placement was a Nike shoe and this Nike placement has endured throughout all the films, while Pepsi has been consistently placed throughout most of the franchise, and thus the films can all be seen as advertisements for other goods. It could be argued that this is a form of economic exploitation that preys on children and teenagers, who are often considered to be a very susceptible media audience.

The youth market is very important to advertisers. Companies such as the Viral Factory do extensive market research in youth culture to identify emerging trends, and then use the media to market the **subcultural** phenomena they have 'discovered'. Their objective is to harness the aura of coolness and create an association between this and a particular brand. Young people, whose incomes are not already committed to things such as home loan repayments, are particularly vulnerable to such strategies because they are perceived to be impressionable and image conscious.

SUBCULTURE ▶

People who share cultural activities such as dress, leisure activities, and social beliefs, that are resistant or opposed to mainstream culture; used mainly in relation to youth cultures.

Why do we teach about the media?   ⏵

Some of the reasons why Michael, Sarah, and I teach about the media demonstrate our contradictory view of the media, our love–hate relationship with them:

1   We all grew up watching television and films, reading, and listening to music. We spent a lot of our leisure time consuming media products. The media were a source of great entertainment and information. Today we still get huge enjoyment from the media. We expect many students also love some aspects of the media. Teaching about the media aims to enhance understanding, appreciation, and enjoyment of the media through understanding how they work.

2   We appreciate the potentially positive social power of the media. Media communication systems are capable of sharing ideas across physical distances and of making them known, despite cultural differences. They are capable of making information and aesthetic forms available in a truly global form to all people and can therefore, in this capacity, be called democratic. One increasingly popular way to gain media traction in order to leverage attention and potential support for social movements and political activism is the use of online petition platforms such as <www.change.org>, <www.getup.org.au>, and <www.moveon.org>. The media have

also been termed democratic because, like a representative democracy, media can provide a voice for the people and can be used to represent the political views of minority groups as well as those of the majority of the population. The media are used to publicise political issues and events, making it possible for pressure groups to unite around a common issue or injustice, thus overcoming the disempowering effects of isolation in ways that were not feasible without mass communication. For the media to be able to fulfil these democratic roles in public life, freedom of expression is crucial.

There are many examples of documentaries that have helped to illuminate issues around women's rights (for example, award-winning journalists Nicholas Kristof and Sheryl WuDunn's 2015 series *A Path Appears*) and environmental concerns, such as *Gasland* (2010), which is an investigation into widespread water pollution from fracking. One of the most prominent examples is the documentary *An Inconvenient Truth* (2006), which has shown the seriousness of climate change. Many politicians and business corporations began to take the problems of climate change much more seriously just a few months after the film's release.

3 We are critical and distrustful of the ways the media are actually working. We believe that in key structural ways, these powerful means of communication are often misused by the people controlling them. Consequently, it can be said that through their use of the media, those people are contributing to many of the problems of our society and helping to maintain a status quo of global social inequality. Teaching about the media can raise awareness of this negative side of the media, and can develop ways of challenging and changing the media at the same time as celebrating their positive aspects. This social concern gives a critical agenda to media studies. It looks forward to social change and it means that media studies operates within a social and political framework.

Understanding the media can help you to develop skills that equip you to work creatively in the media, and can also lead you to a critical awareness of how the media function so you can engage as an informed citizen with the ongoing social debates about the media and the powers they have.

TWO HISTORICAL VIEWS OF THE MEDIA

Such love–hate views of the media are not new. Since the advent of the printing press, commentators and analysts have been putting forward two contradictory views of the media: a utopian belief in the media's positive possibilities versus a fear of and wariness about their dangers. Every new medium has inspired similar debate. The distribution of information through printing supposedly threatened to corrupt, pervert, and destabilise society in various ways, for example, in the nineteenth century by mobilising the working class, uniting them around common concerns, and facilitating the formation of trade unions and lobby groups. The emergence of the printing press also decentralised political power by enabling widespread communication and distribution of information by organisations other than the state and the Church. Some argued that these were positive qualities as they helped society become more democratic and equal. In the nineteenth century, there was also concern about how the reading of romantic novels would influence the minds of young women, who were a huge market for such fiction; Thomas Hardy's novel *Jude the Obscure* (1895), for example, was banned for its moral dangerousness. Others saw the broadening of women's minds as part of the move towards women's emancipation.

We are seeing similar contradictory debates today over satellite communications and the internet, both of which cross state boundaries and are difficult to police, and computer games, which may be excessively violent and encourage teenage lethargy, or, alternatively, may develop swift reaction skills and computer literacy, and engage people much more actively than does television. Currently it is argued that the technology of the internet and mobile phone cameras allow the development of new kinds of journalism, through blogs, citizens' journalism, and cameras that can report images across the globe, which provide far more democracy and diversity within the media. The use of the social networking website Facebook encourages media participation, develops communication skills, and broadens horizons. Alternatively, it is argued that the internet is dumbing down our culture, and is potentially dangerous in that it encourages internet stalking and surveillance, and brings new ailments such as 'internet addiction affliction disorder'. Media fears are based on the political, moral, and cultural damage of which the media are capable. The optimistic flip-side is hope that the media will help solve all our social, political, and communication problems, and lead us into a new utopia.

Current debates about the good and bad aspects of the media echo earlier arguments. Note how easily the following idealistic prediction about the telegraph in the 1840s could be used to describe today's hopes if we substituted 'the internet' for 'the telegraph':

> Universal peace and harmony seem at this time more possible than ever before, as the telegraph binds together by a vital cord all the nations of the earth. It is impossible that old prejudices and hostilities should any longer exist, while such an instrument has been created for an exchange of thought between all nations of the earth (quoted in Czitrom 1982, p. 10).

In contrast, here is the negative view, fearful of the dangers of the new media, from an 1889 article, 'The Intellectual Effects of Electricity':

> All men are compelled to think of all things at the same time, on imperfect information, and with too little interval for reflection … The constant diffusion of statements in snippets, the constant excitements of feeling unjustified by fact, the constant formation of hasty or erroneous opinions, must in the end, one would think, deteriorate the intelligence of all to whom the telegraph appeals (quoted in Czitrom 1982, p. 19).

Once again there are similar arguments being used against today's twenty-first century media. We will examine these long-held fears about the media in more detail.

Fears about political use of the media

Fears about the political ends to which the media can be put relate to the way the media can be used by political parties to control people. While totalitarian fascist and communist states of the 1930s inspired these fears, political uses of the media also occur in democratic societies, where advertising can be seen as a form of propaganda and brainwashing that supports capitalist consumerism, as first shown in Vance Packard's book *The Hidden Persuaders* (Packard 1957). It is often argued that there should be controls placed over the media so they are not misused. Fear that the media may be used for political purposes is one reason many countries insist that the government should not own and/or control the media; this fear also lies behind many of the debates about who has the right to media ownership.

Note, however, that media practitioners often see themselves as political watchdogs, and in this respect are referred to as the 'fourth estate'. The term 'estate' derives from the time of the French Revolution, when the judiciary, the parliament, and the Church were referred to as the first, second, and third estates respectively. The media, as the fourth estate, are a body who can comment on, criticise, and investigate, through free speech, what these other institutions do, which is why freedom of the press is so important.

It was, for instance, the media that publicised the crimes against humanity being perpetrated by the South African apartheid government, prompting the global community to impose sanctions against South Africa and to exert political pressure. The South African government explicitly blamed the press for giving it a negative image overseas and drawing international criticism of the apartheid policy (Fourie 2001, p. 429). The political, cultural, and economic pressures exerted by the global community as a result of this bad press contributed to the downfall of apartheid.

More recently, social networking media have been used to mobilise protesters and to lobby for regime change and democracy in movements such as 'the Arab Spring' (2010–11), the 'Occupy Movement' (2011–), and the 'Hong Kong Umbrella Revolution' (2014). While the use of social networking media in protests is not without criticism about **slacktivism** ◀ SLACKTIVISM (see, for example, Evgeny Morozov [2009] and Malcolm Gladwell [2011]), the 'Facebook Revolution' in Egypt is a noteworthy example. Here, on the 'Revolution Day' Facebook page developed by Egyptian political activists, more than 85 000 people developed a list of demands for the Mubarak regime and pledged to attend antigovernment protests in Egypt in January 2011.

Fears about the media's influence on morals

Sometimes moral fears arise from concern that the media are a corrupting force, particularly in relation to sex and violence. It is argued that people's values can be corrupted by the media they consume. This has led to moral panics and campaigns against too much sex and violence on television. Moral panic tends to focus on the effects of media consumption on young people, because they supposedly have less experience on which to base sound judgment, and less-developed critical faculties with which to position fiction or other media content in relation to external reality. It has been suggested that the cumulative effects of consuming media that contain violent and/or sexualised content are particularly harmful for young viewers, due in part to the tendency of young people to learn by mimesis (mimicking or imitating what they see and hear). Because interactive media forms such as video games require participation in the acts of violence they represent, they are considered especially worrying.

Another perspective on this issue is that the prevalence of high levels of gratuitous sex and violence in the media naturalises such material, making comparable behaviour in real life seem natural, normal, and acceptable. The danger here is that the media may inadvertently legitimate unacceptable ethical positions, such as the use of violence as a method of conflict resolution, or a lack of respect for one's sexual partners (see censorship/effects, pp. 46–8). The flip-side argument in relation to sexuality says that in today's

SLACKTIVISM

A combination of the terms 'slacker' and 'activism'. Slacktivism (also known as 'hashtag activism') refers to the use of the internet to support a social or political cause in a superficial way that requires little effort or risk, such as signing online petitions or using social media to endorse social justice activities. Arguably, this form of activism chiefly benefits the conscience or the self-image of the slacktivist without requiring them to take genuine action to further social justice.

media-world, we are better educated and better informed about all sexual matters than at any other time in human history.

Fears about the media's influence on culture

There are also those who fear that the media devalue culture because what they produce is so trivial or superficial. This is best illustrated in the debates around the relative importance of so-called 'high' and 'low' culture. High culture is supposedly the great art produced by a society, art that is morally uplifting, complex, and serious. It is said to be found in such cultural products as opera, painting, and literature, the understanding and interpretation of which require training and specialist instruction. Low, or popular, culture, on the other hand, is what the masses consume; it is found in magazines, mass-market paperbacks, and popular cinema, and on television. Critics of low culture deride it as morally degrading and simplistic.

Traditionally, low culture has been denigrated as inferior and potentially damaging, and the fact that it was a product of mass media was used to disparage it. Educators thought they needed to protect people against the damaging effects of low culture, so teachers would analyse mass-media products in class, aiming to show students how corrupt, cheap, worthless, and harmful they were. The high–low opposition still informs the way a lot of people think about the media. Such oppositions are partly the product of class-divided societies—high culture is the province of the ruling and middle classes, the bourgeoisie, while low culture is the province of the working class. But it is interesting to note that both right-wing conservatives and left-wing radicals have disapproved of low culture and the popular mass media: the right wing sees the media as offering a diet of cheap, tawdry, corrupt entertainments, while the left wing sees these entertainments as a political sweetener, acting to distract the workers from their political grievances.

Since the 1970s, there has been much study done of popular culture in media studies, mainly due to the need to understand the dynamics of the huge media audiences that are attracted to it—if so many people are consuming media texts, it is important to understand them—but this study is also an attempt to validate popular culture itself, to see it positively and avoid labelling it as something inferior to high culture.

Fears about contemporary consumerism and advertising

It may be that the media in the main simply reflect the dominant values of society, which are based on the values of continual economic growth and consumerism. Advertising is a crucial media form that supports consumerism. Consider the following critique of advertising by musicologist Robert Fink, who claims that because advertising promotes goods, it produces materialism and other potentially negative effects:

> Because it advocates through incomplete truths and deceptions, it creates cynicism. When advertising appeals to mass markets, it promotes conformity; when it appeals to status, it promotes social stratification and class conflict; when it appeals to fear, it promotes anxiety; when it appeals to newness, it creates disrespect for authority; when it appeals to youth, it undermines the family; and when it appeals to sexuality, it creates erotic obsession and dysfunction. Because it appeals to the individual, it makes people selfish; because it must be simple and easily understandable, it deals in social stereotypes and debases language (Fink 2005, p. 64).

It is not necessary to agree with everything in Fink's critique to acknowledge that the way advertising is linked to ever-growing consumerism is of concern, and worthy of note and discussion.

MEDIA STUDIES: DIFFERENT APPROACHES

The first serious academic study of the media began in Europe in the 1930s. Since then media studies has developed in different countries in various ways. We list here some of the most significant approaches and methodologies so as to give an overview of the field of media studies.

The Frankfurt School

The Frankfurt School is the name given to a group of Marxist scholars who first analysed the role of the media in Europe and Germany in the 1930s, and then moved to consider American media in the 1940s and 1950s. As Marxists, they stressed the way the media functioned to subordinate the working class and how they were determined by economic interests. After seeing the political dangers of the media in Nazi Germany, these scholars defined the popular media in the USA as a **consciousness industry** that helped to control the masses. The Frankfurt School was important in that its members produced the first in-depth studies of the media and were the first to see the media as industries. It has influenced many subsequent media analysts.

◀ CONSCIOUSNESS INDUSTRY

Term used by the Frankfurt School to describe how the media function to control the minds and feelings of the masses at the same time as making money.

Effects research

Different strands of research developed in the USA and Europe. In the USA, most media research has been conducted by sociologists and psychologists who were interested in trying to measure media effects. For example, media-effects researchers have conducted empirical research to try to ascertain whether watching violent media causes viewer aggression, using a variety of measures to record affective reactions such as brain activity, heart rate, pupil dilation, and temperature while participants watch a violent film or play a violent video game. 'Affect' is a measurable physiological expression of emotional responses to stimulation. Affective stimuli significantly influence the autonomic nervous system, which regulates involuntary physiological states including heart rate and perspiration. Emotional states like aggression resulting from audio-visual stimuli such as violent films can be indirectly assessed by measuring affect to gauge how the nervous system responds.

Effects research has been carried out extensively, but its results have been contradictory because the effects of media are so difficult to measure. The only conclusion seems to be that it is not possible to measure direct effects because the media are just one component of an infinitely complex chain of causal factors (such as audience members' upbringing, social class, education, personal prejudices, experiences, and so forth). Nevertheless, researchers keep trying, and the era of 'big data' means that their techniques are increasingly sophisticated and backed by funding from major corporations. As media scholars Blake Hallinan and Ted Striphas put it, 'data are an enduring aspect of the media industries. Long before the rise of "big data," studio executives turned to test audiences, ratings, viewer diaries, eye tracking, and unsolicited feedback in an effort to gauge reception of their programming. Industry professionals continue to use these and other resources to guide their decisions about what material to produce in addition to how, and with whom, to populate the content' (2014, p. 14).

And yet a major question remains: how do the media, even if they don't have direct measurable effects, influence the way we think, feel, and behave? Contemporary effects researchers are investigating indirect, cumulative, and long-term media effects that are important to understand. We will not examine effects research in detail in this book, but will return to the central issue of media effects/influence (see especially Chapter 3) since it is of interest on so many levels, from gauging the social impact of controversial media content, such as stereotyping and pornography, through to more pragmatic, profit-driven questions related to advertising effectiveness.

Communication models

A significant field of media research (predominantly of American origin) is interested in explaining how communication in the media works by focusing on forms of media communication (McQuail & Windahl 1981; Fiske 1990, chs 1 & 2). Communications analyst Harold Lasswell worked out a formula (Lasswell 1960) that formed the basis for much subsequent work. It is still useful as a starting point for thinking about what communication is. Lasswell showed diagrammatically how the communication chain points to different areas of media research.

Table 2.2 Areas of media analysis

question	who?	says what?	in which channel?	to whom?	with what effect?
name of media element	communicator	message	medium	receiver	effect
type of media research	control studies	content analysis	media analysis	audience analysis	effects analysis

Source: Adapted from McQuail & Windahl 1981, p. 10

Our main focus will be on what is being communicated in which channel. To explore this, we will use two academic disciplines: semiology and structuralism. Semiology analyses the way communication works through signs and codes; structuralism shows how the ways stories are told, their formal structures, are part of their meaning. We examine these in detail in Parts 2 and 4. Harold Innis, Marshall McLuhan, and Walter Ong are three important North American thinkers who have theorised how the mass media work and communicate. They saw the media as significantly changing society. Innis' great contribution was to analyse communication systems in terms of how they change society's use of space and time, including analysing changing modes of transportation as forms of communication

(Innis 1951). He argued that the means of mediating and transmitting communications shaped history, and this argument was the genesis of the political economy approach to the media.

McLuhan's well-known phrase **the global village** points to the way that media communications unify the world (for further discussion of globalisation, see Chapter 25). Ong, taking a much wider historical view, looked at the way the print media have changed Western society from a spoken-word culture (an oral culture) into a society based on print and literacy. Ong's point is related to McLuhan's other famous catch-phrase 'the medium is the message', which suggests that the medium, or the technology, used to transmit communication (whether print, radio, screen, web, wireless, or via mobile phones) is just as important, if not more important, than the content of the message itself.

◄ GLOBAL VILLAGE

The phrase 'the global village' suggests that the globalisation of communication media has brought the whole world closer together, like a village in which everyone is interconnected.

Content analysis

Alongside effects research, the method known as **content analysis** was developed. Content analysis originated in journalistic research that relied on counting the occurrences of words or phrases. This research method was applied during the Second World War, for instance, to analyse Nazi propaganda publications. Content analysis provides a systematic way to make inferences about patterns of images, printed words, or verbal data in order to describe and quantify their meanings, and interpret their consequences. This research method can be used to reveal cultural patterns, and identify trends in media and communication content, as well as identifying where audiences focus their attention.

◄ CONTENT ANALYSIS

Quantitative measurement of media content.

For media and communication scholars, content analysis can be used to locate and measure patterns in what the media actually produce: so, for example, research on women in relation to the media could look at how much content is given over to women, or what roles women are portrayed as performing. In 2010, the Australian Sports Commission released a research report, 'Towards a Level Playing Field: Sport and Gender in Australian Media', that used content analysis to reveal that women in sport are under-represented in the Australian media. Key findings of the report are that women make up just 9 per cent of all sports coverage in Australian television news and current affairs, and 7 per cent of other sports programming; furthermore, television news reports on female sports are shorter than all other types of sports news.

Another example is the 1992 documentary film *Manufacturing Consent* (a significant analysis of media power). In this film, linguist and philosopher Noam Chomsky looks at US media coverage of East Timor. He does a content analysis in order to support his view that the US media acted politically in the interests of the US government. Thus, in this film, Chomsky combines content analysis with political analysis of who controls the media, their bias, and their self-censorship.

Chomsky argues that during the 1970s, the Indonesian government carried out atrocities on the East Timorese people that were equivalent to those perpetrated by Pol Pot's Khmer Rouge forces in Cambodia also in the 1970s, but that the American media did not report this equally. His content analysis of *New York Times* coverage of these two events between 1975 and 1979, graphically illustrated in the film, is damning: there were 70 column inches of listings in the *New York Times* index referring to East Timor stories compared to 1175 column inches of index listings for stories on Cambodia. Chomsky links this disparity in coverage to the fact that the USA was involved with the Indonesian government at the time and was implicated in arms sales to Indonesia, whereas Cambodia was not a friendly nation:

> The church and other sources estimated that about 200 000 people were killed [in the conflict over East Timor]. The USA backed Indonesia all the way. The USA provided 90 per cent of the arms for the conflict. Right after the invasion [Indonesia's invasion of East Timor] arms shipments were stepped up … There is no Western concern for issues of aggression, atrocities, human rights abuses and so on if there's a profit to be made from them … As the atrocities reached their maximum peak in 1978 when it really was becoming genocidal, [media] coverage dropped to zero in the United States and Canada (Achbar 1995, pp. 102–3).

Chomsky's work is very important in that it demonstrates the way political power can control the media—in this case, largely through not reporting events, rather than misreporting—a finding that is related to study of the political economy of the media; he uses content analysis to support his argument.

Political economy of the media

This approach, derived partly from the Frankfurt School and theorists such as Innis, is concerned with the way the external forces of economics, ownership of the media, and political power impact on media production. The main argument put forward is that the media serve the economic and political interests of whoever owns and controls them—whether this is private individuals interested in profit, or governments interested in political control. The **political economy** approach involves conducting research into who owns and controls the media. It focuses on how industrial mechanisms and imperatives surrounding production, distribution, and exhibition affect the kinds of texts created, the kinds of audiences they reach, and the messages they send. This type of research is often used to show that mass media products embody capitalist ideologies that are then consumed by the mass audience.

POLITICAL ECONOMY ▶

Explains how the media are determined by a combination of economic, social, and political factors, particularly ownership and control of the media.

A simple example is the way in which the production output of the Australian and British film industries has been determined by the domination in the market of the American industry, a domination felt not just in film production, but also in terms of distribution and exhibition. This domination has always had an impact on Australian and British cinema chains, which are more committed to showing American than home-grown products. In Africa, the need for foreign involvement to finance feature films has led to debates about what African cinema really is. *Blood Diamond* (2006), for example, is a political war thriller set during the 1996–2001 Sierra Leone civil war. The film's title refers to the mining of diamonds in war zones that helps fund unrest. This then profits both diamond companies and warlords. Filmed in various parts of South Africa and Mozambique, this Warner Bros film was funded with overseas money, directed by American Ed Zwick, and starred American actors Leonardo DiCaprio and Jennifer Connolly. These foreign influences were deemed necessary to get the film a wide distribution, and to get it made at all. In many African countries, it costs too much to produce local programs with high production values that can compete with the established, well-resourced American studio systems. The varying fortunes of these indigenous industries can be charted in relation to government policies, tax incentives, and investment, rather than in terms of the creative output of filmmakers themselves. Similar studies can be made of Australian and British television productions, which also engage in economic struggle with American products.

One of the major concerns of the 2004 Free Trade Agreement between the USA and Australia relates to issues of cultural production, particularly television, film production, and new media. Many Australians were worried that if Australia did not maintain some restrictions on American products, and if it did not guarantee a certain percentage of television time and cinema releases for Australian products, then it would be swamped by American media. This would mean both a cultural loss in terms of seeing and hearing Australian stories, voices, and content, and an economic and creative loss in terms of losing an industry and outlet for Australian media creators. It has been argued that the great successes of Australian film and television since the 1970s were built on, first, the 1970s restrictions that guaranteed that Australian television advertisements should be made by Australians in Australia and, second, the government support for the film industry. These factors gave the opportunity for many Australians to learn the necessary skills for filmmaking and to make full-length features. This followed a period from the 1950s to around 1970 during which the Australian film industry virtually disappeared under the dominance of the USA. The 2004 Agreement has allowed that a certain proportion of Australian films and television must still be Australian; however, the same provision was not made for any new digital media communication systems that might evolve in the future, and Australian critics of the Agreement fear that this will result in further domination of American productions and furtherance of what is called American **cultural imperialism** ◀ CULTURAL IMPERIALISM (see Chapter 25 for a full discussion of this concept). American formulas and formats still provide the benchmarks that local productions are judged by and try to imitate.

> Imperial domination of the world maintained partly through the dissemination of cultural products. Argues that the globalisation of communication results in domination over traditional cultures, and the intrusion of Western culture and values such as consumerism.

Major concerns relate to the way media moguls such as Rupert Murdoch, Chairman and CEO of News Corporation, control more and more media outlets, and what political restrictions there should be on their media ownership. The problem is that their influence on media output is so great that it increasingly limits our information, and gives them significant political power. Their companies have control over book publishing, other print media, television, and satellite outlets, as well as news, entertainment, sports, and other non-media interests. Note how Murdoch has bought internet sites such as TeamXbox because he knows how important they are to young people. In Australia, the new laws on media ownership enacted in 2006 seem to permit even more media monopolies.

One of the ways satellite television has developed is through buying the rights to major sporting occasions: people who want to see these very popular events have to buy into satellite TV. Consequently, public broadcasting channels such as the ABC in Australia and the BBC in the UK start losing their audiences. Economic issues are also felt in relation to advertising, which is central in media production and threatens, through sponsorship, to exert more control over programming. Sports stadiums and competitions are now regularly renamed in relation to corporations and companies so that television coverage of major events is always announced in terms of the sponsors, who also have to be acknowledged by the winners after matches. Consequently, audiences keep hearing the sponsoring companies' names repeated.

Television researcher Professor George Gerbner, from the University of Pennsylvania, articulates the argument that market forces lead to a standardisation of product:

> we have many more channels than ever before … at the same time ownership shrinks;
> so what happens is fewer owners own more channels and therefore can program the

same materials across many channels; therefore instead of more channels creating greater diversity they seem to be creating greater homogeneity, greater uniformity, greater standardisation and greater globalisation … they can say [to overseas channels] we can sell you an hour's worth of programming for less money than it would cost you to produce your own … this proposition is economically so attractive … it's a standardised, marketing formula [our emphasis] (*The Media Report*, ABC Radio National, 29 August 1996).

There are two major arguments put forward against Gerbner's view that economic control leads to **media homogenisation**. The first is that the market spread of media actually allows opportunities for many different social groups to be heard. People have the opportunity to use the media to their own advantage as there is wider and cheaper access to media production and communication. The internet is regarded as having a huge potential for such democratic and diverse output.

The second argument relates to audiences: ultimately, the audiences—the media consumers—have a big say in what gets produced. If they do not like a product, it will fail, and this forces the media to produce acceptable material. Additionally, audiences can make their own meanings out of texts. They will not necessarily be brainwashed by what they consume.

In relation to claims that media owners such as Rupert Murdoch have too much control, as shown in the documentary *Outfoxed* (2004), John Hartley puts forward a contradictory argument:

> Panckouke was the most important media identity of the French Revolution. Have we heard of this man who owned lots of Parisian newspapers and French media during the French Revolution, or have we heard of the ideas being promulgated in those media by such as Tom Paine and Marat and all the rest of them? The latter. We hear about the ideas, we're interested in the ideas. Ownership in the long run does not determine what it is that these media are capable of doing (*The Media Report*, ABC Radio National, 21 December 2000).

Hartley goes on to argue that, historically, media content exists outside the complete control of those who own and control media corporations and industries. Those who own the media exert economic control, but that does not necessarily translate to the control of meaning and interpretation. These debates about control, effects, and response are central to media studies.

Structural organisation of the media

The way media products are structurally organised affects the way they present information, and this is also an area for media research. Two of the key terms used in this context are **agenda setting** and **gatekeeping**, terms most often used in relation to journalism, news, and current affairs.

Agenda setting refers to instances in which media coverage draws attention to an issue or event, and thereby puts it on the agenda for public discussion and debate. It can be understood as a form of media management or manipulation in which a public figure (such as a politician) might issue a press release about a particular issue, or include it in a policy statement or speech on more than one occasion, thus encouraging follow-up coverage by

MEDIA HOMOGENISATION ▶

Financial pressures and other forces lead all media products to become similar, standard, and uniform.

AGENDA SETTING ▶

The process by which media producers set up the issues—the agenda—that the media will focus on and that audiences will subsequently perceive to be important.

GATEKEEPING ▶

The process of controlling what gets included and whose voices are heard in the media, particularly in the news.

the media. This 'sets the agenda', puts that particular issue on the media agenda, raising its public profile.

Media analyst Joshua Green, in discussing American presidential elections, has shown how clever campaigners specialise in negative advertising. He refers to the tactic of Republican political consultant Lee Atwater 'that a campaign should frame its opponent before the opponent can frame himself' (Green 2004). In the 2016 US presidential race, in an effort to neutralise Hillary Clinton's political experience Republicans have cast her as 'a creature of Washington' and of the Clinton political machinery, more interested in power and prestige than in the hopes and aspirations of everyday Americans. Criticism of her term as Secretary of State is used to underscore this view and to link her to the perceived failings of the Obama administration. The Democrats, in the face of Donald Trump's unpredicted success in capturing the mood of disaffected Americans, have chosen to focus on whether he has the temperament to be Commander in Chief, the credibility to run a national economy, and the decency to advocate for interests other than his own.

It is important to see how different television channels and newspapers watch what their rivals are doing and often feel compelled to take up similar stories, similar agendas, so that they will not be seen as missing out on something.

In Australia, the prevalence of negative advertising in the media could be seen in the 2013 federal election as both major parties addressed citizens' fears and anxieties. There were also attempts to frame the opposing parties and individual politicians, and to fight the election on particular issues. In 2010, Julia Gillard had assumed leadership of the Australian Labor Party from Kevin Rudd, and the Liberals wanted to frame Labor as mutinous and unstable, and Gillard as untrustworthy. This idea was reinforced over the next couple of years, with a focus on Gillard's childlessness and certain parts of the media positioning her as a ruthlessly ambitious unmarried woman. Further fortifying this idea was right-wing broadcaster Alan Jones' now infamous 2012 attack on Gillard (and other women in powerful positions) claiming that women were 'destroying the joint', as though they were not suitable for top positions in public life or office. This caused outrage, and a now highly successful, ongoing online feminist campaign, 'Destroy the Joint', was set up as a reaction to 'the sexism dished out to women in Australia, whether they be our Prime Minister or any other woman'. To date, it has a community of over 75 000 followers and is one of the most visible feminist campaigns in Australia.

The attention to gender that came about due to 'Destroy the Joint' and then Gillard's 'Misogyny Speech' in October 2012 is critical when exploring the later framing of the candidates in the 2013 Australian federal election campaign. Then-Prime Minister Gillard's 'Misogyny Speech' was a reaction to then-Opposition Leader Tony Abbott's alleged sexism. It went viral with over 22 million views within 10 days. Even though later in 2013 Rudd made a comeback as the leader of the Labor Party and ousted Gillard in the lead-up to the 2013 election, in evaluating the positioning of major party candidates in the election campaign, as McLaren and Sawer (2015, p. 686) argue, there was 'unofficial gender-based campaigning'. Accordingly, Rudd and Abbott both used their wives and daughters on the campaign trail, and presented themselves as family men and men who understood women because they had daughters. Labor represented Abbott as an old-fashioned and out-of-touch sexist, and his party as greedily conservative. The Liberals attempted to represent themselves as united and capable against an unstable Labor Party that could not be trusted due to its dysfunctional inner party workings.

The media also participate in agenda setting by giving extensive coverage to certain sensational or spectacular issues and events. A snowball effect can result, as the media coverage of the topic gains momentum and generates the perception that the issue is of great importance, partly because it is getting so much press coverage. When, for example, there was an Ebola virus outbreak in 2014 in West Africa, Western media outlets were complicit in the spreading of sweeping panic. While the outbreak quickly grew into a tragic epidemic, it was largely contained to Africa and the Western media was slow to report on it, until a man unknowingly contracted the virus in Liberia and then travelled to America, where he died. The *Daily Mirror* in the UK reported, for example, a headline: 'Ebola Terror at Gatwick as Passenger Collapses and Dies Getting off Sierra Leone Flight' (4 August 2014). The next day the press revealed that this passenger tested negative for Ebola. Despite the fact that outside Africa there were only four people infected with the disease at the time the newspaper went to print, extensive media coverage in the West of the threat of the Ebola epidemic was engulfing the population of the free world.

Then a viral meme with an image of Kim Kardashian stated: 'More Americans have been married to Kim Kardashian than have died from Ebola.' This meme was not intended to diminish the enormous loss of life in Africa from Ebola but, rather, to provide perspective on the media coverage by pointing out that Kim Kardashian has had more husbands than the number of people who have died from Ebola in the USA: only one American has died from Ebola after being in Africa. The media often seem more interested in a story when it affects 'one of their own', which highlights that 'geographical and cultural proximity play an important role in the selection of news stories' (Cullen 2014).

The media then reported that a wave of panic was spreading in response to the Ebola outbreak in West Africa. The media were creating this wave of panic by putting the issue on the agenda, on the front pages of national newspapers. In America, a few cases of a disease and one death do not constitute a remarkable increase in the risk of contracting the illness. In fact, what increased was the reporting of the risk.

The notion that the structural organisation of media programs and journalism affects the way they present information shows how the media often give more weight to the viewpoints of official institutions than to alternative viewpoints. The news is supposed to be **objective**, to provide a balanced account of issues and events, to air both sides of a debate, and to include diverse perspectives. But the media often privilege certain voices, those of the agenda setters. This is not a deliberate conspiracy, there are various practical reasons for it: the fact that news is deemed to happen in parliament or the law courts, the reliance on official spokespeople and experts to comment on events, and the use of journalists themselves (who select and present the news). All these factors are part of the gatekeeping process.

OBJECTIVITY ▶

Perceiving, reporting, or presenting things from an impersonal, neutral, unbiased perspective.

Many broadcasters, in the interests of keeping their costs as low as they can, rely on news-gathering organisations to supply their stories for them. Agendas are also set in advance: news is often old insofar as journalists go to the people and places where they already know things are going to happen. People who are skilled in dealing with the media often arrange press conferences where they attempt to have the media report their point of view. The way news is organised on a daily basis, with limited time and the need to maintain popular ratings, leads to simplification and sensationalisation of events. Consequently, audiences rarely receive a complex understanding of events with explanations that cover long-term causes: the focus is on what happened today and how the situation changes hour by hour, so that each new bulletin will have something more immediate. In this sound-bite era, the use of striking headlines and good pictures predominates. The Tom Tomorrow cartoon (see Figure 2.1) illustrates these features of contemporary news reporting.

Figure 2.1 Tom Tomorrow cartoon

Source: Dan Perkins 1992

News is also structured on the basis of what journalists call **news values** or **newsworthiness**, a set of values and priorities that have come to be accepted by journalists as common sense in relation to what is regarded as important to be reported. News values, or the features of a story that make it valuable and newsworthy, include calamity, proximity, celebrity, novelty, enormity or severity of impact, relevance, and visual appeal. For example, for the Australian media one person dying in a shark attack in Australia is far more newsworthy than a hundred people dying of cholera in West Africa. Stories with entertainment value and reports about positive breakthroughs or amazing achievements can also make the news.

Much news is bad news, that is, disasters, things going wrong, and problems being highlighted. As a visual medium, television privileges pictures: a story about a whale attacking one of its handlers at a theme park in the USA in July 2004 became an Australian news story, presumably because of its exciting footage, which was easily transmitted from America to Australia. In terms of political or social import, this story had no importance

◄ NEWS VALUES/NEWSWORTHINESS

The elements of an issue or event that make it important enough to report on in the eyes of journalists. Newsworthy features include conflict, relevance, locality, prominence, novelty, and magnitude.

and the handler was not even badly hurt, but it looked good. The fact that today many daily events are recorded on video in America, whereas many fewer are recorded in Africa, simply adds to the preponderance and likelihood of including American news stories, rather than African news stories, in the Australian media.

There is also an emphasis on individuals to personalise stories, which tends to simplify issues—the election campaigns mentioned above, with their excessive focus on the characters of individual leaders, illustrate this. Because of the underlying ethos of individualism in Western society, the media place great emphasis on individuals, and often make use of the personas or images associated with media personalities (such as celebrities, politicians, and newsreaders) in order to encourage the audience to read something more into the story.

Textual analysis and cultural studies

Analysing the media's political, economic, and organisational structures is important, but these approaches don't focus so much on the actual media texts and their meanings. A perceived problem with much cultural studies research examining narrative media is that textual analysis and case studies provide richly detailed analyses of style and meaning in small samples of texts, from which it can be difficult to make well-founded claims about broader patterns or implications for other audiences, texts, or contexts. By contrast, empirical research methods, such as content analyses of large samples, may overlook specificity and detail, and so their capacity to analyse meaning-making within individual texts and readers is weak. Content analysis draws attention to *what* is being presented in the media, but its limitation is that it doesn't interpret *how* events are portrayed, or how individuals actually interpret and respond to them.

This question has been explored more in European traditions of media analysis. Whereas American researchers were mainly sociologists and psychologists, European work came from literary, historical, and philosophical studies, and from traditions of textual analysis. These traditions typically focused on interpreting literature, theatre, painting, music, and so forth, trying to explain their meanings. In the UK, this tradition was significantly developed at the Centre for Contemporary Cultural Studies (CCCS), the so-called Birmingham School. This brought together literary and historical approaches alongside Marxist, feminist, semiotic, and structural linguistic theories, combining a body of critical theory with political concerns. Concurrently with a number of other institutions, the CCCS helped develop and spread the growth of cultural studies, which continues to be influential today.

Like the political economy approach, cultural studies is interested in questions of political power and the social role of the media. A significant area of its work has been in understanding popular culture and issues of representation, alongside examination of the role and position of the audience, and wider contextual studies, so it has wide scope in its analysis. **Textual analysis**—looking at the forms, language, signifying systems, and genres of the media—is one central aspect of cultural studies and this informs much of our work. Detailed textual analysis, sometimes called 'close reading', can take a number of forms. Aesthetic analysis attends to the style of a text, analysing language use, image construction, and the nuances of meaning produced by aesthetic choices such as the connotations of words, the composition of images, and the techniques used in sound design and film editing. Semiotics is an important method of textual analysis that is detailed in Part 2

TEXTUAL ANALYSIS ▶

The process of interpreting and analysing any media text, typically focusing on its form and content, style, and structure.

of this book. Narrative analysis is another type of textual analysis that focuses on larger textual structures, as discussed in Part 4. Media scholars frequently use textual analysis as a research method to reveal the underlying ideological meanings of media texts, and the relationship between representation and reality, as examined in Part 3.

Audience studies

Several of the above approaches are concerned with audiences, either assuming they are being influenced or affected in some ways, or considering their place in the communication chain. Others focus simply on the media institutions and texts themselves. Since the 1980s, many media researchers have argued that the audience area needed developing—they wanted to try to understand how audiences actually do interact with the media—and considerable work has now been done in this field. There is a variety of theoretical approaches to media audiences, which we look at in Chapter 6.

Media education

Since the mid-1960s, media studies has grown in Australia, Europe, Asia, Africa, and America, in schools, colleges, and universities, so that it now stands as an important and popular academic area in its own right. It is possible to find a variety of media courses within tertiary education: mass communications, media studies, cultural studies, film and screen studies, multimedia, journalism, and so on. These are built, to different degrees, on an interdisciplinary method, and present a mixture of critical, practical, and vocational approaches. They use many of the approaches listed above, but add an important element—practical work in teaching people how to be scriptwriters, journalists, filmmakers, and so on. The methods listed above do not include this practical aspect. We believe in the value of practical media work alongside theoretical analysis, and we hope that this book will be of as much value to students who wish to enter the media professionally as to those merely wishing to understand the media.

CONCLUSION

In thinking about media studies and all the approaches mentioned above, we define it as follows. Media studies is the study of

- media technologies
- media texts—their content, production, circulation, and consumption
- the media institutions in which they are produced
- the media's role in society.

This definition encompasses social questions about the media, how people use and understand them (their influence), and technical or aesthetic questions about the ways they communicate (that is, the language of the media). These two concerns—*sociological* aspects (thinking about the social and political roles of the media) and *aesthetic* aspects (looking at and evaluating the artistic merit of texts)—are both central to our field of study. The changing structure and function of the media industries, and the media's political and economic relationships with the public and the nation-state, are very important issues, but we cannot cover all of these areas in one book. For an insightful account of these issues and of how contemporary media 'not only create publics and address markets, they also generate and sustain social networks', we recommend Graeme Turner's *Re-Inventing the Media* (2016). Our focus will be on how to explore media texts, textual analysis, and the media's connection to society.

This chapter has

- defined media studies and explored the contradictory aspects of the media
- considered historical views of the media and recurrent fears about the media
- looked at the development and different approaches of media studies, including the Frankfurt School, effects research, communication models, content analysis, the political economy of media, the structural organisation of media, cultural studies, and audience studies.

? DISCUSSION POINTS

1 What specific media examples can you find to support the argument that the media are good or bad?
2 Can you find any contemporary media news stories or reports that examine the role of the media? What arguments about the media do they put forward?
3 Do the media serve the interests of some social groups in favour of others?
4 How important is it to consider who owns and controls media output when examining its content? (As always, try to give specific media examples to support your argument.)
5 *Mad Max: Fury Road* was made by an Australian director and a substantially Australian cast and crew, with pre- and post-production undertaken on the island continent and location shooting in Namibia. Do you consider it an Australian film? Why?
6 Which approaches that have been developed in media studies do you think are most useful? Why?

SUMMARY

You should now be able to

- consider your own interest in the media
- understand and comment on positive and negative aspects of the media in general
- give your own specific positive and negative media examples
- explain some of the recurrent fears of the media that have been put forward
- define and illustrate subculture, cultural imperialism, content analysis, political economy, media homogenisation, agenda setting, gatekeeping, and news values
- explain briefly the different approaches that have been developed within media studies
- comment on the strengths, weaknesses, and validity of these approaches
- apply different approaches for understanding any one media text.

CHAPTER 3

What Do the Media Do to Us?
Media and Society

Movies don't create psychos, they make psychos more creative.

Scream

This chapter will explore the relationship between the media and society by
- giving an overview of contemporary society
- giving some basic guidelines about how the media work
- exploring how or whether the media affect and influence us
- looking at two specific media examples.

CONTEMPORARY SOCIETY

Change and crisis

We live in a world that is undergoing huge social and political turmoil. Such changes went on throughout the twentieth century, so it is short-sighted to see this as something new. Nevertheless, the rate of change seems to be accelerating. Currently we face the following global issues:

1   There is an ecological crisis of global warming, pollution, and diminishing natural resources.
2   There is a political crisis in terms of power struggles fuelled by ethnic, national, and religious differences, as well as social inequalities; these may be fragmenting individual societies (conflicts in Syria, Congo, Libya, Tunisia, and Egypt, for example), or forming struggles between countries and cultures (ISIS and the Western bloc countries, Afghanistan and the West, Israel and the Palestinians, China and Tibet, for example) or occurring globally, as in the refugee crisis and the so-called war on terror.
3   There is an economic crisis of growth, consumption, and production. This crisis is, of course, linked to the ecological and political power issues.

Inequality and difference

Looking at the world globally, and at individual Western societies, it soon becomes evident that there are major social inequalities. Societies consist of complex networks of groups with different—sometimes competing, sometimes overlapping—interests. Some of these groups are advantaged (in relation to such social goods as housing, education, and life opportunities) by virtue of their birth, their wealth, their class position, their skin colour, and/or their gender. Consequently, there are advantaged and disadvantaged groups in society, or, to put this another way, dominant and subordinate groups. Three major areas of social division are class, gender, and race, although in some contexts religion, age, sexuality, caste, and education can be equally divisive in ways that are often closely related to these three primary categories. Class, race, and gender frequently restrict or create opportunities for individuals and groups to flourish and to attain coveted positions in society.

Since the beginnings of colonial explorations of the rest of the world by Europe in the sixteenth century, there have been major differences in wealth between different countries and cultures. While you may imagine that the world is becoming more economically equal in the twentieth and twenty-first centuries, the opposite seems to be true. The gap between rich and poor is also huge and increasing within Australia, the United Kingdom, and the USA. A report from the International Monetary Fund reveals that the gap in advanced economies is at its highest in decades (Dabla-Norris et al. 2015). According to the Credit Suisse Global Wealth Report (Shorrocks et al. 2015), the wealthiest 1 per cent are now in control of 48 per cent of global wealth. It is estimated that in Britain in the 1970s, 7 per cent of the population owned 84 per cent of the wealth; currently it is estimated that 1 per cent owns 50 per cent of the wealth. While many wars and social conflicts are presented in the media as religious or ethnic struggles—for example, Muslims against Christians, Tutsis against Hutus—these may be better understood as struggles caused by social and financial inequalities.

Maintaining consent in Western democracies

If Western democratic societies are full of social inequalities, why isn't there more social disorder and disruption? Why don't the disadvantaged and underprivileged rebel more often? Why do so many people seem to accept their subordination? There is, of course, some social disruption, particularly crime; however, crime is not usually understood as the actions of oppressed social groups who are struggling to redistribute wealth and have a political agenda. Rather, crime is usually understood as, and presented in the media as, the actions of greedy, deviant, psychologically sick (or evil) individuals. In general, Western democratic societies have found ways to maintain social stability at the same time as maintaining social inequalities. They have succeeded in influencing the perceptions, beliefs, and values of many people by winning their hearts and minds so they accept the status quo (see pp. 186–7). How is this consent maintained? Here are some initial suggestions regarding this complicated question.

- Western liberal democratic systems give everyone the right to vote (in Australia it is a legal obligation). In effect, voting entails delegating power to the political party that best represents and articulates your priorities, values, and beliefs. Because the politicians 'represent' the views of the citizens who vote for them, this system is termed 'representative democracy'. Clearly the media play an important role in the processes of representing and communicating political policies, issues, and so forth. But in practice there are limits to democracy: in most democracies there are only two or three significantly powerful parties, so your voting power is limited to the policies and values they are willing to promote. Because of the need to appeal to the majority of voters, the views of the main parties are invariably relatively conservative, mainstream positions that are often rendered even more general by the media's attempts to cater to the largest possible audience. In the

USA, only about 50 per cent of people eligible to vote actually vote in presidential elections. Ideally voting gives people a say in how their society works; thus the consent of the population is won because people have the sense that they have contributed to and participated in the decision-making processes that structure their society.

- The West is built on an **ideology** (see Chapter 11) of individualism that stresses personal rights, freedoms, and equality. Such beliefs are often legally enshrined in statutory rights and freedoms. This is in contrast to the restrictions of communist countries such as China and other societies such as Burma, which limit individual human rights in the face of collective social good. As individuals, you appreciate the freedoms that Western democracy offers you, and you are encouraged to believe they make the system just.

- Because Western societies are well developed economically, they are able to offer a relatively high standard of living: most people have or have access to a phone, a fridge, a television, a DVD player, and a computer. These societies also have welfare systems: many people receive benefits (in Australia and the UK it is possible not to work and still receive some money to live on, although this is becoming more difficult) and health support. All these factors keep people relatively content and contribute to a belief that Western democracy is the best system available at present. Even if you do not believe in it, it is relatively easy to survive, and it is easier to go with the system than against it.

◀ IDEOLOGY

Ideologies are sets of social values, ideas, beliefs, feelings, and representations by which people collectively make sense of the world they live in, thus constituting a world view. This world view is naturalised, a taken-for-granted, common-sense view about the way the world works.

Such ideas and beliefs are also maintained through a number of social institutions, one of which is the media. The media are a central arena in which consent is won and maintained by representation, agenda setting, and other mechanisms that position certain values, issues, and attributes as being important, desirable, natural, or normal. This argument informs many of the points made throughout this book and is illustrated in numerous examples. It is based around theories of ideology, hegemony, and discourse, which are explored in Part 3.

HOW THE MEDIA WORK

The media show us what the world is like; they make sense of the world for us

The processes of representation, interpretation, and evaluation are absolutely central to the media.

Representation

The media—press, radio, television, cinema, and so on—have become the arenas through which people receive most of their entertainment and information about the world, so they are the primary sources for how we see the world. Most of us have, for example, some idea of what the Himalayas are and what they look like, but this knowledge is most likely gained not from our actual experience of going there, but through representations: reading about them, hearing and watching media stories told about them, and viewing pictures of them.

Interpretation

In their representations, the media give information and then explanations, ways of understanding the world we live in. They take on an interpretative role, teaching us how to make sense of the world, of other people, and of ourselves.

Evaluation

In so doing, the media consistently privilege some issues and identities while devaluing others, thus giving an evaluative framework, a judgmental view of the information about the world that we receive.

These three processes can be understood in relation to gender and ethnicity, or race. The media teach us about masculinity and femininity, what it means to be a 'normal' man or woman; they teach us about race relations, about non-European and European cultures, about the supposedly typical characteristics of these groups. In the social roles that they assign to women and men, and to people of different ethnicities, in the desirable and undesirable stereotypes that they continually present, the media provide a structure, framework, and pattern for understanding ethnicity and gender issues. This is not to say that the media set out with this educational—teaching—agenda in mind, or that they are necessarily even conscious of what they are doing, but the influence they have on us as we grow up, reading and consuming the media, gives us these patterns that explain how we will see ourselves and others, how we will understand gender, race, and our own identities as men or women with particular national, cultural, and religious identities. This is the politics of representation. As film studies professor Richard Dyer says, 'How we are seen determines in part how we are treated, how we treat others is based on how we see them; such seeing comes from representation' (Dyer 1993, p. 1).

Of course it is possible for the media to give many different explanations of the world, many contrasting ways of making sense of masculinity and femininity and other aspects of **identity**, but this book argues that across the major media outlets there is a tendency to give broadly similar views of the world, what we call later a discourse (see pp. 61–2) on masculinity and femininity, that outweighs other viewpoints and sets up a particular view of what 'normal' gendered behaviour is.

IDENTITY ▶

Refers to selfhood, to the characteristics and qualities that uniquely distinguish a person, a group, or a thing from others. The meaning of the term 'identity' is connected to difference (being identifiably unique) and sameness (being identical to oneself, having an essence or personality or qualities that do not change over time).

Media products do not show or present the real world; they construct and represent reality

Many media products represent the real world, but these media products are not the real world itself; they are *representations* or *constructions* of the world. This point is also crucial and is explored in depth in Chapters 4 and 5. Media studies examines how the media constructs reality and then explores the values, beliefs, and feelings that these constructions present to us.

The media are just one of the ways people make sense of the world

The media are not the only social forces to make sense of the world for us, nor do they have total control over how we see and think about the world. They combine with other forces of socialisation. Most significant for children will be the socialisation they receive through their family, religious, and education systems, which teach them how to understand and act in the world. As we grow up, other views about how to behave, about social morality, are disseminated through a whole range of legal, cultural, and political forces. The media provide just one of the arenas in which these views are presented and popularised. The media generally act to reinforce values that are part of the whole society.

The media are created, owned, and controlled by certain groups who make sense of society on behalf of others

Those people who create, own, and control the media are media producers. They are not a totally separate social group, since they are also part of the audience and of society as a whole, but they are a small, elite group, a complex group of people that includes:

- owners and business managers, who are concerned primarily with the need for the media to make profits
- creative personnel, such as writers, directors, cinematographers, and webmasters
- technicians, who run the equipment and machinery.

These categories overlap in a number of ways; for example, many technical jobs are also creative, some managers have creative interests and abilities, and most creators are aware of financial needs and constraints and need to make a living. But note that:

- despite the fact that there is a small, limited number of media producers, they speak to, and on behalf of, the whole society (addressing a broad cross-section of the public)
- those people with the most media power—particularly financial and creative power—are an even smaller group
- those groups that make sense of society on behalf of others are predominantly white, middle class, and male. Without suggesting any conspiracy here, the media have a tendency to make sense of the world from this very particular point of view.

The need for popularity

As an antidote to the notion of a powerful elite in charge of the media, note that the media have to sell themselves successfully to large numbers of the population: they have to win big audiences in order to be economically viable and to survive. This need for popularity complicates, and adds a twist to, the power of the white, middle class males. If people do not like a product, they will look elsewhere for one, so the media must satisfy their popular audience, which is predominantly working class and about 50 per cent female. It could be argued that audiences influence, if not control, media output through their choices of which media products to consume.

When commercial television was first introduced into Western societies, audiences quickly turned to those channels that offered the entertainment they liked best, particularly game shows and soap operas. There was a major move away from public television stations—the ABC in Australia and the BBC in the UK—that offered many programs with middle class and highbrow values. These channels have continually struggled with the need to maintain ratings and present programming that satisfies their mass audiences.

The ABC is still regarded by many as elitist because it privileges high-cultural texts, although it can also be seen as offering an important alternative to mainstream programming. (It also includes many British shows, compared to the predominantly American content offered on commercial channels.)

Analysing the role and position of popular culture in a way that considers its products and the ways audiences, or consumers, use them is complex. The media were described by the Frankfurt School as a 'consciousness industry' that performs a kind of social control in keeping the masses ordered, but some cultural studies critics see them as a potential source of democracy and empowerment for the people.

This contradiction is illuminated by two different approaches to defining popular culture. The first defines popular culture as those cultural pursuits that are *of* or *from* the people, that is, they are produced organically by the people themselves (this definition was most often used when describing earlier folk culture activities such as songs and dances). In a modern context, the notion that popular culture is the culture of the people rests on the idea that ratings and other feedback mechanisms ensure the content of television and other media forms is at least partly determined by what the people (the consumers) want. The second approach defines popular culture as *for* the people, which suggests that something is handed to them that they accept. There is a big difference between that which is *of* and *from* and that which is *for* the people, a difference that is useful in thinking about the power of the media and whether this lies mainly with the producers or with the users/audiences/consumers, whether the content of the media derives from the culture of social elites or from the culture of larger social groups, the people. As usual, there is no simple answer in media studies; elements of both may be found bound together.

THE ACRONYM SEARCH

Looking at the social role of the media means being interested in the social values and beliefs of media texts—their ideology. The acronym SEARCH foregrounds social issues and social differences. Most of the letters stand for a way of socially categorising people, and each category usually includes both the socially advantaged and disadvantaged, as follows.

'S' stands for sex, sexual orientation, and gender. In comparison to women, men are a socially advantaged group in modern societies. Men have more social power and control than women, and there is still discrimination against women. There is also discrimination on the basis of people's sexual preference or sexual orientation—that is, whom they are sexually attracted to. Heterosexuality is seen as the norm, while homosexuality, lesbianism, transsexuality, and bisexuality are seen by mainstream culture as deviant, making those who are not heterosexual another disadvantaged group.

'E' stands for environment. Environment is an element that provides a broader context in which all the key elements in the SEARCH acronym are situated. Our society at present faces a global environmental crisis above and beyond purely human social issues. It's important to see how the media portray the environment today, how they encourage us to make sense of the world ecologically. The media seem to celebrate the natural and non-human world in many ways—notice how often animals are used positively in advertisements. Yet human growth continues to threaten the planet and the media often contribute to this by fuelling consumption. Media advertising encourages us to buy over-packaged, over-processed products that damage the environment, causing waste and pollution in the processes of their production and consumption.

'A' stands for age. Society is made up of people of all ages, but many societies have ageist aspects to them in that the elderly and young people are treated as second-class citizens.

'R' stands for race and religion. The world is made up of different ethnic and religious groups; most modern societies are multicultural or multi-ethnic. Historically, however, some races or ethnic groups have dominated and exploited others, in particular through colonialism and imperialism. Racial inequalities and conflict persist, and we can see the existence of dominant and subordinate racial groups, as well as negative attitudes and stereotypes that are directed at some ethnic groups. Religious conflict is also significant in some cultural struggles.

'C' stands for class. Modern societies have been described as consisting of three classes: the upper or ruling class, the middle class, and the lower or working class. The upper or ruling class is the smallest in numbers and is the most socially advantaged or privileged, while the lower or working class is the largest in numbers and the most socially disadvantaged. Definitions of class are usually framed in terms of the power (and wealth) and/or the cultural values of a person. These definitions are complex and more difficult to use today than previously, as societies have become much more fluid in terms of social class. In other words, it is now less easy to categorise people according to class. Nevertheless, it is worth noting that modern industrial societies, in the wake of increased and continuing high levels of unemployment, now use the term 'underclass' to describe a significant portion of the unemployed population, and it is clear that society still has broad divisions in terms of wealth, money, and wages, as well as what are regarded as acceptable cultural values. So it is still useful to employ this category in understanding society. Australia is significantly different from the UK in relation to class as Australia aspires to an egalitarian ideal of mateship (although this carries an obvious masculine bias); nevertheless, there are still significant differences in terms of wealth and power between different groups of people.

'H' stands for handicap. Handicapped and disabled people (also known as differently abled people—note how different words and labels, *different discourses*, carry different associations) are another social group that are disadvantaged and discriminated against in various ways. Systematic absence from media representations can also be a form of discrimination because it gives the invisible group the message that they are not valued or noticed by society, an attitude that is absorbed by most other people in society.

Other categories (height, weight, hair colour, for example) could be used as markers of normality or deviancy, but these six (sex, age, race, religion, class, and handicap) are particularly useful for drawing attention to social discrimination.

Using SEARCH

We use SEARCH as a tool to search for the assumptions underpinning many conventional views of the world, to wake us up to social inequality and the ecological problems that we must search for ways to resolve. You can use the acronym SEARCH to analyse media texts, and to understand how you and others are socially represented, categorised, and positioned in the following way.

1   Consider how you are placed in relation to these six categories. How does it feel to be in these positions, and how well represented are you in the media?

2   How do the media represent the world in relation to these six categories? Ask the following questions of specific media texts/images, using SEARCH as an approach.

a   How does each media text or image represent the environment, class, race, religion, age, gender, and (dis)ability?

b   What would each media text or image look like to a working class person, a person of non-European descent, an elderly person, a woman, a homosexual person, a person with a disability, and a person concerned with the survival of endangered species?

c   Do the media give a privileged view of some groups over others, showing some groups as advantaged, others as disadvantaged?

3   Look at Figures 3.1 and 3.2. What views of age and disability are presented in these two images?

Figure 3.1 *RED* poster

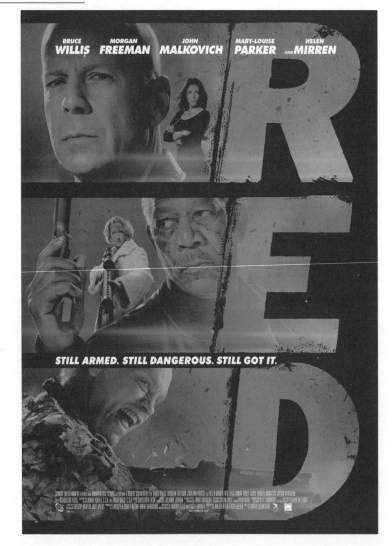

Figure 3.2 'Let's End the Awkward' campaign poster

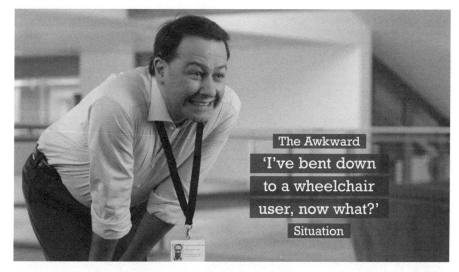

RED (an acronym for Retired and Extremely Dangerous) is a film based on the DC comic of the same name, directed by Robert Schwentke (2010) (Figure 3.1). The film challenges ageist stereotypes and playfully acknowledges previous heroic roles played by its stars as it follows the daredevil exploits of a former black ops CIA agent (played by Bruce Willis) and his highly skilled, lethal accomplices (played by Helen Mirren and Morgan Freeman). The 'Let's End the Awkward' campaign (Figure 3.2) was developed in response to a survey that found most people feel uncomfortable or awkward talking to differently abled people because they are worried about inadvertently causing offence by saying or doing the wrong thing. The campaign, fronted by disabled TV comedian Alex Brooke, targets socially aware young people and shows how to overcome awkward situations such as trying to chat up a deaf person at a bar or crouching down to speak to a person in a wheelchair eye to eye.

An article in the *Australian* titled 'Disability Support Pension Burden Hits $17bn a Year' (by David Crowe, 2 November 2015) brings together identity categories such as disability and age, and implies that people in these sectors of the population are 'burdensome'. On one hand, the article suggests that disability welfare claims must be fraudulent because the proportion of the population receiving the pension has outpaced population growth; on the other hand, it acknowledges that the ageing population and changing retirement ages mean that more people legitimately need the pension. In the public comments posted online in response to the story, religion was also invoked, thereby positioning disability as a threat to society and linking it to multiple forms of prejudice. For example, a person called 'Col' referred to members of a militant Islamic organisation receiving disability support pension payments when he commented, 'I wonder how many people who receive benefits belong to Hizb ut-Tahrir?'

These three examples present radically different perspectives on age and ability: in each instance, the acronym SEARCH can help identify the social role of the media, the assumptions embedded in media texts, and the way the text addresses its audience and positions us in relation to particular identity categories.

MEDIA AND SOCIETY

The big question we keep returning to is how, or whether, the media affect and influence us. We like the way Kerry Millard's cartoon in Figure 3.3 presents both sides of the argument.

Figure 3.3 Millard cartoon

Source: Kerry Millard 1996; published in *Australian Lawyer* November 1996

Do the media reflect or affect the world?

Traditionally, two models have been suggested as ways to understand the relationship between media and society. The first suggests that the media reflect the realities, values, and norms of a society. Thus, if we want to study a society we could turn to its media—its films, novels, television series, magazines, and popular stories—which will reflect to us what people feel and think, how they behave, and so on. But the media themselves do not directly affect society; they simply act as a mirror of society or a window on the world that can be used as a resource to understand the society. The second model suggests that the media do affect what people think, what they believe, and how they behave. The media construct our values for us and have a direct effect on our actions. We will examine both models.

The media as a reflection of society

Do the media change the world?

The main argument against the notion that the media reflect the already-existing norms, values, and realities of society is that the media construct and change events, rather than just reflecting them. Think about events that happen in the real world but are also presented extensively in the media—events such as the royal wedding of Prince William and Kate Middleton, the Academy Awards ceremonies, and sports events like the Olympic Games, the World Cup, and the Melbourne Cup. These events happen independently of the media, but the media build them into something more, into media events, constructing rather than just reflecting them (Ciu 2003).

The Melbourne Cup is an Australian horse race that is celebrated nationally (and, more recently, internationally, thanks to worldwide media coverage) as 'the race that stops a nation'. This is presented in the present tense, as though it has always and will always be true. Historically the race dates back only to the nineteenth century, but more importantly, stopping the nation only became a real possibility once media communication could transmit this event live across the nation, through the telegraph, then radio, then television. At this point the media allow the possibility of a simultaneously shared, national event (the significance of the Melbourne Cup relates to Australia's search for national identity). Events that bring the nation together into what cultural analyst Benedict Anderson (1983) calls an 'imagined community' help Australians to define themselves and their culture. Two national character aspects celebrated in the case of the Melbourne Cup are the triumph of leisure over work and the pleasure of gambling. We can think of few other countries that make a horse race such a significant national event.

The media hype up the significance of such events. Newspapers, radio, and television networks start reporting and speculating on the Melbourne Cup several weeks in advance. (It fits neatly into the annual sports calendar by taking place in early November after the Australian football and rugby seasons have ended, and before the cricket, tennis, and other summer sports seasons are fully underway, so there is plenty of media space available for it.) It becomes a feature on non-sports media programs, a major news event, so that, for example, ABC Radio National news programs actually broadcast from the race meeting. The speculation about who will win the race is linked to gambling and commercialism; participation in the event means being involved in some form of a bet.

Two points emerge from this media event.

1   'Stopping the nation' is only possible via the media, so we can say that the media construct this event rather than reflecting it.

2   If you are a regular media consumer, you should 'naturally' be interested in this event, particularly if you identify yourself as Australian. Indeed, the media suggest that not being interested in the race would mean being un-Australian.

The second point relates to how the media construct and shape our actions, our sense of who we are, our daily and annual routines. This is an example of the way people live in the media-world. The media contribute to the construction of a calendar of annual events. Such constructions are not new: throughout history, societies have organised themselves around cyclical events, mainly religious holidays and festivals linked in some way to the change of seasons, and the practices and rituals of food gathering. These practices have changed with the process of industrialisation so that holidays and rituals are now organised to suit the needs of an industrial society. The biggest annual Western media event is Christmas, but other occasions have also become media events. Valentine's Day, Mother's Day, and Father's Day have all become part of the social and media calendar. These three days are commercialised through the buying and sending of cards and presents, so promotion of them through the media is important financially. Gradually almost every week and every day of the year has become designated as a particular event or linked to a particular cause, and the media are central transmitters of and publicists for them.

Christmas comes earlier each year, occasions such as the Academy Awards—a wonderful piece of media self-promotion—are increasingly big media events. Knowing who the winners and losers are, what they wore, and with whom they attended becomes an important pieces of social knowledge, a sort of **cultural capital**, for social intercourse. Not knowing threatens mild social exclusion. Increased coverage is facilitated by improved technology (satellite link-ups) that allows the instant and cheap transmission of perfect images and sounds from continent to continent in a way not possible only a few years ago.

CULTURAL CAPITAL ▶

Like economic capital (money) and social capital (whom you know), cultural capital (assets such as accent, taste, appearance, clothing, and credentials) positions people in the social hierarchy. Possessing cultural capital functions to maintain and advance social status by delineating social groups and often reproducing social inequalities.

A process of selection is at work here. Some events are not promoted—for example, the African Football Cup of Nations, arguably the third most significant international soccer competition in the world after the World Cup and the European Championship, receives virtually no coverage or news reports in Australia outside SBS, the multicultural television channel. In contrast, American football and world Grand Prix motor racing receive extensive television coverage across the globe. Are these selections made on the basis of audience desires and choice, or on the basis of commercially driven interests? Motor racing was one of the last arenas still available to cigarette advertising and sponsorship in Australia. Why was it allowed to maintain this sponsorship? There are big commercial interest groups supporting and lobbying for media coverage.

Media recordings have also begun to determine how and when real events will take place. The links between sports and media are significant; each lives off and supports the other, a relationship that means sports tailor themselves to fit in with and benefit from media coverage. So, for example, when a goal is scored in Australian Rules football in televised matches, the umpires wait to see a light from the television channel indicating that the television advertisement is finished before restarting the game. Matches are also scheduled over weekends to fit in with and maximise television viewing times. Olympic Games coverage is organised around getting good television coverage and being able to present this across the world for peak-time viewing (in the USA and Europe). Because of this imperative, the marathon has been run at times best suited to worldwide television audiences, rather than athletes.

So far the arguments about reflection have considered how the media influence real-life situations; they cannot mirror or reflect them innocently, since they become part of the events and so change them. When we consider fictions, however, is the reflection model useful? Do fictions show outsiders what life is like in any particular society? Can we gain understanding of the USA, Africa, or Australia by looking at their television dramas? The reflection model is unsatisfactory here because it assumes that media products transparently reveal the truth about any society. Media fictions give us some useful information, but that information will always be limited.

The effects model

What sort of influence do the media have on audiences?

Part of the problem in discussing media effects research is what words to use to describe what the media do to us. 'Effects' is often used scientifically to suggest there is a precise response triggered by the media: we watch something and it makes us do something.

The word 'influence' is more useful in that it allows flexibility: we watch something and it encourages us to do or believe something. The term 'affect' is also useful as it can refer to change in a general sense, or can be used specifically to indicate the physiological dimensions of emotional responses (such as hair-raising fear, or the hot flush of embarrassment or shame).

For example 'neuromarketing' researchers have begun using functional magnetic resonance imaging (fMRI) and other scientific techniques to understand how the brain responds to films, and this media-effects market research is starting to be taken up by filmmakers and marketers to test and refine audience reactions to screen media (Andrejevic 2012). Knowledge about how the brain and the body respond to particular narrative and aesthetic techniques can help filmmakers enhance their craft in order to achieve desired audience responses. Neuroscience is being used for this purpose by 'brain testing' movie trailers for the major studios to maximise excitation, and help distributors market movies more effectively. The Academy of Motion Pictures has shown interest in this type of research by hosting the 2014 event 'Movies in Your Brain: The Science of Cinematic Perception', which brought filmmakers Darren Aronofsky and Walter Murch together with cognitive scientists Uri Hasson, Talma Hendler, and Tim Smith to explore emotional reactions to film, using eye-tracking and fMRI to investigate the effects of frame rate, editing, and visceral images on attention and brain activity.

The argument throughout this book is that the media can and do 'influence' us in many ways, so we generally use that term; however, we sometimes use the term 'effects' to indicate the direct or measurable 'results' of media consumption, such as the measurable changes to audience members' brains and bodies. We certainly need to be aware of the term 'media effects' because it is a key concept in the debates about the media's influence and power. The issue of media effects is also an important consideration in studies of media audiences. For this reason, we revisit the media effects debate in Chapter 6.

Some media-effects researchers have issued strong statements about the dangerous effects of violent media. Bushman and Huesmann, for example, write: 'The correlation between media violence and aggression is only slightly smaller than that between smoking and lung cancer' (Bushman & Huesmann, quoted in Singer & Singer 2001, pp. 234–5), and it is stronger than the correlation between condom use and the prevention of sexually transmitted HIV. Even when carefully designed experiments have been done to back up such claims, it is important to bear in mind the difference between *correlation* and *causation*. A correlation suggests that two things usually occur together, such as excessive consumption of junk food and obesity. Statistically, people who eat more junk food are fatter than people who eat less junk food. This is a strong correlation between a high-fat diet and obesity, but the reason for a particular person being overweight could also be that they have a thyroid imbalance, lead a sedentary lifestyle, or are genetically or metabolically predisposed to have a fuller figure. A causal relationship only exists when it can be proven that out of all the variables that affect people, one variable can be isolated as the culprit that definitely has a particular effect.

The documentary *Super Size Me* attempts to establish a causal relationship between McDonald's, obesity, and other health problems by eliminating all other food from the filmmaker's diet for a month. In the case of the Columbine school shootings, Michael Moore's award-winning documentary *Bowling for Columbine* prompted reflection on the media's role in creating a trigger-happy population in the USA. Moore suggested that by showing so much violence and crime, the media influence people to perceive the world as being a hostile place, to live in a state of fear, and thus to be more likely to own and use guns. However, the media cannot be isolated from other social influences such as family, community, education, and religion, and researchers have been unable to establish a direct causal relationship between media violence and aggression or other effects.

How is the effects issue popularly presented? In 2010, a story in the *Telegraph* newspaper with the headline 'Samsung Warns of Dangers of 3D Television' reported that the Korean electronics firm Samsung had issued health warnings to children, pregnant women, the elderly, and people with photosensitive epilepsy regarding the use of their television sets in 3D mode:

> To view television in 3D, users wear special glasses which bombard the eyes and brain with a succession of flashing images that appear for a fraction of a second. However, the technology puts unusual strain on the body, hence Samsung has advised viewers to take regular breaks to prevent suffering side effects.
>
> Samsung's statement, posted on its website, says: "Some viewers may experience an epileptic seizure or stroke when exposed to certain flashing images or lights contained in certain television pictures or video games. If you suffer from, or have a family history of epilepsy or strokes, please consult with a medical specialist before using the 3D function" (*The Telegraph* 2010).

Scientists have since conducted experiments and found no increased risk of seizures from 3D and, in cases where health effects do occur, they are not related to the subject matter (the content of the 3D film or television program), but rather to its form (the electronic transmission of light signals). Similar effects to those described in the newspaper report on 3D TV and films are found to occur as a result of stroboscopic flashing lights, which can produce epilepsy in some viewers. Indeed, for this reason Gaspar Noé's rape revenge film *Irréversible* (2004) comes with an epilepsy warning, as it includes nauseating pulsing lights and low-frequency sound effects intended to make the audience experience the physical disturbance—fear, nausea, and disorientation—felt by the characters in the narrative. The low-frequency effects that Noé employed are now increasingly common in films like the *Paranormal Activity* franchise, where the demon's growl is reportedly laced with sound so low that it is inaudible. Such sounds (infrasound) naturally occur in natural disasters like earthquakes and cyclones, and have the effect of making people feel cold, frightened, and disoriented. This is an example of the way the media can affect audience members on a physiological level. Psychological and direct behavioural effects of media content are much more difficult to measure.

The media can also produce effects in our behaviour through their technological forms. Our daily habits and lives have changed radically through the increase of media communication systems. The development of the media has made our lives faster, more sedentary, and more domestic: telephone and internet communication enables us to contact each other in an instant, and mobile phones have given teenagers and businesspeople more geographical freedom by enabling easy contact with friends, parents, or business associates when they are outside the home or office. We can deal with problems and communicate feelings across distances in a moment, and people no longer need to be able to do simple arithmetic because they have learnt how to use calculators. The use of word processors has had a major effect on writing practices, making it much easier to produce material that can easily be copied, changed, and rearranged. So the very pattern of our daily lives, in the media-world we live in, is structured differently due to media technologies. This is part of what American communications theorist Marshall McLuhan was getting at when he stated that 'the medium is the message' (McLuhan 1987, p. 7). Rather than concentrating on the content of messages, he wanted people to think about the media's technological forms and how they affect us.

But in relation to the question of effects, affects, and influence, it is the area of media content and the way this is presented that we now focus on in more detail. This is the area that raises most discussion and controversy. Another report in *Forbes*, with the headline 'The Disturbing Internet Footprint of Santa Barbara Shooter Elliot Rodger', shows how this argument is popularly presented, in relation to the tragic mass shooting of college students by the mentally disturbed son of a Hollywood director. The report reveals how media consumption and the use of social media were deeply implicated in these shootings, noting that Rodger posted threatening YouTube videos, subscribed to channels that feature violent media like the 'Red Wedding' slaughter scene from *Game of Thrones*, was a member of misogynistic online communities such as PUAHate.com, and also used computer-mediated communication and news media to publicise his vitriolic autobiographical manifesto:

> Rodger had subscribed to three different YouTube channels that gave advice on how to pick up women and be an "alpha male" … Rodger also authored a 141-page autobiography titled "My Twisted World," which was sent to a local news station. He describes the events of his life since birth, blaming an obsession with World of Warcraft for lack of social development in middle and early high school (*Forbes* 2014).

The implication here is that the media can foster hatred and aggression in susceptible people. Mass shootings are the product of much wider social conditions including gun control laws, and it is these that need consideration. At the same time, the media can be part of these social conditions. Watching news reports about suicide bombers, for example, might conceivably make someone who already feels depressed and disempowered become suicidal or homicidal, for reasons that may be easier to understand than being obsessed with World of Warcraft.

The relationship between the media and society regarding these issues is complex, and the influences on audiences might not always be what is expected. Rodger had publicly identified as an 'incel' (involuntary celibate) and used blogs, social media, and YouTube to encourage hatred of women and to publicise his intention to exact retribution for women's lack of sexual acquiescence. In response to Rodger's horrific actions, another blogger using the name 'Thatincelblogger' wrote:

> He could have flown anywhere in the world with the money he had, there were places where he could have found a good non-feminist wife. I have no idea why he didn't try that. The kid was scum, and so were those he killed. Spoiled, stupid brats. I have no pity for, as one commentator said "blonde sorority sisters in Isla Vista". These girls were bad, immoral trash. And so was he ('Thatincelblogger' 2014).

Should this statement that blondes, feminists, or privileged college students are 'immoral trash' and deserve to die because they choose not to have sex with men like Rodger or 'Thatincelblogger' be considered an act of political communication to be protected by freedom of expression in a democracy? Or is it hate speech that, as public policy scholar Katharine Gelber suggests, 'might harm the democratic conditions that permitted it to be heard' (2010, p. 318)? And what role might media regulations or studies of media effects play in helping to understand and ameliorate the social impact of such offensive language?

At a time when social media and online platforms have given citizens the ability to communicate their personal ideological and political opinions to a broad public, debates about hate speech and offensive language in the media have intensified. By comparison with other potentially harmful or offensive content such as representations of sex and violence, little research has been done regarding the effects of language in the media, and yet tragic cases such as the Santa Barbara massacre indicate the extent to which the media may foster a culture of hatred and violence.

Should there be some forms of media censorship? If so, who should make and control these decisions?

The effects issue is most often raised in relation to questions of sex and violence. The simple hypothesis is that media violence encourages violent behaviour in the audience, and that sex portrayed by the media can corrupt the audience. Even though research about media effects is inconclusive, it is often suggested that specific criminal acts have been prompted by watching media violence or pornography, an argument that is sometimes used in law courts. The logical answer for many people is to limit what can be seen through the use of censorship; however, as the quotation from *Scream* that opens this chapter suggests, the media are not responsible for making people bad. While accepting that the media can influence people and that society needs some forms of censorship, for example, of child pornography, we make the following points against increased censorship and against the use of the effects model to justify it.

1   People have some autonomy (self-control and self-determination) in how they behave; while we may imitate some things we learn from the media—what clothes to wear, use of language, and social interaction—we know what it means to be violent towards someone and are able to be careful about such actions. We are rational beings who can think about and reflect on what we see and do. We understand that media representations, stories, and images of violence are stories or fictions. We can make judgments about what we consume from the media; we do not respond automatically to what we see. We are adept at distinguishing between media representations that contain simulated images of violence (using pigs' blood and prosthetic wounds) and the real thing. Blaming the media is an excuse that denies our responsibility (and is often used to argue for lighter sentences for those charged with violent crimes).

2   It is important that people have access to information about real violence and sexuality because restricting such access and information can be socially and politically repressive. The Vietnam War is a great example of how media coverage can provide society with information that has political consequences. Media coverage of this war was a major influence in turning Americans, Europeans, and Australians against the war. We need to have full access to knowledge of events that have a direct influence on us. Since people rely on the media for information about distant

places and events, control of media representations can be remarkably effective in promoting particular beliefs and attitudes: to a certain extent, the media shape our perception.

There is also a question about how real violence is presented on television. Many people have raised concerns about so-called reality TV programs, such as MTV's *Teen Mom* and *Jersey Shore*, which broadcast their stars' physically aggressive altercations, and shows such as Fox's *Cops*, which deals with footage of actual police business and bad drivers. These types of programs have been criticised for the way they sensationalise violence.

One of the things you will be aware of as a media critic is how the language of the media—camera angles, music, editing, slow motion, and so on—can be used to present and manipulate events in particular ways; this language needs critical analysis.

3   The case around fictional sex and violence raises different questions. Censorship laws in Australia, the UK, and the USA all underwent extensive liberalisation in the 1960s. In South Africa, such reforms had different implications and came later, in the 1990s. Explicit sex and violence have become commonplace in fictional media, helped by improved technology and special effects that have made graphic portrayals, particularly of violence, ever more realistic and detailed. Reactions to this, and campaigns against media sex and violence, have been around since the 1970s, and debate about these issues continues. These developments raise the following questions: do we need censorship? Are there limits to what should be shown? Who should be allowed to see what? What boundaries do we need to draw in order to enable audience members to make informed choices about what they wish to be exposed to without undercutting the political and artistic advantages of freedom of expression and freedom of choice? How do we define the kind of characteristics or landscape that we want to have in the media-world we occupy? Who decides?

In the debate between libertarianism—giving people freedom of choice about what can be shown and seen—and state censorship and control of the media, Jane, Sarah, and I are inclined towards libertarianism. In an ideal world we would not need censorship, but this is not an ideal world; we need to protect people, particularly children, against images that abuse and harm them, or encourage such harm—we need some censorship and restrictions. Two arguments against censorship are made here.

1   The first relates to the value and importance of fantasy. Fictional stories, like dreams, allow us to explore and indulge in fantasies. Dreaming of attacking someone is not the same as doing it, yet many of us do dream of this at some time. Fictions allow us to explore and understand our sexual and violent feelings (see pp. 297–300). Child psychologist Bruno Bettelheim argues for the value of violent fairy tales for children, stating that fairy tales allow a space for the imagination to develop, and that banning fairy tales because they are monstrous and scary would keep the 'monster within the child unspoken of, hidden in the unconscious … Without such fantasies, the child fails to get to know his monster better, nor is he given suggestions as to how he may gain mastery over it' (Bettelheim 1978, p. 120).

2   The second argument suggests that censorship of violence or sexuality won't work. Censorship reflects a belief that if we control media images, we can control human

behaviour; if we stop showing violence, people will stop acting violently. But people act and feel violently towards one another for a variety of reasons. Anger caused by social oppression might be one such reason. The way to deal with such violence is not to censor the media, but to examine what is actually happening in society and try to deal with the deeper causes of anger and violence. Focusing attention on media violence and censorship distracts us from looking at the social problems that determine violence. If the violent feelings are really there, censorship won't make them go away anyway.

The same arguments apply to images of sexuality. In an ideal world, we would spend time understanding people's sexual and emotional feelings, rather than resorting to censorship. The media sometimes celebrate sexual feeling, but they also often point to the sexual problems and repression felt by many people. Censorship or fear of media images of sexuality raises the need to look more closely at our sexual feelings, to deal with these openly in the real world. We might even argue that there is too little sex in the media, too few programs that attempt to bring aspects of sexuality into more open debate.

The media effects debate is a contentious one because it becomes linked to political agendas. Many of those arguing that television violence has dangerous effects on its viewers are seeking to put forward conservative and restrictive censorship legislation. Civil liberty supporters are concerned about the possible erosion of democratic freedoms, so they argue there are no clearly proven direct effects that can be measured, that the media do not have a direct effect. The danger of following this second position is that we lose sight of the fact that in some way, media do affect and/or influence their audiences, although this may be hard to measure and quantify in relation to any individual viewer.

Music therapy is an obvious example. It is based on research showing that music (a form of media) can and does profoundly affect its listeners emotionally, but also in surprisingly physical and psychological ways. In his book *Musicophilia* (2011), physician and author Oliver Sacks explores many case studies where music has been successfully used to produce different feelings and states of mind and being, including helping patients with Parkinson's disease modulate jerky movements, and enabling patients with severe psychological and neurological disorders, including advanced dementia, to reconnect with human emotions and relationships otherwise lost in the course of their illnesses. If music can change or create different moods and feelings for listeners, it seems illogical to claim that audiences won't be affected by other media in some way. After all, why do companies invest such huge amounts of money in advertising and public relations campaigns?

We perhaps need to develop more subtle and sophisticated ways of studying and understanding media effects and influences. Some analysts have used the concept of 'compassion fatigue' to suggest that there is a cumulative effect of seeing so many news reports of world disasters, famines, and human suffering, which has resulted in our turning off some of our emotional responses—our feelings of compassion for these people and events—simply because they are too much, and there are too many, for us to cope with.

We conclude this discussion of the relationship between the media and society with a case study of media images of cigarettes and smoking.

CASE STUDY

The representation of cigarettes and smoking in film and television fictions

There is a clear belief among both tobacco companies and anti-smoking groups that tobacco advertising encourages people to smoke. Once Western governments realised that smoking was definitely harmful to health, they decided to ban cigarette and tobacco advertising in most media; however, it is still possible for people to be seen smoking in films and television dramas. In thinking about the overall question of media influence, we can approach this continued representation of smoking within screen texts in a number of ways: a *quantitative* content analysis to measure how frequently smoking is portrayed onscreen; a *qualitative* analysis to assess what the situations and emotions are when people smoke onscreen; research into the *effects/ influence* of these images; and research and questioning as to *how and why* smoking is included as part of the scripts. As media researchers, you can devise and carry out work in all these areas.

Smoking: quantitative content analysis

Some people are concerned that the simple amount or quantity of onscreen smoking we see is significant.

An extensive content analysis study conducted at the University of California found that 'In films of the 1950s there was an average of 10.7 [smoking] incidents per hour. Pressure from lobby groups saw this figure fall to 4.9 between 1980 and 1982, but by 2002 the total had risen to 10.9'. The study suggests that the recent rise in 'smoking incidents' in films has 'allowed manufacturers to overcome restrictions on tobacco advertising'. Additionally, Professor Stanton Glantz argues that 'This is particularly worrying in the light of research that shows that young people are taking up smoking because of what they see on the big screen' (Glantz 2004).

Smoking: qualitative analysis

What do you feel and think when you see characters in films smoking?

A qualitative analysis would look in more detail at who is smoking, what situations they smoke in, and how this is filmed. The point here is that it's not a question of how many times we see smoking, as it all depends on how each smoking incident is portrayed. Anti-smoking advertisements might well, for example, show people smoking in such a way as to link it with unpleasant behaviour, or sickness and disease.

1 Who smokes? Is it the main characters or secondary characters? Men or women? Young or old people? Healthy or unhealthy? Heroes or villains? Does it make a difference whether the smoking character is a hero or villain? When Charlize Theron's character smokes in *Monster*, it can be argued this is not harmful to audiences because she is playing a psychotic killer whom we are not encouraged to emulate, whereas if James Bond, or the Hobbits from *Lord of the Rings*, or Benedict Cumberbatch as Alan Turing in *The Imitation Game* smoke, this is more dangerous because they are positive heroes whom we are encouraged to admire and identify with (although it's worth noting that audiences often admire villains too and Theron, playing Aileen Wuornos, is in a way the hero of the film).

2 It's useful to examine what prompts characters to smoke, and where and when they light up. Do pleasant or unpleasant things happen to people when they smoke? How are they feeling as they

Continued on next page ▶

smoke? We see Nicole Kidman smoking as Virginia Woolf throughout *The Hours*, and Cate Blanchett smoking as the troubled socialite Jasmine in *Blue Jasmine*, but these portrayals of stressed and mentally unstable smokers might suggest a negative link between stress and mental instability, and smoking. On the other hand, until Pierce (Chevy Chase) 'cures' her with hypnosis, we often see Britta (Gillian Jacobs) in season one of *Community* lighting up in moments of stress as a way of dealing with anxiety, and she is clearly identified as the positive heroine of the series. Audiences might link smoking with this positive character and see it as an action that can help in difficult circumstances. One of the most common clichés links smoking with sexuality and pleasure: sharing cigarettes can be a metaphor for shared sexual attraction.

3   How is smoking filmed? The way we see cigarette smoking presented will also influence us. It is quite common to focus on glamorous close-ups of cigarettes being lit, the flame of the match, the warm glow of the tobacco, or the actual inhalation by beautiful lips. Smoking in these circumstances is foregrounded; at other times, it may be much more in the background. We often see the 'beautiful' visual effects of smoke drifting across the screen, illuminated by subtle backlighting. But we could see nicotine-stained fingers and teeth, an ugly mouth, or harsh lighting—the kinds of images used in anti-smoking campaigns (see Figure 3.4). Whatever techniques are used will associate different feelings with smoking, drawing our attention to it in different ways, and giving it more or less attention.

Figure 3.4 Anti-smoking poster

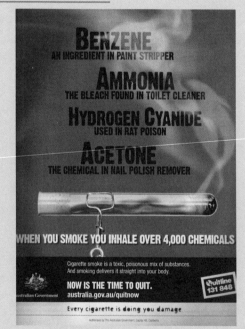

Source: '4000 Chemicals' © Commonwealth of Australia, Department of Health and Ageing; reproduced courtesy of National Tobacco Youth Campaign

All of the above elements need to be considered if we are to try to understand the qualitative associations behind representations of smoking, rather than just quantifying the incidence or prevalence of smoking in popular culture. Government public health campaigns, such as the public service announcement in Figure 3.4, actively work to counteract the influence of repeated and glamorous representations of smoking in the media. Such campaigns provide factual information to audiences so that they are better able to make informed decisions about smoking.

Research into the influence and effects of seeing smoking onscreen

This is an area of audience research, and, as we have already discussed, it is very difficult to prove any simple and direct effects from seeing smoking onscreen since there are so many variables to consider. It might be useful to look at smoking statistics to find out who is smoking and how much. It seems that despite the knowledge about the health dangers of smoking, many young people (particularly a rising number of teenage girls) continue to take up smoking. It's also worth noting that from a marketing point of view, cigarette companies target young people because this is when most people actually start smoking and are at their healthiest, so they really want to make smoking seem attractive to this group.

Why do writers and filmmakers include smoking in films and television?

This is an interesting question. As potential writers and filmmakers, you might consider whether you would include smoking in your scripts. There are a number of possible responses.

1   Realism. Some filmmakers argue that if you are aiming to reflect and portray real life in your dramas, then you have to include smoking since many people do or did smoke. Emma Stone plays the character Grace Faraday in the film *Gangster Squad*, which is set in Los Angeles in the 1940s and 1950s. Most women of her age and class did smoke at that time. Similarly, in *An Education* starring Carey Mulligan as the teenage Jenny Mellor preparing to attend Oxford University in the 1960s, smoking cigarettes depicted sophistication for young women of a certain social class during that time. In *Mad Men*, the American television drama set in the 1960s, smoking is prevalent among many of the characters. Another example is the BBC television drama *Call the Midwife*. It is set in the 1950s and smoking here represents historical authenticity. If you didn't show smoking in these examples, they might seem unrealistic.

Some filmmakers choose not to show smoking in order to be socially responsible. In Lauren Weisberger's novel *The Devil Wears Prada*, smoking is an integral part of the heroine's lifestyle and character from page 2 of the book: 'Attempting to drive this $84000 stick-shift convertible through the obstacle-fraught streets of midtown at lunchtime pretty much demanded that I smoke a cigarette ... I raised a shaking hand to give him the finger and then turned my attention to the business at hand: getting nicotine coursing through my veins as quickly as possible.'

What message does this send to young women reading this?

In the film version, director David Frankel made a positive decision not to have any of his characters seen smoking, as he felt smoking onscreen encourages audiences to smoke. Likewise, Lindsay Doran,

Continued on next page   ▶

producer of the film *Stranger than Fiction* featuring Emma Thompson, chose to depict smoking as unattractive and unappealing, with Thompson's character consistently coughing from smoking. Woody Allen, however, refused to succumb to pressure from the Indian government mandate to show anti-smoking warnings before and during the filming of *Blue Jasmine*. As a result, he did not release *Blue Jasmine* in India.

PRODUCT PLACEMENT

Companies pay film and television producers to include their products in a story as a subtle form of advertising.

2   Money. A second and simple answer is that smoking onscreen is a direct financial result of cigarette companies paying for **product placement**: they pay a film production to include their product onscreen, thereby getting around the advertising ban, and providing film companies with much-needed funds for their ever-increasing costs. Sylvester Stallone has been quoted as admitting that 'As I discussed I guarantee that I will use Brown and Williamson (B & W) tobacco products in no less than five feature films. It is my understanding that Brown and Williamson will pay a fee of $500 000' (Department of Health, Western Australia 2004). Similarly, 'Philip Morris paid $42 000 to have Lois Lane smoke Marlboro cigarettes in *Superman II*' (Department of Health, Western Australia 2004). Product placement for tobacco companies is now being banned, but it remains common for many other products. Some argue that it is more effective and more insidious than direct advertising; since audiences don't realise they are being advertised to, it is more subtle. As audiences increasingly find ways of bypassing adverts—switching the sound down, leaving the room, using video-recording technology that leaves out the ads—product placement is an excellent way for companies to continue advertising. Filmmaking is a costly business, so you might well understand a filmmaker accepting this money. If a cigarette company offered to finance your film, would you take the money?

3   Aesthetics and narrative codes. Smoking is used first as an *aesthetic*, second as a *narrative* device. Aesthetically, smoking has wonderful visual potential. The wispy, semi-transparent movement of smoke or mist across the screen has an enormous atmospheric quality: it creates movement, depth, and mood; it can suggest mystery, horror, or romance. Look at any film by Ridley Scott (or his earlier advertisements) to see how he uses smoke to create atmosphere.

Smoking can also be an excellent shorthand sign system for developing characters and narratives. Since films started, cigarettes, cigars, pipes, and cigarette-holders have been used as props that tell you something about a character and contribute to a story's development. See how Helena Bonham Carter's character in *Fight Club* uses smoking to show her reckless, dangerous, sexual appeal, or how Angelina Jolie's character smokes in *Girl Interrupted* to illustrate her mental instability and edginess. The predominant representations of smoking onscreen in the past have shown it as sexy, cool, and glamorous; there is a culturally coded history, which many people have grown up with, that demonstrates this. The point we want to stress is that filmmakers may use smoking purely as an aesthetic and narrative device that has little to do with actual smoking. You may be against real smoking, but in the narrative world of film, smoking is just a sign system; even non-smokers such as ourselves can enjoy Bette Davis and Paul Henreid lighting up together at the end of *Now, Voyager*.

This example focusing on representations of smoking illustrates that the media's influence on society is complex and multilayered. The media can influence behaviour and attitudes, and these effects need to be considered in terms of media ethics, control, and persuasive impact, in addition to analysing media content.

CONCLUSION

We hope you are beginning to see some of the complexities of the media–world relationship, and the issues of whether and how the media both reflect and influence society. We suggest that Figure 3.5 is a way of understanding this double aspect of the media. In this model, media producers, media texts, and media audiences are separated from popular common sense. The media producers, in constructing their images and stories, are reflecting various social ideas and beliefs that are held by different social groups. The audiences consuming these media texts are partially influenced and affected by what they see. These influences then contribute to the overall social fabric of popular, common-sense ideas.

But media producers, texts and audiences are all part of the social whole; they are not separate entities. The media are one of the social forces that produce popular common sense, the general social beliefs and feelings of a society. In turn, these social beliefs and values influence the media, which reflect them. Like the chicken and the egg, there is no simple answer as to which comes first—media representations or popular common sense—the two are permanently intertwined. What is more, in today's media-world, media images and reality often blur together: we begin to see real events in relation to familiar media images. Thus, the Gulf War was said to look like a video game, and Associated Press news reports of the 2011 Japanese tsunami had headlines such as 'Japan Looks Like "Hollywood Disaster Movie"', stating that the television images 'resemble scenes from a Hollywood disaster movie. Powerful waves, filled with debris. Uncontrolled fires.

Figure 3.5 Model of the media–world relationship

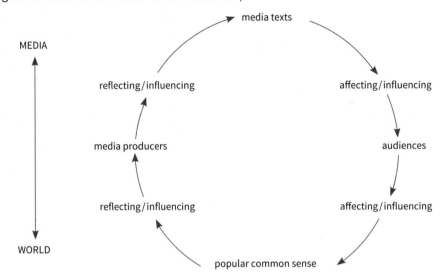

A ship caught in a massive whirlpool' <archive.wbir.com/news/article/161163/16/Japanese-official-says-reactor-not-damaged-after-explosion>.

This chapter has

- considered some of the conditions of contemporary global society
- explored how the media work through making sense, constructing reality, and being popular
- introduced the term 'SEARCH'
- considered whether the media reflect or affect the world
- explored effects models in media studies
- examined media representations of cigarette smoking.

? DISCUSSION POINTS

1 In thinking about popular culture and media products, would you argue that we get what we want, or we want what we get?
2 Do you think programs such as *MasterChef* are *of* the people or *for* the people? What examples would you argue fit into these two categories?
3 Look out for particular media events. How do the media construct them? How involved in these events are you?
4 How would you argue for and against forms of media censorship? What forms of censorship would you argue for (if any), and for whom?

SUMMARY

You should now be able to

- comment critically on the media's role in relation to some of the major crises and conflicts in contemporary society; for instance, discuss and comment on the media's coverage of the conflict in Syria
- explain general principles of how the media function and discuss these principles
- consider the importance and effects of the media's need for popularity
- apply the acronym SEARCH to media representations
- discuss arguments about whether and/or how the media affect and influence people
- define and illustrate the terms 'product placement' and 'cultural capital'
- discuss the pros and cons of media censorship
- analyse fictional representations of smoking.

CHAPTER 4

What's in a Name? Language and the Social Construction of Reality

We don't speak language, language speaks us.

Martin Heidegger

All words are pegs to hang ideas on.

Henry Ward Beecher

This chapter explores how language structures the way we understand the world by
- offering insight into the politics of naming
- demonstrating that language is not natural or neutral
- exploring the ways in which language is a changing site of power and struggle
- looking at examples of language in use in social contexts and in the media.

A central argument of this book is that media representations are constructions based on language. This chapter examines the nature of language, and relates it to ideas about human societies as a whole and to the 'social construction of reality'. What we say about language in general can then be applied specifically to the media.

Here, in a nutshell, are our arguments.

1. Human societies organise and structure the world in particular ways.
2. In so doing, they construct the world and they construct reality.
3. This reality tends to become normalised and naturalised so that it is taken for granted—'that's life'—by the people in that society.
4. We tend to forget that reality has been constructed and that it could be organised differently.
5. We learn about the world primarily through language; thus language is crucial both in this construction and in the transmission of this construction to others.

It is very important to note that this argument means that, like the media, reality—the social world we live in—is also a construction. The naturalisation of social construction blinds us to the fact of human agency in constructing the realities we inhabit. Throughout this book, we ask you to be aware and wary whenever the terms 'natural' or 'normal' are used. These words are often used to naturalise forms of behaviour or social organisation so that people don't question them, but we argue there is nothing natural about the way that human societies are organised. All our actions and behaviours are acted out in social situations and institutions that are the product of human cultures, not of nature. This is not to say that they haven't evolved in relation to natural climatic, cyclical, and geographical conditions, nor is it to say that there is something wrong with these practices, but they are not 'natural' in the sense of being behavioural patterns that inevitably or necessarily arise from human physiology.

WHAT'S IN A NAME? THE LINGUISTIC POLITICS OF NAMING

Does language describe or interpret the world?   (▶)

Language, as the primary means of communication, is the central medium used for the understanding, interpretation, and construction of reality.

It is necessary to consider for a moment the nature of language and the relationship it has to the world. There are two theories for thinking about the relationship between language and the world.

1   Reflective or mimetic. This suggests that language simply describes the world, that it is a method used to name and describe what already exists. According to this theory, all humans see the world in the same way and share the same basic concepts; language is simply a vehicle for expressing these concepts and the world that exists independently of it.

2   Constructionist. This suggests that language doesn't describe a pre-existing world. Rather, it constructs the world through naming it, and constructs the concepts through which we understand life and the world. Thus different languages represent the world in different ways, and speakers of one language understand and experience the world in ways peculiar to that language and differently from the way of speakers of a different language. This is not to deny the reality of the material world, or that it pre-dates language, but to say that it is only apprehended, only understood, once it has been named, or constructed, through language. All knowledge of reality is mediated by language. Our experiences of the world take form only when presented through language.

Christian mythology illustrates the power of the word, of language, as a means of giving life and structure to the world: 'In the beginning was the word and the word was God'. One of Adam's first tasks was to name all the animals and plants, thus giving them substance or calling them into existence. The Bible tells us that language brings things into being. But there is not just one language, not just one way of describing the world. Anyone who has learnt a second language knows that the two languages do not correspond exactly, word for word. Different languages have different ways of describing or naming the world. Inuit language, for example, has as many as twenty-seven words for describing forms of snow, whereas English has just two or three (Hall 1997, pp. 21–44). Reality can be named by language in different ways.

Colour is a good example. Although the spectrum of colours is a continuum along which there are countless variations of colour, through language we name this spectrum and structure it in a particular way. We simplify the spectrum into seven colours, which enables us to handle and describe it, even though we might find it impossible to point precisely to the place where red becomes orange, or orange becomes yellow. But the seven-colour system we use is just one possibility. We could break the spectrum into six colours, combining indigo and violet into purple, or nine colours, adding turquoise or teal, aqua or ochre, and if our language did this, we would even begin to see the spectrum differently. So our words structure the world in particular ways in order to make sense of it.

If the reflective or mimetic method described above was correct, then there would be either one universal language that perfectly described the world, or different languages that corresponded exactly so that there were always exactly equivalent words in every language. This is not the case.

Not only do different languages carry slightly different meanings, but there are also differences in such things as the ways tenses are used, and the use of verbs or nouns to describe things. Different languages structure the world in quite different ways. German, for example, is a gendered language with different words for 'the' depending on the gender, number, and case of the noun. (*Der* is the masculine, singular, nominative form of 'the' used for phrases such as *der Junge* 'the boy'; *die* is the feminine or plural nominative and accusative; and *das* is neuter, singular, nominative, and accusative).

There is an anecdote about a Japanese company that wanted to mount an advertising campaign for selling razors for women to shave their underarm hair. The company used an American advertising agency, which devised a cartoon campaign that featured an octopus shaving under its eight arms. When the commercial was ready, the Americans showed it to staff of the Japanese company. The staff were taken aback and shocked, and refused to accept the campaign. The problem was that in Japanese culture, an octopus does not have eight arms, it has eight legs!

This story illustrates the idea that whatever language we are born into structures the way we see and understand the world. This is the basis of the Sapir–Whorf hypothesis:

> At the heart of the Sapir–Whorf hypothesis is the claim that the very words we speak and the grammatical structures we use actually influence or determine the way we think. In this light, language is not just a means of communicating ideas, it actually helps fashion them (Open University 1981, p. 72).

Do we speak language or does language speak us?

Our view of the world expands as our language capacity expands. We might say that we don't speak language, language speaks us. This, indeed, is one of the main tenets of the work of linguist and anthropologist Edward Sapir and his student Benjamin Whorf, and of structural linguistics. The Sapir–Whorf hypothesis suggests that language constructs our identity, that we are cogs in the machine of language. This hypothesis has been interpreted in two ways:

- our language determines our thinking
- our language merely influences our thinking.

The second interpretation gives us a degree of autonomy. It is worth noting that if we discover new things or new feelings, we have to invent new words in order to describe them, and this gives us further autonomy.

In this book, we accept the constructionist position, as opposed to the mimetic position, and argue that language enables us to think and to understand. It gives shape to our perceptions and feelings by giving them labels. It is a system of *representation*, a term discussed below (see pp. 68–9). The whole process of language is a naming or labelling process that carries profound social and political implications.

Imagine two people engaged in sexual activity. How would you describe or name what they are doing?

- They are making love.
- They have gone to bed together.
- They are having sexual intercourse.
- They are fucking.
- They are fornicating.

All of these describe what is happening, but each carries a different set of connotations, associations, and feelings; they construct different discourses (see pp. 61–2). The first description emphasises the romantic feelings involved, while the second is euphemistic, letting us imagine what is actually happening. The third takes a clinical or medical view, while the fourth has a cruder, more derogatory feeling associated with slang. The last use of language has moral and biblical undertones, suggesting that the two people are unmarried and therefore what they are doing is bad. None of the descriptions is wrong; they all invite us to view and understand what is happening in different ways. There is no way of describing what is happening that does not carry a particular view of the action. Language is not natural, neutral, or static. It is arbitrary, value laden, charged with power relations, and dynamic.

NAMES AS AN EXAMPLE OF CONSTRUCTED IDENTITIES

It may seem obvious to you that your name is part of yourself, but names are given quite arbitrarily and different names may cause us to think differently about ourselves, to see ourselves in a particular way. I, Michael, was born in London, England and most of the kids at my school were white and English. My name, Michael O'Shaughnessy, marked me as an outsider because both my Christian/given name and my surname are particularly Irish. (Note that calling a first name a 'Christian name' places you in a particular cultural and religious tradition, while your 'surname' probably identifies you with your father rather than your mother, thus structuring you into patriarchy.) At school I was called a 'wild Irishman' (in a friendly way). This label, given to me by my English teachers and classmates, reinforced a stereotype of Irish wildness and Irish savagery, which gave me a sense of who I was. I saw myself as having a wild streak and came to see myself as different, as an outsider. Such an identity allowed me to adopt a critical view of England and Englishness at the same time as being a part of that culture. Had I grown up in the same place but been named John Smith or Sebastian Courteney-Smythe, I suspect my character and my values would probably have been markedly different, and in many ways I am pleased with my non-English identity: because the Irish aren't seen as 'Pommies' it feels easier to be an Irish-Australian than an English-Australian (see the discussion on interpellation, pp. 68–9).

People often have a number of different names: first names, diminutives, family names, nicknames, and so on. All of these construct us differently and are used by other people to construct our identity in their eyes. They also allow us a number of different personalities. In work situations, hierarchical positions can be reinforced by the use of names. Because using someone's surname indicates formality and respect, those in junior positions may address those in senior positions by their surnames (although this is, of course, dependent on the culture of the organisation). Conversely, because using someone's first name is a sign of familiarity and informality, those in senior positions may address those in junior positions by their first names. Assistants, for example, are often referred to by their first names. Consider how different names bring out different aspects of our personality.

Sometimes people change their names. Some immigrants to Australia from non-English-speaking countries change their names or adopt different names in order to fit in more easily. Our own experiences with Asian students in Australia have demonstrated that some adopt new or Anglicised first names partly because some non-Asians have difficulty in pronouncing and remembering Asian names. In changing their names, they may also take on new personas, and may discard some of their traditional cultural practices. People who adopt a religious group or cult sometimes change their names to give themselves a different identity that marks them as part of their adopted group.

Ask yourself how many different names you have. In what ways do your names affect your personality? Think of other names you could have. Would these give you a different personality and identity?

In considering the significance of language, we suggest the following guidelines: language is not natural or neutral, but is a site of power, struggle, and social change.

Language is not natural

Language does not simply name the world as it exists, but also constructs a view of the world. You may be already thinking that talking or writing about language is a complicated thing because you have to use language in order to talk about it. As we write this, we are aware of the different ways we could express things and the different meanings that would result. We are also aware that you, as the reader, may want to take issue with some of the things we write. So we want to qualify what we mean when we say language is not natural. We don't mean that it is not natural for humans to speak. Indeed, it seems that one of the defining qualities of what it means to be human is an innate capacity for language. Children have a built-in propensity to learn languages. But there is no normal, right, correct set of words, or way of speaking, that describes the world.

Some theorists describe this characteristic of language by saying that all languages are arbitrary, meaning that there is no necessary connection between the sounds and symbols that make up any language on the one hand and, on the other, the world itself. The symbols and sounds in the word 'thong', for instance, don't have any real relationship with summer footwear except by convention. 'Thong' doesn't look like something that goes on a foot, it doesn't sound like the slapping noise a thong makes on your heel as you walk, and the letters t-h-o-n-g certainly don't smell, taste, or feel like the object with which they are arbitrarily associated. In fact, different cultures use totally different letters, sounds, and words to represent similar forms of footwear: *sandalo* in Italian, *flip-flops* in South Africa and the UK, *jandals* in New Zealand, and *thongs* in Australia, where the thong has a privileged place as a recognised symbol of the relaxed, outdoor Australian lifestyle, to the extent that it featured in the Sydney 2000 Olympic Games opening ceremony. But some cultures whose peoples don't wear thongs have no word to describe them at all. In other places the word 'thong' is used to describe skimpy g-string underwear that nobody would consider putting on their feet, or, with the possible exception of a Brazilian samba carnival, associating with national identity. There are numerous languages that describe the world with their own particular inflections and biases. The idea of bias leads to the next point.

Language is not neutral

Language always carries some associations, connotations, or values with it. We have already seen this with the 'making love' example. Even ordinary words such as 'up', 'down', 'top', 'bottom', 'left', and 'right' carry significant associations. They may be used simply to describe spatial positions. But 'up', 'top', and 'right' also carry positive connotations that relate to a culture that values right over left, and is based on a competitive, judgmental ethos that compares us with others and grades us in hierarchical terms such that 'up' and 'top' are viewed positively, but 'down' and 'bottom' are perceived as negative terms. Even as a named part of the body, 'bottom' carries negative connotations in the way Western culture sees it. In Christian mythology, the left hand is considered to be the 'sinister' hand because of its Latin origin in the word *sinistral* (meaning 'left' or 'left-handed') and because the Devil is supposedly left-handed. The right hand is the 'superior', 'dexterous' (derived from the Latin *dexter*) hand. These words are thus neither innocent nor neutral.

When it comes to more obvious political naming, it is easy to see how the terms 'terrorist', 'guerrilla', and 'freedom fighter' have been used by different political groups to refer to the same people. Similarly, the terms 'boat people', 'refugees', 'asylum seekers', 'queue jumpers', and 'illegals' have all been used to describe people coming from Asia to Australia since 2001, and each of these descriptive terms refers to a different discourse for understanding who these people are and what 'we', the Australian public, should think about them. (Note how 'boat people' is not a term/discourse normally used to describe the arrival in Australia of Captain Cook and his crew, although it could be.) Consider the differences between 'climate change', 'global warming', and 'ecological time-bomb' as ways of describing what is happening to the global environment. In the immediate aftermath of the terrorist attacks of September 11, the Western press and some politicians presented the event linguistically in terms of 'good' and 'evil' (see Figure 4.1).

Note how these words:

- draw on a religious and moral discourse
- construct real events in the same terms as Hollywood adventure films like *Star Wars*
- tend to negate the possibility of any debate or questioning about the meanings and causes behind such actions by simplifying the issues into 'good' and 'evil', black and white terms, thereby sending the message that the only right and logical action is to somehow punish, eradicate, or eliminate that which is 'evil'.

We're not arguing the political rightness or wrongness of these different labels, but noting that the same people can be named in very different ways that have very different meanings, and that all such names carry a political position. The critical term 'discourse' is useful to help understand how language works (see Part 3). Cultural theorist John Fiske argues that a **discourse** offers 'ways of thinking about a particular topic, set within a particular context'. He illustrates this in relation to the occasion when video footage was

◀ DISCOURSE

Discourses are paradigms or ways of understanding that are communicated through texts and language use, and that organise knowledge and social power.

Figure 4.1 Headline from the *West Australian*, 13 September 2001

taken of a black man, Rodney King, being beaten up by four policemen in Los Angeles in 1991, but in court the police were found not guilty, which resulted in African-Americans protesting on the streets.

> Was that a "riot", or an "uprising", or a "rebellion"? If we call it a riot, that puts it in one discursive frame which suggests that it was criminal, it was social disorder. If we call it an uprising, it suggests that it's another discursive frame … it was against something and it wasn't just disorder. So the word "riot" and the word "uprising" come from quite different discourses, ways of talking about an event … No social event proscribes what discourse we use to describe it, it's our choice as users of language. And the way we make the choice of which discourse to put a particular event in, is an extremely important thing to understand (*The Media Report*, ABC Radio National, 7 December 2000).

Consider these three ways of describing the area comprising Africa, South America, and much of Asia: the 'Third World', the 'underdeveloped world', the 'majority world'. There is a major difference between the first two terms and the last. The first two place that world in the negative: if it is third, then it comes after the first two worlds—in the language of hierarchy and the language of competition, which structure much of Western thought, it comes below, it is a loser. Similarly, to be underdeveloped is to be less than, or the negative of, developed. So in this context 'underdeveloped' is a negative term indicating that such areas have failed to meet their full potential, mature, or develop.

The point is that while the terms 'Third World' and 'underdeveloped world' are helpful in some ways in pointing out the discrimination against this 'other' world, they remain negative, and they give a view from the perspective of the minority world. They don't really challenge the structures of power involved; however, to name this area as the 'majority world' is to give it a positive value, because in Western democratic thought, majorities carry rights and power. Naming this area the 'majority world' places the so-called 'developed nations' in a minority position. Suddenly you might see the injustice of a world that is heavily geared towards materially satisfying the minority.

Language is a changing site of power and struggle

Language meanings and associations can and do change over time. We need to realise this so that in any language analysis, we look at the meanings in a historical and cultural context. Feminist author Dale Spender has noted how, in relation to gender, language has a tendency to sexualise and denigrate terms used to describe women (Spender 1980, pp. 16–19). She considers the pairings of a number of oppositions, for example, master–mistress, bachelor–spinster, king–queen, courtier–courtesan, lord–lady. Her findings are that as time passes, either the female terms lose out in terms of their status and value—'lady' now describes ordinary women, whereas 'lord' retains its powerful meanings; 'bachelor' is a social position with more positive value than 'spinster'—or else the female terms come to describe women in terms of their sexuality (for example, over time 'mistress' and 'courtesan' have become words that describe women's sexual position in relation to men).

The label 'queen' has been used to describe and denigrate homosexual men, the implication being that for men to be feminised is a put-down. Note, though, that in the struggle over language, gay men, who first appropriated and reworked the meaning of 'gay' to validate and celebrate homosexuality, have now also reappropriated 'queen' and 'queer' as positive labels of description. 'Queer theory' is now part of media and cultural studies, and fashionable boutiques proudly use the media to advertise 'queen-sized shoes'.

In addition, many women have reclaimed and redefined the diminutive term 'girl', which has in the past been used to refer to mature women in an affectionate way that nevertheless diminishes their social standing (by categorising them with children). Now the term '*grrrl power*', said with a growl, leaves no doubt about the social standing of the women such as Lisbeth Salander, the 'girl' with the dragon tattoo in Stieg Larsson's *Millennium Trilogy*, Baby Doll (Emily Browning) in *Sucker Punch*, and Uma Thurman as Kiddo in *Kill Bill*. If grown women are now being referred to positively with a word that means 'juvenile female', it seems that the term has literally been empowered and redeployed in an assertive way.

This shows that language meanings are not fixed, and can be struggled over by different people and different social groups. Historically such struggles have been very important, particularly those that occur between different ethnic groups. These struggles over language are struggles for power and they are very common.

Who controls language?

In Britain in the eighteenth century, speaking Gaelic in Scotland was forbidden and made punishable. The English were seeking to maintain their rule—hegemony—over the Scots by wiping out Scottish culture and imposing English cultural values through the use of the English language. In Africa, the USA, and Australia, indigenous languages have at various times in the past been banned as part of attempts to destroy indigenous cultures. The English language has been used as a means of establishing power over indigenous populations. Even now the use of Singlish (Singaporean English) or Ebonics (African-American English) is considered to be improper and accrues penalties in academic institutions in Australia, the UK, the USA, and elsewhere.

African writer Ngugi Wa Thiong'o has described how language can be used in struggles for power between different racial or ethnic groups. He talks about how as a child in Kenya, he was forced to learn English, on pain of punishment, in a way that alienated him from his own culture and people by depriving him of the use of his native language, Gíkúyú:

> English became the language of my formal education. In Kenya, English became more than a language: it was the language, and all the others had to bow before it in deference. Thus one of the most humiliating experiences was to be caught speaking Gíkúyú in the vicinity of the school. The culprit was given corporal punishment—three to five strokes of the cane on bare buttocks—or was made to carry a metal plate around the neck with inscriptions such as "I am Stupid" or "I am a Donkey" (Ngugi 1986, p. 11).

Ngugi shows how the use of English as the official language devalued Gíkúyú and made it inferior even in the eyes of those for whom it was a native tongue. As they began to see and think from a European perspective, Africans became alienated from their own cultures, and came to look down on fellow countrymen and women who had not taken up European ways and words. In this way, European economic and political domination—imperialism, the establishment of empire—was supported through language control:

> Economic and political control can never be complete or effective without mental control … For colonialism this involved two aspects of the same process: the destruction or the deliberate undervaluing of a people's culture, their art, dances, religions, history, geography, education, orature and literature, and the conscious elevation of the language of the coloniser. The domination of a people's language by the languages of the colonising nations was crucial to the domination of the mental universe of the colonised (Ngugi 1986, p. 16).

This is not a form of economic imperialism, but cultural imperialism (see Chapter 25). The final irony for Ngugi is that he became a great writer of English whose writing, which has become part of the English literary tradition, is not available to the majority of his own people, who cannot read English. The complications of language are illustrated by Ngugi's history: after his realisations about language and power as a successful writer in the 1980s, he decided to renounce the English language, stating that 'This book … is my farewell to English as a vehicle for any of my writings. From now on it is Gíkúyú and Kiswahili all the way' (Ngugi 1986, p. xiv). However, he later moved to America and once again found English as his main language and the language that would reach a wider audience.

You can look at equivalent struggles over language between Australians of European descent and Aborigines, between non-English-speaking Australian immigrants and English-speaking immigrants, between African-Americans and European Americans, between Native Americans and immigrant Americans. A key question in all these struggles is which language will survive. Even when one language triumphs, as English has done in many situations, there can still be struggles between different kinds of English spoken by different social groups, for example, between cockney English and 'the Queen's English', between 'black English' (or Ebonics) and 'white English', between Australian English, Singaporean English, and white American English, and between English spoken by Aboriginal Australians and English spoken by non-Aboriginal Australians. These struggles are about having power through language; forms of 'deviant' English are often forms of resistance by oppressed social groups.

In 1995, a Canadian radio program about a conference for Native American peoples reported that the contradictions around language were being keenly felt: there was an attempt to maintain traditional languages as a way of maintaining traditional culture—once the languages are gone, the culture will be gone—but there was also a recognition that English had become the language of many of those indigenous groups, so that in a sense it could be seen as their language. Moreover, English was the language that made shared communication between the different groups possible at this meeting (ABC Radio National 1995).

In the 1990s, the South African government decided that its new national anthem should always be sung in the four main languages so as to equally represent the different social groups that make up South Africa.

A further complication arises when we consider that English is increasingly the language of mass communication across the globe (Chinese is the second-most used language). It is certainly the language that dominates computer-mediated communication, especially the internet. Therefore, in order to have one's voice heard in an international forum, being able to speak and write publishable and quotable English is becoming a necessity. Does this mean that the media are contributing to the formation of a monoculture and that the globalisation of communication networks can only be seen in a negative light? We will return to this complex question in Chapter 25.

LANGUAGE AND SOCIAL CHANGE

Can you change society by changing language?   ▶

Awareness of the above arguments about language (arguments that are really about the politics of naming) has led social groups to try to change language use in order to change social behaviour, particularly in relation to sexism. This begs the question: does changing language lead to social change? Will using, say, 'Ms' instead of 'Miss' or 'Mrs', or 'differently abled' instead of 'disabled', change how people think, believe, and behave? While changing language will make some difference, several critics have shown that word changes can be accommodated by mainstream culture without social changes taking place:

> "Ms" was originally intended to be a parallel term to "Mr". However there are lots of studies … which suggest that "Ms" is not being used nor interpreted in this intended way. A study [in Canada] … showed that people had a three-way distinction: "Mrs" was used for married women, "Miss" was used for single women, and "Ms" was being used for divorced women … In Britain it's reported that "Miss" and "Ms" have sort of coalesced so the distinction now is between "Mrs" and "Ms"—"Mrs" signalling a married woman, "Ms" signalling a single woman … the distinction "Ms" was intended to eliminate is still getting expressed but in a different way (Susan Ehrlich, quoted on ABC Radio National 1995).

In many cases, it is not only language but also the medium of communication that determines people's choices about how they represent themselves to others. Many official forms that have to be filled out (particularly those requiring computerised data entry) either neglect to offer 'Ms' as an option, offer it as a restricted option for females over a certain age, or offer it in conjunction with 'Miss' and 'Mrs', rather than using 'Ms' as the default title to designate females as the term was intended to function (the equivalent of 'Mr', which designates all males, married or single, who do not have a specific title such as 'Dr'). Additionally, it seems 'Ms' has now come to take on feminist connotations, while the term 'feminist' itself has now taken on negative connotations for some young women so they do not want to use the term 'Ms' because they do not want to be labelled feminist (although they are clearly the beneficiaries in many ways of the feminist movement). A related phenomenon can be seen in the film *Hot Tub Time Machine* (dir. Steve Pink 2010) in which Craig Robinson's character Nick Webber-Agnew is humiliated by his mates for having a hyphenated surname. The hyphenation of last names became popular so that women did not need to give up their own name when they married: they simply added their husband's last name to their own or their children's names. When a man also adds his wife's last name to his own, however, this is considered to be emasculating.

When George Clooney married Amal Alamuddin in 2014, she adopted his last name. Why do you think George did not change his name? What might have happened if George had changed his last name to Alamuddin to represent his new identity as a married man and his solidarity with his partner Amal?

This example shows that in order to eliminate discrimination against women, there has to be social change as well as language change. Without social change, changing language alone is fighting a losing battle. Nevertheless, language change and language awareness are important parts of raising our consciousness about bias and discrimination, and thus help us move towards social change.

CONCLUSION

This chapter has argued that social reality is constructed and that language, as a system of representation, is central in this construction. Language is not natural or neutral, but carries certain values. It is also a site of political struggle.

The arguments we have made here about language can be applied to the media, even though the media don't always use words—they may use pictures, images, forms of camera movement, editing, or even structural strategies (for example, positioning information that is considered to be most important at the top of a web page). The media's techniques can be understood as the language of the media; the discussion about language in this chapter is relevant to the conventions of journalistic uses of language as well. As critics, you can now begin to deconstruct the language of the media and the ways that stories in the media are written and structured.

This chapter has

- argued that social reality is constructed and that language is central in this construction
- explored the politics of naming

- shown how names can construct identity
- argued that language is not natural or neutral, and that it is a changing site of power struggles
- considered language and social change.

? DISCUSSION POINTS

1 Explain what 'We don't speak language, language speaks us' means. How would you argue for and against this idea?
2 Consider the differences between 'climate change', 'global warming', and 'ecological time-bomb' as ways of describing what is happening to the global environment.
3 Find examples of language that carry particular social or political meanings.
4 Explain and illustrate the term 'discourse' in relation to language use.
5 How many languages do you think will still be used in a hundred years' time? Which will be the main languages used?
6 Can you change society by changing language?

SUMMARY

You should now be able to

- explain the concept of the social construction of reality and the role that language plays in this construction
- explain the reflective, or mimetic, and the constructionist theories of language
- give examples of how language constructs the world
- critically discuss the idea that language is not natural or neutral
- show how language is related to social power
- explain and illustrate the term 'discourse'
- discuss language as a site of social struggle with relevant examples
- consider whether changing language can change society
- argue about whether we speak language or language speaks us
- explain why an understanding of language is important in media studies.

CHAPTER 5

Mediation and Representation

There is no such thing as objective journalism. The phrase itself is a pompous contradiction in terms.

Hunter S Thompson

This chapter will

- examine the meanings of the terms 'representation' and 'mediation'
- give models to illustrate how the media communicate and represent reality
- question the truthfulness of media representational technologies and conventions such as objective journalism
- analyse some specific examples of media representation.

REPRESENTATION

The last chapter argued that language constructs and evaluates the world and reality by naming it. The media constitute a language system, so what we say about language also applies to the media. Language and the media are both systems of representation. 'Representation' is a key concept in media studies. It has three meanings:

1 to look like or to resemble
2 to stand in for something or someone
3 to present a second time—to *re*-present.

Language and media representations do all three.

We know and understand the world through language, through representations. This is not to deny that the real world exists—of course there is reality—but it is to say that all our learning about the world is mediated by language. There is a complex relationship between representation and reality. As Richard Dyer puts it:

> This is difficult territory. I accept that one apprehends reality only through representations of reality, through texts, discourses, images; there is no such thing as unmediated access to reality. But because one can see reality only through representation it does not follow that one does not see reality at all … Reality is always more extensive and complicated than any system of representation can possibly comprehend and we always sense that this is so—representation never "gets" reality, which is why human history has produced so many different and changing ways of trying to get it (Dyer 1993, p. 3).

What Dyer is suggesting here is that when we feel that language and representations don't do justice to our sense of reality, we have to find new ways of representing them, and, indeed, this has been the history of human culture, constantly developing new modes of representation and discovering new ways of seeing reality. Here is another example of how we are not trapped in systems of representation, but can struggle to redefine language to invent new languages. But the central point remains that we still only know reality through representations: 'there is no such thing as unmediated access to reality' (Dyer 1993, p. 3).

Can there be unbiased, objective representations of the world? Michael, Sarah, and I argue no. Because all representations come from humans, they all come from a particular position. So they are relative; they carry the bias of a particular person or group of people, just as this book carries our own biases and positions. How true can representations be? In the end this is something you have to decide for yourself. You may decide that one set of representations are true or that they are more true than others—in other words, that they are the best available so far. As we grow and learn, we find models that best fit how we see and understand the world.

As an example of different and developing ways of looking at the world (very literally in this case), consider the following maps (Figures 5.1 and 5.2).

Which map appears most real to you? Which is most familiar and conventional? What are the differences between them?

Traditional maps have tended to show countries incorrectly in proportion to one another, to the advantage of the European colonial powers while the southern continents are shown far too small. Europe, with its 9.7 million square kilometres, appears to be larger than South America, which is 17.8 million square kilometres, and North America appears to be considerably larger than Africa, which is 30 million square kilometres, whereas in fact North America is smaller (only 19 million square kilometres). Scandinavia, which is 1.1 million square kilometres, seems to be as large as India, which is 3.3 million square kilometres. The new map (Figure 5.2) provides a helpful corrective to the distortions of traditional maps—no less than our world view is at stake. By setting forth all countries in their true sizes and locations, this map allows each one its actual position in the world (*New Internationalist* 1998).

The above points are crucial. These ideas lie behind the important statement given earlier: media products do not show or present the real world; rather, they construct and re-present reality. We will develop this idea by looking specifically at the media apparatus to see how it deals with reality.

THE MEDIA APPARATUS

The word 'media' literally means 'middle'. The media are the things that come in the middle of, or mediate, communication. They are the means through which message senders can communicate to message receivers, or audiences. Anyone wanting to communicate chooses a medium to do so, whether it be spoken or written language, some form of pictorial representation (pictures, diagrams, photographs, films, and so on), or another medium. Figure 5.3 is a modification of Lasswell's formula (see Table 2.2, p. 20).

In this formula, the answers to 'WHAT' and 'by WHAT MEANS', in other words the messages and the modes, constitute today's media. In modern industrialised society, messages are transmitted through the technological means of the World Wide Web, print, film, digital technologies, mobile phones, computer systems, and so on.

Figure 5.1 Traditional world map

Figure 5.2 Arno Peters' non-traditional world map with countries in correct proportion

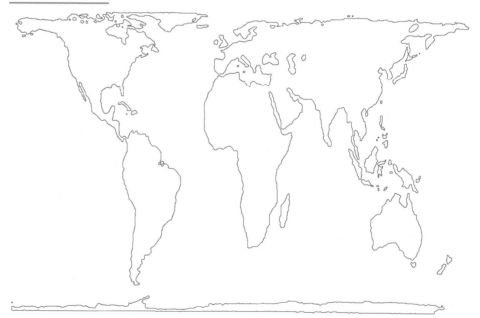

Source: <www.newint.org/issue123/flat.htm>

Figure 5.3 Modification of Lasswell's model of communication

Note how the double arrows in this model recognise that the world impacts on the media, and that audiences are active in making meanings—they don't just passively receive them.

In relation to the visual media of photography, film, and digital cameras, and to the sound-recording media, it has been suggested that they are neutral mechanisms that simply mirror the world, giving us a window or an ear on the world (Figure 5.5).

We stress here the process of mediation: the media stand between us and the world or reality. We can understand our relationships to the world and the media according to the model in Figure 5.4.

Figure 5.4 Model of the media–world relationship stressing the process of mediation

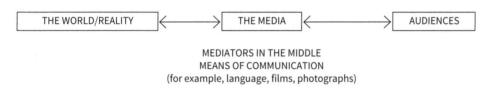

Figure 5.5 Model of the media–world relationship suggesting the media are neutral mechanisms that simply mirror the world

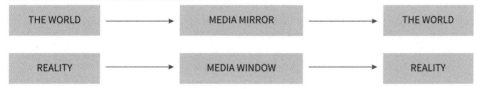

Media studies rejects this model, stressing instead media construction, selection, and interpretation, in order to develop the concept of representation (Figure 5.6).

We need to reiterate this point strongly in relation to the film-based visual media and sound-recording media because of the particular qualities shared by photography, film, digital cameras, and sound recording.

Figure 5.6 Model of the media–world relationship stressing media construction, selection, and interpretation

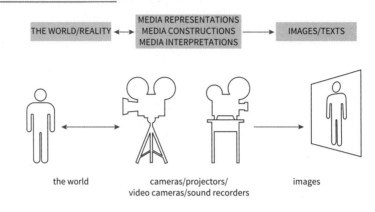

THE MEDIA AND REALITY

Do cameras and media technologies show us the truth?

Many media and artistic representations refer to things from the real world. Novels, plays, poetry, painting, sculpture, photography, film, and digital cameras all aim to re-create objects and people that are part of the world we live in. But photography, film, digital cameras, and sound recording—media technologies—have a different relationship to the real world than do other means of representation such as language, painting, and sculpture. Cameras can reproduce reality in a mimetic way and therefore appear to show us unmediated reality. These media use impressions from the real world and then digitise them, or put them onto film, digital video, or MP3 recorders, to produce images and sounds. Unlike literature, paintings, or sculpture, which are produced by the artist's hands and imagination, photography, film, and digital cameras actually record the reality that is out there. So whereas these new technologies appear to be objective, human eyes, ears, and hands produce subjective renditions of the world. This has tended to make people believe in the realism of these technologically produced images, so that we think we really see or hear the truth when we see photographs and film, or listen to recordings. Because these media depend on a connection between the real world (the referent) and the way it impinges on celluloid or audio-tape through light patterns and sound waves, there is some truth in this belief—but only some. It is crucial to be aware of the fact that these realistic media are constructed as well.

1   For a start, we do not actually see three-dimensional reality; we see two-dimensional images of reality in film and television. When French filmmaker Jean-Luc Godard remarked, 'There are no just images, there are just images', he meant two things: first, he was making a political point that the dominant media images of Hollywood and the mainstream media do not offer a fair or just view of the world in terms of its representation of class and social differences; second, he was saying that images are just that, images—they cannot give us reality, the real thing. Godard also commented that 'A photograph is not the reflection of reality, but the reality of that reflection' (Harvey 1978, p. 71). Belgian surrealist René Magritte drew attention to the illusory nature of images in many of his paintings, including his famous *This Is Not a Pipe*. This painting draws our attention to the fact that the image is simply lines and colours that look like a pipe, but it is not the actual thing to which it refers.

2 Film, photography, and video images only give us a particular or partial view of what we are seeing. We only see from one angle with one view and with particular lighting. We cannot encompass the whole of reality on the screen. There are numerous processes of selection and omission that lead to the way we are shown things and the way different shots are put together. Editing selects and omits material. Choices are made that produce a particular viewpoint, giving a particular meaning to what we see. Selfies are a good example of this (see the case study on pp. 76–8, Self-representation in photographs: selfies). Commentary accompanying images also explains in a particular way what is happening. Sound recordings are equally selective.

3 Images are linked together within bigger systems of narrative and genre, which also affects how we see them. In these systems, the media have tended to hide their own processes of construction. By this we mean that when they show mediated events, they aim to make them flow smoothly without showing the construction that has gone on. All the paraphernalia of representation—autocue, lights, sound, camera equipment, and so on—are hidden from sight. Events seem to unfold naturally, as if they were happening before our eyes. This third point is not so true since the 1990s as it was previously. The media sometimes deliberately reveal their own processes of construction: popular television studio programs show the cameras and behind-the-scenes crew, thus revealing and referring to the recording and constructing processes. Audiences are far more media aware; they enjoy seeing behind the scenes, and they understand that a lot of media manipulation and construction goes on. The growth of media studies has contributed to this.

4 The technology for constructing reality keeps improving. It is now possible, through digital manipulation, to compose photographs that appear real but are not. Documentary theorist Brian Winston comments that 'the technology for digital image manipulation is rapidly becoming a fixture in all newspaper and magazine offices' (1995, p. 5). The consequence is that 'by the summer of 1993, the status of the photographic image as evidence was becoming somewhat tattered' (Winston 1995, p. 5). The consequence of this ability to manipulate photographs is that media reality becomes even more questionable (Figure 5.7).

Figure 5.7 Digitally manipulated image of American President George W Bush

This image was circulated on the internet following the 11 September 2001 attacks on the Pentagon and the World Trade Center.

The rest of this chapter analyses some specific examples of media representation to show how they construct particular views of the world.

CASE STUDY

Families in photographs and paintings

Everyday family photos are media representations/constructions and they are a fascinating source to examine. Our first example compares two representations of the family: one (Figure 5.8) is a family album photo taken in 1960; the other (Figure 5.9) is Thomas Gainsborough's eighteenth-century oil painting *Mr and Mrs Andrews* (c. 1750). Both these images offer particular views of the family.

Figure 5.8 Happy families: a family snapshot

Source: Author's private collection

Figure 5.9 *Mr and Mrs Andrews* by Thomas Gainsborough

Source: National Gallery, London

Figure 5.8 presents an idealised story of the family. It stresses family unity within a patriarchal framework; the five people are working together but are marked out hierarchically in terms of height and age—the male figure, who also has the biggest piece of machinery, is the leader, while the rest of the family are progressively scaled down. The image celebrates the family and the bourgeois values of property ownership and work: there is evidence of the large garden and the process by which it is cultivated and controlled. The audience is invited to celebrate this process of ownership, to witness and congratulate a successful and happy family. It makes an interesting contrast with John Berger's analysis of Gainsborough's painting *Mr and Mrs Andrews* in one of the pioneering studies of media and representation, *Ways of Seeing*.

Berger (1972) argues that in the eighteenth century, oil painting, one of the key media of its day, was a way for the property-owning classes to represent and celebrate their power and ownership. The picture of Mr and Mrs Andrews implies a sense of power over the land that they own. It is a land for recreation—Mr Andrews goes hunting (his gun gives him symbolic phallic power)—and cultivation (we see corn and sheep). But clearly the Andrews take no part in this rural labour—they simply own and benefit from it. In relation to gender, we see a subordinate female figure in terms of height, but also one who is established through costume as a source of visual pleasure and ornamentation.

Continued on next page   ▶

Ownership and commission of oil paintings was only available to a small elite group that could afford them. Photography in the twentieth century, in contrast, set itself up as a democratic medium in terms of its affordability to all and the skill required to do it—anyone can take photos: 'You push the button, we do the rest' says one early Kodak advertisement. But photography is still being used to celebrate official family and property values, and is one of the key mechanisms for documenting a positive account of the family through snapshots of weddings, christenings, and holidays preserved on the mantelpiece, in the family album, and on the hard drive.

There is an alternative view to the official reading of this family photograph and the elements that the photographer has chosen to ignore. I, Michael, am in it and I know the histories behind the image, the realities that were being hidden: the father was having an affair, within a year the parents would be separated, the children were extremely unhappy, and there was always an argument about the children having to do gardening! What this alternative view reveals is the process of construction involved in what we might regard as the most innocent of photographs—the family snapshot: first, in the general ways family snapshots are constructed to celebrate family values, presenting a discourse of the family; and second, in the detail of any particular image. You should be able to see this very clearly when considering how you have been represented and manipulated in any media constructions, since you will be aware of the realities and histories behind the constructions, and of the elements that the camera or the media text has chosen to ignore.

CASE STUDY

Self-representation in photographs: selfies

Selfies are digital self-portraits often taken on smartphones and iPads, mostly for the purpose of being posted to social media sites such as Facebook and Instagram. Selfies have become a ubiquitous cultural practice in recent years due to the prominence of smartphones and the accessibility of wireless networks for instant uploads to social media platforms. While the word first came to light in 2002, 'selfie' officially entered the *Oxford Dictionary* in 2013; it was also the 'Word of the Year' (Oxforddictionaries.com 2015). Selfies can be digitally manipulated and edited within minutes to assist the taker's construction of identity, as well as perhaps to project the image of a particular type of 'lifestyle'. Just as Michael notes in Figure 5.8, there is an 'alternative view' that is being ignored by the photographer in the family photograph and the same is applicable to selfies. Michael, who is *in* the family photograph of Figure 5.8, knew the history and the 'realities that were being hidden'. Selfies may be similarly problematic when read in isolation. Essena O'Neill, a young Australian with over half a million Instagram followers, has experienced a level of celebrity for posting selfies. She recently stated publicly that she felt she had created an 'unattainable' image of 'a perfect life' for her fans and that she had probably taken '100 [selfies] in similar poses trying to make my stomach look good' (Scott 2015). She later changed her Instagram profile name to 'Social Media is not Real'.

Here, in Figure 5.10, our first example of a selfie is of Sarah, one of the authors of this book. It was taken in a relatively ordinary environment, in the mirror at a suburban hairdressing salon on an otherwise uneventful day while Sarah was waiting for hair dye to process with tin foils on her head. She took a selfie with the characteristic gaze directed at the phone camera screen, rather than the mirror. Sarah's facial expression mocks the banality of selfies, but also conveys her boredom with waiting and her feminist disdain for the 'women's magazines' provided to entertain the clientele; it is an intentional play on the popular—arguably generic—selfie 'duck face' or 'trout pout' where many pose in particular ways to perform 'sexy'. In the hairdressing salon, with silver foils in her hair and wearing a shapeless black cape, Sarah was deliberately performing 'unsexy' ironic duck face when she posted this to her Instagram account. She knew this would most likely be 'read' in the way she intended her performance of identity to be read because most of her Instagram followers are other feminists.

Figure 5.10 Sarah selfie

As a form of performative display, selfies are taken in many contexts such as in front of monuments on holidays, at weddings, or in ordinary moments posing in front of the bathroom mirror or at restaurants. They have become popular among world leaders and celebrities. Kim Kardashian capitalised on the trend and published a book of her own selfies, *Selfish*, in 2015. Ellen DeGeneres' celebrity group selfie with Meryl Streep, Bradley Cooper, the Jolie-Pitts, Jennifer Lawrence, and others caused such a frenzy that Twitter crashed (Bacardi 2014). Group selfies have been taken at memorial ceremonies. US President Barack Obama, British Prime Minister David Cameron, and Danish Prime Minister Helle Thorning-Schmidt, for example, came under media scrutiny for taking a group selfie at Nelson Mandela's memorial (Anthony 2013); indeed, this is a type of memorialising of the memorial.

From the banal to the exceptional, according to Jill Walker Rettberg, 'selfies are descendants of visual artists' self-portraits … society disciplines self-representations such as selfies … through ridicule and pathologising' (2014, p. 1). Selfies, routinely labelled narcissistic, are often taken with 'selfie sticks' (collapsible sticks attached to smartphones in order to take selfies from arm's length), which have been labelled 'narcisticks' (Shilling 2015). Selfies are now so pervasive that there have been academic studies on selfie tourism or travel selfies (see Morris, Paris & Pietschnig 2013).

Continued on next page ▶

There have reportedly even been more deaths from selfies than from shark attacks in recent times: in 2015 there were eight recorded shark attack deaths, and fifteen deaths from selfies where people fell from cliffs or were hit by moving vehicles while attempting self-portraiture (Horton 2015). The 'danger' of selfies even prompted the Russian government to launch a 'safe selfie' campaign to raise awareness of the potential for injury or death when taking selfies (Kosoff 2015). Another movement was launched in 2015 called #selfietodiefor (www.selfietodiefor.org); its aims centre on awareness of the potential perils of selfies and its followers pledge to live selfie-less lives. To date it only has just over 300 followers. In early 2016, Mumbai issued no-selfie zones in popular tourist parts of the city due to several selfie-related injuries and three deaths (Sandhu 2016).

Social media, digital cameras, and smartphones assist us in the ease of self-representation, although self-representation—or the distortion thereof—itself is not a new practice. If we think about Frida Kahlo, the Mexican artist renowned for her self-portraiture in her art, often with Kahlo staring unsmilingly at the viewer, we can see that much of her work is arguably about the context: what is behind or surrounding her in her self-portraits. Similarly in selfies, the contextual is often key. Kahlo famously said, 'I paint myself because I am often so alone, and because I am the subject I know best' (quoted in Kettenmann 2003, p. 27). What can Kahlo's self-portraits reveal about the need for connectedness in the selfie era? Is the selfie, as Horning (2014) argues, 'shorthand not just for pictures you take of yourself but instead for one's "self in social media"—one's self commoditized to suit the logistics of networks'? People tell stories through selfies, to each other, for each other, and selfies reflect cultural moments from the ordinary to the grotesque, to the banal and to the extraordinary; however, like any form of representation, they can only ever tell part of the story.

Figure 5.11 displays one of the 'Hey Girl' Ryan Gosling postcards. It says: 'Hey Girl, I tried to take a selfie, but I couldn't take my eyes off you'. The Gosling memes went viral a few years ago and there have been postcards, Instagram accounts, Tumblr sites, and a book *Feminist Ryan Gosling: Feminist Theory (as Imagined) from Your Favorite Sensitive Movie Dude* (2012). The 'Hey Girl' memes are dedicated to photographs of Gosling with pro-women messages created by internet users using Gosling's image. In this postcard in Figure 5.11, Gosling is photographed photographing, rejecting the notion of the 'selfie' because the 'girl' is seen as more interesting to Gosling than himself.

Figure 5.11 Ryan Gosling selfie postcard

CASE STUDY

Representation of queer culture: the Sydney Mardi Gras

Our second example (Figure 5.12), a press photograph and report of Sydney's 1996 Mardi Gras Festival, is an example of mediated and constructed news.

What meanings are being communicated by the photograph, its caption, and the news story? We can divide this into three elements: the photograph itself, the caption, and the written report. Briefly, the photograph appears to celebrate the event in terms of humour and pleasure. Through the humour associated with men dressing up and dancing, it mediates what might otherwise be, for some, a shocking depiction of homosexuality and male sexuality. Media coverage of the Mardi Gras continually negotiates the risk of offending viewers by using humour to offset this danger. Yet while an essential part of the Mardi Gras ethos is poking fun at male power and authority, this text seems to reveal a very different story. After the humorous caption and the positive opening paragraph, the selection of 'facts' reported depict the event in terms of criminality, danger, socially irresponsible behaviour (assaults, littering, drunkenness), and implied public cost (without mention of the huge boost to Sydney's economy that this event brings through tourism). The reference to Clean Up Australia Day in the final paragraph can be read as a veiled moral suggestion that Australia needs to be cleansed of such events. This report thus becomes increasingly negative about and critical of the event, revealing an interesting example of selection and construction.

Figure 5.12 News story about and photograph of Sydney Mardi Gras

Well, hello sailors

A RECORD crowd of 600,000 watched Sydney's eighth annual gay and lesbian mardi gras parade last night.

Police said the massive crowd was generally well behaved.

There were two arrests. One man was charged with offensive conduct and another with four counts of assaulting police.

Fifteen people were taken to hospital and 13 treated for ailments ranging from chest pains to intoxication.

Tons of confetti, bottles and cans awaited council crews on Clean Up Australia Day.

Source: *Sunday Times* 1996

NEWS REPORTING AND OBJECTIVE JOURNALISM

Our third example (below) offers a much more detailed analysis of the way language is used in a short news story, developing ideas from Chapter 4. Many media students aim to enter the media industry and become journalists, so it is important to consider the news media in relation to the power of language. In addition to the politics of naming (see pp. 57–61), and the way reporters present a story according to its news values or newsworthiness, we must also be aware of the conventions of news writing.

Journalists are taught to write from an objective perspective. News reporters do not write from a first-person perspective. In other words, they don't use the pronoun 'I' and they don't directly state their own opinion. In a hard news story, a journalist will never say something like 'I think the new environmental policy is problematic'. This impersonal use of language makes it seem as though nobody is writing the story, suggesting that the story is a collection of facts presented in a neutral manner. The news does not seem to reflect an editorial policy or an economic imperative, or to be a particular journalist's ideas, words, or opinions. It seems to be 'the objective truth'. In this way the media, and the people in control of the media, speak for us all, as though their views are the natural, normal, and factual ones.

BALANCE ▶

Balanced reporting entails the presentation of both sides of an argument, giving them equal space and time.

Journalists are also taught to avoid bias by presenting a **balanced** report. If a journalist is covering a story on a court case, they are obliged to interview both the defendant (or somebody representing the defendant) and the plaintiff (or a spokesperson, such as their lawyer). Similarly, a journalist reporting on an environmental conference must interview politicians from both the government and the opposition to find out about their policies. Representing both perspectives is intended to avoid presenting a one-sided story, which would be considered biased, and so might alienate readers and reduce sales of the newspaper. Conflict is newsworthy, so if the political interviewees agree on environmental policy, the journalist is likely to ask a prominent businessperson or a member of a lobby group for comment. It is assumed that impartially presenting opposing viewpoints creates a balanced report, which suggests that the truth is located in the neutral zone between two polarised opinions, and also that there are only two important perspectives on any given topic. This is not always true: there may be many opinions and many relevant facts, and the 'correct' opinion might not be located in the middle ground.

In the process of trying to write objectively and give a balanced account of the story, journalists include quotes from experts who are authorities in the field or have personal experience of the matter in question. Quotes are reported in such a way as to clearly attribute opinions and ideas to the person who said them, and to clearly separate facts from opinions. If something is presented as a fact, the journalist is supposed to validate it by checking with two other sources to make certain it is correct.

INVERTED PYRAMID ▶

Information is given in descending order of importance, as in a news report.

Journalists and news reporters are taught to begin with the most important points first, the climax of the story at the start, then gradually fill in the context, history, and background, thereby presenting news in the form of an **inverted pyramid**. Media practitioners know that most people don't have time to read a newspaper from cover to cover, or to listen attentively to every news report on the radio, or watch all the news on television. Since readers skim the news, the most important and newsworthy information is presented first. The headline is usually an abbreviated sentence designed to capture attention in fewer than seven words. Unnecessary words such as 'and', 'are', and 'that' are omitted from headlines to make them as concise, informative, and punchy as possible. The first sentence of a news story is called the 'lead'; it is a summary of the entire story. In a typical lead, the journalist tries to answer as many questions about the story as possible in one short sentence. Sometimes journalists attempt to capture readers' attention using some other device, delaying the revelation of the story's main point. This technique, called the 'buried lead', is much more common in feature writing than in news reports. The main questions addressed in the lead are who, what, when, where, why, and how (often referred to as the 'five Ws and an H'). Thereafter, information is given in descending order of importance: the journalist fleshes out the story by providing additional details, quotes, and facts.

While the formula and conventions that journalists follow are designed to make the news as factual and fair as possible, we know that language can never be completely neutral. Analysing a news story may reveal how unintended bias can be encoded in the terminology and structure of a text, even if the author intends to be objective. Many of the features of the media text discussed below contribute to its meaning, but would not necessarily have been intended by the journalist.

CASE STUDY

Analysing the language and structure of a news story

'Saudis Acknowledge Women Exist' is a report from South Africa's *Mail & Guardian* newspaper about gender, law, religion, and power in Saudi Arabia (Pilkington 2002, p. 18). The first sentences of this article read:

> Saudi Arabia is to gender what apartheid South Africa was to race. In public life a woman is almost entirely segregated from men: excluded from the workplace, penned in special "family sections" in restaurants, taught in separate schools and colleges and forbidden to drive.
>
> Under the country's fundamentalist interpretation of Islam, her husband may marry up to four times, but an adulterous woman faces death by stoning. Outside the home she must wear the abaya, a black gown that enshrouds her completely, except for a slit for the eyes.
>
> There are signs, however, that the kingdom is reforming. It is not so much a wind of change as a puff, but it is significant. Women have been granted voluntary identity cards for use in banks and other public places. The card ends the iniquitous legal position in which a Saudi woman simply does not exist. As a child she is a ward of her father, as an adult the ward of her husband and as a widow the ward of her sons.

<www.mg.co.za>

Using our knowledge of the conventions of journalism and of the power of words, we can analyse how the language and structure of this media text position the reader, and encode a particular meaning or a preferred reading (see p. 96) laden with value judgments, rather than objectively informing the reader about recent legislative reforms related to gender equity in Saudi Arabia.

- Context. In relation to its media context, the article appears in the international news section of South Africa's national newspaper, a paper committed to political comment and positive social change. The social and political context of the news story is also important: Saudi Arabia is a monarchy that

Continued on next page   ▶

observes Sharia or Islamic law, which does not give women and men equal rights with regard to issues such as voting, driving, and holding political office.

- Intended or inscribed reader (see p. 92 and p. 152). Consider whom the newspaper wants to communicate with. The way newspapers are organised into national, regional, and international news, and the way the different sections are labelled, do not invite us to see ourselves as members of the global community, or as residents of a particular suburb. In this case, the paper is addressing its readers as South Africans. It is positioning us as South Africans, constructing a South African subject position. This way of communicating has been called 'interpellation' (see p. 152 and p. 168).

- Othering. In doing so, the text is establishing Saudi Arabians as 'Other'. It divides people into two camps: 'them' as opposed to 'us'. The heading and the first paragraph reinforce the 'us versus them' dichotomy established in terms of national identity and context (see 'Binary oppositions', pp. 251–4).

- The headline of the story does not mention the new identity card that offers legal recognition of women's rights to money, property, and independence, which is what the story is about. Instead, the title alludes to the idea that the lack of such rights is like 'not existing' in the eyes of the law. The implication here is that Saudi men must be pretty slow if they've only just realised that women exist. This is implicitly belittling the legal reforms, rather than celebrating them as a positive step. Overstatement of the problem is used to ridicule the new identity card and the legal reforms by making this progress towards a solution seem too limited. (This is a disguised perspective or an opinion, which may or may not be true. Because it is disguised in the language used, readers don't get a chance to question or evaluate it.)

PARADIGM

A set of terms, things, or ideas all based on a common theme or unifying system.

The words that make up the headline were chosen from a **paradigm** of possibilities. By 'paradigm' we mean a set or selection of words that mean similar things and could be substituted for one another. For example, in the headline 'Saudis Acknowledge Women Exist' the word 'exist' was chosen from among many other possibilities. It could have read 'Saudis Acknowledge Women's Rights' or 'Equity' or 'Independence'. Such a headline would have been more informative, but the headline printed in the *Mail & Guardian* was probably chosen to provoke the reader to read further.

SYNTAGM

Syntagm, like syntax, is a term that refers to the structure or pattern of words in a sentence, or things in a sequence.

Syntagm relates to the sequence of words. A different sequence of words would focus on a different aspect of the title as the main subject. Rearranging the sequence of the words, any of the headlines above could have started with the two words 'Saudi Women' (as in 'Saudi Women's Rights Acknowledged'). When we rearrange it like this, we realise that the original headline implies or assumes that Saudi Arabian citizens are all male, and that it is the males who are the subjects making laws and decisions about women. In the original, women are the passive objects of the headline.

Can you think of alternative headlines that would encapsulate the most newsworthy points of the story effectively? Here are a few suggestions: 'Saudi Legal Reform Helps Women' or 'Progress for Saudi Women'. Analyse how each of these headlines and your own headlines **frame** the story in a different way, altering its emphasis and inviting the reader to focus on different aspects or **angles**. Now write your own lead for the story (use present tense and active voice, and avoid writing in the first person). Try to answer as many of the 'five Ws and an H' questions as you can in fewer than twenty-five words, and keep the lead as snappy and interesting as possible to hook readers' interest.

The lead (the first paragraph of the story) creates another analogy, using more oppositions to position the reader on the privileged side of a self–Other dichotomy:

Self	Other
Us	Them
South African	Saudi Arabian
Racism	Sexism
Then	Now
Good	Bad

In other words, the structure of the article encourages the reader to make a negative judgment about Saudi Arabians, and may lead to prejudice and discrimination. This is reinforced by the connotations (see p. 126) or associations of the terminology used in the article.

- Language use. The clothing that Saudi women wear is described as 'enshrouding them completely'. The word 'shroud' has connotations of death and of being wrapped up in a way that constrains movement. The alternative words 'covering them completely' may have been less value laden. Another example of the loaded use of language is the phrase in the second sentence describing women as being 'penned' in sections of restaurants. Because it is usually animals that are kept in pens, this suggests that Saudi men treat women like animals, whereas the article could have said that women were 'restricted to special family sections in restaurants'.

- Structure and hierarchy. Readers notice the headline first and then they pay attention to the first paragraph. As mentioned above, information in news stories is often structured in order of importance (a hierarchy of meaning, with the least important details coming last). The quotes from Saudi men and women offering their own opinions about how the legal reform will affect their lives come near the end of the story, which gives them less chance of being read. News is supposed to give a balanced account of

---

NEWS FRAME

The selection and presentation of stories, issues, quotes, headlines, and images influence the way audiences make sense of the news. The processes of inclusion and exclusion, and the use of language, structure, and emphasis convey values, judgments, and perspectives that determine what the audience will consider important.

ANGLE

In journalism the angle is the central focus or the main idea in the organisation and presentation of a story and its lead.

Continued on next page ▶

different sides of a story in order to maintain journalistic objectivity and to perform the information/education function without bias; however, sometimes a story seems balanced because it includes different views, but it is actually biased because of the way it is structured.

This news story does offer two different perspectives on the significance and magnitude of the legislative reform. In paragraph three, the journalist states that 'the kingdom is reforming. It is not so much a wind of change as a puff'. In paragraph eight, Selwa al Hazzaa, a Saudi woman who is head of ophthalmology at King Faisal hospital in the capital Riyadh, says, 'A huge jump has been made'. The non-Saudi perspective of the journalist is privileged due to its position closer to the beginning of the story.

Another important point, along similar lines, is that two different perspectives are offered about the reason for gender inequality. At the beginning of the article (the top of paragraph two), the journalist writes, 'Under the country's fundamentalist interpretation of Islam, her husband may marry up to four times, but an adulterous woman faces death by stoning'. This statement creates a strong causal link in the reader's mind between Islam and the ill treatment of women in Saudi Arabia. In the very last paragraph of the story, there is a quote from a Saudi woman talking about the Muslim faith: 'There is nothing in the Qur'an that says a woman can't drive or has to have her face covered. This is male domination—not Islam'. Again we have two different perspectives but the one that comes first, which is implicitly privileged due to its placement in the article, is the only one that most people will read if they are skimming the newspaper.

The news report we have been discussing highlights important differences between what the media actually do and what they ought to do. **Normative theories** of the media are theories or approaches that offer an ideal view of the roles or functions the media ought to fulfil in society. The concept of objectivity discussed above includes a set of professional practices based on an understanding of the ideal role that a free press should play in a democracy. The conventions of objective journalism are designed to enable journalists to fulfil this ideal role. For example, a free press ought to cover both sides of an issue or debate in an impartial way, and it ought to act as a watchdog that informs the public about what the government is doing, critiquing the government and sniffing out corruption or discrimination. The media ought to provide a voice for the people and feedback to politicians about what society wants, needs, and thinks.

Due to factors such as accuracy, credibility, and diverse interpretations of information, the media's actual functions might be a far cry from these ideal normative theories. So, for example, in the news report critiquing the treatment of women in Saudi Arabia, the intent was to inform the public about legal amendments and human rights issues, but the actual role that the media played may have contributed to divisive or discriminatory attitudes by creating a binary opposition between 'us' and 'them'.

NORMATIVE THEORY

'Normative' refers to assumed norms and standards of correctness; to ideal views about the role the media should play in society, particularly the functions the press ought to perform.

Through the use of language and the way this text is structured, Saudi Arabians are ridiculed, Othered, and vilified to a certain extent. The news story, which (according to normative theory) is supposed to objectively inform us about events in other parts of the world, has been used to make a religious and political criticism of another culture. Like many readers of this article, we have never been to Saudi Arabia, as a result of which our understanding of the religious and legal rules governing gender relations in that country is largely dependent on media messages. This means that journalists have a very responsible and important position in society because they have the power to frame the way we see or understand world issues and events.

CONCLUSION

As media students, it is your job to be aware of the processes of media construction: to ask how images are being constructed; to consider what view of the world people are being invited to see; and to challenge the reality of these productions. In so doing, you are involved in the process of deconstructing the images and texts you look at.

Let's reiterate why this is important.

1   As potential media producers—writers, editors, camera operators, webmasters, and so on—you need to know the tricks and tools of the trade: how you can produce images and words that will move people to tears, anger, or joy. You deconstruct the media in order to know how to use cameras, lighting, editing, and so on to produce particular effects and meanings. You are learning the aesthetics and technical methods of the media, the language of the media.

2   As critics, you enhance your appreciation of media products through understanding the way they work; you can then communicate this to others.

3   Through deconstruction, you can see the social and political views that are often implicit but not directly stated in media products. You thus reveal the ideological messages and meanings contained in the media, and the ways they make sense of the world for people, through showing the processes of construction. This social, political, and ideological concern is at the heart of this book. Understanding that the media's views of the world are constructions is the key to ideological analysis.

This chapter has

- examined the term 'representation' and its relation to the real world
- emphasised representation as a form of construction
- illustrated the mediating aspect of the media apparatus
- looked at examples of representations of the family, the self, the Sydney Mardi Gras, and Saudi women.

? | DISCUSSION POINTS

1   Watch any episode of a satirical current affairs show and note what examples of media construction it reveals.
2   Analyse the profile picture of the person you have most recently added as a friend or begun to follow on social media. Is their profile picture a selfie? What have they included in and excluded from the frame, and what kind of image do you think they are trying to project?
3   Think of an occasion when you, or your friends or relatives, have been represented by the media. Look closely at these representations and consider how you were constructed in this process. These representations may include visual images and words, either spoken as commentary or as printed text.
4   How would you argue for and against the notion of objectivity within media news reporting?
5   Apply the arguments put forward in the analysis of the 'Saudis Acknowledge Women Exist' news story to a current news story that interests you.

SUMMARY

You should now be able to

- define the terms 'representation' and 'mediation'
- explain how the media communicate and construct reality
- analyse family photographs, selfies, news photographs, and news reports in terms of how they construct reality
- define the terms 'objectivity', 'balance', 'Othering', 'inverted pyramid', 'paradigm', and 'syntagm'
- explain the conventions of objective journalism and reflect on the way they impact on the construction of a news story and position viewers, listeners, or readers to respond to it
- analyse the language use and formulaic structure of a news report.

CHAPTER 6

Texts, Meanings, and Audiences

We must get away from the habit of thinking in terms of what the media do to people and substitute for it the idea of what people do with the media.

James Halloran, *The Effects of Television*

This chapter will

- consider the different factors that affect how people interpret media texts
- examine different theories of media audiences.

Having looked at media and society, and at issues of representation, we can now start to look at media texts and how people interpret them. By 'text' we mean any media item—photographs, advertisements, films, magazines, books, websites, television programs, newspaper articles, and so on. A text must be capable of being reproduced and subjected to analysis. To decode a text is to make sense of it, regardless of whether it has actual writing in it. Textual analysis is a central component of media studies.

Do media texts have single or many meanings?

Later chapters present different critical approaches for textual analysis, but first we need a framework to answer the wider question of whether we can determine what texts mean. There are two main concerns here.

1 Do texts have a single, essential meaning that analysts, readers, and critics are looking for, or can numerous different meanings be found in any one text?
2 What factors need to be taken into account in trying to establish what meanings a given text might hold?

Regarding the first concern, it is widely accepted in media studies that texts carry a number of possible meanings.

We suggest that:

- there is a **dominant reading** or meaning for a text (Hall 1980, pp. 128–38)
- there are different meanings according to the different contexts, critical criteria, and personal perspectives used to approach the text.

These different meanings lead us to the second concern: there are four overlapping factors to take into account:

1 texts—analysis of texts on their own
2 production contexts—the study of how texts are produced
3 distribution contexts—the study of where and when texts are sold or screened
4 audience contexts—the study of how audiences actually use and make sense of texts.

◀ DOMINANT READING

The meaning of a text that is accepted by most audience members and can be determined by examining its textual codes and social/historical contexts.

Each of these factors contributes to interpretations of what a text means. The more that is known about all four, the greater the potential to establish the different possible meanings of any one text, and to give reasons or explanations for these different meanings and readings. Figure 6.1 illustrates this diagrammatically.

Figure 6.1 Model of the relationship between texts, contexts, and audiences

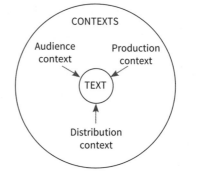

THE TEXT ITSELF

Some people argue that while background knowledge and different contexts may be important, what ultimately matters is the text itself. In many instances this is all that is available. Anyone looking at a text without background knowledge (as is the case for many audiences) can only determine meaning by looking at the text. Textual analysis focuses solely on the textual content and the textual processes used—the language, the way it was photographed, the kinds of camera movements involved, and so on.

However, it is impossible to make full sense of a text (to give it a meaning) in isolation. Texts produce meanings by referring to the world outside themselves and by using pre-existing codes of representation. Audience members have to have knowledge of the real world to which the text refers and knowledge of the conventions of the text's medium (its photographic, cinematic, or televisual codes of representation).

The historical drama thriller *The Imitation Game*, for example, will mean more to people who have some knowledge of the life of Alan Turing, a British cryptanalyst, and the context of Britain's war with Germany in the Second World War because the film is based on Turing's work for the British government during the Second World War when he decrypted German intelligence codes. Similarly, Steven Spielberg's historical drama thriller *Bridge of Spies* won't mean as much to people if they don't know details of the 1960 U-2 spy plane incident during the Cold War. Films also communicate by working with the codes and conventions of narrative films in general, such as the use of continuity editing, and of the historical drama and the war film in particular. When you have some existing knowledge about these events and genres, you can make good sense of such films.

Interpreting the meaning of the text depends on this understanding. In acknowledging these factors, which influence the ways in which a text might be interpreted, we are beginning to refer to the codes and conventions the text is using in its production. Knowing the meaning of the text is dependent on these knowledges. The text's context is also being referred to, but the focus is still primarily on the text. Semiotic and structuralist approaches work in this way (see Parts 2 and 3).

CONTEXTS

Production context (background textual knowledge)

It is helpful to know about the actual processes of the making of a text; this gives clues as to its meaning and illuminates the text in a number of ways.

1 Begin by finding out about the acknowledged motivations of those involved in production. Who wrote, filmed, or photographed the text? What have they said they were trying to do? What have they said about the text? What other work have they done that is relevant? Where several people are involved—as in film and television production, which has producers, directors, cinematographers, editors, music composers, costume designers, and so on—questions can be asked of all of them to find out what interactions went on between them. Try also to explore their unconscious intentions by finding out important personal details of their lives to see if these illuminate the text. The **auteur theory** approach to film studies is an example of this way of reading media products; it focuses on the director as the key figure we need to know about in order to understand the film (Caughie 1981; Cook 1985, pp. 137–46).

    A film's director is considered to be the author of the text and so is assumed to have creative control over the project. Over the course of their careers, some directors develop distinctive signatures, consisting of characteristic styles, favourite actors, themes, narrative structures, or motifs that brand their films. For instance, dramatic lighting, expressionist imagery, and outsiders or alienated characters often played by Johnny Depp or Helena Bonham Carter are recurring motifs in the films of Tim Burton, while in television the showrunner Matthew Weiner has become known for his fastidious attention to period detail and his control over art direction in *Mad Men*. The auteur approach to screen media helps to elaborate on the aesthetic or artistic qualities of screen texts and the context of production, but it neglects to fully acknowledge that screen production is a collaborative process involving creative input from many sources, including the scriptwriter, cast, and crew.

2 Look at the conditions of production. What was being aimed for? What financial or political constraints were involved? Who commissioned the work? Where was it made? What social, political, and historical factors influenced the text? All these factors may have determined the outcome of the final text. Political economy approaches stress these elements.

◄ AUTEUR THEORY

The theory that films are the creative products of film directors and can be interpreted as their personal visions, marked by a unique 'signature style'.

Distribution context

Does it make a difference where and when we read media texts? ▶

Texts do not just appear on their own. They always exist in a social situation and are distributed in a specific context. Because the context of a text influences its meaning, it is important to understand this context to do textual analysis. The two main distribution contexts are space and time: where the text is being read and when it is being read.

Space

Every text appears in a specific media space and in a wider social space. A magazine advertisement appears in a particular magazine and is sold in a particular shop, in a particular location—town, village, city, and so on—in a particular society and country. A television program appears on a particular television channel and is seen in a particular room—bedroom, hotel room, sitting room, lecture theatre, and so on—all of which are specific social locations. These different spaces can influence the text's meaning: whether a particular advertisement appears in a teenage girls' magazine or a men's soft porn magazine, each of which has a different implied readership and a different social agenda, it will take on a different meaning. The same program screened on SBS, the ABC, or Channel 10 in Australia will be affected by the differing ideals of each of these channels and their audiences: multicultural and experimental broadcasting in the case of SBS, social responsibility in the case of the ABC, and commercial success in the case of Channel 10.

Texts are not presented in isolation but are surrounded by other texts—magazine articles, television programs, and so on—that will in turn influence people's readings. Popular television texts used in an academic course will be seen and read differently because of the new context they are placed in. You may be watching *Game of Thrones* at home with your friends for entertainment and relaxation while you eat a Big Mac. Alternatively, you may be watching it in a university lecture theatre as part of a course of study; you may be taking notes. Programs even change meanings depending on who they are watched with—on our own, with friends, with parents, or with strangers.

The importance of context can be easily seen by thinking of clothes as a kind of text. The meaning of articles of clothing will change depending on who is wearing them (man, woman, child) and where they are wearing them (at work, on the beach, at a party). Meanings are affected by and dependent on their context.

Taking this further, it is important to look at the wider social context that any text appears in: images of Katy Perry or Taylor Swift, found all over the world, will have different meanings in different countries. Teenage girls from different ethnic and racial backgrounds in America, Europe, Bali, or Iraq, with different religious, social, and moral codes, will make different readings of the singers' appearances, songs, and performances (Fiske 1989a, pp. 95–113), while males will make another set of readings. The social norms and conventions of any culture will engage in an interplay with texts, and produce different readings and meanings. So the placement of texts within their social and spatial contexts, and their relationship to other texts all need to be considered.

Time

It is useful to notice the time of day that people engage with media texts and consider how that forms part of the context in which texts are interpreted. Many texts are produced to fit specifically with certain times of the day, and are consumed or interpreted at these times. Texts may have a specific time context that contributes to their meanings. Note that the internet is not governed by the usual spatiotemporal conventions. Internet news bulletins, for instance, do not focus on local issues because they can be accessed anywhere in the world, at any time. In fact, many internet users log on at times when there is less traffic.

On another level, we must locate texts in the specific historical times in which they are produced and consumed. Alfred Hitchcock's *Rear Window* was made in 1954 and represents a study of spectatorship at that time. Hitchcock was critiquing the voyeuristic practice of moviegoing and comparing it to spying on one's neighbours through the back window: the protagonist in *Rear Window*, immobilised and confined to his apartment as a result of a broken leg, uses binoculars and a photo-journalist's camera equipped with a zoom lens to intrude on the private moments of his neighbours. In this film the medium is presented as a powerful source of knowledge, but it is also seen as invasive and problematic. The social concerns in *Rear Window* revolve around privacy, reflecting the paranoia in the USA at the time arising from McCarthyism. (In the late 1940s and early 1950s, US Senator Joseph McCarthy instigated the persecution of anyone suspected of being a communist or sympathetic to communist politics, so the fear of being spied on was very real.) When watching *Rear Window* in the twenty-first century, because so much time has passed since the release of the movie, the social concerns it showcases and the technology it uses to explore those concerns may seem trivial or clichéd, yet audiences may also derive pleasure and comfort from a sense of nostalgia, as the story seems to come from a more secure and easier world than ours.

The ending of the film *Fight Club* did not provoke audiences when the film was first released, but after the events of 11 September 2001 television stations withdrew it from screenings because its ending looked so similar to the destruction of the Twin Towers.

You should by now be realising that study of any media text involves a potentially huge and ever-expanding area of knowledge in relation to understanding the terms of the text itself and all the different contexts it might inhabit. Consequently, our readings are never complete; we must be open to finding new factors, such as new background information and different aspects of the social and historical context, which will affect our readings. The more information we have, the closer we get to understanding what a particular text could mean and how it is able to produce such a meaning.

Audience context

How can we analyse and understand media audiences?

All our efforts at finding the meanings of texts may come to grief when we confront the real audience. Theories of the reader or audience suggest that because readers produce meanings and all readers are different, it is possible to come up with many readings and meanings in a text. Any particular reading may only hold for particular individuals. Therefore, any attempt to discover a meaning for a text that holds for more than one reader must rely on generalisations and so runs the risk of becoming overly reductive. While we accept that audiences make different readings, it is still valid to explore texts through examining their textual codes and social and historical contexts in the process of textual analysis. In doing so, we can look for a text's dominant reading. While this is a valuable part of studying texts, it doesn't account for how audiences actually read texts and since, in a way, media texts don't meaningfully exist unless they are being read by someone, this question must be considered.

A large body of work focusing on media audiences acknowledges that the contexts, practices, and processes of reception are just as important in generating meaning as

RECEPTION STUDIES ▶

The study of how audiences actively receive, read, consume, and interact with media texts.

the context of production, the text itself, and the medium by which the message is communicated. This branch of media studies is known as **reception studies**.

The inscribed reader

INSCRIBED READER ▶

An ideal reader who is constructed by the text or who is imagined/ intended by the producers of the text.

When the way audiences engage with media texts is looked at, consideration needs to be given to what communication theorist Paul Willeman has called an **inscribed reader** (Fiske 1987, p. 62). The inscribed reader can best be understood as a receptive member of the target market to which the media text is deliberately addressed. When considering the nature of the inscribed reader of a particular text, ask yourself whether the message seems to assume that the receiver is male, female, wealthy, poor, highly educated, image conscious, young, old, a member of a certain nationality, and so forth.

The actual reader

ACTUAL READER ▶

The real flesh-and-blood individuals who interpret or read texts.

There are a number of ways that actual audiences, or the **actual reader**, can be studied. We can engage in audience research, looking not at texts and the meanings they contain, but at audiences and the meanings they extract from or ascribe to media texts. We need to observe, interview, and interact with audiences as and after they read media texts; we need to watch them watching, or reading, or listening to media texts. We can also develop theories that understand and explain the process of being an audience. These theories examine what is happening when people read texts. You can study your own responses and readings, and compare them with other people's as a way to understand this method. Audience research is a crucial part of media studies, because it completes the circle of text, production, and consumption.

Audience research and theories about audiences

Audience research has understood the audience in two different ways: in terms of effects and in terms of reception. Effects studies (see pp. 19–20, 42–8, 93–4) look at how audiences are directly affected by the media—the media are theorised in terms of making the audience 'vulnerable'. Reception studies, which emerged in the 1970s, look at how audiences are active: in other words, how they use and interpret the media (Cunningham & Turner 2009, pp. 74–6).

Media scholars are not the only people who conduct studies of audiences. Audience research is very significant for the media industries themselves. Companies such as Apple invest a great deal in research that indicates how media consumers might use their products, and organisations such as MTV use focus groups, ratings, and other forms of audience research as a way of finding out how successful they are and for testing new products. Audience research falls into two areas: quantitative and qualitative.

Is it more important to know how many people watch a program or to know what they feel about it?

Quantitative research looks at numbers: for example, how many people watch a particular program (ratings research provides this information). Qualitative research is concerned with how people are actually responding to specific programs: why they like or dislike certain programs, what aspects they respond to positively or negatively, and whether they watch attentively or have media such as television and radio on for the sake of companionship and background noise. This type of qualitative research falls within the reception studies area.

The media try to perfect techniques for measuring the nature of audience response, which they then use as a guide to improving their products. They use preview audiences to test drive films. In these previews, audiences are asked to give their responses to the film. If some parts of the film don't work for enough people, then the producers can change them. The film *Blade Runner* is a well-known example. After initial audience previews, it was decided to introduce a voice-over commentary and change the ending in order to romanticise and simplify the text. At the time, the revised version of the movie proved more popular with the preview audiences. Some years later, the cult success of the movie prompted the release of the 'director's cut'—the version Ridley Scott preferred to that dictated by the producers. This is a common phenomenon now, one example being *Donnie Darko*, but the release of director's cuts still has to be approved by the producers, and they are only released when it is expected that they will make a profit.

Political parties aim to make party political broadcasts that will win the support of the electorate. The preview process for speeches and broadcasts now measures audience response moment by moment, with audiences pressing buttons to indicate their responses when they are asked to choose between such given responses as pleasure/boredom, trust/distrust, and so on. A profile is built up of the most successful kinds of electioneering and this profile is then built into the finished products. Market research is all about measuring the numbers of audience members or consumers, and their likes and dislikes. It is a way of winning markets, and so it can be said that audience research is part of the market economy of the media. Considerable money and effort are put into this work.

In contrast to audience research conducted by commercial interests, audience research conducted as part of scholarly media studies, which is considerably less well funded than its commercial counterpart, claims to come from a disinterested perspective. Effects research, mentioned earlier, devises experiments to test audience responses to programs, including direct measurement of brainwaves and physical reactions, and observation and measurement of actions and behaviours after watching programs. The findings from such research are inconclusive, partly because fear, surprise, and desire can generate similar physiological responses.

How can we understand the relationship between media and audiences? (▶)

There is a variety of ways of understanding the media–audience relationship.

1   Direct effects. The **direct effects** model is sometimes also called the 'hypodermic model' or the 'magic bullet theory of communication', indicating that media producers inject or shoot their intended meaning directly into the audience. The audience absorbs the message like a sponge or as drugs absorbed into the bloodstream. This reflects the belief that the media are capable of radically affecting people's behaviour and beliefs to such an extent that they can be used for the purposes of political propaganda. The direct-effects model of media audiences assumes that media consumers accept the intended meaning encoded in media messages with relative passivity, and that the relationship between media producers and consumers is

◀ DIRECT EFFECTS

The direct-effects model of communication (also called the 'hypodermic model') suggests that the media transmit powerful messages to audience members, who absorb the meaning passively and are strongly affected by it.

predictable and asymmetrical. There is a power imbalance: producers of the media messages have more control over meaning, and the transmission of information is largely one-way, with limited audience feedback or input. This view originated in the 1930s when the media were being used by the Nazis in Germany, by communists in the Soviet Union, and by advertisers and political parties in the USA. This view suggests that if you have control of the media, you can control people's minds, beliefs, and actions according to the process represented in Figure 6.2.

Figure 6.2 Direct-effects model of the media–audience relationship

all-powerful media ——————▶ brainwashing ——————▶ audience

REINFORCEMENT ▶

The media reinforce ideas and feelings that other social institutions are already communicating.

2   Reinforcement. The **reinforcement** model (represented in Figure 6.3) refines the direct-effects approach by suggesting that the media work in conjunction with social forces to influence people when their messages coincide with ideas being produced elsewhere in society—through education, the family, churches, and so on. Media theorist Paul Lazarsfeld's influential audience research suggests that the media are most effective when they work to reinforce existing beliefs, values, and behaviours (Lazarsfeld & Stanton 1949). Lazarsfeld's work indicates that people tend to ignore or resist information that does not reinforce their existing experiences and opinions; however, the media can play a significant role in activating interpersonal channels of communication, especially when messages reinforce the beliefs of opinion leaders, who then pass on the media message to others within their sphere of influence.

Figure 6.3 Reinforcement model of the media–audience relationship

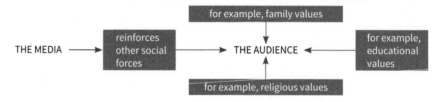

CULTIVATION ▶

The media have a cumulative effect on audiences. Long-term exposure to media cultivates attitudes and beliefs through the persistent repetition of messages and images.

3   Cultivation. A large body of research into **cultivation** suggests that it would be unwise to dismiss the long-term, cumulative effects of screen media on society. In an article entitled 'Cultivation Revisited', media researchers Jonathan Cohen and Gabriel Weimann state that:

One of the more fruitful avenues of research has suggested examining the effects of television on viewers' attitudes and beliefs, rather than on their behaviors. According to cultivation theory, massive exposure to television's reconstructed realities can result in perceptions of reality very different from what they might be if viewers watched less television. In other words, the highly stylized, stereotyped, and repetitive images portrayed on television have been regarded as an important source of socialization and everyday information (Cohen & Weimann 2000, p. 99).

Note that different media texts and genres offer different images of the world. While news, thrillers, and crime fiction may contribute to the development of a 'mean world' perspective, romantic comedies will do quite the opposite.

4   Desensitisation. Another key effect that researchers think the media may have is **desensitisation**. It has been predicted that long-term exposure to certain types of media images can build up tolerance to things that would otherwise be troubling. Repeatedly watching the combination of humour with graphic violence in films such as *Sin City: A Dame to Kill For*, *RED (Retired Extremely Dangerous)*, *Inglourious Basterds*, and *Django Unchained*, for instance, might make us less sensitive to media violence, and less likely to have a shocked response to actual violence, or to perceive violence and aggression as bad. Some researchers go so far as to link media violence to actual aggression in this way:

> The first exposure to violent media can make a person (especially children) anxious and fearful. Repeated exposure reduces these effects and leaves the viewer wanting stronger doses of violence … repeated exposure to violent media, for example, a couple of hours a day for 15 years, causes a serious increase in the likelihood of a person becoming a habitually aggressive person and occasionally a violent offender (Bushman & Anderson 2001, pp. 481–2).

◀ DESENSITISATION

Long-term exposure to media can make audiences progressively less sensitive or responsive to images and messages that made a strong impression when first encountered.

5   Observational learning and cognitive scripts. One of the explanatory frameworks that currently holds most credence regarding the effects of the media on young audiences is the theory of **observational learning** of social behaviour and **cognitive scripts** (see Bandura 1994). This theory suggests that people learn how to behave by observing role models in action and remembering the script that was performed, so that they can play the part later, should a similar situation arise. A script is like a program or narrative that offers ways of behaving or dealing with particular circumstances; it can be derived from witnessing either real or fictional interactions. Research indicates that 'Scripts for behaviour are also constructed early in development, and it is likely that continued exposure to media violence influences the development of aggressive scripts' (Dubow & Miller 1996, p. 136). A script is most likely to be retrieved, mimicked, and progressively reinforced if the situation an individual faces is very similar to the one seen on film or television, if the screen violence is very realistic, if the person identifies with the role model, and if the actor receives positive reinforcement or is perceived as having desirable characteristics, such as being attractive, wealthy, or powerful (Geen 1994, p. 157; Bushman & Huesmann 2001, pp. 236–7).

◀ OBSERVATIONAL LEARNING AND COGNITIVE SCRIPTS

People learn how to behave by observing how their role models act and by remembering the script that was performed so that if, later, they encounter a similar situation they can play the part.

6   Uses-and-gratifications (Blumler & Katz 1974). The **uses-and-gratifications** understanding of the media–society dynamic (represented in Figure 6.4) is significant for having brought the concepts of pleasure and gratification into debate about the media, and it paved the way for more recent research that argues audiences are not just passive consumers brainwashed by media products, but are active participants who make their own meanings.

◀ USES-AND-GRATIFICATIONS

Audiences use the media in unpredictable ways (through selection, interpretation, and integration with other everyday activities) to please themselves, not necessarily as media producers intend them to be used.

Figure 6.4 Uses-and-gratifications model of the media–audience relationship

powerful audience ⟶ takes what it wants from the media ⟶ media

To understand audiences' uses and gratifications, qualitative studies are often carried out through ethnographic work that explores audience responses through a mixture of direct observation, interviewing, and research. This model acknowledges that audience members often use television, radio, and other media as a background to everyday activities, such as cooking, domestic tasks, and studying. In such instances, audiences may gain pleasure from using the media as a form of companionship, but they are unlikely to experience direct effects in response to media content as they may only glance at the television, scan news headlines, or listen inattentively to the radio. The uses-and-gratifications model suggests that direct media effects are impossible to measure due to the infinitely variable, personalised contexts of reception.

Audience research based on an ethnographic model

Stuart Hall (1980) and then David Morley (1992) worked with Hall's encoding/decoding model of communication. This model suggests that different kinds of decoding or readings of media texts are possible, including:

PREFERRED READING ▶

Audiences accept what is being presented without questioning the meaning intended by the media producers.

- **preferred readings**—audiences accept what is being presented without question
- **negotiated readings**—audiences negotiate with the text's intended meaning and accept only some of what is being presented to them
- **alternative/oppositional readings**—audiences read completely against the preferred reading.

NEGOTIATED READING ▶

Audiences accept only some of what is being presented to them.

ALTERNATIVE/OPPOSITIONAL READING ▶

Audiences interpret a text completely against the preferred reading.

POLYSEMIC ▶

A sign that has more than one possible meaning.

The word **polysemic** comes from the Greek words *poly* ('many') and *seme* ('meaning'). 'Polysemic' thus means 'many meanings'. While the polysemic nature (see p. 134) of media texts does provide the possibility for multiple interpretations, these readings 'correspond to the reader's response to his or her social conditions not to the structure of the text' (O'Sullivan et al. 1994, p. 239). Fiske and media theorist Tim O'Sullivan give an example of how these three types of reading might occur in relation to advertisements that depict women in terms of sexual objectification, fashion models, or maternal figures:

> A preferred reading according to the dominant-hegemonic code is to accept and agree with this portrayal as natural, accurate, and attractive. A negotiated reading may be produced by a middle-class career woman who broadly accepts the preferred reading, but "for others, not for me!" She reserves the right to produce her own reading of the ads which corresponds to her social position as an independent woman. An oppositional reading might be produced by a feminist as insulting, degrading, restricting, and proof of men's exploitation of women. The first reading could be produced by women who would buy the products, the second by women who might, if it suited their purposes, and the third by women who would not (O'Sullivan et al. 1994, pp. 239–40).

Morley was interested in seeing how social groups, rather than individuals, make readings, so he looked at trade unionists, young people, and people of colour, expecting to find that they would make readings that supported their own class, ethnic, or youth subcultural values.

The idea of researching audiences as social groups has been productive. An ethnographic approach has been developed by researchers who studied women as audiences of soap operas (Hobson 1982; Brunsdon 1986). A considerable amount of work has been done exploring how women read popular women's texts (such as magazines, melodramas, and romance novels) in a way that makes these texts meaningful to them (Ang 1985, 1991; Radway 1987). This work looks closely at the social circumstances in which women consume the media, and how they relate media texts and technologies to their real lives. Fiske (1989a) has developed the notion of audiences being able to resist what is presented to them. He argues that audiences have considerable power over the texts they consume.

Other researchers have explored audience readings of Madonna, particularly those made by young women, people of colour, and gay people (Schwichtenberg 1993). Richard Dyer and others have looked at how gay and lesbian audiences read the media, as in Dyer's analysis of readings of Judy Garland (Dyer 1987, pp. 141–94). Again, these studies show how audiences make use of texts from their particular perspectives. An extensive audience analysis is found in cultural studies theorist Henry Jenkins' *Textual Poachers*, in which he looks at a whole range of activities and ways of reading by different groups and people, particularly in relation to the *Star Trek* franchise (Jenkins 1992a; Tulloch & Jenkins 1995). The 'poaching' idea suggests more ways of readers altering texts and becoming active rather than passive.

In their efforts to understand how the media influence or affect us, media industries and social researchers will look for new ways of understanding and researching the text–audience relationship.

Audience projections

Do our individual personalities influence our media readings?

We want to introduce a final approach that draws on theories of **projection**. This is a term that was used by psychologists Sigmund Freud and Carl Jung. The central idea is that in texts, audiences see aspects of themselves that they are not consciously aware of mirrored back. This relates to the wider concept that in everything we see around us, we find a reflection of ourselves. Of course, this isn't literally true, but what is being suggested is that the way we see, interpret, and respond to the external world and to other people is a reflection of our own unconscious, internal state. Another way of putting this is that we project ourselves onto the world and other people. This is a basic tenet of much work in the fields of psychology and psychotherapy.

I, Michael, realised this when I started listening closely to what I and others said when we were interpreting media texts. I understood that I was projecting myself, my view of the world, onto the text. In preparation for a course on melodrama, I watched D W Griffith's short film *Mender of Nets* with two friends. Discussing the film afterwards, each of us had a very different reading of the ending, in which the actress Lillian Gish is left on her own. One of us said with optimism, 'Ah well, she's learnt a lot. It will be better next time'. The second said despairingly, 'Of course, relationships never work'. The third reflected that 'All men are bastards!' These three readings (all of which fit the text) reflected the views on relationships that we three held at that time. We had projected ourselves onto the text.

Consequently, if you are trying to understand how audiences read texts, you can use the idea of projection and argue that any one person's reading of a text is a reflection of themselves: that is, they project their own ideas and feelings onto the text. Our conscious

◀ PROJECTION

People project their own unconscious feelings onto other people or objects; they see in objects and other people aspects of themselves reflected back.

and our unconscious feelings and beliefs are reflected in the way we interpret a text. This is a simple but also quite startling idea.

This approach takes us into analysis of how the mechanisms of cinematic identification work for individuals rather than groups, and begins to tap into our unconscious readings, which are notoriously difficult to ascertain.

A COMMON STUDENT QUESTION ABOUT TEXTUAL ANALYSIS

Students analysing texts often raise significant issues, as expressed in the following question.

Did the producers consciously intend to create the meanings we see in texts?
Aren't we reading too much into texts?

Finding out the intentions of the producers of media texts is of some use, particularly because the intention to sell, persuade, or entertain is usually profit driven and guided by vested interests on the part of the media producers. It is a good idea to be mindful of who might benefit from a text being interpreted and responded to in a particular manner, and it is worth searching for published interviews that may reveal authorial intentions. However, the meanings audiences draw from texts are not necessarily derived from, or even related to, understandings of the intentions of the texts' producers.

In relation to the common student question 'Aren't we reading too much into texts?', there is a useful distinction between reading things into a text (projection) and reading things out of a text (exegesis). If the interpretation comes purely from the reader, then that particular reading may be of little value in determining the meaning, although it tells you interesting things about the reader. You can ensure that a particular reading is coming out of a text by paying close attention to the codes and conventions, structure, and composition of the piece, by acquiring knowledge of its cultural context, and by checking to see if the meaning you derive from the text resonates with other readers.

CONCLUSION

Text, context, and audience all need to be taken into account when trying to analyse the meanings of texts. Media meanings are dependent on the text itself, on its context, and on its audience. As we take account of more and more aspects, we aim to get closer to seeing the potential and actual meanings of a text. There won't be one simple answer to what a text means, but we argue here that some readings and meanings are more complete than others.

This book offers a variety of approaches for reading texts: semiological analysis; analysis of narrative structure; mythological analysis; sociocultural analysis; political economy approaches; and ideological and discourse analysis. In your work, you will gradually become able to use all these approaches in the study of any one text. As long as you make clear what aspects of the text you are focusing on—whether this be background information, textual codes, social and historical context, or actual audience research—then you will be able to support the readings of texts you make and the meanings you see in them.

This chapter has

- explored the potential meanings of texts
- considered the importance of text, contexts, and audiences in these meanings
- looked at various theories of media audiences, including direct effects, reinforcement, cultivation, desensitisation, observational learning and cognitive scripts, uses-and-gratifications, ethnographic research, and projection.

? | DISCUSSION POINTS

1 How can the contexts of space and time affect readings of media texts?
2 Do you ever see situations where you, or other people, appear to be behaving by following a media script (for example, imitating characters from *The Simpsons*, *South Park*, or *The Big Bang Theory*, or saying in an American accent 'd'oh!')? What effects are these behavioural scripts having on social interaction?
3 Which of all the approaches to audience studies discussed in the chapter do you find most useful and why?
4 What are the strengths and weaknesses of these different approaches?

| SUMMARY

You should now be able to

- explain the difference between a media text and its context
- explain what different factors need to be taken into account when reading a media text
- explain, with examples, why these factors are important
- explain the difference between the inscribed reader and the actual reader
- explain the terms 'dominant/preferred reading', 'negotiated reading', and 'alternative/oppositional reading'
- explain the differences between quantitative and qualitative audience research, and what is valuable for each kind of research
- give an overview and explanation of different audience theories and research methods
- explain the terms 'textual analysis', 'auteur theory', 'reinforcement', 'uses-and-gratifications', 'cultivation', and 'desensitisation'
- explain and illustrate how the theory of projection relates to audiences.

CHAPTER 7

New Media and Technological Development

We've entered a new era of virtuality, where the interpenetration of a plethora of communications media, from CCTV and mobile phones to webcams and cable channels, has created an environment in which never before have so many watched so many others, doing so very little.

Will Self, quoted in *The Media*

This chapter will
- identify the characteristics of new media
- consider the implications of technological development and its relationship to social change
- present a case study of television (TV), algorithmic culture, and surveillance
- define technological determinism and the digital divide
- consider positive and negative aspects of technological change, including algorithmic culture and surveillance.

Technological development is nothing new: it has been happening since sticks and stones were first fashioned into rudimentary tools. It is the accelerated rate of change in recent years and its powerful impact on the role of the media in society that interest us here. This chapter explores technological developments in the media, and considers some positive and negative aspects of these developments.

At the end of the nineteenth century, the technologies of film, photography, recording, telegraphy, and telephony were radically changing practices and patterns of human communication and behaviour. At the time people didn't know how these technologies would affect business, social relationships, and political communication. We are in a similar situation at the beginning of the twenty-first century with the latest media technologies.

DIGITAL MEDIA ▶

Media such as digital video games, the internet, and other forms of computerised media that mathematically process and convert whatever information needs to be represented into numerical form. The information can then be manipulated, reproduced, converted, shared, and transmitted in versatile, swift, immaterial ways.

ANALOGUE MEDIA ▶

Analogue media such as photography, print, and radio use material processes and mechanical modes of representation to transcribe and transmit content in forms such as physical data or electrical signals.

CHARACTERISTICS OF NEW MEDIA

The term 'new media' is often used very loosely, but it is worth pausing to consider what this means. Generally, new media refer to **digital media** as opposed to **analogue media**. Analogue media encode information such as sounds or images into an 'analogous' form, such as printed words or painted pictures, transcribing the original into a physical representation. Analogue media can be objects such as books, photographs, and magazines, or the information can be further converted into a signal, such as light and soundwaves, which can be projected or broadcast to many recipients, as is the case with cinema, television, and radio.

Digitisation encodes information in numerical form (such as the binary system of zeros and ones used in computers). This mathematical information is a symbolic representation of the original data, just as paintings and typed words are symbolic representations; however, digital data can be stored, processed, compressed, manipulated, and multiplied far more readily, as it is not bound to any physical artefact. Digitisation has revolutionised the ways information is mediated, modified, organised, produced, reproduced, distributed, and consumed. Wireless technologies such as satellite signals, cellular telephony, Bluetooth, and cloud-based storage further liberate the transmission of information from material and mechanical constraints such as telephone lines and electric cables.

Digitisation has been described by sociologist and media theorist Manuel Castells (2000a, p. 2) as a 'universal language' that is able to unite different communities around the globe, and can customise and integrate the production of words, sounds, and images. New media or digital media are characterised by interactivity, immateriality (or virtuality), non-linearity and hypertextual networks, convergence, and decentralisation.

INTERACTIVITY

All media texts and technologies are interactive to a certain extent, in that people take an active role in textual production and interpretation; however, the term 'interactivity' is usually used to refer to forms of communication in which the audience is able to use technology to manipulate the structure, sound, or image of the text itself. In this sense, interactivity is a property of the medium of communication that empowers the user.

Where conventional media allow media consumers agency in the way they receive and interpret media messages, digital technologies enable reciprocal, two-way communication, with a very fast feedback loop that promises to change the asymmetrical power relations of mass communication by giving citizens more choice and control. Interactivity can take different forms, offering different degrees of participation. Navigation through, say, a website or a series of sites involves choosing an individual pathway by clicking on hyperlinks to different sections of information according to the media user's needs and interests. Interactivity may also involve contributing to media texts, such as blogging, chatting online, vodcasting, podcasting, editing a collaboratively authored webpage such as Wikipedia, or shopping online and uploading consumer reviews on sites such as Amazon and the Internet Movie Database (IMDB). In virtual environments, such as digital game worlds, users may experience a more immersive, participatory form of interaction (see below) in relation to virtual reality and immateriality.

IMMATERIALITY AND VIRTUAL REALITY

Digital media texts are 'dematerialised', as Lister et al. (2003, p. 16) put it, meaning that they are liberated from their physical form: for example, in semiotic terms the 'signified' content of a photograph or book is separated from the 'signifier' (the film negative or the paper) that carries this content. Immateriality (or virtuality) affects the way media users experience the media in that we no longer necessarily come into contact with a physical object, such as a book, a DVD, or a vinyl record, but it also affects virtual experiences of space, time, motion, and our own identities. We navigate the virtual 'desktop' on our computer screens to access cyberspace, which is a virtual space entered through a virtual 'window' on our screens. Via the mouse or touchscreen, we use virtual tools such as scissors, pencils, paperclips, and paste analogous to tools on our actual desk, and we open portals similar to actual windows to access external spaces and places that hold information we want. Each of these virtual spaces or objects has a material counterpart or reference point. In this sense, everyday life is lived to a large extent in immaterial screen space, which can be understood as a form of virtual reality.

Once in cyberspace we might 'visit' sites such as YouTube and 'open' other windows to view video clips, or we might immerse ourselves in a virtual reality construct, such as *EVE Online*, *IMVU*, or *Blue Mars*, which are furnished with interactive avatars, graphic interfaces, and even their own economies. These virtual worlds involve another level of immersion in virtual reality—a simulated reality in which fantasy identities can be constructed without the need for the user's physical body to bear a close relationship to the identity projected to others. This liberating aspect of new media has been lauded as a harbinger of equality. Race, sex, and disability, for instance, are rendered invisible so racism, sexism, and discrimination on the basis of physical disability are, theoretically, eliminated and online communities are organised according to the shared interests of disembodied participants.

To a certain extent, the rise of Twitter and Facebook has overshadowed involvement in virtual worlds. Sometimes people forget that screen media space is not just a virtual world—it has an interface with reality. For instance, Kanye West is an American rapper, fashion designer, and producer married to Kim Kardashian. West is a prolific tweeter and has over 19 million followers. Endorsements by celebrities such as West, including retweeting on Twitter, are highly sought after by companies and for promoting social issues, political agendas, or even other celebrities. West's tweets have become notorious for being banal as well as ridiculous and entertaining; nonetheless, they have great potential for reach. These tweets have become comic fodder. For example, classical singer Josh Groban performed a stunt on an episode of TV show *Jimmy Kimmel Live* to 'advertise' his new (fake) album 'The Best Tweets of Kanye West'. In the skit, Groban put music to and sang in the style of West's typical tweets, such as: 'Do you know where to find marble conference tables? I'm looking to have a conference … not until I get the table though'; 'Fur pillows are hard to actually sleep on'; 'Man, whatever happened to my antique fishtank?'; and 'Classical music is tight, yo'. While West seemingly tweets whatever comes into his mind, his tweets are not without ramifications. He is often embroiled in Twitter rants about other celebrities such as Taylor Swift that enrage her fans, and his 2016 tweet 'BILL COSBY INNOCENT!!!!!!!!!!' created an online backlash, with many angered that West was seemingly defending actor Bill Cosby, who has been publicly accused of sexually assaulting more than fifty women during the course of his career.

Many other celebrities have also faced consequences for their inappropriate or thoughtless use of social media. For example, actor Ashton Kutcher was forced to apologise after a late-night tweet to his 8 million followers declaring that the sacking of Joe Paterno was an 'insult' to his legacy; Paterno was fired from his role as the longstanding Penn State National Football League coach after he was implicated in a cover-up of alleged sexual assault of young boys. Kutcher and then-wife Demi Moore were high-profile and vocal advocates against child sex trafficking, and the ill-informed tweet meant Kutcher's credibility came into question. After public apologies, Kutcher declared he would hand over the management of his Twitter account to an agency.

The blurring of the boundaries between the real and the virtual is increasing as more convincing simulations of reality are made possible, and as media use penetrates ever more aspects of everyday life, thereby enabling a seamless interface between mediated and actual spaces, experiences, and modes of communication.

NON-LINEARITY AND NETWORKS

New media functions on the principle of networks, rather than linear or hierarchical structures. Conventional media are often organised in such a way as to encourage audiences to follow a linear, one-way path through information. We are, for example, meant to listen to a radio interview from start to finish. Some conventional media, like books, offer more ways of manipulating the order of information, such as using the index to skip to the page of interest. New media are characterised by much higher degrees of non-linearity and indexicality, and are often structured as networks. Thus, once it is digitised, a radio interview transcript or a film can be organised into chunks of information that users can navigate in much the same way they navigate a book index, and can use an internet navigation bar to locate information and jump directly to a point of interest.

This non-sequential way of organising and accessing digitally encoded information in new media is termed **hypertext**. The prefix 'hyper' refers to something that exceeds or extends beyond given limits, as hyperlinks take a user outside or beyond a given web page. In *New Media*, Lister et al. define hypertext as:

> a work which is made up from discrete units of material in which each one carries a number of pathways to other units. The work is a web of connection which the user explores using the navigational aids of the interface design. Each discrete "node" in the web has a number of entrances and exits or links (2003, p. 24).

This principle of networked information originated with the development of the internet in the 1960s because the US Defense Department wanted to establish a computer system that could withstand a nuclear attack, rerouting packets of information through independent pathways to avoid losing data if the centralised computer system was destroyed. Not only are the internet itself and the individual websites that comprise it organised according to this non-linear network principle, but hypertextuality is also increasingly coming to characterise contemporary forms of storytelling (see the section on media convergence below).

CONVERGENCE

Media convergence is a trend in which different media sources, such as newspapers, telephones, stereos, radios, and televisions, merge or converge so that they can be accessed together by the one multipurpose device. A smartphone can be used to access email and use internet applications, navigate, take digital photos and videos, and listen to music, watch television, and read the newspaper. Convergence affects media consumption, media distribution, ownership, and production. **Multiplatforming** refers to the same media content (for instance, a news story) being distributed across several different media forms or platforms: the same news story can be accessed in a newspaper, on the radio, on television, and online in print, audio, or audio-visual form.

Multiplatforming itself is possible not only because of technological convergence and the flexibility enabled by digitisation, but also because of the conglomeration, or convergence, of ownership whereby one media corporation owns websites, newspapers and magazines, radio stations, games divisions, and television networks. This form of convergence of media ownership and control is described as **vertical integration**. For instance, before splitting into News Corp (publishing) and 21st Century Fox (screen

◀ HYPERTEXT

Chunks of text or data connected by electronic links in a networked database. Hyperlinks enable the user to navigate through information along multiple, non-linear pathways.

◀ MULTIPLATFORMING

A process of media convergence that involves distributing branded content across multiple outlets; for instance, the narrative and characters of a film or television franchise can be distributed as films, novels, games, soundtrack CDs, and other merchandise, including clothes.

◀ VERTICAL INTEGRATION

This term describes a concentration of power when a media company owns various parts of the production, distribution, and exhibition chain, for example, printing presses, magazine companies, content providers such as photographic databases, the distribution vehicles, and retail outlets.

media) in 2013, Rupert Murdoch's media giant News Corporation owned some eight hundred media companies spanning print, music, sports, games, film, and TV. Vertical integration differs from **horizontal integration**, whereby a media company owns several different types of the same part of the production process. Disney, for example, also owns Pixar and ABC Television, and controls a significant share of Hulu. In order to avoid creating corporate monopolies that limit fair competition and diverse outputs, regulations have been put in place to control convergence of ownership, as when Hollywood studios were prevented from owning the theatres that exhibited their films. But with just six big media conglomerates controlling 90 per cent of American media production, there is a significant impact on the variety and choices available to audiences.

HORIZONTAL INTEGRATION ▶

This is a form of convergence of media ownership in which a corporation owns several companies involved in the same aspect of media production.

In terms of media production, convergence is having a noticeable effect on storytelling and communication strategies. The advent of blogs has shifted conceptions of news from an authoritative, 'objective', or balanced account of issues and events to more subjective commentary that blends journalism with journal writing. The popularity of home cinemas with surround sound and widescreen high-definition digital television (HDTV) is narrowing the distinction between film and television. Furthermore, the ways that multiplayer online games such as *World of Warcraft* and game consoles such as Xbox, PlayStation, and the 3D, remote-control features of Nintendo's Wii can explore space and narrative in digital games have also influenced the ways scriptwriters have developed narratives in films such as *Inception*, *Need for Speed*, *Assassin's Creed*, and *Warcraft*, and in the disjunctive chronologies and interwoven storylines of television programs such as *Ringer* and *The Walking Dead*.

This last example, *The Walking Dead*, demonstrates clearly how pervasive media convergence and trans-media storytelling are becoming in the growth of franchises. This American horror-drama television series is based on a comic-book series of the same name. Not only utilising the television medium, *The Walking Dead* has a strong online presence. For example, its website's landing page is interactive for fans with forums for chats, games, videos, and links to all of its social media channels. *The Walking Dead*'s 'Story Sync' gives viewers the opportunity to interact as they watch the television show by voting in snap polls or weighing into discussions about the action. As Jenkins says, 'few watch television in total silence and isolation … And, for a growing number of people, the water cooler has gone digital' (2006b, p. 26). So it has not only reached millions of fans through the television; its reach has extended (in)to online media, comics, games, and graphic novels, for example. It has such an active cult fan base that the activity surrounding the series has itself been channelled into a video game series. *The Walking Dead* video game series are interactive graphic adventures, and provide an example of trans-media storytelling that combines techniques of television narration with interactive, immersive gaming conventions, demonstrating multiplatforming and media convergence.

According to screen theorist Jason Mittell:

> ARGs [alternate reality games] are an interesting cult phenomenon taking advantage of the ubiquitous role media play in our daily lives. Typically ARGs are launched subtly with a few well-placed clues (or "rabbit holes"), leading players into a trail of websites, phone numbers, newspaper ads, and physical events that posit an alternate immersive reality with embedded mysteries and puzzles. An ARG by its definition must operate in secret, as the goal is to obscure the boundaries between an emerging storyline and real life (<http://flowtv.org/?p=165>).

Mittell (2006) points out the contradiction of asking audiences to believe in and participate in an alternate reality that they have already conceptualised as fictional on television. Some examples include *The Lost Experience* (from the television show *Lost*), *Why So Serious?* (an ARG that promoted the feature film *The Dark Knight*), and *Cloverfield* (also a film of the same name). While this creates a tension between the two media, ARGs can also be symbiotic because they feed back into a television series, for example, and provide new story threads when producers tap into the ideas and theories users are discussing online.

As these news and entertainment examples suggest, convergence of media technologies can lead to a standardisation of content that decreases the substance and the efficiency of communication, but it can also enrich communication by providing more options for senders and receivers of messages, and by enabling the creation of multimodal texts that combine a variety of media forms.

DECENTRALISATION

Decentralisation refers to the dispersal and personalisation of new media in contrast with conventional media, and to the higher degree of market segmentation and fragmentation that characterises new media. There has been a shift from a centralised, one-to-many mass communication or broadcast system, in which one source or input signal is transmitted simultaneously to many recipients, to a networked, many-to-many model of media production, transmission, and consumption in which there are multiple inputs, outputs, and connections. The media have been integrated into and dispersed throughout many aspects of everyday life and, as Lister et al. write, 'Consumption of media texts has been marked by a shift from a limited number of standardised texts to a very large number of highly differentiated texts. The media audience has fragmented and differentiated' (2003, p. 30). These changes to texts and audiences mean that for some media, such as subscription television, the business models and industry goals have shifted considerably: subscription television is not reliant on audience ratings to secure advertisers in the same way as broadcast television. The goal of cable stations such as HBO and Showtime is to achieve high levels of audience loyalty to at least one quality television series so that people will continue their monthly subscriptions.

In addition to the dispersal of audiences and corresponding changes in the industry, media production has become decentralised in that ordinary citizens have become producers of blogs, digital videos, and other media. Formerly media production required expensive capital, such as a printing press or a broadcast licence, whereas now it only requires access to a computer with an internet connection or a modern cell phone to record and disseminate text, images, and sounds. Such digital media are called 'prosumer' technologies because they equalise the power balance between media producers and consumers, in some cases eliminating the distinction between them altogether so that people using such technologies are termed 'produsers' (producer-consumers). However, as discussed below, the participatory and democratic freedoms that such media technologies offer are counterbalanced by the potential for technological developments to be used for surveillance and other mechanisms that limit the freedoms of citizens.

The most radical recent advance in the decentralisation and dispersal of new media involves ongoing developments in multimodal wireless communication technologies that are 'diffusing around the world faster than any other communication technology to date' (Castells et al. 2007, p. 1). To give an example of the blinding speed at which new media are spreading, market research forecasts that the growth in mobile data traffic in Sub-Saharan Africa will be twenty times as high in 2019 as it was in 2014; whereas in 2015 there were some

635 million mobile phone subscriptions in Sub-Saharan Africa, 'This is predicted to rise to around 930 million by the end of 2019' (Ericsson 2014). As mobile phones become more sophisticated, and the cost of wirelessly accessing the internet decreases and download speed increases, high levels of cell phone penetration may enable developing nations to leapfrog ahead without having to invest in costly fixed-line infrastructure, or personal computer hardware and software, particularly if wi-fi systems are also set up to provide the possibility of free access to digital information in public places. Other wireless technologies and cloud-based services such as Bluetooth and AirDrop enable digital information to be shared very easily, leading to further levels of dispersal and interconnectivity.

CASE STUDY

Television, algorithmic culture, and surveillance

In the second decade of the 2000s, television has transitioned to digital form and streamed video content has become an increasingly popular way to watch television. Because of differences between film and television (such as image resolution, the size and shape of television screens compared to those of cinema, distractions in the domestic environment of television reception, and the constraints of shooting schedules, budgets, and the studio environment), television has traditionally had a more limited audiovisual style. Most television productions emphasise close-ups, and use less mobile framing and less sophisticated layers of sound than feature films. The introduction of HDTV, which compresses more data into an audiovisual image, has made the style and quality of television productions more cinematic. More television shows and feature films are being shot in 3D or on high-definition digital video instead of celluloid—such as *The Great Gatsby* (dir. Baz Luhrmann 2013) and *Gone Girl* (dir. David Fincher 2014)—and films are using serialised narratives to capitalise on allegiance to characters in a way similar to television (such as superhero film franchises). HDTV can be filmed and watched in widescreen format, and LCD screens and home entertainment systems with surround sound and digital game interfaces are very popular. These developments demonstrate the convergence of film and television, but television is also converging with the internet.

Increasingly, subscription to multiple-channel cable and satellite television, the streaming of television episodes online via sites such as ABC iview and YouTube, and the use of iTunes and Netflix to globalise the release dates of popular television series all mean that people are increasingly able to access the programs they want whenever they want. This shifts power away from the linear, centralised scheduling timetables of the television networks. Whereas television used to **broadcast** material designed to appeal to a broad, nationwide audience, now producers can operate on **narrowcast** principles, targeting specialist markets, niche interests, and dispersed global audiences.

BROADCAST

A means of media transmission that makes information available to a broad spectrum of the population.

NARROWCAST

Narrowcast media transmission caters for small groups of people.

Hulu, iTunes, Netflix, and services such as TiVo and Foxtel's IQ demonstrate how technological developments are accelerating media convergence, and changing relationships between media producers, consumers, and technologies. Online streaming services such as Netflix and Hulu can offer every episode of a series on demand, and are capable of scanning available program selections to search for those featuring actors on a user's wish list, or using their own initiative to suggest new programs a user may enjoy, based on previous viewing preferences.

The ability of this technology to collect information about its users and create consumer profiles is similar to the ways Facebook's facial-recognition software allows automated identification and tagging of photographs, and Amazon gives customers personalised notifications of new releases, based on their searches and sales history. However, consumer profiling raises concerns about **surveillance** and privacy, because media producers can use such details as ammunition for aggressive marketing strategies, and government agencies or other groups can coopt facial-recognition software for purposes such as surveillance. Even wearable technologies, biosensor products, and smart media technologies like FitBit and GoogleLens are now used to surveil consumers and report on their vital signs and behaviour, while facilitating brand engagement and targeted advertising. Since websites like Amazon and services such as Netflix can hold information such as credit card details to foster online commerce, and interactive media are designed for two-way information flows, concerns about confidentiality are very real results of technological convergence. Indeed, services such as YouTube collect and sell information about consumer preferences to television networks so that they can target the audience more effectively.

The global reach of surveillance is so extensive that in order to house and process the mountains of data sourced by eavesdropping on citizens' telephone calls, intercepting texts and emails, and tracking people's movements using CCTV, their cell phones, credit cards, and smart objects like Google Glass and Apple Watch, America's National Security Agency has built a 140 000 square metre facility in Utah to store information. The location and inner workings of this data centre are supposed to be secret, but the Domestic Surveillance Directorate website (https://nsa.gov1.info/index.html) cordially invites visitors to 'Learn more about our secret surveillance activities' and conveniently provides 'Direct access to leaked information related to the surveillance activities of the U.S. Intelligence Community'. This site is a parody of the National Security Agency, which would never mount a placard outside its flagship building telling citizens 'if you have nothing to hide, you have nothing to fear', but it contains richly informative content derived from leaked government documents, news media, privacy groups, and government websites.

Increasingly, the **algorithms** of major media companies not only surveil audiences, they are also shaping culture and taste, using mathematical and computerised statistics to interpret and predict the enormous variability of personal and demographic preferences for film, television, music, books, and

SURVEILLANCE

The term 'surveillance' derives from Latin and French words for 'survey' (to oversee; to have a comprehensive view) and 'vigil' (to be watchful); hence it has connotations of watching over a person in a controlling manner. Academics such as Michel Foucault have examined how regimes of discipline and punishment function through self-surveillance, as well as through public punishment and the architectural designs of prisons (such as the panopticon, in which prisoners are always visible to an unseen guard in an all-seeing guard tower). Contemporary surveillance also has connotations of both counter-terrorism security protocols and voyeurism.

ALGORITHMS

Rule-based calculations or step-by-step mathematical or computational information processing: 'a set of mathematical procedures whose purpose is to expose some truth or tendency about the world' (Striphas 2015, p. 405).

Continued on next page ▶

games. New media scholars Blake Hallinan and Ted Striphas define algorithmic culture as 'the use of computational processes to sort, classify, and hierarchize people, places, objects, and ideas, and also the habits of thought, conduct, and expression that arise in relationship to those processes' (2014, p. 3).

Netflix originated in 1997 as an online selection and postal DVD service. It was co-founded by two software engineers, Reed Hastings and Marc Randolph, who developed a system for users to rate the DVDs they watched. This ratings system fed into the Netflix algorithm, which predicts what content users might enjoy, based on what they have liked and what other audience members with similar preferences have watched and enjoyed. Netflix is now global, with distribution rights in 190 countries, and since 2013 has been using its algorithm to predict what audiences will like, and to develop original, data-driven film and television content such as *Orange Is the New Black* (2013–), *Narcos* (2015–), *Daredevil* (2015–), and the comedic Western *Ridiculous 6* (dir. Frank Coraci) based on Adam Sandler's global popularity and trends indicating the return to popularity of the western genre. Netflix Chief Content Officer Ted Sarandos explains that the development of original content is important not only because it enables the company to use its algorithm to identify and meet audience desires directly, but also because Netflix holds copyright and has control over exhibition and distribution of that content worldwide (2016). Traditional television and film production companies do not usually allow a film to be made available online at the same time that it is released in cinemas, nor do they permit an entire TV season to be released all at once.

The Netflix algorithm seems almost utopian in its ability to identify what media audiences want and to deliver it to them whenever they want it. However, there are also less altruistic factors driving the Netflix business model and algorithmic culture more generally, because this form of data gathering is also an integral component of surveillance culture. In previous decades, audiences watched films and television; now, they also watch us. In addition to recording user ratings of TV shows and films, Netflix tracks the times of day or night when users watch, what kind of screen they use (tablet, laptop, phone, or TV), and where. Netflix also monitors viewing behaviour such as stopping, rewinding, and fast-forwarding to find out where people's attention flags if they don't watch an episode all the way through. Netflix is now using this detailed information about viewing practices and preferences to support the development of original series, as well as recommending films and television programs to subscribers (Hallinan & Striphas 2014, p. 12).

As sociologist Pierre Bourdieu explains, our personal tastes and preferences are central to our identities as individuals and as members of particular social categories:

> Taste classifies, and it classifies the classifier. Social subjects, classified by their classifications, distinguish themselves by the distinctions they make, between the beautiful and the ugly, the distinguished and the vulgar, in which their position in the objective classifications is expressed or betrayed (Bourdieu 1986, p. 6).

Netflix, Amazon, Apple Music, Spotify, and Pandora identify and predict 'likes' and trends, and so curate cultural content in ways that shape people's choices and tastes. Striphas refers to this as 'the offloading of cultural work onto computers, databases and other types of digital technologies' (2015, p. 395). This not only has implications for understandings of culture and creativity, but also raises questions about aspects of choice and identity being shaped by and transformed into data, analytics, and technological rather than sociocultural networks. As media students and researchers, we need to think critically about these transformations in the mediasphere, asking:

What happens when engineers—or their algorithms—become important arbiters of culture, much like art, film, and literary critics? … What is at stake in "optimizing" would-be cultural artifacts to ensure a more favorable reception, both by human audiences and by algorithms? (Hallinan & Striphas 2014, p. 15).

To what extent do you think we are delegating the tasks of taste-making and cultural authorship to algorithms and algorithmic media? Is it problematic that our media culture and the people, commodities, and ideas contained therein are being curated, classified, and ranked by automated algorithmic processes and crowd informatics?

(▶)

IMPLICATIONS OF NEW MEDIA

Technological determinism is the belief that technological innovation reshapes social life and drives social change. Marshall McLuhan, who is famous for saying that 'the medium is the message', could be described as a technological determinist. In other words, the technological medium itself is of paramount importance because the means used to communicate a message has a social logic that informs the way we think, the way we represent things, and the way we perceive and extend ourselves into the world, which implies that new forms of cultural interaction come into being as a result of technological change. We are beginning to see ourselves as global citizens in part because new communication technologies have enabled us to network and relate to each other in this way. Two examples are how the internet facilitates instantaneous global communication, and how Slingbox technology enables US cable-television subscribers to access and view their cable service anywhere in the world that a satellite uplink is available.

The concept of technological determinism also suggests that different media also lead to different ways of organising knowledge and power. Communications theorist Neil Postman claims that all technology has an 'embedded ideology' that comes encoded with a value system or 'an ideological bias, a predisposition to construct the world as one thing rather than another, to value one thing over another' (1993, p. 13). Print media, for example, privileges sight, literacy, education, and print media producers, correlating with a fairly impersonal, linear, rational way of thinking and relating to others. Newer media forms, such as wireless mobile communication and computer-mediated communication, offer increasing interactivity, autonomy, and choice on the part of the user, as well as unprecedented personal control over the production, manipulation, and distribution of content.

The weapon of mass distraction image (see Figure 7.1) illustrates different possible positions in relation to technological determinism and the reciprocal influence of media technology on society. It shows a human brain literally plugged into a television set, suggesting that humans are both the power source and the creative input that

◀ TECHNOLOGICAL DETERMINISM

The view that technological innovation reshapes social life and drives social change. Technology determines how society functions, rather than society determining how technology should be developed or used.

Figure 7.1 Weapon of mass distraction

Source: Courtesy of *Laugh It Off*

fuels the development of media texts and technologies, but also that the media distracts us from real-life concerns and determines, to a certain extent, what we think about.

With regard to technological determinism, Castells' position is that there is a two-way or dialectical interaction between technology and society: 'Technology does not determine society: it embodies it. But nor does technology determine technological innovation: it uses it' (2000a, p. 5), which suggests that technology and society are mutually constitutive, rather than one being driven by the other. Without necessarily taking a technological determinist stance, it is clear that media digitisation does have a number of social, political, legal, and economic implications that are worth considering. These include the digital divide, democratisation, issues to do with media piracy, copyright law, and corporate monopolies, and changes in social behaviour related to new ways in which the media are involved in everyday life.

THE DIGITAL DIVIDE

At present there exists a digital divide, an economic division between the people who have access to new media and those who do not, and a skill division between those who are comfortable with new media and those who are not (see p. 6). As Castells writes, 'While technology per se does not determine technological evolution and social change, technology (or the lack of it) embodies the capacity of societies to transform themselves' (2000a, p. 7). Globally, there is a broad economic division between north and south global hemispheres, between developed and developing nations, and between rich and poor nations. Access to computer technologies, the internet, and mobile phone technology is predominantly available to the better-off. This is not just experienced internationally, but also within countries where some people have access to new technologies but many don't (such as the poor, the elderly, and those living in isolated rural areas). As Castells writes:

> Differential timing in access to the power of technology for people, countries and regions is a critical source of inequality in our society. The switched-off areas are culturally and spatially discontinuous: they are in the American inner cities or in the French *banlieues*, as much as in the shanty towns of Africa or in the deprived rural areas of China or India (2000b, p. 33).

The danger is that the digital divide can increase the ever-widening gap between the haves and the have-nots, but as the technology develops and its prices drop, it becomes more readily available; there is evidence that the new technologies are being eagerly taken up across the globe. People with low incomes, say, may find purchasing a computer prohibitively expensive, but they can budget for a mobile phone with prepaid billing: 'The availability of prepaid systems has made it possible for the global telephone divide to be narrowed more rapidly than the internet divide' (Castells et al. 2007, p. 32). At the same time as this is happening, wireless technology is facilitating the interchange of ideas and goods, and therefore technological developments have the potential for increasing global equality.

The skill division is predominantly generational. Marc Prensky has described 'two tribes' of digital users: 'digital immigrants' and 'digital natives' (Prensky 2004). Digital natives, everyone under twenty-five and a lot of people aged between twenty-five and forty, have grown up with computers, video games, and the internet; they have no fear of these technologies, and turn to them first as sources of entertainment, information, and communication. The new technologies are not second nature to digital immigrants, who include older people, even if they do manage to use such technologies. (There is a third group that simply avoids, fears, and doesn't know how to use the technologies—but these technophobes will soon die out!)

A potential impact of projects that aim to bolster the use of information and communication technologies (**ICTs**) among older people, poor people, and those who live in the developing world is that they make the developing world a more substantial target for marketing, and for the dispersion of Western ideologies. However, when marginalised groups are neither represented in nor adequately served by the media, and not afforded equal access to it, the resulting inequity constitutes a danger to democracy:

◀ ICTs

Information and communication technologies, such as computers.

> The ability to communicate is a basic human right that is denied to some according to their ability to gain access to technology. Without basic telecommunications services, groups are not able to fully participate in the global economy, participate meaningfully in political discourse, or even socially interact with the global village (Snow 2001, p. 21).

DEMOCRATISATION

Despite these digital divides and the concentration of media ownership in the hands of a few multinational corporations, there is an overall media trend towards democratisation—increased access to information and participation in communication—that continues the trends of the media developed since the advent of printing. The internet is the major element here. Its ability to cross national boundaries, to enable two-way interactivity, to sort information at incredibly high speeds, and to make massive amounts of information available is simply phenomenal.

Democratisation is not just seen in terms of receiving information. It is now possible for anyone to become a media practitioner and publicise their point of view, which takes the democratic right of freedom of speech to new levels. Anyone with fairly basic technical skills can set up their own websites or make their own movies; in developed nations, these skills are now taught in primary schools. The digital technologies of audio-visual recording and editing also make it possible for people to make and distribute their own films or music CDs to a standard never before achieved. In addition, the use of blogs, whereby individuals can set up their own World Wide Web personal communication commentaries, has challenged the standard journalistic outlets of press, radio, and television. As Jenkins writes:

> Bloggers are turning the hunting and gathering, sampling and critiquing the rest of us do online into an extreme sport. We surf the Web; these guys snowboard it. Bloggers are the minutemen of the digital revolution … Blogs are thus more dynamic than older-style

home pages, more permanent than posts to a net discussion list. They are more private and personal than traditional journalism, more public than diaries (Jenkins 2006a, p. 179).

People turn to blogs as sources of information that may not feature the news values and conventions of balance that characterise conventional journalism, but can instead offer diverse perspectives and a richness of context, commentary, depth, and detail in reportage. By extension, blogging is often referred to as 'citizen journalism' as it bypasses the media gatekeepers (examples of this are numerous in relation to unauthorised photographs and documents regarding the Iraq war being leaked and discussed on the internet via WikiLeaks and other sites). Wikis and blogs are particularly important self-publishing tools in contexts where the media are controlled by the state, such as in China; however, as discussed below, the WikiLeaks phenomenon demonstrates that it is also important for citizens to be able to access and publish information independently even in democratic countries that enjoy freedom of the press.

An obvious and direct aspect of the democratisation attributed to new media is that interactive media restructure the power relations of political communication. In addition, networks, according to media analyst Terry Flew, 'facilitate a politics beyond the formal political sphere' (2005, p. 57). The internet is increasingly used as a tool for political communication that extends beyond, and often undermines, traditional sources of political authority, rendering politics more participatory. One of the big benefits of new media in the political sphere is that voters can use it to speak to politicians directly. For example in 2007, YouTube users posted videos with questions to US presidential candidates, who were asked to respond live on CNN. In one of these videos, a snowman and his little snow child ask candidates how they will combat global warming (see Figure 7.2).

While social media facilitates expanded avenues for connectivity, it also pressures users with what Kate Crawford describes as 'a new kind of noise problem' (2010, p. 65) and reveals 'the human limits of attention' (2009, p. 532). Digital technologies are providing not only the means for production and connection, but also an environment that fosters a collective between those who are engaged and, as Peter John Chen argues, 'at the grassroots level, we have also seen the way a range of applications of the internet have affected the political world' (2011, p. 1). This has implications for various parties including the electorate, politicians, and the media. The advantages of using interactive and personalised modes of address to actively engage voters in political communication are now well understood by politicians, and voters use social media to subscribe to political campaigns and follow their progress.

Kevin Rudd and Tony Abbott used YouTube channels, Twitter, and Facebook during the lead-up to the 2013 Australian

Figure 7.2 Billiam the Snowman, YouTube video image

Source: Nathan Hamel & Greg Hamel of Kotas

federal election to address young voters, hone image-management strategies, and disseminate political advertising, with varying degrees of success. It is important to note that while Twitter has a relatively small percentage of users in Australia of around 10 per cent (Bruns & Burgess <www.cci.edu.au/node/1358>) and Facebook use is much higher, Twitter is an important tool for journalists, who are reportedly among the most active groups on Twitter (Mullin 2015). This means that Twitter is a critical platform for politicians to engage with. A Twitter hashtag (#) is used to group tweets about a particular topic. In Australia, the #auspol hashtag groups discussion about Australian politics. It is among the most popular Twitter trending hashtags globally, making it into the top 30 Twitter trends, and in 2014 it was the top Australian trend (Peatling 2014). Kevin Rudd was well known for taking social media seriously, and ran a presidential-style election campaign in 2013, even flying in members of Obama's digital team to assist. He followed Obama's example by appearing on 'Ask Me Anything' (AMA) on popular social media site Reddit to answer questions for an hour; this attracted around 10 000 comments. Rudd also capitalised on the selfie trend, ostensibly to demonstrate that he is an 'every man', by posting a picture of himself with a shaving cut.

Although politicians can effectively use new media to establish greater public profiles, these can also be used to undermine politicians and political parties. Before the 2013 election, a number of anti-Abbott and anti-Rudd Facebook pages were set up, and many satirical political advertisements were made and posted online. There was a large selection of these easily available on YouTube, and also shared on Facebook and Twitter. A prominent Labor parody of a Liberal Party ad in 2013 was the centre of controversy, with the Liberal Party lodging a copyright complaint that resulted in the ad's removal from YouTube. The video was a spoof of the Liberals' first 2013 election ad campaign, 'New Hope'. This ad discusses Australia as being filled with opportunity; however, the Labor parody voice-over says 'Australia has always been a land of opportunity, and the Liberals have an opportunity to take power again. And we'll do anything it takes to get there. We'll say we're in it for the kids, but we'll actually cut the schoolkids' bonus'.

A now common feature of the political landscape is weighing in on political issues using video-sharing technology, cartoons, and memes, for example. Two popular identities have won Walkley Awards for their creative political parodies. Huw Parkinson, who won a Walkley in 2015 (<http://www.rabbitandcoffee.com/>), creates video mash-ups of political figures inserted into popular films and TV shows, and *First Dog on the Moon* cartoonist Andrew Marlton won a Walkley in 2012 for his clever use of humour to highlight political life in Australia (<www.firstdogonthemoon.com.au>). The political organisation GetUp! created a controversial video in the lead-up to the 2013 Australian federal election where it criticised billionaire media mogul Rupert Murdoch's alleged agenda-setting and censorship in his major newspapers, which were used to run an anti-Labor campaign. The ad featured an actor holding a Murdoch-owned newspaper, the *Courier Mail*, with an anti-Rudd headline, to which he responded: 'Don't let the crap decide your vote … Stand up for what you want. Tell Rupert, "We'll choose our own government".' The actor then used the *Courier Mail* to clean up dog faeces (<www.getup.org.au/campaigns/media/murdoch-ad-update/why-we-were-banned>). The video ad was censored by commercial TV Channels 7, 9, and 10.

GetUp! is not a political party, but it is a youth media, non-partisan lobby group that has been a significant force, and has used the media in powerful ways to communicate information about the policies of each of the major parties in Australian politics. The democratic aspects of social media largely stem from users generating their own content (rather than only receiving content from established media organisations). Sites such as YouTube, Facebook, and Twitter enable ordinary people to broadcast their opinions and connect with like-minded people throughout the world. While some political clips on YouTube are humorous and slick, other YouTube postings simply show videos documenting politicians making promises, contradicting themselves, or making discriminatory comments; the YouTube community then engages with and comments on the footage. Such online videos demonstrate the democratisation of new media because their content makes a statement about the importance of free speech and two-way political communication. The form in which such political communication is disseminated shows the power of 'prosumer' technology and its impact on national politics (Wood 2007).

The negative side of this democratisation is put forward by Andrew Keen in his book *The Cult of the Amateur: How the Internet is Killing Our Culture* (2007), which warns of the economic, cultural, and legal problems of digital piracy, ill-informed, amateur self-broadcasting, and the unreliability of information posted online by anonymous persons claiming to offer expert opinions. Once again, some commentators view the new media with fear.

ECONOMIC AND LEGAL CONSEQUENCES: PIRACY, COPYRIGHT, AND COPYLEFT

The ease of producing, transforming, and sharing knowledge on the internet has prompted debates about authorship, piracy, and the rights of content creators, versus the responsibility to protect the freedoms of user communities and the public interest in maintaining the internet as a shared resource or an 'information commons', a term coined by Stanford law professor Lawrence Lessig.

Some argue that software developers have intellectual property rights as well as the rights to protect and profit from their own ideas by means of copyright licences. There is also the argument that copyright protection helps maintain industry standards. Microsoft dominates its market, which means it has become the standard and the majority of consumers are obliged to use Microsoft-compatible software. Because of the large number of Microsoft users, Microsoft products make money and therefore more are developed, continuing a cycle that keeps Microsoft on top. Apple also holds an increasing share of the market and the same principles apply in relation to Apple products. One criticism of these types of monopolies is that they limit innovation, yet they are also seen to offer users the advantage of uniformity among the choice of available products, which prevents the potential confusions and incompatibilities that might arise from multiple, competing software architectures.

Alternatively, proponents of open source media, also known as the 'freeware' movement, argue that the advantages of an industry standard can be achieved by freely sharing software code, rather than using copyright laws to protect it. The open source movement draws on a global pool of talent to exchange and build on ideas based on what is called the 'copyleft' system, which permits users to copy, modify, change, and sell open source programs as long as they pass on the same rights to others and publicise their own code too (Hassan 2004, p. 119). Nobody owns or authors open source code such as the Linux operating system; instead, a number of users add to and improve it incrementally, continually sharing the code they use to modify it so that issues of incompatibility do not arise. Flew observes that the open source movement has practical and philosophical advantages:

> In contrast to the rationalistic, individualistic, and materialistic subject of liberal economics and those who participate in commodity production in order to promote their personal economic wealth, open source taps into the strong wellsprings of giving, reciprocity, status acquisition through giving without material reward, and creative altruism that have been a part of internet culture long before it was discovered by business (Flew 2005, p. 220).

It is interesting to speculate about how the characteristics of the internet and the patterns of interaction it has fostered may ultimately influence law, social relations, and business.

As discussed above, the global, networked, information-sharing characteristics of the internet make it difficult to regulate and protect intellectual property, and relatively easy for users to copy and disseminate media content, and to evade national territorial jurisdictions and legislation. These economic and legal consequences of new media also impact on the music industry, most famously in the meteoric rise and fall of the file-sharing site Napster and subsequent commercialisation of MP3 technology through the Apple iTunes pay-per-song online music store. Today, peer-to-peer (P2P) file-sharing, MP3s, iPods, and services such as Spotify pose a significant challenge. The ability to upload, download, exchange, store, and create your own music and music libraries is threatening to make the CD industry and music radio stations redundant.

The term for this process is **disintermediation**. This means eliminating the intermediary, which translates as cutting out the middle man, namely, in the case of music, the record company. If people are getting access to music straight from the musician, bypassing the need for a producer, a manager, and a commercial distributor, the question is how the music industry will survive and how musicians themselves will be able to make a living. Some artists, such as Pearl Jam, sell tickets to live concerts and uplink those concerts to the web as a response to widespread bootleg recordings (Flew 2005, p. 97). On the other hand, new media occasionally create marketable musicians, such as teenager Justin Bieber, who became an international pop sensation (injecting millions of dollars into the music industry) after a talent scout discovered videos of him performing on YouTube.

In addition to the challenges faced in the music industry, the strike by the Writers' Guild of America (WGA) in Hollywood in 2007–08 hinged on screenwriters' rights to and payment for the dissemination of their material online. Almost a decade since the last film and television writers' strike, WGA candidates for the US election in 2016 are reportedly issuing another strike threat over new media, for example (Robb 2015). These concerns about the unauthorised dissemination of material online are not restricted to entertainment media. WikiLeaks is an organisation that releases private and classified information online—particularly information about governments and their actions. Such information is acquired through anonymous sources, ostensibly in the democratic interest of freedom of information. After WikiLeaks made secret US diplomatic cables public, the US Justice Department opened a criminal investigation into the organisation and its director, Julian

◀ DISINTERMEDIATION

To bypass intermediaries, such as publishers and distributors, in order to transmit media directly from the creator to the consumer via self-publishing tools and techniques.

Assange. Nevertheless, Assange has not been prosecuted in any country for WikiLeaks publications, and it is difficult to find criminal charges that apply to the republishing of material that others have obtained. Assange and WikiLeaks have many supporters, as well as detractors, around the world, and the international debate WikiLeaks has stimulated highlights the many issues regarding online information-sharing that will need to be resolved in the coming decades.

SOCIAL BEHAVIOUR CHANGES

It is important to consider the ways in which new technologies may be changing social behaviour. Some people have criticised digital games as forms of technology that discourage children from developing their physiques through exercise, or are morally dangerous because of their emphasis on sex and violence. Others, such as Prensky (2004), argue that in fact these technologies are developing a whole set of new and valuable skills, including advanced motor-coordination skills that enable young children to develop the reaction responses and skills needed by jet pilots, and the ability to multitask, which enables children to receive and act on many different information sources at the same time. All these new technologies and the possibility of online shopping are also affecting how retailers operate; overall, more people will be able to find their work and their entertainment in the private space of the home. Certainly, the introduction of computer tablets has had far-reaching impact on the print media publishing industry, and on the ways in which people read and consume traditional media such as music, magazines, books, and television.

The new technologies are also influencing how we relate to and communicate with each other, in both positive and negative ways. While some internet relationships are reportedly successful, others suggest that there is a large discrepancy between meeting someone in cyberspace and meeting face to face. Worse than this are the practices of internet predators in stalking or luring children or teenagers into sexual situations. Blogging, SMS, cell phone videos, online video publication, and emailing all enable playful communication, but have also enabled anonymous and painful sexual harassment and bullying, as well as providing ways to publicise these serious issues. While interactive media have many positive uses, misuse can have devastating outcomes, including suicide by teenagers who are persecuted by peers who bully and humiliate them online, such as when, in 2012, 15-year-old Canadian Amanda Todd suicided after being cyberbullied and pressured into exposing her breasts online. Prior to her death, Todd created a YouTube video using a series of flashcards to tell her story of being harassed online. After her death, the video went viral and was viewed over 17 million times. This in turn opened up a national discussion on the criminalisation of cyberbullying. Taiwanese entertainer Peng Hsin-yi suicided in 2015 after enduring sustained cyberbullying. Peng left a note stating that she hoped her death would bring public awareness of cyberbullying. In Australia, a highly publicised case of cyberbullying was linked with suicide when celebrity Charlotte Dawson took her own life in 2014. Dawson was a vocal public campaigner against cyberbullying because she had endured relentless anonymous online attacks. Media scholar Emma Jane calls this type of cyberbullying 'e-bile', which she defines as 'the extravagant invective, the sexualized threats of violence, and the recreational nastiness that have come to constitute a dominant tenor of Internet discourse' (2012, p. 2). Dawson's death prompted calls around Australia for tougher legislation against cyberbullying.

Research into the social differentiation of wireless uses and users suggests that women largely use mobile media such as cell phones for remote parenting and social connectivity, men use such media for business and status, and adolescents use them for social networking and entertainment (Castells et al. 2007, p. 46). Each demographic has its own goals and codes of etiquette: adults switch their phones to silent during meetings, and consider it rude when someone accepts a call during a business or social engagement and annoying when their own phone rings repeatedly, whereas young people who are not yet fully in the workforce consider it rude to switch off phones and reject calls, and consider that the number and frequency of communication exchanges signal popularity and status. Preferences for different styles of communication also follow interesting social patterns across age, gender, and nationality. Young people who have grown up with the internet and mobile phones (digital natives) report suffering withdrawal symptoms when their phones are lost, stolen, or broken, and experiencing internet addiction affliction disorder (IAAD) when denied internet access. Furthermore, research suggests that 'Americans prefer asynchronous communication methods such as email and voice-mail, because they are considered more efficient, keeping things brief, leaving users in greater control', and they use hands-free sets rather than SMS because they usually drive instead of using public transport (Castells et al. 2007, p. 37). It is interesting to test such research by thinking critically about how and why you, and the people you know, use new media.

CONCLUSION

This chapter has examined the defining characteristics of new media such as digitisation, interactivity, virtuality, non-linearity, decentralisation, and convergence, and has developed a framework for thinking critically about technological developments by considering the positive and negative impacts they can have on society. While there has been considerable negative publicity about, for example, violent digital games and their links to aggressive behaviour, many games involve exciting interaction through the internet with other players, thus helping to develop cooperative social relations. Many online games also encourage participants to develop technical skills, manual dexterity, and conceptual agility. The technology therefore has the potential for positive human development but, inevitably, it also involves a commercial dimension: gaming is a multibillion-dollar facet of the media entertainment industry that generated US$91.5 billion in 2015. When critiquing the role of the media in society, it is important not to lose sight of who benefits from new media technologies and content.

Understanding the implications of technological developments in the media has also necessitated coming to grips with concepts such as algorithmic culture, democratisation, and the digital divide. It is important to remember that the benefits of new media are unequally distributed around the globe. Some countries with low levels of PC penetration have astoundingly high levels of wireless internet technology uptake (Japan, for example). Elsewhere, high levels of laptop ownership and readily available wireless connection inhibit interest in mobile phones and mobile internet access; furthermore, in some regions people don't have access to new media at all (Castells et al. 2007, p. 36). In summary, we need to draw together different aspects of studying new media technologies, texts, and modes of production, distribution, and consumption in order to consider how new media might affect social behaviour now, in the future, in our own communities, and around the world.

This chapter has

- examined the key characteristics of new media
- introduced the concepts of technological determinism and algorithmic culture
- discussed the implications of new-media technologies such as the digital divide, surveillance, copyright and piracy concerns, and social behaviour changes.

? | DISCUSSION POINTS

1 In what ways are new media more democratic than conventional media?
2 Who, if anyone, might benefit from, and who might be responsible for, the digital divide and algorithmic culture?
3 Consider why fan communities form around particular digital games and game consoles such as Xbox, Wii, and PlayStation. What advantages and pleasures do these games offer in terms of virtuality and interactivity?
4 What impact do you think massive mergers, such as Google purchasing YouTube, might have on the production and consumption of online video? Would smartphone technology have developed and dispersed so swiftly if iPhone had merged with Android and Samsung Galaxy?

SUMMARY

You should now be able to

- give examples of the impact of digitisation on media production, consumption, and distribution
- list and explain five important characteristics of new media
- analyse new communication technologies, and assess their relationships to social change and democratisation
- evaluate how the digital divide and algorithmic culture impact on your community and the communities of others.

PART 2
Pictures: Semiotic Analysis

Whoever controls the media—the images—controls the culture.

Allen Ginsberg

Overview

Part 2 begins to look at media texts in detail. The focus in the first chapter is on still images, mainly advertising photographs, and the methodology used is semiology or semiotics. After an explanation of semiology, we will illustrate its use as a method of textual analysis by working through a number of examples, and we will then broaden out the discussion to consider representational strategies in television and internet advertising.

CHAPTER 8

Semiology

Let's refer to the US marines we see in the foreground as "sharpshooters", not "snipers", which carries a negative connotation.

Fox News internal memo, quoted in *Outfoxed*

This chapter will

- explain how to use the semiotic method to analyse media texts
- define key terms and techniques used in semiotic analysis
- offer examples using semiology to analyse the signs, codes, and conventions with which media texts communicate
- outline how the modality or truth status of a text influences meaning and interpretation.

Semiology, also known as semiotics, began as a method for analysing language. It is now used for analysing how all sign systems work. It explores the logic and methodology behind communication, and shows how we can understand systematically, through the semiotic method, what communications mean. It is concerned with meaning and with the ways in which meanings are produced and transmitted.

SEMIOLOGY ▶

Semiology (also called semiotics) is the science of signs, or the study of signs and sign systems.

Semiology suggests that all communication is based on sign systems that work through certain rules and structures. Language (words) is the most important and dominant sign system for humans, but the world is full of other sign systems—traffic lights, road signs, navigation bars in a website, editing and photographic conventions in film and television, mathematical symbols, clothes, hairstyles, hand signals, Morse code, and so on. All forms of the media are sign systems. All systems can be analysed using semiology.

Semiology originated as a means of understanding language. One of its founders was linguist Ferdinand de Saussure, who taught semiotic analysis in a general linguistics course in 1906 (Saussure 1974; Culler 1976; Gordon 1996). Another pioneer of the study of signs and sign systems was Charles Sanders Peirce, who sought to understand non-language sign systems (Peirce 1958). Peirce founded the American tradition of semiotics when he developed an early account of 'sign theory' and various categories of signs in the 1860s. The methodologies of Saussure, Peirce, and others have been used as a means of analysing media products (Hawkes 1977, 1996; Fiske 1990; Hall 1997). Roland Barthes' book *Mythologies* (Barthes 1973) was one of the most significant applications of semiology in media studies, and, despite its age, it is still a readable and relevant text.

How do signs communicate?

The communication model of signs can be understood according to Figure 8.1.

Figure 8.1 Communication model of signs

SENDER ⟶ MESSAGE/SIGN SYSTEM ⟶ RECEIVER

Any message, any meaning, can only be communicated through signs and a sign system. The sign is the central aspect of semiology. A **sign** is any signal that communicates something to us. The nature of the sign can be understood in two similar ways:

1   Signs work on the basis that the sign stands in for, or represents, something else—the meaning, concept, or idea to which it refers.
2   Every sign consists of a signifier and a signified, as Figure 8.2 illustrates. The **signifier** is whatever material form is used to convey meaning: letters, images, sounds, and so forth. The **signified** is the concept that the images, sounds, or letters communicate.

◀ SIGN

Communicates meaning by standing in for or representing a thing or an idea.

◀ SIGNIFIER

The visible, tangible, or audible aspect of a sign that carries the meaning.

◀ SIGNIFIED

The thing or idea that a sign refers to.

Figure 8.2 Relationship between sign, signifier, and signified

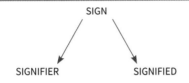

Using the first way of understanding the nature of signs (point 1 above), we can see that the letters d-o-g make up the word 'dog'. This formation of letters constitutes the sign that stands in for, or represents, the idea of a four-footed canine mammal.

Using the second way of understanding signs (point 2), we can illustrate the distinction between signifiers and signifieds by once again thinking of the sign 'dog'. The signifier is the letters d-o-g arranged into the word 'dog' (or the signifier could be a picture of a dog). The signified is the idea or concept of a dog (see Figure 8.3).

Figure 8.3 The sign 'dog'

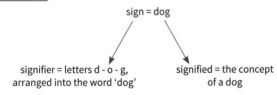

An example that shows the distinction between signifier and signified is a picture of a man offering a woman a rose, as in the reality TV program *The Bachelor*. The gesture can be understood as a sign. The rose here is the signifier, and what is signified is the man's love for or attraction to the woman. Roses do not necessarily signify love, which means that the gesture (sign) is based on a shared code, or convention, that roses can stand in for, or represent, love.

This may seem a slightly complicated way of understanding messages, but it is useful for media study because it draws our attention to the processes of representation or signification involved in the actions of the media: all media messages, all their signs, work on the basis of something standing in for something else; all signs include a signifier and a signified. This helps us see the construction involved in media messages, and reminds us that what we are seeing is not 'reality' (although it may resemble it) but signs and signifiers that aim to represent the real world.

There are numerous aspects to semiological analysis. In exploring how signs communicate, how semiology works, we will focus on the following key points, which are explored in more detail below.

- Signs communicate through codes and conventions.
- These signs and conventions are culturally shared—they depend on cultural knowledge.
- Signs communicate through systems of difference.
- Signs communicate through denotations and connotations.

SIGNS COMMUNICATE THROUGH CODES AND CONVENTIONS

All sign systems have a set of elements that are combined according to certain rules, codes, and conventions. The English language is based on twenty-six letters, which can combine into words and grammatical patterns. We have to learn and understand the correct codes in order to communicate: the letters d-o-g, for example, are the code for describing a certain group of four-legged, furry creatures. Sentences are put together according to the conventions of grammar. The words **code** and **convention** are key words in media study.

CODE ▶

Codes are standardised formulas for communicating meaning.

CONVENTION ▶

Conventions are methods of organising signs to communicate meaning in ways that become habituated and widely shared over time.

All media messages use codes and communicate through conventions. These codes and conventions are sometimes difficult to spot because we become so used to them that we decode them automatically, without noticing. For instance, it seems perfectly obvious that the most important part of a print media text should be written in the largest and boldest font, with less important information in smaller, finer print. The typeface is chosen according to a code of priority and prominence. It is also conventional to organise this information with the most salient points displayed at the top and centre of the text. The fact that such codes and conventions are used to determine font styles and sizes becomes unnoticeable: we decode the underlying message about the text's relative importance without realising it and tend to skim over small print, assuming it is unimportant (sometimes to our own detriment).

Email and SMS messages communicate using a special code that is more informal and abbreviated than commonly used written language usually is, making use of emoticons and acronyms. Emoticons are graphic representations of emotions, used in communication that is not face to face. For instance, ':-)' is the emoticon code for smiling. Acronyms and abbreviations are a concession to the small screens of mobile phones, and the quick style of communication that is being used. Thus, in SMS conventions, vowels are sometimes omitted, so 'text message' becomes 'txt msg'. The sounds of certain letters and numbers can also be used to substitute for longer spellings, for instance, the use of brevity conventions of SMS or email, the way the phrase 'Great, see you later!' can be translated into the code 'gr8, cu l8r!' This code is sometimes referred to as 'digital literacy' or 'net-speak', and was incorporated into mainstream language use and media advertising in the early 2000s. Towards the end of the decade, it lost its freshness and popularity as mobile phone users increasingly adopted predictive text, a quick, automated way of writing messages without having to manually spell out words letter by letter. The informal, abbreviated net-speak code is occasionally still used in online chat and email, where predictive text is unavailable. Mobile phones have affected communication in many ways, especially by encouraging brevity and informality.

CODES AND CONVENTIONS DEPEND ON CULTURAL KNOWLEDGE

Sign systems will only work successfully with people who know and share the same codes. For example, a retired person who used to work as a secretary and has never used a mobile phone is not likely to understand the 'gr8, cu l8r!' message, but they might be able to use and understand shorthand, another code that involves brevity conventions for quick communication. Different languages are a good example of different sets of codes and conventions used to represent or stand in for the world. The letters d-o-g are signs in the English language code. French uses the letters c-h-i-e-n to refer to canines. All languages have different words. To understand these different signs, you have to have learnt the code (the language); however, cultural knowledge is something more than simply knowing what the code means. It is being aware of all the things that might be suggested by the code. The following points elaborate on this.

SIGNS COMMUNICATE THROUGH SYSTEMS OF DIFFERENCE

One of Saussure's central points in analysing language is the understanding that words don't mean anything on their own. Their meanings depend on the fact that words are part of a system of difference: they only take on meaning in relation to other words. 'Up', for example, means nothing unless we can relate it to the word and concept 'down'. We can only understand what dogs are in relation to our knowledge of other animals—cats, wolves, horses, and so on—from which we know they are different. The red of a traffic light means nothing in itself; it is only in relation to the context and code of red as opposed to green as opposed to amber that we make sense of it through a system of difference.

SIGNS COMMUNICATE THROUGH DENOTATIONS AND CONNOTATIONS

Signs work on two levels of meaning: denotation and connotation.

Denotation

To consider what a text denotes is to analyse it on a purely descriptive level without delving into what it might imply. It is simply to ask 'What is there?' **Denotation** attempts to describe without comment, evaluation, or judgment the contents of an image. At this level, signs are as close to value-free as possible. On a denotative level the American flag, say, is a rectangular shape consisting of horizontal stripes of red, alternating with stripes of white,

◀ DENOTATION

Denotation is what Barthes calls 'the first order of signification'. It is the most obvious level on which a sign communicates and it refers to the common-sense meaning of the sign. The denotative meaning can be expressed by describing the sign as simply as possible.

with a smaller rectangle of blue in the upper left-hand corner. The blue rectangle contains white star shapes, also arranged in horizontal rows.

Connotation

Semiology suggests that all signs carry with them a set of **connotations** or associations, that is, they will remind the viewer of certain feelings, beliefs, or ideas that are attached to the signifier. It is our task, when analysing images semiologically, to ask what are all the possible connotations associated with any particular sign or element in the image. Objects, colours, clothes, words, print styles, lighting, camera angles, body language, and so on can all carry connotations.

To return to our example of the American flag, we might note that the flag is associated with (has symbolic connotations of) patriotism, liberty, and justice, at least for most Americans. We would also note that stars are associated with excellence, celebrities, heaven, dreams, and so on. The blue rectangle represents the sky, which, through phrases such as 'free as a bird in the sky', has connotations of freedom (liberty). Each star also represents an individual state in America, and the fact that they are grouped together, instead of being dispersed at random all over the flag, has connotations of unity.

A similar way of describing this mode of analysis, and an approach you may have come across elsewhere, is symbolism, which suggests that particular objects or images carry symbolic meaning. The colour red symbolises passion, danger, and sexuality in Western culture. (Note that in China, red signifies good luck and prosperity; it also signifies communism, a further illustration that symbols are culturally specific.) Peirce also gives the term 'symbolic' a more specific meaning, which we will discuss when we elaborate on different types of signs.

Connotations are associative meanings that the viewer or audience perceives in an image, and they work on two levels: individual and cultural. For the purposes of this book, we are only interested in the cultural level, and the way connotations help us see the interaction between the sign and the values of a culture, but we do need to understand both levels.

1   Individual connotations. The experiences we have in life as individuals shape our ways of seeing the world and our responses. This works in all aspects of our lives, including our responses to images. If, for example, the first time a young girl smells a rose is also a time that she has an upsetting experience (perhaps at a funeral), the smell or sight of roses may subsequently serve to remind her of, or suggest to her, sadness. Seeing roses may continue to carry this individual connotation for this girl, so that seeing roses in a media text would produce connotations of distress rather than love or romance. While it is important to acknowledge the presence of these individual connotations and look out for them when we analyse the meaning of images, they are not useful for semiotic analysis because they are not connotations normally shared by other people.

2   Cultural connotations. This second level of connotations points to the way that different objects carry associations and connotations that are shared collectively by many people in a culture. So, for example, a gift of roses is culturally acknowledged as carrying romantic connotations. Fiske's analysis of the meanings attached to jeans points to the different connotations—such as freedom, youthfulness, and

equality—associated with jeans by groups of people (1989b, pp. 1–21). Being aware of these connotations will make us aware of the cultural meanings in images.

Connotations will not be the same for all cultures, which is why it is important for us always to think about an image's context and the cultural knowledge that different audiences will have. Neither will connotations always be shared by all people in a culture, but as long as we can see that they are shared by a significant number of people, they will be important in analysing the possible meanings of any texts.

Commentary

Lady Gaga made headlines when she wore a dress, hat, purse, and shoes fashioned from raw red meat to accept an award at MTV's Video Music Awards in 2010 (Figure 8.4). This was obviously an outfit meant to make a statement, and it did so largely through connotations that meat has in Western society. Gaga said she wore the dress as a form of protest against the US military's 'Don't ask, don't tell' policy, which barred openly gay people from the US army and upheld that people could be discharged from military service if they were discovered to be gay. According to Gaga, she wore the meat dress to promote the idea that if 'we don't fight for our rights, pretty soon we're gonna have as much rights as the meat on our bones'. This intended meaning may not be obvious and Gaga herself noted that there are many possible ways the dress can be understood; that is, it has a number of connotative meanings.

Figure 8.4 Lady Gaga and the meat dress

One powerful interpretation connects the outfit with animal rights activism. In many parts of our culture, cow meat is a substance that is usually cooked and consumed, and a beautiful woman clothed in raw meat seems bizarre or even disgusting. Using meat as clothing in this way creates an association between raw meat and the other parts of animals that people wear regularly, such as leather and fur. Those viewing the dress might question whether wearing raw meat is really that different from, or any less inappropriate than, wearing other parts of an animal. From this point of view, the meat dress signifies animals being murdered for fashion and communicates the associative meaning (the connotation) that this is wrong.

It is worth noting that real meat was used to create Gaga's outfit and the animal rights group People for the Ethical Treatment of Animals (PETA) criticised her for dressing in animal body parts. This response indicates they understood the dress to signify that it is okay for animals to be killed for fashion. Nevertheless, PETA also reported that Gaga's meat outfit encouraged lots of people to download a copy of a vegetarianism manual from their website, which suggests that many people did decipher the message to be that humans should not exploit animals.

Other interpretations of Gaga's meaty attire relate to the representation of women. On one hand, the outfit could be understood to reference the unrefined, animalistic nature of carnal desires, and to therefore make a statement about the female wearer's 'raw' sexuality. On the other hand, it could be seen to have connotations regarding women being treated as 'pieces of meat'. When people looked at Gaga at the awards show, they saw a famous female body in a slinky, revealing dress. However, it was a body literally covered in meat. Potentially, this suggests that when women are ogled and evaluated for attractiveness, they become like a piece of meat—graded for 'quality' in contexts such as nightclubs, which are often referred to as 'meat markets'. By Gaga choosing contentious and lifeless meat as fashion, she arguably 'parodizes the event in which women who are role models for many other women try to look their best and bring to perfection an industrialized, objectifying image of themselves' (Rozmarin 2011, p. 473). A standard line that celebrity women are asked on the red carpet by the media is: what are you wearing? In 2015, a successful campaign was endorsed by many celebrities. It was called #askhermore 'to call out sexist reporting and suggest ways to re-focus on women's achievements' <http://therepresentationproject.org/the-movement/askhermore/#sthash.P8UQNat1.dpuf>. Was Gaga's meat dress also an earlier activist statement against this sort of superficiality about celebrity women's appearances?

All these interpretations are affected by the context of who made these garments, where they were worn, and by whom. Lady Gaga's outfit was created by a famous fashion designer, Franc Fernandez, and it was worn at an A-list red carpet event by Gaga, who is widely known for her unconventional, statement-making fashion. Such a context allowed for someone wearing an outfit made of raw meat to be understood as making an artistic display. Does it mean that the potential to politicise the issues is diminished because we have grown to expect excess and shock from Gaga?

Think about what a meat suit or meat dress would signify if you made it and wore it to the supermarket. What connotations would a meat outfit have then? What other connotations might Lady Gaga's meat dress carry in various contexts?

ICONIC, INDEXICAL, AND SYMBOLIC SIGNS

Peirce's analysis of signs introduces further categories into the analysis of signs by splitting signs into three types: **iconic**, **indexical**, and **symbolic**.

Iconic signs are signs that resemble that which they signify. All photographs or film signs are iconic in that the image literally looks like what it refers to. Similarly, paintings or diagrams that look like what they signify are iconic. The sounds of the wind whistling or wolves howling in a horror film are also iconic signs, because the recorded sounds resemble noises that the wind or real wolves actually make.

Indexical signs are signs that indicate or point to something else. (The index finger is the one we use for pointing, and a book index points us back to a page reference.) So a knock on the door, for example, is a sign that indicates someone wants to come in, smoke indicates fire, indicator lights on a car flicker to signal that the car is going to turn. Thermometers, speedometers, analogue clocks, and graphs are all examples of indexes because they indicate, point to, or measure temperature, speed, time, and so forth. The relationship between an indexical sign and its signified has been termed an 'existential', or physical, connection.

Symbolic signs are signs that stand in for, but have no resemblance to, their signified. The most obvious example is language, which uses symbols, letters, and words to stand in for what is being described. Similarly, road signs and mathematical signs are usually symbolic. The important point here is that there is no necessary connection between sign and symbol; the signs are, in Saussure's words, **arbitrary signifiers**.

An easy way to remember these different kinds of signs is to think of your computer screen. The image of the printer on your tool bar is called an icon because it looks like a printer. The arrow-shaped cursor that appears when you use the mouse to pull down a menu and select a file, tool, or function is literally pointing you to further information, so it is an indexical sign. Website addresses are indexes that point you to a webpage's location on the internet. The sound that indicates that you have new email and the beep that computers make when you hit the wrong key are also indexes because they prompt you to check your inbox or point out that you have made an error. Nearly every key on your computer keyboard has a symbol on it. The $ sign doesn't resemble money; it is simply a symbol that stands for money.

Look around you and identify examples of iconic, indexical, and symbolic signs. It is most likely that you will be able to see examples of iconic and symbolic signs in most social situations. Note that a sign can belong to more than one category.

◄ ICONIC SIGN

The relationship between the signifier and the signified is based on likeness or resemblance.

◄ INDEXICAL SIGN

The relationship between the signifier and the signified is one of indication, direction or measurement, sequence, or causation.

◄ SYMBOLIC SIGN

The relationship between the signifier and the signified is arbitrary (there is no natural link) and is based on culture, context, and convention.

◄ ARBITRARY SIGNIFIER

Arbitrary signifiers have no logical connection to their signified. The signifier does not look or sound like the signified, nor does it point to the signified in a causal or indexical fashion.

? CLOTHES AS SIGN SYSTEMS

As a way of applying semiological analysis, try the following exercise. You may find it useful to read Fiske's analysis of the meaning of jeans as preparation for this (1989b, pp. 1–21).

As we have seen with Lady Gaga's meat dress (Figure 8.4), an item of clothing can be a powerful signifier. The clothes we wear every day also act as sign systems to tell other people and ourselves who we think we are. They don't just keep us warm or comfortable, they give messages about ourselves. Arrange with a friend to semiologically analyse each other's appearance, that is, look at the clothes each of you is wearing as signs and signifiers. What do they signify? What do they connote? You can include hairstyles, make-up, and any jewellery

Continued on next page ▶

in this analysis—they are all sign systems. Try to apply all the relevant concepts: look for iconic, indexical, and symbolic signs in your clothes; and understand how systems of difference work by imagining different kinds of clothing, different colours, and each of you wearing the other's clothes. Consider how all these things would change the meaning of the clothes.

You might also consider dress codes and conventions, and how they relate to context, social class, and the economics of the fashion industry. Consider each item of apparel as a sign, and break it down into signifier and signified (for instance, jeans are a signifier, and the idea or meaning that is signified by wearing jeans may be youth or freedom).

THE LANGUAGE, OR CODES, OF VISUAL IMAGES

When analysing how meaning is constructed in photographs and still images, we must consider the codes of technical representation and the codes of content.

Codes of technical representation

In different media there are different codes and conventions at work, as we indicated above in our discussion of text messages and the use of particular font sizes in print media. Other codes and conventions are used in images and screen media, including conventions such as continuity editing (see p. 227), which govern how different shots should be combined in film and television. When a dialogue scene is being edited, the shot–reverse–shot convention is an editing pattern used to show the speaker, then the reaction of the other person. When there is a significant transition in time or space in a film or television text, such as a flashback sequence, it is conventional to use a dissolve or a fade, instead of a straight cut. Camera angles are also used according to conventions, such as when a low-angle shot (looking upwards) is used to make a figure seem powerful or dominant.

We can analyse the significance of the photographic codes in any image by asking the question: *how* has it been photographed? The answer may include any of the following elements: camera angle, framing and cropping, focus, film stock (black and white, or colour), and lighting. All these contribute to the meaning of the image. We can look at each of them and ask what is denoted and what is connoted: for example, the use of soft backlighting to produce a halo effect around a person's head will have certain connotations, and the use of top or side light to create a heavy shadow over their eyes, or to cast half of their face in shadow, will have different connotations. These lighting codes can make a person seem angelic, brooding, and inscrutable, or sinister and deceitful, as though they have a shadow side or something to hide. Similarly, grainy images and hand-held footage are part of a technical code of realism that is often used in documentary-style programs or photojournalism to give a sense of immediacy and authenticity.

Codes of content

We can also analyse any image by asking the question: *what* has been photographed? The answer may include any of the following elements: objects, settings, clothing or costumes, body language, body position, and colours. All these elements contribute to the meaning of the image, as they denote and connote something. Fashion photography relies on long-standing conventions of composition to show off the clothing and the model's body to best advantage, and this in turn often draws on body language, poses, and photographic codes of representation that are common in soft porn. Thus advertising can borrow pornographic codes of representation to help create a feeling of desire surrounding the fashion item on display.

You are already familiar with many of these codes of technical representation and codes of content, probably without realising it. Semiotic analysis slows down the process of automatically decoding or interpreting these codes and asks how the meaning was constructed. Codes of technical representation and codes of content both need to be considered when analysing any image. We need to ask how each of these elements contribute, as signs and signifiers, to the meaning of the text. This will be explored, with detailed examples, in the next chapter.

Modality

The final semiotic term we want to introduce is the concept of modality. **Modality** is a term originally used by linguists to refer to words that qualify the degree of certainty expressed in a statement (words such as 'maybe' or 'might' are called modal auxiliaries). In language, modality markers are the utterances that tell a reader or listener how sure the writer or speaker is that what they are saying is true. If I say, 'Umm, I think it might rain tomorrow, don't you?', I am making a low-modality statement. The modality markers 'umm', 'think', 'might', and the question mark indicate that I am not certain whether it will really rain. In contrast, the following statement is high modality: 'It is definitely going to rain tomorrow.' Modality is an important concept in semiotic analysis because it indicates what the dominant view of reality is, and it indicates who we are most likely to believe or trust. In the example above, we are likely to believe the person who sounds most certain. Note how high-modality language is used in news reports: statements are not qualified, they are asserted as fact, which leads us to believe that the journalists have carefully researched the story and thoroughly checked the facts.

The concept of modality can also be applied to visual texts: 'In a commonsense view, "realism" in the visual code corresponds to "truth" in the verbal code: a realistic visual representation is also likely to be seen as true' (Hodge & Kress 1991, p. 130). Cartoons and animated films are low-modality texts, whereas live action is more realistic and therefore has a higher truth status. The grainy or informal image of a snapshot or a home video, the hand-held footage in a documentary, and the black-and-white pictures in a newspaper are all high-modality texts. Modal markers and codes of technical representation, such as composition, lighting, camera technique, and film stock, tell us we should believe that these images represent real people and events. The airbrushed, Photoshopped, posed, and professionally lit images in a fashion magazine have a weaker relationship to reality than the snapshot or news photo, but they are higher modality than a cartoon sketch or a computer-animated image of a talking animal such as Mickey Mouse or Nemo.

Modality works to position media consumers in relation to media texts by inviting us to agree with and believe in the views represented in the media message to a greater or lesser degree. According to social semioticians Bob Hodge and Gunter Kress, 'Social control rests on control over the representation of reality … Whoever controls modality can control which version of reality will be selected out as the valid version' (Hodge & Kress 1991, p. 147).

◄ MODALITY

A measure of the degree of certainty or realism associated with an instance of communication.

CONCLUSION

In this chapter we have investigated how signs can be broken down into signifiers (images, words, or another medium carrying a message) and signifieds (the meaning or concept that is referred to), and we have introduced different types of signs: icons (signs that resemble), indexes (signs that indicate), and symbols (arbitrary signs). We have established that signs communicate through systems of difference, and through denotation (the descriptive or literal level of meaning) and connotation (the associative level of meaning), as well as through accepted codes, conventions, and modality markers.

There is more to semiology and you can explore the topic through further reading, but the outline above will give you enough to start engaging critically in some close textual analysis of images.

This chapter has

- explained what semiology is and how to use it to analyse media texts
- defined key semiotic terms and techniques related to the types and components of signs and codes of communication
- offered examples of semiotic analysis to show how signs make meanings
- introduced the concept of modality or truth status.

? DISCUSSION POINTS

1   What are Peirce's three categories of signs? What examples of each can you see around you right now?
2   How do codes of content differ from codes of technical representation on cell phones?
3   Consider how modality influences whom you believe or trust in a television show, news broadcast, or magazine article.
4   If the very next person you see were to ask you on a date, what would the exact words of your response be? Which parts of your reply might be termed 'modality markers'?

SUMMARY

You should now be able to

- explain what semiology is
- outline the steps or techniques employed to analyse media images using the semiotic method
- define the following terms: 'signified', 'signifier', 'denotation', 'connotation', 'index', 'icon', 'symbol', 'code', 'convention', and 'modality'
- apply these terms in an analysis of a media image of your choice.

CHAPTER 9

Reading Images and Advertisements

There are no just images, there are just images.

Jean-Luc Godard

This chapter will

- demonstrate the semiological approach by analysing a number of case study images
- explore the interplay of words and images, and consider how audience, context, and intertextuality can affect meaning and interpretation
- analyse the relationship between signs, social contexts, and ideology
- evaluate the strengths and limitations of semiology.

What follows is a series of examples, exercises, and case studies that use semiology to analyse different images (Figures 9.1 and 9.2). Each analysis raises questions for you to answer and is followed by a detailed commentary on the image in question. The examples at the beginning of this chapter use photographs, particularly advertisements. Later in the chapter we move on to consider new-media advertising, looking at how these media forms address the audience differently and use varied strategies of representation to catch and hold attention, and to persuade people to purchase products and buy into the particular lifestyles and values promoted in the commercials.

Advertisements are a rich source for semiotic analysis: they usually combine images with written text, are very carefully put together so as to have maximum effect on an audience, they are a form of propaganda but will only work if they give audiences some form of pleasure, they are ubiquitous in Western culture, they often reveal important ideological attitudes, and, because they are static, they are often easier for media students to analyse than moving images. Do not, though, assume that advertisers themselves know or care about semiology. Although some might (particularly advertisers who have studied communication or media studies), they do not need to know the theory of semiology in order to design advertisements. Semiology is primarily a tool of analysis, not of media construction.

MEANING AND INTERPRETATION

Print media images represent a moment frozen in time, and often invite us to imagine a larger story of which the single moment is a part, a story in which we might be able to imagine ourselves participating in some way. A particularly useful question to ask about any image in order to reveal something of its intended meaning is: what is the **implied narrative** of the image? This involves asking what you think has just happened in the image and what is going to happen next: in other words, what story is the image telling? We can also ask where the viewer or interpreter of the text is positioned within the implied narrative. Are we one of the characters? Are we being asked to enter into the story world in a particular role?

◀ IMPLIED NARRATIVE
The story that a picture suggests, including the events that may have happened immediately prior to the moment in the image, and immediately afterwards.

Many advertisements invite us to take an imaginary role in the implied narrative of the text, and to play out a version of that role in real life by purchasing the product.

Media texts and images can imply different things to different people in different contexts. Texts are open to many interpretations due to the polysemic nature of images and the ways in which differing contexts, audiences, and connotations can influence meaning. 'Polysemic' means 'many meanings'. In addition, the meanings of signs and texts depend on cultural knowledge of other texts circulating in popular culture. In this sense meaning is

INTERTEXTUALITY ▶

The process of knowingly borrowing and referring to other texts, or interpreting one text in the light of other related texts.

constructed **intertextually**, in connection with the meanings of related texts. Intertextuality means that some signs extend beyond themselves, incorporating references to other texts on which their meaning in some ways depends. Shows such as *Community* rely heavily on intertextuality as they constantly refer to other media texts. From its very first episode, *Community* playfully invokes knowledge of other television series and famous films such as John Hughes' teenpic *The Breakfast Club*. Without knowledge of the intertexts, one would have no idea why the character Abed suddenly says things that seem out of character, weaving in lines of dialogue from popular films. The 'Modern Warfare' episode references just about every action movie from *Aliens* to *The Matrix*, and Abed throws in a line about the sitcom *Friends* for good measure: 'To be blunt, Jeff and Britta is no Ross and Rachel. Your sexual tension and lack of chemistry is putting us all on edge, which is why, ironically, and hear this on every level, you're keeping us from being friends'. *Community*, in turn, is mentioned by characters in other television shows such as *30 Rock* and *Cougar Town*. Due to the polysemic nature of media texts, audiences would come up with different meanings for Abed's words (and perhaps be very confused) if they didn't recognise the intertextual references that form part of a pop-cultural role-playing game. Another prominent example of allusion to other media texts to invoke intertextuality within its narrative is American fantasy-horror television series *Supernatural*. In the pilot episode alone, references are made to the 1960s/70s sitcom *The Brady Bunch*, to *The X-Files*, and even to the cartoon *The Smurfs*.

In print media we often don't have the benefit of as much narrative context as television series or movies contain, so there need to be other ways of narrowing the possible meanings

ANCHORAGE ▶

Anchorage limits polysemy by articulating the preferred meaning of a text, as a caption labels an image.

of images. Image captions work as a form of what Barthes calls **anchorage** (Barthes 1977; O'Sullivan et al. 1994, p. 13): this ties down or anchors the image to a certain meaning for us, thereby reducing the polysemic possibilities; it also shows us how to view it. News presenters on television are often referred to as 'news anchors' for the same reason: they introduce, interpret, and explain the images we see. Thinking about how words, captions, and titles anchor the meaning of images to one particular interpretation is an important step in semiotic analysis, focusing on the relationship between words and images. Words often crystallise the more nebulous meanings or connotations that images convey.

Notice how, for example, the captions change the meaning of the pictures of water in Figure 9.1, even though the pictures themselves remain exactly the same.

Without any accompanying captions, the top images of the dripping tap and the glass of sparkling water could be interpreted in many ways: as a symbol or implied narrative of slow and steady progress in which a glass is filled drop by drop, or as promoting mineral water, or as advertising the services of a plumber who fixes dripping faucets. The first image of the tap is labelled 'commodity' and the first image of the glass of water is labelled 'luxury', and then the captions are reversed when the images are repeated. These words anchor the meaning by telling us how to think about the water in the images. The text to the right shows the HSBC logo, which restricts the meanings of the images further and indicates it is an advertisement for a bank, not a plumber or a soft drink. These captions, together with

Figure 9.1 HSBC commodity/luxury advertisement

A basic essential?
Or a more refined taste?

At HSBC, we hear the views of over
125 million customers worldwide.
And the subject of water is definitely hot.

From farmers to fitness fanatics,
everyone has different needs.

It's our awareness of many different
perspectives which helps us keep the
debate flowing.

yourpointofview.com

The world's local bank

Source: HSBC Bank Australia Limited

the claim that 'It's our awareness of many different perspectives that keeps the debate flowing', show that the images are part of an advertising campaign for a bank, and that the advertisement is deliberately playing with the ideas of polysemy and anchorage to make us think carefully about our views and assumptions. In the global context of pollution, climate change, and pervasive commercialisation, water can be a luxury and a commodity, a basic essential, and, in the case of brands such as San Pellegrino sparkling mineral water, a luxury commodity for people of 'refined taste', as the small print suggests.

We can now use the techniques of semiology and the concepts of implied narrative, polysemy, intertextuality, and anchorage to analyse how words and images work together to construct meaning in media texts. The object of such analysis is to raise awareness of the possible meanings that can be produced through analysis of signs and signifiers, photographic codes, and cultural codes of understanding. This will equip you with the skills to decode what the different signifiers represent, and will enable you to give a detailed argument to support your findings. It is also important to consider who the audience is, and how the cultural and social position of the reader affects meaning.

Analysis of the surgeon image and its caption

We will analyse a photograph (Figure 9.2) of a surgeon operating by posing a number of questions about the image, and thinking through the three different elements of text, audience, and context. We will consider who is being addressed and what kind of a text this looks like. We don't know what the context of production or reception is, or what the photographer intended the text to mean, so we will have to make an educated guess by paying careful attention to the text's signifiers, codes, and conventions. To begin the analysis, do the following.

1   Write down your immediate reaction to this image. How does it make you feel?

2   Write down what type of photograph you think this is, where it might be found, and who might have taken it.

3   Write a brief caption to go with the image of the surgeon.

As media analysts, we need to unpack the signifiers and assumptions that prompt such interpretations, and ask what semiological codes and conventions lead to these readings, and what cultural knowledge is required to read the image in this way.

Common responses suggest that people feel uneasy, threatened, or disturbed by the image of the surgeon. People also tend to think that the image may be a news image, or a still from a low-budget horror or science-fiction film.

Figure 9.2 Surgeon operating

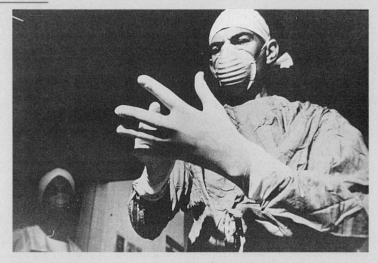

Source: British Film Institute

Text

The image is read through its signs and signifiers, content, codes, and conventions. We have focused on four key aspects of the image in order to tease out the factors that influence interpretation.

1   Photographic composition and conventions. The most important factors here are the lighting, the camera angle, and the camera lens. The low angle puts us, as viewers, into a subordinate position because we are looking up at the doctor, who therefore seems dominant. The camera lens is a wide-angle lens, which has the effect of distorting our vision so that the hand is made to appear unnaturally large in relation to the rest of the body. The size of this signifier emphasises its threat to the viewer. Furthermore, the lighting is harsh and it shows part of the hospital in shadow. This plays on the way in which darkness is associated with fear, the unknown, and other negative connotations.

2   The type of photograph. Is this photograph coded as a family snapshot, an art portrait, a news photo, or an advertisement? There are conflicting signifiers here, which complicates our analysis. Some signifiers connote reality, and some suggest that the image does not represent a real surgeon performing an operation. The fact that it is in black and white, and the stark lighting, connote documentary realism, but the photographer has framed the subject artfully (rather than snapping the photo spontaneously). The photographic code of black and white can signify reality, or it can locate the photo in an era prior to the availability of colour photography. We often associate black-and-white photos with evidence or facts. They have a high modality (a close connection with reality and authenticity) because newspapers have traditionally contained black-and-white photos, and because they are often used in documentaries (to show evidence of a bygone era); however, as colour printing processes become less expensive, and more prevalent in newspapers, black-and-white photography is more often understood as serious art photography. Because the composition of the photograph suggests that it has been staged instead of snapped, we might assume that it is art or a professional publicity still, rather than a photo documenting a real operation.

3   The photographic content. The signs and signifiers of the surgeon: the mask, and gloves. We recognise that the costume denotes a doctor, a surgeon. Doctors connote, among other attributes, illness, healing, medicine, and science. Surgeons have threatening connotations for many people because surgery is generally undertaken when something is perceived to be seriously wrong with a patient. Signifiers such as the surgical mask and latex gloves carry a number of connotations. The mask, as well as making the doctor anonymous, hidden, and impersonal, connotes danger and warfare through its similarity to gas masks and to the mask worn by Darth Vader in *Star Wars*. The latex gloves connote the need for protection against germs; they also make the doctor seem even more impersonal. Doctors put on gloves when they are going to do something to the bodies of patients, so the gloves also signify the threat of invasion of the body.

4   The setting. As a sign, the hospital operating theatre is a place that connotes sickness and life-and-death situations—consequently, it is a place of anxiety. The setting can be thought of with more favourable connotations—the hospital is, after all, potentially a place offering health and care. But in relation to this image, we tend to foreground the unsettling connotations because of the photographic codes—the way the image has been photographed.

Continued on next page   ▶

This analysis aims to develop your semiological analytic skills and to demonstrate the importance of considering who the audience is. Interpretations will depend on the cultural and social position of the readers, and on the assumptions about the audience that are embedded in the text.

Audience

Consider who the implied reader is, and how the audience is positioned or addressed by the image, by constructing a story about the image of the surgeon, and suggesting what may have happened immediately before and after the photograph was taken.

In addition to drawing on understandings of textual conventions and thinking through how the audience is being addressed, we can supplement our interpretation by imagining the story, context, and relationships in which an image is located. Question how the viewer is situated in the image and its implied narrative.

The low camera angle from which the photograph of the surgeon is taken puts us in the position, the point of view, of the patient, and we are thereby invited to identify with the patient. The audience members are positioned as vulnerable to and in need of medical intervention, so the inscribed reader is someone who might need to have surgery themselves. With a different camera angle and point of view, such as an over-the-shoulder shot, the inscribed reader would alter, perhaps addressing medical students and showing how to perform a surgical procedure.

The image shows the surgeon's hand reaching towards the camera, suggesting that he is in the middle of an operation. The lighting is stark and the lens makes the hand unnaturally large and overwhelming, suggesting that the surgery is serious and life-threatening. Perhaps the patient has just been rushed into the emergency room and the doctor is fighting to save the patient's life. This is not the only story that can be associated with the photograph—you may have come up with different implied narratives. The implied narrative that we have constructed draws on the codes, conventions, and culturally specific connotations discussed above, and it assumes that the text is addressing a particular audience. We could make further inferences about the inscribed reader if we had additional information about the context of the image, how and why it was produced, and how and where it is intended to be received.

Images are often polysemic; thus, the surgeon might be performing an autopsy in a morgue, delivering a baby, demonstrating a procedure for medical students, performing a minor, elective surgical procedure such as rhinoplasty, or even acting in a film about a mad scientist. But the capacity of images to carry a number of meanings does not suggest images can mean anything at all. Images and texts are open to an infinite number of possible interpretations, but they have a more limited number of plausible interpretations. The figure in this photograph is clearly meant to be a doctor, not a lawyer. He is wearing hospital garb, not a tie and a pin-striped suit, and is in an operating theatre rather than a courtroom. These things are denoted; hence there are limitations to polysemy.

Context

Consider how the context of the image and its relationship to other similar images influences its meaning. We have been working with the assumption that the photo exists in the context of a newspaper feature article or a science-fiction film, based on a number of signifiers that suggest this. In different contexts of reception, our understanding of the inscribed reader and the meaning of the photograph would shift substantially. The way we interpret the meaning of the photograph would alter radically if, for example, the context of reception was a medical textbook, an advertisement for latex gloves, or a religious anti-abortion publication. Notice how information about context affects our understanding of the inscribed reader and the meaning of the text.

Intertextuality

We read the image of the surgeon in relation to other images with which we are familiar. Thus our readings are dependent on our cultural knowledge and are constructed intertextually (in conjunction with the meanings produced in related texts).

The image of the surgeon takes on disturbing connotations through cinematic conventions. It is similar to the kind of images we see in black-and-white science-fiction films. A recurrent conventional figure, or sign, in such films is the mad scientist or doctor. This figure has featured in movies and popular literature since the days of Mary Shelley's *Frankenstein*, and more recently films such as *Prometheus* (2012) and *Sunshine* (2007). The photographic codes complement this: horror and science-fiction films use similar conventions of harsh shadows and distorted camera views to create disturbance.

Captions

Captions anchor the image to a particular meaning, narrowing the polysemic possibilities. Refer back to the caption you gave this image and reflect on how it expresses your initial interpretation.

The photo is actually of Dr Christiaan Barnard, who performed the world's first heart transplant operations in the late 1960s, and the original newspaper caption was 'Hands that save'. This draws our attention to the way captions and context can give a particular meaning to an image, as well as to the way a photograph can convey an attitude to its subject matter. In this case, in contrast to the caption's words of hope, the photograph seems to reflect the unease that some people felt about heart transplants at the time (1967). Heart transplant operations were new and unsafe, and some people questioned the morality of performing them. Thus we can see connections between the image and the fictional figure of the mad scientist who is understood to be mad because they usurp the powers of God and nature.

When analysing the relationship between words and images, think back to what you have learnt about connotations and paradigms (see p. 82). Remember that the author of the text could have chosen many different words from a paradigm or set of possibilities. A technique that semioticians sometimes employ to decode the meaning of a text makes use of paradigms and connotations to consider what the text leaves out, and why. Think of different terms that could have been used in the caption for this photo, and suggest why they were not. The caption could have read, for instance, 'Doctors who save', or 'Scientists who save', or 'Hands that heal'. This last caption has a similar denotation to 'Hands that save', but it would have changed the connotative meaning because healing implies a natural process in which the body gradually restores itself to health. The term 'healer' and the phrase 'healing hands' can also be used to refer to New Age or mystical techniques, rather than scientific or medical treatments. Such connotations would detract from the intended emphasis on the skill of the surgeon and the technological advancement signified by the new heart transplant procedure. 'Saving' as opposed to 'healing' implies an active agent intervening in a life-and-death situation. It also includes a spiritual connotation but a more Christian one, since God or Jesus are often referred to as 'saviours'. Thus the caption 'Hands that save' works effectively to link the medical discourse to the discourse of heroism and the ideology of a god-like individualism (instead of associating Dr Barnard with mad scientists or mystical healers). The words in the caption reinforce the photographic code of the low camera angle to enhance the sense of power associated with the surgeon.

Continued on next page ▶

ADVERTISEMENTS AND IDEOLOGY

We will now take semiotic analysis a stage further. The concept of ideology will be discussed fully in Part 3, but it is important to introduce it here. What is the ideological meaning of the images you are looking at? Ideology (see p. 33) means a set of values, beliefs, and feelings that, together, offer a view of the world. Each image contains an implied view of society, of the world, and of our roles in it. You can analyse advertisements with this in mind. Barthes demonstrates this in his essay 'Myth Today' (1973, pp. 109–59). Other theorists, such as Hodge and Kress, suggest that sign systems are the ways in which social groups can communicate ideas about how society is structured, what values are preferred. The dominant social groups can use sign systems to give messages that support their values and their domination. In their book *Social Semiotics*, Hodge and Kress write: 'In order to sustain these structures of domination the dominant groups attempt to represent the world in forms that reflect their own interests, the interests of their power' (1991, p. 3). By this the authors mean that it is in the best interests of the dominant group (the wealthiest, most privileged, and most powerful people, such as those who own the media and have political influence) to represent the world in a way that legitimates and reinforces their own position or ideology. In a capitalist society where money is power and success is measured by the accumulation of material objects, the media function to create desires for products that are associated with the trappings of success. Advertising and other media texts that represent the lifestyles of the well-to-do invite us to agree that it is desirable to buy into a materialist, consumerist lifestyle and the value system that goes with it. The ideology of affluence that is often communicated in commercial media suggests that owning products that make you look and feel more like the wealthiest members of society is a way to link your own identity to this concept of success. When we buy into this belief system, we implicitly agree that material wealth is an appropriate measure of success; therefore we consent to the ideological values of economic growth and consumerism.

If this seems to be a complicated way of understanding how ideology is communicated in media images, it may help to think back to the SEARCH acronym introduced in Chapter 3 (pp. 36–8). Remember that beliefs related to class, race, age, sexuality, and so forth are represented in media texts, and that such representations communicate ideological values about what is natural, good, normal, and desirable. We will consider the ideology presented in the following advertisements.

CASE STUDY

Colorbond fencing advertisement

Consider the advertisement for Colorbond fencing (Figure 9.3). It includes a wealth of semiological detail for analysis, but we want to go to the heart of the ideology that it presents. Advertisements often work by showing ideal characters in ideal situations. When you are considering this image, ask yourself what is ideal about the situation depicted.

Figure 9.3 Colorbond fencing advertisement

This Colorbond advertisement idealises family life and property ownership, and, through that, marriage and heterosexuality. What is unusual about that? you might ask, for surely these are perfectly normal and healthy ideals. They certainly are 'normal' and this is what we want to explore—the way this image conjures

Continued on next page ▶

up a whole story, implies and supports a whole lifestyle, and thereby presents an ideological construct. We will demonstrate how this is implicit in the image, which is supposedly concerned with selling fencing.

The Colorbond advertisement offers us two images, a past and a present, which together construct an implied narrative. This narrative is about the positive rewards of following a traditional suburban family lifestyle, a normal or ideal pattern of life. The top image implies the new suburban home of a young family: the fence, lawn, and tree signify a suburban backyard, and this is consolidated by the puppy (the family pet), clothes on the washing line, and what seems to be a child's sneaker in the puppy's mouth. The tree is a sapling, newly planted, which, together with the general emptiness of the rest of the back yard, implies a new garden and, by implication, a new house. The contrast between the established trees over the fence in the bottom picture and the absence of anything over the fence in the top picture suggests that the first picture is depicting a new housing estate where nothing has grown very tall yet—an estate from which the vegetation has been removed for a fresh start. This suggests two complementary stories of what has happened in the past. The first is a romance: a young couple met, fell in love, got married, had a child, and bought a house. The second is a story of enterprise and solid financial investment in property: a housing estate in an expanding suburb was being sold and occupied by property owners, who were contributing to the prosperity and development of Australia.

The second picture in the Colorbond advertisement expands on these narratives. The passage of time—ten years—brings things to fruition. The garden has grown (witness the tree) and industrious gardening by the owners of the property has produced a much more picturesque setting (although we don't see the labour, just the finished product). Beyond the fence, we see signs that this same process is happening all around, as the gardens of neighbours are also blooming. Humans are out of sight in both images, but the implied stories of marriage and children, and of domestic success and modest prosperity, allude to the absent characters in these stories. There is also a suggested narrative of the future: a story of continuing prosperity and growth.

These scenes imply that progress and happiness can be found in the domestic lifestyle of the suburban quarter-acre block, in a country that is still young but is growing ever more beautiful and prosperous. The Australian ideological dream of domestic bliss is thus encapsulated in these images. The advertisement offers its audience the pleasure of putting these connotations together, in the same way as a jigsaw puzzle offers entertainment. It shows us parts of the implied whole, which is a common way for signs to work; a sign suggests something more. In semiology this is described as **metonymy** (O'Sullivan et al. 1994, pp. 181–2). If someone says 'I'll take the wheel' they mean that they will drive the car, and in this context one part of the car (the steering wheel) is a metonym for the entire vehicle and the act of driving it. Similarly, in the 'Hands that save' caption of Figure 9.2 above, 'hands'

METONYMY

Metonyms are signs in which one part or element stands in for or represents something larger.

is a metonym. Part of the body—the hands—stands in for the whole person (Dr Barnard) and for his actions (performing surgery).

Behind the metonym of the fenced garden standing in for a larger ideal or ideology of family values, heterosexuality, and home ownership is the assumption that this is the desirable lifestyle. Here, the aspect of private property is crucial. The central sign is the fence and the accompanying caption: 'Only a Colorbond fence will look as good in ten years' time as the day it was put up'. The fence confirms ownership of property, which is the confirmation of success in white, Western, Australian culture. The fence divides up the land, apportioning it out to those who have the money to purchase land. In doing so, the whole capitalist ideology of Western culture is encapsulated. It is not problematised or questioned; it is normalised.

We can see this normalisation process at work by thinking about how else land could be treated. Think about Aboriginal culture's view of the land: it is not to be owned; we are simply the caretakers of what is there for everyone to communally use. White and Aboriginal views about land and ownership are two quite different ideologies. The image in the Colorbond advertisement supports the white view of land as something to be divided up and privately owned. While it could be said that caretaking is going on in relation to this land, it is caretaking within a European garden tradition—the flowers and plants, planted in such an orderly way, are not native to Australia, and they are watered with reticulated water, yet this artificially created culture is shown as normal. Note also the biblical connotations carried by gardens in the Western tradition: the association with the Garden of Eden enables a reading of the domestic garden as an idealised paradise, a place of rest and recreation, an escape from the demands of work.

While the fence recedes in terms of visual prominence in the second image, being more covered up and masked by the new growth, it is still there as the marker of boundaries. It continues to confirm property ownership, which is the confirmation of success in white, Western, Australian culture.

Yet there is, in this advertisement, a hint of something that might disturb its domestic paradise. The caption 'Only a Colorbond fence will look as good in ten years' time as the day it was put up' draws our attention to the other side of the passage of time—decay. While the garden grows, the owners are growing old. The Colorbond fence does not age. Ageing and decay are the shadow side of the garden's growth. We call it the shadow side because of our culture's refusal to accept decay and ageing as part of the processes of nature. Ageing is rarely celebrated in Western culture. People seek to hold onto youth and, in an ageist culture, the elderly are often held up for ridicule. This advertisement raises the spectre of decay and old age but, instead of drawing our attention to the problem of an ageist culture, it affirms the ideology of finding ways of avoiding age and decay. It attempts to show that ageing and decay can be defeated in the process of raising a family and owning private property.

The advertisement makes sense to us as an audience because we understand how its signs and signifiers relate to myths of the ideal nuclear family. At the same time, it also confirms these ideological values through its narrative. We are so imbued with these ideals that on seeing this advertisement in our day-to-day lives, we probably would not consciously see all that we have discussed (any more than the advertisers deliberately intended the ideology). Ideology is sometimes difficult to see because it is so obvious to us, which means that you will need to look carefully to discover what ideological assumptions are being confirmed in any advertisement you analyse. You will see many images that link together elements of property owning, marriage, and, by implication, families in similar ideological constructions.

ANALYSING NEW MEDIA ADVERTISEMENTS

In addition to considering ideology in advertising, it is also crucial to consider how media technologies and media audiences factor into the meanings of texts. Reading images depends on more than a nuanced knowledge of semiotics; it also depends on a contextual awareness of how audiences use the media, and how media producers and advertisers target audiences. In addition, as discussed in Chapter 7, theorists such as Marshal McLuhan have argued that the medium itself sends a message. It is important to question how different advertising mediums invite different representational techniques and give different messages to media consumers. The luxury car industry has invested extensively in innovative ways to reach its market, moving beyond print, radio, and television advertising, and sponsorship initiatives to pioneer new forms of internet advertising that foster a sense of personal investment in the product. Initially, internet advertising impacted on print advertising revenue more than on television advertising, but as technology advances and the target demographic for television and print advertising moves online, this is changing.

Online advertising was initially characterised by pop-ups and sponsored sites, in which a small window would appear when a visitor accessed a web page, or a host site such as Google or Amazon would priority-list certain links at the top of the screen or down the sidebar. With the increasing efficiency of pop-up blockers, banners and other strategies have become more popular. Banners are animated or graphic advertisements that cannot be blocked or deleted by visitors to a website. Online advertising is advantageous in that it accesses an international market in a relatively inexpensive manner, and it is possible to plant ads on sites that are likely to attract interested clientele in the target market. Google's purchase of YouTube has also had a significant impact on online advertising practices:

> If the pre-Google era of YouTube is characterized by amateur-produced videos in an ad-free environment, the post-Google purchase stage is characterized by professionally generated videos in an ad-friendly environment. Because of YouTube's popularity, industries have shown a deep interest in monetizing it. Since being purchased by Google, YouTube has adopted a new e-commerce model; it puts banner ads in videos or in YouTube pages and shares the revenue with the copyright holders of the videos (Kim 2012, p. 56).

Both internet pop-ups and banners have subsequently influenced television advertising strategies. The station and program logos that appear in the corner of the television screen, and the ads for upcoming programs or goods and services that pop up or scroll along the bottom of the screen are called 'bugs' in the USA and **digital onscreen graphics (dogs)** in the UK and Australia (Copeland 2007, p. 273). These branding and advertising mechanisms, and the terminology associated with them, are derived from internet advertising. Pop-up and banner style advertising and product placement techniques are used on television to ensure that viewers do not change the channel when an advertisement appears, because the ads appear onscreen while the main program is still showing. Ironically, new media advertising techniques that were originally designed to give users more interactive choices have developed into strategies to force us to view ads.

Whereas car companies like Nissan reportedly spend $25 million to advertise a new-release vehicle and Mercedes-Benz creates interactive ads using social media like

DIGITAL ONSCREEN GRAPHICS (DOGS) ▶

Dogs or 'bugs' often take the form of station logos or other information added at the bottom of the frame during post-production. Such graphics can brand television programs and the networks on which they screen, and they can prevent piracy, advertise the next program, or offer viewers extra information.

Instagram to invite potential customers to design and customise their dream machine, Tesla has no paid advertising campaign. Distinctively, Tesla relies on contacts with key journalists who write stories and create buzz about elite electric cars that drive themselves. More surprisingly, though, the absence of any Tesla ads has prompted advertising schools like Miami Ad School and fans of the brand to create advertisements for free on behalf of the company. For instance, YouTube user 'Everdream Pictures' posted a charming and clever aspirational commercial for Tesla called 'Modern Spaceship', directed by Joe Sill and Andreas Attai, and produced by James Khabusi and RJ Collins. The ad shows a young boy playing with rocket ships and space helmets that he has made with cardboard boxes and tinfoil. When he is 'ready for takeoff' he runs into the garage and looks at his father's Tesla with all the awe and triumphal music of Elliott gazing at ET's spacecraft. In a wonderful fantasy sequence, his father joins him in the garage and, instead of reprimanding him for trying to drive the car, puts on a cardboard space helmet and climbs into the passenger seat as the car launches silently and smoothly into outer space. Another highly professional fan-made Tesla ad by Parachute and director Sam O'Hare features magical CGI fireflies who swarm together to create an electric car. Both ads were featured in *AdWeek* and both achieved considerable coverage on Twitter (Nudd 2015). What better way to get free creative input than to allow fans to celebrate the brand they love?

Internet technology has become so accessible that more affordable cars such as Volkswagens can successfully target a broad demographic in yet more inventive and interactive ways. In an appeal to interactivity, the 'VW Bug Configurator' online campaign not only allows prospective buyers to use an online 'configurator' to customise their dream car's colour and features, it invites them to take their vintage or sporty custom-made car on a virtual test drive. In 2015, VW created a video ad that went viral due to its humorous use of the Golden Sisters—elderly YouTube personalities Mary Bartnicki, Josie Cavaluzzi, and Teresa Dahlquist. Viral advertising relies on audiences actively engaging with ads and spreading them through their social networks (see Chapter 13 on culture jamming). The Golden Sisters proved to be enormously popular and very effective at dispelling 'old wives' tales' about diesel engines being dirty and smelly as they gossiped and squabbled in a VW. In the 'Three Old Wives Talk Dirty' ad one of the sisters even held her snowy white scarf over the VW exhaust to prove how clean the diesel emissions were. Unfortunately for VW, the 2015 emissions scandal, in which the company was found to have falsified emissions data for its diesel engines, meant that the cute ladybug configurator was overshadowed by negative press, and the 'Clean Diesel' ads themselves came to be considered 'old wives' tales' and were deleted by VW.

These innovative advertising strategies demonstrate that as media technology changes, it leads to different patterns of media consumption and to changing strategies in the advertising industry; however, many of the semiotic strategies used by advertisers and many of the underlying ideological messages remain the same.

WHY USE SEMIOLOGY?

What are the advantages and limitations of using semiology as a methodology for text analysis?

Advantages of semiological analysis of media texts

1 The first advantage is practicality. Semiology is a helpful method for taking images apart. It gives a set of guidelines, checkpoints of things to do when we face an image, and serves as a guide through the maze of meanings. When we get stuck, we can go back to check connotations, or codes, or ask what is being signified. It can also be usefully applied beyond media texts to any cultural sign system, such as the wearing of clothes, or the organisation of social space in buildings and architecture.

2 Semiology is a method that stresses the relation of one text to others and to society as a whole. Its insistence on cultural codes and conventions encourages us to make links and comparisons with other texts and other genres, and leads us to see meaning as socially produced. Semiology's insistence on connotations draws attention to the way texts relate to wider social meanings, and to the role that readers and audiences play in constructing meanings. In doing so, semiology draws attention away from individual authors and their creative 'genius' and intentions. One of Barthes' famous essays is entitled 'The Death of the Author' (1977, pp. 142–8). This movement away from the emphasis on authorial intent and ownership of a text can be seen as a strength or weakness, depending on one's point of view. This is one of the distinctive features of the methodology of semiology: it does not focus on the intentions of individual creators. At times we find it useful to return to individual authors, but whatever your viewpoint, this is one of the distinctive features of the methodology of semiology: it is not interested in the intentions of message creators.

3 Semiology's insistence on breaking the sign into signifiers and signifieds, showing how something always stands in for something else, prises texts away from the notion that they are unproblematic reflections of reality. By continually asking what is being signified by a particular sign, we realise that texts are constructions of meaning, rather than transparent reflections of reality. Stuart Hall puts it this way:

> Saussure's great achievement was to force us to focus on … how language actually works and the role it plays in the production of meaning. In doing so he saved language from the status of a mere transparent medium between things and meanings. He showed instead that representation was a practice (Hall 1997, p. 34).

This is particularly important in relation to photography, film, and digital cameras, because they can so easily appear real, unmediated, and unconstructed. Semiology helps remind us that they are not, that they are constructions.

4 The way Barthes used semiology—seeing signs as wider systems of social myths—enables us to analyse ideology in media texts.

Limitations of semiological analysis of media texts

1 Semiology is just one approach to texts and the media. It does not cover everything and therefore we need other approaches alongside it.

2 The project or dream of semiology as a science of signs has been productive, but it has also led to the main fallibility of semiology. In the end, semiology's acknowledgment of polysemy, and its awareness that cultural knowledges, contexts, and audiences are elements that need to be taken into account in understanding meanings,

actually leads to the realisation that there are too many variables. We can point to significant probabilities and preferred meanings of texts, but other possible readings also have to be acknowledged. Philosopher Jacques Derrida adds to the semiotic method by introducing the concept of **différance**, an ongoing process of signification in which each sign or signifier refers to something else with which it is associated, and so on, so that the meaning will always be incomplete. Thus the term *différance* indicates that a sign is meaningful because it differs from other signs (black gets its meaning in relation to other colours because it is distinct from other colours), and because meaning is indefinitely deferred through the process of association (black is associated with darkness, which is associated with mystery, which is associated with suspicion and crime, and so on). Ironically, the science of signs has proven that we can't find the absolute meaning. So we have to go beyond semiology as a way of understanding media.

◄ *DIFFÉRANCE*

Refers to an endless chain of signification in which each sign or signifier is linked to or associated with something else, so that the complete or final meaning is infinitely deferred.

3   Saussure focuses on the rules of language and sign systems (he calls the abstract, formal system of rules and conventions **langue**). While this is useful, it does not take into account the concrete processes of language that Saussure calls **parole**, a term that refers to actual instances of speech and language use that is necessarily dynamic, contextual, and transient rather than predictable or rule-bound. Even the sign systems themselves can change over time, so it is best to be wary of a cogs-in-the-machine view of communication wherein language and its rules, and signs and their meanings, are fixed in time. The rules of language do not control language users; rather, it is the other way around. The reality is that people can break and change codes, struggle over meanings, and exert some autonomy over and through the systems: we can speak language. Because languages change meanings over time, there is more flexibility than is allowed for in Saussure's approach.

◄ *LANGUE*

Langue is the fundamental structure that underlies and governs language and expression.

◄ *PAROLE*

Parole is a particular instance of language use or expression, when the underlying rules (*langue*) are put into practice.

CONCLUSION

This chapter has explained techniques for reading images and advertisements by working through a series of examples, analysing their implied narratives and intertextual meanings, and examining the influence of text, audience, and context on meaning and interpretation. We have considered the advantages and limitations of using semiology to decode the ideological meanings of images, and to examine how broadcast media and internet advertising campaigns address and engage their target audiences. As long as we are aware of these limitations and of other possible approaches, semiology should still be a helpful and ultimately useful means to an end, that end being understanding media texts and, by extension, understanding the place of media in society.

This chapter has

*   showed how to use semiology to analyse media images
*   discussed the relationship between words and images in media texts
*   considered how the medium of representation (print, television, or internet, for example) affects meaning, and how the audience, the context, and intertextuality affect meaning and interpretation
*   analysed the ideological meanings of signs
*   weighed up the advantages and limitations of semiology.

? DISCUSSION POINTS

1   Do you think we contribute to stereotyping when we interpret social signs and form assumptions about people based on the connotations that their appearance and possessions carry?

2   Choose an image from any magazine and work out who the inscribed reader is, and how the spectator is positioned or addressed.

3   Find an advertisement that is available in several media, such as a movie trailer and a poster for the same film. In what sense can these types of publicity material be considered metonyms? Analyse whether the two versions address the audience differently and use different codes of representation.

SUMMARY

You should now be able to

- discuss the relationship between words and images in media texts
- use semiology for decoding the ideological meanings in media texts
- explain and apply the following terms: 'polysemy', 'metonymy', 'anchorage', and 'implied narrative'
- employ these terms and techniques in an analysis of an advertisement, discussing how the reader is positioned in relation to the text
- evaluate the strengths and weaknesses of semiotics as an analytic tool.

CHAPTER 10

Model Essay: Semiotic Analysis of an Advertisement

Historians and archaeologists will one day discover that the ads of our time are the richest and most faithful reflections that any society ever made of its entire range of activities.

Marshall McLuhan

This chapter will

- use semiotic terms and techniques to analyse an advertisement
- analyse the relationship between image, text, intertext, and context
- consider how the reader is interpellated
- interpret possible ideological meanings in the text
- demonstrate the development of an argument, and the use of quotations to substantiate or clarify points in an essay.

What follows is an example of how to write an essay using semiotic techniques to analyse an advertisement. It includes in-text references and a bibliography. The bracketed references in this essay refer to books listed in the essay's bibliography, rather than the references of this book. In academic essays it is important to give evidence of reading and research. Always include references to and terminology from the course material in the unit you are studying, and define key terms and concepts with care. It is also advisable to include and discuss quotes from other academic books and articles to support, clarify, and substantiate your ideas. Academic essays should also feature a clear **introduction**, a **thesis statement**, a **conclusion**, and an alphabetised bibliography or reference list.

◀ INTRODUCTION

The introduction of an essay should include an outline of what you aim to achieve (state essay topic, objectives, and the text you are analysing) and how you intend to achieve it (your methodology and structure).

◀ THESIS STATEMENT

The part of an essay that outlines the central argument is called the thesis; it should be briefly stated in the introduction, and developed throughout the essay. You should also consider possible objections and counterarguments (the antithesis) in order to weigh up different points of view and defend your ideas.

◀ CONCLUSION

The conclusion of an essay should summarise the key points and briefly discuss their significance, with reference to the objectives stated in the introduction.

ESSAY TOPIC

Undertake a semiotic textual analysis of an advertisement, showing how meaning is constructed. Consider signs, signifiers, connotations, codes, and anchorage, as well as the possible ideological meanings of the advertisement.

Figure 10.1 Hahn Loveboobs advertisement

Source: courtesy of Andrew Disney at Lion Nathan

Advertisements exist as a means of selling products (see Figure 10.1) by creating an association between a brand and a desirable lifestyle or identity. Within media images of and messages about products, lifestyles, and identities, many ideological messages are encoded. Here, 'ideology' can be understood as 'the practice of reproducing social relations of inequality within the sphere of signification and discourse' (O'Sullivan et al. 1986, p. 107). O'Sullivan et al. claim that ideology is communicated through signs, including advertisements, and that ideology serves the interests of the wealthiest, most powerful groups in society. More generally, ideology can refer to any world view or set of assumptions and beliefs that are taken for granted as being natural and normal, but that are actually socially constructed. Ideology is not neutral; it is always implicated within power relations that privilege certain people over others. However, texts can contain resistant ideologies that challenge the dominant ideology. Feminist ideology, for instance, challenges the privileged position of men within the dominant patriarchal ideology.

Using semiotic analysis to decode its meaning, this essay aims to denaturalise the ideological messages in a Hahn beer advertisement. The Hahn advertisement appeared in the *Weekend Australian Magazine* in the *Australian* national newspaper in March 2007; it was also screened simultaneously as a television advertisement and publicised on the Hahn website. Following the semiotic method, I will work through denotations, connotations, context, intertextuality, and the way the text addresses its audience, to support the argument that the image reinforces patriarchal ideology, but it also communicates more subtle ideological messages about gender, class, consumerism, and age.

Bob Hodge and Gunter Kress, authors of *Social Semiotics*, write that

> Semiotics has been defined as "the science of the life of signs in society" … In its terms everything in a culture can be seen as a form of communication, organised in ways akin to verbal language, to be understood in terms of a common set of fundamental rules or principles (Hodge & Kress 1991, p. 1).

Semiotic analysis was originally developed by Ferdinand de Saussure to analyse language. As Hodge and Kress suggest, semiotic analysis can also be used as a means of understanding communication such as media texts.

The first level of signification considered in semiotic analysis is denotation, which means 'the commonsense, obvious meaning of the sign' (Fiske 1990, p. 91). On a denotative or descriptive level, the advertisement depicts a heart-shaped figure with two dots drawn in the sand, captioned with text above and below the image, and accompanied by a picture of a Hahn Super Dry beer bottle on the lower right. Even if it isn't noticed at first, the sand drawing also denotes breasts, or 'boobs'. The beer bottle is surrounded by pale lines that radiate outwards. The caption above the heart shape reads 'When women think of …' and the caption below it, written in text that is upside down, reads 'Men think of …'. Beside the picture of the beer bottle are the words 'Super honest. Super refreshing'. The Hahn web address <hahnloveboobs.com> is visible in small print in the lower corner beside the beer. There is also a small image of a bottle top at the bottom left of the advertisement containing a message to drink responsibly, in the form of another web address <www.drinkaware.com.au>.

In addition to denotative meanings, elements in the advertisement also communicate connotations or associations. Connotations operate at the second level of signification and depend on cultural knowledge. For example, the heart has connotations of sweethearts, romance, and love due to cultural knowledge of Valentine's Day gifts and cards. Additionally, the lines that radiate outwards from the Hahn logo have connotations of rays of light, suggesting that the beer itself is an energy source, or that it has super powers. This reading is reinforced by the repetition of the word 'super' in the text on and near the bottle, and by association with the visual style of superhero comic books, in which similar radiating lines often suggest power. The halo effect of the rays also has religious connotations, and the golden colour of the bottle and its silver label carry connotations of something precious.

The advertisement contains what semiotician C S Peirce described as iconic, indexical, and symbolic signs (1958). The photograph is an iconic sign because the images resemble sand and beer. Iconic signs such as

Continued on next page ▶

pictorial images have a 'likeness' to the 'thing, person or place being represented' (Dyer 1982, p. 124). The internet address is indexical, because it points or directs us to a location in cyberspace. Symbols are signs that 'have no logical connection between the sign and what it means' (Crow 2003, p. 33). The letters H-A-H-N are symbols that are understood to refer to the brand name of the beer through linguistic conventions.

The meanings of different components of the advertisement can be decoded when we consider the target audience of the image, the context in which the image is located, and the intertextual relationship the image has with the simultaneous television and internet advertisements for the product.

We can determine who the intended reader of the advertisement is by considering who it is implicitly addressing. According to Fiske:

> One of the most ubiquitous and insidious ideological practices is what Althusser calls "interpellation" or "hailing". All communication addresses someone, and in addressing them it places them in a social relationship. In recognising ourselves as the addressee and in responding to the communication we participate in our own social, and therefore ideological, construction (Fiske 1990, pp. 174–5).

Following Fiske's claim that all communication addresses someone, the beer ad addresses Hahn's target market, which seems to be men aged 18–38. Although it acknowledges what women think and feel, the advertisement primarily invites viewers to link the male desire for a voluptuous woman with the desire to buy Hahn. It is designed to be easy for male viewers to put themselves into the picture. By interpellating viewers into a youthful, masculine, heterosexual identity, it is implied that this subject position is normal and natural. People from all demographics were exposed to the advertisement on Australia television and magazines, and it was publicised globally online. But a wealthy female connoisseur of fine wine, a gay man with little interest in women's breasts, or a Muslim who abstains from alcohol would probably not feel the advertisement addressed them; hence they wouldn't necessarily accept the social position or internalise the ideology that the text assumes.

Advertisements use established conventions of signification such as metaphors, metonyms, and symbolism to construct meaning. The 'boobs' and the sand are metonyms because, 'metonymy works by associating meanings within the same plane. Its basic definition is making a part stand for the whole' (Fiske 1990, p. 95). Sand is a metonym because it is just one part of the surf, sand, and sun that beaches entail and that, in the context of both the advertisement and Australian culture, connote the outdoor lifestyle, fun times, and holiday romance or summer fling that might be enjoyed on the beach. Similarly, 'boobs' is a metonymic signifier for a sexually desirable woman. Boobs are a part of female anatomy that stands for the whole woman, literally reducing her to a body part: boobs are an object of desire, just as beer is. Interpreted in this light, the advertisement provides an example of sexual objectification and commodification in which the woman is 'constructed as an object for the "look" of the male spectator' (Walters 1995, p. 51).

An implied narrative underlies the advertisement and helps make sense of the text, just as interpellation positions us in relation to the text. The composition of the advertisement places the viewer close so we look straight down on the heart, and see the grainy texture of sand and droplets of condensation on the beer bottle. The implied narrative is that the viewer is the person on the beach who has just drawn in the sand and who is within reach of the bottle of beer. That person is not pictured in the print advertisement, which invites everyone who sees it to insert themselves into the narrative. Those who visit the website or see the television advertisement know there is a larger intertextual, implied narrative suggested by the image. In the screen versions of the advertisement, a young, attractive, white man and woman are on the beach together. The curvaceous, bikini-clad woman draws a heart in the sand and gazes adoringly at her partner, indicating that she loves him. Her love interest is standing opposite her where the camera (and therefore the audience) is positioned. As he looks down at her message he sees an inverted heart; he also sees her cleavage, so he places two dots representing nipples in the heart. This suggests that instead of loving her, he loves boobs. This implies conventional ideologies of femininity and masculinity in which women are interested in love and romance, whereas men are interested in having sex.

The meanings of the heart in the sand and the beer bottle are anchored by the words written on the advertisement. According to Fiske, the term 'anchorage' describes the 'function of words used as captions for photographs' (1990, p. 110). Fiske points out that visual images are polysemic (they have many possible meanings), so words can be used to anchor the meaning of an image by reducing the range of plausible meanings. On a denotative level, the word 'boobs' ensures that the audience knows the symbol in the sand is meant to represent breasts rather than a heart or a beach bum, which are other meanings that viewers might form in the absence of any caption to anchor the image. The word 'refreshing' has connotations of something new and revitalising, which is consistent with a surfie, youth-culture lifestyle devoid of worries about serious things such as responsibilities or commitment.

The playful, youthful associations with surfie boys and beach babes links with other ideological messages related to age and class. The humour of the wordplay about 'love' and 'boobs' and Hahn being a 'refreshing' drink for 'refreshingly honest' young people is directed at those who might see political correctness as a false or dishonest veneer that covers over what people really think and feel. It also targets people who use the word 'boobs' to describe breasts. Signifiers in the advertisement suggest that sexism is permissible within the context of a young, male, lower middle class subculture. Beach sand, boobs, and beer are not generally used to advertise expensive beverages, or venues in which wealthy, mature, professional people might nibble seafood salads and sip chardonnay. Hahn is not a costly boutique beer, so it is affordable for young consumers who do not have much money. Hence, although the images may be desirable to individuals from a range of social circumstances, the connotations operate predominantly within a class-specific context that primarily targets readers of a certain age and gender. The process of interpellation is, however, also more complex, as the ad addresses a secondary audience of young, postfeminist women who accept contemporary sexuality and gender roles, and are neither offended nor threatened by ironic, playful forms of sexism.

The fact that the advertisement is primarily directed at a young, male audience is precisely what invites a tolerant, humorous reading or response. In Australia, if not elsewhere, there is a cultural stereotype of young men being playful, harmless larrikins and easygoing pranksters. Youth makes their actions and attitudes seem more excusable. There is a permissiveness associated with late adolescence (even if such behaviour persists into middle age) that is best summed up by the saying 'boys will be boys'. Within this ideology or view of masculinity, it seems acceptable and natural for 'boys' to make fun of political correctness. This ideological perspective turns the serious issue of sexism into a good lark, or something they'll grow out of, a natural and playful rebellion against adult relationships and responsibilities.

The reading that patriarchal ideology is endorsed and privileged is supported by textual evidence, such as codes of representation that suggest some messages in the text are dominant, others subordinate. Hodge and Kress claim conventions organise signs and help us to interpret them 'via codes which organise signifieds and signifiers' (1991, p. 262). One common way of organising signifiers is by placing them in a hierarchy. In the

Continued on next page ▶

Hahn advertisement, the text is arranged so the most important messages are the largest, and nearest the top of the page. The instruction to drink responsibly is written in the smallest font at the bottom of the page, and is literally marginalised (printed near the margin), so as not to discourage consumption. The woman's viewpoint is written the right way up at the top of the page (which initially implies the female perspective is 'right', or important), whereas the man's viewpoint is upside down. This means viewers of the advertisement have to turn the page around and literally see the world in a new way, from a masculine perspective, to be able to get the joke about the inverted heart's resemblance to breasts. The phrase 'Men think of … [boobs]' ultimately has priority because, when we turn the page around, it is upright at the top of the page and it makes a lasting impression, reinforcing a heterosexual, patriarchal ideology.

The advertisement makes a mild sexist joke, but in doing so it invites viewers to see the situation from the woman's point of view as well as the man's, and it depicts women as being subjects with thoughts and feelings as well as being sexualised objects. The advertisement explicitly states, 'Women *think* …' and it is clear in the television advertisement that the woman also *feels* miffed when her boyfriend responds to her romantic gesture with a crude joke. The 'Super honest. Super refreshing.' tagline suggests that she ultimately accepts that his masculine perspective on sexual relationships is different from hers, and sees it as refreshingly honest.

In conclusion, I have shown the Hahn advertisement has connotations of youth, sexiness, and fun in the sun that, by association, make the product desirable. It is important to stress that the advertisement only works for those who have the relevant cultural knowledge and share the belief that such things are desirable. The advertisement is open to oppositional readings, especially by those outside the target market. A reading is 'oppositional' when 'the audience disagrees with dominant values expressed within the preferred reading of the text' (Bell et al. 1999, p. 21). Feminists, for instance, may interpret the advertisement as gender discrimination, not harmless fun. Deeply religious or conservative people may view sexual references and alcohol consumption as problematic.

The Hahn advertisement shows dominant patriarchal, consumerist ideologies maintaining their privileged place, but these ideologies are not entirely accepted as natural and normal. They are represented as being in dialogue with other ways of seeing the world, such as feminism and messages about responsible alcohol consumption. Indeed, the advertisement literally interpellates viewers into different subject positions, encouraging us to see the world from different points of view and to acknowledge diverse perspectives and interpretations.

Bibliography

Bell, A, Joyce, M & Rivers, D 1999, *Advanced Media Studies*, Hodder & Stoughton, London.

Crow, D 2003, *Visible Signs*, AVA Publishing SA, Crans-près-Céligny, Switzerland.

Dyer, G 1982, *Advertising as Communication*, Methuen, London.

Fiske, J 1990, *An Introduction to Communication Studies*, 2nd edn, Routledge, London.

Hodge, R & Kress, G 1991, *Social Semiotics*, Polity Press, New York.

O'Sullivan, T, Hartley, J, Saunders, D & Fiske, J 1986, *Key Concepts in Communication*, Methuen, New York.

Peirce, C S 1958, *Collected Papers, 1931–58*, vols 7–8 (ed. Arthur Burke), Harvard University Press, Cambridge, MA.

Walters, S D 1995, *Material Girls: Making Sense of Feminist Cultural Theory*, University of California Press, Berkeley.

CONCLUSION

This model essay has demonstrated how to analyse an advertisement's components, considering the intended market, the context, and the signifiers, connotations, codes, and conventions that create meaning. It exemplifies how to define key terms and concepts, incorporate quotations to support ideas, and construct an argument about the ideological messages in a text. These techniques can also be applied to other texts, such as magazine covers, DVD covers, and websites.

This chapter has

- shown how to set out an essay using semiotics to analyse an advertisement.

? DISCUSSION POINTS

1   Can you find any elements of the Hahn advertisement that have not been discussed in the essay, or aspects that you would interpret differently?
2   How might your own experiences and ideas influence your interpretation of the advertisement and affect the argument about its meaning?
3   Consider how the elements in the SEARCH acronym (sex and sexuality, environment, age, race and religion, class, and handicap) relate to signifiers in the Hahn advertisement and to your own reading of the ad.

SUMMARY

You should now be able to

- write your own essay, using semiotics to analyse a media text.

PART 3
Making Sense: Discourse, Ideology, and Hegemony

It's all around us, here even in this room. You can see it out your window, or on your television. You feel it when you go to work or go to church or pay your taxes. It is the world that has been pulled over your eyes.

Morpheus, *The Matrix*

Overview

Part 3 extends the process of semiological analysis by exploring the concepts of discourse, ideology, and hegemony. After reading this part, you should be able to use all three concepts in your analysis of the media, media texts, and the relationship between the media and society.

CHAPTER 11

Discourse and Ideology

Surely one of the most visible lessons taught by the twentieth century has been the existence, not so much of a number of different realities, but of a number of different lenses with which to see the same reality.

Michael Arlen

This chapter will

- give definitions of discourse and ideology
- illustrate how these terms describe all human communication and are also concerned with social power
- consider Western discourses of criminality
- discuss the importance of beliefs, feelings, actions, and common sense in relation to ideology
- explain and illustrate the concept of 'unconscious consciousness'
- consider whether it is possible to have no ideology
- show how discourses and ideologies are embedded in language, texts, institutions, and identities
- introduce the key terms 'interpellation', 'identity', and 'subjectivity'
- analyse media texts that demonstrate ideology and interpellation at work
- consider how our identities and subjectivities are constructed.

The terms 'discourse', 'ideology', and 'hegemony' relate to the work of three important theorists: Michel Foucault, Louis Althusser, and Antonio Gramsci. These terms are first, concerned with the way any ideas and values are felt and expressed in a society, and second, concerned with issues of social power.

The work of these theorists argues that power is unequally distributed in society—there are dominant and subordinate groups—and that this power is partly maintained and reproduced by the circulation of ideas and beliefs. These ideas and beliefs are circulated through language and texts via the media and social institutions such as the family and the education system. These terms have been enormously influential in the development of media and cultural studies. They are complex: they contain various possible meanings and can be interpreted in many ways. Alongside their use in the work of Foucault, Althusser, and Gramsci, they have been the subject matter of numerous essays, articles, and books, and have formed the theoretical basis for much media analysis.

We use the terms 'discourse' and 'ideology' first as terms for discussing how ideas and values are presented in the media. We use the term 'discourse' to refer to the ways in which these ideologies are *communicated*, and 'ideology' as the main way of discussing issues of social power and the media, whereas 'hegemony' (which will be discussed in Chapter 12 and in subsequent chapters) refers to the ways in which ideologies are *negotiated*, maintained, and disputed.

DISCOURSE

We have already used the terms 'discourse' and 'discursive frame' in relation to language as demonstrated by John Fiske (pp. 61–2).

'Discourse' comes from the French word *discours*, which means 'dialogue, speech, or conversation'. Its simplest meaning is the articulation, voicing, or putting forward of a point of view. This act of articulation is usually part of an exchange of ideas among several speakers or social groups. Each group develops its own jargon and methods of encoding and communicating knowledge. This knowledge is shared among members of the group, hence discourse relies on collective understanding. Thus discourse is a social process of constructing meaning within a mutually understood set of rules. In this sense discourse is quite a neutral, descriptive, or innocent term: as humans, we need discourses to communicate with each other.

Note that discourses find expression in texts and other communicative practices as well as in speech. The term 'discourse' typically refers to the collective discussion or interplay of meanings and ideas circulating around a particular subject, incorporating these different modes of expression and instances of communication.

Foucault's theory of discourse is that societies tend to bring together a range of voices, ideas, and beliefs into overall discourses that offer ways of understanding the world (Fiske 1987, pp. 14–15). Any society has a number of discourses by which it makes sense of the world and which we can study by means of Foucault's techniques of **discourse analysis**.

◀ DISCOURSE ANALYSIS

Explores the ways in which power and knowledge are communicated through texts, language use, and systems of thought.

What are the main Western discourses of criminality? ▶

Foucault has used the notion of discourse to examine how societies understand and make sense of sexuality, madness, and criminality (Foucault 1981; Rabinow 1984; Fillingham 1995). He argues that a range of ways of thinking (discourses) are brought together to make sense of these areas, and that these discourses can and do change over time. In relation to crime and criminality, for instance, he sees how medical, legal, religious, and moral discourses define criminality and criminals and suggest ways of dealing with them. Medical discourses define criminals in terms of being sick or healthy, and if they are deemed sick then they need curing and rehabilitation; religious and moral discourses define criminals in terms of being good or evil, deserving reward or punishment; and legal discourses define criminals as a danger to other people and, being concerned with the preservation of people's safety and property, decide what courses of action to take to prevent further crimes. Thus we can see three kinds of possible treatment for criminals, based on three discourses for understanding their actions: *rehabilitation* or cure for their sickness; *punishment* (which could take various forms) for their evil deeds; and some form of *restriction* (for example, the removal of limbs or imprisonment) to prevent future crimes.

You are probably aware that elements of all three of these discourses—medical, religious, and legal—are present in the way societies construct prisons and use imprisonment today. Prisons are simultaneously supposed to be instruments of rehabilitation, punishment, and crime prevention. Which of these predominates in practice?

For Foucault, discourses are always linked to what he calls 'disciplinary power' in that they are 'concerned with the regulation, surveillance, and government of, first, the human species or whole populations, and second, the individual and the body' (Hall 1994, p. 123). They are, in other words, the means of organising and transmitting social control.

In this sense discourse is a less neutral, innocent term, as it is involved in maintaining social power.

Foucault suggests that at different historical moments these discourses cohere in different ways: religious and moral discourses used to be the dominant ways of understanding criminality (see Foucault 1979). Now legal and medical discourses carry more weight. There is a continuous struggle between competing discourses, each of which attempts to instate itself as the overall discourse for making sense of a particular aspect of the world. Because this model understands that the dominant discourse changes over time, it incorporates the possibility of social change. New discourses can emerge that challenge existing power relations. This is the major difference between discourse theories and theories of ideology, which seem to suggest a much more fixed view of how society works.

The second major difference between discourse and ideology is that discourses tend to be modes of thought, speech, or expression, whereas ideologies can be these things as well as being material in the sense that they can be found in buildings or activities. Rosary beads and crucifixes, for example, are part of the ideology of Roman Catholicism but not part of the discourse of Roman Catholicism, whereas Scorsese's films, in which these material objects frequently appear, are part of that discourse because film is a mode of expression. Discourses do, of course, result in material practices—the kind of prison that a society builds will depend on its discourse of crime and criminality—but discourses remain modes of thinking and speaking, modes of expression.

Discourses of criminality in *Orange Is the New Black*

In Netflix's critically acclaimed and most-watched television series *Orange Is the New Black*, the lead protagonist (Piper Chapman) is a privileged, wealthy, liberal, educated WASP (White Anglo-Saxon Protestant) woman who plays a convicted felon sentenced for carrying a suitcase of drug money for her then-girlfriend, who was an international drug smuggler. The offence had happened a decade earlier, and by the time of Chapman's arrest she was engaged to a man and living quietly among New York's upper middle class. This is perhaps the first clue to the way in which the show attempts to dent stereotypes around discourses of criminality: it centres on a white, middle class woman who was seemingly living a 'normal' life. Further, the female characters on the show come from a range of gender orientations, social classes, and ethnicities. There are blacks, whites, transgender, lesbian, and Hispanic people represented. Accordingly, the diversity in other discourses around class, race, and sexuality allows *Orange Is the New Black*, at times, to defy some assumptions often present in criminality discourses.

However, it is important to consider whether stereotypes are not being maintained just because there is a level of visibility and representation. So, while *Orange Is the New Black* does disturb the exclusion of women in dominant discourses on criminality, it also constructs a view of prison life that centres on a white woman and a particular view of femininity, and can be therefore be read perhaps as reinforcing racialised stereotypes within criminality discourses about people of colour. What this means is that there are contradictory discourses at play within the show, and it is necessary to consider how discourses around power, gender, race, class all tie in to/with the criminality discourse.

Within contemporary Australian media, many news reports focus on the length or severity of sentences imposed on criminals, how appropriate these are, and what the effects are on the victims of crime. Embedded within these reports and discussions you will again find various discursive positions in relation to crime.

IDEOLOGY

Ideology is a complex term. Within media studies it is defined as follows. Ideologies are sets of social values, ideas, beliefs, feelings, and representations by which people collectively make sense of the world they live in, thus constituting a world view. This world view is naturalised, a taken-for-granted, common-sense view about the way the world works. It is important to note that this definition is linked to, but somewhat different from, one that you may already have come across; within politics, the term 'ideology' is often used to refer to a set of deliberately formulated, coherent, rational ideas that are used as ways of defining how society can be organised, such as a conservative, or socialist, or eco-friendly, or fascist ideology, which can be personalised as a Cameron ideology, an Obama ideology, a Turnbull ideology, and so on. When used in this way the term 'ideology' usually suggests that the ideas are in some way unrealistic, rigid, and dogmatic. Our definition of ideology extends its meaning beyond the rational to include feelings, and beyond a narrow political view to consider all aspects of the world.

Every person has a set of values, beliefs, and feelings that make sense to them and enable them to function in the world. Whatever we do—whether it is donating money to a charity, angling for a promotion at work, inviting someone to go to a concert, or watching television—it not only has to make sense to us in some way, but also enacts the way that we make sense of our world. Our actions arise from our view of the world, and they act out our values, beliefs, and feelings, fleshing out the fact that, say, we believe it makes sense to help those less fortunate than ourselves, or to compete with others in order to become successful, or to initiate a relationship by going on a date rather than by means of an arranged marriage. Since the way we conduct our lives is an interconnected social practice, this stresses that people make sense of the world collectively. In all societies there are shared values, beliefs, and feelings that govern how people act and live together, a shared common sense. Institutions such as schools and television contribute to this interconnectedness, since they provide forums for a wide range of individuals to receive the same message. If an ideology is to have a significant social impact, it must be shared and agreed on by a large group of people, which is why the mass media are so important in communicating and reinforcing ideologies.

Beliefs and feelings in ideologies: 'unconscious consciousness'

Our definition stresses that beliefs and feelings are important to any ideology. This takes us out of the realm of the purely rational and conscious; people's ideologies are connected to their hearts as well as their heads, and ideologies are not consciously thought out. They operate at the level of what Althusser calls 'unconscious consciousness'. This is a very useful concept. We perform many human actions without being conscious of our motives.

We do not always think carefully about what we are doing; many of our social actions are imbued with beliefs, feelings, and values, and are performed with unconscious motives.

A simple example illustrates this. What happens when you and a person of the opposite sex approach a door together? Who goes through first? Does either of you hold the door for the other or invite the other to go first? Does either of you immediately go in front of the other? Watch other people and yourself in this situation. Normally, you would do whatever you do without much conscious thought, but behind the choices you make lies an ideology of gender relations (and/or age).

There are a number of different possibilities:

- the man holds the door open for the woman, who goes through
- the man opens the door for the woman, who then invites the man to go through
- the woman maintains or quickens her pace while the man slows his, allowing the woman to arrive at and go through the door first
- the woman holds the door open for the man; and so on.

Tradition has women going first. How can we understand the ideology of this? The following are different interpretations of what this means in terms of gender relations:

- it shows male respect for and deference towards women
- it allays male insecurities about their own social skills, since men who open doors for women are sending women into environments first so women will ease the way socially for them
- it suggests that although women go first, men control the action by opening the door
- it relates to a medieval ideology and code of chivalrous behaviour.

Most of these views suggest that men control what happens. While these explanations allow for the possibility that women might take positive action in advancing towards the door first, and might even enjoy being shown respect, they can still be seen as accepting the notion of male power. People wanting to challenge such behaviour might deliberately break the convention by having women wait for men to pass through first, or by taking turns in going first. This may seem a trivial incident, yet it is an aspect of day-to-day gender relations. Now that you have read this, the next time you come to a door with someone of the opposite sex you will be conscious of what is happening, which will encourage you to reflect on which gender ideologies and relations are implicit in such actions. It may also make you wonder what to do next!

The point is that in many areas of life, people act at the level of unconscious consciousness; they do and say things without thinking about their motives, or their unconscious assumptions and ideological world views.

The consequence of living and behaving through unconscious consciousness is that certain patterns of behaviour become naturalised, defined as part of human nature, regarded as common sense or the way things are. These behaviour patterns are not seen as ideological by those who practise them. Indeed, they are not even thought about much, which relates back to our ideas about language and the social construction of reality: neither language nor social organisations are natural; both are constructed, even though both are often regarded by people as natural and normal. We have already suggested that you should think carefully whenever anyone suggests that the way humans act is normal or natural. If someone says to you that something is just human nature, look for the ideological implications in the action they are describing. Remember that the consequence of naturalising behaviour is to naturalise and thereby hide ideology. In this way ideology is capable of reinforcing existing power relations and social structures in a manner that inevitably works to the advantage of one group (the dominant group in that context), and disadvantages others by making them seem abnormal, different, or deviant.

WHERE ARE DISCOURSES AND IDEOLOGIES FOUND?

The previous sections of this chapter defined discourse and ideology, and suggested that it is difficult to see these clearly because they are naturalised, common-sense ways of understanding the world. To try to make the concepts easier to understand and identify, we can ask: where are discourses and ideologies embedded? Can we see them? What examples will illustrate them?

There are three places to look for and find ideologies:

1   in language, texts, and representations
2   in material institutions
3   in our heads and hearts (our subjectivities and our identities).

Discourses and ideologies in language, texts, and representations

Language, texts, and representations are the most significant sites for media studies. In our analysis of language (pp. 61–2) and advertisements (p. 140), discourse frameworks and ideological meanings have already been mentioned. To see these in media texts, simply ask the following question of any text you analyse: what are the values, beliefs, and feelings that inform the way this text makes sense of the world?

CASE STUDY

Children's early readers—ideology at work

Look at children's early readers as an example. The books children are given to learn to read are a fascinating repository of ideological meanings and discursive frameworks, and are particularly interesting because they are one of the early media sources that socialise children. The *Key Words Reading Scheme* (Murray 1964, 1990),

Continued on next page ▶

first published in 1964 and better known as the Ladybird *Peter and Jane* books, is a readily accessible example. Try to locate copies of these books to look at. They are obviously outdated in some ways (and a new series, *Learn to Play: Tom and Kate,* was published from 1990) but the *Peter and Jane* series was still being published in 2014 and may well be familiar to you. All countries and all school systems have some equivalent to these books, such as the *Dick and Dora Happy Venture Readers* in Australia, and the *Dick and Jane* series in America.

A close look at the illustrations and text from these books reveals a number of significant ideological, discursive aspects.

The first point to make is that they present one family—Peter and Jane and their parents—as the ideal, natural, normal family. This family discourse is imbued with a particular set of ideologies, the most obvious being its ideologies of class, ethnicity, and gender. Peter and Jane's family is the nuclear family: mum, dad, two children, and pet dog. The home is middle class and suburban. The illustrations show a detached home (which signifies middle class in the United Kingdom) and a sizeable garden, and, combined with the storylines, the series depicts a family with enough money to buy good toys and go on regular holidays. The family members are white, though later editions of the series include some people of colour as background characters.

The values of the children are conformist in relation to two institutions: the police and schools. In *Boys and Girls* (a title that seems interested in setting up difference and delineating acceptable behaviour for the two genders) the text reads: 'Peter and Jane like the school.' In *Things We Like* the text reads:

> Look, Jane, that is a Police car. It says POLICE on it. That is the Police Station. I like the Police, says Peter. They help you.
> Yes, says Jane. The Police help you.

Without wishing to denigrate the institutions of the police and education, it is clear from the perspectives of class and ethnicity that the police and schools may have very different meanings for, say, Aboriginal children, black South Africans, African-Americans, or black Britons living in inner-city areas, where the police, for example, may not be seen so simply as 'good' but as agents supporting the dominant white middle class.

It is in the gender area that the stereotyped ideology is most apparent in these books. The boy is always older than the girl, thus validating male power through age. Jane also looks up to Peter. This is literally so in a number of illustrations that depict Jane in physically lower positions, often sitting rather than standing. This age hierarchy continues in the narrative, in which Peter is the main character. He is given more actions to do, whereas Jane is often given a supportive role, praising and validating Peter's behaviour. She acts as cheerleader for his football exploits: 'Peter has the red ball. He plays with the boys with the red ball.' Jane looks on. 'That was good, Peter, says Jane. That was good.' Jane also tends to serve Peter: 'I want a cake, please, says Peter. A cake for me, please, he says. Here you are, says Jane. Here are some cakes.'

Both children are socialised into helping with domestic chores, which encourages ideals of pride in property and reinforces the notion that good behaviour is rewarded. But these chores are clearly divided on the basis of gender: boys work outside the house, girls work inside. 'Here we are at home, says Daddy. Peter helps Daddy with the car, and Jane helps Mummy get the tea. Good girl, says Mummy to Jane. You are a good girl to help me like this.' The mother is depicted in the home more than the father, who goes out more: 'Peter and Jane are in the car with Daddy. They like it in the car. Mummy is at home.'

All of these gendered differences are presented as normal, and thus ideologies of gender, class, and ethnicity are naturalised. Children do not necessarily internalise these values when they read the books, but if they do not, they will not find themselves reflected in these stories. And children whose families are different from this normal, ideal family may perceive themselves as different, as not fitting within the norm. Children who are not white, middle class, and living with happily married parents are not being addressed. Either you take on these values as normal, or there is no space for you in the narrative.

You can do a similar ideological analysis by looking at the children's reading books you had when you were growing up or children's television programs. Educational programs such as *Sesame Street* and *Play School* present a more modern world than the world of Peter and Jane but they still carry ideological meanings. Entertainment cartoons such as *The Simpsons*, *South Park*, and *Angela Anaconda* also present various ideological views of the family and children.

We have used childhood in relation to readers to show how people from a young age are ideologically socialised and to encourage you to reflect on your childhood experiences. But the point is that all media texts, all forms of language and representation, carry ideological meanings; many of our examples throughout this book aim to show how they work.

In relation to how children grow up within ideological frameworks, Barthes went beyond texts when he analysed children's toys. He saw that toys were also instruments of socialisation, determining how children would see and understand the world. Toys, like media texts, are socialising agents. They help children to learn what their role in society might entail, and they enable them to practise playing that role. Dolls, trucks, tea sets, and toy medical instruments enable children to imitate adult behaviour and practise adult roles, while children's media texts model adult roles and enable children to explore these possibilities via the mechanisms of identification and fantasy. As Barthes says, 'The fact that French toys *literally* prefigure the world of adult functions obviously cannot but prepare the child to accept them, constituting for him, even before he can think about it, the alibi of a Nature which has at all times created soldiers, postmen and Vespas' (1973, p. 53). This leads us directly into more material areas of ideology, which are explored next.

Ideologies in material institutions

So far in this chapter, we have spoken of ideology in terms of representations; however, ideology can also be seen in actual material institutions and human activities. Most obviously, this can be seen in the buildings that structure our lives, marking out our territory, determining how we can behave and act in the world. In Australia the idealised quarter-acre suburban block is a space for families to grow up and socialise in; in the UK, semi-detached or terraced houses do the same. These architectural arrangements confirm that we live in family-based spaces. Our houses structure some space as communal and social, for the whole family; other spaces in houses (bedrooms, toilets, bathrooms, and so on) are defined as more personal and private. Many Western cultures structure their buildings around the culture and ideology of the family, so that it seems perfectly normal and natural to live in these separate spaces rather than in more communal forms. Visit any new housing estate and you will see how the structure of rooms is built around adults' and children's spaces. Familial ideology is embodied and naturalised through architecture.

These architectures do change. Feminists have noted how, with the gradual emancipation of women since the nineteenth century, kitchen and cooking areas, which were once separated and placed in inferior positions at the back of houses, have become bigger, more central, more comfortable, and more communal, showing the increased status of the activities conducted in them and the sharing of domestic activities with men.

CASE STUDY

Educational buildings as an example of ideology in material institutions

As a more extended example, it is interesting to look at educational buildings to see how the organisation of interior spaces has a built-in ideology of education.

Write down your thoughts on what ideology of education is built into lecture theatres and then read the following commentary.

Lecture theatres are built for one-way transmission: knowledge is given out from one person, one source, to many people. Those seated are invited to look at and interact with the lecturer, not each other. They are invited, by the desks attached to the seats, to take notes, thus validating what the lecturer is saying. Apart from the taking of notes, the theatre is essentially a passive learning place—the students remain seated and don't talk—and one in which students absorb information and knowledge from the lecturer, the overheads, the screen, and the whiteboard. Education is focused on the mind and rationality rather than the body and feelings.

First, this suggests that knowledge is not to be gained experientially but by accepting views from authority. It sees knowledge as rational rather than emotional. It suggests that knowledge is there to be transmitted to students, rather like pouring knowledge from a jug into the students' upturned mouths. In this process, the lecturer is given power and a voice: the lecturer speaks, students listen; the lecturer may stand and move about, students remain in their seats; the lecturer can survey all of the students at once.

Second, lecture theatre education is like mass production in factories. Many students are dealt with at one sitting and are regulated through the timing of lectures. No attention is paid to whether the time of the lecture is a good time for learning—education is controlled by the demands of time-and-space management, as in a factory, only here the product is students' minds, not cars or televisions.

You could argue that what education and the lecture theatre teach, what the ideology of education is, is that students have nothing worth saying. Education teaches you to be silent, to respect your elders, to keep still, and to ignore your body, your emotions, and your experiences.

Imagine for a moment a round building in which students sit on cushions arranged in a circle, all on one level, where before students start learning, they enhance their concentration through meditation. You can see how such a building and its organisation of space would embody a different ideology of what knowledge, learning, and education are.

We have painted a somewhat one-sided view of the lecture theatre here. It does have an element of performance and pleasure built into it: like a theatre for plays, it is an auditorium (literally, 'a place for hearing'), with fairly comfortable seats and a stage for the lecturer to perform on. In addition, music, videos, and films can be transmitted. There are ways of using the space that challenge some of the aspects described here; however, inviting student response and interaction, while possible within the space, is not what this building has been constructed for. It does not reflect the ideology of education that has informed its architecture.

The material institutions we live in organise us in terms of space and time, and this reflects the ideology of our culture. This is not to suggest that there is a conspiracy to socialise us; rather, these architectural patterns have evolved as a way of fitting in with the dominant trends of a society. They become so much part of our everyday landscape that they seem quite normal to us. We lose sight of the process of social construction—until we see another way of doing things, and realise that our own way is not the only or the natural way.

Ideologies in our heads, hearts, subjectivities, and identities

Are our identities ideological? ▶

While texts and discourses exist outside us, ideology is internalised by us. If we accept values such as those represented in the *Peter and Jane* books, then we carry those ideologies as part of who we are. The idea here is that our identities (our concepts of who we are) are, like language and ideologies, constructed, which was discussed in Chapter 4 when looking at our individual names (pp. 59–60). This is quite a challenging belief because it causes us to question ourselves. What this suggests is that our personality, our individual identity, and our subjectivity have been produced by a number of external factors. Our ethnicity, class, religion, and gender are, once again, the most obvious. Ask yourself: would you be a different person if you were of a different nationality, or if you were from a different class, or if you were of the opposite sex? Would you be different if you had been born in a different century? How would you be different? By asking these questions, you may begin to get a sense of the constructedness of your own identity.

Identity can also be formed by things such as height, weight, attractiveness, and so on. All these factors go towards who we are and how we think of ourselves. Would being fatter, thinner, or more attractive, or having a name such as Sunny or Mohamed change how you feel about yourself and how you are perceived by other people? So, in our identity we internalise particular ways of thinking, feeling, and believing; we take on particular ideologies. One of the most interesting aspects of the new-media technologies is in relation to identity. This is expressed by the *New Yorker* cartoon (from 1993 by Peter Steiner) that says, 'On the Internet, nobody knows you're a dog' below a picture of a dog working on a computer. Many people who play internet games or indulge in internet chat construct for themselves a new personality, an *avatar*, that expresses new parts of themselves. The possibility of playing with identity is seen as one of the most exciting aspects of the new technologies.

Interpellation

INTERPELLATION ▶

A process in which we internalise
ideologies as a response to being
hailed or addressed.

We can understand this process by using the term **interpellation** (see also the advertisement analysis, p. 152). For example, my teachers 'hailed' or 'interpellated' me, Michael, as 'the wild Irishman' and I accepted this, recognised myself, and internalised the ideological values of the wild Irishman as my identity. Althusser also uses the term, arguing that 'the process of internalising ideologies', which we have been discussing above, 'is facilitated through interpellation' (Althusser 1977, pp. 162–70; O'Sullivan et al. 1994, pp. 155–6). This 'hailing' has the effect of putting us in our place or positioning the addressee in relation to the addresser.

Gender is central to identity, and gender socialisation is one of the earliest processes of interpellation. Try to remember, or imagine, how people talked to you when you were young and how much they encouraged you to see yourself as either a boy or a girl. ('It's a boy' or 'It's a girl' may have been the very first words spoken in your presence.) To confirm this gender identity, you probably adopted certain kinds of appropriate male or female behaviour. Simply being labelled as 'boy' or 'girl' may determine your behaviour to some extent. Note how you yourself might talk differently to boys or girls, thus interpellating them in different ways. Think of the following popular nursery rhyme that contrasts 'typical' good or bad gender characteristics:

Sugar and spice and all things nice, that's what little girls are made of.

Slugs and snails and puppy dogs' tails, that's what little boys are made of.

The rhyme interpellates us at an early age with male or female characteristics; if we want to prove by our behaviour that we are typical boys and girls, we behave accordingly.

Look at any newspaper and note how it interpellates its readership into particular subject positions. Do you notice that different sections of the newspaper seem to be addressing different social subjects? The sports section hails the reader as male, the social pages hail the reader as female, the finance section positions readers as anonymous but tends to locate them within a privileged, well-educated class. What are the specific differences in these modes of address? Do journalists speak to the public differently, depending on whether they assume that they are addressing a male or a female, a professional, or a tradesperson? You might also notice that the local news section and the world news section locate the reader within a particular national identity, assuming allegiance to and interest in that nation's celebrities, issues, and events. For world news, the same event will be reported differently in different countries, in a manner that is geared to position the audience to respond in certain ways, depending on whose interests are at stake.

Nationality and interpellation

National identity is also crucial in our understanding of who we are. In South Africa, new ways of describing citizenship and the nation emerged after the first democratic elections in 1994 in the form of slogans such as 'the new South Africa' and 'the rainbow nation'. These phrases assume that all South Africans share a desire to distance themselves from the divisive past of apartheid, and they address and interpellate citizens as members of a unified but diverse and colourful group with a hopeful future.

In Australia, because the history of white settlement is relatively short, many Australians feel that establishing a national identity is a crucial task. Phrases such as 'un-Australian' (used to describe certain activities, such as snobbishness, being pretentious, cheating, or betraying the code of mateship) and 'a fair go' are typically Australian. They mark out the territory of what 'we', as Australians, understand as acceptable behaviour; when we are spoken to using these terms, we are interpellated as Australians.

The media work as a hailing, interpellating system. The way they address us (their **modes of address**), constantly interpellates us—as family, as citizens, as children, and so on. This is particularly true of television and radio, where there is often a 'direct address' by announcers to 'you', the listener. Such modes of address give us our identities and subjectivities.

◄ MODE OF ADDRESS

Refers to the way a text speaks to or addresses its audience.

CASE STUDY

Interpellation in sports coverage

It is useful to examine how the pronouns 'us' and 'we' and the possessive 'our' are used in the media as forms of interpellation. During the Sydney 2000 Olympics, the *Sydney Morning Herald* headline on the day of Cathy Freeman's 400 metre final was 'Race of *Our* Lives' (emphasis added); when Australia recorded an amazing Test cricket win over Pakistan in 1999, the *West Australian* headline was '*WE* DID IT' (Figure 11.1; emphasis added). Who is being interpellated in these headlines? Who is being included within 'our' and 'we'? Are you included? Who is being excluded (since any notion of an inclusive we/us always implies an excluded them/Other)? And what ideologies and discourses of identity are being constructed and circulated here?

The Freeman caption occurs in the context of the Olympic Games. As this competition is held between nations, Freeman's race is Australia's race and the 'our' of the caption assumes all readers to be Australians (although many non-Australians would have been in Sydney at the time). What is significant here in the construction of Australian national identity is that Freeman, an Aboriginal woman, becomes the leading symbol and representative of Australia. The caption thus includes and unites Aborigines and non-Aborigines, men and women, together as 'us', as Australian. It could be argued that the reverence and adulation shown by the Australian media and people to Freeman go against the norm of discrimination against Aboriginal people, and were part of a public relations campaign attempting to show the rest of the world that Australia was a well-integrated, non-discriminatory, multicultural society. Alternatively, it may be seen as a powerful symbol and example of reconciliation, and a challenge to discrimination.

The cricket headline example, in the context of the other words and photographs of the front page, has further complexities. The 'we' here could again be seen as referring to all Australians, but as it is a picture of two white men, it could be seen as interpellating just white, male Australians or even just white, male, cricket-loving Australians. There is a further complexity in that the 'we' may refer only to Adam Gilchrist and Justin Langer, and since these men both played for Western Australia, the 'we' comes to mean Western Australians in opposition to other Australians; the headline can thus be read within a context and history of interstate rivalry

Continued on next page   ▶

Figure 11.1 Front page coverage of an Australian test match win over Pakistan

Source: *The West Australian* 23 November 1999

within Australia. The implied and excluded 'them' is most obviously the Pakistani cricket team, but this could be widened to all Pakistanis, all non-Australians, or all non-Western Australians. The headline is thus not as inclusive of all Australians in its interpellation as is the Freeman headline. The other words and images are interesting in the way they provide further narrative threads and interpellated positions.

The reference to the players' wives seeks to interpellate and include female readers (though within a heterosexual and competitive discourse).

The image of mateship and teamwork draws on earlier 'digger' ideologies of Australian warriors (the two sporting heroes may be viewed as similar to the young male heroes of the film *Gallipoli*) that naturalise the idea of inter-nation conflicts between 'us' and 'them'. This is supported by the caption 'How the Test Was Won', which is a wordplay on 'How the West Was Won', a celebration of the subjugation of the indigenous peoples of the USA.

Finally, the caption 'The Match that Stopped the Nation' refers us to the Melbourne Cup horse race, thereby making this event equally significant and nationally inclusive. The words 'we', 'us', and 'our' thus become rich, interpellative mechanisms worthy of detailed analysis.

We hope you can come to an understanding of this process of interpellation, and can see how it may relate to your own identity in terms of nationality, gender, ethnicity, and so on. If you have never been in a situation in which your identity has been challenged, for example, by moving to a new society or by changing your name (or even by going to the gym, which tends to change body image), the process of interpellation may be difficult to see. While your national identity, your personal name, and your body shape may seem to be natural parts of you, try to see these as parts of your constructed subjectivity, and be aware of how the media will address messages to specific aspects of your identity for marketing purposes or to serve other vested interests. Also, please note that throughout this book, we use our own structures of interpellation in the way that 'we' address 'you'.

NOTIONS OF IDENTITY AND SUBJECTIVITY

Are we cogs in the machine, or do we have free will?

'Identity' and **subjectivity** are terms often used in media studies. They are partly interchangeable: both refer to the way we understand who we are—our identity—and the position from which we look at and understand the world—our subjectivity. A key question for both is: are these natural, or are they socially constructed? And this raises another question: are we defined and determined by forces outside of us—like cogs in a machine—or are we self-determining, autonomous individuals with free will? We live in a culture that stresses individuality, encourages us to believe that every person has unique qualities, and puts forward the view that we have control over who we are, what we do, and how others see us, but this view is questionable.

On the one hand, Western culture glorifies the individual and understands much of what happens to the world in terms of individual actions (see Chapter 23). News stories and political events are presented to us as the stories of individuals—politicians, businesspeople, criminals, and so on—and what they do. Entertainment, sports coverage, films, and television programs focus on individual stars and personalities. These media products are often also packaged in terms of the individual stars they feature. Magazines gossip about the private lives of individuals. History is often presented and taught in terms of key individuals. Even media studies sometimes stresses the individual role of media

◄ SUBJECTIVITY

Pertains to an individual's personal thoughts and experiences, their own—subjective—way of seeing the world, as distinct from general or universal experience, and objectivity.

moguls, such as Bill Gates, and influential film directors, such as James Cameron or Tim Burton. These characteristics of the media relate to the ideology of individualism that permeates Western culture.

On the other hand, the nineteenth and twentieth centuries produced numerous academic and theoretical perspectives that show the opposite—that individuals are not in control of their own destinies, that we are subject to forces beyond our individual, conscious control. Challenges to the view that individuals have control over their own destiny have come from several major sources.

1. Darwinian theories of evolution and survival of the fittest suggest that we are determined by our genetic and biological evolution, which determines what we do and who will survive.

2. Marxist theory sees class struggle and economics as the motor and determinant of history (it holds that we act in accordance with these impersonal forces). According to **Marxism**, it is the actions of whole groups or classes, not the actions of individuals, that change the world. The following passage paraphrases Marx's view that humans have only a limited degree of autonomy: People make history, but only on the basis of conditions that are not of their own making (see Marx [1852], 1948).

3. Freud, the father of psychoanalysis, and his followers argue that we are determined by our unconscious, driven by our basic drives towards survival and pleasure. We act on the basis of these unconscious desires and the fears associated with them, rather than on our conscious choices.

4. B F Skinner and other behaviourist psychologists suggest that all human activities are simply determined responses to external stimuli: in other words, we do not act, we react (see Skinner 1976).

5. Saussure and some other linguists suggest that language determines who we are, what we think, and how we understand the world; rather than saying 'we speak language', we could say 'language speaks us'.

6. More recently, feminists have put forward the view that gender is the key factor determining who we are and how we behave.

7. Those working on the problem of racism have proposed that ethnic origins are the most important factor dictating behaviour and identity.

8. The theory of memes, developed by scientists such as Richard Dawkins and Susan Blackmore, argues that humans evolve through imitating others, that successful memes—patterns of behaviour—are passed on from one person to another and thus become part of who we are, our identity.

So we have two polarised positions. The first sees humans as possessing individual autonomy and free will—the ability to make our own choices and determine our own destiny. The second sees humans as cogs in the machinery of biology, psychology, history, and culture.

The term 'subjectivity' draws attention to our autonomy, and to the fact that our actions are predetermined or subject to influences beyond our conscious control (Fiske 1987, pp. 48–61). The word 'subject' (derived from a Latin word that means 'thrown under') is about us having power: in grammatical terms, English sentences are built around the structure subject–verb–object: someone or something (subject) does

MARXISM ▶

The theories developed by Karl Marx, including that the struggle between different groups in society (classes) brings about historical change, economic needs are the most important factor in determining people's behaviour, and what people think and believe is controlled, often unconsciously, by the dominant social groups.

something (verb) to someone or something (object). Similarly, to 'subject someone to something' is to have power over them. On the other hand, we talk of people being subjects of kings and queens: as subjects we are under the power of other people and other forces. When we think of our own subjectivities, it is helpful to see both the autonomous power we have (the fact that we have our own way of seeing and operating in the world) and the determined quality of our identity or subjectivity (the way it has been shaped by outside forces).

CONCLUSION

We do not have a definitive answer to the question: do humans have free will, or is their behaviour determined? (although we hope you noticed that we have presented most of the nineteenth- and twentieth-century theories that challenge human autonomy in terms of the individuals who pioneered them). However, we do question the notion that individual identity is something existing outside culture. It is useful to see the ways in which individual identity is actually a social construct. Discussing this, cultural theorist Kathryn Woodward states:

> Identity can be seen as the interface between subjective positions and social and cultural situations … Identity gives us an idea of who we are and of how we relate to others and to the world in which we live. Identity marks the ways in which we are the same as others who share that position, and the ways in which we are different from those who do not (Woodward 1997, pp. 1–2).

Woodward stresses the role of 'symbolic systems'—the media, images, and language—in contributing to our identities: 'Representation as a cultural process establishes individual and collective identities, and symbolic systems provide possible answers to the questions: Who am I? What could I be? Who do I want to be?' (1997, p. 14).

We argue that ideologies are found within these symbolic systems (and in material systems such as buildings), and that these are therefore an important aspect contributing to the construction of our identities and subjectivities. Understanding this is a form of consciousness raising (raising awareness of social and political issues) that can give us more power and awareness in terms of understanding ourselves and others, and can help us to decide how we would like to act in future. Seeing how we are determined by the ideology we were born into, seeing how our behaviour has been shaped since birth (when people first start telling us who we are and how we should act), can give us a broader set of social choices about who we want to be and what we can do in the future. We can break out of earlier ideological constrictions.

We can never fully escape the framework of our own perceptions of the world. Ideology is constituted by and concealed in our world view, and in language. Trying to see ideology and step outside it or look around it is like trying to see contact lenses when we are looking through them. In *The Matrix*, when Morpheus offers Neo the choice to understand what the Matrix is or remain in a world of dreams and illusions, and when he later shows Neo 'the construct', the way he describes the Matrix also works as a good description of ideology: 'The Matrix [ideology] is everywhere, it's all around us … it is the world that has been pulled over your eyes'. It is possible for us to become aware of our ideologies, to become conscious of our unconscious consciousness, and sometimes to make changes to our world view and how we live in the world, but we will still always have a set of values, beliefs, and feelings that guide our behaviour, determining how we think, feel, and act, even if they are new. Our ideologies may change over time, and you will probably be aware of changes you have gone through in your own life. But in losing one ideology or world view, we replace it with another. This is not a bad or a good thing; it is just the way things are. Ideology as a world view simply describes the state we live in.

In this sense ideology is a neutral term, a description of how people will always function on the basis of their world view. We should also note that in any society, different groups may have quite different ideologies that may be contradictory. So there is room for a variety of ideologies, different world views, that we expect to find in the media. It is useful as a critical term as a way of picking out the naturalised world view, the common-sense assumptions that lie behind any media text.

This chapter has

- defined the terms 'discourse' and 'ideology'
- examined discourses of criminality
- explained and illustrated unconscious consciousness
- shown that discourses and ideologies can be found in language and representations, material institutions, and individual identities and subjectivities
- defined and illustrated 'interpellation'
- examined issues of individual identity.

? | DISCUSSION POINTS

1   Think of films and television shows that explore criminality and punishment, such as *True Detective*, *Orange Is the New Black*, *Wentworth*, *Sherlock*, *Hannibal*, *The Wolf of Wall Street*, *American Hustle*, or *American Gangster*. What discourses surround the issues of crime and/or imprisonment in each of these?

2   Apply your understanding of the term 'discourse' by identifying and discussing the different discourses used to communicate about and make sense of drug use in television series such as *Weeds*, *Breaking Bad*, *Sons of Anarchy*, *Mad Men*, and *Misfits*, and films such as *The Wolf of Wall Street*, *Pineapple Express*, *Fear and Loathing in Las Vegas*, *Trainspotting*, and *American Gangster*.

3   Look at the architectural plans for new public buildings or houses. What ideology or ideologies are they constructing?

4   Consider how many different names you are known by. What are the ideological implications of these different names, and how do they contribute to your own identity and subjectivity?

5   Look for examples of interpellation in the press, magazines, and television, and discuss how these work.

6   Examine ways in which the media interpellate people into identity categories.

7   Discuss the validity of theories that suggest individuals do not have autonomy.

SUMMARY

You should now be able to

- explain what the terms 'discourse' and 'ideology' mean
- discuss different and changing discourses of criminality
- explain unconscious consciousness
- show how natural, common-sense ideas and actions are ideological
- consider the ideologies of gendered behaviour
- discuss where you can find discourses and ideology
- find examples of ideology in symbolic systems—language and media representations—and in material institutions
- define interpellation and show how media texts interpellate audiences
- find examples of media interpellations
- reflect and comment on how these concepts relate to your own sense of identity and your social position
- explain briefly how and why individual identity can be understood as a social construction
- denaturalise ideology by identifying areas in your everyday life and surroundings where assumptions about social values are present.

CHAPTER 12

Dominant Ideology and Hegemony

The ideas of the ruling class are in every epoch the ruling ideas.

Karl Marx

This chapter will

- introduce dominant ideology theory
- explain how repressive and ideological state apparatuses work
- explain and illustrate the terms 'ideological work' and 'incorporation'
- show the limitations of dominant ideology theory
- suggest that the media are sites of contradictory ideologies
- introduce the liberal pluralist model of society
- introduce and illustrate the concept of hegemony
- examine the discourses and ideology of Christmas.

The focus of this chapter is specifically on issues of social power in relation to ideology and the media. It will look first at Althusser's dominant ideology model, then question and modify it, and then introduce Gramsci's hegemony model.

DOMINANT IDEOLOGY

Is there just one ideology or are there many ideologies?

So far we have talked about ideology and ideologies, which may have prompted you to ask if there is just one ideology or are there many? We argue here that there are numerous ideologies. Each social group has its own way of thinking, feeling, believing, and making sense of the world. It is possible to talk about ideologies (or discourses) of masculinity and femininity, of Australianness, Britishness, or Asianness, of blackness or whiteness, of teenagers or senior citizens, of middle and working classes, and so on. In this sense we have used the term simply as a description of how people always think and feel through ideology, and in recognition of the existence of different ideologies.

We now want to introduce and consider the idea of a 'dominant' or 'ruling' ideology, as suggested by French Marxist philosopher Louis Althusser (1977, pp. 147–8).

This use of the term is Althusser's way of understanding how social power is maintained in society by the dominant social groups. Althusser, following on from Marx, suggests that each society has a **dominant ideology**. Marx, in an earlier version of this idea, talks of the 'ruling ideas' of a culture, suggesting that when the proletariat or the subordinate group internalises and accepts the ideas of the ruling class, they form a kind of 'false consciousness'.

The dominant ideology—comprising a set of shared feelings, values, beliefs, and so on—is shared by the majority of people in a society, thus making it dominant in two senses. First, it is dominant in numerical terms. Second, it is dominant in the sense that it

DOMINANT IDEOLOGY ▶

A world view that supports the ruling class as dominant, the status quo, yet is shared by the majority of people.

tends to support the interests of the dominant, ruling groups. We are interested in the way dominant ideas, beliefs, and values, which support particular groups in society (whites, the middle class, men), come to be accepted and believed by many people in society. We are also interested in the way the media contribute to this acceptance.

Below are some relevant extracts from the works of Marx and Althusser. They are complex and densely packed with concepts and ideas, but this density means they are rich with meaning and import.

First, here is Marx discussing ruling ideas.

> The ideas of the ruling class are in every epoch the ruling ideas: in other words, the class that is the ruling material force in society is at the same time its ruling *intellectual* force. The class that has the means of material production at its disposal has control at the same time over the means of mental production, so that in consequence the ideas of those who lack the means of mental production are, in general, subject to it. The dominant ideas are nothing more than the ideal expression of the dominant material relationships grasped as ideas and thus of the relationships which make one class the ruling one; they are consequently the ideas of its dominance. The individuals composing the ruling class possess, among other things, consciousness, and therefore think. In so far, therefore, as they rule as a class and determine the whole extent of an epoch, it is self-evident that they do this in their whole range and thus, among other things, rule also as thinkers, as producers of ideas, and regulate the production and distribution of the ideas of their age: thus their ideas are the ruling ideas of the epoch (Marx [1846], 1974, p. 64).

Marx, as you can see, stresses ideas but sees these as determined by material forces, that is, the forces of economic ownership and production.

Althusser's wider concept of ideology takes us a stage further in the argument about how societies adhere to values and ideas supporting the dominant groups, and how ideology is not worked out consciously or conspiratorially.

> It is customary to suggest that ideology belongs to the region of "consciousness" ... In truth, ideology has very little to do with "consciousness", even supposing this term to have an unambiguous meaning. It is profoundly *unconscious* ... Ideology is indeed a system of representations, but in the majority of cases these representations have nothing to do with "consciousness" ... they are perceived-accepted-suffered cultural objects and they act functionally on men via a process that escapes them. Men "live" their ideologies ... *not at all as a form of consciousness, but as an object of their "world"*—as their *"world"* itself ... The ruling ideology is then the ideology of the ruling *class*. But the ruling class does not maintain with the ruling ideology, which is its own ideology, an external and lucid relation of pure utility and cunning ... the bourgeoisie has to believe in its own myth before it can convince others (Althusser 1977, pp. 233–4).

Althusser's concept of ideology thus goes beyond pure ideas and consciousness to the way in which people believe in ideology. He sees ideology as an unconscious force that people live, rather than see: it is lived 'as their "*world*" itself'. Both these extracts argue that ruling ideas or ideology are so deeply embedded in our society that they are shared by almost everyone and seem totally normal.

We can see similar ideas in the film *The Matrix* when Morpheus suggests that the constructed world of the Matrix has been used to blind Neo to the truth (see p. 177). When Neo asks 'What truth?' Morpheus replies, 'That you are a slave, Neo. That you, like everyone else, was born into bondage, kept inside a prison that you cannot smell, taste, or touch. A prison for your mind.' The Matrix, like the dominant ideology, has been accepted as good and natural even though it may not benefit the majority of people. The force of the dominant ideology, or the illusion of the Matrix, prevents individuals or groups from questioning or challenging those in power, or overthrowing the system that exploits them.

As another example, think how unproblematically people accept the basic notion of private property, the notion that individuals can claim exclusive ownership over all kinds of goods and land. Private property is so taken for granted in Western society that it may seem ludicrous to challenge it, and, indeed, it may seem as though everyone benefits from it because everyone owns something. We certainly do not want our precious possessions taken away from us. But private property has evolved in societies where ownership of property is predominantly in the hands of a minority. According to a study by the World Institute for Development Economics Research of the United Nations University, the richest 2 per cent of adults in the world own more than half the world's wealth (Davies et al. 2008, p. 7). Who really benefits from the system of private property, a system well maintained by laws and law-enforcement bodies? (Some offences against private property in Western cultures are traditionally subject to punishments greater than those meted out for some assault offences; for example, fraud can attract a harsher penalty than rape.)

What happens to this common-sense ideology when we say 'All property is theft'? This saying, attributed to French philosopher Pierre-Joseph Proudhon and taken up by Marx, asks us to rethink and re-evaluate the social conditions of property. To say I own something is to deny others the right to share it: it is to steal it from them. How much of our own property have we actually made ourselves? Have we really stolen it from someone else? Compare this ideology with Aboriginal ways of relating to material things, or to the African concept of *ubuntu* (which refers to community and shared responsibility in terms of child rearing, social welfare, and so on). Ideas of community, sharing, land guardianship, and communal ownership offer a very different possibility, a different way of organising how we live in the world and use its resources.

This is not to say that private property is wrong. Rather, it is suggested here that this ideology, which is shared by most people in the West, may actually be most beneficial to those who traditionally have owned the most. This dominant ideology (dominant because it is supported by most people) supports the dominant (socially powerful) groups. What we want to do here is to shake up your common sense, your accepted values, just to show that there are other points of view.

In these times, as the world's resources are depleted, questions relating to the desirability of our system of private property may be particularly urgent. The ultimate aim of our consumerist society is for everyone to possess their own car, fridge, electrical goods, and so on. The economic growth of our society is built on this attainment of an ideal and comfortable style of living. If this were achievable it would be wonderful, but the possibility of planetary survival, given the continuing explosion of private ownership of consumer goods, is questionable. The Latin word from which the term 'consume' derives—*consumo*—means 'to destroy', the implication being that consumers are destroyers. The ecological crisis may reach a point at which society will have to find some new way of living, some new ideology, in order to survive.

RSAS AND ISAS

Why do subordinate groups accept the power of the dominant groups?

Althusser wanted to understand how ideology was transmitted socially, how it was that people took and accepted the values of the dominant groups even if these views might not be in everyone's interests. He suggested two sets of mechanisms that achieved this: repressive state apparatuses (RSAs) and ideological state apparatuses (ISAs) (Althusser 1977, pp. 133–48).

RSAs

RSAs are mechanisms that are called into play to force people to conform to the dominant ideology. They are used deliberately, to control, punish, and coerce people who attempt to challenge the system. They are primarily the institutions of the law, the law courts, the police, the prison system, and the army, all of which are used to deal with people who trouble and disrupt society. RSAs do not work ideologically on people's feelings and beliefs; they work directly through force (including force of law) and, when necessary, through punishment. They are only deployed for extreme forms of social disorder, such as crime or mass protest. In the media, censorship laws and policy restrictions on media ownership provide this form of control.

◀ RSAs

Repressive state apparatuses—the institutions of force that societies use to control people, for example, the army, police, law courts, and prisons.

ISAs

ISAs, of much more interest to media studies, are the institutions through which people are socialised into accepting the dominant ideology. ISAs do not force people; they work more like hypnosis, convincing people or winning their consent to the dominant ideology. Althusser identifies key institutions that carry out this socialisation process: religion, the family, the education system, and the media.

◀ ISAs

Ideological state apparatuses—the institutions of socialisation and persuasion that societies use to control people, for example, religion, family, education, and media.

The media are now very important; in many ways they have taken over the central role once occupied by the Church, which has declined considerably since the nineteenth century in many countries (although fundamentalist churches still have significant influence on small groups of people). Together with the family and the education system, the media offer ways of understanding and making sense of the world and of ourselves. They explain how people should think, act, and feel. It is important to note that these institutions may not always agree: religion, education, and family ideologies may at times conflict with each other and with the ideologies presented in the media.

The media as an ISA

How do the media work ideologically? What values and beliefs do they construct as normal, natural, and desirable? How do the media work in relation to the dominant ideology? These are major questions in media studies and there are no simple answers; indeed, they are the subject of much debate in media studies. We will outline some of the main positions below.

Althusser's basic argument is that the media tend to support the dominant ideology. They do this by producing programs and products that support the values of white, patriarchal, capitalist culture; however, to do this successfully the media have to overcome two problems.

1   In order to win support for the dominant ideology, the media must also win the support of subordinate and minority groups in society (women, indigenous people, the working class, and so on). They must come up with products that give these groups pleasure, since these groups comprise the bulk of the audience.

2   The media are often drawn to addressing social tensions, focusing on social conflict and problems. News and current affairs, for example, focus on moments of social disruption and conflict, 'bad' news. Drama, fiction, and films are nearly always based on conflicts between characters and between value systems. Police dramas, for instance, one of the major prime-time genres of popular television, always focus on moments of, and places associated with, social breakdown. They choose to explore crime, and, consequently, at some level, consider the social causes of crime, touching on poverty, inequality, unemployment, drugs, and so on—major social issues that threaten to disrupt society. Situation comedies focus on the family and gender relations, and thus draw attention to the battle of the sexes and the breakdown of the family unit.

Thus the media often draw our attention to social problems. But this does not mean that they call into question the ultimate desirability of the current social system. What is of interest here is how these programs deal with and resolve the social issues raised while still supporting the dominant ideology. Television news, by providing a forum and mouthpiece for dominant institutional voices, ultimately reassures and normalises every disruptive act, thereby allaying our fears about the stability of our world. Police dramas, while they depict poverty and crime, and raise them as potential social problems, tend to turn criminals into psychopaths, sick individuals not like us (thereby reassuring us that we are not like criminals), and the police into figures that we identify with. Situation comedies, while they do raise issues relating to the family and gender relations, relieve our tension through the safety valve of humour. In all these examples, we can say that the ways the media deal with the problems constitute ideological work: ultimately, their resolution will not disturb society. Rather, they allow the predominant ideology to be maintained.

How do the media do ideological work?

We will now explore three ways in which the media do this ideological work.

1   By masking and displacing social issues and problems

As discussed above, the media can hide or avoid social problems. This happens in a number of ways.

*   Some issues are simply avoided or rendered invisible. These are the issues that do not get media coverage at all. Some social groups are notably absent from certain types of media representations: popular drama rarely features Aboriginal culture, differently abled groups, gay culture, and so on. Such groups are often marginalised through their exclusion.

- Social difference is masked or displaced by interpellations that address all social groups under a unifying label. The three most common interpellations or forms of address used by the media are to address the audience as 'family members', 'citizens of a nation' (for example, Australians, South Africans), and 'members of the public'. Sometimes we are addressed as all three at the same time. These labels and interpellations are not false. We are all family members, citizens of a nation, and members of the public. But these labels—which are used to unite us, to bring us together as equals, and to suggest that we share the same aims, needs, and desires, and the same views about the ideal family and national goals—also mask and displace differences: differences between white and Indigenous Australians, between rich and poor, between two- and one-parent families, between men and women, among others. These interpellations focus on some parts of our identity rather than others: 'family member' focuses on our family and domestic identities rather than on our working identities as trade unionists, factory workers, office cleaners, company managers, and so on. Social differences, particularly those relating to class and ethnicity, are dissolved into the unities of domestic and national identity. The media thus favour interpellations that unite us rather than those that highlight social difference. The common family address heard on television—'You and your family'—assumes all viewers watch as parts of families, thereby excluding viewers who are not 'family viewers'.

- Social problems and contradictions are often masked or displaced by being understood in personal or psychological terms or within a moral framework of good and evil, rather than in social terms. Police dramas are a good example of this. A criminal's behaviour is often understood as the result of individual personality disorders: the criminal has a psychological problem. The social causes of crime, such as unemployment and drug trafficking, which have the potential to portray this criminal as typical of a social group, are displaced in favour of personal, psychological explanations. When you next watch television, listen to the radio, or read a newspaper article, see how the social problems being raised are addressed. Are they explained as the result of social causes, or are they personalised in terms of individuals with particular personal problems? Consider how contemporary television series represent drugs and drug-taking: Netflix's *Narcos* is a good example of a series that focuses on individuals caught up in the problems of drugs and drug trafficking. The series tells the true story of Pablo Escobar, a billionaire drug kingpin from Colombia. While Escobar was the leader of the Medellín cocaine cartel, the audience is able to align in some small way with him due to the reason he did this: for family; he was born into poverty. While his actions left devastating consequences, drug trafficking is placed in a wider social context, drawing attention to social problems around border control, addiction, and gang warfare. Mainstream police procedural dramas such as *True Detective* and *The Mentalist*, or reality programs such as *Border Security: Australia's Front Line*, on the other hand, align the audience with the law enforcers, and remain focused primarily on the regulatory and judicial context.

2   By incorporating or containing other ideological positions

Rather than attempting to disallow or even censor dissident ideological voices, the media sometimes neutralise these voices by allowing them space but containing them within the overall system. Since the end of the Second World War, youth cultures in Western societies have threatened to disrupt ideologies of how youths should behave. Popular artists such as rappers Eminem and P Diddy and comedian Sacha Baron Cohen have managed to amass huge fan bases because they actively resist the dominant order. These prominent figures in youth culture undermine what they see as political correctness and set out to alienate members of 'nice', 'responsible', 'mature' social groups. As Nick Hornby, author of the novel *High Fidelity*, argues, by contrast with the violent misogyny of Eminem's rap collective D12, whose bestselling album *Devil's Night* contains lyrics such as 'Independent women in the house/show us your tits and shut your mother f—ing mouth', the 'sonic ferocity', obscenity, and nihilism of groups such as the Sex Pistols and Nirvana seem 'thoughtful and politically engaged' (*The Weekend Australian*, 3–4 November 2001, pp. 4–6). But all these figures are allowed some space in the media and are thus made acceptable.

Some attempts are made to curtail youth movements through legal and police action focused on drugs and youth gatherings (the RSAs at work), but the movements are often better contained by allowing them to continue within the confines of the society: in other words they are accommodated, or **incorporated** or **recuperated**, or contained within society in such a way as to defuse their radical potential.

INCORPORATION OR RECUPERATION ▶

The processes by which dangerous, rebellious, radical ideas and movements are made acceptable not by banning or criminalising them, but by partially accepting them; 'incorporated' means, literally, 'taken into the main body'.

The challenges thrown out by youth cultures are incorporated into an ideology that recognises teenage years as a natural time of rebellion—this is what it means to be a teenager, so it is acceptable. Popular music is incorporated into the music industry, television shows such as *Rage*, and radio station playlists (radio announcers provide the music with a context and accompanying commentary that give it a safe, socially acceptable interpretation). The new technologies of popular music—iPods, MP3 players, mobile phone ring tones, and peer-to-peer file-sharing (P2P)—construct music in terms of fashion and technological sophistication, rather than a voice of social challenge. Significantly, the 'noise pollution' associated with youths playing music on large, portable 'boom boxes' in public in the 1980s has been effectively neutralised by the introduction of personalised musical devices with headphones.

These days, owning certain portable technologies and using them to consume music in public can function as a generational marker. For example, Apple products such as MacBooks, iPods, iPads, and iPhones are now seen as fashionable accessories, a trend reinforced by slick advertising and clever product placement in films—in 2014, Apple topped Brandchannel's product placement rankings with appearances in nine of the top thirty-five Hollywood films (Fingas 2015). While music technologies also have business applications and are being taken up by older people too, part of the appeal of Apple products is their strong association with youth culture and members of Generation Y, or the 'Millennial Generation'. The commercialisation and popularisation of elements of youth culture defuse them of their radical challenge.

In relation to who has the right to speak on the media, democratic societies have actually encouraged 'other' voices: for example, television channels such as Australia's SBS and the UK's Channel 4 are understood to be forums for the articulation of marginalised positions. But it can be argued that these forums again function to incorporate these different voices (rather than allowing them to fulfil their radical potential) by including them as a minority part of the mainstream, thereby preventing the social groups represented from feeling left out and causing social disruption. Similarly, while mainstream television channels occasionally present challenging programs that question the dominant ideology, their very positioning within normal television schedules—surrounded by advertisements, trailers, and other non-challenging programs—functions so as to neutralise their messages, which get lost by being incorporated into the overall output of television and by the way in which audiences have been encouraged to be passive spectators.

We can even see incorporation at work in narrative structures—the way stories are put together (see p. 235). Many popular fictions are drawn to social problems. Initially a narrative may give support to a radical point of view, but then the way that the narrative is structured and resolved neutralises this point of view. Thus, as a whole, the narrative incorporates or contains radical positions, which is why we stress the importance of narrative structure in relation to ideological meanings.

RESIDUAL, DOMINANT, AND EMERGENT DISCOURSES

In his analysis of media, society, and ideology in *Marxism and Literature*, cultural theorist Raymond Williams has described three different kinds of discourse: **residual discourses**, **dominant discourses**, and **emergent discourses** (Williams 1977b). These are very useful terms for media analysis. Today many texts explore the ways in which men and women relate. For women, this is often presented as a question of how to balance desires for relationships, children, work, freedom, and independence; for men, it is a question of how to balance their traditional masculine qualities of assertion and aggression with a more caring, emotional masculinity, and to balance their desires for relationships and independence. Williams would see this in terms of residual, dominant, and emergent discourses of femininity and masculinity. Residual discourses might relate to women's desires to be swept off their feet by a knight in shining armour, a man who would save and look after them, or to men's patriarchal belief in their right to treat women as property. Dominant discourses relate to the ideas and beliefs about masculinity and femininity that are currently shared by most people in Western societies—beliefs that women and men are equal but different, and that this equality should be reflected in equal opportunities, equal wages, and shared domestic responsibilities. These discourses emerged from the 1960s onwards influenced by what was then the new and emergent discourse of feminism. Current emergent discourses of femininity and masculinity might suggest that women and men can live separately, or that children can be brought up perfectly well by same-sex couples.

In relation to media texts, Williams argues that it is possible for all three discourses to be present in a text at the same time, which brings us back to incorporation. You can probably find films and media stories in which women say that they want to have their independence but also want to get married and have children—*No Strings Attached*, *Switch*, *Knocked Up*, *He's Just not That into You*, *Pitch Perfect 2*, *Trainwreck*, and many other films and television programs are good examples of this. It quite often happens that the emergent discourses— for example, the desire for independence or to explore different sexual experiences—end up being subsumed into the more traditional, residual, and dominant discourses of monogamous marriage, children, and family. The narratives thus include the three kinds of discourse but, although they allow the women to explore new possibilities at first, they end

RESIDUAL DISCOURSE

Set of ideas and beliefs from the past that are still accepted by some people.

DOMINANT DISCOURSE

Contemporary ideas and beliefs shared by a majority of people.

EMERGENT DISCOURSE

New ideas and beliefs held by a few people at first, and then gradually becoming accepted by more people.

up placing them back in traditional roles, and in this sense they once again incorporate and contain these new aspects of femininity.

3   By giving audiences texts that are pleasurable

There is one more crucial aspect of the media to be noted here: pleasure. Most people use the media for pleasure and relaxation, so the media work hard to give us pleasures. As audience members and consumers, our feelings of pleasure (our emotional responses) may be more important than our ideological understandings of the media—if we enjoy a program, who cares what its ideology is? Ultimately, this attitude is crucial for the media to win our support. Fiction stories offer the pleasures of suspense, excitement, spectacle, chases, emotional involvement and identification with characters, humour, and so on (see Chapter 19). Most advertisements, films, and television programs offer us the pleasure of looking at and identifying with the beautiful people and objects that are portrayed. Such texts subtly seduce us into conceding that they represent ideal types and desirable commodities, and believing that if we purchase the products or emulate the people represented, we will be more like the models or actors and will find pleasure, happiness, and desirability. If a media text such as an advertisement for fast food offers us pleasure, it is hard to resist. Try telling a child with a sweet tooth and a desire for a cute toy that comes with a Happy Meal that hamburgers and milkshakes are unhealthy and ideologically unsound. In consuming the product we may also consume the ideologies it presents.

THE LIMITATIONS OF DOMINANT IDEOLOGY THEORY

This description of how the media work ideologically contains many useful insights. Using the terms and methods given above to unpack the ideological work of the media will reveal a lot, but there are problems associated with this model too.

Throughout this book we have stressed the contradictory nature of the media, its good and bad possibilities (see pp. 12–13). The dominant ideology model, while useful, ultimately runs the danger of seeing the media purely in a bad light and allowing no possibility for alternative positions.

First, the model is too simple in the way it suggests ideology is just administered by the dominant groups and accepted by the masses. It paints ideology as too much of a one-way system. It suggests that the dominant ideology is always imposed from above and accepted unproblematically by people. This does not account for people who refuse to accept these values, or for the two-way struggle that goes on between dominant and subordinate groups in establishing social values. Ideology can easily be thought of as an all-powerful force that the media wield to induce conformity, and that the ruling members of society use to brainwash and subordinate the rest of us, but this is not strictly the case. People are not sheep helplessly herded about by ideological forces. Just as media audiences do not passively accept and absorb the intended meaning of media texts (see pp. 95–6), individuals and groups do not always accept or conform to the dominant ideology. More importantly, it is possible to have many different ideologies, many different world views, any of which can challenge the dominant ideology.

Second, the argument about incorporation given above is too rigid: you can argue that democratic societies are able to neutralise any dissident voices through incorporation, but it can also be argued that rather than being neutralised, radical ideas are actually being popularised and are thus beginning to shift the overall ideology of society. The dominant ideology model doesn't allow for the fact that there are people working in the media who challenge the dominant ideologies. It is important to remember that the media, and their producers and consumers, are capable of representing and engaging with alternative ideas: ideological assumptions and norms can be challenged and changed. Films such as *An Inconvenient Truth* or *The Eleventh Hour*, for example, have been able to challenge the dominant ideology in relation to issues of climate change. As John Hartley has argued in analysing media representations of ethnicity and Aboriginality:

> if we accept that the media … encourage racism in certain of their ways of reporting the world, then we have also to believe that they can influence … for positive change as well as negatively … that the media are forces for progressive social change as well as for negative social stereotyping (Hartley & McKee 1996, p. 73).

The theory of dominant ideology is thus too rigid and simplistic. It does not allow for contradictions and variations within the development and establishment of ideology.

Third, media technologies are now more accessible, so people can write their own blogs, produce their own videos, CDs, and so forth, which means that the media are no longer so controlled by elite groups.

We want you to be aware of situations in which the media are an expression of the dominant ideology, but also to see them as a site for competing and contradictory ideologies, as well as a place where you as journalists, filmmakers, or scriptwriters can do positive and creative work. Taking account of these criticisms, there are two other models of society for thinking about how the media work ideologically.

LIBERAL PLURALISM

The models of society discussed so far suggest an imbalance and struggle between dominant and subordinate groups. The **liberal pluralist** model of society, probably the viewpoint of most Western democratic countries, offers a different perspective. A pluralist society has many different social groups, and therefore exhibits a plurality of many different voices that may have different social perspectives and positions, but within a democracy all are allowed to speak and will have some access to the media. This suggests that different social positions simply coexist alongside others, in the same way that, say, people of different ethnic backgrounds coexist. According to this view of society, everyone has a chance to produce media products within the free marketplace of the media and audiences are free to accept whatever views they wish to. This pluralist position argues that we all have the right and opportunity to speak, and that within society we are all equal.

We value the opportunities of democracy and see the possibilities for the media to present many different voices and a whole range of sometimes contradictory ideological viewpoints (including our own), but we still return to an overall view that society and the world as a whole are unequally positioned. Gramsci's model of hegemony is a way of acknowledging these imbalances and understanding how the media can be a site of competing ideologies and discourses.

◀ LIBERAL PLURALISM

A liberalist pluralist society is one that includes many different social groups with different viewpoints; they all have the liberty and opportunity to speak out.

HEGEMONY

HEGEMONY ▶

Power and leadership maintained through processes of struggle and negotiation, especially through winning the consent of the majority of people to accept the ideas or ideologies of the dominant group as common sense.

The word **hegemony** comes from *hegemonia*, the Greek word for 'leader'. Theories of hegemony were developed by Antonio Gramsci, a leader of the Italian Communist Party in the 1920s and 1930s who was imprisoned by the fascist Mussolini regime.

Hegemony is a way of understanding how one social group maintains its ultimate power over subordinate groups. Power and control are exercised through influence, persuasion, and struggle. The concept of hegemony explains why oppressed groups don't revolt: their ideas, needs, or interests are being represented or recognised by the system to a certain extent, enough that they consent to their place in society. So when we speak of the maintenance of hegemony, we are referring to a way of maintaining power, but we also acknowledge resistance to the exercise of that power.

The major point about hegemony is that it suggests that maintaining power over others is always a process in struggle: it is never stable, it involves participation and negotiation on both sides, and it is a two-way process (in contrast to ideology, which tends to be perceived as a one-way process, imposed from the top down). It is in this two-way process that people can use the media in ways that can challenge the dominant ideas and ideology.

How is hegemony maintained? ▶

Just as Althusser recognises the power of RSAs to maintain social control, Gramsci acknowledges that coercion—force—is one method that can be used to maintain power and leadership. This was particularly the way that authoritarian states such as the Soviet Union, fascist countries including Second World War Italy and postwar Spain and Portugal, and the South African apartheid regime maintained power by using institutions such as the police, the law, and the army, all of which have the capacity to enforce compliance and punish dissidents (see p. 179). But Gramsci is most interested in how hegemony is maintained through consent.

Consent as a method of maintaining hegemony parallels the way in which ISAs are maintained. Gramsci sees consent as the basis of the social organisation of the democratic societies that predominate in Western culture. The notion of hegemony as maintained by consent brings us back to a question posed at the beginning of this book: how do the media win support for their representations?

It can be seen how hegemony works by imagining an example of it at a micro social level: the interactions of a parent and child. The parent holds the main power (in the same way as the dominant groups in society hold power) over the child, yet cannot always make the child do what the parent wants. Children have wills of their own, and parents constantly have to resort to bribery or blackmail ('You can watch television if you do your homework'), or to the granting of concessions ('You can have half of the sweets now and half later') in order to get their way. (They could use force as well, but this would not win consent.) Parent and child are involved in a process of negotiation and struggle.

At a macro social level, similar negotiations and struggles go on between bosses and trade unions, political parties and lobby groups, men and women, whites and Aborigines, and so on.

Gramsci's theory of the continual negotiation and struggle between dominant and subordinate social groups suggests that there must be some positive reward for the subordinate groups in order for them to accept their social conditions: Western democracies, for example, must offer enough freedoms, pleasures, comfortable lifestyles, and media entertainments for members of subordinate groups to accept the status quo.

The big question is whether these rewards and concessions will result in only small and gradual changes that actually leave the dominant powers still in control, or whether they can lead to fundamental social change. In relation to gender, ask yourself whether, despite all the changes and concessions won by women and feminism, the hegemony of men, of patriarchy, is still maintained. In relation to halting climate change, will gradual changes that allow us still to operate within a culture of economic growth and consumerism work, or will we need to adopt fundamentally different ways of living? We cannot give a definite answer to these questions, but there is one other aspect of Gramsci's theory that is useful for understanding how the media work: the idea of **counter-hegemony**. People working within the media (and elsewhere) can attempt to challenge the dominant ideology, as Hartley suggested above, by working to produce a counter-hegemonic world view (see Chapter 13).

◀ COUNTER-HEGEMONY

A world view or activity that is in opposition to and challenges the dominant world view.

The aim is to get popular support for a new discourse or ideology that will challenge the status quo. It is this possibility for change and contradiction that takes us out of the impasse of a dominant ideology imposed from above. Such counter-hegemonic activities are explored in the next chapter. Once again, it is important to note that the internet and digital communication have opened up many new channels of communication that provide an increased means for people to engage in communication struggles.

CASE STUDY

Christmas ideologies, discourses, and hegemonic struggle

By now you should be beginning to see the complexity of ideology and hegemony, and their potential richness as ways of understanding how societies work. What follows is one last example: Christmas. By analysing the contradictory ideologies and competing discourses of Christmas, we will illustrate how ideology is rarely simple, and how hegemonic forces win our consent by incorporating conflicting ideologies and offering us various pleasures associated with media consumption.

Most societies are based on a set of contrasting and competing ideologies or discourses. Some of these will be very old, others more recent; some will be current, others will relate to the emerging values of new groups in society (as Williams suggests with his categorisation of residual, dominant, and emergent discourses; see p. 183).

Christmas is an example of this complexity. While Christmas is not actually a media text, within Western cultures it can be considered a media event, and it is certainly a social and cultural phenomenon that creates a great deal of media attention—including advertising blitzes, Christmas songs and carols on the radio and in the shops, and special cinema releases and television programming. More recent Christmas films include

Continued on next page ▶

Nativity 2: Danger in the Manger starring David Tennant, *A Very Harold and Kumar Christmas*, and *A Very Murray Christmas*. Older Christmas-themed movies get played on television at this time of year too, such as *It's a Wonderful Life*, *Love Actually*, *The Polar Express*, *Home Alone*, and even *The Grinch* and *The Nightmare Before Christmas*. Many television series have Christmas specials, even the residents on Ramsay Street in *Neighbours* encourage Christmas festivities, and news programs follow stories about Christmas celebrations and Santa sightings. All together, Christmas becomes a media event; a media event is something that, like the Olympics or an election, overshadows and disrupts normal programming, and involves a bevy of special features and interviews across a number of media forms.

It is useful to consider Christmas, which derives from Western cultural traditions, in relation to other religious traditions. Holy days and the texts, rituals, and celebrations through which they are communicated are elements of religious discourse. In this respect, Christmas coexists with holy days that are relevant to other religions: Hindus and Jews celebrate different versions of the festival of lights, called Diwali (for Hindus) and Hanukkah (for Jews); Muslims celebrate Ramadan and Eid-ul Fitr. Each religion can be understood as a value system, a way of making sense of the world: an ideology. Depending on where you live, Christianity may not be the dominant religious ideology, but you will still almost certainly be exposed to the media hype surrounding Christmas. You might think holy days would not be easily commercialised. Ramadan involves regular intervals of prayer and a strict period of fasting from dawn until sunset, followed by Eid-ul Fitr (feasting and celebration at the end of the month of fasting). Fasting is accompanied by other forms of voluntary deprivation (donating money to the poor, and giving up pleasures and luxuries such as going to the cinema). This custom is intended to make people value and give thanks for what is normally taken for granted, and to foster compassion and understanding for those who are less fortunate. However, Christmas has been almost totally commercialised and is gradually being exported throughout the world. Although there are some underlying similarities, Ramadan is in many ways the complete opposite of the excess consumption that characterises Christmas. Shopping centres may raise banners saying, 'We wish our Muslim customers well during the holy month of Ramadan', but they rarely advertise a 'Ramadan sale' and Disney does not produce animated films teaching children about 'the spirit of Ramadan'.

Christmas was established as a major festival in the West in the nineteenth century, particularly in the USA and Victorian England. Many of the traditions and rituals of Christmas were formulated then, and have persisted and developed since. Five distinct ideological strands or discourses that converge in Christmas as a cultural experience are identified below.

1 Christianity. Christmas is of course a religious celebration of the Christian faith. The word derives from a church service (Mass) that celebrates the birth of the central figure of the Christian religion, Jesus (Christ), and it honours a more minor figure, Saint Nicholas (Santa Claus). As such, it emphasises love, spirituality, new birth, and the giving of presents to express our love and care for one another.

2 Magic and myth. Father Christmas, or Santa Claus, is part of the magical discourse of childhood in which fantasies of generous elves and flying reindeer are played out against the fairy tale backdrop of the North Pole. Children are persuaded to be good by being told that Santa needs little helpers, and that Santa won't bring gifts to naughty children. For many children, Santa is the central figure of

Christmas and opening presents is the main event. Bible stories, baby Jesus, and attendance at church are becoming, for children, a subsidiary or residual discourse.

3   Saturnalia and pagan festivals. Christmas is founded on and related to older religious festivals, for example, Greek and Roman festivals of Saturnalia (a winter celebration for Saturn, the Roman god of agriculture, a time for wild revelry prior to the deprivation, frugality, and cold of winter), and pagan celebrations that celebrate death and rebirth in the depth of winter and the move towards spring. The natural symbols of these festivals—trees, holly, mistletoe, and so on—connect with the fact that the religions associated with these older festivals involved worship of the Earth and nature. Historically, Christianity incorporated these symbols partly to help establish itself as a successor to pagan religions. ('Festival' derives from the Latin word *vale*, which means 'farewell', and 'fest' from the Latin word for feasting, so it literally means 'farewell to feasting'; similarly, 'carnival' derives from the Latin words for 'farewell' (*vale*) and 'flesh' (*carne*), thus meaning 'farewell to the flesh', because there will be little meat to eat until new animals are born in spring.)

4   Saturnalia allowed great indulgence, as do many holidays that today are seen as pleasurable breaks from work rather than times of religious contemplation (holy days). Saturnalia also involved a social topsy-turviness—the turning upside down of normal cultural values and conventions. This occurred in such practices as role-reversal games (such as the rich serving and feeding the poor). Christianity won its audience over to the Christian story partly through maintaining and incorporating these other traditions and their pleasures. Saturnalia and other pagan traditions are still fundamental to Christmas. They have been blended with the religious story, even though they conflict with the religious meaning of Christmas in some ways. The holiday period allows for excessive partying, drinking, and merry-making, alongside observance of Christian religious ceremonies and the notion of giving to others and to the poor. While the contradictory nature of these elements may involve clashes between religious observance and general celebration, they tend to coexist reasonably well.

5   Family. Christmas has become a time for celebrating and honouring the family, one of the cornerstones of modern society. The ideal is for everyone to spend Christmas Day with their families, an ideal that is lived out by many, but of course it breaks down for those people who do not have a family or do not live near their family. In reality it also often provokes major stress among families. Christmas is a time when there is a rise in marital and family breakdowns, as well as suicides. Thus, as the holiday attempts to cement the ideology of the family, it also makes the cracks in the structure all too visible.

6   Consumerism. While all four aspects—Christianity, magic and myth, Saturnalia, and the ideal of the family—are still central to Christmas, it has now become primarily a celebration of capitalism and materialism. Christmas is the time for a mass celebration and frenzy of consumerism, a mass spending of money. Christmas has become progressively more commercialised, such that the spending of money and the selling of goods are now the predominant feature of Christmas. It is often said that Christmas

Continued on next page   ▶

begins earlier each year, which is a reflection of the fact that the success of Christmas is measured, to a large extent, by shop sales. In 2015 Christmas goods, decorations, and music were being displayed in shops in September.

These five ideological aspects blend. It is difficult to take any one position on how to judge Christmas because all five contradictory aspects are in play at once. Presents, for example, are inscribed into all the discourses: they can be seen as an expression of our Christian love and charity to one another, they magically appear, they offer great pleasure, indulgence, and enjoyment, and the biggest presents are usually given to family members at present-giving rituals focused on family gatherings. And presents cost money—the more expensive the present, the better it is deemed to be. Nearly everyone can find something positive in the present-giving aspect of Christmas, which accounts for its popularity. Those who decry Christmas—because it is too commercial, or because they are disgusted by the waste of money involved, or because they are atheists and disagree with the promotion of religion, or because they are Christian and disapprove of the orgy of indulgence that occurs—risk being labelled Scrooges and being seen as outsiders.

Many Australians still hold onto old traditions that are linked to their British heritage, some of which, particularly the tradition of roast turkey and Christmas pudding, and the emphasis on winter, are clearly out of place in the Australian climate. But there is increasingly a move towards champagne breakfasts on the beach, and picnics with cold meats, salads, and summer puddings, which is an attempt to construct new traditions and new ways of celebrating that take Christmas into another dimension. Some clever entrepreneurs are encouraging the celebration of Christmas in July as a way of connecting Christmas with winter and getting people to spend even more money on celebrations. It will be interesting to see how multicultural Australia develops Christmas rituals.

In this example of Christmas as a repository of different ideologies and discourses (residual, dominant, and emergent), contradictory aspects are at work, but they can exist relatively comfortably side by side. Similar contradictions can be found in media texts. The idea of contradictory ideological aspects and the attempt to understand how they work together are central to this book. You may well find traces of new and old ideological positions, and traces of progressive and conservative discourses, within the same media text. You will begin to see how different ideological elements interact, how they are linked, and how they are often cemented over (or sugar-coated, as is Christmas) with the promise of pleasure.

The discursive struggles and contradictions can also be seen in terms of hegemony. Different people find different ways of negotiating the Christmas event, but most people consent to imprudent financial and dietary splurging during the festive season as the media constantly foregrounds the pleasures of giving and receiving, goodwill, and togetherness. Those who resist Christmas and refuse to buy into the consumerist ideology that has become so central to media representations of Christmas become outsiders, Grinches who must be persuaded of the value of Christmas and reincorporated into the dominant order.

The movie *The Grinch* (based on the book *How the Grinch Stole Christmas* by Dr Seuss) is a good example of hegemony at work, because it gives space to and incorporates resistance to the ideology of Christmas, particularly the materialistic aspect. In the end the Grinch is won over, he accepts Christmas, but rejects its materialism: 'Maybe Christmas,' he thought, 'doesn't come from a store. Maybe Christmas … perhaps … means a little bit more!' He is then rewarded by love and acceptance: 'The Grinch's small heart grew three sizes that day!' But this acceptance of the spirit of Christmas barely masks the materialism that is still the predominant discourse of Christmas.

CONCLUSION

In this chapter significant similarities between dominant ideology and hegemony have been noticed in that both operate through a mixture of coercion and consent; the limitations of dominant ideology, and how hegemony introduces a more flexible system of struggle and negotiation than the rigidity of dominant ideology have also been noted. It is useful to relate the processes of hegemonic negotiation back to the idea of ideological work (pp. 180–4), and to see ideological work—masking, displacement, incorporation—as similar to the hegemonic processes of winning consent.

We have noted how media texts can include contradictory discourses, radical and conservative aspects, residual and emergent discourses at the same time, and the importance of pleasure within media texts as another way of winning audience consent.

You should now be able to use theories of discourse, ideology, and hegemony as a way to unpack the complexities of media texts, and their often contradictory messages and meanings. Instead of seeing texts as having total control over audiences, the concept of hegemony fits in with media theory that understands that audiences can do things to texts in the readings they make of them and the pleasures they derive from them, and that media practitioners can also challenge the dominant ideology.

This chapter has

- defined dominant ideology, ISAs, and RSAs
- explained and illustrated ideological work and incorporation
- defined the terms 'residual', 'dominant', and 'emergent discourses'
- considered liberal pluralism
- defined and illustrated hegemony.

? DISCUSSION POINTS

1 How often do you notice the media addressing or interpellating its audience—you—as a member of a particular nation, or as a family member? Collect examples of these interpellations.

2 What are the similarities and differences between dominant ideology and hegemony theories?

3 Consider *Archer*, *South Park*, *The Biggest Loser*, *Redfern Now*, *Upper Middle Bogan*, *The Voice*, and *Orange Is the New Black*. Are these programs products of the dominant ideology, examples of programs presenting counter-hegemonic values, or products that demonstrate that we live in a liberal pluralist society?

4 Find examples of residual, dominant, and emergent discourses within the way Christmas is represented in the media.

SUMMARY

You should now be able to

- explain and critically comment on Althusser's theory of dominant ideology
- explain what ISAs and RSAs are and how they operate
- explain the concept of ideological work in the media and give examples
- define and illustrate 'incorporation'
- explain briefly the theory of hegemony and compare it to dominant ideology
- explain the concept of a liberal pluralist society
- explain the concepts of residual, dominant, and emergent discourses, and find examples of these in relation to discourses of gender in media texts
- analyse how media texts reinforce, challenge, or negotiate the dominant ideology
- analyse the discourses of Christmas within your society.

CHAPTER 13

Culture Jamming and Counter-hegemony

> "Culture Jamming" sticks where rational discourse slides off. It is, simply, the viral introduction of radical ideas. It is viral in that it uses the enemy's own resources to replicate itself—corporate logos, marketing psychology, clean typography, "adspeak". It is radical because—ideally—the message, once deciphered, causes damage to blind belief. Fake ads, fake newspaper articles, parodies, pastiche. The best CJ is totally unexpected, surprising, shocking in its implications.
>
> <www.abrupt.org/CJ/CJ.html>

This chapter will

- discuss ways in which media consumers can actively and creatively engage with the media, considering issues such as technology, humour, and legality
- outline some objectives of media activism
- offer a working definition of culture jamming
- analyse several examples of culture jamming
- explore the strengths and limitations of culture jamming as a counter-hegemonic discourse.

This chapter considers ways in which media audiences and media consumers can actively and creatively engage with the media and challenge dominant ideologies with a counter-hegemonic discourse.

Culture jamming is understood as a mode of resistance to the norms and conventions of mass culture that exposes and opposes the media's underlying power structures and ideological messages (Klein 2000). The term 'jamming' can refer to an obstruction, that is, the equivalent of a traffic jam for the media; it can also reference a more playful, spontaneous form of improvising and engaging with the media, as when musicians jam together. Culture jammers use their familiarity with the codes and conventions of advertising and other forms of communication to throw a spanner in the production of meaning by creating spoofs, defacing texts, and thereby subverting the intended meanings of the media texts that they choose to rework. Often they actively try to denaturalise the media images that we see every day by making us notice and question their underlying messages.

The objectives of culture jamming often include consciousness raising (raising awareness of social and political issues), as well as using the media to criticise dominant culture and the media themselves. Culture-jamming techniques can also be used simply to be clever or funny, without a political or critical motive. While purely comedic reworking of brands and ads may or may not be classified as culture jamming, the use of the communication techniques and styles associated with the movement for the purposes of product promotion is definitely not culture jamming, as our discussion of the Diesel example below demonstrates. An actual ad cannot be an instance of culture jamming. The co-option of jamming strategies such as satire and graffiti into commercial branding

◄ CULTURE JAMMING

A form of media activism that subverts and reworks the intended meaning of existing media texts, or parodies major corporations, public figures, and their media images.

is discussed later in this chapter, but bear in mind that culture jamming is a form of communication that can come only from outside commercial culture, not from inside the media industry.

What follows are several examples of culture jamming and a discussion of the issues that they raise:

- graffiti campaigns conducted by feminists and anti-smoking activists
- an email exchange that developed into an online campaign against Nike's employment policy regarding the manufacture of merchandise in free-trade zones
- recent innovations involving YouTube remixes, contagious media, and social networking
- university-based brand activism, critiques, and legal issues
- graffiti and street art
- the co-option or recuperation of communication strategies used in culture jamming back into mainstream advertising as a strategy to sell soft drinks and fashion merchandise.

MEDIA ACTIVISM ▶

Activities involving individuals or lobby groups that attempt to change the way in which the media work, or that use the media to make a social or political statement.

Culture jamming emerges out of a tradition of **media activism**, dating back to the 1970s, that addresses images in billboards and outdoor advertisements. In the 1970s, feminists unhappy about the sexual objectification of women started to paint slogans and captions on images of women used in outdoor advertisements. Such political graffiti drew attention to the sexism in these images and in so doing challenged patriarchy. To point out the harmful effects of smoking, anti-smoking campaigners adopted similar tactics, painting captions on cigarette advertisements. Both campaigns, in conjunction with political lobbying, appear to have had some effect in terms of bringing about changes to representations of women in advertising, limitations on cigarette advertising, and harsher regulation around smoking. This form of communication uses existing media texts (which normally reinforce the dominant ideology) to make an ideological critique.

The use of humour to engage with serious issues is a distinctive feature of culture jamming. As Henry Jenkins points out, 'Jokes tend to cluster around points of friction or rupture within the social structure, around places where dominant social discourse is already starting to give way to an emergent counter-discourse' (1992b, p. 251). This is the case in relation to the use of humour in instances of culture jamming related to the disruption of gendered and racial power relations, and even serious political issues such as terrorism.

The Diesel spoof (Figure 13.1) shows how culture jammers have exposed the way that advertising offers tantalising images of unattainable perfection that serve to fuel consumption. Diesel's famously ironic and cryptic advertising campaigns frequently appear to criticise media messages, social norms, and the process of advertising itself. Note that we might call Diesel's uses of irony in its original ads examples of postmodern media culture, but it would not be accurate to call them culture jamming since they originate within the media industry and motivate consumption. While the original Diesel 'Successful Living' and 'Happiness: Sponsored by Diesel' campaigns make fun of the notion that a corporation can brand anything, even an emotion, the 'Inadequacy is fuelled by Desire' jam playfully points out how Diesel is complicit in the same cycle of consumption that it critiques. The image shows an ordinary young couple frolicking in an artificial paradise, literally burning with desire for Diesel clothes. The text of the Diesel jam bluntly states: 'INADEQUATE is how the media make you feel so that you desire what they are selling.'

Typically, the advertising industry relies on the fact that most people compensate for the feeling that they can't measure up to the ideals of beauty and wealth embodied by models in ads by buying products that are supposed to make them look and feel better. *Laugh It Off*, the authors of the culture jam, seem to be urging media audiences to 'slit desire in the

Figure 13.1 'Inadequacy is fuelled by Desire'

Source: Courtesy of *Laugh It Off*

throat and break capitalism's kneecaps' by refusing to consume such products, even by doing 'textual violence' to brands by defacing advertisements. Because the majority of culture jamming opposes aspects of the dominant culture, it is sometimes referred to as a counter-cultural activity, or as a counter-hegemonic discourse. If capitalism and consumerism are part of the dominant culture, as expressed and promoted through the mass media, and if our consent for these ideologies is won by offering us the pleasures of consumption and the illusion of enhanced desirability, then it is clear why texts such as the Diesel jam can be considered to be counter-hegemonic. The discourse of mass culture speaks to us about consumption and appearance, and the counter-cultural discourse of culture jamming speaks about refusing to consume, and refusing to be seduced by images that offer unattainable, unhealthy, or unethical ideals. It is the form of communication (appropriating mass media texts and technologies), as well as the content of individual messages, that makes culture jamming subversive.

TECHNOLOGY

The content or message of media texts can communicate ideological values. In what sense can media technologies also be influential in challenging or reinforcing social norms and power dynamics?

Email and other forms of computer-mediated communication (CMC) have been celebrated as being both democratic and empowering mediums of mass communication because they enable individuals and small groups to get their message out to large numbers of people without having to contend with restrictive policies and regulations, or prohibitively expensive equipment and production costs. The world-famous 'McLibel' case, in which a handful of media activists used the internet to publicise a legal battle against McDonald's, was run on a second-hand computer in a rented room. CMC is also characterised by a direct feedback loop in which the senders and receivers of messages can exchange views and negotiate meanings.

While there are feedback mechanisms with traditional media such as newspapers, radio, and television, CMC is structured to facilitate a two-way flow of information, rather than the asymmetrical transmission of information in which the sender and receiver are separated by space, time, and an imbalance of communicative resources. In traditional media, audience members lack control over the means of transmitting messages, a gap that can only be bridged by initiatives such as phone calls or letters to the editor, or formal processes such as media research, ratings, and opinion polls. Mass media producers have an impersonal relationship with those who receive their messages, and media consumers have less power and agency in the communicative exchange: consumers control the interpretation of the message, but they don't have access to the means of constructing their own media products and sending responses straight back to the producers. In online communication, the sender and receiver are connected by wireless technology or the network of phone and cable lines that links their computers to one another, so it is possible for the communicative exchange to retain some interpersonal characteristics. This in itself can be empowering for media consumers, because they can make their point of view known and communicate it to other individuals with whom they have some personal connection.

For example, fans and critics of the popular fantasy franchise Harry Potter interact with each other using digital media, including online fan fiction and video spoofs to express not just their opinions about the narrative, but their views on its gender politics. In particular, the YouTube video *If Hermione Were the Main Character in Harry Potter* (2015) intercuts footage from the Harry Potter films showing Hermione fighting gender-based oppression for witches and wizards, and destroying the patriarchy. Similarly, spoofs of the film *Fifty Shades of Grey* abound, including a trailer in which Ellen DeGeneres casts herself in the role of leading lady, and a very artful stop-motion YouTube video by 'Shakycow' called *Barbie's 50 Shades of Pink* (2015), which uses Barbie and Ken dolls to enact the trailer, with Barbie playing the role of the domineering, wealthy entrepreneur and Ken the naive college student. The irony of Barbie performing a playful, feminist critique of contemporary popular media culture simply by playing herself enacting the leading man's role in a romance will not be lost on viewers.

CASE STUDY

Use of email as a subversive technology

While he was a student at the Massachusetts Institute of Technology, Jonah Peretti made a statement against Nike's employment policies by putting in a routine request to have his sneakers customised. For a fee of $50 Nike offers to personalise its products by stitching a word or phrase under the Nike swoosh logo. This service, called 'iD', is part of a branding exercise that relates Nike to freedom of choice and freedom of expression by encouraging customers to 'build' their own shoes. Noting the irony of this slogan in light of the conditions that employees who actually do build Nike shoes reportedly endure in free-trade zones, Peretti chose the word 'sweatshop'. In the email exchange that followed, Nike cancelled Peretti's order on the grounds that 'sweatshop' was 'inappropriate slang'. The ensuing email exchange spread spontaneously after Peretti forwarded it to friends who were interested in the subject, and they passed it on to their friends. Initially, everyone received the email exchange from someone they knew. Eventually, the exchange circulated around the globe, and became part of a broader media campaign against the negative aspects of globalisation in general and Nike's alleged labour practices in particular.

In the following correspondence between Peretti and Nike, none of Nike's messages address the issue of whether the company engages in unethical labour practices. For Peretti, Nike's refusal to engage with the issues he was raising was worse than an admission of guilt because it meant that no headway could be made.

Dear NIKE iD,

Thank you for your quick response to my inquiry about my custom ZOOM XC USA running shoes. Although I commend you for your prompt customer service, I disagree with the claim that my personal iD was inappropriate slang. After consulting Webster's Dictionary, I discovered that "sweatshop" is in fact part of standard English, and not slang. The word means: "a shop or factory in which workers are employed for long hours at low wages and under unhealthy conditions" and its origin dates from 1892. So my personal iD does meet the criteria detailed in your first email.

> Your web site advertises that the NIKE iD program is "about freedom to choose and freedom to express who you are". I share Nike's love of freedom and personal expression. The site also says that "If you want it done right ... build it yourself". I was thrilled to be able to build my own shoes, and my personal iD was offered as a small token of appreciation for the sweatshop workers poised to help me realize my vision. I hope that you will value my freedom of expression and reconsider your decision to reject my order.

Thank you, Jonah Peretti

From: "Personalize, NIKE iD" <nikeid_personalize@nike.com>

To: "Jonah H. Peretti" <peretti@....>

Subject: RE: Your NIKE iD order o16468000

Dear NIKE iD Customer

Regarding the rules for personalization it also states on the NIKE iD website that "Nike reserves the right to cancel any personal iD up to 24 hours after it has been submitted". In addition, it further explains: "While we honor most personal iDs, we cannot honor every one. Some may be (or contain) others' trademarks, or the names of certain professional sports teams, athletes or celebrities that Nike does not have the right to use. Others may contain material that we consider inappropriate or simply do not want to place on our products. Unfortunately, at times this obliges us to decline personal iDs that may otherwise seem unobjectionable. In any event, we will let you know if we decline your personal iD, and we will offer you the chance to submit another." With these rules in mind, we cannot accept your order as submitted. If you wish to reorder your NIKE iD product with a new personalization please visit us again at www.nike.com

Thank you, NIKE iD

Continued on next page ▶

Peretti has since gone on to co-found the *Huffington Post* and he is CEO of BuzzFeed, an online media business that tracks internet trends and internet memes, which are images, videos, or phrases that catch on and spread like wildfire online. Read about Peretti's five tips to make content go viral at <http://techcrunch.com/2010/08/13/five-viral-rules-video>.

Culture-jamming exercises

Print media

- Select an ad, a brand, a slogan, a magazine cover, or some other form of print media text that sends a message you disagree with, or promotes a product, ideology, or ethic you object to, find hypocritical, or find humorous.
- Write down the intended meaning of the text, where you found it, its intended effect, and its inscribed reader and target audience.
- Use marking pens, collage, or software such as Photoshop to manipulate the image, and rework or challenge its meaning (for example, add or delete text or images, write speech bubbles or captions).
- Write down what your new intended meaning is, what effects you hope your jam might have, where you would like to publicise it, and whom you would like to see it. (Sharing images on Instagram or Facebook is one of the easiest ways to self-publish.)
- Show your jam to someone in the original target audience and ask them what it means to them.

Broadcast media

Take a television or radio advertisement and make up your own alternative or subversive soundtrack to replace the original.

Wireless communication, vidding, and social networking

How might you use your mobile phone, YouTube, Twitter, or Facebook as culture-jamming technologies for the purposes of media activism or political communication?

CASE STUDY

Universities and students—media, law, and humour

Around the world, many media students and media consumers have put the steps in the culture-jamming exercise above into practice, and university campuses have become flash-points for questioning, challenging, critiquing, or playfully poking fun at media culture, brands, and tertiary institutions themselves. Brands have become part of the cultural vocabulary, and are used to comment on images, identities, and social exclusion that may be tacitly employed in commercial branding campaigns seeking to associate a product or company with its target market. For example, the University of Queensland (UQ) carefully cultivates its image as a prestigious, world-class university that consistently ranks in the top three tertiary institutions in Australia and the top 50 to 100 universities globally. Along with its being an established sandstone institution with beautiful gardens, lakes, and stately buildings that make it an Antipodean equivalent of the so-called Ivy League universities in North America, this has arguably created perceptions of elitism and social exclusion as the university seeks to attract the very best students in Australia and a wealthy, well-educated class of international students. In 2015 anonymous culture jammers replaced the university's logo, a gold coat of arms, with the yellow logo for the Mexican taco chain Guzman y Gomez, featuring two happy, chubby Mexican men. This hack appeared whenever anybody searched for the university online and saw the UQ Wikipedia page or any number of university ranking pages listing the 'Guzman and Gomez University' as Queensland's flagship research institution. You might interpret this as free advertising for the taco franchise that had recently opened on campus, or as a comical message about social inclusiveness.

That same year UQ rolled out its 'Create change' ad campaign, which featured attractive, well-groomed students and alumni in labs and locations across the beautiful campus being trailed by glittering clouds of something signifying inspiration, or perhaps as a callback to Obama's campaign slogans, 'change we can believe in' as we 'walk into the future'. We can't show you these images because the university did not grant permission to reproduce them, since it was discovered that the clouds of inspirational fairy dust contained unwanted icons. Bored students waiting at bus stops plastered with large 'Create change' posters found dozens of flying penises hidden in the fairy dust and promptly posted pictures of them on Facebook. The campaign was quickly dubbed 'Where's Willy?' in social media and the popular press, in homage to the 'Where's Wally?' books that invite people to search for the tiny figure of Wally hidden in a crowd. Rather than being pleased that students were studying the campaign images so intently, and the press was effectively giving UQ free advertising and establishing a strong link between the university's brand and youth culture, the university was concerned about brand tarnishment and insisted that the advertising agency clean up and replace all of the images.

Even culture jams that are intended to be humorous run the risk of attracting legal consequences if the messages are taken too seriously. Some corporations have defended themselves against culture-jamming activities by invoking international legal precedents to prevent brand parody on the basis of copyright infringement and brand tarnishment. In some cases culture jamming can also attract charges of **defamation** if untrue allegations are made or implied, and if an individual's or corporation's reputation and livelihood are damaged by the jam. Culture jammers who have been sued for their activities have used **freedom of speech** as a defence against the charges of trademark and copyright violation, defending their right to create messages that use brands and logos to make people question the media.

DEFAMATION

Defamation involves publicising information that is untrue and so injures someone's reputation, or if it is deemed to be not in the public interest for that information to be published.

FREEDOM OF SPEECH

The right to express opinions publicly without interference from government or other sectors. This right is subject to legal limitations that restrict the publication of material that incites hatred or violence, or is defamatory.

Our final example in relation to university culture, students, and social activism that we would like you to consider reveals the damaging potential of unauthorised media. In January 2016 an online article titled 'How the Extremist Right Hijacked "Star Wars," Taylor Swift and the Mizzou Student Protests to Promote Racism' led with the following statement: 'As online platforms like Twitter and Facebook become increasingly important for the dissemination of breaking news, extremist leaders are recognizing the power of subverting mainstream coverage in the service of their own agendas' (Hankes 2016, n.p.). The article goes on to recount the proliferation of racist memes, tweets, and images, before detailing the spreading of false 'eyewitness' reports of student protests, and the creation of fraudulent 'White Student Union' Facebook and WordPress sites for universities around the world, including UQ and the University of California, Berkeley. Such sites were not authorised by the universities involved or their student unions, and in most cases were not created by students who attended these universities, yet they generated a great deal of media publicity and the anonymity of online media production made it easy for racist political messages to proliferate. The perpetrators of these messages openly encouraged their followers on social media to use disposable mobile phones and create 'sock puppet' accounts registered to fake identities to avoid being censored by Twitter and Facebook, so as to 'strike out on their own and impersonate people of color and women in order to conduct "culture jamming"' (Hankes 2016, n.p.).

Think carefully about the 'Where's Willy?/Create change' campaign and the 'White Student Union' case. A graphic designer doing contract work for UQ's advertising firm reportedly hid the flying penises in the UQ ads and had moved on to other work by the time they were discovered. Since these images were technically produced by an advertising company, can the so-called 'dicks at UQ' images be considered culture jamming? What about the bogus 'White Student Union' Facebook sites? Are they just trolling campaigns, or are they a form of culture jamming? If your university has one of these, what might you do about it? ▶

PARTICIPATORY BRANDING, SOCIAL MEDIA, AND ALGORITHMS

The strategic use of social media by major brands conducting participatory advertising campaigns in contemporary youth culture means that we need to question what advertising is, what culture jamming is, and what they are becoming. As Nic Carah and Michelle Shaul argue in their critical analysis of algorithms and advertising, 'Brands are a critical part of the ongoing experimentation that underpins the development of mobile social media platforms like Instagram' (2016, p. 69). Until Facebook bought it in 2012, Instagram did not demarcate advertising images from other content and it did not earn advertising revenue, but recently select brands like Smirnoff Vodka have begun paying for sponsored posts, and experimenting with ways to embed their brand identity in users' accounts and activities. In other words, 'Branding on Instagram relies on the active participation of users, who present their bodies as images' (Carah & Shaul 2016, p. 70). For example, Carah and Shaul detail how Smirnoff embedded itself in the 2014 Splendour in the Grass music festival by constructing a glamorous cocktail bar, with artists painting evolving murals on the walls, beautiful models circulating among and posing with the patrons, and novel props and photo opportunities, to encourage users to post images of themselves drinking Smirnoff on Instagram, branded with #vipublic. 'Activation,' they write, 'is the marketing industry term for the real-world spaces created by brands to embed themselves within cultural events and practices', so the Smirnoff cocktail bar functioned as a '"set" or "stage" for the production of brand images. As consumers and cultural intermediaries at brand activations post images via their own social media accounts, they attract the attention of their own followers. Their use of hashtags places the brand within a wider flow of images related to their own bodies and identities' (Carah & Shaul 2016, p. 74). Predictably, people tend to play out fairly standard scripts when presented with such an ideal stage to perform on, and most participants posted images of themselves posing like models, leading Carah and Shaul to conclude that 'Algorithms appear to enhance the capacity of media to reinforce discursive norms' (2016, p. 83).

If social media provide ample opportunities for brand engagement, and brands are actively courting the audience's participation in the construction of narratives and identities, why is it that consumer behaviour appears to be becoming more predictable in some ways than it was in the era of analogue advertising, when it was much harder to interact with or potentially jam a Smirnoff TV ad or billboard? ▶

Carah argues that 'culturally embedded and participatory forms of branding became integrated with the predictive and analytic capacities of social media' (2015, p. 1). He explains that Instagram's and Facebook's algorithms recognise users, respond to their preferences, and adapt in order to keep them engaged for as long as possible by suggesting that they explore more content: in an addictive cycle, the longer users participate, the more the algorithm learns about them, and can target them and sustain their attention more effectively. Facebook and Instagram 'work with major brands to integrate data from the social media platform with companies' internal marketing data in order to determine how engagement online is translated into sales' (Carah 2015, p. 13). These participatory advertising strategies harness social media, relying on consumers' creativity and communication to make members of the brand's target market visible as data and as promotional media content (Carah 2015, p. 15).

In the past, culture jammers have responded to the symbolic and ideological content of advertising campaigns, and spoken back to tag lines and slogans written by people in advertising agencies; how do we now respond to the marketing endeavours of the computational programs that watch us and record our social and media activities? ▶

CASE STUDY

Banksy—street art, anonymity, and culture jamming

Accessible, affordable, interactive media technologies have enabled culture jamming in its different forms to spread across the globe, informing far-flung groups of people about common concerns. Arguably, some stencil art, such as that by French graffiti artist Blek le Rat, by American Shepard Fairey, who created the Barack Obama *HOPE* poster in 2008, and by 'anonymous' British street graffiti artist and political activist Banksy, offers an innovative form of cultural resistance to neoliberal globalisation.

Banksy has an international reputation for his prolific and subversive art in public spaces. His work has been appearing since the 1990s; however, he came to mainstream recognition in the early 2000s. His disruptive culture jamming has materialised, often illegally, all over the world, and, to date, his identity remains unknown despite his living in the surveillance society that he highlights repeatedly in his work. Banksy offers social and political commentaries, and dark humour through his stencil art, often with slogans, on walls and bridges, and in unknown alleyways, refugee camps, and the urban streets of cities across the world. The themes of his work are consistently anti-establishment, anti-capitalist, and anti-imperialist. The art offers critiques of poverty, war, the treatment of refugees, consumerism, and greed, for example. Consistent in his cultural activist graffiti are representations of rats, members of the British royal family, policemen, and children.

Banksy has produced a film, *Exit Through the Gift Shop* (2010), and a documentary, *Banksy Does New York* (2015), was made about his city-wide, month-long residency in New York City. Over the course of a month, Banksy would create a new nightly work of art around the city, and a hunt for Banksy, the enigma, would ensue. The documentary was not only made with footage from the official film crew, but it was user-generated and crowd-sourced, as the locations where Banksy would spraypaint were secret, and so reliance on passers by to find and comment on the art was critical. 'Dismaland' was another Banksy project. It was a temporary theme-park display of satirical works and sculptures set up for one month in England in 2015. It featured approximately sixty artists Banksy invited, and it was described by Banksy as a 'family theme park unsuitable for children' (Canter 2015). It was an apocalyptic take on Disneyland, with displays such as Cinderella mangled in a pumpkin carriage crash. This was perhaps a reference to Princess Diana's death, as a dead, blonde princess spilling from the carriage was shown with a paparazzo shooting continuous photographs at the crash scene, at night.

Another theme in Banksy's work is rats. Blek le Rat started spraypainting rats around Paris over twenty years ago, with the idea that rats will outlive the human race. Banksy has followed in this tradition. This is a powerful symbol for social commentary in terms of street art. Rats are commonly viewed as needing to be exterminated, much like the art that is 'illegal' and that authorities have attempted to clean away from the streets. This work is referenced in the reboot of the *X-Files* (2016) in an episode titled 'Home Again'; when officious bureaucrats intent on 'cleaning up the streets' are cruel to Philadelphia's homeless, an anonymous but phenomenally successful street artist known as 'Trashman' creates a stencil artwork that comes to life and avenges social injustice. Like rats, much street graffiti is seen as dirty and its removal by authorities is an attempt to sanitise, yet rats—and street art—keep coming back. Banksy works have been subject to defacement and removal by authorities such as local councils.

Do you think this matters? Is street art meant to be ephemeral?

Here in Figure 13.2 is one of Banksy's subversive, iconic works, 'The Spy Booth'. It depicts three spooks wearing sunglasses and trench coats with listening devices at a phone booth. In 2014 it appeared on a house near GCHQ (Government Communications Headquarters), the UK's intelligence and security agency. It appeared just months after whistleblower Edward Snowden, a former CIA (Central Intelligence Agency) agent, copied classified information from the NSA (National Security Agency) in order to disclose information about global surveillance to the media.

What do you think Banksy is conveying in 'The Spy Booth'? Do you think it is linked to the Snowden leaks, or is it just coincidental? If you think about other Banksy pieces, can 'The Spy Booth' be read as consistent with some of Banksy's broader context of cultural activism? Is it more powerful read in conjunction with the themes of his other works?

However, it is arguable that some street art, such as Banksy's, is not always as subversive as culture-jamming agitation as it was first intended. As a form of resistance against neoliberalism, his work has been adapted and co-opted by neoliberalism itself to become viewed by members of the elite as desirable commodities to 'own'. Celebrities such as Kate Moss, Brad Pitt, Angelina Jolie, and Christina Aguilera have purchased Banksy's work at auctions; socialites and businesspeople rush to purchase Banksy originals. Banksy himself, however, finds this trend ridiculous, as the social class boundaries that street graffiti artists such as him originally sought to challenge maintain hegemonic power structures. After an auction at Sotheby's in London in 2007 where Banksy works sold for over six figures each, the elusive artist updated his website with a statement about the commercialisation of his art: he posted an image of an auction at which people were bidding on a large painting in a gilt frame featuring the words 'I CAN'T BELIEVE YOU MORONS ACTUALLY BUY THIS SHIT'. In 2014 this artwork sold at an unauthorised retrospective at Sotheby's for £10 000. Banksy rarely speaks to the media; however, he made contact with a journalist in 2013—through a publicist—and discussed his concerns about his own 'success' as an artist. Despite his anonymity, he is a celebrity, and despite his anti-commercialism, his work has been commodified. He has anonymously held shows where he has sold art for millions of dollars, and he has entered media culture by writing books and making films. Banksy is reportedly worth US$20 million and he says that:

> there's no way round it—commercial success is a mark of failure for a graffiti artist. We're not supposed to be embraced in that way. When you look at how society rewards so many of the wrong people, it's hard not to view financial reimbursement as a badge of self-serving mediocrity (Hamilton 2013).

Does Banksy's culture jamming have significance as a single piece, or is its power in the collective works and the identity that has been attributed to him? Do you think Banksy's culture jams are diluted because they are now popular among the rich and powerful he seeks to satirise? It may seem obvious at first, when we look at the works Banksy has produced, but let's think about this more: who is Banksy's target audience and has it changed with his celebritisation, even if he is self-reflexive and critical of this?

Continued on next page ▶

Figure 13.2 Banksy's 'The Spy Booth'

LIMITATIONS OF CULTURE JAMMING

Adbusting is a particular type of culture jamming, also known as 'subvertising'. There are a number of criticisms of adbusting and related forms of culture jamming.

◀ ADBUSTING

Adbusting involves modifying advertisements to undermine their intended meaning (for more information see <www.adbusters.org>).

1   First and foremost, adbusting works within the system that it is attempting to critique. It is still a form of advertising, and it runs the risk of reinforcing brand recognition for the companies it is trying to undermine. In other words, the cleverer the graffiti, the more negative publicity that it generates, and the more likely people are to remember the brand in question when they walk into a shop—and that is one of the major goals of advertising.

2   The controversy that surrounds a brand or corporation as a result of media activism can end up making the product seem more desirable, particularly to members of the youth market who wish to be identified with controversial and radical positions.

3   There can be serious legal implications. Culture jammers can be sued for brand tarnishment, brand infringement, copyright violation, and even defamation.

4   The use of controversy and humour can serve to focus attention on the ad, not the issue, or it can trivialise the issue.

5   Developments in media technology can be considered a strength and a weakness of culture jamming. The Nike email example (see pp. 196–8) raises questions about the subversive potential of digital image manipulation and online media activism. The internet is largely dominated by the English language and it requires computer literacy, which, in turn, requires training and technology. So, despite being a more democratic medium in which more people are able to become media producers, CMC is still exclusive to some degree.

6   Organisations such as Adbusters and *Laugh It Off* have been called hypocritical for jamming ads and printing the jams on calendars, stickers, clothing, and other commodities that they then proceed to sell. Even culture jamming has been incorporated as an advertising strategy. Once marketing strategists realised that it was perceived as cool, they began to construct ad campaigns that appealed to the consumer's awareness of the very process of advertising. In Australia a brand of beer called Piss developed cult status when it launched the no-frills ad campaign 'Buy Piss, Drink Piss, Get Pissed'. This was successful (irrespective of the taste of the beverage itself) because it did not involve inflating the price of the product with expensive advertisements, and pricey graphics on the labels and packaging. This campaign is not a *bona fide* jam, but it made its mark precisely because, like culture jamming, it was perceived to be honest and upfront about marketing mechanisms, instead of trying to seduce the consumer with desirable but unattainable images.

A further example of the impact that counter-hegemonic movements have had on advertising can be found in the way that political activism has been exploited to market fashion merchandise to young consumers. The anti-corporate, anti-globalisation movement, for example, has been co-opted to boost the sales of American Apparel, a company whose advertisements claim that the brand is 'sweatshop free' and 'environmentally friendly'. In this way advertising and culture jamming can be understood as forms of political communication, but we can also see how social and political issues are themselves becoming commodified. Of course people do have to make a living and if they are doing so in environmentally friendly ways, it is a positive step.

As journalist Meg Carter points out, the communication styles and methods of counter-culture and mainstream culture are rapidly converging: 'Sony, Diesel and Puma have appropriated the communication tactics of political activists by taking their advertising onto the streets, emulating the look of flyposting in their legitimate ads, and using typography or imagery inspired by graffiti' (2004, p. 24). The examples above illustrate recuperation or incorporation as discussed previously (see p. 182).

Recuperation involves the conversion of subcultural signifiers such as fashion garments, accessories, hairstyles, slang, music, etc. into mass-produced commodities (see Hebdige 1979, p. 94). Body piercing and tattooing stopped being challenges to social norms when it became possible to buy do-it-yourself removable Celtic armband tattoos and adhesive pseudo navel rings from any novelty store. Something so common and commercially available no longer signifies anything remotely cool, angst-ridden, or rebellious: it now signifies conformity. The homogeneity of mass production undermines any possibility that such objects could articulate a unique identity or a radical lifestyle statement. The other part of the process of recuperation involves the 'labelling' and redefinition of 'deviant' practices (Hebdige 1979, p. 94). This second mode of recuperation is exemplified when the police or the media refer to graffiti as 'aerosol art' instead of 'vandalism', and when Banksy's images find their way onto cute 'Banksy Does New York' gift cards that tourists can buy as souvenirs. In the process of recuperation, we see mass culture incorporating and repackaging the less threatening aspects of subculture.

The most extreme instance of this is the appropriation of culture jamming itself by government agencies. In 2011 the British intelligence agency MI6 hacked a terrorist website (the Jihad magazine *Inspire*) that instructed people how to build pipe bombs by redirecting those who attempted to download the instructions to a site that gave lessons on baking cupcakes ('Terror Trap Takes the Cake'). Who would have thought government counter-terrorism agencies would co-opt counter-cultural media strategies to fight subversive acts of terrorism with a sense of humour?

Despite the limitations of culture jamming as noted above, it has been a very significant form of challenge to dominant ideology and the power of the media. If it has been recuperated, there may be some new form of media resistance that will emerge in the future as subversive uses for new technologies continue to be discovered.

CONCLUSION

This chapter has examined the use of conventional and new media technologies for media activism and counter-hegemonic purposes, and it has discussed issues related to copyright law and the use of humour that arise in culture jamming. Part 3 has focused more broadly on the ideologies and discourses of the media, looking at the media as an instrument of dominant ideology, and as a hegemonic instrument of contradictory and alternative ideologies. These issues are explored further in Part 4, where many of the aesthetic practices of media storytelling are also considered.

This chapter has

- defined the term 'culture jamming' and explained some of its objectives and techniques
- analysed the intended meaning, inscribed reader, and potential effects of some culture-jamming initiatives
- investigated the subversive potential of media technologies and discussed how they might be influential in challenging social norms and power dynamics
- evaluated the strengths and limitations of culture jamming.

? | DISCUSSION POINTS

1 Do you think the use of humour trivialises serious issues, or makes them more memorable?
2 Counter-cultural communication strategies can be used for exploitative purposes as well as to initiate positive social, political, and environmental changes. Is it possible for media texts such as advertisements to promote progressive ideas and ideals as well as selling goods and services?
3 Are there any circumstances in which you think that culture jamming should be illegal?

SUMMARY

You should now be able to

- discuss the objectives of media activism
- define the term 'culture jamming'
- analyse the strengths and limitations of culture jamming
- evaluate the effectiveness of culture jamming as a counter-hegemonic discourse that challenges dominant ideology
- using culture jamming as a tool, apply what you have learnt to respond to the mass media and create your own media jam.

PART 4
Stories: Approaches for Narrative Analysis

The truth about stories is that that's all we are.

Thomas King *The Truth About Stories*

Overview

Part 4 builds on the concepts of semiology that were discussed in Part 2, and the critical terms 'discourse', 'ideology', and 'hegemony' that were introduced in Part 3.

Here we will look into stories, one of the oldest and most common forms of communication and entertainment. Stories engage audiences through their exciting and involving narratives. A number of different ways to approach and understand how stories communicate to us will be offered. Fictional stories found in feature films, television series, and serials will be analysed, as will stories and narratives constructed in factual programs, documentaries, reality TV, and video and internet games.

CHAPTER 14

Genres, Codes, and Conventions

Sex, money, and violence. That's all we ever see.

Anon.

This chapter will

- consider the meaning of the term 'genre'
- examine the western genre
- consider the way media codes and conventions can evolve.

GENRES

What are genres? How and why have they evolved? What is genre theory?

The quotation opening this chapter is a comment by an elderly Eastern European man who was discussing cinema at an evening class that Michael once ran. The man's words point to the fact that cinema and television have a tendency to tell the same stories over and over again. This repetition and familiarity are found in terms of content—the subject matter of sex, money, and violence, for example—and in terms of the way this content is put into different types of familiar stories, or different genres. It is probably obvious to you that whenever you go to the cinema or switch on the television, you can easily and quickly identify what type of film or television story you are watching, which demonstrates the skills you have developed as a viewer to recognise the codes and conventions of a particular genre, and their predominance within the media. Let's start our examination of storytelling by examining the term **genre**.

GENRE ▶

Groups of texts that share a set of conventional characteristics such as content, narrative structure, and visual style are classified as textual types or genres.

Within media studies, the term 'genre' was first used as a means of critical analysis in relation to film, and then television. It has been and can be used in relation to literature and other arts, and also in relation to video games, magazines, and other media forms. It is a term that was first used by media analysts but is now also used by audiences in everyday conversation about the media. An explanation of how it was first developed in relation to film and television will be given, and the way the study of genre is relevant to media texts, industries, and audiences will be discussed.

People can often quickly classify any film or program as belonging to a particular genre—horror, musical, sitcom, crime, soap opera, and so on—by recognising similarities, familiar codes, and conventions. Genres are useful for

- producers, who make and sell their product by identifying it as part of an already successful, and therefore marketable, generic formula
- film and television makers, who can communicate easily and quickly through these formulas, and can also work creatively within the form
- audiences, who use genre as a basis for their choice of films or television programs, and as a key to understanding them.

The constituencies represented in Figure 14.1 (the film and television industry, filmmakers, and audiences) can all use genres and generic formulas beneficially.

Figure 14.1 Uses of genres

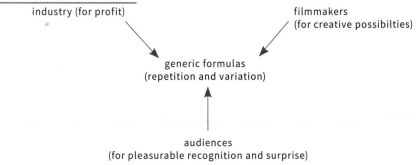

Genres evolved initially through the film industry. Producers wanting to make money realised they could capitalise on a successful film by offering viewers something similar, more of the same. Of course it had to be different in some ways, but featuring the same actors, stars, and/or the same kind of story with some new developments—a crucial pattern of repetition and variation—were the main methods adopted by the industry. This practice developed with the very beginnings of silent cinema and it can already be seen to be successfully operating by the 1920s. It continues today, as successful films and characters return time and again to the screen—James Bond, Harry Potter, Batman, and Hugh Jackman's character Wolverine in *The X-Men* franchise, to name a few. Genre study began in the 1960s as a way of studying and understanding Hollywood films. It showed several things.

- Most genres are immediately identifiable through their familiar **iconography**, that is, their recurrent use of visual images: the western genre features the iconography of cowboys, hats, guns, horses, cattle, wagon trains, saloons, frontier settings, and so on. Some genres will also have their own visual style, such as the extreme camera angles and harsh lighting style of ***film noir***.

- Genre stories work through repetition of familiar plot lines.

- Genres were economically beneficial for the film studios as a way of organising the production, distribution, and exhibition of films.

- Genres were initially critically regarded as cheap and valueless, a cinematic form of pulp fiction, the name given to trashy dime novels and magazines that would be literally pulped if not sold. Quentin Tarantino deliberately used the term in *Pulp Fiction*, his celebration of cheap generic elements. Later, though, critics began to see value and complexity in these generic stories.

- Many directors—in the western genre, John Ford, Howard Hawks, and Sam Peckinpah, among others—worked within these generic plots to produce their own deeply crafted and often complex visions of American society; later, critics of genre began to celebrate and validate these.

◀ ICONOGRAPHY

Visual images (icons) associated with a particular genre that are repeatedly used.

◀ *FILM NOIR*

French for 'black film'; black-and-white thrillers or detective stories made in the 1940s and 1950s conventionally featuring low-key lighting, retrospective voice-over narration, flashbacks, suspicion, intrigue, crime, urban settings, and *femmes fatales*.

- Genres continually evolve. Alongside the repetition of familiar codes and conventions, variations on the genre are introduced that give a new inflection, and often a new direction, to the genre (see discussion of the western below). *Film noir*—those complex and dark thrillers made in black and white in the 1940s and 1950s—returned in the 1970s, 1980s, and 1990s, having evolved into colour films; they still influence many films today. Thus a genre can continually develop to encompass new elements and produce new meanings.

CORE PROBLEMATIC ▶

Central problem or opposition that a genre explores.

- Genre theorist Steven Neale suggests that genres focus on a **core problematic**, an issue of social importance that the genre explores (Neale 1980). This problem is often structured as a dramatic conflict with two sets of competing values in opposition. In the family melodrama genre, for instance, there is a central opposition between the main character's desire for individual freedom versus the need to fulfil expected social and familial roles and duties. This is particularly the case for women but can also be experienced by men, as in *American Beauty*. This simple but effective device of oppositional values (binary oppositions) is discussed in more detail below (pp. 214–16), but it's useful to mention now as part of the conventions of genre.

The Eastern European man who complained about the constant diet of 'sex, money, and violence' saw commercial cinema as cheap and trashy, as promoting American capitalist ideals, and, most importantly, as formulaic, repetitive, and obvious. We may well ask why people watch genre films when the nature of the formulaic plot means that it is generally fairly easy to predict how the story will end. At one level this sense of obvious knowingness provides its own pleasures. Those who watch genre films often find a sense of satisfaction in being able to predict what will happen next, and they take pleasure in having these expectations subverted, manipulated, or confirmed. The Drew Goddard and Joss Whedon horror-spoof film *The Cabin in the Woods*, starring Chris Hemsworth, was successful because it made the characteristics of the genre explicit and reworked them playfully. Avid consumers of certain genres such as horror and science fiction also become adept at spotting intertextual references to other films and recognising the familiar iconography and conventions that characterise the genre, and they enjoy this sense of expertise.

But more importantly, the way Hollywood keeps returning to the same issues is actually a potential way of talking about and confronting some of the major human concerns, conflicts, and problems that society faces. The constant diet of sex, money, and violence provides the opportunity for exploring these fundamentally important concerns. Genres such as the western and the gangster film have been understood as a way for American society to reflect on itself, its history, and its development, a way of America talking to itself.

How has genre theory developed?

Genre theory for popular cinema was established at a time when most films were easily placed in a few key genres: western, gangster, and musical. Since then, a number of things have happened.

1   The advent of television has widened the scope of film culture and has established a whole new set of television forms or genres—game shows, current affairs programs, situation comedies, soap operas, reality TV, and so on.

2   Cinema has helped to nurture a generation of media watchers who are incredibly knowledgeable and sophisticated as viewers. Television, VCRs, and DVDs have enhanced media literacy by recycling older films that would, prior to television, have disappeared from general public viewing after their initial release. This generation of media watchers has seen an enormous amount of popular film and television that spans a considerable historical time period. While they may not have studied the media, they know a good deal about media texts, techniques, and technologies, and, in particular, they know about genres. Program makers need to be aware of the skills of their audience: they must provide novel material that continues to enthral and entertain them, but they can also rely on the audience being able to appreciate, if not actually analyse, quite complicated variations on genres.

3   The consequence of this has been what is called **generic hybridisation**. This hybridisation can have a number of effects: it can broaden the market appeal by attracting audiences who like different genres, it can unsettle audience expectations and provide fresh pleasures and surprises, and it can challenge cultural norms and ideas by reworking the conventions and characters that are usually used to convey the dominant ideology. James Cameron's generic hybrid *Avatar* attracted fans of science fiction, action, adventure, fantasy, family films, thrillers, and romance. *Kill List* blended elements of action, war, gangster, crime, war, suspense, and horror genres. Examples of hybridity on television include *Embarrassing Bodies*, a high-rating, BAFTA award-winning series about people with medical issues, often of a taboo or sexual nature, that combines a documentary style with the interwoven storyline structure of soap opera and content similar to that of a medical investigation drama. *Archer* and *Drawn Together* are both animated genre hybrids, and *Guardians of the Galaxy* blends the western genre with science fiction and fantasy. These are all groundbreaking series in terms of the way they play across genres, but generic hybridity happens on more subtle levels too. A mystery thriller, comedy, romance, and police-procedural drama series such as *Castle* is a hybrid that incorporates the narrative structure of an investigative crime series. The series primarily follows the work of Richard Castle, a best-selling murder mystery novelist who works with the NYPD to help solve unusual crimes in New York. Here, Castle functions as both novelist and detective to solve crimes.

◀ GENERIC HYBRIDISATION

Generic hybrids are texts that blend the codes and conventions of two or more genres to produce a new combination.

To show how you can start thinking about genres in more depth, comment is made below on one popular genre: the western.

The western

The western is probably the most well known of all genres to come out of Hollywood. While the western is partly an attempt to look at, explore, and understand America's own past, that exploration has a mythic quality, that is, it tells us more about America's ideas about itself than the actual realities of American history. Many critics argue that although set in the past, the stories are often related to contemporary events. The myth of the western and the heroic cowboy also speaks to people from many different cultures; in this sense it has had a universal appeal. The popularity of the genre has inspired many interesting books and articles about the western.

Jim Kitses argues that there are several key oppositions that mark out the central themes and core problematic of the western: the wilderness versus civilisation, the individual versus the community, nature versus culture, the west versus the east (Kitses 2004). These oppositions are played out through violent conflict that is enacted across the frontier, the boundary that separates civilised society, and law and order, from the freedom of the wilderness or paradise that lies beyond the frontier. Stories are often about either the hero's establishment of law and order in this wilderness (the bringing of civilisation to the west), or the hero's escape from the constraints of civilisation to live life more fully outside the law and society (often also a journey of self-discovery for the hero). The idea of crossing the frontier, of going west to a 'manifest destiny', is central to American culture. This goes back to the very formation of America by European colonists, who sought freedom from the political and religious constraints of Europe. The ideal of the USA as a land of freedom and opportunity is encapsulated in the continual search for new frontiers, new freedoms. (Science-fiction films, which portray space or cyberspace as the final frontier, continue this tradition and the connection between the two genres is evident in hybrid films such as *Cowboys & Aliens*.) The western traditionally explores the historical period when America established its new civilisation beyond the frontier, roughly from 1860–90.

Table 14.1 gives examples of Kitses' binary oppositions.

Table 14.1 Kitses' oppositions

THE WILDERNESS	CIVILISATION
The Individual	**The Community**
freedom	restriction
honour	institutions
self-knowledge	illusion
integrity	compromise
self-interest	social responsibility
solipsism	democracy
Nature	**Culture**
purity	corruption
experience	knowledge
empiricism	legalism
pragmatism	idealism
brutalisation	refinement

THE WILDERNESS	CIVILISATION
savagery	humanity
The West	The East
America	Europe
the frontier	America
equality	class
agrarianism	industrialism
tradition	change
the past	the future

Source: Adapted from Kitses 2004

The beauty of this schema is that it can be interpreted in many different ways, which makes it a rich framework for storytelling. The wilderness, for example, can be seen positively as a paradise of freedom and beauty as opposed to the restrictive and corrupt world of civilisation, or negatively as a savage and brutal world in need of the restraining control of civilisation. The history of the western shows significant changes in its representations over time, one example being the way Native Americans were portrayed initially as savage redskins or Indians (opposed to the cowboys), but gradually came to be represented more positively as humane, intelligent carers of the land, as seen in *Dances with Wolves*. Other critics have regarded the western as a blank canvas on which a whole multitude of stories can be presented, giving it great diversity.

All of the above description shows how the western worked through patterns of repetition and variation, and established codes and conventions that enabled filmmakers an opportunity to develop their own concerns, and provided a formula that was easily followed by audiences and easily produced by film studios. Its popularity at the box office made it a money maker.

The western was extremely popular from the earliest days of silent film with films that included *The Great Train Robbery*. It developed its own iconography (as mentioned above), familiar plots, and stars such as Roy Rogers, and reached a high point in the 1940s and 1950s through the films of John Ford that featured, among other stars, John Wayne and Henry Fonda. Films in this period explored new psychological aspects, but after this period the genre lost some of its popularity. In the late 1960s, when US film censorship regulations were relaxed, the western was reinvented by filmmakers such as Italian Sergio Leone, who made what came to be called 'spaghetti westerns' (often shot in Spain), and Sam Peckinpah. Leone used Clint Eastwood as an antihero, and he and Peckinpah introduced much bleaker, more extreme representations of violence and moral ambiguity that challenged many of the earlier ideals and reworked the western conventions. Their films were also seen as commentaries on the political events and culture of the 1960s and 1970s, such as the Vietnam War.

Westerns then declined in popularity, apart from occasional films such as *True Grit*, *Django Unchained*, *The Unforgiven*, *The Hateful Eight*, or *The Homesman*, but many films continued to reference western themes, such as *Serenity*, *No Country for Old Men*, and *Cowboys & Aliens*, each of which took aspects of the western and reworked them in a contemporary or furturistic setting, illustrating genre hybridisation: *Serenity*, a space-western film by Joss Whedon, drew heavily on western iconography, particularly the landscape. This futuristic science fiction–western hybrid film also embedded the use of speech associated with westerns, as well as the political and historical environment, but radically altered the time to a future frontier, while retaining the typical western narrative as post-civil war. *Cowboys & Aliens* was a science-fiction–western film set in 1873. It revolved around an outlaw, a wealthy cattle owner, and a traveller who rallied together to attempt to save a group of people in an Arizona town from alien abduction. The Coen brothers' film *No Country for Old Men* was based on the Cormac McCarthy book of the same name. It was a type of modern western with mythological themes juxtaposed across the Texas landscape. *No Country for Old Men* updated the typical western film slightly, as the film is not set in the old west, but rather 1980. The Coen brothers subverted formal expectations within *No Country* by abstaining from a salient musical score. This allowed for a focus on the material components.

In 2005 *Brokeback Mountain* broke new ground by presenting an explicitly gay cowboy story (many earlier westerns had homoerotic elements, as did the recent Jesse James film; see below). Television series such as *McLeod's Daughters* and *Deadwood* heralded a potential revival of the genre. The extreme language of *Deadwood* meant that it was not broadcast on free-to-air television stations in Australia, but it nevertheless established a popular following through cable and DVD rentals. *Deadwood* mixes aspects of soap opera with western themes, and goes further than Leone and Peckinpah in highlighting the grim brutality of frontier life. Its success may have prompted big film productions that brought films such as *The Assassination of Jesse James by the Coward Robert Ford* into cinemas in 2007 and, more recently, westerns such as the Coen brothers' remake of *True Grit* (2010). The Jesse James film was a big-budget film starring Brad Pitt. It was a long film that was very much a psychological character study, rather than an action-packed adventure, but it featured familiar western imagery and plot lines—hats, guns, horses, the wide open landscape, train robberies, gunfights. It also reworked the Jesse James story, which had already been the subject of over thirty feature films. Critics noted that the film could be interpreted as a study on the theme of celebrities and their fans, which linked it to contemporary twenty-first century culture and another example of how a western can be used to deal with contemporary concerns (see Chapter 23).

The film poster (Figure 14.2) contains significant western elements: the gun, holster, and belt, the clothes, particularly Ford's hat, the landscape, and the print font of the film's title, which is similar to that of old 'wanted' posters. Yet the poses of the characters suggest contemplation and introspection rather than action, and thus point to the main themes of the film and suggest a difference from more typical action westerns. The advertising caption, 'A MASTERWORK!', also seeks to elevate the western to the status of art, beyond the pulp-fiction aesthetic of many westerns.

Figure 14.2 *The Assassination of Jesse James by the Coward Robert Ford* poster

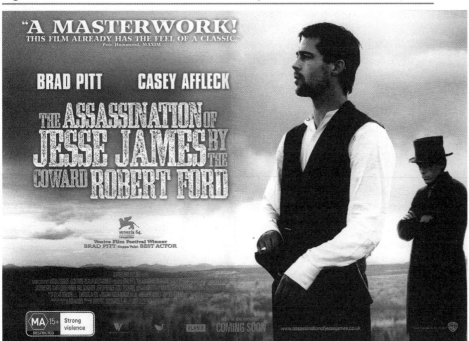

While these new westerns have been moderately successful, it seems unlikely that there will be a return to mass production of the genre. For contemporary audiences it is perfectly possible to watch and enjoy new westerns without extensive knowledge of the genre, but insight into the genre's familiar codes and conventions can heighten appreciation and understanding.

CODES AND CONVENTIONS

Can the meanings of media conventions change over time?

Genres work on the basis of codes and conventions that are easily recognised by the audience, mainly because of their familiarity. This is evident in our earlier discussions of semiology (pp. 124–5) and media images of smoking (p. 53). Can the meanings of film codes and conventions change through time? Can they be reworked so that they are not necessarily fixed to one meaning? James Dean and Judy Garland are now widely recognised as gay icons, though they would not have been understood as such by mainstream audiences when their films were first released. In this case the cultural context has changed radically, and this has resulted in a rereading of classic texts in light of discoveries about the private lives of the stars, and public perceptions of what forms of sexuality are deemed acceptable or even cool.

The history of art and cultural production is a history of people finding new styles, new aesthetic conventions, and new means of representation and expression. It is also replete with examples of people rediscovering and reworking old styles into something new—neoclassicism, neorealism, postmodernism, and so on. Each new style is seen initially as an aesthetic breakthrough, as unconventional and challenging. Such innovations supplant more traditional, conservative styles and are often rejected by some people because they are too radical. In time, the new style becomes familiar and conventional, so that eventually it does not have the same impact and its meaning changes. It becomes traditional and clichéd, and in time more new styles and conventions emerge that offer further breakthroughs.

A good example of the way conventions can change in the way they are used is found in the evolution of the filmmaking style known as **montage**. In the 1920s, Russian filmmakers such as Sergei Eisenstein and Dziga Vertov developed a stylistic form of editing known as Soviet montage. Montage is the practice of joining or editing short pieces of film together as the basis for telling stories. First used in the 1920s, it was designed to complement the revolutionary ideals of the communist revolution, and was theorised as a film style that was radically different from the conventional techniques of the capitalist Hollywood filmmaking system. Today the aesthetic techniques of Soviet montage continue to thrive, but they are no longer the exclusive province of radical filmmaking. On the contrary, montage has been taken over by mainstream filmmakers, and the best place to see it in action today is in advertising or on MTV (which is really an extended advertisement for the music industry)—the most potent forms of capitalist screen production.

What we can see from this is that a particular film style or convention does not guarantee particular kinds of political or social use or meaning. Forms and conventions can be used in different contexts to give them different meanings. This is very important in film and video because many new techniques are often developed for radical and innovative purposes. Like Soviet montage, they may be used originally to challenge the dominant system, but they can then be appropriated by the dominant system, which uses the same technique in a non-challenging way. This can be seen as another instance of hegemonic recuperation (see p. 182). The most innovative television advertisements often borrow techniques, styles, and conventions from experimental, radical filmmakers. The surrealist films of Czech animator Jan Svankmajer challenged the conventions of his society, but his techniques—and, indeed, he himself—have been used by advertisers to sell commodities.

MONTAGE ▶

Montage (the French word for 'editing') refers to two specific ways of joining together shots from different spaces and times—MTV-style collage of images set to music, and/or Soviet montage or political montage using Sergei Eisenstein's technique of juxtaposition.

Koyaanisqatsi

Filmmaker Godfrey Reggio is an interesting case of someone who was very aware of conventions and how to use them. He was the director of the films *Koyaanisqatsi* and *Powasqaatsi* (similar to *Baraka*). In his previous work, which aimed to raise public awareness about the abuse of young people, he used advertising billboards, where he employed 'conventional techniques in an unconventional way' (Reggio 1990). In other words, he took the apparatus of capitalist advertising to promote radical, socialist ideas.

Reggio (1990) has stated that in *Koyaanisqatsi* and *Powasqaatsi* he was 'trying to let people see from another point of view things that we see every day—looking for things people have seen zillions of times to see them afresh, from another point of view'. He hoped that his images would shock and disturb viewers, making them question where modern society is going. He wanted to do this as spectacularly as possible, partly to attract the audience, but also to draw attention to the way our society is becoming increasingly fascinated by spectacle and images. He used the techniques of time-lapse photography to critique modern-day industrial societies. By speeding up the action, the humans who are portrayed appear as insects or robots, functioning unthinkingly, automatically. This technique also shows the city as an animated, live creature, whose arteries pulsate with the red and white corpuscles of speeding car lights replayed in fast motion. When it was first released *Koyaanisqatsi* was an unusual film to watch. It gave audiences pleasure but challenged the dominant ideology. Since then, the techniques that Reggio used to critique society have once again been appropriated by advertisers to celebrate modern societies: accelerated images of urban societies are constantly used as trailers to promote commercial television stations and programs such as *Las Vegas*, or as advertisements to sell gas and electricity.

Paradoxically, it has now become somewhat conventional to use unconventional images to try to create audience interest. In the 1990s, some of the advertising campaigns for the Benetton clothing company were similar to Reggio's work in that they used unusual, shocking images such as portraits of convicted murderers and serial rapists on death row. This form of campaign aims to raise awareness of issues such as the death penalty at the same time as heightening consumer recognition and awareness of the Benetton brand. The tension between these two objectives (one humanitarian, the other profit driven) has led to accusations that Benetton is guilty of the commodification of social issues.

Juice magazine caused a stir when it featured photos of supposedly murdered corpses (as if taken by police photographers) in clothes advertisements with the words 'Fashion to die for' (Figures 14.3 and 14.4). These styles and the images associated with them were attempts to break taboos of what is acceptable.

The development of cartoons over the past fifteen years shows a similar tendency to challenge conventions. When *The Simpsons* was first produced (in 1990) it was considered too shocking to be broadcast on British television. The 'Itchy and Scratchy' cartoons within the show were considered particularly gruesome. Gradually, *The Simpsons* has become more and more accepted and popular, and less shocking, but newer cartoon shows such as *American Dad* and *Archer* have pushed the boundaries further in terms of what is conventionally acceptable and funny.

Figures 14.3 and 14.4 These fashion spreads in *Juice* are examples of heroin chic

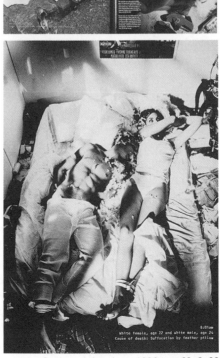

Source: *Juice*, June 1996, pp. 62–3, 66

Dogma 95 (spelt 'Dogme' in Europe) is a recent film movement that deliberately defines itself in opposition to mainstream filmmaking practices, by attempting to challenge the dominant ideology. Members of the Dogma collective sign a vow of chastity that is a set of realist rules or conventions based on the Dogma manifesto, among them that Dogma filmmakers vow to avoid the high-budget illusions of commercial Hollywood cinema by shooting on location using hand-held digital video, natural light, and available props. They don't use special effects, non-diegetic music, fancy editing, or genre formulas. They aim to get back to the essence of filmmaking as compelling storytelling, rather than focusing on filmmaking as a commercial venture. Those who make Dogma-style films feel that mainstream filmmakers have their artistic integrity compromised by commercial constraints. Directors, for instance, are sometimes compelled to use a certain star in order to obtain financial backing for a film, or are asked to change an ending or cut a scene to get a broader age rating so more people will see the film. Another Dogma rule states that, in recognition that film production is a collaborative process, film directors don't get credited as the author of the film. In a sense, Dogma filmmakers are making an ideological statement resisting capitalism and individualism through their aesthetic choices, conventions, and filmmaking practices.

TELEVISION GENRES

While the concept of genre works for both film and television texts, there are important differences and some genres are medium specific. Reality-based programming such as news, documentary, lifestyle shows, game shows, and reality television typically don't translate well to film. There are exceptions, such as feature-length documentaries, the *Jackass* movies, and films about reality television (*The Truman Show*, *American Dreamz*) or news broadcasting (*Morning Glory*), but film lacks the sense of immediacy and 'liveness' that these television genres rely on. Imagine going to the cinema once every few weeks to watch the news, or spending nine or ten hours in the cinema watching a fortnight's worth of *MasterChef* or *The Bachelor*. Television also operates on the basis of a predictable schedule organised around the assumption of a general audience that may include people of all ages; hence the restrictions of scheduling family-friendly content also impact on what genres are developed for television, and how audiences use genre as a concept that guides viewing choices.

The different schedules and time scales of film and television production, and the size and nature of the stories told relate to a key difference determining the genres found in each medium: narrative structures. Film genres tend to feature closed storylines that are resolved by the end of the film, whereas television genres tend to be open narratives developed in episodic instalments each night or each week, which means that certain genres, such as romantic comedy, that lead inevitably towards a closed ending aren't well suited to television: as soon as the couple forms, the incentive to keep watching the series would evaporate. Furthermore, serial television genres, such as medical dramas like *Nurse Jackie*, *The Night Shift*, *Grey's Anatomy*, and *House*, that lack a strong central storyline and are constantly introducing new characters and dilemmas, have few corollaries on the big screen.

The closest examples of an ongoing narrative in genre film are film franchises and sequels, such as the James Bond films and the *Pirates of the Caribbean* series. The enormous popularity of such series suggests a degree of convergence between film and television, and changes in audience and industry practices that impact on genre. Film sequelisation capitalises on the addictive desire to know what happens next when a story ends with a cliffhanger; it also harnesses audience allegiance to characters such as Captain Jack Sparrow or James Bond. The film industry uses these attributes, which are associated with the serialised narratives of television genres, to enhance the appeal of the action blockbuster genre—a genre that is exclusive to the cinema due to its massive budget and the need for big stars, location shooting, and special effects.

Because television is consumed mostly in private homes equipped with devices such as DVD recorders and remote controls, television audiences need to be able to recognise genres much more swiftly as they channel surf and search for something to watch. Neale describes this as the 'rapid deployment of genre-recognition skills' (2001, p. 4). This need for clear branding of genres has led to the increasing use of sonic branding, with theme songs and canned laughter frequently used to signal genre, and visual branding, using digital onscreen graphics such as program and channel logos popping up at the bottom of the screen. Changes in the media industry and audience practices since the 1980s have also seen the growing popularity of cable and satellite television, and with this the emergence of genre-specific channels such as the Sci-Fi Channel or Animal Planet to cater to true genre enthusiasts.

CONCLUSION

Most films and most television programs fit into a specific genre, and operate under similar principles to those outlined above, such as the use of repetition and variation, and of familiar plot lines or structures. Genre theory can also be applied to computer games, distinguishing particular types of game and the codes and conventions within which they operate, and noticing how they themselves often draw on the pre-existing imagery of popular cinema genres. Knowledge about genre should give you greater insight into cinema, television, and all the uses of the language of the moving image that are discussed in the next chapters.

This chapter has

- defined genre and its main characteristics
- noted the importance of repetition and variation within genres
- discussed the western as an example of genre
- examined how codes and conventions can change their meanings
- distinguished how genre functions differently for film and television industries and audiences.

? | DISCUSSION POINTS

1 How much is your own media consumption based on genre?
2 Apply Kitses' oppositional table (Table 14.1, p. 214) to any western.
3 Watch a Dogma film such as *The Idiots*, *Celebration*, or *Italian for Beginners*. Consider how a mainstream Hollywood director such as Steven Spielberg would have filmed the same story, and how the experience of spectatorship differs. Why might Dogma filmmakers want to challenge Hollywood norms?

SUMMARY

You should now be able to

- define genre
- explain why genres are so popular
- identify the iconographic characteristics of specific genres
- show how genres operate on the principles of repetition and variation
- discuss generic features of the western
- use Kitses' oppositional table (Table 14.1, p. 214) to analyse a western
- define and illustrate the term 'generic hybridisation'
- use genre theory for analysing films and television programs
- comment on how filmic codes and conventions change over time.

CHAPTER 15

The Language of Film: *American Beauty*

I'm trying to find a way of making every frame, every shot in the movie, tell the same story.

Sam Mendes, director, *American Beauty*

This chapter will

- give a detailed analysis of a short sequence from the film *American Beauty*
- explore the conventions and language of film narrative
- focus specifically on the use of *mise en scène*, cinematography, editing, and sound
- help you with your own film or television textual analysis assignments.

Before reading this chapter, watch the opening two minutes of the film *American Beauty* and if possible view the whole film. It will be useful if you can refer back to this sequence using a DVD as you read the analysis below.

Having explored aspects of genre, the aim of this chapter is to show you how to go about a detailed textual analysis of a short sequence of film, video, or television by exploring the four elements of the 'language of film' (Bordwell & Thompson 2004): ***mise en scène***, **cinematography**, **editing**, and **sound**. Each of these aspects needs to be looked at closely. While this chapter focuses specifically on a feature film, the analytic techniques presented will be useful for analysing any media moving-image form.

The way film language is analysed here should be helpful in showing how you could approach an assignment or essay in which you are required to undertake a close analysis of cinematic style.

For this kind of detailed sequence analysis, you should transcribe what happens in every shot within the sequence, as demonstrated in the shot list at the end of this chapter. To transcribe a sequence, you will need to watch the sequence several times over, pausing repeatedly to take notes. It is helpful to watch once with the sound muted so that you can focus closely on the *mise en scène* (content of the shot), cinematography (how content is filmed), and editing. Then listen to the soundtrack without looking at the image, so as to focus on sound. Next, watch the vision with the sound up and note the relationship between sound and image. Later, add in extra details such as shot duration, and make notes about lighting, performance, and your responses to each shot. Finally, reflect on the significance and meaning of the different aspects that you have transcribed, and the relationships between them. Try to consider the impact that the different techniques have, as well as thinking about what the director's intentions might have been.

AMERICAN BEAUTY

The film *American Beauty*, directed by Sam Mendes, scripted by Alan Ball, with cinematography by Conrad Hall, was made and released in the USA in 1999. The film starred Kevin Spacey as Lester Burnham, a middle-aged family man re-evaluating his life. Annette Bening played Carolyn, his ambitious wife, and Thora Birch was Jane, his sullen teenage

◀ MISE EN SCÈNE

A French theatrical term meaning literally 'placed in the scene'. *Mise en scène* refers to what has been filmed: settings, objects, costumes, actors, and the way these are visually arranged and lit.

◀ CINEMATOGRAPHY

The processes of filming the *mise en scène*—how things are filmed. This includes the angles (for example, high or low) and positioning of the camera (for example, long-shot or close-up), focus and framing, any camera movements (for example, pan, track, zoom, or tilt), any special camera effects (for example, slow motion or time lapse), the film stock used, and processing methods.

◀ EDITING

The process of joining or splicing together separate pieces of film, separate shots. Edits may cut directly, dissolve, mix, fade, wipe, etc.

◀ SOUNDTRACK

The recorded combination of human voices, sound effects, and music.

daughter. Mena Suvari played Jane's beautiful friend, a cheerleader called Angela. This chapter will consider in detail how the film's *mise en scène*, cinematography, editing, and soundtrack contribute to the construction of meaning and emotional impact, by analysing a two-minute sequence starting immediately after the film's title. We will consider this with reference to typical film and narrative conventions.

According to Quentin Tarantino, 'In the first ten minutes of nine out of ten movies the movie tells you what kind of movie it's gonna be. It tells you everything that you basically need to know' (cited in Smith 1994, p. 42). Like many other films, the opening of *American Beauty* is very important because it is designed to establish the narrative world, introduce the characters and issues, and capture the audience's attention so that they want to keep watching. The film actually begins with a short sequence in which Jane, Lester's daughter, is talking and being videoed by her boyfriend, Ricky. Our analysis starts after this as the title of the film appears.

The film's title

American Beauty was successful at the box office and with critics, winning five Oscars. 'American Beauty' is the name of a particular rose, and roses and rose petals were significant images in the film, but the film's title can be read as being about contemporary American society and values in general, and about the nature of beauty. There are many films exploring such issues, supporting or questioning the ideals of America and the American dream; these often focus on single individuals or families as a way of personalising the issues. However, a title such as 'Meet the Burnhams' or 'Lester's Life' would have lost this general social aspect. Such explorations of family relationships and human desires can also be relevant to many non-American audiences. Note that the film was directed by Sam Mendes, an Englishman, who felt it was relevant to his own life and states in the director's commentary on the DVD that the theme of the film was that 'Beauty is found in the places you least expect it'.

Mendes regarded the film as a satire but also as 'something far more haunting and poetic' (Mendes 2004). He saw it as a film in which all the main characters are 'trapped in prisons of their own making at the beginning and then gradually escape ... It becomes a rites-of-passage story for all of them' (Mendes 2004). Mendes also comments that he tends to read scripts in visual terms, that is, he finds visual means to interpret the script: 'I'm trying to find a way of making every frame, every shot in this movie tell the same story' (Mendes 2004). This draws our attention to the visual combination of cinematography and *mise en scène*, and we aim to explore how he uses these to tell the story.

Shot 1, the first shot after the film's title—*American Beauty*—is important visually and for its soundtrack; it lasts a long time, 22 seconds, and acts as a conventional **establishing shot** to show us Lester's neighbourhood. It is an aerial shot: the camera slowly moves down from the sky to focus on Lester's street. It allows us to see the whole of Lester's community, suggesting that the film is about an individual—Lester and his family—and a neighbourhood typical of many American suburbs. From the trees we can see it is autumn or winter, a time of death. Note also that this shot is repeated but in reverse at the end of the film (see also narrative structure on pp. 249–52). To make the introduction of this shot smooth, it fades in so the scene gradually appears before us, rather than plunging us straight into the action. In contrast, at the end of the film there is a direct cut to a black screen and silence, which Mendes hoped would be conventionally jarring for the

ESTABLISHING SHOT ▶

A wide or long shot conventionally used to show the whole of a location or set so that we can see and understand the space the action is taking place in. Normally followed by shots that are closer to the action.

audience, his 'final attempt to keep the audience on the wrong foot'. This, and all quotes from Mendes used in our analysis, can be found on the director's commentary on the *American Beauty* DVD.

This aerial, overview, bird's-eye view is typical of many films but it is particularly apt for this film: its view from the heavens is linked with Lester's voice-over, which is speaking after his death—maybe from heaven. The camera is positioned at a high angle, looking down on the action in many instances throughout the film, reinforcing the sense that Lester is a disembodied spirit looking back on his life. In terms of *mise en scène*, it is worth noting that the suburb is full of houses that look very similar and the colour is somewhat muted. These aspects of *mise en scène* suggest a community of dull conformity and order.

Music and sound

The soundtrack combines two main elements: music and Lester's voice-over. The music starts just before the image appears. This is a conventional narrative device. We are used to seeing images and hearing music together and, though the music is often **non-diegetic sound** (that is, sound added from a source outside the story world, as opposed to **diegetic sound**), audiences are happy to hear the music as emotionally appropriate to the visuals.

◄ NON-DIEGETIC SOUND

Sound that comes from somewhere outside the story world, such as the musical score, which the screen characters cannot hear.

The music is very carefully woven into this opening sequence to give us a sense of rhythm and to highlight key points in the script. It combines subtly with Lester's voice-over and the cutting between shots, as if punctuating the sequence, alerting us to what is most significant. There is one central musical phrase that is repeated forty times, in ten cycles (or verses) of four. There are several pauses and variations so that it retains audience interest, but once we have heard the first cycle we can anticipate the music quite predictably.

◄ DIEGETIC SOUND

Sound that comes directly from the fictional world (the diegesis) of a screen text.

Repetition is a common device in music, particularly in the increasingly popular minimalist music of the late twentieth and early twenty-first centuries. Constant repetition can produce a sense of timelessness, finding beauty in something very simple. This might be linked to the neighbour Ricky's ideas of beauty in the film, shown in the sequence where he has filmed a bag blown by the wind repeatedly going round in circles (like this music). Alternatively, the musical repetition might be equivalent to the repetitious vicious circle and dullness of Lester's suburban life.

The first musical pause comes straight after Lester says, 'This is my neighbourhood'. There is a single high note played as the cycle ends, as if to give a musical full stop, while we take in what we are hearing and seeing. The second pause coincides with Lester's own dramatic pause after his comment, 'In less than a year I'll be dead.' This is a striking statement and it sets up one of the major narrative questions and audience hooks: how, when, and why will Lester die? To give more emphasis to this statement, the audience also has the first cut in this sequence, to shot 2 (the overhead view of Lester in bed), with the sound of the ringing alarm clock. Cutting in this way doesn't just move the narrative forward: it highlights the drama. The jarring clock counterpoints Lester's alarming statement and is a symbolic wake-up call.

After he stops the alarm there is a wonderful addition to the music soundtrack: a brief descending, coming-down sound that is finished with a single low, thudding bass note, on the first beat of the next cycle. This coming-down sound complements the visually descending camera movement and angles. It also parallels Lester's own spiritual and emotional state as he is coming down to earth and realising the inadequacies of his life.

Shot 3 is a dog's-eye view of Lester's feet and his slippers from under his bed. The low-level camera works with the music to show that Lester is, at this point in his life, feeling as low as he can go. Because the shot size has moved from the first extreme long shot through tighter framing to a close-up, this sequence draws the audience into increasing intimacy with the character as Lester's voice-over invites us into his suburb, his home, and now his emotional life.

The musical phrase begins its third cycle and Lester resumes his monologue. As this cycle is coming to an end, Lester makes another dramatic comment: 'In a way I'm dead already.' This time the music doesn't pause, but to highlight the drama the next cycle is played an octave higher to lift the drama and intensity (a quick drumbeat is added to the music), and played with no voice-over; we are simply able to observe Lester (shots 4–6) and enjoy the music. As the cycle ends, Lester says, 'Look at me', and this leads directly and powerfully into the next, the fifth cycle, which is highlighted by the bass note on the first beat, but also a brief rising sequence leading into the first beat.

The beginning of the sixth cycle coincides with a shift from Lester, inside the house, to Carolyn, his wife, outside the house. There is no pause in the music, but to parallel this shift in location and character the music changes by adding another descending sound, by using a string instrument rather than marimba, and by lowering the volume. The change and development in the music help us follow the change and development of the narrative.

Film music is rarely analysed in great depth, but can be hugely important in creating atmosphere and in highlighting, complementing, and developing the drama and the narrative.

Lester's voice-over

Lester's voice-over introduction provides important narrative information and gives us a particular viewpoint, or sound-point, from which to understand this story. It also draws on the *film noir* convention in which the main character tells events through voice-over, relating events in flashback form and so constructing a circular narrative that ends where it started. *American Beauty* is thus linked to the *noir* themes of mystery, murder, darkness, and circularity. The specific idea of a character giving their life story after their death is found in *Sunset Boulevard*, the *film noir* that Ball and Mendes were both conscious of; cine-literate audiences would also note this reference.

The use of voice-over encourages audiences to form a specific affinity with the character who is speaking. By hearing how Lester sees the world, we too begin to see and hear things from his point of view (this is also visually encouraged in shots 13, 15, and 16, which show Lester watching and listening to the other characters). Thus an identification and sympathy are established with Lester right from the start, but through *film-noir* conventions we are used to such characters being doomed and/or flawed. If we just saw him being a loser at the beginning of the film, we might not value him; if we heard about him from his wife's point of view, we might see him differently, but because we hear his point of view (and clearly he has some self-awareness about his own limitations), we are invited to be on his side. Mendes comments that there is 'something so wonderfully lonely about the voice that hovers over the film … a loneliness that is present in much of the movie'. The voice-over sets up this mood, working with the bird's-eye view of the camera to create a sense that Lester is somehow alienated from his own life. This loneliness is also established in the way that Lester is isolated in screen space. In the opening sequence he is not interacting with anyone and he is often alone throughout the film.

Cinematography, *mise en scène*, and editing

Shot 2 is an overhead shot of Lester in bed. It is significant both cinematographically and in terms of *mise en scène*. Overhead shots are not used often. They do not represent a normal, human point of view or perspective. The view relates to the previous shot, which was also high up, so it is a continuation of this god-like, aerial perspective and gradually moving to earth. But conventionally, this viewpoint, particularly within the home, is disturbing and disorienting. It signifies that this domestic home is out of balance: something is wrong, dysfunctional. In terms of *mise en scène*, it shows a man alone in a double bed. This also says something about his relationship with his absent partner—he is alone. The distorted shadow of the lampshade on the left also expresses the disturbance of his domestic life. Colour is important here: Mendes remarks that 'the story is told in terms of colour'; the film has a 'muted palette' and is 'very monochromatic, blues and greys, probably the most colour you see for the first half hour, apart from the red of the roses' (Mendes 2004). In this opening sequence, there seems to be a contrast between the outside of the house and inside. From the outside Lester's life appears to be shiny bright and picture perfect, as represented by the bold colours, particularly green, red, white, and blue in the exterior shots, but from the inside his house looks and feels gloomier, more shadowy. This shot shows the monochromatic muted palette with the blue sheets, paralleling the depressing tone of his interior monologue; both suggest the dullness and shadow quality of Lester's suburban life.

At the end of shot 2, Lester starts to roll over and we cut to a close-up of him completing this movement and then facing the camera, still placed above him, with considerable shadow cast across his face, again emphasising the darkness of Lester's life. This camera position is not so strange as we are now close to Lester's face. The editing sequence has thus moved us in three successive shots from extreme long establishing shot, to long shot, to close-up. This is a typical and conventional method of camera storytelling. Film theorists David Bordwell and Kristin Thompson (2004, p. 310) note how standard editing techniques, known as **continuity editing**, developed as a way of making stories unfold seamlessly, a way of smoothing out the potential disruption of editing from one space to another.

The use of 'match-on-action' (see Bordwell & Thompson 2004, p. 315), wherein a movement or action is started in one shot and completed in the next, is one such technique: here, Lester's rolling movement is the action that is matched between the two shots to provide continuity and smoothness between shots. Because we are watching Lester move, we aren't disturbed by the cut; indeed, we may not even be consciously aware of it. Meanwhile, the look on Lester's face, which we can now study closely, confirms the midlife crisis and dysfunctionality already indicated by his comments on his own deadness, and by the cinematography and *mise en scène*.

Shots 4–6 continue to focus on Lester; they show him putting on slippers and in the shower. The slippers connote dullness and lack of glamour, while the dog's-eye view from under the bed might signify a sense of unease, of something watching and lurking unseen in suburbia, as well as showing the final coming down to earth of this sequence. In terms of colour, the shower shots use dull blues and greys though the camera movement gives

◄ CONTINUITY EDITING

A system of editing, established in Hollywood by about 1920, for telling stories smoothly. It uses particular techniques and conventions for filming within a scene such as the use of establishing shot, use of shot–reverse–shot, eyeline match, match on action, observance of 180 degree rule, and continuity of action, sound, and lighting.

some dynamism to the shots. 'Moving pictures', as cinema has been called, are about movement that provides spectator interest. Filmmakers create movement either by having something move within the scene—Lester rolling over—or by moving the camera, as in shots 1, 5, 6, 7, 10, 12, and 15. The shower shot also has a certain shock value in showing Lester jerking off, masturbating, confirming his anti-hero status. The *mise en scène* places Lester behind the glass door and the frames of the shower, contributing to Mendes' aim to find a visual way of showing Lester's imprisonment, the first of a visual 'series of jail cells'. We see this again in shots 13, 15, and 16, which show Lester behind the prison bars of the window. This is a great way of visually signifying that the often-idealised domestic home is actually a prison, trapping Lester, while the glass barriers illustrate the way he is separated from other people.

Shot duration often decreases and the pace of editing will increase in order to heighten suspense around the climactic moments in a scene, sequence, or story, a form of **rhythmic editing** or **rhythmic montage**. In this sequence the first and last shots are quite long (22 and 20 seconds), which gives a sense of balance and the time to take in these important shots. The overall pace, with several of the shots lasting about 5 seconds, is typical of contemporary commercial cinema editing. As cinema has developed, the speed of editing has increased. Audiences are stimulated by constant change and are also quick readers of visual images. Commercial cinema and television, with the need to please audiences, have increased the pace of their editing, which is one reason that older films seem slower to us: in terms of editing pace, they usually are.

> RHYTHMIC EDITING OR RHYTHMIC MONTAGE ▶
>
> Rhythmic editing means the pace of editing—how long each shot lasts.

Cutting the rose

Shot 7, the extreme close-up of the red rose, is very significant. It is the rose of the title and red (in complete contrast to the dull blues and greys) is the most important colour in the film. Red was a major element in the advertising posters, which showed the image of the rose petals that are also central to Lester's sexual fantasy. It is the colour of blood, which is shown dramatically at the end. Throughout the film, sexuality, passion, beauty, anger, and death are all linked by the colour red. The camera tilts down until the rose is cut. This downward movement is again linked to Lester's description of his own life and all the camera movement that has gone before, paralleling Lester's comment: 'It's all downhill from here.' The next shot reveals that it is Carolyn, Lester's wife, who has cut the rose, so the rose leads us into the next sequence of the narrative. The red rose thus acts in terms of developing the narrative, what comes immediately before and after, and in setting up an important **motif** that will be developed later in the film.

> MOTIF ▶
>
> Any significant element (an object, colour, place, sound, camera movement, or angle) that recurs or is developed throughout a film.

But it has further meanings. To emphasise its power, the shot is an extreme close-up that fills the screen in sharp contrast to all the earlier colours: no words are spoken over it and there is no background distraction: we are totally focused on the rose. This technique of blurring out the background is used again in the cheerleaders' sequence when Lester fantasises about Angela: as we go into extreme close-up of Lester's face, the background of other spectators has just become black; similarly, when the camera focuses on Angela, the other girls have disappeared and the gym background has been darkened. Since she is heavily associated with the rose petals, it is worth noting the similarity of technique in these two sequences that are connected to the American Beauty rose. Note also that the focus used in this close-up is very sensitive to any change in focal distance so that, as the camera tilts down, it has to pull focus: this takes the petals out of focus but brings the stem, which we are now looking at, into focus. This could represent a movement in our attention from petals (seductive beauty) to thorns (the dangerous power of the femme fatale), or from the beautiful façade of Lester's life to the fact that his life is about to be nipped in the bud, or it could simply be a way of directing our attention to the act of cutting that takes place next.

The cutting of the rose is particularly important when we consider it in relation to editing or montage. The Russian filmmakers and theorists of the early twentieth century argued that when any two images are shown one after another, viewers will link them, seeing a relationship and producing a reading or meaning based on this relationship. Sergei Eisenstein claims that the editing process is central to the composition of meaning in a film because spectators form 'associative links' between shots (Eisenstein 1992, p. 147). 'Montage,' he writes, 'is an idea that arises from the collision of independent shots' (Eisenstein 1992, p. 140). Eisenstein describes one kind of editing process as **intellectual editing** or **intellectual montage** whereby two linked images produce a concept or idea.

The first image here is of Lester masturbating, the second of Carolyn cutting the rose; thus a link is created between Lester's upstanding penis and the full-bloom red rose (even though Lester's penis is not actually visible, but is purely imagined). In terms of intellectual montage, Carolyn's action, cutting the rose in this next shot, can then be understood as a form of symbolic castration, and, as we quickly come to realise, this is a good description of the current marital relationship between Lester and Carolyn, in which he has been emasculated within the domestic setting and Carolyn has become the dominant partner. This is a good visual illustration of how filmmakers can convey a huge amount of information about characters in a single image or action. In the briefest of moments, Carolyn's castrating character and her relationship with Lester are encapsulated.

Shots 7–9

In the three shots (7–9) that introduce Carolyn, we have another typical narrative film convention. Whereas the first three shots of the film moved from establishing long shot to close-up, here we have the reverse: close-up, where we are unsure exactly where we are but interest is created by the close-up itself, and by the questions—Where are we? Who is cutting the rose?—leading to mid-shot and then establishing shot, which places Carolyn in the garden, in front of her house.

There are several other points of interest in these shots. In relation to editing, note the technique of smoothly linking two shots by placing the main focus of visual interest in these different shots in the same area of the screen or frame; this is a form of **graphic editing** or **graphic montage**: in shot 7 the rose and its stem are placed just to the right of the centre of the frame, so that is the area we are focusing our attention on; the next shot (8) has Carolyn standing in exactly the same area of the frame or screen, so we are immediately focused on her. You can find other examples of this technique, most notably the cut from the aerial shot 1, where the main visual focus is on a small part of Lester's street, between the two rows of houses; this is exactly the same space on the screen that Lester's face is in for shot 2, so our eye is already focused on this spot, making the transition and narrative easy to follow.

In relation to framing (cinematography) and *mise en scène*, note how the establishing shot 9 places the camera directly at right angles to the street and garden fence in front of us. This position can be described as theatrical in that it replicates a front-on position

◄ INTELLECTUAL EDITING OR INTELLECTUAL MONTAGE

Two images linked together produce an idea or concept.

◄ GRAPHIC EDITING OR GRAPHIC MONTAGE

The linking of two separate shots through visual similarity or contrast.

in relation to the action, a position similar to the best seat in the house of a theatre, from where one looks at right angles to the stage. Some commentators have noted Mendes' main work as a theatre director and how at times he treated scenes almost as though they would be played on a theatre stage. One obvious example is the dinner-table sequence between Lester, Carolyn, and Jane. Once again the camera and audience are positioned at right angles, this time to the table. The resulting images are quite two-dimensional, quite flat, lacking any depth, which could be part of Mendes' satirical technique at this stage in the film to make Lester's home life seem flat.

Two other aspects of *mise en scène* worth noting are Carolyn's costume and the white picket fencing around the houses. Carolyn's costume is a grey, businesslike suit. It immediately tells us something about her character—she is a businesswoman, rather than a housewife. White picket fences are standard and stereotypical signifiers of idealised American dream homes, seen in countless films and television programs. Their appearance may be read satirically or ironically—that is, rather than seeing this as a perfect home and community, it is all too good to be true, so much so that we wonder about the problems lying beneath the surface.

SOUND BRIDGE ▶

Sound is used to link two separate shots.

At the end of shot 9 we hear the sound of a dog barking. This is an example of a **sound bridge**, which smoothly leads us to the next shot, where we see the dog. It also shows how off-screen sound works to extend the boundaries of screen space, helping the spectator to imagine an entire world that exists beyond the borders of the frame. Camera movement is motivated by the movement of the dog, so it is subordinated to narrative. This again is conventional in mainstream feature films and one way in which the 'cinematic apparatus', defined by Jean-Louis Baudry as 'the ensemble of equipment and operations necessary for the production of a film and its projection' (1992, p. 693), is often made invisible for the spectator. This means that all the processes of filmmaking—cameras and their movements, lighting, editing, sound booms, microphones, and so on (the cinematic apparatus)—are used to tell the story, but we as the audience are encouraged to focus on the story and not consciously notice any of the camera and sound-recording technology. The apparatus operates virtually invisibly; the skill of the filmmakers is in maintaining this invisibility. When this apparatus is accidentally revealed—seeing the sound boom or a continuity error, for example—the cinematic illusion is destroyed, often provoking laughter.

End of the sequence

The appearance of the dog, Fitzy, leads to the introduction of Lester's gay neighbours. There is satirical humour here: first, in their stereotypically camp concern with the dog's behaviour; second, in the fact that this conventional and normal neighbourhood can include gay men as part of that normality (their costume, too, is a very conformist style and colour); and third, in the clone-like naming of both of them as Jim, which draws attention to stereotyping since it represents gay men as a type, rather than as individuals. Such stereotyping is foregrounded and denaturalised throughout *American Beauty*, but it is also reinforced in problematic ways. Homosexuality and the dangers of its denial and repression will be a major theme in the film as represented by the neighbours just about to move in on the other side of Lester's house; indeed, the film might be seen as an exploration of aspects of masculinity since the male characters are the major figures in the film. (As a writer-producer on the TV series *Six Feet Under* and *True Blood*, Alan Ball also explored issues around homosexuality and death.)

The final shots (13–16) further demonstrate Lester's imprisonment, and his estrangement from Carolyn and the rest of the world. Shots 13 and 16 both show Lester framed/imprisoned by the window. This sequence encourages us to observe Lester, as well as, through editing, to see the world through his eyes. In shot 13 he is seen watching and so we assume that the next shot will be his point of view. We are thus being stitched, by the editing and cinematography, into seeing the world through Lester's eyes, which we do in shot 16 as he looks out of the window.

Shot 16 is the most cinematographically complex shot in the sequence; it combines with sound manipulation to further draw us into Lester's world. The shot begins with the camera tracking from left to right as Jim and Carolyn meet. This movement allows it to frame Lester in the background between Jim and Carolyn. Initially, Jim and Carolyn's trivial conversation dominates the shot—they are in the foreground, Lester is in the background and out of focus, and at first we probably don't notice him. Gradually, this situation is reversed using three separate techniques. First, the camera slowly zooms in on Lester until Carolyn and Jim are excluded from the frame. Second, at the same time it does a literal change of focus, so that Carolyn and Jim go out of focus while Lester becomes clearly defined. And third, to complement this visual change, there is an equivalent pulling focus in the soundtrack as the sound of Carolyn and Jim's conversation fades away while Lester's voice comes back into prominence. Thus we have come back to Lester's point of view, which is where we started with his voice-over. This short sequence has introduced major aspects of Lester's life and now the story can begin.

Table 15.1 Shot list for opening sequence of *American Beauty*

1	22 sec.	Music: Fade-in of extreme long shot (ELS): aerial view of Lester's neighbourhood; camera slowly descends; voice-over and music.
2	10 sec.	High-angle long shot (LS) Lester in bed, alarm clock ringing; switches off alarm and begins to roll over; coming-down sound effect; music, and voice-over.
3	7 sec.	High-angle close-up (CU) Lester; match on action as he rolls over; music starts with higher pitch.
4	3 sec.	CU slippers. Low-level 'dog's-eye view' shot from under the bed.
5	4 sec.	CU shower and Lester's face, camera pans left to right; shower sounds.
6	13 sec.	Medium shot (MS) Lester showering; camera continues to pan left to right and creep zooms in slightly; music develops; shower sounds.
7	4 sec.	CU rose tilt down; rose goes out of focus; focus on stem being cut, background out of focus.

(Continued)

Table 15.1 Shot list for opening sequence of *American Beauty* (Continued)

8	6 sec.	Medium close-up (MCU) Carolyn (wife) lifts up rose (she is in same place on screen as rose was in previous shot).
9	5 sec.	LS (establishing) Carolyn in left corner; 180 degrees—white picket fence—dog barks at end of shot, sound bridge.
10	2 sec.	CU rapid pan right to left; picket fence and dog.
11	4 sec.	LS Jim 1 at gate of fence with dog.
12	7 sec.	LS Jim 2 at door: camera pans right to left to two Jims and dog.
13	3 sec.	MCU Lester framed behind window.
14	3 sec.	LS of Jim approaching Carolyn.
15	20 sec.	MS Carolyn and Jim meeting; camera tracks forward and pans right to left to CU of Jim and Carolyn. Between them, in the background, Lester watches from the window and the camera slowly zooms towards him as his voice-over (V/O) begins, pulling focus from Carolyn and Jim to Lester.
16	6 sec.	CU behind Lester out of window to Carolyn and Jim.

CONCLUSION

In this analysis we have aimed to show how carefully a film sequence can be crafted. We have deconstructed the sequence, examining all the aspects of film language that communicate to us. This is a skilful example of film narrative and storytelling, producing a sequence that will engage its audience and which will then give an interesting view of contemporary American and Western families and society. We can learn a lot about how to make films and how they communicate to us through such detailed analysis. Further features of the film's narrative will be explored in subsequent chapters.

This chapter has

- demonstrated how to analyse a short film extract
- explored the language of film.

? DISCUSSION POINTS

1   What view of the American family does *American Beauty* present?
2   What is beautiful in *American Beauty*?
3   What other examples can you find of significant uses of *mise en scène* or cinematography in *American Beauty*?

SUMMARY

You should now be able to

- define and use the terms '*mise en scène*' and 'cinematography'
- explain the terms 'continuity editing', 'rhythmic', 'graphic', and 'intellectual editing'
- show how all of the above can contribute to a film's meanings and emotional effects
- be aware of how sound and music communicate in screen texts
- notice conventional techniques of narrative filmmaking
- do your own detailed analysis of any film, television, or DVD sequence.

CHAPTER 16

Narrative Structure and Binary Oppositions

We mostly understand ourselves through an endless series of stories told to ourselves by ourselves and others. The so-called facts of our individual worlds are arbitrary, facts that fit whatever fiction we have chosen to believe in.

Jeanette Winterson, *Art Objects: Essays on Ecstasy and Effrontery*

This chapter will

- define narrative
- explain and examine how narratives are structured
- examine the importance of the structural position of characters in narratives
- look closely at the significance of narrative endings
- explain and examine the term 'binary oppositions' in relation to narrative
- look at the way couples are represented in narratives.

This chapter will explore the narrative structures of fiction films and traditional television narratives.

THE IMPORTANCE OF NARRATIVE

What are narratives and why do we like them?

NARRATIVE ▶

A sequence of events taking place over a given period of time that are linked, mainly through cause and effect.

Narratives, or stories, are a basic way of making sense of our experience. This is a cultural process shared by all societies; humans understand and relate experiences through stories. When people talk about things that happen, both in fiction and in real life, they put these experiences into a story or **narrative** structure with a beginning, a middle, and an end. We have fictional stories, but we also have feature stories about current affairs in the newspaper, documentary stories, and sports stories. When we relate our own daily experiences—'How was your day at work?'—our accounts often come out as stories.

But stories and narratives are something more than this sequence of events. It is very normal to ask: what's the theme of the story? or, what's the moral of the story? This idea of stories having a moral, a point, or a lesson to teach goes back to stories such as Aesop's fables, biblical stories, myths, and legends, and is just as relevant today in media narratives. All these stories can be considered as means by which societies talk to themselves. They look at certain human issues and questions, and, by the end of the narrative, a solution, resolution, or overall message about the problem has been presented. Family sitcoms, for example, show us how to relate to teenage siblings or deal with parents; programs such as *Degrassi: Next Class*, *Pretty Little Liars*, *Awkward*, and *Gossip Girl* show us how to live out young adult sexuality and explore relationship issues. The logic of storytelling is to communicate some message, some point, and any good analysis or reading of that story will aim to try and understand what those messages are.

The aim of this chapter is to analyse how stories work by looking at their structure. The first stage will be to identify the components of any story's structure. The second, more significant, stage is to see how the narrative structure relates to and affects the meaning of the story. The argument being made here is that the way a story is told or structured will affect how it is understood. When analysing the relationship between narrative structure and meaning, a detailed transcript, as was done for *American Beauty* in the previous chapter, would not be useful. It will be more helpful to make a rough map of the whole film, break it down into scenes, and note the function of each scene and character in the overall story. This technique, known as a 'plot segmentation' (Bordwell & Thompson 2004, p. 93), gives a film analyst an overview of how the story is organised in time, space, and causation. A plot segmentation of *American Beauty* would foreground the circular nature of the narrative, and would establish the relationships between the different storylines and characters.

NARRATIVE STRUCTURE AND STRUCTURALISM

The approach offered here is based on **structuralism**. Structuralism was developed in the field of anthropology, particularly by Claude Lévi-Strauss (1978), for analysing many aspects of human society, such as kinship patterns and cooking practices. It has also been used to study myths, and has been applied in many other academic areas. In media studies, structuralism is used to analyse narrative. Its broad aim is to go beneath the surface of any media text to see how the story structure contributes to meaning.

◄ STRUCTURALISM

A method of analysis that involves looking for and examining the underlying structures of meaning in language, social relationships, narratives, and so forth.

Can we identify specific structures in stories and are these structures important? ▶

The importance of narrative structure is made clearer if we distinguish structure from content. A useful example is to look at how gay characters have been represented in films. This is well documented in Vito Russo's book *The Celluloid Closet* (1981), which provided the basis for an excellent documentary film. He argues that most early representations of gay characters were negative, in that they laughed at and demeaned homosexuality, or showed gay characters as deviant and criminal. Russo argues that from the 1970s on, films sympathetic to or supportive of gay characters began to appear, but he draws attention to the way these characters are positioned or structured in the narrative. He finds that however sympathetically the gay characters may be portrayed, more often than not the story provides an unhappy ending for them, as is the case in *Dallas Buyers Club*, for instance. At the end of his book, Russo includes, alongside a bibliography and filmography, a necrology that charts the various endings assigned to gay characters, drawing attention to the predominance of unhappy endings for them: suicides, madness, solitude, imprisonment, death. The crucial point is that the narrative structure shows that gay characters will end up unhappy no matter how sympathetically they are portrayed. This is a damning conclusion. We can still see this tendency in films such as *Free Fall*, *Weekend*, and *Passion*, which do not have happy endings. Even *Carol* ends with just a glimmer of hope that the two women will find happiness together after a legal battle that ends with Carol losing custody of her young daughter.

Popular television series such as *Modern Family*, *Pretty Little Liars*, *Greek*, *Faking It*, *The Fosters*, and *RuPaul's Drag Race* are making homosexuality an accepted part of mainstream popular culture by making fun of it, celebrating it, and exploring (or exploiting) its dramatic potential with a range of ongoing stories, both sad and happy. The extended narratives of television mean that there isn't closure or resolution to the stories of many of these characters until the entire program is axed. This means that television has the potential to depict a wide range of possibilities, to open issues for ongoing discussion rather than closing the subject with a definitive ending. In some ways the ongoing storylines of television are closer to real life than the neat resolutions offered in many films because television always leaves us with new dilemmas, challenges, and questions.

HOW DOES NARRATIVE STRUCTURE DETERMINE MEANINGS?

Narrative pattern

There is a basic structural pattern to narratives. According to cultural theorist Tzvetan Todorov, all narrative is a movement between two equilibriums:

> At the start of the narrative there is always a stable situation ... something occurs which introduces a disequilibrium, a disturbance to this situation ... At the end of the story, the equilibrium is then re-established but is no longer that of the beginning (Todorov 1975, p. 163).

The equilibrium established at the end is a form of resolution of the questions, enigmas, and desires that have been introduced by the disturbance. This can be expressed diagrammatically (see Figure 16.1).

Figure 16.1 Basic structural pattern of narratives

The disturbing incident at the beginning of the story catalyses changes for the main characters, and often also sets up a goal or objective that the protagonist strives to attain. This creates a narrative question in the reader's or audience's mind that draws us through the story: we continually wonder how the protagonists will deal with the trials and tribulations they face. Of course, the central narrative question is only answered at the end of the story when the major crisis is finally resolved, but before that point we are seduced further into the narrative world as the main characters encounter obstacles, turning points, complications, and conflicts that threaten to prevent them from attaining their objectives. These dramas need to be overcome before a new equilibrium can be attained, and before the audience can feel a sense of narrative closure.

Consider how this works in the film *Legally Blonde*. The opening credits sequence shows Elle (Reese Witherspoon) in a stable and very positive situation. She is highly successful, adored by her women friends, and seemingly adored by her boyfriend. We see all this and hear the song 'Perfect Day', which confirms her happiness and stability. The stage is set for her prospective engagement. The disruption comes quickly (as in most films and stories, so as to immediately engage the viewer/reader) when she is dumped by her boyfriend and this then sets up a twofold goal, or enigma: her goal to get into Harvard and her goal to win her boyfriend back. Audience members want to know whether she will succeed in these goals. As the narrative proceeds these questions begin to be answered—we learn fairly soon that she does get into Harvard, so the question then becomes will she succeed there, and then later she gets involved in a particular court case and we want to know the outcome of that. New characters are introduced, and new disruptions and questions are set up.

All these questions reach a resolution at the end. The ending finishes off the story and provides a new stability, as well as answers to the central narrative questions.

There are several important consequences of the basic narrative structure. First, it suggests that all problems and disruptions must have a resolution, an answer, which means that narrative as a formal structure is a reassuring and comforting structure: even if the ending is potentially unhappy (in films that end with the death of the main characters, for example, such as *The Assassination of Jesse James* or *American Beauty*), at least it is resolved. This does not fit with our experience of real life: we know that the resolution to a problem often raises new problems, choices, or questions, and that there is rarely a definitive ending to situations or disruptions. Narratives, however, serve to put a reassuring frame on the way we see and structure life.

Second, because there is closure to the story, audiences are invited to do nothing more than feel an emotional response. The closure suggests finality, which means that the audience is not invited to act, to do something in response, even if it is a confronting story. This is an issue that some storytellers have wanted to challenge by creating stories that do not have closed narrative structures (see discussion of Brecht, pp. 291–2).

Third, the way stories are told suggests the inevitability of the outcome—there are no other possible solutions, it had to end that way. But it is possible to produce narratives that suggest a range of different outcomes and narrative possibilities. Films such as *Predestination* do this, while *Bill and Ted's Excellent Adventure* provides a humorous example with three possible endings. While such narratives are rare in film and television, a branching narrative structure that invites audience interaction and participation by offering choices among multiple pathways, settings, and character traits is increasingly common in computer games, interactive television, and other variants of computer-mediated communication. DVD releases of films often include as a special feature scenes that were not included in the final version, or an alternative ending that was shot but not used. This draws our attention to the fact that narratives are constructed, not inevitable outcomes.

Q&A—What importance do questions have in narrative structure?

Narratives are essentially driven by questions and answers that hook the audience into the narrative—we want to know what happens next. All narratives set up key puzzles or questions. There tend to be one or two major questions and a host of smaller ones, and each one is answered at some stage. This is what Barthes (1974) has called the 'hermeneutic code' because the word 'hermeneutic' refers to enquiry and interpretation. The British Film Institute has described the way audiences are involved in film narrative as follows:

a   The viewer is prompted to ask questions—for example, Who dunnit?, Who is this mysterious stranger?, Will they fall in love?

b   He/she watches on, confident of getting an answer eventually.

c   The film, meanwhile, lays down in the viewer's path a series of false trails, dead ends, and delays, keeping us from the answer—just yet.

d   The film introduces smaller questions that get answered quicker.

e   The film also leaves 'lying around' certain clues, hints, and tantalising revelations about the original 'big' question. These lure the viewer onwards.

f   The viewer predicts, from time to time, answers to questions and then adjusts these predictions according to new evidence and re-predicts until he/she reaches the conclusion with a start of surprise or satisfaction of expectations fulfilled.

(British Film Institute, *Teaching Notes on Narrative*, unpublished)

Q&A in *American Beauty*

The big question, as discussed previously, is how and why will Lester die? As the narrative progresses it becomes clear that someone will kill him and the question then becomes a 'who-will-dunnit'? Can we pick the killer? We are given some very obvious suspects, particularly his wife and his daughter's boyfriend, so we keep trying to decide between these different characters and their motives. We change our prediction that Carolyn will kill him when she herself hears the shot. There is also a major question about whether Lester can find a happier way to live. These two questions persist throughout the film. Alongside this are the numerous smaller questions, such as: is Ricky, the neighbour, a dangerous psychopath? Will Lester's daughter, Jane, get together with Ricky? Will Lester and Angela get together? Will Carolyn sell a house?

The narrative sets up a suspenseful question—for example, will Lester lose his job?—that it then answers quickly, in this case 'Yes'. But this sets up new questions: what will he do now?

This ongoing process of asking and answering questions leaves us both satisfied and wanting more: we become involved viewers, emotionally, imaginatively, and intellectually engaged with the story world, rather than distanced from it as we might be while watching an **avant-garde** film that encourages us to question the institution of cinema and the dream-like stories it offers. We can see here that film audiences are active participants in the process of making meaning. Our imaginations, intellect, and other faculties are constantly stretching to find answers to the questions raised over the course of the narrative, and to relate what is happening in the story to our own experiences and knowledge of the world. We must also consider the possibility that media audiences are passive to the extent that they tend to become immersed in the narrative world, and are not encouraged to question the capitalist, consumerist values that underlie many mainstream cinema texts and the versions of reality they construct.

AVANT-GARDE ▶

Literally means 'advance guard'; refers to cultural products that are seen as unconventionally new and different from mainstream culture but which will supposedly lead cultural developments forward.

The structural position of characters

How are characters structurally positioned in narratives, and how does this positioning contribute to meaning?

There are six useful questions to ask about any narrative.

1   Who and/or what makes things happen in the narrative (social and psychological determination)?

2   Whose point of view do we see and hear things from, and in what sequential order are events presented to us?

3   What structural roles do people have in the narrative?

4   What is the dominant discourse or the hierarchy of discourses?

5   Are women positioned differently from men in the narrative?

6   What does the ending tell you about the ideology of the film?

The answers to these questions carry consequences in terms of the text's meanings.

1   Who and/or what makes things happen?

Events may be driven by the actions of impersonal forces such as tornadoes and earthquakes, by social forces such as poverty and war, or by humans, either in groups or as individuals. Whichever of these determines events, most mainstream narratives focus on individual humans and how they respond to these events.

The Day after Tomorrow: *is this film concerned with global warming or human relationships?*

When viewing *The Day after Tomorrow*, are audiences more interested in how the main characters deal with the new ice age and how it is affecting their interpersonal relationships, or are they concerned with how this is affecting the global population? Audiences are normally encouraged, by the way events are filmed and the way the story is presented, to take up a position of identification with the main characters, or to empathise with them. Furthermore, audiences are usually invited to understand these characters psychologically rather than socially, that is, audience members are encouraged to ask what makes the characters tick as individuals. Instead of being given a larger social, political, and economic context from which to make sense of their lives, we are given psychological reasons from their past and present lives for the way characters feel and act.

Popular narratives tend to privilege, or at least show more interest in, the psychological over the social, which relates to the whole ideology of individualism that permeates Western society. We can see this at work in the type of history that we are taught. Traditionally, history has been presented in terms of key historical figures, personalities who made history (the kings and queens version of history). We have learnt about individuals—Queen Elizabeth, Christopher Columbus, Joan of Arc, Nelson Mandela, Jandamarra (an Aboriginal freedom fighter of the Bunuba people who resisted colonial settlement of the Kimberley region in Western Australia in the 1890s), Captain Cook, Hitler, and so on—rather than about major economic shifts and changes.

Film and television narratives have this same interest in individuals, maybe because it is easier to represent and understand individuals—they can be made memorable by being endowed with interesting characteristics—than it is to represent and understand social forces, which are more complex and abstract. In the case of film, it became clear early on that audiences were interested in individual actors (stars). This may be related to the size of the screen and the use of close-ups that enlarge the human face to huge proportions. The interest in individuals crosses most areas of the media, and the industry has actively constructed and encouraged this fascination with individual stars, directors, and media personalities as a marketing device. News stories, for example, are often structured around key individuals, and sports coverage focuses on stars and personalities (see Chapter 23), and it is often easy to think of film history in terms of individual directors rather than in terms of movements in film.

Most film narratives focus on one or two major characters. Our attention is held by them being made into interesting characters—attractive, witty, cruel, loving, and so on—and by having stars, who are themselves often charismatic, fascinating, and well-known people, play these parts. But more important than this is the general pattern of narrative that shows main characters going through an individual process of change, growth, and development: paralleling the narrative pattern of stable situation–disruption–new stable situation, there is usually a pattern of character change (see Figure 16.2).

Figure 16.2 Narrative pattern and character growth

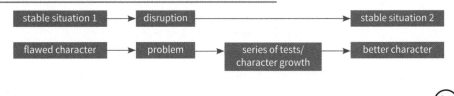

What happens to main characters in the course of a narrative? ▶

Major characters are initially presented in narratives as having some kind of flaw in their character or an emotional problem. The film then provides a situation that tests them out: they have to work through a series of problems and in so doing resolve their own character flaw—they go through a process of moral development and character growth. Characters do not always get better; some remain flawed and end up unhappy—Citizen Kane, for one, never learns from his situation, though we as the audience can learn something from observing his failure to change.

Television protagonists present a different kind of narrative development in relation to character and character flaws. In television series and serials, characters may follow extended character arcs, developing and changing over a long period of time. In a long-running soap opera such as *The Bold and the Beautiful*, a character may move from evil to good and back again, and develop many relationships and goals along the way. In such cases a particular character's learning curve and a particular narrative question may be extended over several episodes or even several series, rather than being resolved in a single episode or text. Alternatively, television characters might just go on exhibiting the same flawed character throughout a series. This is particularly true for situation comedies, or shows such as *The Simpsons*, but such characteristics are also found in many dramas in which the main characters exhibit the same flaws week after week. Homer Simpson's gluttony and ruthless politician Francis Underwood's evil scheming in *House of Cards* are but two. The witnessing and playing out of these flaws is central to audience pleasure without any need for them to be resolved.

In *American Beauty*, Lester is seriously flawed, but by the end of the film he has transformed himself and his whole way of being. In *The Day after Tomorrow*, one of the main characters is a father who neglects his son. The onset of an ice age makes him realise this, testing him to change his behaviour, to become a good father and thus a better person. The drama of global warming and ice age disaster becomes a backdrop for a feel-good story about family relationships. The narrative focuses more on the characters' growth than on the social problems that provoke it. This is the danger of narratives that focus on these individual psychological stories: wider social and political issues become background, one example being the trivialisation of global warming. Some people argue that the narrative hook of individuals and their psychological stories gives the opportunity to examine the serious issue of global warming being discussed in the popular media that we might otherwise ignore. Yet another argument is that the family concerns of *American Beauty* and *The Day after Tomorrow* relate to wider social concerns felt in Western society about masculinity (*American Beauty*) or father–son relationships (*The Day after Tomorrow*), and that these in themselves are important social issues.

The question posed here is this: does the stress on individual growth and resolution relegate social issues to second place in mainstream narratives? Most films and television programs privilege the psychological over the social. They may include both, but they focus mainly on individual characters.

Narratives do not have to work like this. The Soviet montage film movement of the 1920s–30s concentrated on social groups and issues, rather than heroic individuals with whom audience members could identify on a personal level. These films often used untrained actors to play nameless characters who embodied or typified a particular social class or identity.

In terms of gender, *Kill Bill* provides an interesting example of the balance between social and psychological issues. The film raises social issues that are significant for women, such as rape, respect in the workplace, mentorship, solidarity (or lack thereof), and child rearing. But does it raise awareness about the position of women in society, or does it just focus on the desires, challenges, and motivations of exceptional individuals? Feminist film critic Angela Martin (1979) asks the following question of feminist film studies: 'Are we looking for images of real women or films which are really about women?' She is distinguishing between films that show individual women understood in psychological terms and films about the social conditions that women in general endure. The latter puts more stress on the social problems experienced by women and the need for these to be changed if women's lives are to be improved.

The final point to make is that, if you stress social causes and problems in a narrative, then the narrative's answer to these will be in terms of social issues and contexts; if you stress psychological causes and problems, then the narrative's answers will be to work on people's individual characters, and the social problems will thus become a background to the psychological problems. This is particularly significant in relation to how we are invited to understand texts that represent crime and criminality. If the narrative presents criminals as produced by social forces, and if the narrative focuses primarily on these forces, then the logic of the story is that we must change society to solve the crime problem. If, however, crimes are committed by psychologically deviant individuals who need to change their characters, then the solution suggested by the narrative is that we must change the individuals. The social issues again recede into the background as the individual issues are foregrounded. Perhaps the best film narratives combine individual psychological issues with social concerns as equally important and interlinked, as do *Carol* and *Biutiful*.

2 From whose point of view do we see and hear things? What is the order of events?

▶ **Point of view** is an important cinematic term that raises questions about where the viewer is positioned in relation to the screen characters and the narrative world, and about how the text addresses its audience. It stresses the way audiences are invited to view and hear events. Often films and television programs encourage identification with a main character, particularly through the device of first-person, voice-over narration, as in *Jane the Virgin*, or by point-of-view shots that encourage us to see things from the perspective of the main character, as in *The Diving Bell and the Butterfly*. Close-ups are another technique that literally bring us into intimate proximity with screen characters and can invite a sense of identification. (Note how rare it is for minor characters to be filmed in close-up, and how rarely the camera will position the audience in line with their audiovisual or subjective point of view.) In these ways we may be invited to sympathise with characters even if they are murderers or criminals. Alfred Hitchcock's famous film *Psycho* uses certain techniques to encourage the audience to sympathise with the character of Marion Crane, who has stolen $40 000, and to see events from her point of view. Her murder in the film shocks audiences because a strong identification has been established with her, but the film then goes on to establish sympathy with her murderer by showing many events from his point of view.

Most narratives invite viewers to identify with characters and to be emotionally involved with the events shown. Emotional involvement comes about because audiences are encouraged to enjoy being close to (simulated) exciting events. In the cinema we can almost feel what it is like to go on a rollercoaster ride, to fly in an aeroplane, to be part of a bank robbery, to make love, to be in a fight or a car crash, and so on. These virtual experiences are dependent on camera work, editing choices, and sound techniques, all of which draw us into the action, making us feel part of the events being portrayed. This encourages a viewing experience based on strong emotional responsiveness; such emotional viewing experiences are often more stimulating than a detached, intellectual appraisal of the same issues and events.

It is, however, possible to present events in different ways. Some narratives invite detachment rather than identification. In order to facilitate detachment, these films may use long shots (to encourage the audience to distance themselves from the action) and slower editing. They may also avoid presenting events from the point of view of any particular character. All these techniques are designed to encourage the audience to be critical and detached in their viewing, and to make them aware of the construction of the film itself, unlike the techniques of traditional Hollywood cinema, which try to convince the audience of the realism of the story. You can find excellent examples of this detached style of viewing in several of Peter Greenaway's films, including *Drowning by Numbers* and *The Cook, the Thief, His Wife and Her Lover*, or in the documentaries of Peter Watkins (*Edvard Munch* and *The Freethinker*).

Can you think of other examples?

Analysis of the narrative structure of *Elephant*

In the film *Elephant*, Gus Van Sant was responding to the Columbine High School massacre. As Van Sant says in the 'Production Notes Press Release Kit' for *Elephant*: 'American school shootings had reached an all-time high. I wanted to make something that tried to capture the atmosphere of kids going to school in that time.' He uses several structural techniques that are significant in the way we view the film and that make it different from many mainstream films.

- In terms of cinematography, Van Sant uses long tracking shots, in which the camera follows students walking around the school. There are very few cuts and often little action other than the students walking through hallways. Occasionally, the film goes into slow motion for a few seconds and then resumes normal speed. All this creates the following possible effects for audiences: the lack of action and continual tracking shots encourage us to become fascinated with simply observing the school environment (which Van Sant wanted to communicate), and build a sense of suspense as we wait for something to happen. The camera technique adopts a similar camera style or convention used in many contemporary documentary films (see p. 275) and thus gives an added sense of realism. The lack of editing, shot–reverse–shot, and point-of-view shots encourages audiences to watch with more distance rather than become emotionally identified with any characters.

- The film has no main characters; rather, it introduces and weaves its narrative around a number of different school students, giving no one predominant point of view, which allows us to observe a group, a general social situation. This is a technique found in other films, particularly those of Robert Altman such as *Short Cuts* or *Gosford Park*, or the more mainstream *Love Actually* (dir. Richard Curtis), but it is still not the normal film narrative convention.

- The consequence of the previous two points is that we are given no strong point of identification—we begin to see the world through multiple points of view.

- In terms of narrative structure, the events are not presented in a simple sequential series of events. Although the film focuses on the events of one particular day, starts at the beginning of the day, and finishes with the shooting, it includes several flashback elements and also shows us some events more than once but from different perspectives. Consequently, we see the boys who will do the shooting entering the school early on, but we have to wait to see what will happen. This waiting to find out what will happen is complicated because most audiences, aware of the real events of Columbine and elsewhere, will know what is going to happen. Therefore there is not a sense of suspense and uncertainty about what will happen; there is foreknowledge. We watch the events and the characters knowing what fate is in store for them.

- These structural cinematic and narrative techniques are used for a purpose: Van Sant had no simple answer to explain the Columbine and other high school shootings. Whereas most mainstream films want to give us a clear point of view from which to understand events, Van Sant wanted to make a

Continued on next page   ▶

film that raises questions, provokes discussion, and points out the problems and contradictions of contemporary students' experiences. He used the title *Elephant* believing it referred to the parable in which a group of blind men try to identify what an elephant is by just feeling one part: each man—after feeling just an ear, or leg, or tail, or tusk, or trunk—thinks he knows what he is feeling, but he doesn't. *Elephant* is 'about a problem that was hard to identify, because of different ways of looking at it', according to Van Sant's production notes and press kit. Whereas most narratives work in terms of explaining events in terms of cause and effect, this film refused to do this. As Van Sant says, 'We didn't want to explain anything.' He didn't want to find 'an explanation for something that doesn't necessarily have an explanation', which is particularly challenging in this film because so many people in the audience will be looking for some explanation, some simple way of making sense of such terrible events.

THE NARRATIVE ORDER OF EVENTS

The most straightforward narrative sequence presents events in a strict chronological order. But this sequential narrative doesn't show everything—it cuts out time to leave out the boring bits, and only focuses on certain people and events. Only occasional narratives, like the television series *24* (in which an entire 24-episode series covers just one day in the life of a counterterrorist operative) or the experimental film *Timecode*, show events in real time, but these examples also only show scenes from particular points of view.

Many films—*Elephant* is one—break up the chronological sequence of the narrative, flashing back, or forward, or retelling events. This can have important consequences for how we interpret the film. These kinds of structural positionings are crucial in constructing our responses to any narrative, and it is important to be aware of this process of construction.

3   What structural roles do people have in the narrative?

The way characters are positioned in the narrative tells us something about how audiences are expected to understand them. Consider, for instance, how many mainstream films and television programs consistently portray people of colour in minor roles, as Chris Rock pointed out at the 2016 Academy Awards when he playfully suggested that there should be an Oscar category for '"Best Black Friend". The winner, for the eighteenth year in a row, is Wanda Sykes!' Later in this chapter the different kinds of structural roles assigned to men and women in narratives are discussed. Many films invite us to be, for example, interested in the male hero's search for knowledge by providing us with information about what he thinks and feels: we are invited to identify with him. In contrast, we are often invited to watch female characters without knowing their personalities: they tend to be more objects of visual pleasure whose structural role might be to sing songs or perform strip routines: the audience is encouraged to objectify them. Similarly, male characters are often set at the centre of a film, while women serve secondary support functions, such as wife, mother, or mistress. In this way women are structured as supports or appendages to men. In this chapter we also examine the way characters are structurally positioned at the end of narratives. This positioning encourages us to understand the character in a particular way (as discussed above in relation to gay characters). Analysing the structural position of characters requires us to think not so much about what characters do as about their positions in the narrative.

4　What is the dominant discourse or the hierarchy of discourses?

To develop the idea that characters' structural positions in narratives contribute to meaning, let us consider the terms 'dominant discourse' and 'hierarchy of discourses', as used by cultural theorist Colin MacCabe (1974). In a film or television narrative we are presented with a number of different discourses that explain or comment on the situation. Most obviously, there are characters' voices. Thus in *American Beauty* we have the voices of Lester, Carolyn his wife, Jane his daughter, Angela, both Jims, Ricky, Ricky's father, Ricky's mother, and so on. Each of these characters have quite different ways of making sense of the world and speaking about it—different discourses, coexisting alongside each other. MacCabe argues that a narrative will organise these voices into a particular hierarchy, so that one voice is heard as more important, more truthful than another. For example, we hear both Ricky's and his father's competing discourses about homosexuality and drugs, and we also hear Carolyn's and Lester's perspectives on the same subjects.

Whose voice do we most believe in and trust?　▶

Our job as film analysts or audience members is to work out whose voice, whose discourse, the film presents as most truthful: the hierarchy of voices must be determined. In this case Ricky's view of the world is clearly seen as superior to that of his repressed and violent father. In general the film uses our allegiance with particular characters to discredit negative discourses in which homosexuality is viewed as sinful or abnormal, and it mocks the legal, medical, and moral discourses that condemn recreational drug use.

　　MacCabe suggests that in addition to the discourses of the characters, we must pay attention to the discourse of film language. By this he means that the things that comprise film discourse—camera style, lighting, editing, music, and so on—invite us to see and hear things in a particular way, and contribute to the way we position people in the discourse hierarchy. Thus, in *American Beauty*:

- the camera and lighting show Angela as sexy in the way they frame and light her body
- some of the lighting on Ricky's father portrays him as potentially sinister, while the way he and his wife are positioned in terms of *mise en scène* shows us how dysfunctional their marriage is
- music and sound play a crucial role in the moment when Ricky first videos Jane, an act that could be presented as voyeuristic, intrusive, and perverted but the music soundtrack is gentle and mystical, and it is this that tells us that what Ricky is doing is fine and romantic.

MacCabe's argument is that viewers make sense of all these competing voices, linking and comparing them until they are arranged into a hierarchy that finally produces a dominant discourse, the discourse that will ultimately give us the truth about events. Of course different audiences may make different readings, but we argue that it is possible to look at the film's arrangement of the different discourses, and, from that, deduce what audiences are being invited to think and feel. Viewed in this manner, it makes sense to ask: what does the film think about what it is showing us? Or, what is its project? (What does it project to us on the screen?) Looking at the film's hierarchy of discourses and seeking out its dominant discourse become a way of understanding what the overall film is presenting and how this is inscribed into its narrative structure. These are useful questions that will shift our attention away from our own personal reactions. Asking these questions is similar to looking for a film's preferred reading (see p. 96). You can investigate the dominant discourse of any text by asking

1   What or whose different voices or discourses are presented?
2   How would you order them in a hierarchy (which is most persuasive)?
3   What is the dominant discourse?

At this point it would be easy to fall into the intentionalist position and argue that the dominant discourse is that held by the director (what the film thinks is what the director thinks). While the view of the director is significant, there is a dominant discourse in the text that is the product of not only the director's intention, but also of a host of factors beyond this.

5   Are women positioned differently from men in the narrative?

Many critics have suggested that recurrent patterns are apparent in the structural roles usually given to men and women. Table 16.1 below suggests some of the main roles, characteristics, and functions that men and women tend to have or fulfil in narratives, as well as some of the gender lines that transect different genres.

These are generalisations and do not apply to all narratives but they show tendencies in the representation of men and women. We briefly mentioned above the difference between identification with men and objectification of women. This is a useful distinction that draws our attention to how we watch films. We sometimes ask students to list their favourite male and female stars. We then suggest that for heterosexuals, their favourite same-sex stars represent the kinds of women or men they themselves would like to be, the kinds of women or men they identify with; favourite opposite-sex stars represent the kinds of women or men they desire, the kinds of women or men they objectify. This points to two major viewing pleasures we are offered and experience as film viewers—the opportunity to imagine oneself as an all-powerful fantasy figure (the character we most identify with) and the opportunity to gaze erotically on a beautiful fantasy figure whom we desire and objectify.

Table 16.1 Structural roles of men and women in film—oppositions

Male hero	Female heroine
identification	objectification
narrative movement and control	narrative stasis and spectacle
primary characters	secondary characters
active	passive
feelings expressed by external actions	feelings expressed by displays of emotion
strong	weak
work or other public world	home or other private world
investigators	investigated
known	unknown
westerns, thrillers	melodramas, musicals

Film theorist and filmmaker Laura Mulvey notes these two different kinds of viewing pleasure, and in one of the most influential pieces of feminist criticism, describes the way women and men are presented in films:

> Woman as Image, Man as Bearer of the Look: In a world ordered by sexual imbalance, pleasure in looking has been split between active/male and passive/female. The determining male gaze projects its phantasy on to the female figure, which is styled accordingly. In their traditional exhibitionist role women are simultaneously looked at and displayed, with their appearance coded for strong visual and erotic impact so that they can be said to connote to-be-looked-at-ness. Woman displayed as sexual object is the leit-motif of erotic spectacle: from pin-ups to striptease, from Ziegfeld to Busby Berkeley, she holds the look, plays to and signifies male desire (Mulvey 1985, p. 304).

She continues, arguing that in many mainstream films audiences are invited to identify with men and objectify women, regardless of whether they are male or female. Thus female audiences are asked to look through a male perspective, to see things through men's eyes. Mulvey demonstrates that identification with male heroes is produced primarily through narrative position and editing techniques: in the narrative men are often the major characters—they are introduced at the beginning of the story, we know the most about them, and they are involved in unravelling the enigma in the story. Through editing and camera position we are often encouraged to see the things they see, and thus we are stitched into their point of view. All these elements create a position of identification. Often these techniques will be employed to full effect while female characters perform actions—dancing, singing, and so on—that invite the camera, the male characters, and the audience to take pleasure in looking at them. Author and critic John Berger sums up the differences between the portrayal of men and women:

> One might simplify this by saying men act and women appear. Men look at women. Women watch themselves being looked at. This determines not only most relations between men and women but also the relation of women to themselves. The surveyor of woman in herself is male: the surveyed female. Thus she turns herself into an object—and most particularly an object of vision: a sight (Berger 1972, p. 47).

This explains the uncomfortable relationship between female subjectivity and personal appearance, and it foregrounds the point that being looked at is a passive subject position. This relates to the idea of narrative stasis: the narrative pausing to enable spectators to dwell on the spectacle of the female form. While female characters may function to provide visual pleasure and create desire in film narratives, the male actor's deeds and actions are usually what drive the plot forward. We can see all this in the relationship between Lester and Angela in *American Beauty*: the way he gazes at her, the way she 'stops' the narrative in the cheerleading scene, the way we are much more involved in Lester's thoughts and actions.

Mulvey's work, along with the work of other feminists, draws attention to the politics of looking and the emphasis on visual appearance that is associated with women in film. Table 16.1 also suggests that women are often secondary or subordinate characters in films, that men are more important. This is normally the case for genres such as westerns, thrillers, science-fiction films, and crime movies. Content analysis reveals that, on the whole, there are more major roles in film narratives for men than for women. However, there are genres where women often take the primary roles—notably musicals, melodramas, and soap operas—but, as the table suggests, these roles tend to operate differently from male roles. Often the women playing such roles are being reactive (they respond to events rather than initiating actions), the focus is on feelings rather than actions, and the settings tend to be the private, domestic world of home rather than the professional, public world of work.

You may think that these observations refer to the kinds of media texts produced in the past, and that the situation is now different because there are many films and television shows—*Girls*, *House of Cards*, *The Good Wife*, *How to Get Away with Murder*, *Kill Bill*, *The Honourable Woman*, *The Hunger Games*, and *True Grit*, to name some—that have women as central and strong characters. Even so, it is still worth considering how our attitudes (and the attitudes of established media producers who are currently in positions of power and making decisions about media content) have been, and are still being, influenced by the cumulative impressions of masculinity and femininity that we have acquired throughout our viewing histories. Many films in which women take a prominent role, such as *The Proposal* starring Sandra Bullock as an assertive boss, are still romantic comedies, in which the ultimate goal of the main character is to find a love interest.

Most of the changes in the way race and gender are represented are very recent, and figure in only a small proportion of media texts produced globally. The emergent trend to include strong female characters is a marketing device that still frequently positions the value of these characters in relation to their physical appearance. Even in texts such as the *Charlie's Angels* franchise, the women are not the most powerful characters in the narrative: they all defer to their boss, Charlie, and their appearances are still of central importance.

You may be interested in the Bechdel Test (originally formulated by Alison Bechdel in 1985), which looks at film content in relation to gender bias: to pass the test, a film has to include at least two female characters, who have a conversation, about something other than a man. A surprising number of popular films fail this test, including all the *Lord of the Rings* trilogy and all the *Star Wars* films, but all four of the *Hunger Games* films do pass the test.

6   What does the ending tell you about the ideology of the film?

Consider the importance of narrative endings and resolutions, which are an essential part of the narrative pattern. Endings are significant in determining a narrative's ideological meaning. There are different ways of ending stories. Let's explore this further.

Note at least three different possible types of ending: closed/circular, closed/progress, and open or unresolved (Figures 16.3–16.5).

Figure 16.3 Closed/circular ending

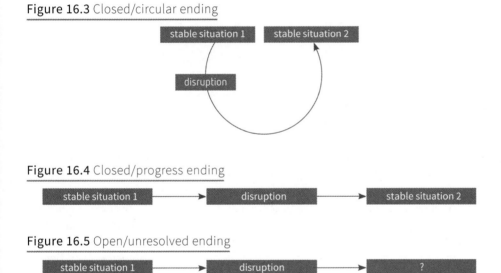

Figure 16.4 Closed/progress ending

Figure 16.5 Open/unresolved ending

Most narratives are closed in that they answer all the questions set up in the narrative and they resolve any problems that the film sets up. The closed/circular ending (Figure 16.3) is one that ends where it started. This seems to be a very common cinematic device (much more so than in novels), where shots at or near the end echo or directly repeat the opening shots. *Fight Club* is a good example of a film in which the opening shots are seen again near the ending of the film. Seeing these same shots signals to the audience that the end is coming. It may have some connection with the way in the past cinema-goers would pay a single entry fee that would allow them to stay in the cinema and watch the movie being screened again. Audiences could enter at any time and stay for as long as they wanted. The normal point of exit would be when you reached the 'this is where we came in' moment, indicated by the repetition of images that occurred at the moment of arrival.

The circular characteristic is found particularly in flashback films, which start at one point in time, go into the past, and then return to the original point for the ending—*Citizen Kane* and *Never Let Me Go* are good examples. The ideological point about such narratives is that, in a sense, they don't go anywhere, they don't progress, and they just bring you back to where you started. This suggests that progress is impossible, that it is impossible to change things. The status quo is thereby reinforced. This view of society is fatalistic and conservative. However, the cyclical, flashback narrative structure can also indicate other things. The structure of a film can make a statement that the issue at the heart of the film is unresolvable, or that it is a problem that tends to resurface; a pattern that repeats itself over and over again in families, in individuals, or in society. *Nil by Mouth* and *The War Zone* are examples of narratives that deal with the cycle of domestic violence and family abuse, and both are structured to avoid closure and progress. An open or unresolved ending can leave the audience with the responsibility for defining their own ideas and positions, and can even encourage us to take action. Films that work with time-loop paradoxes frequently have a circular narrative structure too (*Inception*, *X-Men: Days of Future Past*, *Terminator*, and *Source Code*). Few films have a truly cyclical narrative structure that denies the audience a satisfying sense of closure. *Inside Llewyn Davis* and *Memento* are films that leave the audience at the beginning of the narrative, freshly engaged with exactly the same questions that they began with. But in each case we have more knowledge about the characters and their situations, and as a consequence we move on to a deeper level of questioning. In such films the narrative structure is indicative of the philosophical enormity of the unanswerable questions about identity and memory with which they grapple.

The flashback form was popular in *film noir*, which shows humans trapped in a hostile universe. These films suggest that whatever humans do, they are doomed to their preordained ending. Similar circular patterns can be seen in many cartoons and situation comedies today.

In contrast, closed/progress endings (Figure 16.4) allow for progress and change. Things are not as they were at the beginning (whether happy or unhappy), which suggests that humans can change their life situations. This relates to the process of moral change and growth that main characters go through. It is a pattern that is usually positive—characters learn and become better people during the narrative—and it suggests that we can move on from the status quo.

When watching a film or television program, try to determine whether, and how, it reproduces these closed or circular and closed or progress patterns.

MAINSTREAM AND NON-MAINSTREAM CINEMA

Mainstream Hollywood cinema tends towards closed endings; however, films can be open or unresolved, which is sometimes the case in relation to mainstream cinema. The horror genre—films such as *The Conjuring*, and those in the *Resident Evil*, *Paranormal Activity*, and *Final Destination* franchises—has traditionally had open endings. This is not only so that there will be room for a sequel (though this is commercially sensible) but more because the horror genre is meant to disturb us. Part of the power and the pleasure of horror films is that they allow us to experience, in a safe cinematic setting, fear and to confront things that frighten and fascinate us. But the nature of fear is about being unsafe, and it is important for the success of the genre that the endings of the stories leave open the possibility for the horror to return. Refusing the comfort of a closed ending allows the narrative structure to create disturbance. Critics have suggested that at times of moral and social uncertainty, commercial films may not offer clearly resolved endings (Wood 1986), but non-mainstream narratives are the usual place to find more open endings.

Non-mainstream narratives with open or unresolved endings are often found in so-called arthouse films, a type of film that is more intellectually oriented than commercial cinema. Arthouse films frequently present a challenge to the audience, and to the dominant order and accepted norms of society. They often aim to say something meaningful, and many have a slower editing pace and a more consciously artistic approach. Endings can be deliberately ambiguous, inviting spectators to think reflectively about what they have seen, to puzzle out the meanings, and to explore the moral and social dilemmas raised. Art films may thus reflect more of the uncertainties of real life; they certainly don't offer us easy answers and are not so comfortable and reassuring, as discussed above with *Elephant*. *Birdman*, *Black Swan*, *Inherent Vice*, and *Trance* are good examples of films that unsettle and challenge the audience because they deal with disturbing subject matter in complex ways without presenting characters to whom the audience can easily relate.

In relation to endings, think about how characters are positioned at the end of narratives. Most obviously, consider whether they receive rewards or punishments, happy or unhappy endings. This gives a good indication as to whether their actions and behaviour are legitimated.

Binary oppositions

We can develop narrative analysis further through the application of **binary oppositions**. These are used by many critics (Kitses 2004; Turner 2006, p. 104). You can see them at work in Table 16.1 (p. 247), in Kitses' western oppositions (Table 14.1, p. 214), and in our analysis of language (p. 83). You may well have encountered them elsewhere. The concept of opposition or duality is fundamental in the organisation of language, as it is in Western philosophical thinking as a whole. Aristotle expressed this when he stated that 'Everything is either A or not A'. He used opposition or negation as a means of definition, a use that is apparent in language; as discussed in relation to semiology, words don't mean anything on their own—they have meaning in relation to other words (through systems of difference). Each word or concept is defined by its opposite and only makes sense if we understand its opposite as well. 'Yes', for example, is understood in relation to 'no', 'right' in relation to 'left' or 'wrong', 'up' to 'down', 'light' to 'dark', 'good' to 'bad', 'black' to 'white', 'masculine' to 'feminine', and so on. We make sense of the world through oppositions. As Hartley puts it, 'Such binaries are a feature of *culture* not *nature*; they are products of signifying systems, and function to structure our perceptions of the natural and social world into order and meaning' (O'Sullivan et al. 1994, p. 30).

So we, as humans, create these categories. 'Binary' is derived from the Greek word *bio* meaning 'two'. It is about splitting or pairing things into twos: positive and negative, yes and no, and so on. It is the basic numerical system used in computers. All computer decisions are based on asking and answering yes/no questions. Whichever answer is chosen will lead automatically to the next stage of computation.

This system of duality has been challenged by those who argue that it creates separation and does not adequately represent reality. While, for instance, male–female is one of the central binaries that we use today (and also that we use throughout the book), the fact is that, biologically, this opposition may not adequately describe reality. First, there is no absolutely clear dividing line, since it is possible to be hermaphrodite (male and female). There are also numerous gradations or variations of what is male and what is female. The chromosomal and hormonal differences used to biologically define male and

BINARY OPPOSITIONS

A means of cultural classification that splits the world into sets of dualistic opposing categories, such as male and female, black and white.

female difference show that nearly all men have some female chromosomal or hormonal elements, while nearly all women similarly have male elements. Few people are one hundred per cent male or female in these terms. Thus, biologically, the categories of male and female are more fluid than Western culture has traditionally recognised; the lines of difference are not so clear-cut and we see this fluidity recognised today with intersex and transgender people.

Note that binary oppositions such as male and female, right and wrong are hierarchical: one term is often privileged over the other, and the devalued or negative term tends to be defined in relation to the dominant category. The male–female opposition has been objected to because 'male' is taken as the primary category against which 'female' is defined. As Graeme Turner writes:

> Assuming male and female are opposites means that, automatically, women are what men are not; if the male is strong, then the female must be weak, and on it goes … we can see the accretion of negatives on the female side as a necessary product of the assumption that male and female are opposites. To continue the chain is to end up with good (male) versus bad (female) (Turner 2006, p. 104).

The binary system and way of categorising the world also implicitly condones adversarial or oppositional ways of thinking, in which there are rigid, mutually exclusive discursive positions and winners and losers of debates, instead of negotiated compromises and flexible positions that entail mutual incorporation of different perspectives. We can see how our political systems often work in this way and how the media, in their ways of reporting events, nearly always frame things in terms of opposition and conflict. These may be very limited, and limiting, ways of seeing the world.

Let's return to the use of binary oppositions in narrative analysis. Narratives are organised around conflict and opposition, which are fundamental to narrative interest. There has to be some kind of struggle, some disruption that sets up conflict. The conflict is most obviously between individual characters, but this will also indicate conflict between different value systems. Indeed, the overall structure of all narratives can be seen as involving the resolution of conflict between two opposing forces. The term **dialectical synthesis** refers to a discussion or argument between two competing or opposing sides. In a philosophical argument or an academic essay, these two sides are called the thesis (what is being argued for) and the antithesis (the counterclaims, or alternative points, perspectives, views, and voices that are being argued against the thesis). In a narrative, the thesis and the antithesis relate to whatever binary opposition structures the story contains, and, just as in an argument or essay, each side must engage with the other and be able to explain or understand the opposing point or perspective in order to be able to refute or incorporate it. When the two sides come to terms with each other, the dialectical synthesis, or narrative resolution, is reached.

DIALECTICAL SYNTHESIS ▶

Two opposing forces (such as good and evil, or thesis and antithesis) generate conflict or debate that is resolved when the two sides come together in a form of synthesis.

We can discern many different oppositions within the structure of a single narrative. Jim Kitses was one of the first media critics to use oppositions in his illuminating analysis of the western (see Table 14.1, p. 214). He suggests that the western is replete with general oppositions such as wilderness versus civilisation, and antagonistic characters such as cowboys and Indians, outlaws and lawmen. In specific films these general categories would be linked to the personal and individual stories of particular characters; for example, John Wayne or Clint Eastwood as the heroes would be aligned with either nature or culture, or with values such as self-interest and individualism, or social responsibility and community. Kitses' list of binary oppositions is enormously helpful in relation to the western genre, as already discussed. It is also useful as an example of this structured system of oppositions; we can apply it to other genres and narratives.

Note, first, that in the system of binary oppositions, when we make a list it is important to see vertical connections between all the categories listed on either the right or left side of the table; in the above example, 'the west', 'wilderness', 'individual', 'freedom', and so on are all linked in some way—they are literally on the same side of this opposing equation—which shows how the dramatic conflict contains a whole series of elements on each side.

Second, oppositions can be observed between particular characters, between different human characteristics, between different settings or even colours, and so on. These then cohere to provide a central opposition between two different value systems. Analysis of this opposition leads us to a deeper understanding of what the film is essentially concerned with.

Third, ultimately the film must find some resolution between these oppositions, and fourth, the richness of this system is that while there is usually some sense of right versus wrong, good versus evil (so that one side of the oppositions is preferred), it is not absolutely clear-cut good and bad. In the simplest of dramas—films such as *Star Wars* and *The Lord of the Rings* trilogy—this might be the case, but even in these films there are complications. 'Evil' Darth Vader turns out to be 'good' Luke Skywalker's father; Gollum in his split personality shows aspects of good and evil, and the power of the ring brings out the dark sides of good Bilbo and Frodo. Other narratives show more complex ambiguities between good and evil, between the two oppositional sides, and the resolution often shows the need to combine elements or to have some crossovers between the two sides. Over time, value systems change so that in the opposition cowboys versus Indians, for example, there has been a gradual change from seeing the cowboys as good, the Indians as bad, to the reverse. The same basic binary opposition is used but with different inflections.

Once again, the idea of dialectical synthesis can help us to understand how resolution is reached. Just as the thesis and the antithesis must be brought together into a synthesis, the protagonist and the antagonist in a story typically need to take on aspects of each other's value systems and character traits in order for the conflict between them to be resolved. Western cowboy heroes, for example, often bring civilisation and community to the wild west frontier, but paradoxically their ability to enforce law and order is dependent on the strength of their individualism, and they themselves remain free (outside or beyond the law) in the wilderness. In order for a cowboy hero to defeat the Indians, he frequently needs to acquire traditional Indian skills, such as tracking and hunting, and often he understands Indian culture and language better than characters such as the settler or the merchant, who are totally aligned with civilisation and the east.

You should find a clear set of oppositions in almost every mainstream narrative you analyse, and finding it will provide a key to understanding and interpreting the story and its structure.

Some films, such as Darren Aronofsky's Academy Award-winning feature *Black Swan*, are explicitly structured around binary oppositions to the extent that the theme of the narrative *is* duality. Even a brief narrative extract such as the film trailer shows that the oppositions between the black swan's power and the white swan's purity, sexual experimentation and sexual repression, insanity and sanity, are structuring themes. The film's ending makes a powerful, if heavy-handed, statement about the negative consequences of failing to achieve dialectical synthesis or a harmonious balance of opposing traits within the self.

Look at Gordon Bennett's *Altered Body Print (Shadow Figure Howling at the Moon)* (Figure 24.1, discussed on pp. 399–400) and consider how he is using binary oppositions.

Coupling endings

How many film and television narratives end with coupling? ▶

We will extend this analysis of the resolution of binary oppositions to looking at how film and television narratives often work by focusing on couples, one particular binary, and using these as a central part of the narrative. It has been suggested by philosopher Stanley Cavell that cinema is a machine for making couples. This is because many film endings lead to romance and actual or potential marriage or remarriage. The final result of all the narrative drama, tests, tension, and suspense is for a man and woman to get together as a heterosexual pair. While this is obviously not true of all films, it is common. The predominance of successful coupling as the desirable end-product of narratives reproduces an ideology of heterosexual, monogamous romance and marriage, which goes back before cinema to other storytelling traditions, and to plays and novels. It is encapsulated in fairy tales, which invariably begin with the introduction, 'Once upon time there was a …' and end with the phrase 'and they lived happily ever after' (suggesting a heterosexual couple who have just married).

Happy endings with successful coupling were the norm for Hollywood films from the 1930s to the 1950s. Movies with happy endings are still being made and they are now often referred to as feel-good movies, but since the 1960s there have also been more unhappy, unresolved endings. The earlier films can be seen as a reflection of the optimism of American society and the durability of the family unit from the 1930s to the 1950s; films from the 1960s and after reflect the increasing instability of and uncertainty about social values, and the fact that the family unit has been under considerable pressure in the past four decades.

Couple endings can have many variations: examples include tragic endings in which the couples separate or the failure of the couple to come together. Many westerns end with the male hero walking away alone into the sunset, continuing on his journey or quest, and remaining outside society and marriage. Non-heterosexual couples are another possibility: male buddies, female buddies, gay and lesbian couples, and family couples such as estranged mother and son, or father and daughter.

CONCLUSION

We have described narrative as a pattern of dialectical synthesis structured around the resolution of binary oppositions and shown that this pattern affects meanings. Understanding these structures is another way of seeing how texts work and interpreting them. Close examination of how characters in texts are positioned, how they are presented to audiences, and where characters are at the ends of texts can reveal the ideological meanings and social values of a text. The focus here has been on fiction, but the same analytic methods can be applied to non-fiction texts such as documentaries, news, sports, and quiz and chat shows, as the following chapter on non-fiction texts demonstrates.

This chapter has

- defined narrative and narrative structure
- argued that narrative structure can determine meaning
- examined the structural positioning of characters in narratives
- considered the importance of narrative endings and resolutions
- defined and illustrated the term 'binary oppositions' in narrative.

? DISCUSSION POINTS

1   How are crime, criminals, and policing usually presented and resolved in film and television narratives? In social or psychological terms? From the point of view of criminals or law officers? What are the ideological implications of different narrative structures?

2   Find a film that breaks up the chronological narrative sequence. First, rearrange the plot segments into their chronological order. Then compare these two different ways of presenting the narrative, and consider how the non-chronological sequence changes the way we understand and respond to the narrative.

SUMMARY

You should now be able to

- explain the importance and prevalence of narrative
- define and illustrate the terms 'narrative structure' and 'binary oppositions'
- show how narratives work through a structure of disruption, narrative questions, and resolution
- discuss the ways in which characters are structurally positioned in narratives and the consequences of this
- explain and illustrate the use in a narrative of flaws in major characters
- explain and illustrate the ideological implications of narrative endings
- give examples of non-mainstream narrative techniques
- explain and illustrate the term 'hierarchy of discourse'
- compare the different ways men and women are positioned in narratives
- draw up a list of binary oppositions for any film or television text and consider how these are worked through and resolved.

CHAPTER 17

Digital Television and Interactive Narratives

> I like the idea of a continuing story ... and television is way more interesting than cinema now. It seems like the art house has gone to cable.
>
> David Lynch, *Screen Rant*

This chapter will

- consider the key distinctions between film and television narratives
- introduce the different eras of development in television and changes in image culture
- focus on narrative complexity in contemporary television
- examine different forms of streamed video
- discuss pornography in the media
- examine how narratives are structured in computer and internet games.

While the previous chapters focused on traditional dramatic narrative forms with a particular focus on cinema, this chapter explores emerging and evolving narrative forms such as streamed television and interactive games. It will question the extent to which structuralist narrative approaches can be applied to these texts, and will examine how audience behaviour and preferences are changing in relation to technological developments and changes in the media industries.

TELEVISION NARRATIVES

Television is a narrative form that originally had close ties to radio, theatre, and cinema, but it has evolved in the context of rapid economic and technological transformation. The evolution of television can be traced through three distinct eras. TVI lasted from approximately 1948–75; TVII ran from about 1975–95; and we are now in the era of TVIII. In the early years of television (TVI), audiences were restricted to fixed schedules on a limited range of local or national broadcast channels. The second period (TVII) was characterised by greater consumer choice due to industry deregulation, the possibility of recording programs on VCRs and watching them later, and the proliferation of cable and satellite channels that catered to niche audiences (Nelson 2007). TVIII is the digital era, which television scholars Glen Creeber and Matt Hills describe as 'television's present state and beyond; a time of increased fragmentation, consumer interactivity and global market economies' (2007, p. 1). This era is characterised by user-generated content, the streaming, downloading, and multiplatforming of content, and binge-viewing of multiple episodes when an entire season is released at once by streaming subscription services such as Netflix. Indeed, Netflix predicts that as broadband becomes faster and less unreliable, traditional forms of television will soon be replaced by personalised video-on-demand services available via internet TV apps because 'people love TV content, but they don't love the linear TV experience, where channels present programs only at particular times on non-portable screens' ('Netflix's Long-Term View', <http://ir.netflix.com/long-term-view.cfm>).

In what ways are television programs different from films that we watch in the cinema? ▶

Most of what we have said about narrative in Chapter 16 applies to film but only partially to television dramas, which are equally important media texts. The first major difference is the context of reception. In contrast to the private, darkened space of cinema, the much smaller screens on which we watch television were initially introduced for domestic and family viewing. The television set was originally in the collective family space, the living room, to be viewed by all members of the family, often together, and quite possibly engaged in other activities at the same time. This togetherness is now fragmented, partly by programming schedules, which mean that different family members can watch at different times of the day, but also by the increasing number of screens or platforms on which television can be watched and the cheaper prices of these screens: we now find television sets in rooms other than communal family rooms, such as bedrooms, where television can be watched more privately. The phrase 'Netflix and chill' became a euphemism for hooking up with your boyfriend or girlfriend in 2014, by which time watching television had become an intimate, personalised experience. The screens on which we watch television have also changed dramatically in recent years: mobile viewing on small tablets and laptops is now widespread, as is the home-theatre experience, with large screens or data projectors and surround-sound systems that offer an experience closer to cinema.

The second major difference arises from the domestic context of television consumption: television tends to be more dialogue-driven and is divided into short, self-contained segments so that the storylines can be followed by someone who is not giving the screen their undivided attention. The structure of televisual narratives invites a different kind of engagement, and different interpretive practices arise from the context of reception. With the exception of binge-viewing practices, instead of *gazing* intently at the screen as we do in the cinema, television audience members *glance* at the set while they are going about other everyday activities such as studying, ironing clothes, making lunch, or talking on the phone. These different viewing patterns also relate to the differing content and styles of the two media. Television texts often focus on everyday life and family concerns, and they are watched routinely in private or domestic circumstances. Because it is historically situated in the home, television also has a tone or mode of address that is more conversational than that of film (figures on television tend to address or acknowledge the viewer as a participant, sometimes implicitly including them as part of a live studio audience). In contrast, film maintains a sense of voyeurism and generally does not acknowledge the audience explicitly (for example, screen characters rarely look directly at the camera or acknowledge that they are performing a role or being watched).

There are also major differences between television and film in relation to narrative structure. Television's predominant form is episodic or serial in structure. Whereas cinema offers films that are complete narratives in themselves—one-offs, usually with closed endings—television offers programs in which the narrative continues week after week, either as serials, in which the story carries on and develops from one episode to the next, or as series, in which there is some development from one week to the next but each episode has its own particular story. Situation comedies operate in this way. Many series today combine complete stories in a single episode alongside a continually developing narrative, such as the 2016 reboot of *The X-Files*. Television's most extreme form of the continuous series is the soap opera. Programs such as *Neighbours* (screening since 1985) and the record-breaking British soap *Coronation Street* (screening since 1960) go on for decades due to soap opera's serialised, open-ended, never-ending narrative structure.

Media convergence and other changes to the television industry, particularly the fact that audiences can now use their televisions as a portal to access the internet instead of relying on local broadcast channels, mean that television narratives now also continue on multiple platforms and even in entirely different media forms. For instance, the storyline of *Jessica Jones* extends well beyond the television screen: the character originated in Marvel's *Alias* comics and lives on in screen-based tie-ins and crossovers, including connections with Spider-Man and the Avengers in the Marvel cinematic universe, role-playing games such as *Marvel: Future Fight*, *Luke Cage*, and *The Defenders* Netflix series, and a planned movie appearance.

There are practical and economic reasons that these serialised, multiplatform narratives are developing in the television industry. The need to win regular audiences was met by regular broadcast programming—same program, same time each week. Now television creators continue to capitalise on the established familiarity with characters and settings that brings audiences back to programs they like, even when viewers stream, download, or record the program, or when the narrative extends across different storytelling platforms. The formulaic format predominates in television schedules for non-fiction programs as well: game shows, travel programs, sports and cooking shows, even the news and weather reports are all programmed in regular weekly or daily episodes, and are now frequently accompanied by companion websites that offer supplementary material. The aim is to build up a loyal audience.

Complex television and streamed content in the digital age

The 1990s saw the advent of new and more cinematic forms of programming, and, with them, new modes of viewing. Series such as David Lynch's *Twin Peaks* (ABC 1990–91; Showtime 2017), Chris Carter's *The X-Files* (Fox 1993–2002, 2016–), and Joss Whedon's *Buffy the Vampire Slayer* (WB 1996–2003; UPN 2001–03) brought the focus firmly onto young audiences, dedicated and even fanatical viewing patterns, and the cult of the creator. Cult television typically features 'a coherent and well-populated fictional world, deep backstory, offbeat and charismatic major characters, metatextuality, "mythic" themes and plots and the extension of the cult fiction across a full range of media and merchandise products' (Gwenllian-Jones 2003, p. 174). Cult television programs are often fantasy or science-fiction series set in complex narrative worlds with 'narrative enigmas that are central to each programme's character-based and fantasy-based format' (Hills 2004, p. 513).

The 1990s cult series that helped to change televisual storytelling from self-contained episodes to the more narratively complex serial form all originated on network television, but their success has proven to be extremely influential in terms of more recent developments in subscription television, film, and content streaming. This is evident in the return of *The X-Files* for two movies (1998; 2008) and a tenth season in 2016, *Twin Peaks*' cinematic prologue *Twin Peaks: Fire Walk with Me* (1992) and the continuation of the series in 2017, and also the enormous popularity of *The Avengers* franchise that Whedon helms and that is feeding back into television production via *Agents of SHIELD* and Marvel offerings on Netflix. Each of these series was under the creative control of a strong writer-producer, known as a television showrunner, and each benefited from the development of strong online fan communities.

TV production strategies are changing to facilitate creative synergies between film and TV, and technological change is influencing the narrative and aesthetic models that television creators adopt. Netflix's data-driven production strategies identified that audiences want to be able to 'binge' on long narratives with sustained character development in a show with a cinematic style and big-name stars. TV is a mode of storytelling that requires ongoing commitment from the actors and showrunners who carry the show and develop its signature style, which is arguably why the British mini-series model and shows like *Sherlock* with very few episodes per season are gaining traction in the global media industry. This format is used by high-end shows like *True Detective* and *Fargo* to ensure commitment from A-list actors for just one short season of a TV series, after which the series changes actors for a new season designed as a prequel or featuring a different case or location.

Parallel with this, there is an increasing trend to brand television series with the name and signature style of auteur film directors such as Jane Campion (*Top of the Lake*), the Coen brothers (*Fargo*), David Lynch (*Twin Peaks*), and David Fincher (*House of Cards*). These developments don't signal the emergence of a new form of authorship for high-end streamed and subscription television content as much as they indicate an emerging 'novelistic-cinematic' type of television storytelling developed for a flexible, user-centred, online exhibition mode that synthesises multiple authorial voices and creative input from predictive AI algorithms, actor-producers, film auteurs, and television writer-producers.

Greg Metcalf discusses these changes to televisual storytelling in his book *The DVD Novel: How the Way We Watched Television Changed the Television We Watched* (2012), analysing the complex interplay of technological change and changes in cultural modes of narrative production and consumption. His discussion of how television episodes are now scripted much like 'chapters in a season-long novel' instead of episodic or never-ending stories applies directly to shows like *House of Cards*. This Netflix series even titles its episodes 'Chapter 1', 'Chapter 2', and so on, which is fitting since the show is adapted from a BBC mini-series (1990) that was itself based on a novel (by Michael Dobbs 1989), both also titled *House of Cards*. Both David Fincher and David Lynch have spoken publicly about television being the most exciting form of audio-visual storytelling today, akin to a new realm of independent film production in terms of the degree of innovation and experimentation that is taking place, and the creative challenges of complex, character-driven narration. These kinds of shows are created and consumed more like extremely long films than a series of one-hour stories, a phenomenon that television scholar Jason Mittell explores in *Complex TV: The Poetics of Contemporary Television Storytelling* (2015).

Changing modes of TV production and consumption

The Netflix model, which is characterised by the production of increasingly complex and sophisticated television narratives, is not the only way in which television storytelling and viewing have transformed in the digital age. For instance, Amazon's original content-production strategy harnesses the creative and critical power of media consumers by allowing anybody to submit a script or concept video for consideration using the company's free online Storywriter and Storybuilder tools. Once an idea for an episodic series has been picked up for Amazon's development slate, Amazon Studios asks its online user base to review promotional material and the pilot episode in order to test the content and tailor it to audience desires. To an even greater extent, the production of original and remixed video content by audience members rather than professional filmmakers has also been facilitated by online video platforms such as Vimeo and YouTube.

Largely fuelled by the introduction of YouTube in 2005, people now regularly make videos to go directly onto the internet that can be viewed on computers, tablets, and mobile phones. The nature of this form of online digital video storytelling is different yet again from film and television because, even with increased bandwidth allowing much faster rendering and download times, and higher resolution digital video, internet narratives are still often compressed into short sequences of about five minutes. As media scholar Jin Kim states, 'YouTube has come to represent what video on the web looks like: short, mostly humorous and easily accessible … Responding to professional video services in mainstream media, YouTube also offers full-length episodes of television shows' (2012, p. 54). Not only do platforms like YouTube allow users to publicise their videos to a wide audience and to develop their own video channels with subscribers, but these internet productions are also changing narrative form and arguably demonstrating the increased democratisation of new media and the transgression of boundaries between media producers and consumers.

However, while YouTube may embody the user-oriented, information-sharing ideal of the democratisation of digital media, and its blurring of distinctions between media production and consumption, it simultaneously (and less obviously) enforces the legal and economic interests of traditional commercial media companies. YouTube has sophisticated content-surveillance technologies that identify copyright material, and it has contractual arrangements with most major music and screen media corporations that enable those content providers to have a video removed or to allow it to remain online in return for a share of YouTube's revenue from advertising (Bajde et al. 2015, p. 299). Since being purchased by Google in 2006, YouTube has been under increasing pressure to bow to the demands of media corporations to protect copyright and control content distribution and use, and it has shifted from being a site largely stocked by free, user-generated content to one that exhibits and sells professionally generated content such as television episodes, music videos, and even films (Kim 2012, pp. 53–5).

Kim points out that 'Rather than competing with each other, narrowcasting YouTube and broadcasting television utilize each other. Media convergence comes about because people use YouTube as a stepping-stone to mainstream media, and the mainstream media use YouTube to promote their programs, especially in "webisode" format' (2012, pp. 55–6). For example, YouTube users with their own channels and subscribers post video reviews of BBC's *Sherlock*, the official promotional video for Sherlock's season-three return after he faked his death in season two takes the form of a seven-minute mini-episode or webisode ('Many Happy Returns' 2013), and YouTube also features the BBC's extended trailer for the special episode set in Victorian times ('The Abominable Bride' 2016).

In the second decade of the twenty-first century, network television, subscription television, commercial online streaming services, and user-generated content on YouTube all coexist, with major media companies using YouTube as an additional content exhibition and distribution channel, but they also conflict in terms of intellectual property rights and revenues (Kim 2012, p. 57). As Kim summarises:

YouTube-inspired online video services such as hulu.com, and traditional broadcasting channels (e.g. NBC, CBS, ABC) adopted online video streaming … Big media have adopted YouTube strategies, and solved technical issues that YouTube had, such as the length of files, revenue and video quality. As online video services were becoming more popular, the media industry came to recognize two potentially advantageous characteristics of streaming video services: re-transmission channels and interactivity-based advertisements (Kim 2012, p. 58).

Film, TV, and the internet shape structures of perception and attention, with cinema and long-form 'cinematic-novelistic' television narratives inviting an attentive, sustained, and contemplative gaze, whereas other televisual forms like commercial network television and YouTube's short videos fragment attention and command little more than a distracted glance as we consume bite-sized narratives. Fashion media theorist Elizabeth Wissinger argues that there has been a shift in contemporary visual culture and that the age of social media is the age of the 'blink', in which brief flickers of sensational imagery that aren't even organised into narratives command even shorter attention spans (Wissinger 2015, p. 18). For example, as Nic Carah writes, 'Instagram is a media device designed for glancing, directed by the swiping and tapping of the user's finger on the screen of their smartphone' (Carah & Shaul 2016, p. 72). The fleeting televisual glance of YouTube and Instagram lives side by side in media culture with the more contemplative cinematic gaze, and the swift, jumpy, volatile blink of apps like Snapchat that are shaping new regimes of attention.

PORNOGRAPHY

Pornography is not often used as a topic for analysis in formal academic studies. There is some significant research by leading scholars such as Linda Williams, author of *Hard Core* (1989) and *Porn Studies* (2004), and Alan McKee, Kath Albury, and Catharine Lumby, who conducted the *Porn Report* (2008), and in 2014 *Porn Studies*, a quarterly peer-reviewed academic journal, was established by Routledge, followed by Sullivan and McKee's *Pornography: Structures, Agency and Performance* (2015). However, pornography is important for a number of reasons: because of its ubiquity, because of its importance in driving media technological change, and because of its significance for sexuality and in relation to censorship, and in relation to issues discussed above—genre, narrative structure, binaries, and coupling endings.

1   Within the media industries, pornography is a very significant player. While it does not figure on free-to-air television (although explicit sex-service adverts appear on late-night television) or screen in mainstream cinemas, it has its own outlets through satellite and cable television channels, sex cinemas, so-called men's entertainment magazines, DVD hire and purchase, and, most importantly, the internet. Economically, porn is very big business and it is being widely distributed and consumed. While porn does not receive the media attention that popular cinema does and it is difficult to obtain accurate figures, globally porn is estimated to be a $97 billion industry, according to Kassia Wosick, assistant professor of sociology at New Mexico State University (Morris 2014, n.p.). This rivals the Hollywood film industry's annual US box office revenue.

2   Pornography has always been an important player in the development of media technologies. No sooner was photography developed in the mid-nineteenth century than thousands of pornographic photos were being distributed; the potential economic profits from such photos drove the improvements in photographic techniques and processes. The economic profit motive is the essential driving force behind pornography, which has also been influential in determining how media technologies develop and prosper. In recent years, internet, telephone, and text technologies have been used in the pornography and sex industries, again making huge profits and driving the development of these technologies. Advances in computer graphics and animation, using techniques such as human capture in films like *Beowulf*, are also being exploited by pornography. Feminist author and screen theorist Barbara Creed (2003) points out that there is enormous potential to use digital stars in the porn industry because little talent is required, and physical perfection and contortion are easier to create than convincing performances. It is increasingly possible to simulate sexual representations without using actual humans.

3   Regulation of the media industries is another area in which pornography sparks debates. Representations of sexuality are one of the two major concerns about censorship (violence is the other). Different countries have different legislation about sexual representations and about actual sexual behaviour. In Canada it is legal for teenagers to have sexual contact from the age of fourteen, but it is not legal to make and show explicitly sexual media programs for people under the age of eighteen. Yet despite pornography's legal prohibition to people under the age of eighteen, the reality is that young people can and do get access to pornography, which becomes one of the main arenas for them to learn about sexuality. Some campaigners in Canada are anxious that, while teenagers are taking in the messages of pornography, they cannot legally provide teenagers with positive and helpful media messages about sexuality.

In terms of censorship, the history of pornography over the last forty years has been one of continual struggle and debate; it appears that explicit material keeps breaking the barriers of what is acceptable and what can be portrayed. Some people argue that for men and women, and for different sexual orientations, pornography has allowed significant freedom and explorations offering liberation from sexual repression; others see it as exploitative and abusive to women and young people, and still others see it as corrupt for everyone. Around the world, media regulations generally prohibit showing genital arousal on television or in mainstream cinemas. This means that erect penises are not shown, but because female genital arousal is less visible, it is acceptable to show naked women. This leads to systematic inequity in terms of the sexualised objectification of women and men.

4   Pornography is one of the sites where men and women learn about sexuality, so it is important to ask what kinds of messages and information are being presented. Textual analysis is one of the means by which this can be done; genre studies, narratology, and structuralism are others. Narrative structure can be described in sexual terms: like striptease and sexual behaviour, it provides a structure of enticement, excitement, tease, questions, and answers, which is linked to the final goal of narrative resolution, or sexual satisfaction. This is most often represented in

terms of male climax, or orgasm. Such climax can be said to parallel the narrative climax of films. In terms of binary oppositions, the most obvious opposition is the relationship between men and women, masculine and feminine. There is of course homosexual pornography, but much of this can also be analysed in terms of oppositional roles: subservient and dominant, for example. Given that most pornography is geared towards moments of sexual resolution, how are these resolutions presented in terms of the male–female opposition? Is there, for example, an equality of male–female relations in terms of power, pleasure, and how they are visually presented, or are there significant differences? Overall analysis of the genre, its structure, and its oppositions can provide insight into the ideologies of masculinity and femininity, into gender relationships, and into ideologies of sexuality and sexual behaviour.

COMPUTER AND INTERNET GAMES

Cinema was the predominant media entertainment in the first half of the twentieth century; television was in the second half. While both media are still very important in the twenty-first century, they also compete with digital games and internet interactions. People are now spending more time in front of computer screens, and devices such as iPhones and iPads, than television or cinema screens. The new kinds of media entertainment offered by computer games and the internet share some similarities with cinema and television but also introduce some differences, so it is worth considering the extent to which games draw on the characteristics of Hollywood productions.

Can the narrative analytic frameworks set up in this chapter be applied to the new media? Do they operate as narratives and follow the conventions of genre? Do they position audiences in certain ways? Do they work through binary oppositional frameworks? What new elements do they introduce?

Narratives

A key difference between films and games is 'the relative importance of narrative structure or narrative development' (King & Krzywinska 2002, p. 21). The most obvious use of narrative in many games involves

> cut-scenes [that are] short, pre-rendered audio-visual sequences in which the player usually performs the role of a more detached observer than is the case in the more active periods of gameplay. Many games use cut-scenes to establish the initial setting and background storyline … Cut-scenes are also used at varying intervals throughout many games, to forward the storyline (King & Krzywinska 2002, pp. 11–12).

The cut-scene narrative component of games often looks more cinematic than the rest of the game, but lacks the distinctive quality of interactivity and functions more like gift wrapping, to lure the player into the interactive game activity. Once players are immersed in the game, the story tends to unfold in real time. Unlike film narratives, which routinely skip over slow-moving or non-essential action, games seldom use ellipses and they tend to involve extended periods of gameplay, often using a repetitive and episodic structure.

This generates a sense of immediacy that differentiates game narratives from film narratives and perhaps brings them closer to the narrative structures typical of some television genres that present events in real time.

The narrative structure of digital games operates on at least three levels and is partly based on the same principle as genre: repetition and variation within a three-act structure organised around a beginning, middle, and end. On one level, the expository cut-scene storyline elements of game narratives are predetermined and repetitive. On another, in the extended second act that involves active gameplay, the player controls variables in the narrative and becomes the author of their own storyline each time they play. As new-media analysts Geoff King and Tanya Krzywinska put it in *Cinema/Videogames/Interfaces*, digital games often invoke the cause/effect structure of narrative, even if it is not linear:

> moments of the most heightened and intensively interactive gameplay often entail features such as cause/effect relationships and linear progression (although the latter, in particular, is far from always guaranteed: it is quite possible to regress, to lose ground, during activities such as combat or the negotiation of difficult terrain) (King & Krzywinska 2002, p. 24).

On a third level, players can also become creators or authors of the games they play by substantially contributing to the text as they create mods and skins. Mods are game modifications that involve creating new spaces and scenarios; skins are customised character appearances.

Most computer games do have an end in sight, which means there is some kind of goal involved for the participant, often a competitive one that involves playing against either the computer or other participants. This also makes the games close to the narratives of sports. But there are significant differences between the narratives of computer games and film or television narratives.

First, the narrative of each game is likely to be slightly different every time you play (a form of generic variation), whereas an individual film is the same every time you watch it. There is in general more fluidity to outcomes within the game world.

Second, endings can happen in very different places. A game where you are fighting against some killer opposition, for example, can result in your being killed—game over—very quickly. One of the narrative pleasures of games is that you can get better and go further, kill more opponents, score more points, last longer in the game. Thus, as the narrative lasts longer and its resolution changes, it can progressively get better.

Third, for some games this can mean an almost infinite regression: once you can win at one level, then you can go to the next, and so on. With some games you will finally be able to win every time at every level; when you do, it's time for a new game. With others you might be in a system where you are always trying to beat your best score and thus you could go on playing forever—there is no ultimate narrative resolution.

Another type of game, such as the *The Fast and the Furious* Nintendo and Wii games, and the *Mad Max* or *The Walking Dead* computer games based on popular films and television series, relies on players' intertextual knowledge of backstory, an established fictional universe, and familiar characters. In the multiplayer Xbox game *South Park Let's Go Tower Defense Play*, irreverent in-jokes and controversial narrative lines are directed at fans of the *South Park* TV series.

Despite these similarities between film, television, and digital games on the levels of narrative and genre, there are also significant differences. In film the conventions of the action genre dictate that Robert Downey Jr's character Tony Stark will overcome insurmountable obstacles and live through to the end of the *Iron Man* films. Similarly, in the *Deadpool* movie (from the Marvel universe), we know that Deadpool/Wade Wilson, played by Ryan Reynolds, will triumph. By contrast, the digital games based on the *Iron Man* film franchise or the *Deadpool* game work within the same genre but, though they are modelled closely on sequences from the films, operate according to different conventions and expectations. Players expect to die many times before ever completing the game, or even to play as a War Machine fighting against Stark, or Deadpool fighting Ajax, which leads to a higher degree of uncertainty and suspense:

> The fact that the experience of games can entail large measures of anxiety and uncertainty—to an extent not usually found in the cinema, because of its particular narrative regime—has been linked by some commentators to the role they might perform in the socialization process for adolescent males. Playing a game … to achieve mastery in the face of the stresses and anxieties it creates, is seen as one way of practicing the "performance" of dominant versions of masculinity (King & Krzywinska 2002, p. 53).

In addition to similarities and differences in the social functions and narrative structures of film, television, and digital games, games can also be understood in relation to genre. Games can easily be based on the settings, characters, motives, and contexts of popular genres since action, fantasy, and science-fiction genres come with their own established sets of rules, conventions, and expectations that fill in a lot of the backstory and 'offer instantly recognisable frames of reference that allow gameplay to proceed with only minimal elaboration of the specific scenario' (King & Krzywinska 2006, p. 55). *IMVU* draws on conventions of the soap opera genre, and the *Who Wants to Be a Millionaire* and *Deal or No Deal* games are directly based on the television game shows of the same names. These can often be played on PC, Mac, iPads, iPhones, or Android devices. Further, as King and Krzywinska point out, teleportation is an accepted convention of the science-fiction and fantasy genres; hence, while it is not out of place in the futuristic, military, first-person shooter *Doom* and the massively multiplayer online role-playing games (MMORPG) *Black Desert*, *League of Legends*, and *Archeage*, it would be incongruous in the badass gangster underworld of *Grand Theft Auto*, *Sleeping Dogs*, or *Saints Row*.

Most of the games discussed so far are goal-directed and thus have similarities to narratives requiring resolution. But many other games, such as the virtual worlds of *IMVU*, and internet chat rooms provide worlds where people can visit and play in a virtual space that isn't so goal oriented or geared towards narrative resolution. The choices and variety of possibilities are more like those you face in daily life—Where do I want to go today? Who do I want to visit?—but in a virtual world. The narrative resolutions here are simply dependent on how long you want to play. It's more like having a telephone conversation with someone: the narrative will depend on your interactions, your mood, time constraints, and so on. But whereas in a telephone conversation you just speak to one person, with multiple user domains (MUDs) and internet games and chat, you have many more people. Part of the excitement here is meeting new people (perhaps a parallel to the idea of variation described here as one of the pleasures of genre narratives). Your participation will have a narrative closure that occurs when you decide to leave the game or online environment. Even though your departure may be triggered by your feeling some kind of resolution, some satisfaction in what you have done, this is not really the same as the ordered narrative resolutions of film and television fictions.

Binary oppositions in games

Many games are based on oppositional structures: you play against the game itself or against other players. The structure is most obviously one of goodies versus baddies, heroes versus villains, so binary structures are central to how the games are presented. There are two things to point out here. The first is that while there is a similarity to film and television narratives in this structure, the big difference is that the games tend to construct a much more black-and-white world. The games do not have the oppositional subtleties or complexities that can be found in the best film narratives, which allow for more crossovers and interconnections between the two sets of oppositions. But the games certainly encourage participants to see the world in quite simplistic, binary, oppositional terms.

The second point is that these oppositional structures carry ideological positions. In the USA, when army recruitment was falling early this century, the army decided to offer a free computer game that simulated army action. The game was widely distributed and proved highly popular (mainly with boys and young men), and army recruitment figures substantially improved. The excitement of simulated war games, in which no one was really injured or killed, led to an increase in those volunteering for armed service. This simulated game also depicted an enemy who could be seen as related to the USA's wars in Iraq and Afghanistan, and on terrorism. In contrast to this, Arab countries in the same period recognised that most computer war games presented Arab figures as the baddies, so they started to produce games that featured Jewish figures as the baddies and Arab figures as the heroes. The problem with any of these oppositional war games is that they can easily demonise particular social or racial groups.

Interactivity and first person—alternative narratives

Computer and internet games offer other significant differences from film and television narratives. They introduce a high degree of interactivity and they do so from a first-person perspective. Interactivity means that you, as participant, are involved in the game, its narrative, and how it unfolds. This makes two differences from film narratives: first, some games allow the possibility for different narrative developments, since you can choose at various stages what direction the narrative can go in. Thus there are numerous possible narrative developments and different possible resolutions, unlike in film narratives, which generally move towards a single, fixed ending. So, once again, game narratives are more fluid, more open.

Second, because you as participant are involved in making choices and decisions about what should happen, you become an active author of the game rather than just a receiving reader as you are in film narratives, which means you are much more directly involved. Digital games require intervention, not just interpretation, and this shifts the emphasis away from narrative. Players must respond to events in a manner that affects what happens on screen, something not usually demanded of readers of books or viewers of films. Success often depends on rapid responses, effective hand-eye coordination and learned moves or skills effected through devices such as joypads and keyboards, or puzzle-solving skills (King & Krzywinska 2002, pp. 22–3).

This involvement is also from a first-person perspective, again a major difference from film and television narratives, which you watch from the outside, from a third-person, observer perspective. One of the major pleasures of computer and internet games is that you get to enter the drama, the game, the narrative itself, in a much more involved and active position. The impression of aliveness and presence in the game world arises from the experience of inhabiting and exploring a digital landscape, acting as a central figure in the narrative. As King and Krzywinska write:

> The possibility of seeming to move "inside" the fictional world on screen is sometimes seen as a defining characteristic of games, especially those based recognizably on individual films, franchises or film genres. The player can, at one remove, "become" the central figure in a cinematic environment, following and extending the kinds of experiences offered in film (King & Krzywinska 2002, p. 4).

The *District 9* online game, for example, can be played as either a human or an alien. In the *Defiance* multiplayer game, the player can choose to be either a human or an 'Irathient' (a humanoid alien species). The world of the film is extended in terms of both interactivity and variation of perspective/allegiance. This first-person perspective is linked to the possibility of exploring different aspects of your own personality as you can construct new identities for yourself, particularly in the form of avatars, the form and identity that you decide to present yourself as in the game. While films and stories have traditionally offered readers or viewers the chance to identify with different characters—to imagine yourself as Chris Hemsworth being Thor or as Natalie Portman being Jane Foster in *Thor: The Dark World*—computer and internet games offer you even more freedoms to explore and discover different parts of yourself in active participation.

FILM, TELEVISION, AND GAME CROSSOVERS

Digital games form a multibillion dollar aspect of the entertainment media industry, and tie-in games are valued highly in Hollywood as a way of capitalising on existing film audiences and attracting new audiences, particularly in the lucrative youth market. The opening sequence in which Daniel Craig in his role as James Bond pursues his target across vertiginous rooftops in *Casino Royale* was clearly designed with the game tie-in in mind; in fact the series of 007 games released since 1995 helped broaden the audience to include a whole new generation of Bond fans, according to King and Krzywinska (2002, p. 8). The tie-ins between cinema, the internet, and games are perfectly illustrated by the websites of popular films such as *Thor* and *Deadpool*, which not only invite you to navigate a variety of windows of information into the individual films, but offer an opening into the broader Marvel universe, consumer purchases, and gaming interactivity.

In addition to this, computer games, television, and cinema are all mutually influencing each other: computer games have been influenced by cinema's and television's visual and narrative styles. In order to make computer games more and more attractive, they improved their graphics and sound quality, and the complexity of their narratives. The result is that games can now offer visual and aural pleasures that are coming closer to those offered by cinema and television. While computer games are often spin-offs from films or television programs, cinematic styles are now changing in response to the technologies of the computer games. Animation techniques, which form the basis of most computer games, have developed and become increasingly popular in the cinema, as can be seen in *Guardians of the Galaxy*. Films such as *Dawn of the Planet of the Apes*, *The Hobbit: The Desolation of Smaug*, and *The Life of Pi* adopted motion-capture animation techniques or visual manipulations that made them look more like computer-game graphics than traditional realist cinema. Narrative sequences in cinema now sometimes resemble sequences from games in the way the camera can move through space, turn corners, and negotiate movement through buildings. A film such as *Warcraft* plays on this in the way many of its action sequences involve protagonists moving with impossible dexterity and speed in the virtual world of the computer game on which the film itself is based.

It can be argued that, to a large extent, the interactive and immersive experiences of gameplay offer alternative and complementary pleasures to those offered in film and television narratives. There are similarities in the narrative structures and actions of game worlds and of cinematic and television worlds, as well as significant differences. Perhaps narrative theory can never fully encompass the differences between identification with characters and active participation as a protagonist, nor can it account for the kinaesthetic, experiential, and technological dimensions of gameplay.

CONCLUSION

This chapter has considered whether and how the approaches to narrative that apply to traditional media such as film can be applied to digital television, and computer and internet games. We have explored how technological developments in the television industry are associated with radical changes to televisual form and content, and with significant differences in the ways that audiences engage with television. In particular we have tracked the shift from commercial network broadcast television, which was fragmented by advertising and consumed according to a set schedule, through to current uses of video-streaming services such as YouTube and Netflix. The chapter has also investigated the proliferation of pornography on the internet and the popularity of interactive video game narratives.

This chapter has

- compared television and film narratives
- examined the impact of the internet in terms of pornographic narratives
- considered narrative in computer and internet games.

? DISCUSSION POINTS

1 Television has been described as a domestic medium. Does this claim still have currency in the era of TVIII? How do changing television technologies, exhibition formats, and reception modes affect audience responses?

2 Online pornography is increasingly able to simulate sex using computer-generated 'actors'. The more this occurs, the more it will raise interesting questions as to what is acceptable and legal: while the use of real humans for pornography may in some cases be exploitative, abusive, and illegal, how, for example, will we deal with exploitative and abusive representations that don't use real people?

SUMMARY

You should now be able to

- discuss some of the key similarities and differences between film and television narratives
- consider how narrative structural analysis can be used for analysis of computer and internet games.

CHAPTER 18

Documentary and Reality TV

> Reality television is not the end of civilisation as we know it; it is civilisation as we know it.
>
> Germaine Greer, *Media Studies: The Essential Resource*

This chapter will

- apply narrative structure and binary opposition analysis to non-fiction television
- consider the development of documentaries and reality TV
- problematise issues related to truth and realism
- demonstrate how concepts such as discourse and generic hybridity relate to reality-based media
- discuss responses to reality TV.

While previous chapters focused on fictional entertainment media, this chapter looks at a variety of reality-based programming ranging from television news through documentaries to examples of reality TV. It will demonstrate how structuralist narrative approaches can be applied to non-fiction texts, and will examine how the concepts of modality and generic hybridity relate to reality-based media. We will question why reality TV became so popular, and why it has given rise to social controversy and panic about moral degeneration.

NON-FICTION TELEVISION: NEWS

Since television began it has produced many non-fiction programs; the most prevalent have been news, current affairs, documentaries, sports, quiz shows, and chat shows. In recent years television has been inundated with reality TV programs. The analytic tools used in the previous chapter—narrative structure and binary oppositions—can be applied to all these programs. To exemplify this we will look at news and sports programs.

The news is broadcast several times a day. In narrative terms it is not a 'sequence of events taking place over a given period of time that are linked, mainly through cause and effect' (see p. 234); rather, it is the putting together of a whole series of different events and stories. But these different events are contained and positioned within a narrative format. The overall nature of this format is to take the disturbances of world events and present them in a way that is ultimately reassuring and/or entertaining (see Chapter 2 for discussion of gatekeeping and agenda-setting).

The news is presented by newsreaders whose familiar faces and voices are the channels or discourses through which all news is filtered to us. They represent the dominant discourse and deliver the news with clarity and certainty. News presenters are usually authoritative, attractive, and well spoken. No matter how disturbing the events are, the studio presence of the newsreaders creates a distance between us and the raw reality and gives a sense of familiar comfort. The news is structured with a beginning, a middle, and an end. The structure is normally a series of headlines that act as the disruption of our stable situation, as in fictional narratives. The lead stories are then elaborated on in more detail and presented in order of importance, followed by other, non-headline stories. The sequence conventionally ends with sports stories and sometimes a feel-good story about animals, celebrities, or children, thus moving us from disturbing political and social events, often heralded by some stirring music, to pleasurable and positive, reassuring events. Finally, the newsreaders sign off and wish us a good evening or say goodbye. Often headlines are repeated but by this stage they have been made familiar and acceptable; they are thus contained within the format of the news. All of this leads us in the end to reassurance, closure, and acceptance (stable situation 2), a state that requires us to do nothing.

Peter Watkins draws attention to the similar structure of news presentations, what he calls their 'monoform', which treats all stories in the same way:

> This same method of story-telling is used night after night, year after year, no matter what the emotional demand of the theme or subject being presented. The repetitive, split-second similarity in the way that it organises sounds and images blurs the distinctions between different themes and subjects, and between what might otherwise be entirely different emotional responses to them. There is no allowance for differentiation of information, whether about a terrible air-crash, or a man who has painted his pet elephant pink. Both stories are presented via the same grid-lock and narrative structure … This repetitious story-telling pattern, linked with the fact that it is closed (has no space for the audience to reflect or intervene), and that it usually consists of a dense, non-stop bombardment of violent juxtapositions of image, sound and conflicting themes, has had a devastating effect on society (Watkins 1997, p. 6).

Watkins sees this sameness in the manner of representation as extending beyond news coverage to all areas of the audiovisual media (see <www.mnsi.net/~pwatkins> for information about Watkins' films and his extremely critical views about the media).

Documentary theorist Bill Nichols, looking at the form and structure of news coverage, suggests that the point of view constructed for audiences is a position of 'viewer-observer', a position that means people are detached from the news coverage. Consequently, 'News reportage urges us to look but not care, see but not act, know but not change. The news exists less to orient us towards action than to perpetuate itself as commodity, something to be fetishised and consumed' (Nichols 1991, p. 194).

The entertainment factor of news is present in the way that the headlines can also act as narrative teasers—a glimpse of some exciting images, or a few words that set up a story with 'More of that later'. In the world of ratings and audiences, television news has to sell itself in order to win its audience through a discourse of entertainment and pleasurable viewing. To do so, news stories invariably use a binary discourse to construct and explain events. This 'exciting' conflict between opposing parties or individuals is the overriding structure for nearly all stories.

SPORTS AND QUIZ SHOWS

One of the dominant features of television discourse is the use of **direct address**, a person speaking to and facing the camera: they bid us good morning or good night and wish us a safe weekend on Fridays. These voices are more intimate and directly connected to us

◄ DIRECT ADDRESS

Direct address to camera is when the person onscreen looks straight into the camera as though they are looking at and addressing the audience directly. This breaks the conventions of cinematic realism by acknowledging the process of filming; it also substitutes a different sense of realism, intimacy, and immediacy.

than other voices in fiction films and television programs. They are allowed to look at the camera and hence directly at us; they are the mediators for other people, whom they introduce, frame, and question, and they comment on what we have just seen or heard. The faceless voice-overs that announce programs are also privileged discourses. Like the voice of God, they emerge out of nowhere and speak with authority.

There is a structural similarity in the format of a whole range of non-fiction programs that are introduced and fronted by professional television presenters. These programs also work in terms of narrative structures, as seen in sports programs and quiz shows, two of the most popular areas of television programming. Sports events themselves are clearly based on a narrative format setting up a conflict–opposition, usually between two individuals (boxing, tennis) or two teams (netball, football), sometimes between groups of individuals (running, swimming). The final whistle, or the end of the match or race, determines the narrative closure, by which time the question of who will win will be satisfactorily answered. The actual sport is mediated and developed by commentary, pre- and post-match discussion and analysis, and interviews with and stories about individual players, programs that build up and prepare us for coming events. All these extra-event elements can be analysed to see how they construct events and narratives in particular ways. You may notice some particular features, for example, the partisan, nationalist nature of commentary so that an event such as the Olympics is mediated by whichever country is broadcasting: Australian coverage is obsessed with Australian participants and how many medals Australia has won. The commentary also expresses the value systems endorsed by the sport: strength, physicality, and determination in many 'masculine' sports, grace, beauty, and dexterity in more 'feminine' sports, and cooperation in team sports.

Analysis of the history of sports coverage shows that more and more entertainment factors have been introduced into sports coverage, such as the music and dance opening extravaganzas of the Olympic Games and the World Cup, the use of classical music theme tunes to go with those events, the use of increasingly fashionable sports clothing, personal and emotional stories about the competitors, the ever-developing use of new camera technologies, slow motion, new camera angles, instant replays, and the creation of sports stars and celebrities. All these aspects have widened the appeal of sports, so now there is something of interest for all spectators. The narrative strategy of waiting for the final result of a sports competition is the perfect audience hook.

A similar narrative hook is found in quiz shows. Here there is an added element in that audiences can be surrogate participants, can try to answer the questions themselves and then wait to see if they are right. Quiz shows build up suspense and excitement through the use of music and delaying the revelation of the right answer; they create emotional interest by finding out competitors' personal stories. Sports and quiz shows work because the final outcome is always unknown: our desire for narrative resolution and closure is central to our involvement, and we won't get it unless we watch until the show ends. Quiz and sports programs present a world view of competition, success, and failure. The added ingredient in quiz shows is often the possibility of winning huge sums of money, luxury travel, or expensive consumer goods. In this way the shows support a materialist, consumer-driven, capitalist view of the world: money equals happiness. Both these types of programs are mediated by professional commentators or quiz show hosts who guide us through the events.

DOCUMENTARY

Documentaries have always been an important part of film and television. When film was invented at the end of the nineteenth century, two distinct strands of filmmaking evolved. One used film to tell spectacular fictional stories about individual characters; these developed into Hollywood feature films. The other used film to record or document reality, as seen in the first short films by the Lumière brothers (1895) such as *Workers Leaving a Factory* and *Train Arriving at a Station*. Both strands continued, but fiction and spectacle were, and remain, commercially dominant.

The term 'documentary' is used because film is a kind of document, a record of reality, but also because it derives from the Latin word *doceo*, which means to 'warn or advise'. Documentaries are often a kind of warning or advice about important world issues. MTV's reality-based television documentary series *Catfish: The TV Show* (Ariel Schulman, Yaniv 'Nev' Schulman, and Max Joseph, 2012–) is a good example of this: like the documentary film on which the TV series is based (*Catfish*, dir. Henry Joost and Ariel Schulman 2010), it warns of the potential for deception, delusion, and misrepresentation when people form relationships via online dating or social networking media. The documentary film exposes the false Facebook profiles of a small-town housewife and in doing so it reveals damaging personal information about her and her family. Although the premise of the TV series is that a person becomes suspicious about someone with whom they have an online relationship, and contacts MTV to investigate their partner's identity and set up a face-to-face meeting, the producers often 'reverse engineer' episodes by establishing contact with the deceitful partner first and then approaching the naïve partner with an offer to investigate the relationship. Both the film and television versions of *Catfish* have been accused of staging or reconstructing the order of events and manipulating vulnerable subjects, which raises issues about the ethics of documentary filmmaking.

Documentary ethics: do documentaries exploit their subjects?

We identify two major issues about documentary. The first is the question of documentary ethics and whether documentary makers exploit their subjects. This is an important issue that you might consider if you are making documentaries yourself: how are you treating your subjects and what will happen to them as a result of being filmed? Who has power in the filming situation? Craig Gilbert, producer of *An American Family*, comments: 'We are using human beings to make a point ... we are "exploiting" them to make our films ... and the fact is that our incomes and our careers often depend on our ability to conceal the truth of this exploitation from our subjects' (Gilbert 1988, p. 293). Is the very act of pointing a camera at someone and shooting them a form of exploitation or intrusion? In Australia the family who was filmed in the documentary series *Sylvania Waters* (1992), when reality TV was just emerging, ended up publicly burning the videotapes of the series and condemning the producers for exploiting them. In the documentary *Crumb* (1994), an account of cartoon artist Robert Crumb, his brother, Charles Crumb, was filmed discussing and exposing his own private life. Did he realise what he was letting himself reveal when he was being interviewed? The intimate and rather pathetic details of his life were then broadcast in cinemas in a sequence that was

◀ DOCUMENTARIES

Films and television programs about real-life situations.

presented in such a way as to make audiences laugh at him. Shortly after viewing the film, he suicided. The whole issue of victimisation and exploitation by the media is very important in texts dealing with real people rather than paid actors.

Do documentaries capture reality and tell the truth?

The second issue is focused on the perennial questions of the truth status of documentaries: can they actually tell the truth, the whole truth, and nothing but the truth? Do they capture reality? Can they offer an unbiased, objective view of the world, or just a partial truth? Do they show or construct reality? From all that was said in Part 1 about the media's construction of reality, it will be clear that we don't think documentaries can be simple, unbiased windows on the world; even though visual and sound-recording techniques offer the possibility of recording and capturing reality unlike any previous aesthetic techniques, there is always a process of construction (selection and framing of events, editing, point of view, commentary, and so on), and these constructions will always come from a particular position. Documentary maker and producer John Grierson's comment on the problem of documentary and how it 'captured reality' is that filmmakers engage in 'the creative construction of actuality'. Grierson acknowledges and embraces the fact that filmmakers interpret and construct events—'actuality'—in particular ways. Documentarists have developed various approaches, styles, and conventions in their work, and all of them have to deal with the issue and problem of how to capture reality.

Documentary history: Flaherty and Vertov

Robert Flaherty made films from the 1920s onwards and is sometimes regarded as the father of documentary filmmaking. He used his movie camera as an anthropological tool to document his studies of Inuit (Eskimo) communities while he lived in their midst. *Nanook of the North* (1922) is his most renowned film. Flaherty faced issues about documentary ethics and truthfulness. Sometimes he would stage aspects of the situation that he was filming, such as asking hunters to use traditional weapons to harpoon seals instead of using their guns. Sometimes he would ask his subjects to undergo dangerous tasks for the benefit of his films. This technique documented traditional practices and made the films appear more authentic, but it was not an accurate representation of Inuit hunting practices in the 1920s. Flaherty's aim was to record the experiences, cultural practices, and living conditions of these remote communities in an honest manner that represented the essence of real life, even if it didn't mirror it exactly as it happened.

In contrast, Russian filmmaker Dziga Vertov, who was working around the same time as Flaherty, firmly believed that filmmakers should not manipulate events for the camera. He was opposed to the nostalgic and theatrical illusions presented in fiction film and wanted to use film to expose social reality, even to expose the reality of the filmmaking process itself. His most famous film is *The Man with a Movie Camera* (1929), which incorporates newsreel footage and shots of the process of filming and editing. Vertov saw the movie camera as a mechanical eye that was capable of looking at reality in a way that human beings cannot. He celebrated the camera as a new machine: 'I am eye. I am a mechanical eye. I, a machine, am showing you a world the likes of which only I can see … My road is towards the creation of a fresh perception of the world … more perfect than the human eye' (Edwards 1985, p. 45). Vertov felt it was important that the film audience was made aware of the filmmakers' interventions in the production process as decisions were made about selecting and editing footage.

Cinéma vérité and observational documentary

The earliest documentaries were what Nichols calls '**expository**, voice of God' documentaries. In these a commentator explains everything that is happening for the viewer. During the 1950s film equipment technologies developed that made camera and sound equipment lighter and more user-friendly; consequently, filmmakers could more easily and unobtrusively follow people around and record their actions and words. This gave rise to a radical change in documentary and catalysed movements in the USA and Europe, known variously as **cinéma vérité**, **direct cinema**, fly on the wall, or observational documentary. Documentarists such as Richard Leacock, Don Pennebaker, the Mayles brothers, Frederick Wiseman, Jean Rouch, and Roger Graef believed that with the new technology, documentaries really could capture what was happening. Once it had, then the results could be shown to the world.

Cinéma vérité literally means 'film truth', though ethnographic filmmaker Jean Rouch prefers to translate it as 'cinema sincerity'. He is said to have invented *cinéma vérité* when he was on location, filming in a remote area, and accidentally knocked his camera tripod into the river. From that point on he had to hold the camera when filming, creating the unsteady footage and mobile framing that we now associate with documentary realism. Rouch found that this mode of filming gave him a more spontaneous, intimate relationship with the people and events he was filming (Rouch 1995). It also allowed the footage to be less staged or controlled, because the camera could be situated amid the action and respond dynamically to changes. Up to this point cameras had always been placed on tripods, largely because they were too heavy and bulky to carry. The development of lightweight 16 mm cameras and portable sound-recording equipment, such as the Nagra tape recorder, and later super 8 and inexpensive home video cameras, personalised movie making, rendering it accessible to more people and so changing the conventions and aesthetic outcomes of filmmaking. Technological advances in filmmaking were swiftly transferred to television, with the emergence of British televérité current affairs shows such as *World in Action* (1962), which capitalised on the introduction of 16 mm cameras (Sexton 2003).

In *cinéma vérité* films, the camera is imagined to be an eye that views and records life itself with as little contrivance, intervention, illusion, or manipulation as possible. The conventions of *cinéma vérité* include hand-held footage, minimal editing (long takes in chronological sequence), and the absence of non-diegetic music or voice-over narration. The films of *cinéma vérité* are not staged and scripted fictions—they contain actual people in actual settings rather than actors in studios. Rouch sees *cinéma vérité* as a form of expression in which the filmmaker says to the audience, 'This is what I saw. I didn't fake it, this is what happened. I didn't pay anyone … I didn't change anyone's behaviour. I looked at what happened with my subjective eye and this is what I believe took place' (cited in MacDonald & Cousins 1996, p. 265).

The main difference between *cinéma vérité* and its US counterpart, direct cinema, is that the latter assumes the camera can capture an objective record of events. Rouch acknowledges that the camera can't capture objective truth because the filmmaker is always making decisions about what to focus on and what to ignore, and because only

◀ EXPOSITORY DOCUMENTARY

A voice-over commentary explains what we see, thereby controlling our viewpoint.

◀ *CINÉMA VÉRITÉ*

French for 'cinema truth'. A documentary style developed in France in the 1950s and 1960s, *cinéma vérité* is similar to direct cinema, fly-on-the-wall documentary, and observational documentary, but the filmmakers participate more directly and self-reflexively in the narrative.

◀ DIRECT CINEMA

The North American corollary of *cinéma vérité*, direct cinema has an observational style, but does not involve interviews or intervention by the filmmakers.

one particular version or perspective on reality can be recorded. In addition, knowing you are being observed or filmed changes behaviour, resulting in what Rouch calls 'provoked reality'. As such, this filmmaking is more like a fly in the soup (affecting reality) than a fly on the wall (watching but unnoticed). To add a self-reflexive, participatory element and another level of realism, Rouch would often ask the people he filmed to watch the footage and comment on it. He then used their own commentary to explain the images, instead of using the 'voice of God' expository narration.

Despite the continued popularity of this observational style, its limitations are recognised and today we have a fascinating contradiction around documentary. Documentary's realist premise—that it can innocently, impartially, and objectively record the world—has been challenged: it is accepted by many that documentaries can't capture unmediated reality. Therefore, if all representations are constructions, documentary filmmaking should be discredited. But this realisation can free up documentary filmmaking from its link with realism: in its documentation of the real world, it can use many techniques and include all manner of representational modes. Consequently, we have a flowering of documentary practices that are not restricted by the need to capture pure truth; instead, documentarists can experiment with numerous ways of presenting reality and capturing different truths.

'Some form of truth is the always receding goal of documentary film'

Taking this contradiction further, Linda Williams has asserted that 'some form of truth is the always receding goal of documentary film' (1993, p. 20). In saying this she seems to recognise that documentary can never capture pure truth or objective reality since it is always relative and getting away from us; nevertheless, documentarists still seek a truth. She thus recognises the impossibility of finding absolute truth but insists on the importance of attempting to find partial truths about the world. This perhaps explains how many viewers are caught between their own sophistication and cynicism about the media whereby they can dismiss television and films as constructions, hype, biased, and so on, but at the same time they are still fascinated by the possibility of seeing reality captured by film or video and are thus drawn to documentaries and reality TV.

Given this fascination with reality, the availability of increasingly sophisticated film and video technology, and a range of exciting stylistic possibilities, there has been since 1990 an amazing increase in documentary production, exhibition, and popularity. Today documentaries are often screened in mainstream and arthouse cinemas, and there are many documentaries on television that are gaining big audiences.

Documentary styles and conventions

You can use your knowledge of semiotics to analyse the codes and conventions of reality-based screen texts. It is easy to identify documentaries because they use familiar signs and conventions, such as the jerky, hand-held camera, low-resolution or poorly lit images, interviews where people speak directly to the camera, interviews that hide the identity of the speaker, subtitles used over poor-quality sound recording, surveillance cameras, voice-over commentators giving matter-of-fact observations, use of archival footage, re-enactments, and so on.

Over time these signs and conventions have developed different connotations of authenticity. Often when a technique is used for the first time—such as hand-held cameras—its originality gives it an added reality quotient, a greater degree of authenticity, and we don't see it as a convention; however, the more it is used, the more familiar and conventional it becomes, so that gradually it loses its strong realistic authenticity and we are more aware of processes of construction.

As documentary analysts Jane Roscoe and Craig Hight point out in their book *Faking It: Mock-Documentary and the Subversion of Factuality* (2001), distrust of special effects and cinematic illusions arises from technological advances that allow digital image manipulation and computer-generated imagery to produce fakes that look astonishingly real. This threatens the truth status of images that we would previously have accepted as documentary evidence; hence technological developments have led us to question the concepts of truth and reality. Perhaps the popularity of reality TV is both a symptom and a cause of this escalating distrust of the media and the uncertainty about what we can count on, what we know, and what counts as knowledge.

GENERIC HYBRIDITY

Generic hybrids (see p. 213) are texts that blend the codes and conventions of two or more genres to produce a new combination. If we think of documentary and news as genres, then we can see that these core types of non-fiction texts have spawned many new crossbreeds. The sheer diversity of generic hybrids emerging from the documentary tradition is made possible because documentary filmmaking itself has always encompassed a wide range of styles, techniques, and topics.

The boundaries that once separated documentary from feature film, information from entertainment, fact from fiction are now much more blurred or fluid. Documentaries such as *Sherpa* (2015), *Dreams of a Life* (2011), and *The Look of Silence* (2014) have moved closer to traditional forms of entertainment: they tell narrative stories, they often focus on key individuals and personalities, and they use humour, suspense, exciting pictures, catchy soundtracks, and all the standard techniques of dramatic storytelling (all of which is partly driven by economic imperatives). Fictional films and television shows often use documentary techniques in relation to camera work and visual style. You may have noticed that contemporary films will often move into black-and-white footage or use unsteady, hand-held cameras in sequences that aim to convey a sense of immediacy or authenticity. Documentary filmmaking techniques, associated with factual representation rather than with fiction, are used extensively in films such as *District 9* (2009), *Europa Report* (2013), *The Big Short* (2015), *Cloverfield* (2008), and *Monsters: Dark Continent* (2014).

The hugely successful but very low-budget horror films *Paranormal Activity*, *Paranormal Activity 2, 3, 4* (2007–15), and the latter two films in the series, *Paranormal Activity: The Masked One* and *Paranormal Activity: The Ghost Dimension*, and also *The Blair Witch Project* employ documentary-style footage and subject matter especially effectively. Each of these horror films is supposedly filmed by the characters themselves as they document their experiences of creepy phenomena, and each is shot almost entirely using hand-held cameras. This technique places viewers right in the middle of the action when, for example, the terrified students in *The Blair Witch Project* (1999) run through the dark forest, and the camera jerks and shakes along with them. Or, as the couple in *Paranormal Activity* set up their camera with night vision, then go to bed, we watch as they sleep unaware of what's creeping into their bedroom. It also makes these events seem much more realistic (and therefore more frightening), because we are used to shaky home videos recording things that really happen to us and our friends and family.

This documentary style is also evident in the streetwise look of recent films dramatising real events (*Snowtown*, 2011, *The Hurt Locker*, 2008, *America: Imagine the World without Her,* 2014), and in many advertisements and programs, such as *Jersey Shore* and *UnREAL* (2015–), which use documentary styles and technologies to create a realistic effect. The producers of *UnREAL* felt that presenting a parodic commentary on a reality TV show such as *The Bachelor* (2002–) as if documenting a real-life situation on the set of that show would give the program power and realism. Other films actually mix fiction and documentary. *True Stories* (1986), a brilliant play on the blurred line between fact and fiction, is one such film. The most significant mixes of fiction and documentary are mockumentaries, which form a whole genre on their own.

Mockumentaries

This Is Spinal Tap (1984) is one of the most well-known early mockumentaries. It imitated the style and conventions of music documentary but was actually about a fictional rock music group. (So successful was the film that the group did actually get asked to play concerts and thus developed a real music career.) The main pleasure for audiences is the humour of the film, based on sending-up—mocking—of the genre, which is dependent on the audience's knowledge of rockumentary conventions. Casey Affleck's film about Joaquin Phoenix's faux rap career, *I'm Still Here* (2010), involved an elaborate, long-running hoax in which Phoenix publicly announced his change of career from film actor to rapper, cultivated dishevelled hair and clothing, and, to all appearances, descended into a life of undisciplined drug use and debauchery for the year during which Affleck filmed him. Phoenix remained in character during public appearances as audiences laughed at his attempts to rap. Humour is a major factor in many mockumentary films, such as *What We Do in the Shadows* (2014), *Borat* (2006), and *Brüno* (2009). It is also apparent in mockumentary television series such as *Modern Family* (2009–), *Parks and Recreation* (2009–15), *The Thick of It* (2005–12) and *Utopia* (2014). Additionally, as these titles suggest, there is pleasure in seeing people who could be like us, the audience, on screen.

But humour is not the only factor behind mockumentaries. Some of the earliest examples of fictions using a documentary, realistic format were not comic at all. Orson Welles' famous 1930s radio broadcast of *War of the Worlds* was presented as a real live-news story. So convinced were some people by the realism of the broadcast that they started to flee New York in the belief that aliens were invading. Peter Watkins developed the form most powerfully in *Culloden* (1964) and *The War Game* (1966). *Culloden* was a documentary about an eighteenth-century battle between Scotland and England that re-enacted the battle as if a television reporting crew was on hand to film the events and interview the participants. No viewer would actually have thought this possible, but it gave the historical events a contemporary immediacy and invited viewers to be aware of the conventions of documentary reporting. *The War Game*, shot in documentary format, was an imaginary look at what might happen in the event of a nuclear war in Britain. The realism of the events was deeply disturbing, so much so that the BBC banned the film, arguing that people would be confused by the documentary format and believe it was real.

Roscoe and Hight have argued that, while there is humour in the mockumentary form, it also has a serious function in that it challenges viewers about the boundaries between fact and fiction. By making the documentary conventions visible, it encourages viewers to realise that all documentaries are constructions, 'thus questioning and challenging documentary's authority' (Roscoe & Hight 1997, p. 78), which otherwise tends to be accepted at face value. Another kind of pleasure for audiences may come from their attempt to sort out documentary from mockumentary, testing their ability to interpret signs and signifiers. Have you ever seen a program where you are not clear at first whether it is a real documentary?

Self-reflexive documentaries

Many filmmakers are themselves aware of the limitations of the media and their ability to capture truth. Rather than making mockumentaries, they continue to make documentaries but within what Nichols has called a 'self-reflexive' mode (Nichols 2001, p. 125). This **self-reflexivity** invites audiences to be aware of the processes of construction and to question what is being presented. Our attention may be drawn to the filmmaker's presence and involvement in the project, encouraging the viewer to question the film's truth, as do the films of Michael Moore and of Nick Broomfield, who are active participants in their own films; or attention may be drawn to the filmmaking process itself (as Vertov and Rouch did) as a way of exploring the whole issue of film truth and reality.

SELF-REFLEXIVITY

The process whereby media texts self-consciously refer back to themselves, often drawing our attention to their construction.

The 2007 Australian documentary *Forbidden Lie$*, about Norma Khouri, who authored a novel purporting to document the honour killing of a Muslim woman, uses highly self-reflexive techniques to problematise the constructed nature of truth and fiction, revealing that the filmmaker herself was seduced by Khouri's lies. Near the end of the film, the actress playing the part of the woman who was allegedly killed opens her eyes and looks directly at the camera, shattering the illusion of the re-enactment, and the false backdrop depicting a home environment in which Khouri is being interviewed is abruptly moved away and revealed to be a studio set.

Errol Morris' film *The Thin Blue Line* (1988) is another excellent example of the reflexive documentary style. This mystery enquiry is focused on interviews with two men involved in a murder. In its search for truth and reality, the film reveals that all we have are ways of representing, re-enacting, and reconstructing events. It shows how our lives are so imbued with media realities that it has become difficult to tell if we are living life or watching a movie. Crossing the boundaries of *film noir* and documentary, *The Thin Blue Line* combines a mixture of elements into a tense and pleasurable narrative that includes stylised interviews, reconstructions, clips from fiction films, slow-motion footage, an absorbing music soundtrack, and a plethora of different voices, or discourses, that cannot be placed into a simple hierarchy. There is no overall dominant discourse, no expository voice of God or commentary that makes the subject of the documentary clear. In this way meanings are more open and are dependent on readers. The film challenges the certainties of realist texts, making it difficult to discern preferred readings. One of the main insights is that ultimately we may not be able to know the world, that we may not be able to find 'the truth' (Williams 1993).

In addition to labels such as 'self-reflexivity', terms such as 'raw' and 'cooked' are sometimes used to describe different styles of documentary filmmaking. Raw documentaries are those in which cameras are given to ordinary people to record stories with minimal manipulation or artistry (it is this type of documentary that is mimicked by the *Paranormal Activity* films). The presentation of unrefined live-action footage is increasingly apparent online, with the growing popularity of video-sharing and video blogging (or 'vlogging'). Many people now own portable digital recording devices or mobile phones that can record good-quality videos, so they are easily able to shoot an event or blog entry and publish it on social networking sites such as YouTube without much editing. In contrast, cooked documentaries are those that employ elaborate techniques and have high production values, such as the spectacular cinematography in *Touching the Void* (2003), which uses actors to simulate and reconstruct the experiences of the protagonists some twenty years after the events.

Documentary is a rich form that has evolved through various stages in its attempts to record reality, and offers a perfect arena for you to consider all the questions about media truth, objectivity, bias, and construction that were raised in Chapter 5. Additionally, documentaries have often relied on narrative and have been based around conflicts, so you can fruitfully apply binary oppositions and narrative structure as tools for analysis in the same way as can be done for fictional stories.

REALITY TV

REALITY TV ▶

The general premise is that reality-based programs portray people who are not actors saying lines that are not scripted in situations that are drawn from real life but often are constructed and filmed in a manner designed to capture a sense of authenticity, immediacy, and realism.

While documentaries have become ever more popular, the most significant development in television production of the past few years has been the growth of so-called **reality TV**. Following on from the phenomenal success of *Big Brother* and *Survivor* around the turn of the century, there was an amazing expansion of programs.

There are various forms of eliminatory competition (*Australia's Got Talent*, *Britain's Got Talent*, *Dancing with the Stars*, *The Bachelor*, *The Biggest Loser*, *The Voice*, *Project Runway*, *America's Next Top Model*, *My Kitchen Rules*) and makeover programs (*Extreme Makeover*, *Ladette to Lady*, and *Revenge Body with Khloe Kardashian*). The competition game-show formats are distinctive because of the level of audience participation and interactivity they invite via the internet, telephone, and merchandising.

Drama has also been harnessed to documentary to produce generic hybrids such as docudrama and docusoaps, and shows documenting danger and crime. These forms of reality television have capitalised on the successful formula of soap opera by focusing on emotional dramas played out between characters that the audience can identify with. To hook the audience, they often draw on the cliffhanger format of ongoing storylines and a kind of voyeuristic fascination with other people's crisis situations.

There have also been programs that have documented the humour and spectacle of the world, often using amateur or surveillance footage. The strain of reality TV that blends comedy and documentary strategies has a long history. It was originally called comedy *vérité* (Mills 2004) and it evolved out of candid moments caught on experimental film and funny responses in vox pop news surveys to include programs such as *Candid Camera* (screening intermittently since 1948) and *Funniest Home Videos* (1989–).

Reality TV is characterised by the following:

1 Originality and unpredictability. This appears to be a new form of television, both in its use of ordinary, non-actor people, but more so in its presentation of a staged, yet still documentary, reality. Initially, *Big Brother* (2000–) and *Survivor* (2000–) were so absorbing partly because audiences had seen nothing quite like them before.

Part of the appeal of reality TV is its unpredictability and spontaneity. While we don't know what will happen in traditional fictions, we do know that there are some controlling forces—writers, producers, and directors—who will shape the material. With the reality TV shows, control is there in the format of the program—one person eliminated each week, for example—but who that is can be quite unpredictable.

2 Authenticity. Reality TV programs have developed out of technological possibilities that make it possible to, for example, record the activities of *Big Brother* housemates from many different angles for 24 hours a day. In terms of the aesthetic style of reality TV and the way in which it cues an audience response, media analyst Morwenna Crago notes that '*Big Brother*'s unself-reflexive unveiling of the "workings" of the documentary process is specifically designed to produce authenticity, just as the proponents of *cinéma vérité* thought it would be possible to display the "truth" of their own observation, guaranteed in some way because we, the audience, could observe them apparently in the act of observing' (2002, p. 113). Most other reality TV shows also rely on certain characteristics to give the impression that what we are viewing is genuine and unplanned (for example, *Gogglebox*). Crago (2002) refers to these characteristics as 'the aesthetics of authenticity', which include:

- display of the televisual apparatus on screen (visible microphones, etc.)
- liveness and immediacy of the action
- surveillance-style footage
- shaky, hand-held cinematography when contestants are asked to make video diaries
- metadiscourse surrounding the show constructing it as a lab experiment, a nature study, a confessional, and a competition—all established material for documentaries, talk shows, and news reports
- subtitles and voice-overs that tell us what really happened if the sound or lighting quality aren't great or an action is obscured
- action and dialogue being unscripted, and the contestants or guests not trained actors.

The authentic is fascinating (even when people aren't doing anything much) because it is real. As with gossip, we are intrigued by the ordinary and the private. Some webcam sites that simply document people doing totally mundane, everyday but private activities have achieved similar popularity. There is a fascination with human emotions and the psychology of private life, and these shows seem to offer the possibility of really seeing inside people as we look in on human experiments in a laboratory situation.

3 Economics. The production costs of reality TV programs are much smaller than those of fiction or costume dramas. The main costs are recording technologies and limited set construction; there are few actor costs (presenters do still play a significant role), no scriptwriting costs, no costume costs, and so on. Furthermore, some significant costs will be met by commercial companies in return for product placement. *MasterChef* (2010–) ensures that its sponsors' kitchen products are visible and that the contestants use them while cooking. Similarly, contestants on the renovation program *The Block* use the many sponsors' products in their DIY, and *Project Runway* requires contestants to create

their designs with the help of certain computer products, highlighting their advantages and capabilities. In other reality TV shows, people working for particular companies are the feature of the program, which serves the commercial interests of these companies as well as the shows' producers. For example, shows such as *Undercover Boss* (2010–), *The Apprentice* (2004–), and *Jerseylicious* (2010–) are an effective form of advertising for the companies on which they focus. When the US version of *Undercover Boss* featured 1-800-FLOWERS, the florist franchise went to number one on Google Trends within a few hours of the episode airing. *Jerseylicious* focuses on the owners of the renovated Gatsby Salon in New Jersey and the show has proved to be a very successful advertisement for the now extremely popular salon. Built-in product placement such as this bypasses the threat of audiences who use their remote controls to skip over commercial breaks. Finally, there is considerable money to be made by the telephone networks when shows depend on audience participation by phoning or texting in to the programs. Given the ratings success of reality TV, all this has meant a big challenge to the continuation of expensive drama productions.

4   Democratisation. Just as media technology has increasingly given people the chance to produce their own media products, reality TV has increasingly offered spaces for non-actors to appear on screen and become famous as television personalities or celebrities (see Chapter 23). Quiz shows were one of the first television formats that did this, but reality TV has taken it to new levels: it suggests a revaluing of the ordinary, everyday working class in relation to the privileged, fantasy space occupied by the middle and upper class characters that populate many fictional film and television texts. Furthermore, reality TV invites a high degree of participation and interactivity through gossip, phone and internet voting, and official show websites that feature updates, discussion boards, quizzes, games, and contestants' blogs, as well as tie-ins such as *The Biggest Loser*'s online 'Diet Club', which people can join to lose weight along with the show's contestants. This means that reality TV offers media audiences more control and input than do carefully scripted, pre-shot programs. There is also a possibility of identification with and celebration of the participants, who show that almost anyone can break into the media world. In a sense we could say that reality television is celebrating a more democratic ideology than are fictional texts.

5   Escapism. Reality TV is in fact an extraordinary escape from reality. Rather than using the current media technology to really investigate the realities of our contemporary world, most reality TV offers us an escape from reality that is far too mundane or grim to be considered.

6   Cultural dumbing down. The fact that many programs feature ordinary people (as opposed to skilled actors) just 'being themselves' (as opposed to acting in a complex fictional narrative) has made some commentators deride the programs and the audiences who watch them. They see both as evidence of the dumbing down of television. These programs have attracted controversy and criticism for their celebration of low culture and the grimier aspects of humanity. Prominent authors, such as Salman Rushdie, have launched scathing critiques of reality TV on the grounds that its popularity reflects the moral degeneration of society:

Add the contestants' exhibitionism to the viewers' voyeurism and you get a picture of a society sickly in thrall to what Saul Bellow called "event glamour". Such is the glamour of these banal but brilliantly spotlit events that anything resembling a real value—modesty, decency, intelligence, humour, selflessness; you can write your own list—is rendered redundant. In this inverted ethical universe, worse is better. The show presents "reality" as a prize fight and suggests that in life as on TV, anything goes (cited in Rayner et al. 2004, pp. 127–8).

Nevertheless, others have argued that reality TV entices audiences with drama, passion, and intrigue, and presents us with an understanding of contemporary cultural issues in much the same way that Shakespeare's (high culture) plays did in the sixteenth century. From this perspective, reality TV is both popular and socially useful.

7   Ideology of competition. Rushdie and other critics see reality TV as promoting a ruthless kind of social Darwinism, an ethic of survival of the fittest, in which back-stabbing competitiveness gets rewarded onscreen while invasiveness and gossip are indulged in by off-screen viewers, for whom television provides a distraction from important and valuable concerns or pursuits. While the programs give us a chance to see, explore, and understand human emotions, these are often presented within situations and structures of competition, hierarchy, rewards, failure, and success. Rather than have a program just watching a group of people interacting, the programs usually ask people to compete against each other. It is as if this is the natural order of the world and that competition, not cooperation, is human nature.

Reality television programs stress the value of image and appearance for social success. These programs don't have to work in these ways: the reality series *Extreme Guide to Parenting* (2014) took American families and got them to explain the rationale behind their parenting choices, which include child hypnosis, coddling, and push-parenting. The results, directly confronting the extreme opposites of wealth and lifestyles, were fascinating, particularly as the American families dealt with some of their own prejudices, weaknesses, and inadequacies, inviting audiences to see their everyday life and values in a new light.

CASE STUDY

UnREAL and reality TV

In his work on the ethics of reality TV, Christopher Meyers states, 'The structure of most reality TV programs depends on the tension between humiliation and praise, which places the burden on the virtuous viewer, who can, and should, essentially "work around" those ethical problems, focusing on the playful or educational or social aspects of a show while also being repulsed by the humiliation' (2012, p. 21) This is particularly evident in makeover and dating reality TV programs such as *Snog, Marry, Avoid* (2008–11; which was remade in the USA as *Love, Lust, or Run*, 2015–) and *Tough Love* (2009–13), the latter of which features a dating 'boot camp' with host Steve Ward. In *Tough Love* single women are ritually humiliated and punished for

Continued on next page   ▶

their dating shortcomings by Ward: 'The women are monitored and physically punished (via electronic shock) for a number of "dating crimes", such as talking about their career' (Taylor 2012, p. 125).

The Bachelor is the flagship show that epitomises this form of reality TV dating competition. The franchise has been running since 2002, with over twenty seasons and multiple spin-offs such as *The Bachelor in Paradise* and *The Bachelor Australia*. The premise of *The Bachelor* is that a single man dates multiple women who live under the same roof. While they compete for his attention over a series of weeks, he eliminates those he finds less attractive until he eventually identifies his chosen one and presents her with a red rose to signify his love. Following allegations of sexism due to the polygamous and patriarchal nature of the show, a sister series *The Bachelorette* was introduced. (Quips that a series called *The Spinster* would not have been well received merely underscore the allegations that gave rise to *The Bachelorette*, which typically features one of the popular but unsuccessful female contestants from a previous season of *The Bachelor*.) Television scholar Dana Cloud's investigation of the sustained success of *The Bachelor* suggests that these kinds of reality TV shows depend on a complex form of ironic investment by viewers:

> the irony bribe is a strategic mechanism of a cultural text that invites audiences to identify with the pleasures of the reaction against the taking seriously of a patently ideological fantasy (such as faith in true love as a source of women's agency). Ironically, the irony bribe naturalizes the worldview of a hegemonic text in the process of denaturalizing it (Cloud 2010, p. 415).

It is precisely this quality of ironic distance and affective investment that prompted the development of a clever dramatic spoof of reality television dating shows: *UnREAL* (Marti Noxon & Sarah Gertrude Shapiro 2015–). *UnREAL* is a knowing, cleverly scripted, behind-the-scenes parody of supposedly unscripted reality dating programs such as *The Bachelor* and it features a show-within-the-show called *Everlasting* on which multiple women vie for the everlasting love of a Prince Charming figure. Writer-producer Shapiro was a producer on *The Bachelor*. Her work examines 'female social hierarchy and the role of the media in creating it' (Shapiro 2013). After *The Bachelor*, she used kickstarter funding to make a short film called *Sequin Raze* that purported to show her experience of what it was really like behind the scenes on *The Bachelor*, and on the strength of the short film's success she initiated *UnREAL*. The series focuses on the way that reality TV production staff engineer what Rouch would term the 'provocation of reality' by 'casting' contestants as either 'wife material' or 'villain', and cruelly maneuvering them into these scripted roles to amplify the drama of the competition.

Shapiro is very aware of feminist issues and concerns related to appearance and surveillance, and part of the appeal of her show, in addition to its deliciously despicable protagonists, is that it makes the audience think seriously about these issues. She reveals:

> I chose Reality TV as the stage on which to explore these themes because of its ever presence in our current cultural conversation, and the multiple layers intrinsic in crafting a show within a show. Like Foucault's Panopticon, if we internalize the gaze of the camera then we are never alone, we are always performing, always ready to be seen and judged. Living our lives on an imaginary Reality show, obsessively self-documenting and rating ourselves, grappling for acceptance, power and control (Shapiro 2013, n.p.).

This acknowledgment of our complicity with surveillance culture and patriarchal society is part and parcel of the show's knowing address to its audience, and a cornerstone of its appeal. It relies on the audience's familiarity with reality TV shows like *The Bachelor* and *Big Brother*. Cloud argues that in *The Bachelor*, the pressure on women to disclose, the assumption that 'men act and women appear,' and the suppression of female sexuality all contribute to *The Bachelor*'s normative, moralistic view of romance and femininity, and could lead to *The Bachelor*'s audience internalising patriarchal attitudes (2010, p. 422). Think back to the discussion of dominant ideology and hegemony in Chapter 12, where we introduced Louis Althusser's concept of the ideological state apparatus—institutions of socialisation and persuasion that societies use to control people (such as religion, family, education, and media). Ideologies are sets of social values, ideas, beliefs, feelings, and representations by which people collectively make sense of the world they live in, thus constituting a world view; this world view is naturalised, a taken-for-granted, common-sense understanding of the way the world works. *UnREAL* is poised to expose and make the audience question these ideological attitudes and norms, while also questioning the ruthless, self-serving engine of capitalism that drives these shows to see individual participants as instrumental to the producers' financial success. In this sense the series functions as a critique of the illusion of realism, as well as an ideological critique.

In *The Reality of Film: Theories of Filmic Reality*, Richard Rushton critiques arguments that orthodox cinema and television drama provide 'illusions of reality' (2011, p. 20). He problematises the idea that in 'breaking down such illusions, counter-cinema provides a path to a more genuine reality, a reality freed from illusions' (Rushton 2011, p. 21). Instead, he believes that films and television series 'make available concepts, feelings and ways of seeing and relating to the world that contribute to what we understand as reality' (Rushton 2011, p. 7). From this perspective, the TV series *UnREAL* can be understood in relation to the history of realist screen conventions and can be seen to function as a critique of the illusion of realism. Authenticity in film and television is not easy to create, and realism can be seen as a set of techniques or conventions employed in the service of convincing spectators into thinking that what they are watching is, *in some way*, true to life.

CONCLUSION

Reality TV and documentaries continue to thrive. It will be fascinating to see how they develop in future. They share several characteristics with fictional films and television, and thus can be analysed in similar ways. While they present us with views of reality, it is important to be able to see and show the various ways in which they are constructions of reality, to be able to deconstruct them, and to ask what values and ideologies they represent.

This chapter has

- considered the structure of non-fiction television—news, sports, and quiz shows
- given a brief history of documentary
- considered problems of ethics and truth in relation to documentary
- discussed mockumentaries
- discussed reality TV and dramatic parodies of reality TV shows.

? | DISCUSSION POINTS

1   Compare and contrast television news broadcasts from different channels on the same day. How similar or different are the structure and order of stories? How different are their presentation? What elements of entertainment and what binaries of conflict can you find in the stories?

2   Watch any sports and/or quiz program and analyse the verbal discourse of the commentators and/or quiz show hosts. What discourses of nationalism, gender, and the family do they construct?

3   Go through a week's television programming and identify how much of it can be classified as reality TV. Write down a list of reality-based TV programs and then divide them into different groups or categories. Briefly note your responses to these programs. What do you like or dislike about them? Can you write a definition of reality TV that encompasses all of your examples?

4   Why are reality TV programs so popular?

5   Do you agree with Rushdie's criticisms of reality TV?

6   If you have watched any episodes of *The Bachelor* or related reality dating shows, describe your attitude as a viewer and explain how it relates to Dana Cloud's argument about investment and detachment in her article 'The Irony Bribe'. Discuss what irony means and how it applies to *UnREAL*. How do you think viewer attitudes to shows like *The Bachelor* and to value systems such as feminism and materialism might alter after watching *UnREAL*?

SUMMARY

You should now be able to

- apply narrative structure and binary oppositions to non-fiction film and television
- analyse the verbal discourse of sports commentators and quiz show hosts
- define the term 'documentary'
- discuss documentary ethics and documentary truth
- give a brief history of the development of documentary
- comment on the generic developments of documentary and reality TV
- discuss the ways in which these programs are authentic and/or constructions
- apply concepts such as discourse, modality, and generic hybridity to reality-based media
- debate the pros and cons of reality TV and suggest reasons for its escalating popularity.

CHAPTER 19

Why Stories?

Oh blessed art, how often in dark hours when the savage ring of life tightens around me have you kindled warm love in my heart and transported me to a better world.

Franz von Schober, *The Music Show*, ABC Radio National, 2004

This chapter will

- examine the pleasures readers get from stories
- look at some specific theoretical approaches to stories and fictions
- consider the relationship between real life and stories.

THE PLEASURES OF STORIES

Franz von Schober's words are addressed to music but could be applied to many artistic forms, including literature, film, and television fictions. They lead into consideration of the questions: why do people watch film and television narratives or read stories? What do they get out of these experiences?

These are big questions that have produced volumes of theoretical work. The simplest answer is that people get various pleasures from watching and reading narratives. But how do we define and explain these pleasures? We will consider a number of possible viewpoints on this, drawing on various writers and critics.

FICTIONS AND REALITY

Do fictions have any connection to our everyday lives?

Von Schober's words suggest a split between reality—'the savage ring of life'—and fictions (art)—'a better world'. We can understand the connection between reality and fictions in two different ways. The first suggests that fictions occupy a completely different space: the space of imagination, fantasy, and unreality; places of escape, where we find consolation from everyday problems. The second argues that while fiction might offer a particular kind of experience, there are always connections between fiction and reality. They allow us to see a wide range of human characters and experiences from across the globe. Even though they might be about imaginary characters (Harry Potter, Elsa from *Frozen*, Don Draper, Hannah Horvath), fantasy creatures (dragons in *The Hobbit*, the kraken in *Pirates of the Caribbean*), and constructed stories (the television series *Dr Who* or the film *Inception*), and even though they can be set in the future (*Moon*, *Star Trek*) or in invented places (Pandora, Gotham City), they are always connected to and have something to say about our world and ourselves. Like fables, they have a human, moral point to make. Every fiction deals with real concerns as diverse as relationships, history, social conditions, or emotional states.

They are ways of exploring real-life issues at the same time as they allow us to exercise our imaginations; they also enrich our experiences.

This has already been demonstrated in the discussion of genres, such as the western, that explore American culture, allowing the USA to talk to itself about itself (see genres, pp. 213–17). We have also shown this in the discussion of representations of coupling, the family, and sexual expression, subjects that feature in many narratives.

It has been argued that narratives are always related to the historical and social moment of their production. *Ten Canoes*, a film that is set in a timeless past, can be understood in relation to contemporary Aboriginal culture and concerns; Australian films made in the 1970s that look back at Australia's past actually reflect and deal with concerns of the 1970s. *My Brilliant Career*, a film ostensibly about feminist issues in 1900, arose out of and reflected the concerns of Australian feminists in the 1970s. *Sunshine*, set in the future, was a reflection of current concerns and anxieties about climate change and technological change. Furthermore, when we turn to stories that are in some sense fantastic and unreal—myths, legends, fairy tales, science fiction—we can connect these to an internal or psychic reality. Jungian author Robert Johnson reports on a schoolboy giving a definition of myths as 'Something that is true on the inside, but not true on the outside' (Johnson 1987, p. 2). A myth is true: it is not true in the outer, physical sense, but it is an accurate expression of a psychological situation, of the inner condition of the psyche. Similarly, Bruno Bettelheim argues that children know fairy tales are not real but recognise on some level that these stories have internal, human truths they need to learn to help them grow up happily: 'The child intuitively comprehends that although these stories are *unreal*, they are not *untrue*; that while what these stories tell about does not happen in fact, it must happen as inner experience and personal development' (Bettelheim 1978, p. 73).

Fictions can be compared to dreams. According to Sigmund Freud and other psychoanalytic thinkers (Freud 1976a; Ullman & Zimmerman 1979), dreams are messages about our real-life selves. Fictions are also messages about our world (or about the world of the authors of the fiction). Creators use fiction as a way of talking about issues that concern them in real life. In this way, fictional texts and the real world are inextricably linked. This link is part of the media–world connection. Our pleasure in fictions derives partly from the fact that we learn something from them, that we gain insight and understanding into how people, society, and ourselves as individuals work. There is thus an important relationship between the fictional and the real, between texts and society.

We will further explore how fictions work by looking at a number of theories that aim to understand what happens in the viewing, reading, and listening process.

ARISTOTLE, CATHARSIS, TRAGEDY, AND COMEDY

CATHARSIS ▶

The expression and release, or purging, of emotions by audiences at the climax of a tragedy or drama.

The classic model of what happens when someone consumes a fictional text is found in Aristotle's analysis of Greek tragedy. He suggested that the experience enables people to feel extreme emotions, particularly fear and terror, provoked by the story, and then at the end to experience a purging of these emotions in a moment of **catharsis** or emotional release (Wellek & Warren 1976, p. 36; Benjamin 1977, p. 38). More recently, the catharsis hypothesis has been used by media effects theorists to suggest that sometimes watching violent films is a good outlet for our aggressive impulses, allowing them to be safely explored and contained in the fantasy space of the cinema, instead of being played out in real life.

Audiences experience the feelings and dilemmas of characters through identification with them. They can understand extreme situations that they might never experience in their own lives. As audience members experience and therefore begin to understand the world inhabited by the characters, they empathise with them, and this empathy makes them develop as people. 'The function of literature … is to relieve us … from the pressure of emotions' (Wellek & Warren 1976, p. 36). Notions that texts serve to release pent-up emotions have also been applied to comedy. Some theorists argue that in letting out air, laughter acts as a release valve and is therefore a form of relaxation. Laughter is increasingly being seen as therapeutic (Koestler 1975; Powell & Paton 1988), an activity that makes us healthier. Generating laughter is a common aim of media comedy fictions, which are very popular.

There are other ways in which comedy is a release or safety valve. Freud suggests that comedy allows us to speak about social taboos and repressed topics, particularly sexuality. It is a way of speaking the unspeakable (Freud 1976b).

There is debate over whether the function of comedy as a safety valve is socially progressive or reactionary. It can be progressive (that is, it can contribute to social change and development) by raising issues that would otherwise not be dealt with. But it can also be reactionary (that is, it can help to maintain the social status quo) because once there has been a release of tension, there is no need to deal with the social problem that produced the tension. Some comedy shows extend the boundaries of what is socially acceptable and break social taboos: when shows such as *Girls*, *Little Britain*, *The Fosters*, and *South Park* first appeared, audiences were divided on whether they were funny or unacceptable. Author and philosopher Umberto Eco saw the potentially anarchic quality of comedy when he described it as 'the ultimate subversion of authority' in his novel *The Name of the Rose*.

A key question is: does humour contribute to social change, or do people continue to accept the things that they laugh about and enjoy the release of tension rather than taking social action? At its best, comedy can raise our awareness of social ills and can thereby contribute to social change. Laughter can make serious material seem harmless; it can be a subversive agent of social change, or a mechanism for trivialising significant issues.

While comedy, which invariably laughs at someone, can satirise those in power and authority, it has often been turned on minority or oppressed social groups—Irish people, Poles, Aborigines, Jews, non-whites, women—in a racist and sexist fashion. A useful question to ask about comedy and jokes is: who is the joke against? Answering this will begin to reveal its progressive or reactionary tendencies.

How soon after a serious event is it acceptable to make jokes about it? Can you remember when you first heard a joke about the September 11 attacks and what your reaction to this comedy was (see Figures 19.1 and 19.2)?

Figures 19.1 and 19.2 Joke images circulating by email after the September 11 attacks on the World Trade Center and the Pentagon

Source: Anonymous

MARXISM AND BRECHT

Thinking about comedy and catharsis as emotional release leads to the question of whether media texts should provoke audiences to social action. Marxist ideas are relevant here.

Marxist interpretations of literature and film endeavour to show how narratives reveal the struggle between social groups and classes, and how the stories of individual characters are part of these struggles and of the changing economic forces that determine our actions. It is possible to carry out Marxist analyses of films and literature produced by non-Marxists or writers who lived before Marx: Marxist interpretations exist of the works of Shakespeare, the Brontë sisters, Balzac, and other writers. There are also Marxist analyses of films, cultural theorist Fredric Jameson's (1977) examination of *Dog Day Afternoon*, for example.

Marxism's answer to the question 'why do we need stories?' is that they show us what is wrong with our society and they point to a better world. Viewed in this light, they are part of a revolutionary movement in that they contribute to social understanding and social change. According to Marxists, in a classless society people might actually no longer need stories or art, because life would be perfect. There would be no more fictions. Austrian author Ernst Fischer writes of the Dutch artist Piet Mondrian, who held Marxist views: 'Reality would, he believed, increasingly displace the work of art, which was essentially a substitute for an equilibrium that reality lacked at present. "Art will disappear as life gains more equilibrium"' (1963, p. 7). According to Marxism then, stories are signs that things are not perfect.

One of the most influential Marxist practitioners and theorists was playwright and poet Bertolt Brecht. He challenged the worth of theatre as catharsis, arguing that this form of emotional involvement and release

- encourages acceptance of life as it is
- privileges emotional response over intellectual insight and understanding
- contributes to maintaining the status quo rather than provoking social change (Willett 1964; Benjamin 1977).

In Brecht's view, a narrative might explore social problems, but if it works through emotionally involving its audience, the final result is the banality of a good cry, or a comment such as: how terrible, how terrible things are, but that's life. According to Brecht, theatre that works through emotions fails to provoke audiences to action: the only thing such texts might prompt audiences to do is go for a drink after the show.

Brecht argued that it is the way stories are told, their form and structure (the final narrative closure, the level of suspense, and so on), that produces these effects, and therefore viewing pleasure. He wanted to challenge narrative inevitability and reassurance (see p. 237). He argued for a different kind of storytelling, **epic theatre**, that would produce 'pleasurable learning' (Willett 1964, pp. 72–3), learning that would allow audiences to see the world in a new way, revealing new truths. I (Michael) first came across this kind of learning when I saw the 7.84 Theatre Company in the United Kingdom. Its name referred to the statistical distribution of wealth in Britain in the 1970s, a time when 7 per cent of the population owned 84 per cent of the country's wealth. My view of the UK as a basically egalitarian, democratic society (which is how it was then, and still is often, presented in the media) was shaken by this wider social truth. In Australia, which is often referred to as a classless society, the current figures for wealth ownership are virtually the same. Learning the following facts was a similarly shocking revelation for many: 'In some states in Australia, between 50 and 60 per cent of all children in custody are aboriginal, although they represent less than 4 per cent of the juvenile population', and 'The United States consumes 33% of the world's resources' (*New Internationalist* 1997, p. 6).

◀ EPIC THEATRE

A form of storytelling or theatre developed by German playwright Bertolt Brecht that challenges conventional storytelling forms by encouraging audience detachment and understanding, rather than emotional identification.

What would be important to Brecht about these statistics is that, rather than focusing on individual, psychological concerns, they reveal certain deep-seated political truths about society: they uncover the inequality of social structures. He sought a theatrical form that could encompass such teachings while still involving the audience and in doing so broke away from the emphasis on psychological concerns that, as we have seen, is the dominant form of mainstream media (pp. 239–41). Brecht's most famous technique for achieving this aim was the use of **Verfremdung**, which has been translated as 'alienation' or 'distanciation'. *Verfremdung* techniques are theatrical devices, now sometimes called Brechtian devices, that interrupt the realistic flow of the narrative in such a way that audience members are jolted out of their emotional involvement with the exciting narrative, or out of their identification with the main characters. Such techniques aim to make audiences think critically about what is happening by putting them in a distant or alienated position.

VERFREMDUNG (DISTANCIATION, ALIENATION)

Aesthetic techniques that make the audience step back from their emotional narrative involvement to a more critical position, which often enables them to see familiar things in a surprising new way.

Advocates of this technique argue that such reflection leads to insight, understanding, and ultimately acceptance of the need to act. Moreover, it is argued that this learning process is pleasurable for oppressed audiences since it contributes to their liberation. Whereas catharsis produces a pleasurable emotional release that occurs while the audience is watching the play, the release that is provoked by a Brechtian work comes afterwards, from doing something about problems raised in the text. An example of the stress on social factors and *Verfremdung* is found in the film *Kuhle Wampe*, scripted by Brecht (1932). A man suicides by jumping from a high building because of his poverty and unemployment. The camera doesn't show him jumping or falling to his death so as to shock and excite us. It just shows him leaving his watch behind (saving what is still valuable for his family) and then gives the grimly ironic caption: 'One less unemployed.' Clearly a good way of dealing with unemployment figures! The man thus represents a social group rather than a psychological type, and the audience is encouraged to view the event with critical distance rather than emotional excitement. *Dogville* is an interesting contemporary film that also adopted some of these Brechtian techniques.

These revolutionary ideas were very influential on a group of film and television makers in the 1960s and 1970s. The most famous of these was French film director Jean-Luc Godard. Godard tried to incorporate Brechtian devices into his films in order to make spectators think critically, come to new understandings of society, and be provoked into social action. Filmmaking and film going became an actively political pastime, rather than a purely pleasurable recreation.

MYTHS ▶

LÉVI-STRAUSS AND THE PURPOSE OF MYTHS

Stories that often feature ancient gods or fantasy creatures, that recount how a society evolved. At a rational, scientific level they are fantastic, impossible, and unreal, but they may contain social and psychological truths and insights that offer symbolic resolutions to real issues or questions.

Another approach to narrative is found in the structuralist work of French anthropologist Claude Lévi-Strauss, who examined the role of **myths** (one of the earliest forms of stories) in 'primitive' cultures (Lévi-Strauss 1978; Turner 2006, p. 103). He argues that myths serve an important function for these societies. In his book *Mythologies* (1973), Barthes also uses the term 'myth' to refer to the ideologies that lie behind cultural signs. Myths dealt with the central problems and contradictions felt by a culture; in story form (often stories about gods or heroes) they played these conflicts out to a resolution that gave societies some sort of framework for how to live. Media analyst Graeme Turner explains myth as follows:

> Within myths, contradictions and inequities which could not be resolved in the real world were resolved symbolically. The function of myth was to place those contradictions— between humans and the natural environment, for instance, or between life and death—as part of natural existence. Myths negotiated a peace between men and women and their environment so that they could live in it without agonizing over its frustrations and cruelties (Turner 2006, p. 103).

Lévi-Strauss' theory stresses the play of binary oppositions as structures that set up and resolve contradictions. The result is not social action, but social peace and acceptance of the status quo. Our discussion of contemporary media narratives and their resolution of oppositions relating to contemporary social concerns—the desire for marriage and family versus friendship and multiple partners, for example—suggests that media narratives can be seen, using Lévi-Strauss' terms, as forms of contemporary myths.

The idea of rites of passage is worth mentioning here. Rites of passage are traditional points or periods of significant change in a person's life—birth, marriage, and death are the most obvious, but many societies also have traditional rites that help mark the transition of young adults from childhood to adulthood. These are often described as death and rebirth rituals or as initiation ceremonies—a symbolic death is experienced that allows new life to come forward at the same time as another stage of life is left behind. Modern and postmodern Western culture has lost many of these traditions, although remnants of them can be seen in many of the adolescent activities of teenagers involving sex and drugs; for example, the schoolies' week celebrations that Australian school leavers indulge in— traditionally, a week of relatively excessive holidaying and partying—are a kind of initiation into, as well as a challenge to, adult life.

While there may be an absence of formal rituals in real life, film, television, and fiction narratives fill some of this gap by providing numerous examples of rites of passage and initiation stories. *The Maze Runner*, *Insurgent*, *The Perks of Being a Wallflower*, *Beautiful Creatures*, and *Blue Is the Warmest Colour* are all examples of coming-of-age films. Historian Mircea Eliade expresses this well when he writes about the appeal of fairy tales:

> It is impossible to deny that the ordeals and adventures of the heroes and heroines of fairy tales are almost always translated into initiatory terms … initiatory scenarios … are the expression of a psychodrama that answers a deep need in the human being. Every man wants to experience certain perilous situations, to confront exceptional ordeals, to make his way into the Other World—and he experiences all this, on the level of his imaginative life, by hearing or reading fairy tales (Eliade 1963, quoted in Bettelheim 1978, p. 35).

This holds true for many other film, television, and written narratives.

ENTERTAINMENT, ESCAPISM, AND UTOPIA: MUSICALS AND SOAP OPERAS

The pleasures we get from media products are often described as escapist, while the texts themselves are belittled as just entertainment. Saying something is 'escapist' or 'just entertainment' is a way of dismissing it. These disparaging terms are presented as self-evident—it is assumed that they don't need explanation, that we know what they mean. This does not do justice to the terms. Film studies professor Richard Dyer has written most illuminatingly about the term 'entertainment', analysing its history, development, and meanings (Dyer 1992). He has also written about popular genres that are often dismissed as escapist, particularly musicals and soap operas (Dyer 1981; Dyer et al. 1981).

To describe a media text as escapist is to suggest that the people watching it are avoiding reality, that they are not facing up to the real world. It suggests that the text is unrealistic, that it promotes irresponsible avoidance of social problems. Escapist entertainment is often contrasted with realistic stories that explore the grim realities of life and so are deemed to be more worthy and valuable. We don't agree with this characterisation of popular entertainment as simply escapist. Dyer has suggested that many cultural products have a utopian element to them: they point to the possibilities of a better world (as suggested by the Marxist analysis of media texts).

There is a long and respectable tradition of utopian writing and visions. The utopian vision of a perfect world can inspire readers with hope and optimism, and can give a blueprint for how they would like to live. It is something to work towards; it suggests the possibility of social change (in contrast to many realist stories that simply confirm how terrible life is, rather than positing an alternative). These escapist visions involve an escape to something as well as an escape from something.

Dyer suggests that the musical and the soap opera can present ideal values and ideal ways of living (what we escape to) that are in direct contrast to the realities of everyday life (what we escape from). The musical offers the following ideal qualities as a response to their mundane, everyday opposites:

- abundance *vs* scarcity
- energy *vs* tiredness and exhaustion
- community *vs* isolation and alienation
- transparency in human relations *vs* human deviousness
- intensity of experience *vs* lacklustre lives and boredom (Dyer 1981).

In classic films such as *Singin' in the Rain*, and modern versions of the musical such as the films *Burlesque*, *Nine*, *The Sapphires*, *Pitch Perfect 2*, and *Bran Nue Dae*, as well as the musical TV series *Glee*, the musical provides all five elements of contrast between the ideal world that we escape into and the everyday world. Particularly in spontaneous song and dance numbers, musicals offer the open and simple expression of intense and exciting feeling (often love, joy, and friendship), and there is a great outpouring of energy and movement. Even in the musical biopics *The Runaways*, *Behind the Candelabra*, and *Control*, bleak films that undermine the conventions of the musical genre, these contrasts between social realism and the transcendent, uplifting possibilities of music are apparent. Typical musicals show people brought together in a sharing, caring community where there is plenty of material and emotional sustenance for everyone (in fact there is often an abundance of it). *Glee* encapsulates this function of the musical, as the show revolves around a group of high school outcasts who are brought together by their Glee Club, where they find solidarity and friendship, and can sing their troubles away. This contrasts with the dull grind of daily life, where people work hard for a living but often don't have enough, materially or emotionally, where human relations may be unclear and conducted with ulterior motives, where people are stressed, tired, or bored, and where many live isolated and alienated lives.

The documentary *Amandla* gives an account of how popular music and song were major factors in developing and supporting the revolutionary struggle of the African National Congress against apartheid in South Africa. *Amandla* is not a musical but it shows how the utopian aspects of music, far from being escapist, were directed specifically into commenting on and changing social realities for the better. Perhaps it is important that this popular culture musical form and expression was not broadcast by the media, but sung and participated in by people in the streets—an example of popular culture created by the people, not for the people (see p. 36). The grassroots nature of the *toyi toyi* dance and protest songs shown in *Amandla*, rather than being broadcast to the entire nation, enabled it to operate under the radar and thereby avoid possible banning. This meant that music could be used to communicate political messages from township to township across the country. In some ways the use of music as a form of political expression and social commentary continues in South Africa today through the subcultures of hip-hop and *kwaito* music.

All this is to illustrate that so-called escapist entertainments have a connection to our real lives and can offer something positive. There can of course be a negative side to entertainment. Some game shows and gambling (especially as presented in lottery advertisements) offer magical fixes to our scarcity problems, but these fixes promote the same consumerist values on which much of our culture is built. (Interestingly, research has shown that many lottery winners actually end up losing friends and most of their money, and fighting with their families, ending up little better off than before.) Game shows and lotteries operate like the circuses provided by Roman emperors, as devices to keep people happy and distracted from social and political problems. You may want to question these forms of entertainment, but entertainment that is simple and easy to watch, and accessible to many people, should not be denigrated as a whole for these reasons. Examine each example to see what is being presented. In so doing, you may find valuable elements, as Dyer has pointed out.

The utopian visions provided by the media give us pleasure and are sources of aspiration and inspiration. The flipside to this is the media's presentation of dystopias or dystopic views of the world, stories of social breakdown, decay, and apocalypse (*Divergent*, *Mad Max: Fury Road*, *Blade Runner*, *The Matrix*, *Elysium*, and *The Hunger Games*, for example). These dystopic texts also relate to our present world. They provide us with warnings of what could happen to us.

In *The Pleasure of the Text* (1975), Barthes adds another dimension to thinking about audiences and our responses to fictions when he discusses the pleasures of reading fictions. He uses the French word ***jouissance*** (bliss), which he distinguishes from ***plaisir*** (pleasure).

Barthes is aiming to convey a difference between *plaisir*, which is straightforward enjoyment of fictions that don't really have a deep impact on us, and *jouissance*, a disturbing yet blissful experience that produces an extremely heightened response. This may be experienced with fictions that have a potentially life-changing impact on us, making us see the world anew.

◀ *JOUISSANCE*

A French word, one meaning of which is 'bliss or ecstasy'; much more powerful, and sometimes more disturbing, than *plaisir* (pleasure).

◀ *PLAISIR*

French for 'pleasure'; the kind of enjoyment derived from fictions that do not have a strong or enduring impact.

To clarify this, try to make a list of fictions that you have simply enjoyed and fictions that have thrilled you with *jouissance*. Compare your list with a friend's list and try to explain to each other what the nature of the *jouissance* impact was on you.

REALISMS

REALISM ▶

Objects in art—paintings, sculpture, literature—that appear true to real life and the aesthetic methods or styles used to create them. Realism, the dominant aesthetic in painting and literature in the nineteenth century, aimed for verisimilitude and focused on the lives of ordinary people.

The aesthetic tradition that seems closest to real life is the mimetic tradition of **realism**. In contrast with escapist entertainment, mimetic cultural productions aim to imitate reality, to produce narratives and stories that are recognised as realistic.

This mimetic tradition started with Greek culture, and the history of mimetic art is a history of continually evolving styles and methods used to reproduce reality. The styles evolve partly because people's perceptions of reality are always changing, so reality is impossible to capture. 'Realism' is an important critical term in relation to nineteenth-century painting and literature, and twentieth-century film and television. Raymond Williams has explained the different elements that make up realist texts:

- ordinary people, particularly the working classes, as subject matter
- serious treatment of their lives
- contemporary social contexts (Williams 1977a).

The fact that working class people were finally being represented in these ways was itself a major factor in audience pleasure: the pleasure of people seeing themselves seriously represented, recognising their own lives and society. Film theorist Roy Armes makes the important distinction between realism as an aim or attitude (aiming to tell the truth, to show things with verisimilitude so that they look very similar to what we see in our daily lives) and realism as a method or style (a set of artistic or stylistic conventions that try to achieve this aim) (Armes 1971). Because there are numerous, changing ways of seeing the world, there are also many realist styles or sets of conventions (realisms). Neorealism, Soviet realism, Dogma 95, *cinéma vérité*, direct cinema, naturalism, kitchen-sink realism, social realism, magic realism, and dirty realism are all used to describe styles or tendencies in literature, and in film and television products. As each new style appears, it wins an audience because of its freshness and stylistic innovations.

Films with a high degree of verisimilitude—for example, the films of Mike Leigh—are perceived to be more accurate representations of society, and so are therefore often interpreted as offering productive, instructive social commentary. The connections these styles forge with real-life issues and their seriousness mean that they have tended to be given more cultural weight than escapist entertainment. Because they appear realistic, it is sometimes easy to forget the construction involved in their representations.

FANTASY

In contrast with an understanding of fictions that sees them as imitations of real life, the use of the term 'fantasy' to describe and analyse fictions draws attention to dreams, imagination, the subconscious, and story worlds that differ significantly from everyday experience. Links have traditionally been made between films and dreams. The description of Hollywood as a dream factory points to the desirable aspects of Hollywood films (they provide wish fulfilment, as do dreams) and their unrealistic nature, living in a dream world.

Fantasies are essentially unreal, the product of our dreams and imaginations, but this is one of the most exciting things about film and television stories: they give filmmakers and audiences a chance to live out their wildest and most extreme fantasies. This has been the source of some controversy, particularly in relation to representations of sex and violence. Some people argue that these representations are dangerous and have the potential to corrupt us or lead us to commit violent acts. Others reject this, saying that

1   we are capable of recognising that we are not seeing real events
2   these stories allow us to safely work through difficult aspects of ourselves, and our society.

The second point is an argument that it is important to allow violent representations because they give us a chance to explore and understand our own violent tendencies. Very few people are murderers, but many of us, at some point in our lives, dream of or feel like killing or attacking someone. Looking at and understanding these dark and repressed sides of ourselves enable us to cope with them. Denying us the opportunity to explore them will repress them further, and that could be harmful. Stories allow us to play out, in our imaginations, a whole set of possible actions, to test them out, to see what happens if …

Literary theorist Rosemary Jackson describes fantasy as 'the literature of sub-version' which 'attempts to compensate for a lack resulting from cultural constraints; it is a literature of desire, which seeks that which is experienced as absence or loss' (Jackson 1981, p. 3). This is similar, in some ways, to Dyer's view of the utopian musical. Jackson sees media texts that portray extreme human behaviour as explorations of areas and desires that society normally represses.

Illuminating what happens when our fantasies are played out on screen, film theorist Victor Perkins describes audiences as 'participant observers' (Perkins 1990, ch. 7). He notes that the language of film, the way stories are told, enables audiences to feel as if they are participating in the events on screen, thus involving them in extreme actions and intense emotions—killing, being killed, making love, chariot racing, and so on. At the same time, we still know we are in the cinema; part of us remains detached and observes what is happening on the screen, and in ourselves, as we experience these situations. We are simultaneously participants and observers. The cinema becomes a playground where we experience all sorts of emotions and actions, and at the same time reflect critically and rationally on how it feels and on what the consequences are for ourselves and others. This testing ground provides a significant arena of pleasure and learning.

We have already referred to Bettelheim's argument that violent fairy tales are actually good for children as a way of letting them face and explore their own violent capacities (see p. 47). On ABC Radio National's *Media Report*, Robert Kee, a noted Hollywood scriptwriter, discussed the social role of dark media fantasies with interviewer Donna McLachlan:

McLachlan   What is your feeling about the kind of depth and strength of some of these monsters that are appearing on screen, *American Psycho*, and Hannibal Lecter, and so on? Is it disturbing, do you think, that there is that portrayal of the monster, or is it healthy?

Kee   Oh, it's very healthy. Human beings are angel and devil, and a perfect balance of the two. And the fascinating thing about human beings is you never know from one day to the next which you're going to get. I mean, on Monday they build Notre Dame Cathedral and on Tuesday Auschwitz, and which is it going to be? And you only need to pick up a newspaper from one day to the next, and you see this constant manifestation of the deep evil in human beings. And what all of us try to do, of course, is deny it exists in us. It's that backpacker serial killer over there, it's not me. But every time you cut somebody off in traffic, every time you slam a door in somebody's face, every time you're rude to a clerk, every time you take advantage of somebody, there's a little bit of evil seeping out of you, and you enjoyed cutting that guy off in traffic, and don't deny it. And so if we turn our backs on the dark side of our nature, if we just try to avoid it and insist it doesn't exist, it's going to sneak up from behind us and swallow us whole.

And art, which has the power to illuminate these dark corners of human nature, can make us understand that it's us, and it's in our nature. It doesn't mean that we're evil ourselves, that we're going to be overcome by our own evil nature, but it's always there, and the power is there, and as long as we understand that and are aware of it, then we can keep ourselves in balance and go round being a decent human being (Kee 2001).

Stories that go beyond everyday realism—horror movies, the surreal explorations of film directors such as David Lynch, and films that show unrealistic possibilities—allow audiences an even wider testing-out of human feelings and experiences. Films such as *Black Swan*, *Fight Club*, *The Matrix*, *Crouching Tiger, Hidden Dragon*, *Edge of Tomorrow*, and *About Time* can be understood (like myths discussed above, pp. 292–3) as allowing audiences to explore their inner world, their psychic processes, or as symbolic of external social situations. The fantasies they portray—having a real-life double (*Black Swan*, *Fight Club*, *Gone Girl*), living in a computer-generated reality (*The Matrix*, *The Avengers*, *Iron Man*, *Prometheus*, *Her*), being able to fly (*Crouching Tiger*), living the same day over and

Figure 19.3 Cartoon illustrating consequences of denial of our shadow selves

"One does not become enlightened by imagining figures of light,
but by making the darkness conscious." C.G.JUNG.

Source: Ron Pyatt 1990

over (*Edge of Tomorrow* and *About Time*)—enable the main characters to explore internal psychological states and allow the audience a space to consider what it is to be human.

It is worth noting that these kinds of fantasy explorations seem to be one of the pleasures offered within the virtual world of computer games and the internet. The opportunity to construct their own avatar and enter a virtual world that is not subject to the natural laws of physics or the real world gives participants the opportunity to explore their fantasy worlds.

THE HERO'S JOURNEY: JOSEPH CAMPBELL

Joseph Campbell, who was a professor of mythology and theorist, described general, recurring patterns in all forms of storytelling. Campbell is not the only one to have sought out such general patterns. The structuralist work of folklorist Vladimir Propp, who analysed the common characteristics of fairy tales, is most well known in media studies (Propp 1975; Turner 2006, pp. 98–102). He looked at fairy tales and concluded that a recurrent pattern involving set characters and plot actions forms the basis of all fairy tales. According to Propp, these characters are the villain, the donor (the provider), the helper, the princess (or the person who is being sought), the princess' father, the dispatcher, the hero (or the victim), and the false hero. Film narratives have been subjected to Propp's analysis and have revealed similar set characters: 'A list of the main characters in the original *Star Wars* movie fits Propp's eight spheres of action quite neatly' (Turner 2006, p. 102).

Table 19.1 Propp's spheres of action and *Star Wars* character types

the villain	Darth Vader
the donor	Obi-Wan Kenobi
the helper	Han Solo
the princess	Princess Leia
the dispatcher	R2-D2
the hero	Luke Skywalker
the false hero	Darth Vader

Source: Turner 2006, p. 102

Propp's structure comprises six stages:

1 preparation
2 complication
3 transference
4 struggle
5 return
6 recognition.

Propp's work can be understood as an elaboration of Todorov's narrative structure (p. 236) and can be fruitfully applied to many film texts. A humorous email (Figure 19.4) circulated across the globe was claimed to have been found in the dustbin of *Harry Potter* author J K Rowling. It draws attention to the structural similarities of many stories.

Figure 19.4 Humorous *Harry Potter* email

Harry Potter and the Philosopher's Stone
~~Star Wars A New Hope~~: synopsis

[*Harry Potter*] ~~Luke Skywalker~~ is an orphan living with his uncle and aunt on the remote wilderness of ~~Tatooine~~.

He is rescued from [*Muggles*] ~~aliens~~ by wise, bearded [*suburbia*] ... ~~Ben Kenobi~~ [*Hagrid*], who turns out to be a ~~Jedi Knight~~ [*wizard*].

[*Hagrid*] ~~Ben~~ reveals to [*Harry*] ~~Luke~~ that [*Harry's*] ~~Luke's~~ father was also a ~~Jedi Knight~~ [*wizard*], and was the best ~~pilot~~ he had ever seen.

[*Harry*] ~~Luke~~ is also instructed in how to use [*a magic wand*] ~~the Jedi light sabre~~ as he too trains to become a ~~Jedi~~ [*Quidditch player*].

[*Harry*] ~~Luke~~ has many adventures in the ~~galaxy~~ [*Hogwarts*] [*wizard*] and makes new friends such as ~~Han Solo~~ [*Ron*] and ~~Princess Leia~~ [*Hermione*].

In the course of these adventures he distinguishes himself as a top [*Quidditch Seeker*] ~~X-wing pilot~~ in the ~~battle of the Death Star~~ [*Quidditch match*], making the ~~direct hit~~ [*catch*] that secures the ~~Rebels~~ [*Gryffindor*] victory against the forces of evil, [*Slytherin*].

[*Harry*] ~~Luke~~ also sees off the threat of ~~Darth Vader~~ [*Lord Voldemort*], who we know murdered his ~~uncle and aunt~~ [*parents*].

In the finale, ~~Luke~~ [*Harry*] and his new friends ~~receive medals of valour~~ [*win the House Cup*].

All of this will be set to an orchestral score composed by John Williams.

Source: Anonymous

Propp's work does not go much beyond discovering and describing these patterns. Campbell's approach is similar in that he too looks for structural patterns in myths, fairy tales, and stories from all over the world, but Campbell progresses beyond this to explain what this structure means for human beings. In this way, his work has a similar aim to the work of Lévi-Strauss in understanding the role and meanings of myths and stories in human society.

Campbell gives a very different view of the media to the approaches that we have presented in this book. Much of our analysis has stressed the social construction of representations. We have presented methods for deconstructing texts, a process that makes us aware of the ideological and social meanings inscribed in them, and reveals that the media are produced by dominant social groups in such a way as to reproduce the dominant values of society.

Campbell draws on a quite different theoretical framework. His theories are greatly influenced by the work of Jung, and his aim is much more a celebration of media texts than a warning critique. Campbell stresses the universal aspects of human nature and societies. He suggests that there are similar universal human patterns and truths found in the myths, legends, and religious beliefs of all cultures, and argues that the stories in them present a blueprint that shows us how to act in the world to find enlightenment and fulfilment, and achieve our human potential. He argues that they have a dominant pattern or structure, which he calls 'the hero's journey'. Campbell's ideas can be found in his books and in video interviews (Campbell 1972, 1988a, 1988b, 1991; Golden 1992).

The hero's journey involves a hero who goes through tests, struggles, and problems on the way to achieving their goal. Campbell suggests that this structure provides a framework that shows us how to act as humans if we are to realise our heroic potential. According to Campbell, we are all (men and women) heroes with the potential to find our heroic fulfilment. To do this, we have to undertake a hero's journey by 'following our bliss'. This idea of following your bliss is crucial to Campbell's work. He suggests that each of us can find something that truly moves and touches us. Only by following our bliss can we realise our potential, our happiness. He notes, though, that many pressures of contemporary society, such as trying to survive economically and to conform socially, do not encourage this. We are thus faced with the challenge of deciding whether to do what society pressures us to do or follow our own spirit. Earlier, Campbell argues, so-called primitive societies were more able to encourage people to do this than modern industrial, secular, capitalist societies, which have lost this capacity.

The stages of the hero's journey outlined by Campbell in his book *The Hero with a Thousand Faces* (1972, pp. ix–x) are:

1 departure
   - the call to adventure
   - refusal of the call
   - supernatural aid
   - the crossing of the first threshold
   - the belly of the whale
2 initiation
   - the road of trials
   - the meeting with the goddess
   - woman as the temptress
   - atonement with the father
   - apotheosis
   - the ultimate boon

3   return

- refusal of the return
- the magic flight
- rescue from without
- the crossing of the return threshold
- master of the two worlds
- freedom to live.

Campbell elaborates on each of these stages, finding examples of them in a multitude of stories. He suggests that, like ancient myths and stories, film and television narratives are our modern myths in that they include and illustrate these same heroic structures. This is graphically illustrated in many films and stories, such as *Beowulf*, *Star Wars*, and *The Matrix*. In fact, George Lucas' *Star Wars* franchise and George Miller's *Mad Max* films are directly based on and inspired by Campbell's theories. The popular success of these films suggests that they resonate deeply with the beliefs and feelings of audiences.

Originally, Campbell built his theories on analysis of pre-existing myths and stories. Now there has been an interesting reversal. Lucas and Miller knew about Campbell's work and used it in constructing their stories. In Hollywood today many scriptwriters learn about Campbell and use his ideas and narrative formula as a basis for writing their stories (Vogler 1992).

Campbell has been criticised for his Jungian position and the way that his theories can be aligned with an ideology of individualism. The universalist aspects of his theories are seen by some as deriving from a Western perspective that fails to see and acknowledge the differences between cultures. The focus on the hero supports a typical American ideology of individual power, rather than acknowledging the importance of society as a whole. We can see how some of his ideas have been taken up, appropriated, by big business in their advertising campaigns, with slogans such as Nike's 'Just do it', advertisements that present and celebrate ordinary people as heroes, or encourage us to follow our bliss.

Australian playwright David Williamson offered this Australian critique of Campbell's ideas when asked if he thought American film producers rely on Campbell's notion of the hero's journey:

> I think that they do very much have that story structure firmly in their heads, that the hero must start out, must go through a series of challenges, each of which he or she overcomes, and becomes a better and stronger person at every turning point, and finally ends up the film a true hero. Now I think Australia and Australian writers tend to believe that this is a falsified picture of life, that life proceeds more often according to the neuroses theory where people keep making the same mistakes over and over again—which is more conducive to a comedic approach than a heroic, dramatic approach …
>
> Many of us, it's my observation, don't conform to the hero's journey in our lives, we battle on, we get through our lives and we do tend to make the same mistakes time and time again, however well-meaning. Yes, so I, if anything, would tend to satirise the hero's journey rather than take it seriously (ABC Radio National, *Big Ideas*, February 2004).

Whether you like Campbell's theory or agree with Williamson, it is clear that Campbell's ideas have been very influential in film and television production over the past thirty years.

PSYCHOANALYSIS

Sigmund Freud and Carl Jung developed psychoanalytic theory in the early twentieth century. Within media and film studies **psychoanalysis** has been used in two ways: first, to explain the psychological pleasures of the viewing experience; and second, as a method for interpreting stories to show how stories often illustrate psychoanalytic truths.

The pleasures of viewing and looking at images on screens

Freud argues that one of the key human drives or desires is the desire to look (Mulvey 1989). This desire, called **scopophilia**, is a source of great pleasure and satisfaction. One aspect of scopophilia is voyeurism, the desire to look secretly at events, to spy on people, which can be seen as one of the pleasures offered by film and television texts. Audiences indulge in the fantasy that the actors on screen are real people acting out their lives before cameras, seemingly without realising those cameras are there. Audiences watch these events unfold, often from a darkened auditorium. We choose to believe that we are being permitted to see the most intimate aspects of these lives, beyond what we experience in relation to most people we actually know. Films such as *Rear Window*, *Blue Velvet*, *Disturbia*, and *American Beauty* consciously explore these pleasures. Voyeuristic vision is characterised by distance (the observer is separated or concealed from the observed in some manner) and secrecy (the observed is not aware that they are being watched and does not consent to it). The combination of distance and deception leads to a sense of control and objectification. In *American Beauty*, Ricky films Lester and Jane without them knowing he is playing the role of a peeping Tom, a voyeur. The use of point-of-view shots and long shots conveys the distant, controlling nature of voyeurism.

The pleasures of identification and objectification (see pp. 246–8) can also be said to be built on scopophilia, as we either psychologically identify with characters onscreen or turn them into visual objects of desire. Fetishistic scopophilia develops this look of desire. It is more to do with being absorbed in the pleasures of looking, rather than controlling or objectifying what the viewer is looking at. The huge size of the cinema screen is tailor-made for objective and fetishistic looking. Often the object that is being fetishised (frequently a part of the body) takes on huge proportions and is fragmented, so it fills the screen in close-up and overwhelms the viewer with its desirability. This is a different experience from the scopophilic pleasure derived from voyeurism. In *American Beauty*, when Lester watches Angela perform her cheerleading routine at the sports stadium, his gaze is fetishistic and scopophilic. Angela is filmed in slow motion; the camera fragments her body and moves into close-up, even though Lester is actually seated some distance from her. The use of close-ups and slow motion conveys the overwhelming and obsessive nature of fetishism.

Freud argues that men desire women but also fear them because their lack of a penis poses the 'threat of castration'. The fetish object results in the 'disavowal of castration': it is a substitute for the missing penis, it fills the gap in a reassuring way, but it then becomes the focus of sexual excitement. It can take on disproportionate importance because it is taking the place of something that is deeply desired. A fetish for silk, velvet, or fur, for instance, may be a reassuring substitute for the feeling of skin or hair. The film *There's Something about Mary* depicts the villain as having a fetish for the shoes worn by Cameron

◀ PSYCHOANALYSIS

Psychoanalysis, as developed by Sigmund Freud, argues that people are motivated by their unconscious, that there are several developmental stages people go through as they grow up, and that psychoanalysis can make people aware of their unconscious conflicts, fantasies, and desires (which are attributed chiefly to the development of the sexual instinct) through the free association of ideas, analysis, and interpretation of their dreams.

◀ SCOPOPHILIA

From the Greek; love of looking, a basic human drive.

Diaz's character. A shoe fetish is often explained as based on an analogy between the action of a foot slipping into a shoe and sexual intercourse.

Freud and Jung both make interesting comments on the psychological value of phantasies (the dreams people have and the daydreams they indulge in). Freud suggests, rather negatively, that 'A happy person never phantasies, only an unsatisfied one', which perhaps suggests that only neurotic people would want to watch films or read stories. Jung argues, much more positively, that phantasy is 'the creative activity whence issue the solutions to all answerable questions; it is the mother of all possibilities' (1923, p. 573).

Psychoanalysis as an interpretive method

Psychoanalytic interpretations of stories suggest that the way characters behave can be understood in psychoanalytic terms. Psychoanalysis argues that humans go through patterns and stages of development as they grow up, develop, and mature. Negotiating these stages is crucial to our health and emotional and psychological growth. We can see a direct parallel in this process of negotiating struggles and growth with our previous discussion of how characters in narratives go through a process of moral growth (pp. 240–1). Oedipus is the most famous specific example. Oedipus, in the Greek play *Oedipus the King* by Sophocles, kills his father and marries his mother. Freud used Oedipus' name for his theory of the Oedipus complex: the unconscious desire that male children have to kill their father so they can replace him and have sex with their mother. The play, Freud thought, was about the struggle of the Oedipus complex. It is possible to interpret many texts in a Freudian way: to understand some male rivalries as symbolic struggles with the father, some male attractions as symbolic desire for the mother.

Filmmaker Alfred Hitchcock consciously used Freud's ideas in *Psycho*, in which Norman Bates cannot come to terms with his own sexuality because of his connection to his (dead) mother; it is this that leads him to become a murderer. Such films demonstrate the failure to successfully overcome psychological problems, whereas films such as *Analyse This* or *The Day after Tomorrow* show characters successfully negotiating psychological struggles. David Lynch explores aspects of the unconscious and Freudian desire very explicitly in *Blue Velvet* and *Lost Highway*. Freud theorised that everyone represses many of their desires but no matter how hard they try, these **repressed desires** will come back in some disturbed form to trouble them.

REPRESSED DESIRE ▶

The act of repression forms the unconscious. Forbidden material (Oedipal desire, for example) is rejected from conscious thought, but not destroyed. It is stored in the unconscious from where it continues to produce effects.

Critics, including Robin Wood, have interpreted horror films as illustrating this mechanism of repression where the monstrous characters represent the return of repressed desires (Wood 1986). Freud also theorised all people as having three layers of personality—the id, the ego, and the super ego. Individuals in real life struggle to find a balance between their id (the force that seeks to satisfy all of their desires without concern for anyone else) and their super ego (the parental, moralistic controlling force that won't permit pleasure)—a balance in which the aim is for the ego to achieve progressive conquest of the id. Similarly, we can interpret film narratives as representing this struggle, where different characters represent the different forces. The pleasure we have as audience is in seeing these psychological dramas being acted out. Many cartoons can be easily interpreted in this way: Bart and Homer in *The Simpsons* seem to represent the id, while Marge and Lisa are much more like the super ego. Homer, because he is an adult, has to try to hold down his id instincts. In *South Park* the children mainly represent the id, while several of the adults (though not all) are more the super ego. One of the pleasures in cartoons for children is the amount of space given to id characters. Bettelheim (1978) argues that fairy tales work in this way too, telling stories about these struggles so that 'as stories unfold they give conscious credence to id pressures and show ways to satisfy those that are in line with ego and superego requirements'.

You don't need to consciously understand Freudian theory to understand what the story is presenting. However, filmmaker and playwright David Mamet writes: 'I would suggest that those who are interested [in filmmaking] might want to do some reading in psychoanalysis, which is a great storehouse of information about movies' (1991, p. 7). Mamet sees psychoanalysis as a tool for understanding human character that can be used by writers or filmmakers, even by readers of texts. Freud once wrote that he had discovered nothing about human personality that writers and artists hadn't already known about and demonstrated. Whether or not Freud's ideas are right, they have become part of popular common sense so that today psychoanalytic ideas inform many media products. Most people know something about his ideas of the unconscious, the Oedipus complex, Freudian slips, and so on. *Analyse This* is a good example of a film that explains some aspects of psychoanalysis but wouldn't be so popular if audiences didn't already understand the basics.

The application of psychoanalytic theory, mainly deriving from Freud and the subsequent work of psychoanalyst Jacques Lacan, to media studies is too complex to pursue here, but there is a body of reading and other research you can follow up (Lapsley & Westlake 1989, ch. 3; Kaplan 1990; Leader & Groves 1995).

READING AS A TRANSFORMATIVE EXPERIENCE

We have given a brief summary of some approaches for understanding what happens when people view or read fiction and have argued that there is always some connection between real-life events and fiction. But the difference in our experience of these two realities has also been acknowledged. We want to reflect now on what the viewing experience is like and how this compares to real, everyday experiences. My brother has asked me, Michael, why I watch so many films, and he suggests that part of me is missing out on real life. His comments suggest that I am having surrogate experiences through these films rather than actually doing the things myself, as though reading about or watching real life is not the same as actually living it. Similarly, I am surprised at how many people watch sports events rather than participating in the sports themselves—it seems to make sense to say that participation is more pleasurable than observation. Part of me agrees with my brother, and as I get older it seems more important to experience many things for myself rather than reading about or watching them.

But the experience of viewing fictions is not just surrogate experience. It is an intense form of human experience, a part of real life that yields profound pleasures and insights. These can be compared to those found in meditation, ritual, and mysticism. The origins of fiction and stories lie in myths and religious rites; stories serve direct spiritual ends. The fiction experience invites us into an altered state of consciousness, a different way of being, that can be more intense than many real-life experiences. It may be deeply spiritual, filling us with wonder and revelation, thereby helping us in our everyday lives; it gives space and time for contemplation, allowing us to put our lives in perspective, and it may help to recreate us, as suggested by the word 'recreation'. Just as our dreams are sometimes more intense than our daily experiences, so too being immersed in fictions can stimulate our hearts, minds, and emotions in extraordinarily fulfilling ways. While the fiction experience seems to be about external events—it comprises stories happening to other people—it actually allows us to go on an inward journey. As we consume fictions, we leave behind the mundane practicalities of everyday life to travel deep into the heart of ourselves, discovering our core beliefs, feelings, and desires.

THE IDEOLOGICAL VALUES OF STORIES

This mystical view of stories and fictions sounds very positive, but stories still carry values or ideologies. Indigenous Canadian writer and scholar Thomas King illustrates this well: he argues that stories are fundamental in explaining how people and cultures operate—people learn about themselves and their culture through stories. He examines two different creation myths, the Christian myth of Genesis—Adam and Eve—and a Native American creation myth. King argues that these kinds of stories form the basis for people's understanding of humanity, the Earth, and the universe. He compares the two myths and finds some fundamental differences:

> The elements in Genesis create a particular universe governed by a series of hierarchies—God, man, animals, plants—that celebrate law, order, and good government, while in our Native story, the universe is governed by series of co-operations ... that celebrate equality and balance (King 2003, pp. 23–4).

He concludes from these differences:

> So here are our choices: a world in which creation is a solitary, individual act or a world in which creation is a shared activity; a world that begins in harmony and slides towards chaos or a world that begins in chaos and moves towards harmony; a world marked by competition or a world determined by co-operation (King 2003, pp. 23–4).

We can express this through another binary table.

Table 19.2 Differences in Christian and Native American genesis stories

Christian	Native American
hierarchies	equality
law and order	cooperation
individual god	many gods
harmony to chaos	chaos to harmony
competition	cooperation

King suggests that both these stories construct reality but notes that one story—the Christian myth—has become dominant so that its reality (hierarchical, competitive) has become dominant, while the indigenous world view of equal cooperation is subordinated. He asks whether Western culture in general 'has fostered stories that encourage egotism and self-interest' (King 2003, p. 26). The point King is making is that stories construct human value systems, ideologies, so people need to look closely at what those are. And if, as he says, you are unhappy with your value systems and 'want to change society, then change the stories you tell'.

CONCLUSION

This chapter has explored the question of why people read and watch stories, what pleasures they take from them, and what values and meanings stories can carry. It has done this by offering a number of theoretical and critical perspectives that suggest some answers to these questions.

The chapter has also looked at

- the connections between fiction and stories and the real world
- tragedy, comedy, and the theory of catharsis
- Marxist approaches, with Brecht as an example
- entertainment as escape or utopia, with musicals and soap operas as examples
- the role of myths, first from Lévi-Strauss' perspective, and then through the ideas of Campbell and the hero's journey
- the different approaches of realism and fantasy
- psychoanalysis as a method for analysing stories and the pleasure derived from them
- stories as a mystically transforming experience
- the ideological values of stories.

? | DISCUSSION POINTS

1 Why do you read or watch stories? What kinds of stories do you like? Why?
2 Look at one or more of the following comedies: *South Park*, *Little Britain*, *The Simpsons*, *Fahrenheit 9/11*, *Super Size Me*, *Bridesmaids*, or *Legally Blonde*. Consider what, if any, social ills they are dealing with, whether they are contributing to social change, and who or what is being laughed at.
3 Think of examples of film or television narratives that have had a major impact on you in some way. Why and how did they do this? Describe the different reactions they produced in you.
4 Discuss the pros and cons of realism and fantasy as storytelling forms.
5 How valid and useful do you find the theory of the hero's journey?
6 How valid and useful do you find psychoanalysis as an approach for understanding stories?

SUMMARY

You should now be able to

- comment on and discuss the relationship between fictional texts and the real world
- explain and apply all the approaches listed in the conclusion in relation to understanding how stories work
- define and illustrate the terms 'catharsis', *Verfremdung*, 'myth', and 'realism'
- comment on the ideological values of stories.

Part 4 has given you a whole series of ways for analysing and interpreting texts and stories. These are presented in summary form in Figure 19.5. This will be a useful guide and checklist for any text analysis you are doing.

Figure 19.5 Media studies methodologies as applied to *American Beauty*

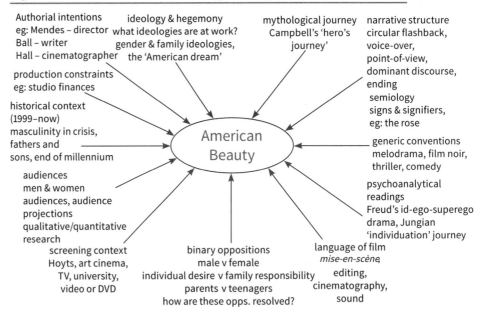

PART 5
Media and Identity: Representation, Impact, and Influence

Representation as a cultural process establishes individual and collective identities, and symbolic systems provide possible answers to the questions: Who am I? What could I be? Who do I want to be?

Kathryn Woodward *Identity and Difference*

Overview

In Part 5, the concepts of ideology and discourse will be used to examine media representations of gendered and ethnic identities. Stars and celebrities will be used as examples and consideration will also be given to how gender and ethnicity are experienced in the real world. Hopefully these chapters will have some personal relevance to you in understanding your own identity as female or male, your ethnic identity, and your own personal interest in stars and celebrities.

CHAPTER 20

Feminism, Postfeminism, and Ideologies of Femininity

> Feminism has fought no wars. It has killed no opponents. It has set up no concentration camps, starved no enemies, practised no cruelties. Its battles have been for education, for the vote, for better working conditions, for safety on the streets, for child care, for social welfare, for rape crisis centres, women's refuges, reforms in the law. If someone says "Oh, I'm not a feminist", I ask "Why? What's your problem?"
>
> Dale Spender, *Man Made Language*

This chapter will
- differentiate between sex and gender
- outline the nature/nurture debate
- discuss patriarchy and feminism
- consider the development of feminism and postfeminism
- analyse textual representations of women to show how femininity is constructed in the media.

The role of the media in identity formation is complex and contested. Rather than claiming that particular media texts have direct effects on the way we see ourselves and others, this chapter and the chapters that follow will consider the media as agents of socialisation, carriers of culture, and ways of communicating ideology. After introducing some key terms related to identity and gender studies, feminism and ideologies of femininity will be discussed, and a range of texts that illustrate how women are constructed and represented in the media will be analysed. The analyses focus on the contradictory ideologies and discourses of femininity found in advertising imagery since the 1990s. The aim is to see how certain ideological shifts have occurred in response to feminism and how these have both progressive and regressive potential. As such, this is a good example of ideological work, of the struggle over the maintenance of male hegemony, and of the simultaneous appearance of different ideological positions in the media. These points extend the discussion of ideology, discourse, and hegemony found in Part 3.

SEX AND GENDER: WHAT'S THE DIFFERENCE?

In thinking about the categories of male and female, masculinity and femininity, it is useful to make a distinction between two defining terms: 'sex' and 'gender'. Sexual difference is a biological distinction based on male and female genitalia, and chromosomal and hormonal differences. Gender is about social and cultural roles, personality traits, and behaviours that are deemed socially acceptable for men and for women in relation to concepts of masculinity and femininity. Gender study arises from concerns about the relative social positions of men and women, and about the social inequalities and the social struggles between them. Our interest in the question of gender comes from the fact that sex and gender are two of the most important ways that humans classify themselves and other people.

Gender issues also intersect with sexual desire and sexual expression. Sexuality, in Western culture, is often connected with heterosexuality, love, marriage, and the family. The social institutions of marriage and the family are ideally meant to include, and to be the natural outlet for, sexual feelings and sexual expression. The dominant ideology has been that people find love and sexual satisfaction in monogamous relationships and in families, although the reality is that these social institutions coexist with other forms of sexual and emotional relationships. An explanation of gender identity, sexuality, and social experience enhances our understandings of ourselves, our families, and our roles in the communities and social structures in which we live.

BIOLOGICAL ESSENTIALISM *VS* THE SOCIAL CONSTRUCTION OF GENDER

The nature/nurture debate asks: which factor has the strongest influence on the development of gender identity—nature (biological and genetic factors) or nurture (social expectations)?

One of the major arguments about gender is between essentialist definitions of gender and the view that gender is a social construction. The **biological essentialist** position sees gender as being based on genetic, biological, and psychological differences. It holds that men and women are essentially (inevitably) different in their biological and emotional make-up, and that this determines how they feel and act. An essentialist would argue that due to hormones and physiology, women are naturally more nurturing and gentle because they are built to breed and care for children. Men are naturally more competitive, aggressive, smart, and powerful because of testosterone and a stronger musculature that enables them to protect their mate and young. Essentialism naturalises dominant ideologies of gender, heterosexuality, and patriarchy. It reduces everything to inescapable binary oppositions with no possibility of change, deviation, or development.

In contrast, the **social constructionist** position sees gender characteristics as a consequence of how people are socialised. Even as children, males and females are treated differently, and encounter attitudes and beliefs (some present in media texts and narratives, some directly experienced through social interaction) that shape our expectations of how we should behave and what we might achieve. A constructivist would argue that it is these social pressures, not the particular physiology or aptitudes that we are born with, that primarily influence the formation of adult identity. A cultural studies approach to media analysis aims to deconstruct identity and subjectivity. It shows that who we think we are is a result of a series of interpellations, discourses, and social structures into which we are born: ethnicity, class, and gender position, alongside nationality and language, structure people's identities and subjectivities. Through analysis these identities are questioned, destabilised, and undermined, challenging 'common-sense' assumptions about what is normal or natural. You might ask yourself to what extent you think that your own sexuality and your identity as a woman or a man are biologically determined or influenced by your family, culture, and education. Transgender further complicates conceptions of identity (see Figure 21.11 on p. 342).

◄ BIOLOGICAL ESSENTIALIST

The belief that the physical body—the hormones, inherent instincts, and genetic predispositions etc.—defines the essence of identity and determines personality characteristics, behaviour, and abilities.

◄ SOCIAL CONSTRUCTIONIST

Sees identity as constructed by external social forces such as the media, family, education, religion, and expectations of community members.

Essentialist and constructivist perspectives can also be extended to include race and sexuality, and to support or undermine stereotypes and generalisations associated with these aspects of identity. This complex debate about biological essentialism and social construction cannot be resolved here. Our approach is to accept elements of both, but to stress the influence of socialisation.

GENDER, QUEER THEORY, AND THE FLUIDITY OF IDENTITY

Judith Butler is a theorist who was influential in extending feminist analysis into a new field called 'queer theory'. Butler argues that all gender behaviour is 'performative' (1998). Men and women learn to embody gender roles through 'the structure of impersonation by which any gender is assumed … Gender is a kind of imitation for which there is no original' (Butler 1998, p. 722). However, this does not mean that we are always performing gender as though we are actors in a play, nor does it mean that we consciously enact femininity or masculinity. Instead, Butler is arguing that the requirements of our role as a girl or boy, then later as a woman or man, are ingrained in us from birth. One of the first things said when a baby is born is 'It's a boy!' or 'It's a girl!', and from that moment on we are conditioned to behave in a manner that 'matches' our sex—females are expected to be feminine, and males are expected to be masculine. For Butler, this conditioning means we are constantly repeating the behaviour and actions that society tells us 'belong' to the body we inhabit (female or male). We are all doing a gender, rather than being a gender. For Butler, 'doing gender' in this way is actually what creates our identity and sense of self, and there is no essential reality behind these roles. Women and men are socialised into a compulsory performance of normal gender roles that they must perform on pain of ostracism, violence, punishment, and repression. Two questions are crucial here: first, what range of roles and identities are available for women and men? And second, are these roles performative, or is there something that makes women essentially feminine and men essentially masculine?

Deborah Cameron (2007) cites the contemporary popular idea that 'men are from Mars and women are from Venus' as an idea that supports the myth of gender difference—that men and women are different beings from alien planets and therefore speak different kinds of language. Cameron points out that the reality is that we live in a society and time in Western cultures where differences between men and women have actually become less and less marked over the past forty to fifty years; consequently, no group of women and men in history has ever been so similar as affluent Western men and women are, sharing the same educational opportunities, career opportunities, aspirations, and values. She believes that the myth of profound difference is being used to reassure people that gender difference does still matter. She argues that in people's minds, gender does still make a difference and is very important to our sense of identity, our social relations, and our sexual relations; people don't want to think it's just a trivial difference, such as being left- or right-handed. But Cameron doesn't accept that there is a profound difference. The debate surrounding biological essentialism and social construction also relates to questions about sexuality: are people born heterosexual, homosexual, or bisexual, or do they acquire a sexual orientation during the course of their life, and how does sexuality relate to gender behaviour?

These questions affect everyone in a very personal way because our gender identity and our sexual identity are fundamental to how we understand ourselves. Many people are very passionate about their stance on the matter, which is reflected in public debate about these issues. For example, when Lady Gaga's song 'Born This Way' was released, it was widely interpreted to be promoting the notion that people are 'born' gay or straight, in the same way people are born blue-eyed, black-skinned, Chinese, or Italian. The popularity of the song prompted a number of people to weigh in on the essentialist versus constructionist debate in public forums such as blog sites and newspaper columns. The tensions between essentialism and constructionism became apparent in these discussions, which represented the differing positions on the topic. Some argued that people are indeed born gay or straight, and many of them held this idea up as another reason that gay people should not be persecuted for their sexual orientation—these people took the stance that you can't help who you are if you are born that way, and people should not be discriminated against for things out of their control. Others asserted that nobody is 'born' gay or straight, because all sexuality categories, including heterosexuality, are socially constructed. (Importantly, this is a different position from one that maintains heterosexuality is the norm and homosexuality is an aberrant 'choice'.) Still others upheld that there are both essential and constructed elements of gender and sexuality. Similar discussions took place in the mediasphere when Caitlyn Jenner came out as a transgender woman in 2015 (see Figure 21.11 in Chapter 21).

You, as readers, might note that we, as authors, have stressed gender differences throughout this book. Do you think this means we are supporting the myth of difference, the oppositional duality of men and women, or are we drawing your attention to the way the media and culture construct these differences for us?

PATRIARCHY

Society is based not just on different genders but also on unequally positioned genders: masculinity and femininity are differently valued. **Patriarchy** is a system based on the law of the father. This is so in two ways: first, through lineage (children are given their father's family name rather than their mother's); and second, through the legal and political institutions that, although no longer given over into the exclusive power of men, have developed as male institutions. In the past women could not hold political office, they were excluded from voting rights (women won the right to vote only after protracted struggle), they had lesser legal rights, and married women were regarded as the property of their husbands. Religion is one of the last major institutions still divided over the issue of whether women have the right to hold positions of power, as evident in the news article about gender equity and Islam ('Saudis Acknowledge Women Exist' discussed on pp. 81–3), and the struggle of women to be ordained in the Anglican and Roman Catholic churches.

Historically, most cultures have privileged men with greater rights than women, and most continue to give them greater benefits in terms of power and wages. This denigration of femininity, alongside the inequality in power between the sexes, can lead to a sexist, **misogynist** society, as well as to a rejection of men's own gentler characteristics. In Australia in 2012, then-Prime Minister Julia Gillard delivered a powerful speech directed at then-Leader of the Opposition Tony Abbott accusing him of 'misogyny'. This speech went viral and was reportedly downloaded 22 million times in the first ten days. Some argue

◀ PATRIARCHY

A social structure in which the father or a male figure is the leader and descent is reckoned on the male line. Masculine power and authority dominate social, political, and economic institutions, thereby oppressing women.

◀ MISOGYNY

Hatred of women and femininity (literally, 'hatred of the womb').

that Gillard's speech was a turning point in how we use the word 'misogyny', as it brought discussions about gender and sexism into the everyday public discourse in Australia. It also provoked the Macquarie Dictionary to widen its definition of misogyny from 'hatred of women' to include 'entrenched prejudice against women'.

FEMINISM ▶

FEMINISM

The movement for women's equality and liberation.

Feminism has had an enormous impact on society. Initially feminists fought for women's social, legal, political, and economic rights, and attempted to understand how the construction of femininity is related to the status of women. This altered understandings of gender roles and identities, and led to important social changes that had far-reaching impacts on women and men.

Feminism should be understood in the context of a long history of patriarchy and the oppression of women that stretches back through the centuries. The history of feminism has many stages, sometimes described as first-wave feminism, second-wave feminism, and third-wave feminism. First-wave feminism can be traced back to the late eighteenth century but was at its peak between 1880 and the 1920s, during which time the focus was on legal advances in the public sphere. The emphasis of the first wave of feminism was on attaining full citizenship, legal equity, and recognition that women should have the same rights and opportunities enjoyed by other citizens, including the right to vote. The efforts of early feminists such as Mary Wollstonecraft, author of *A Vindication of the Rights of Woman* (written in 1792), included the struggle for emancipation and suffrage (the right to vote). In the nineteenth century and the early twentieth century, first-wave feminism involved novelists such as George Eliot (a woman) and Virginia Woolf, and political theorists such as John Stuart Mill and his wife, Harriet Taylor Mill, all of whom raised questions about women's rights, duties, and responsibilities. *Sufragette* (2015) is a film that dramatises the first wave of feminism, focussing on working-class women around 1912 in Britain.

The most well-known strand of feminism, now known as second-wave feminism, emerged in the late 1960s and it has had enormous influence on Western society. Where the earlier feminist movement had concentrated on gaining equity for women in the public sphere, the second wave of feminism acknowledged that the oppression of women in a patriarchal system also extends to the private sphere, including personal relationships. This insight is expressed in the slogan 'the personal is political', marking a shift to include concerns such as domestic violence, women's reproductive rights (abortion and contraception), childcare, relationships, the body, emotions, and sexuality. The second-wave feminist struggle against sexual oppression and harassment focused on the exploitation of women through sex, and on how women's bodies and appearances are controlled and valued. Consciousness-raising groups raised awareness of the ways in which women (as well as men) have internalised patriarchal expectations, and sought to liberate women from preconceptions of how they ought to behave. Feminist analyses of the media also critiqued the way women tend to be visually represented as sexual objects, developing a body of theory to analyse and understand this practice (see, for example, Mulvey's work in the field of feminist psychoanalysis and film studies, pp. 247–8).

Since that time and particularly since the 1980s, there have been many new developments and debates in relation to the social roles of women and men, and the construction of gender and sexual identities. Different strands of feminism have developed, and there have also been reactions against feminism. *Backlash: The Undeclared War against American Women* is the title of a book by feminist author Susan Faludi. This book looks at developments, particularly in the USA, that suggest patriarchy has been fighting the advances that women have made over the last few decades (Faludi 1992). Faludi cites the men's movement and commentators such as Robert Bly as part of this backlash, and points to the misogyny in films such as *Fatal Attraction* (1987) and *Basic Instinct* (1992) as further examples. The backlash has been successful insofar as feminism has taken on negative connotations, including, ironically, that feminists are unfeminine (hairy, power-hungry, butch lesbian separatists who aim to oppress men). This perception has led some women (and men) to reject feminism.

The advertisement shown in Figure 20.1, which is aimed at men, is deliberately politically incorrect and as such can be seen as part of the backlash against feminism. The caption 'What's wrong with this picture?' implies that there is nothing wrong with the fantasy that women should look sexy while devoting themselves to domestic labour for men who ogle their bodies and laze about on the couch. The punchline 'You never mix your whites with your coloureds' jokingly suggests that the only thing wrong is that the woman hasn't sorted the laundry properly. It combines a knowingness about feminist debates around the unequal division of domestic labour and the sexual objectification of women with the suggestion that men have certain instinctive, essential, sexual drives that can only be satisfied by treating women as objects of visual, and ultimately sexual, pleasure. Note that the context of reception also influences interpretation of the image in significant ways. In South Africa, for instance, a country sensitive to racial discrimination, the advertisement would be read within the discourse of gender politics and political incorrectness, but the punchline takes on added significance.

Figure 20.1 Advertisement for *RALPH* magazine

Source: *RALPH* magazine

'Third-wave feminism' tends to be used as an umbrella term to describe an era of feminist thinking that has developed since the 1980s. While first- and second-wave feminism stressed the construction of femininity and fought for equality with men, some third-wave feminists argue that there might be important differences between men and women (and between women), and that traditional feminine qualities and characteristics need to be revalidated and endorsed. The intersection of contemporary feminist theory with a body of theory by and about lesbians has been particularly productive in this respect, in that it recognises that women's desires do not necessarily revolve around men, marriage, and family. Many third-wave feminists have also acknowledged that although patriarchy privileges men, men seem to suffer from it in various ways too. Many men have come to feel the privilege of paid employment (being, or having to be, the breadwinner) and the exemption from parenting duties as a burden in the first instance and a sacrifice in the second.

Third-wave feminism has explored the fact that much first- and second-wave feminist theory was the product of the white, middle class elite and that did not understand or include the experiences of women of colour. The African-American feminist theorist bell hooks spells her name with lower-case letters to signify the fact that she is a member of a doubly marginalised group and that being a woman of colour differentiates her experiences from those of white women. Feminism, hooks claims, should be opposed to all systems of domination (including oppression on the basis of race, class, sexuality, and gender; see hooks 2000). This careful attention to difference, diversity, and the historical or contextual specificity of women's experiences is a core characteristic of third-wave feminism, and it arose from feminist critiques of homogeneity that date back to civil rights movements in the 1960s and 1970s. The third wave of feminism is also characterised by a focus on youth movements and issues, and a critical resistance to earlier codes of feminist behaviour or appearance (for example, body hair as a symbol of resistance to patriarchal norms).

POSTFEMINISM

POSTFEMINISM ▶

The term can be used to suggest that feminism is in the past, outdated, no longer relevant to contemporary gender dynamics. Alternatively, postfeminism can refer to a postmodern approach to feminism and/or contemporary critiques of earlier feminisms.

The term **postfeminism** is often used in relation to theories and ideas that reject much of earlier feminist orthodoxy and/or that embrace a postmodern approach to feminism (see Chapter 24 for a discussion of postmodernism). There are many definitions of postfeminism; however, the most common ones involve a tension between two different understandings. On the one hand, postfeminism is associated with antifeminist discourse and with the sense that we have entered an era after feminism in which resistance to patriarchal oppression is no longer necessary. On the other hand, postfeminist theory is a sophisticated postmodern or poststructural critique of earlier approaches to feminism that are seen as being extreme, essentialist, caught up in dualisms, or flawed and misguided in other ways. Interestingly, feminism has had such an impact on both the media and society that its fundamental insights and goals have, in many ways, been internalised and affirmed in both these strands of postfeminist discourse. Some postfeminists take the benefits of first- and second-wave feminism for granted: it is from a position of increased equity and changed attitudes that they are able to critique earlier feminist positions. Postfeminism is thus distinct from feminism in the 1960s and 1970s and challenges this feminism, but at the same time it is still built on and linked to earlier feminist movements.

THE LIMITATIONS OF SECOND-WAVE FEMINISM

Postfeminist theory articulates the limitations in earlier feminisms, which can be broadly categorised as follows.

Second-wave feminism and sex

Recent feminist theory suggests that earlier perspectives on sexuality were restricted and restrictive. In the struggle to shift definitions and representations of women away from the purely sexual, second-wave feminism objected strongly to media texts in which the female body was sexualised. These feminists argued that such representations interpellated the audience into a masculine subject position, encouraging viewers to take pleasure in the controlling, possessive gaze and to participate in the process of sexual objectification. These critiques of objectification still have force and we may still rightly object to women being reduced to images that sell commodities by making men think about sex. The danger in this is that the attempt to control objectification also censors women's efforts to represent and express their own sexuality, or to enjoy media representations of female sexuality. While this aspect of second-wave feminism can be seen as repressive of women's sexuality, it should be noted that women's magazines today do not display any such aversion to sex or sexuality. They are full of articles, information, stories, and pictures that explicitly explore issues of female sexuality.

There is currently a host of new possibilities for women in terms of the expression of sexuality (Tasker & Negra 2007; McRobbie 2009; Taylor 2012). The opening up of these possibilities is partly related to the reappropriation or reclaiming of particular signifiers of femininity. Wearing make-up, for example, may at first seem to undermine the feminist position that a woman's worth is not located in her appearance or in her status as an object that is sexually appealing to men, but postfeminists may wear make-up in a way that draws attention to the artifice involved in beautification, inviting the viewer to recognise that a mask is being worn. Make-up can thus be worn with irony, humour, and playfulness, and thereby become part of a game that involves playing with identity and celebrating femininity. This play with identity challenges essential notions of the self and makes it acceptable, in feminist terms, for women to create different identities for themselves through make-up, hairstyles, and clothes. Apart from giving women the freedom to be ironic and knowing about their assumption of feminine identities, make-up can also be used as an instrument of power in relation to men, allowing women to assert their sexual attractiveness as power over men. Some recent advertising campaigns for make-up (see, for example, Figure 20.2) show it being worn aggressively rather than enticingly.

Another form of asserting a postfeminist position, or 'girl power', is evident in a clothing brand called Bad Girl, marketed using a logo with a halo over it (subverting the good girl–bad girl division by celebrating the deviance of the bad girl). In her influential book *Bad Girls: The Media, Sex and Feminism in the 90s* (1997), postfeminist theorist Catharine Lumby explores the positions of a new generation of feminists in debates about pornography, censorship, and the media. Signs of oppression (such as the label 'bad girl', or even images of sexism and objectification) can thus be reclaimed and reused by the oppressed group, in this case women, as a sign of power and agency. For more recent developments in this area of scholarship, see Angela McRobbie's critique of postfeminist culture and promiscuity in

Figure 20.2 Advertisement for 17 Cosmetics

The caption reads: It's not make-up. It's ammunition. 'I'm the last bird you'll peck on the cheek, mate.'

Source: 17 Cosmetics 1998; photograph by Mosche Brakha

The Aftermath of Feminism (2009) or Anthea Taylor's *Single Women in Popular Culture: The Limits of Postfeminism* (2011).

Valuing differences between women and men

The second general limitation of second-wave feminism has been seen as its approach to questions of differences between men and women. Over time feminist theorists have attempted to understand what constitutes women's identities, and to explore the issue of whether gender identity is essential or constructed (Butler 1990). Postfeminists and third-wave feminists develop the point about the construction of femininity further, suggesting that all gender roles for men and women are socially constructed, and that gender categories are themselves subject to question.

Class and ethnicity in feminism

Postfeminism challenges the perceived dominance of white, middle class voices in second-wave feminism by taking care to include a range of women's voices and positions. The experiences and concerns of a black, or so-called coloured, South African woman will have similarities with, but not be identical to, the experiences and concerns of a Māori woman, a well-off Singaporean businesswoman, and a white female academic from California or London. Each of these women will experience patriarchy in distinct ways, and no woman can speak for all of them.

FEMINISM TODAY

Earlier feminism was not a simple, unified set of ideas. It was a variety of evolving positions that, despite sharing the overall objective of developing women's lives for the better, differed on how this was to be achieved. Many current female students are members of third-wave feminist and postfeminist generations; they were born into a world where they are treated differently from the way their mothers were treated, and they have opportunities that their mothers never had (male students have also been affected by these new ways of living). It is interesting that many people take these 'new' rights for women—the ones that first- and second-wave feminism fought for—as given and many do not want to label themselves as feminists. While they are the product of feminism and support many of its ideals, they also challenge it. These contested ideas about femininity and feminism emerge in a variety of media texts.

Lady Gaga is one example of a contemporary female icon who adheres to social expectations regarding sexualised femininity but also pushes the boundaries of how a female can and should be understood. Gaga is slim and attractive, and is widely known to have had plastic surgery to make her face more traditionally appealing. Like many other female pop stars, most of her songs are about romantic relationships, sex, and nightclub culture, and she often reveals a lot of skin in her video clips. In these ways, Gaga can be seen to have moved away from the older ideals of feminism to prioritise beauty and sexual relationships with men. However, this does not mean that Gaga is antifeminist, but rather that she is third-wave or postfeminist. She extends the perimeters of what is acceptable regarding female representation, and therefore opens up new possibilities for how women might be valued and how they might express themselves.

First, she is known for her eccentric, artistic fashion, which is frequently 'unsexy' (for example, see the discussion of Gaga's meat dress on pp. 127–8, Figure 8.4). Second, her music videos include the energetic group dances and provocative posing that are now commonplace in this medium, yet they also feature elements that are confronting and subversive, for example, glasses frames made from smoking cigarettes, lurching dancing, coffin pods for 'monsters', swallowing of rosary beads, and simulated birth scenes complete with goo. The third point relates to the persona she has built up. Gaga has labelled herself 'Mother Monster' and calls her millions of fans her 'little monsters'. In this way she is a self-proclaimed 'Lady' and 'Mother', but she merges this with ideas about monstrosity. Hence Gaga can be seen to embody accepted forms of sexualised femininity but she also exaggerates and subverts these, creating a spectacle and asking us to reflect on her as an artist. It is interesting to think about the different reactions people have had to Lady Gaga; to what extent are their responses influenced by older notions of femininity and womanhood?

Earlier feminist concerns and struggles produced many social changes that are now part of the media landscape and that feature in contemporary life for women:

- equal rights in terms of pay and job opportunities
- challenges to sexual discrimination and sexual harassment
- acceptance that women can enter any field of work
- acceptance that having children does not preclude full participation in the paid workforce and in public life generally, because caring for children should not be just women's work but a shared parental and social responsibility
- increased maternity benefits
- more freedom in terms of marriage and divorce
- a greater understanding and privileging of women's feelings, skills, and sexualities.

This rosy picture should not disguise the fact that women are still discriminated against in numerous ways: women's political power, in terms of parliamentary representation, is low, and struggles around equal pay, childcare facilities, violence against women, and general misogynist tendencies continue.

CASE STUDY

Women and advertisements

Advertisements featuring and addressed to women are a good place to look at media ideologies and discourses of femininity. The following examples (Figures 20.3–20.5) show some contradictory aspects of the construction of femininity in the contemporary, postfeminist era. Take a few minutes to look at each and consider what in them is significant in relation to constructions of femininity.

Some of the advertisements appear to offer women some pleasure and some power, and thus appear to have progressive aspects, while at the same time being traditional and patriarchal; others present a postfeminist perspective. While you are reading these advertisements, remember to think about:

Mode of address
Mode of address (see p. 169) refers to the different ways in which a text speaks to or addresses its audience. In this advertisement, who is speaking to whom?

Pleasure
One of the ways in which hegemony works is through winning the consent of subordinate groups and persuading them to accept their position by offering certain pleasures. Numerous pleasures for women are made available in these advertisements. Can you recognise pleasures we have not discussed?

Advertisement 1

Ideological contradictions and ideological work are demonstrated well in the Continental Slim-a-Soup advertisement (Figure 20.3). This advertisement plays with the theme of women's sexuality and sexual freedom, but it goes on to place severe limitations on it and finally channels women's desire into more traditional avenues.

Figure 20.3 Continental Soup advertisement

Source: Continental Brand Foods

Continued on next page ▶

Women's desire

Women's desire is foregrounded through the sexually appealing image of the man. The female audience is invited to take sexual pleasure in objectifying the man, thus acknowledging active female sexuality.

Restrictions on women's desires

Having invited women to take sexual pleasure in viewing the man, the advertisement then negates this through a focus on health discourses and by playing on the guilt associated with contravening social norms related to body shape and passive sexuality. Safe sex is a major issue confronting us today. This advertisement advocates safe sex as no sex. Instead of tackling safe sex in terms of safe sexual practices, women are encouraged to displace their desire back into the safer arena of food. This displacement is reinforced by making viewers feel guilty. Guilt has traditionally been used by Christianity (and other religions) to suppress sexuality for men and women. The West represses sexuality in many ways but at the same time, through advertising and other popular media products, consistently foregrounds sexual desire. This is one of the fascinating contradictions of Western culture. Sexual advertising may work because people are sexually repressed, since desire works on the basis of absence or lack. If people were sexually happy, these advertisements, which seem to be offering us sexual satisfaction through the purchase of goods, would not work. People would not need to buy the goods because they would already be sexually satisfied. Consequently, advertisers need people to be sexually repressed. This advertisement suggests that if the narrator followed her sexual desire, she would feel guilty.

Food

This advertisement proposes that the substitute for sex is food. The ice cream is presented as desirable (including the phallic chocolate wafer) but while female desire is acknowledged, it is simultaneously dismissed. Ice cream, like sex, will not be good for the female reader (even though she might want them both). Vegetable soup, however, will be. Again this draws on a health discourse (of nutrition). While it is undoubtedly true that vegetables are healthier than sweets, the real reason women are being asked to reject ice cream is because of physical appearance. The suggestion is that consuming ice cream will make women fat and as a result they will not conform to (male) ideals of femininity. There is indeed an interesting reference to size in the advertising copy ('and because size really does matter'), which, while it is partly a joke about how women may enjoy sex with well-endowed men, is also a subtle reminder to women to be conscious of their own size, weight, and appearance. Consequently, the narrative resolution and structure of this advertisement are to present various forbidden pleasures for women that are then finally denied, in the guise of a health discourse, in favour of traditional values.

The advertisement offers aspects of a progressive discourse about women's sexuality, but then incorporates them back into a traditional view of feminine roles and ideal femininity.

Advertisement 2

This advertisement (Figure 20.4) was intended to show that fashion is something that is in your blood or under your skin—a sense of style that is innate and distinctive, like the fashionable clothing produced by the Young Designers Emporium; however, a number of key signifiers in the ad work to convey a more unsettling message about women, vanity, and physical appearance. The Jupiter Drawing Room, the advertising agency that created the image, noted that they were playing on an awareness that the youth market tends to be attracted to things that shock their parents' generation. Another advertisement in this series depicts a young woman drawing a red ribbon out of her wrist, with the caption 'In your blood.' The configuration of the initials 'Y D E' on the page reads 'DYE' or, phonetically, 'die', thus connoting death and creating an association between death and the fashion industry, in which fabric and coloured dyes are so important. Presumably, Young Designers' clothes are desirable enough to die for, if you are the kind of person who has an innate sense of style, a person who has fashion 'in your blood'. The resemblance between the red fabric or ribbon and blood reinforces the connotations of death, leading critics to interpret the advertisements as images of suicide. These oppositional readings are extreme, but a semiotic analysis does reveal links between the image and the phrase 'fashion victim', and between that phrase and many other media representations of women as victims (victims of violence and crime and sexual abuse, victims in slasher films, and so on).

The phrase 'fashion victim' and the advertising image itself are particularly powerful because the woman is deliberately cutting herself, and this connects to social realities in disturbing ways. For many women, being a fashion victim and obsessing over appearance not only hurts the bank balance, but can also lead to plastic surgery, eating disorders, and other forms of self-harm. This is related to the actual site of the cut on the body of the woman in the image, and to the tape over her breasts (which is similar to the kind of tape models use in fashion shoots). The 'wound' is over her uterus, a part of the body associated with uniquely female forms of

Figure 20.4 Young Designers Emporium advertisement

Source: Jupiter Drawing Room advertising agency,
South Africa

Continued on next page ▶

power and creativity. While it is true that many young women channel their creativity into designing their own clothing or style, and into many areas other than family and children, the image looks like an attack on the heart of femininity itself, in the form of abdominal surgery (like a caesarean or hysterectomy).

The Young Designers Emporium advertisement makes a radical statement asserting the importance of the traditionally feminine preoccupation with fashion and style by suggesting that such interests are not superficial but actually run deep under the skin and in the blood as a creative force. While validating fashion as a serious interest, the image is simultaneously sending a negative message to and about women, and thus it communicates contradictory ideologies of femininity.

Advertisement 3

"No one I would have rather shared my VS v-card with;)

> This show is genuinely a dream come true. Can't thank you enough" – *Gigi Hadid to Kendall Jenner, on Instagram, after their first runway appearance together for Victoria's Secret.*

<www.instagram.com/p/97ozTrDCX3/?taken-by=gigihadid>

Advertisement 3 (Figure 20.5), while not a traditional advertisement, is an image featuring models and best friends Gigi Hadid and Kendall Jenner after their first runway show for Victoria's Secret, an American lingerie company. It is important to read this image in a broader context, because Hadid's and Jenner's backgrounds arguably play a part in their roles as Victoria's Secret models: that is, they are able to project images that are seen as desirable not only for what they look like, but for who they are, and for a particular lifestyle they project. Jenner is the daughter of Kris and Caitlyn Jenner and a sister of the Kardashians. Hadid is a model and television personality. Both Jenner and Hadid have reality TV experience: *Keeping up with the Kardashians* (Jenner) and *The Real Housewives of Beverley Hills* (Hadid's mother is one of the stars on this reality TV show). Hadid and Jenner are 'it girls' in the current postfeminist cultural climate, and they represent an image of 'girl power' that is assumed will inevitably transition to 'empowered' womanhood. They represent what Amy Shields Dobson describes as the 'interconnected values signified in girl power narratives … namely consumerism, visibility/image circulation, and "celebrity"' (quoted in Harris (ed.) 2008, p. 126). The most elite Victoria's Secret models are known as the 'angels'. The social power that is attached to being an angel can be observed in the high visibility of former angels such as Karlie Kloss, Claudia Schiffer, and Miranda Kerr. In Figure 20.5, Jenner and Hadid are smiling widely at their 'achievement' as they have both literally and figuratively spread their (Victoria's Secret) wings: one of the highest 'honours' in the modelling world. Jenner and Hadid are wearing their Victoria's Secret attire (lingerie), resplendent with the requisite angel wings, while dressed also as fairy-butterfly insects, albeit in tight and restrictive corsets representing control of the self and also presenting an image of 'ideal' femininity.

Our culture unavoidably, and unfortunately, valorises some voices, sexualities, lifestyles, and bodies—those who are already profiting in a neoliberal climate financially, often significantly enhanced by their media engagement: white, middle class, as well as the very wealthy, youthful, able-bodied, and heterosexual. Thus the 'ideal' subject is, for example, someone who projects a particular version of success, such as that embodied by Hadid and Jenner: the young, thin, empowered, celebrity 'it girls' whose lifestyle allows them to attend parties with other celebrities, and whose 'dreams' to become Victoria's Secret models came true. Their individual cultural capital was already high before they ventured into the 'elite' world of

Victoria's Secret modelling; together, however, they are a powerful force for marketing success. They both epitomise what is valued in, and aligned with, both postfeminist and neoliberal logics: agency/choice; autonomy/self-control; self-discipline (thinness); self-governing; self-improvement and entrepreneurialism resulting in career success; and individualised self-promotion, which they do through their social media channels and in celebrity appearances. Thus Jenner and Hadid embody a rhetoric of choice and empowerment: they can *choose* to be self-objectifying, sexually appealing, and delicate—but girlish—butterfly angels to sell products in their lingerie modelling careers, but they can *also* project autonomy by being able to pay their own way in life and make their own career choices within a culture where being so thin that you boast a 'thigh gap' holds currency. So there are ambiguity and tension at play, as this image demonstrates.

Figure 20.5 Kendall Jenner and Gigi Hadid

Source: www.instagram.com/p/97ozTrDCX3/?taken-by=gigihadid

There has been a backlash against the unrealistic bodies (and lifestyles) that Victoria's Secret advertises. For example, the advertising campaign that Victoria's Secret ran to promote a range of bras called 'Body' used toned, slim models and used the tag line 'The Perfect "Body"' in front of nine tall, slim, fair, underwear models and one tall, slim, darker skinned model in 2014. A social media campaign was soon launched (#iamperfect) to draw attention to irresponsible marketing. In this campaign, women of all shapes and sizes from all around the world used Change.org and social media such as Twitter to petition Victoria's Secret to change the advertisement. With over 33 000 signatories, the campaign was successful and Victoria's Secret changed the tag line to 'A "Body" for Every Body'.

What significance do you think 'angel wings' have in terms of models promoting underwear in angel wings for Victoria's Secret? Do you think this means that the ideal (young) woman—the postfeminist subject—should be 'angelic' and 'pure'? What is the ideal postfeminist subject, and why is it problematic?

The danger with postfeminism's devil-may-care attitude about gender and sexuality, evident in some postfeminist media texts, is that it assumes that gender relations and the power dynamics they entail are issues that have been resolved, rather than being ongoing concerns linked to race, class, and other forms of identity and oppression. Many of these postfeminist media texts depict assertive female characters who don't care about issues such as sexism because they already have the benefits of equal opportunity.

CONCLUSION

These are complex advertisements in their mixture of discourses and the way they present different aspects of ideologies about femininity. Many contemporary advertisements offer something positive to women but ultimately reassert aspects of traditional femininity. In this way we can see a hegemonic struggle taking place: women win something, but the traditional roles and power relations are not ultimately shifted. Others are more obviously challenging. Significantly, in modern advertising we can see evidence of a heightened degree of awareness about the problems inherent in the objectification of women, the denigration of traditionally female spheres of interest, and the representation of women in passive or stereotypical roles. Feminist critiques of the media and society have caused us to question the commodification and objectification of the female body, denaturalising patriarchal ideology. Even though sexist representations are still present in the media, media producers and media audiences now recognise that they are problematic, and audiences are more likely to view such images with humour, irony, or a critical eye rather than accepting them unquestioningly. These images enable us to use the critical tools of ideology, hegemony, and discourse as a way of understanding what they are doing.

In relation to the wider social hegemonic struggle between men and women, Cameron (2007) voices an interesting perspective. Over the past fifty years in Western culture, women have won more and more power and equality, and are now present in more aspects of the public sphere than ever before, including in the media, where many women have important jobs. Consequently it could be argued that, as women achieve power and bring their feminine values into the public arena, society is gradually being feminised. But Cameron suggests that actually the opportunities that have opened up for middle class, educated women, which in many ways make their lives more like men's, depend on a focus on individual achievement and individual freedom, whereas women's lives in every social class used to revolve around their domestic, reproductive, and caring responsibilities, carried out in the community as well as the home. So in order for women to take up positions of power, they have to become more like men, and therefore society has been masculinised because the values that people are living by are symbolically or traditionally masculine values, such as being focused on the individual or on getting ahead.

This chapter has

- outlined major terms and concepts for understanding gender
- considered the issue of biological essentialism versus social constructionism
- traced the history and developments of feminism
- examined in detail how women are represented in advertisements
- considered the social role of women from a hegemonic perspective.

? DISCUSSION POINTS

1 Discuss the pros and cons of the nature/nurture debate in relation to the construction of femininity and masculinity.
2 All gender behaviour is performance. Discuss.
3 How valid do you find third-wave feminism's criticisms of earlier feminism?
4 What's wrong or right with contemporary representations of women in advertising? Discuss, with examples.

SUMMARY

You should now be able to

- articulate your own position in the nature/nurture debate
- explain the arguments about gender between biological essentialism and social constructionism
- explain the difference between sex and gender
- define the terms 'patriarchy', 'feminism', 'misogyny', and 'postfeminism'
- outline the main concerns of the three waves of feminism, and explain how and why feminist concerns have changed over time
- analyse how the different discourses of femininity present in media texts relate to patriarchal or feminist ideologies, and to changing perceptions of gender roles.

CHAPTER 21

Ideologies and Discourses of Masculinity

Homo sapiens—male *n.* once dominant species on planet Earth, entered into swift decline in latter half of 20th century due to social, environmental and economic factors. Now confined almost exclusively to research-based sanctuaries around the world.

Encyclopedia Britannica 2090

This chapter will

- examine dominant masculinity and other variations
- consider the crisis of masculinity
- analyse media representations of men.

Representations and ideologies of masculinity have already been discussed a number of times (seeing *American Beauty* and *The Day after Tomorrow* as films that explore contemporary masculinity). In the last chapter we examined feminism and ideologies of femininity, and now we look at discourses and ideologies of masculinity in media representations and in real life. Our interest is in how these relate and how they contribute to masculine identity. It will also be useful for you to think about your own views of men and masculinity. What do you like best and what do you like least about men and masculinity (in the real world)? Which male film stars, pop stars, and television personalities do you like most, and what characteristics do they have that you like? Think about how your answers relate to the rest of this chapter.

INTRODUCTORY POINTS

Patriarchy and masculinity

The previous chapter argued that we live in a patriarchal society. The dominant values of patriarchal society are linked to values encouraged in men and masculinity. Western society encourages competitiveness and individuality. It also encourages aggression and violence as ways of solving problems. All these values are central in the way we work, in the economic sphere, in terms of our education system, the way we interact socially, and in the ways boys are socialised into becoming men. You could say that warfare is the ultimate problem-solving device of patriarchy. Our culture still tends to validate such male characteristics, while at the same time denigrating female characteristics and femininity.

Dominant and alternative ideals of masculinity

Just as with ideologies and femininities, we should remember that there is not only one version of masculinity but many possible variations of male behaviour: there are many masculinities. A short list of male stars demonstrates some different styles of masculinity: Johnny Depp, Seth Rogan, Brad Pitt, Jay Chou, Floyd Mayweather Jr, Chris Hemsworth, Robert Downey Jr, Dwayne Johnson, Kanye West, Leonardo DiCaprio, and Jake Gyllenhaal all offer something different. Different ethnic groups may have different masculinities: African-American masculinities, for example, may be different from white masculinities.

However, as with ideology and femininity, there is a dominant ideal of masculinity. In the 1980s this ideal was epitomised by stars such as Arnold Schwarzenegger and Clint Eastwood, both of whom represented strength, toughness, attractiveness, heterosexuality, and whiteness. These ideals are still found at the beginning of the twenty-first century—but there are many other possibilities and the ideals are being questioned. The ideal version of dominant masculinity presents a problem for real men because it is so difficult to attain. Many comic actors draw attention to the impossibility of achieving perfect masculinity and point to its ridiculousness, but heroic film texts still predominate.

Alongside the media ideals, there are also dominant versions of masculinity and femininity lived out in the real world, which is less clear-cut, but we argue that as a consequence of our socialisation and upbringing, men and women are likely to develop certain patterns of typical behaviour. While the behaviour of some women and men will not conform to these patterns, it is still possible to see general tendencies in masculine and feminine behaviour and identity in how men and women act and feel.

Masculinity in crisis

Since the 1970s masculinity has become an issue in Western culture; people speak of masculinity being in crisis, which suggests that the old masculine ideals are no longer universally accepted and that people have begun to question what it means to be a man. Bookshops have sections on men's health and men's issues, universities have courses in men's studies, and there is extensive research related to masculinity. Jokes are made about and against men in the way they used to be made against women. Essentialist notions of identity are being challenged and people are beginning to realise that if gender roles are socially constructed, they do not necessarily have to accept or respect the roles, values, and expectations that have been associated with masculinity. This crisis was prompted by two movements: feminism and the gay rights movement. Feminists, having first looked at and questioned the construction of femininity, then began to problematise masculinity, seeing it too as a social construction and also challenging some of the values associated with masculinity. Consequently, some men began to question and look at their own masculine identities.

Figure 21.1 is the opening text from an article published in *Cleo*. The article imagines a world in which men have become redundant. The text is a mock encyclopaedia entry on *Homo sapiens*. This article is typical of media products that comment on or make reference to a crisis in masculinity.

Three waves of critical masculinity studies

In parallel with the growth of feminism, the gay rights movement challenged the oppression of lesbians and gay men by heterosexist society. The gay movement offered many insights into both homosexual and heterosexual masculinity, and challenged some of the stereotypes of so-called normal masculinity. Most recently, a body of work called queer theory (see p. 314) is continuing this task in different ways.

Feminism and the gay rights movement challenged normal masculinity and suggested new possibilities for masculine identity. Researchers such as Tim Edwards identify three

Figure 21.1 Extract from an article in *Cleo* magazine

"homo sapiens - male *n.* once dominate species on planet Earth, entered into swift decline in latter half of 20th century due to social, environmental and economic factors. Now confined almost exclusively to research-based sanctuaries around the world."
Encyclopedia Britannica, 2090

WARNING: ENDANGERED SPECIES!

MEN

Source: text from *Cleo* May 1998; photograph by Jasmine Martin

waves of masculinity studies, similar to the three waves of feminism. In *Cultures of Masculinity* (2006), Edwards states that the first wave studied the social construction of sex roles; since the 1980s second-wave masculinity studies or the so-called 'men's movement' have been exploring masculinity further and critiquing the limitations of the sex-role paradigm. The second wave was characterised by the work of Robert Bly (*Iron John* 1990), Steve Biddulph (*Manhood* 1994; *Raising Boys* 1997), and Raewyn (previously known as Robert) Connell (*Gender and Power* 1987; *Masculinities* 1995). This wave looked to find ways of changing and revalidating masculinity.

The third wave of critical masculinity studies is influenced by concepts drawn from queer theory such as performativity and by poststructuralist ideas about normativity. As a result, by the start of the twenty-first century, masculinity was in question. It is now seen as more fluid than ever before, in the sense that there are more options available for men as to how to be masculine. The damaging nature of patriarchy to both women and men has been acknowledged, and attempts have been made to find new versions of masculinity that challenge the oppression and sexism of patriarchal masculinity. And as Deborah Cameron argues (see p. 328), the social gap and differences between women and men in Western culture have become much smaller.

With awareness of the crisis of masculinity, many popular films, television programs, newspaper and magazine articles, and advertisements address the question of what it means to be a man today. Gay culture has become much more acceptable and has influenced ideals of masculinity.

The points above suggest that masculinity is not only in crisis but is also a problem for our society. Critiques of patriarchy have in some cases implied a vilification of masculinity. As a man, how do I, Michael, feel and write about this? In many ways I am critical of masculinity and patriarchy, and I recognise ways in which men are sexist and oppress women. I would like to see social changes. But I am also sympathetic towards men's position in our society. I think it is important to see that men too have suffered under patriarchy, in trying to live up to its limiting and impossible ideals. Men's failings hurt themselves as well as others, and these are predominantly the result of society, not biology. But criticism alone won't always help matters; we need to understand the processes that have produced patriarchy and we need to make changes in masculinity. At the same time, I want to validate the positive aspects of masculinity alongside the positive aspects of femininity; I see them as complementary.

MEDIA REPRESENTATIONS OF MASCULINITY

To develop all these issues, we will now look at various media representations of masculinity. Comments will refer to media representations and to masculinity as lived in the actual world.

What kinds of masculinity do the media offer?

Masculine characteristics

Power is the major attribute that is seen as the key signifier and definer of masculinity, in the media and in the real world. Masculinity is achieved by having physical (see, for example, Figure 21.2) and/or social power.

The valuation of physical power can be seen in sports, in stars such as Sylvester Stallone and Arnold Schwarzenegger, and in films such as *The Expendables* and *Beowulf*, a valuation that is confirmed in countless media narratives in which the hero proves himself and wins the day through physical contest. The message 'might equals right' still predominates in texts that conclude with fighting. Male body attractiveness is also often linked to developed muscularity.

The ideal male also has social power, meaning wealth and influence in the world of business. Richard Gere's character in *Pretty Woman*, Michael Douglas' character Gordon Gekko in the *Wall Street* films, and Daniel Craig as James Bond are typical.

Figure 21.2 Advertisement for Levi's Jeans

DO YOU FIT THE LEGEND?

Source: Levi's Jeans 1993

Their desirability is linked to social power—in this way power functions as an aphrodisiac. Like Craig's, Gere's beauty is expressed through his clothes, which are, significantly, professional clothes (he wears business suits and ties), thereby linking male identity to the professional world. Men are often defined by their jobs: a successful man is a man

Figure 21.3 Advertisement for Van Heusen shirts

Source: Van Heusen Company 1985

who does well professionally. This locates masculine identity in the public world of work, rather than the private world of domesticity (the feminine world). Men who are purely domestic are not considered real men.

Figure 21.3 is an advertisement for men's shirts. The caption of the advertisement (not shown)— 'There's a decision-maker inside all our shirts'—draws attention to the rational qualities of the well-dressed man depicted, whose professional skills confirm his successful male identity.

Male power inevitably involves power over something or someone, or both. This includes men's power not only over women, but also over other men, over the environment, and over themselves, which is linked to the fact that male relationships are often competitive or controlling. Masculinity is consequently not just a problem for women, but also for men and the environment as a whole. The ability to control (controlling others and self-control) is linked to power and rational abilities. Thus control is a defining feature of ideal masculinity.

Women, in contrast, are conventionally given power in representations in just one way: they have sexual power that they can use over men, as demonstrated by Jennifer Aniston's *femme fatale* character in *Derailed*. This has positive aspects in that it acknowledges female sexuality and in the simple fact that women are shown as having a measure of power. But it also has negative aspects: it reduces women to their sexuality (we cannot see them as separate from it), it encourages us to see women primarily as sex objects, and it denies women other forms of power. The logic is that the only way women have power is through their sexuality, which encourages women who want power to learn to use this attribute in a manipulating way, rather than attempting other ways of gaining power. In addition, this trend devalues women who are not stereotypically sexy, and it diminishes the worth of attributes such as intelligence, eloquence, practicality, agility, humour, and kindness.

Men and women together

Since masculinity and femininity partly define themselves in relation to each other— masculinity defines itself in relation to femininity, and vice versa—it is useful to look at images of men and women together and to consider the limitations of oppositional thought. Such representations tend to highlight the binary opposition that makes discourses of masculinity and femininity work. Men and women are often represented together in a context of heterosexual coupling. Consider the way men and women are coupled in Figures 21.4–21.6. What power relationships are established? Who looks or is looked at? Who has the dominant discourse? What different, complementary, opposite, and desirable characteristics are depicted for women and men?

Figure 21.4 Advertisement for Creda heaters, c. 1980

Source: General Domestic Appliances

Men together

Many media representations present stories about men relating to other men. Two themes predominate: struggle and friendship between male buddies. Many stories show both: male rivalry turns to male friendship when the protagonists find themselves fighting

Figure 21.5 Biff cartoon 1989

Source: Mick Kidd

Figure 21.6 Advertisement for Pino aftershave

Source: Vidal 1995

HOMOPHOBIA ▶

Fear of same-sex intimacy, though most commonly used to refer to men's fear of homosexuality and emotional closeness between men.

alongside one another or against each other. Depicting male characters fighting alongside one another allows them to be physically close and provides a situation in which each can earn or win the respect of the other, which leads to friendship. Other narratives involving fighting encourage men to distrust each other or to see other men as rivals, or present the playing out of father–son relationships.

These hero stories can be seen as dramas of masculinity. The stories are about men finding their true masculinity, their masculine identity, as in the film *300*. The process of testing they go through initiates them into masculinity. Traditionally, westerns and gangster movies have validated typical masculine characteristics (in stars such as John Wayne and Clint Eastwood), but many stories today carry an interesting tension as to whether they are celebrating or critiquing masculinity. Films such as *The Departed*, *Gangs of New York*, *Reservoir Dogs*, *Fight Club*, *The Fighter*, and *The Assassination of Jesse James by the Outlaw Robert Ford* seem to revel in moments of male aggression and male power, and at the same time show how futile and destructive—to self and others—such masculinity is. These films can be read as celebrations and critiques of masculinity.

Homophobia is fear of same-sex intimacy. Men's fear of intimacy with other men is often a fear of homosexuality and it is often expressed in an aggressive manner. The media only depict intimacy between men in certain situations: war films when a buddy is dying, sports after goal-scoring exploits, and other dramas in which men fight, drink, or joke together. Buddy films contain an interesting tension: they validate male friendship but reject any homosexual possibilities. Male bonding has also been interpreted as a rejection of femininity and hence as part of misogyny. Yet some critics argue that these buddy movies unconsciously suggest strong love and homoerotic attraction between men. They argue that the male stars are filmed in such a way as to make them visually attractive not only to female characters in the film and women in the film audience, but also to male characters in the film and men in the audience. The actual narrative structure may deny or disavow male attraction, but the way it is filmed suggests **homoeroticism**.

The central relationship in the Australian film *Chopper* (dir. Andrew Dominik) is between Mark 'Chopper' Read (played by Eric Bana) and his best mate, Jimmy (played by Simon Lyndon). In one scene the depth of emotion between these two men erupts into physicality and Chopper is stabbed by his friend—the two are gripped in what looks like a dying embrace as Jimmy plunges the knife into Chopper's torso again and again. 'If you keep stabbing me I'm gonna die, mate,' Chopper says without any evidence of anger. The two characters lock eyes and it looks for a moment as though they are about to kiss. It is an ambiguous cinematic moment, charged with a twisted kind of homoeroticism. This theme is repeated in the relationship between Jesse James (Brad Pitt) and Robert Ford (Casey Affleck) in *The Assassination of Jesse James by the Outlaw Robert Ford*, Dominik's next film.

Look at the images of male bonding in the Ella Baché sunscreen advertisements in Figures 21.7–21.8. Is this bonding depicted as powerful, ridiculous, or homoerotic?

◀ HOMOEROTICISM

Sexual desire between same-sex couples, though most commonly used to refer to men; also often refers to the pleasure received in gazing at an attractive member of the same sex in sport, film, etc.

Figures 21.7 and 21.8 Elle Baché sunscreen advertisements

Source: Ella Baché

Men and feelings

It has been suggested that men learn to hide their feelings (or that they don't have many feelings) and that they learn to value rationality over emotion. In reality, men's feelings are repressed in many ways as they grow up.

The most obvious example is the way that men have been taught not to cry; however, this does not mean they do not feel. It just makes the realisation and expression of feeling more difficult. While women are encouraged to show their tears but not their anger, men are encouraged to hide their tears but show their anger. The socialisation of boys teaches them that anger and aggression are legitimate feelings for men: it is OK to be angry; indeed, anger can confirm masculinity. This is shown repeatedly in media representations. Traditionally men have not been encouraged to discuss their feelings and traditionally they are not represented as doing so. Instead, their feelings are expressed through violent action.

Male violence

Male violence has two aspects: destruction of others and self-destruction.

Destruction of others

Male violence towards women, children, and other men is prevalent throughout the world. It occurs in private and domestic spheres and in public spheres (including large-scale armed conflict). Anger may sometimes be a useful and appropriate response for men and women, but how that anger can be appropriately expressed is a vexed question. The male solution—fighting—permeates all media, which may help to endorse this behaviour for individual men and promote it as the best way of solving social problems. The ubiquity of violence as a problem-solving strategy endorses warfare as a legitimate problem-solving strategy, which is not to argue a direct-effects response mechanism: the argument here is not that men see violence on television and imitate it; nor is it an argument for repressive censorship of media violence. Both these views are too simplistic. Rather, we want to draw your attention to the issue of male violence, and to media representations of male fighting and anger towards others. Hopefully this will make you think about what model of masculinity the media offer us and how this might relate to the way men act in the real world. We think the question of how to work with male anger and violence is one of the major social issues the world faces at present.

Self-destruction

Violent actions are not always towards other people. Many male feelings of anger are, masochistically, turned inwards (there is an ironic similarity between the words 'machismo' and 'masochism'). The culture of pain and **masochism** is found in everyday images of masculinity, such as the King of Shaves advertisement (see Figure 21.9), which implies that men suffer self-inflicted pain and discomfort every day as part of the price they pay to embody an acceptable (clean-shaven) image of masculinity.

MASOCHISM ▶

Pleasure (or perverse sexual gratification) felt when experiencing pain, humiliation, or deprivation. The term is derived from the name of erotic novelist Leopold von Sacher-Masoch.

The discourse of masochism is prevalent in sport, one of the defining arenas of traditional masculinity. Sport is often presented as an arena of endurance: 'no pain, no gain', 'when the going gets tough, the tough get going', and so on. (It doesn't have to be this way, but typically male sport is understood in terms of power, strength, and competition—winning and losing—rather than grace, elegance, transcendence of time, beauty of the human form, and so on.)

The following comments by professional sportsmen show sport as a regime of endurance and punishment for the body.

Your thigh muscles swell up as if you were going to burst. You zig-zag along. The whole body is under terrible pressure (P Trentin, cyclist).

The feeling of lack of air is terrible. You think you're going to pass out—that you're not far from dying. It's true, you say to yourself, maybe that's what dying feels like (B Thevenet, cyclist).

Up to the middle of the race the fatigue increases. You're practically dead but you have to carry on. To reduce the pain you think about how much the others are suffering. Your thighs swell up, your arms hardly make it and your back stops responding. When you get to 1500 metres you tell yourself that if you had any sense you'd stop there and then.

But you have to keep going. Right up to the end the burning sensation gets worse—you feel as if your whole body is on fire from head to toe … rowing involves 100% effort and that means 100% pain (Y Fraysse, oarsman) (Brohm 1978, p. 25).

Figure 21.9 King of Shaves advertisement

Source: 'Bloody murder' advertisement for King of Shaves, courtesy of Paul Irwin, Director of Creative Partners (Aust)

What these quotations demonstrate is that the body is being disciplined and controlled. Pleasure is not involved or, if it is, it is the pleasure of pain—masochism.

Boxing is a sport in which the competitors deliberately inflict and suffer pain and serious physical injury. The image of Vitali Klitschko's battered face (Figure 21.10) shows these wounds being borne with stoic resolve. The implied narrative suggested by the low-angle shot, the boxer's proud expression, and the caption is that Klitschko has been rejected by his girlfriend because he lost the fight; it also reinforces the idea that real men don't cry or require sympathy when disappointed or hurt in any way. This illustrates how the media can function to reinforce the dominant discourse of masculinity, and how women are or can be complicit in supporting notions of ideal masculinity.

Images of masochism and brutal physicality feature prominently in films directed by Martin Scorsese, such as *The Departed* and *Raging Bull*. In *Raging Bull* Robert de Niro plays the part of boxer Jake La Motta. He typically invites people to attack and hurt him, which reaches its climax when he beats his own head and fists against a brick wall. This self-destructive violence is directed specifically against the head, the source of rationality and control. Film theorists such as Yvonne Tasker have noticed how many male film heroes

Figure 21.10 Boxer Vitali Klitschko

The caption reads: 'Pucker up, sweetie. Vitali Klitschko after being pummelled by Lennox Lewis can't understand why his beloved Olga won't give him a sympathy peck on the cheek.'

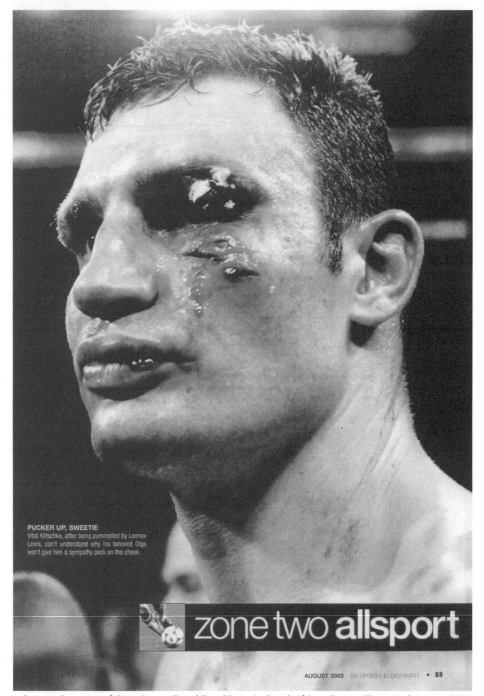

Source: Courtesy of Getty/ImageTouchline Photo in *South African Sports Illustrated*, August 2003

undergo testing rituals that involve extreme pain and often body wounding (Tasker 1993). This certainly relates to male initiation ceremonies of many traditional cultures. Such ceremonies test young men by inflicting pain on them. It also resonates with Robert Bly's idea that masculinity is about wounding (Bly 1990). Clearly, masculinity and pain are strongly linked. Pain is a way in which men can express their feelings.

The film *Fight Club* explored similar themes. Here the pleasure, emotional release, and bonding found in fighting with other men were initially shown as beneficial and health restoring (despite the physical injuries involved) for Edward Norton's spirit and for those of many other men. This is contrasted with the self-help support groups shown earlier in the film. It is noticeable that the character played by Meatloaf, who had lost his testicles to cancer (the threat of castration is a recurrent theme in the film) and grown breasts, thereby becoming emasculated or feminised, found more benefit in this ultramale brotherhood than in the support groups. The film seemed to be suggesting that fighting is better than hugging! It appeared to resonate with male audiences, and it may be that this reassertion of the value of traditional male expression and aggression is part of a reaction against the influences of feminism and the emergence of the sensitive New Age man. As film critic Amy Taubin argues, in dealing with issues of masculinity the film is another example of homoeroticism:

> Shot in a wet-dream half light that gilds the men's bodies as they pound each other's heads into the cement, the *Fight Club* sequences are a perfect balance of aesthetics and adrenaline; they feel like a solution to the mind/body split (Taubin 1999, pp. 16–18).

Men in frocks

A number of comedy films feature men cross-dressing—men wearing women's clothes—to disguise themselves as females for a period of time, tricking all the other characters around them but making audiences laugh at the 'absurdity' of a man trying to be a woman. Films that follow this pattern include *Some Like It Hot*, *Tootsie*, *Mrs Doubtfire*, *Sorority Boys*, *White Chicks*, and the three *Big Momma* films. In the *Big Momma* franchise, Martin Lawrence plays an FBI agent who disguises himself as the large, elderly matriarch 'Big Momma' to go undercover. These films have been critically ridiculed but made millions at the box office. Like Robin Williams' character in *Mrs Doubtfire*, Lawrence's character crosses boundaries of age as well as gender when he transforms into 'Big Momma'. A significant percentage of these films' humour derives from the visual comedy of what appears to be an old lady with the physical capabilities of a young, fit man. Nevertheless, the main source of comedy the films rely on is a man, with 'manly' interests and urges, presenting as a woman—a masquerade that inevitably leads to comical mix-ups and misrecognitions. Such texts are interesting because they present a transgression of dominant masculinity. Note the following points.

1   This transgression is threatening to the establishment because it blurs the normal gender definitions that give people their identity and that are used in the support of patriarchy.

2   Men in drag are often represented humorously, thus making the situation less threatening. The male figures are made to appear ridiculous. Some argue that the laughter generated by such representations is directed against femininity, in that

femininity is being parodied. If this is so, then this would make these texts misogynist. Others argue that the humour arises from the fact that these texts reveal that gender identity is a construction or a mask and, as such, they challenge patriarchy.

3   In these films the male characters find that assuming a female persona means they can express their feelings better and be more emotional, and their time spent as a woman gives them insight into the challenges women face (such as sexism in the workplace).

4   In films such as *Tootsie* and *Mrs Doubtfire* where the cross-dressing character is also a trained actor, the 'skill' it takes for these male characters to impersonate women is emphasised; therefore it is masculine skills that are being applauded, rather than feminine attributes.

5   The transgression of gender norms in these films is temporary. With rare exceptions— *Some Like It Hot*—the cross-dressing characters revert to their original gender by the end of the film. In having the main characters reassume their masculine identity, they *ultimately* reassert normal gender positions in their narrative structure, thus avoiding any possibility of gender uncertainty.

It is also important to note that cross-dressing is distinct from transgender, which refers to those who identify with a gender other than the one they were assigned at birth. In early 2015, after much earlier speculation, the media intensely reacted to former American Olympic champion and television personality (*Keeping Up with the Kardashians*) Bruce Jenner coming out as a transgender woman, Caitlyn Jenner (see Figure 21.11). In accordance with well-timed media management, a new Twitter handle @Caitlyn_Jenner

Figure 21.11 Caitlyn Jenner

Source: Alamy/Richard Levine

was created at the same time as the *Vanity Fair* cover and article were released. Jenner set a Guinness World Record, amassing over 1 million Twitter followers in four hours, surpassing the previous record set by President Barack Obama <www.guinnessworldrecords.com>. Films that explore the lives of transgender characters—including *The Crying Game*, *The Adventures of Priscilla, Queen of the Desert*, *Dallas Buyers Club*, *Predestination*, *52 Tuesdays*, and *Transamerica*—are distinct from the types of cross-dressing comedies such as those mentioned earlier. Rather than presenting gender-crossing as funny, these films address the struggles faced by those who do not fit the restrictive male-masculine, female-feminine mould. When a male in women's attire can *pass* for a biological female, this is more disturbing for some people than when ineffective cross-dressing leaves no doubt as to their biological sex. In such situations there is uncertainty about the stability of gender categories.

Cross-dressing is usually considered more transgressive when men dress as women than when women dress as men. There are some examples of film comedies in which a girl disguises herself as a boy, including *Victor Victoria*, *Just One of the Guys*, and *She's the Man*, but the gender-crossing they feature is not deemed to trouble gender categories to the same extent as in male cross-dressing films. You may wonder why this is the case.

One suggestion is that because masculinity is valued more highly than femininity in patriarchy, women dressing in men's clothes is seen as a positive thing, whereas men dressing as women are seen to be losing power and authority. Men dressing as women are seen to be devaluing themselves and, more importantly, masculinity (and consequently patriarchy). This makes cross-dressing a subversive act that can be a powerful attack on patriarchy.

How do you read the image of the Vanity Fair *cover that was the first to 'reveal' transgender celebrity Caitlyn Jenner in Figure 21.11? What can this image more broadly tell us in terms of the reader being positioned in the frame as well? What do you think it means that Caitlyn chose* Vanity Fair *in particular to present herself to the world? How do you read the cross-dressing images shown in Figures 21.12 and 21.13? Are they humorous, or serious? If humorous, then who or what are we being asked to laugh at?*

Figure 21.12 Advertisement for 17 Cosmetics

Source: 17 Cosmetics 1998; photograph by Mosche Brakha

Figure 21.13 Advertisement for Ursa computers

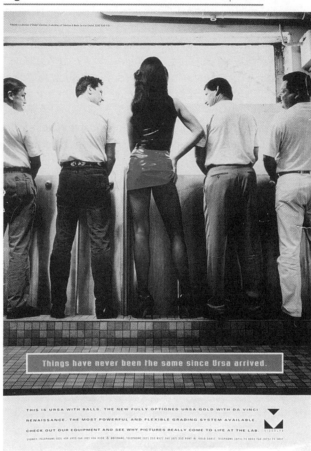

Things have never been the same since Ursa arrived.

Source: Videolab 1995

Gay representations

There have always been underground films, stories, and magazines made by and about gay men, including the films of Kenneth Anger and the novels and plays of Jean Genet. There have also been many gay filmmakers and stars working in apparently heterosexual films. Their work in mainstream film has often been read from a gay perspective by gay audiences, as exemplified in Vito Russo's book *The Celluloid Closet* (1981) and in the documentary it inspired. Mainstream films overtly about gay issues tended to pathologise gay characters as sick or criminal, as Russo argues, but since the growth of the gay rights movement, there have been more films celebrating gay men (and lesbian women) and providing much more optimistic resolutions, such as the films of Pedro Almodovar. And now there are several instances of gay representations on popular television (see pp. 235–6).

Men advertising hygiene products, cosmetics, and fragrances

The cosmetics market, traditionally aimed at women, has realised it has a huge potential male market. In order to win this market, it has to overcome the perception that the purchase and use of cosmetics are feminine activities. Focusing on men looking and smelling desirable may risk making them seem effeminate, so advertisers also need to focus on more traditional male qualities. Shaving advertisements are a rich source to examine. At the same time as stressing how attractive shaving can make men, the advertisements manage to maintain the ideal of masculine strength and proximity to physical danger by showing razors as instruments of technological power, capable of providing dangerously close shaves. Many are framed in terms of competition (beating rival products), and many link shavers to sports activities and achievements in sport.

Advertisements for perfumes marketed at men are similarly linked to physical activities. Such advertising strategies ensure that men wearing male perfumes are not challenging traditional masculinity and the virility with which it is associated; rather, these advertisements suggest that by wearing male perfumes, men are strengthening their traditional masculinity. The imagery of the advertisement for XS (Figure 21.14), a perfume produced by the house of Paco Rabanne, emphasises phallic strength. One of the most successful advertising campaigns in recent years has been for Old Spice shower gel for men, starring Isaiah Mustafa as 'The man your man could smell like' if only he used Old Spice. The Old Spice ad (Figure 21.15) appealed to both men and women with its knowing, humorous representation of gender ideals, and it went viral on YouTube, becoming one of the most viewed commercials in history. Interestingly, 'The man your man could smell like' doesn't have to do much in these advertisements to assert his masculinity: all he does is wear Old Spice in a shower, on a yacht, on a beach, on a horse without his shirt on … This ad presents a fresh take on the long-standing strategy

Figure 21.14 Advertisement for Paco Rabanne XS perfume

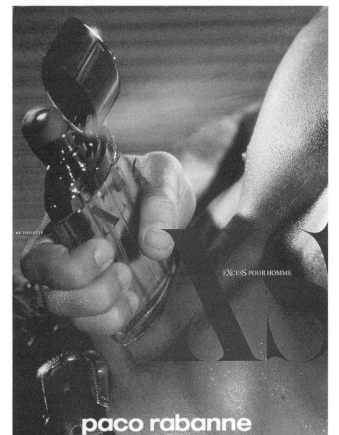

Source: Paco Rabanne; published in *Cleo*, September 1994

Figure 21.15 Advertisement for Old Spice: 'The man your man could smell like'

Source: Courtesy of the Advertising Archives

Figure 21.16 Advertisement for Lynx/Axe: Happy Women's Day!

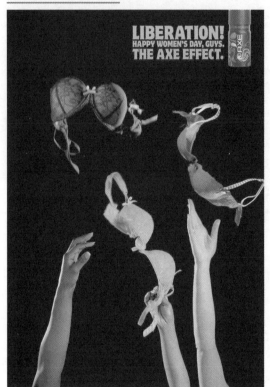

Source: Courtesy of Lowe Bull advertising agency, Johannesburg

of Old Spice's rival company, Axe (also known as Lynx), which specialises in advertisements that show 'the Axe effect', which involves women tearing off their clothes when they catch the scent of Axe on a man. Figure 21.16 uses the caption 'Liberation! Happy Women's Day, guys' and an image of women throwing their bras in the air. It recuperates the concept of women's liberation and its association with 'bra burning', defusing its threat to men by playfully turning it into yet another opportunity for men to think about naked women and sex. Even though women take on a more traditional masculine quality in the way they respond sexually to the scent and rush out to purchase Old Spice or Axe for their partners, men still have the overall power. In the past few years it has become much more acceptable for men to care about their appearance, as shown in **metrosexuality**.

Metrosexuality doesn't designate a different kind of sexuality so much as it refers to a market consisting of urban, open-minded men who pay attention to fashion and appearance, and look just gay enough to attract the attention of men as well as women. David Beckham is the most well-known metrosexual example, as he blends traditional masculine sporting prowess with concern for fashion, appearance, and occasional cross-dressing—a good example of the blending of residual and emergent discourses (see pp. 183–4 and 384–5).

METROSEXUALS ▶

Young, stylish, urban men who care about and spend considerable money on their appearance, and are attractive to women (and, often, to other men).

Male pin-ups

Since the mid-1970s, representations of the naked male body as an object of desire have become more frequent (this may be partially linked to the increased visibility of gay culture). Richard Dyer (1982) was one of the first critics to explore this phenomenon. Representations of naked men have often been a source of humour (in contrast to representations of naked women). It is as though humour is being used as a way of defusing feelings of unease about the portrayal of naked men, a tendency still evident in films such as *The Full Monty*, which ultimately refuses to show 'the full monty' (full frontal male nudity). But while humour still persists in some representations of male nudity, many are now explicit about showing the male body as an object of desire; these representations aim to provoke not laughter but desire. Such images have become very common, and demonstrate that there is a trend towards men being seen as objects of the sexual gaze. In this context, it is interesting to note that the advertisement for Wolf shoes (Figure 21.17) attempts to combine humour and sexual desirability.

Many critics have argued against the portrayal of women as sexual objects in the media. How do you assess the fact that men are now being portrayed in similar ways in stripper films such as *Magic Mike* (dir. Steven Soderbergh 2012), starring Channing Tatum and Matthew McConaughey, and *Magic Mike XXL* (dir. Gregory Jacobs 2015) with Tatum and Joe Manganiello? Is this an example of equality? Does it validate the active sexual desire of women and gay men? Does it denigrate men by making them sexual objects? Does it threaten men who can't live up to these visual ideals? In what ways are male pin-ups and male exhibitionism different from the portrayal of females as sexual objects? Do male pin-ups work? Are they amusing or sexual?

Explore these questions by collecting and examining media images of men as sexual objects. How do you and your friends feel about these images? Is there a difference between male and female attitudes towards them? Note particularly how imagery of strength, work, and sport, as well as the fact that male models tend not to look at the camera, may help to maintain masculine identity. Note, too, the considerable emphasis on the body and skin, including the taut muscularity and smooth hairlessness of the bodies depicted (simultaneously suggesting masculinity and femininity). Keeping these questions in mind, look at Figure 21.17, and also Figures 21.7 and 21.8, in terms of how they represent male power and desirability.

Then look at Figures 21.18 and 21.19, which are images from a campaign for Kolotex hosiery that promote Voodoo Control pantyhose. The image in Figure 21.18 was the first image to appear

Figure 21.17 Advertisement for Wolf shoes

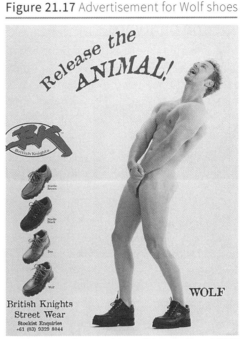

Source: Intransit International 1998

Figures 21.18 and 21.19 Billboard advertisements for Voodoo pantyhose (Kolotex hosiery)

Source: Oddfellows Billboard Advertising 1998

on billboards. How do you read this image, in which there is a combination of humour and sexual desirability? After a couple of weeks, the second image (Figure 21.19) was revealed to show the woman. How do you read Figure 21.18 in terms of issues of the relative power of men and women, and in relation to Figure 21.19?

Voodoo pantyhose

The following quote is from Janet Hogan, the managing director of Oddfellows Billboard Advertising, the advertising agency behind the campaign for Voodoo Control pantyhose. It is a good example of how authors' intentions can be important in the construction of meaning, how images are produced in relation to contemporary ideas about sexual representations, the changing roles of men and women, and how audiences can read texts:

> In keeping with past Voodoo advertising, the billboard for Voodoo Control pantyhose was designed to reinforce Voodoo's positioning as the pantyhose for women in control; women who believe that promoting their sexuality does not in any way compromise their liberated status.
>
> The campaign has been so hugely successful … because it deliberately challenges political correctness and recognises that the vast majority of women aren't hung up over gender stereotyping. Most think the whole issue of gender politics is boring, academic, counterproductive and out of touch with everyday women. They enjoy risqué advertising and the irony and humour implicit in the role reversal strategy which underpins Voodoo marketing.
>
> To create maximum impact and intrigue, the ad was designed in two stages: a teaser ad followed by a reveal of the product.
>
> The first stage shows on the left hand side a scantily clad male trying to cover himself with a piece of cloth. The message on the right: "Ladies, please control yourselves" leaves the audience to assume that the fellow is struggling against some overzealous females trying in vain to disrobe him.
>
> With the reveal, Stage 2, it becomes clear that it is in fact him pulling on the cloth, engaged in a sort of sexual tug of war with a woman wearing Voodoo Control pantyhose. The gold cloth pulled tightly around her waist and thighs emphasises the firming, flattering quality of Control top pantyhose.
>
> It is up to the reader to read as much or as little as she/he likes into the ad.
>
> Most consumers would undoubtedly read very little. They simply respond to the cultural cues present.
>
> On one level the ad is simply a sexy demonstration of the product being advertised. On another, the struggle between the sexes; a (vulnerable?) male trying to dominate the female, but unable to.
>
> If she epitomises the role model most modern women aspire to: feminine, strong, and ultimately in control, the ads epitomise the complexity of contemporary sexual mores, where really anything goes. Indeed, Voodoo is being rewarded with massive sales by the majority of women who are grateful that someone has dared to take on the thought police and do it with style and humour (correspondence to author from Janet Hogan, Managing Director, Oddfellows Billboard Advertising July 1998).

Images of masculinity in sports stars

Sporting heroes provide important role models, particularly for young men; therefore the kinds of cultural values, ideologies, attributes, and practices that sport promotes have considerable social significance for the construction of a dominant masculinity. In the poster of Breyton Paulse (Figure 21.18), a key player in South African rugby (he played right wing for the Springboks, the Stormers, and the Western Province), we see a rare instance in which the passionate expression of emotion is legitimated for men and between men. Paulse is well known for his fearlessness and expertise on the rugby field, and for his genuine warmth and dedication to community organisations and to his fans. Despite his relative lack of stature, his courage and endurance earn him the reputation for having a 'giant heart', and his commitment to the game warrants the tag 'THAT'S PASSION'. This emotive aspect is framed within the discourses of science, technology, and military strategy that reassert the masculinity of sports stars and sports fans, and distance them from the feminised connotations of words such as 'heart' and 'passion'. The picture features numbers quantifying Paulse's vital statistics, distinctive blue lighting often found in science-fiction films or emanating from computer screens, and a background image of an eye-like vortex lined with a spiral of vectors. These aesthetic elements of the picture signify that sport involves a passionate dedication that is measured, strategic, and calculated.

The fact that the sportsman in Figure 21.20 is pictured wearing a kind of body armour that offers a degree of protection in his dangerous contact sport links sport to warfare. This association is not uncommon. Some theorists have argued that sport is a ritualised form of warfare that promotes and naturalises an adversarial ideology, framing masculinity within an overarching discourse of calculated capitalist competitiveness:

> Sport makes competition appear natural and thoroughly human ... The increasing importance of the media as the carrier of this

Figure 21.20 Rugby player Breyton Paulse: '1.72 metres, 78 kilograms, and 1 giant heart ... THAT'S PASSION'

1.72 METRES, 78 KILOGRAMS, AND 1 GIANT HEART...
THAT'S PASSION

Club Newlands

Source: courtesy of Club Newlands

sporting discourse makes the two institutions mutually convergent with capitalist ideology (Cunningham & Miller 1994, p. 66).

The image in Figure 21.21 of North Queensland Cowboys captain Jonathan Thurston sharing a moment of parental intimacy with his daughter in the midst of his team's celebration of their inaugural NRL (National Rugby League) grand final win captured the attention of the Australian public. Thurston was the crowd's hero, having kicked the golden point field goal in extra time to defeat the Brisbane Broncos. But the image's popularity was about more than being a long-overdue winner, or a highly skilled Indigenous footballer, or a father. Rugby league is replete with variations of those stories. It's the juxtaposition of the toughness—mental, physical, and historical, for Thurston to make it to that moment— and the tenderness of a man whose attention turns to his daughter in the midst of the masculinist celebratory rituals of laps of honour and hoisted trophies.

Figure 21.21 North Queensland Cowboys captain Jonathan Thurston

The picture, posted to the NRL's official Instagram account and captioned 'Dreams do come true', received almost 15 000 likes and 300 overwhelmingly positive comments, making Thurston a hero for the NRL also. Its image as a 'family code' of football has been tainted in recent times by allegations of sexual impropriety and drug-taking by enough of its players for the management and the public to question the culture of the code— particularly its attitude to women. The image of an avowed family man, and a proud and successful Indigenous Australian who has upheld the 'traditional values' of the code, was a counterpoint to criticism in a crowded football sports market vying for the loyalty of women and families.

Do you think an image such as the one of Thurston with his daughter
(Figure 21.21) represents a particular form of masculinity that sports fans may
also admire or seek to emulate? What ideologies do you think this image of the
captain of an NRL team brings together?

▶

If we think through the different aspects involved in sport, we can see that a range of values and seemingly oppositional ideologies are brought together in this discourse of masculinity.

Table 21.1 Sporting discourse of masculinity

competitiveness	AND	cooperation
individualism	AND	team spirit
brawn	AND	brain
discipline	AND	heroism

All of these values are harnessed to masculinity and are often framed in terms of heroism and service to one's country.

Because sports stars represent their countries in international competitions, their bodies are inscribed with the discourse of nationalism and the ideology of patriotism. The figure of the sports star provides a symbolic synthesis for the ideological tensions between these different value systems. In being a fan of any individual sports star, boys and men can admire, participate in, internalise, and then propagate the masculine values they represent.

CONCLUSION

This chapter has defined the main characteristics of dominant masculinity but argued that there are other models of masculinity to be found in media representations and the real world. It has been argued that masculinity is in crisis and has been going through significant changes over the past thirty years. Correspondingly, so have media representations of men. Look out for traditional representations of dominant masculinity as well as new and changing representations, such as the image of the sensitive New Age guy (SNAG), the metrosexual, and representations that reflect the crisis of masculinity.

In the last decade or so, films and television programs have tended to deal more sensitively with male issues, with relationships between fathers and sons, and with men's emotions and vulnerabilities; advertisements play with role reversals and documentaries focus on male issues. The influence of gay culture has affected many areas of mainstream masculinity through areas such as clothing styles and popular music. All these factors have affected our ideas about sexuality and gender. Many young people are now much more fluid in their understandings of and feelings about gender and sexual identity.

The changes in masculinity dovetail with changes in femininity: both areas are going through processes of exploration and development. Women may be more conscious of this through feminism's direct impact on their lives, while men's awareness of how these issues impinge on them is more recent. In discussions among students, there has been a broad trend towards women saying that while they feel oppressed in many ways and are critical of media representations, they actually enjoy being women. In contrast, men, who tend not to have the same complaints about their place in society and the way they are represented in the media, often feel confused about being men. It is as though contemporary male roles are more uncertain than current female roles. Whereas women feel they have something to gain from these changes, men may sometimes feel threatened. We should strive to create a climate in which both women and men feel they have much to gain from such changes.

This chapter has

- outlined the main characteristics of dominant masculinity
- noted that there are alternative ideologies of masculinity
- considered the crisis of masculinity
- noted the significance of feminism and the gay rights movement in relation to masculinity
- analysed media representations of masculinity
- considered the representation of male sports stars.

? | DISCUSSION POINTS

1   Do contemporary media representations reflect a crisis of masculinity?
2   Consider how the media represent men together. How many times are men subjected to tests that prove their masculinity? Pay special attention to father–son relationships. Are these representations celebrating or critiquing traditional masculinity? Look for any homophobic and homoerotic tendencies.
3   What ideologies of masculinity do sports stars encapsulate?

SUMMARY

You should now be able to

- discuss traditional and contemporary ideologies and characteristics of masculinity
- discuss the crisis of masculinity
- explain how social forces, such as patriarchy, feminism, and the gay rights movement, have influenced masculinity
- comment on and illustrate the importance of power in relation to masculinity
- discuss media representations of male violence and male feelings
- find examples in the media of different ideologies of masculinity
- comment on media representations of male cross-dressing
- define and use the terms 'homophobic', 'homoerotic', 'masochism', and 'metrosexual'
- find media examples to illustrate these terms
- analyse media representations of male sport
- use the theory of residual, dominant, and emergent discourses to analyse media representations of masculinity.

CHAPTER 22

Ethnicity, Ideology, and the Media

Why aren't there no brothers on the wall?

Spike Lee, *Do The Right Thing*

This chapter will

- examine media representations of ethnicity
- consider the significance of absence of representation
- give an overview of European and majority-world historical relationships
- explore the terms 'Eurocentrism' and 'Orientalism'
- examine discourses of ethnicity using binary oppositions and stereotypes.

Let us start with three points about ethnicity.

1   Like gender, ethnicity and nationality are major ways humans classify their own and other people's identity: 'I'm Australian', 'I'm Aboriginal', 'I'm Asian', 'I'm Indian', 'I'm Zulu', and so on.

2   The world is divided into different and unequally positioned ethnic groups and cultures; there are many inequalities of power and wealth between these groups, who are, consequently, often in conflict internally and with other ethnic groups.

3   The media are important in giving us constructions, images, and representations—discourses—of ethnic difference. As such, they offer us ways to understand ethnicity and ethnic issues.

In this chapter, we refer to images and ideologies of ethnicity in the media, as well as to how ethnicity is lived and experienced in the real world. While we use the terms 'ethnicity' and 'race', it is important to point out that there is a major problem with the term 'race'. Not only is it without scientific basis, but because it suggests biological differences, using it is also tantamount to accepting the proposition that these essential differences exist. To speak of ethnic groups and ethnicity, on the other hand, is to refer to cultural differences between social groups. While we do not accept the baggage associated with the term 'race', it is used occasionally because it is so much a part of common-sense understandings and definitions.

REPRESENTATION OF ETHNIC GROUPS AND ETHNICITY

How important is ethnic invisibility—absence of representation?

Consider the significance of the following scene from the film *Crash* (dir. Paul Haggis). This film is set in multiracial Los Angeles. It explores tensions between a number of ethnic groups, focusing mainly on the struggle between African-Americans, Iranians, and Latin Americans.

We follow the story of two African-American youths, who share a meal in a diner and banter about the racial politics of tipping the waitress; then they squabble about whether an uptight, wealthy white woman, played by Sandra Bullock, is racist because she exhibits fear and aversion when she sees them approach. Then they draw a gun and hijack her car. This film puts issues of representation and biased perception right at its centre. Representation is an important political issue. It is important for ethnic groups to be represented in the media in ways that honour diversity instead of stereotyping groups of people. African-Americans, like Australian Aborigines, have consistently been denied their own images, stories, representations, histories, social customs, and rituals, and until this matter is redressed, the lack will continue to contribute to ethnic and racial inequality. It is necessary to fight for these representations.

As film analysts Robert Stam and Louise Spence have argued, a structuring absence is when the lack of images of people of colour defines white people as the central, natural identity category; absence of representation 'is as bad as distorting stereotypes' (Stam & Spence 1983, p. 7) and can be even more problematic than negative representations. The absence of diverse representations of African-Americans in the media affects the way African-Americans see and understand themselves (remember Ngugi's argument that indigenous Africans have been deprived of their own language and thus their cultural identity; see p. 64). *Crash* is itself a representation that gives a voice and a face to African-American points of view, and Haggis' film is one of a number that have emerged from Hollywood since 1990 suggesting that African-Americans are beginning to gain a foothold in Hollywood from which to represent themselves (Bogle 1973; Diawara 1993; Reid 1997). This shift is also evident in the acknowledgment of African-American film stars at the Academy Awards in recent years.

The other major concern is the misrepresentation of ethnic groups. It is important to see who is accorded the right and the ability to make representations, who has access to the media. The tendency within Western culture has been for media representations to be produced by whites, and thus most epitomise a white view of the world and of other ethnic groups. This is explored further after consideration of the black–white opposition and the historical realities on which relationships between people of colour and whites have been built.

As you read through this chapter, remember that skin colour is not the only thing that makes race and ethnicity visible in public space or in media texts, and race and ethnicity are multifaceted aspects of identity and culture that cannot be reduced to binary oppositions like black and white. For example, many Asians do not identify as either black or white, religious affiliations transcend racial and ethnic categories, and accents can make race and ethnicity audible even when skin colour or clothing does not make them visible. Television shows such as *Homeland* and *The Honourable Woman* offer complex representations of religious and cultural allegiances and identities. In *Homeland* Sergeant Brody (played by English actor Damian Lewis) plays an American Marine who is taken captive in the Middle East and converts to Islam, adopting the distinctive garments and prayer mat. In *The Honourable Woman* fair-skinned American actor Maggie Gyllenhaal plays Jewish businesswoman Nessa Stein, who wears the headscarf when visiting Palestine and who gives birth to a son, Kasim Halabi (Oliver Bodur), who is raised by her Palestinian friend, Atika Halabi (Lubna Azabal).

In contemporary media culture, representations of Islam are particularly important to consider. As Halim Rane, Jacqui Ewart, and Mohamad Abdalla note, there has been 'no minority religious community [that] has captured media headlines as Muslims have in the West' since the beginning of the twenty-first century (Rane, Ewart, & Abdalla 2010, p. ix). For instance, in 2014 there was a seventeen-hour siege at the Sydney Lindt Cafe where a lone gunman was alleged to be carrying out a terrorist act in the name of ISIS. Even though this was later proved a false claim, in the aftermath many Muslim listeners contacted radio stations and social media saying they were too frightened to use public transport for fear of being identified with terrorism. A young Muslim woman was seen removing her head covering on public transport, and this act resulted in a viral movement called #illridewithyou where many Australians offered to travel on public transport with Muslims in a show of solidarity.

BLACK–WHITE OPPOSITIONS

Ethnic conflicts have existed throughout history. Many wars that have complex economic and social causes are also cultural conflicts between ethnic groups. Ethnic conflict is involved in many of the armed conflicts around the world today. Central to the argument about representations of ethnicity is the idea that whites and people of colour have fundamentally opposed natures. This apparently simple opposition is actually complex. The descriptions 'black' and 'white' do not do justice to the multiplicity and range of different ethnic groups. But because they are popular labels, they are useful for understanding the discourses surrounding ethnicity.

Issues of ethnicity and their representation are further complicated by other factors, including education, age, gender, attitude, location, and circumstance. Class, too, can significantly influence relations between different ethnicities, though it does not determine them or how films portray these matters. For example, in both *Crash* and *The Blind Side* Sandra Bullock plays an upper class white woman who encounters lower class black men, yet these interactions play out very differently in each film. In *Crash*, as described above, her character anxiously clutches her husband's arm when they pass two black men while walking at night, and her fears are confirmed when the men steal her car. In contrast, Bullock's character in *The Blind Side* comes across a young black man with nowhere warm to sleep and her first response is to invite him to stay with her and her family. This film explores the tensions that arise as the poor black man becomes a member of the wealthy white family.

Table 22.1 Black–white oppositions

white	black
white	people of colour
European descent	non-European descent
West	East

The opposition black–white carries within it notions of inequality, subordinate and dominant groups, and of groups that are different and opposed to each other, which points to the idea that ethnic groups are in conflict over power. The white–black opposition can be expressed in various ways, all of which point to its historical origins.

The last two sets of oppositions—European descent–non-European descent, and West–East—draw attention to the history behind these oppositions: the realities of global European expansion since the fifteenth century. Note that once again this oppositional form of thought polarises groups in extreme ways that make it seem as though there is no middle ground and they have nothing in common. In actuality, each of these pairs of terms is situated on a continuum with subtle gradations of difference linking the extremes at each end.

THE HISTORY OF THE WEST AND 'THE REST'

The historical relationship between Europe and the rest of the world has a number of elements, all of which demonstrate European domination of other cultures.

Exploration and discovery

These were, and still often are, the terms used to describe the invasion of other lands and cultures by Europeans. The Americas, Africa, and Australasia were said to be discovered, despite the fact that they had indigenous populations at the time of the so-called discovery.

Extermination

In colonised lands, the colonisers employed repressive policies against the indigenous peoples, and in many cases virtually exterminated them.

Colonisation

Europeans started to settle and live in these 'new' lands, setting up a number of European colonies, such as in the Americas and Australia.

Colonialism

Colonialism refers to the acquisition and maintenance of colonies. Colonialism involved control and domination of the indigenous populations, who were subjected to laws originating in Europe. Colonialism was established in, among other places, Africa, the Middle East, India, Pakistan, and parts of the Asia–Pacific Region.

Exploitation

The prime motives behind colonisation were the exploitation of the natural resources of colonised lands (through mining and agriculture, for example), the exploitation of the labour of indigenous peoples (particularly through slavery), and the opening up of new markets for European goods. In more recent history, the USA's economic domination of some countries, particularly in Latin America, has been called neocolonialism (new colonialism). One instance of this domination is cigarettes and tobacco, which are being subjected to increasing regulation in the West but aggressively promoted in the majority world (also called the Third World), thereby providing new markets for tobacco and cigarette companies. The wealth and dominance of Europe and the USA (also called the First World, developed nations, the minority world, and the Western world) are largely built on the exploitation of the wealth, labour, and resources of these other countries.

The relationship between the majority world and the minority world has been described in ways that make the exploitation involved in this relationship invisible. First, the term that the United Kingdom used (in 1949) in relation to many of its empire and former empire states was 'the Commonwealth' (meaning the wealth held in common by all the nations). The idea as it was expressed was one of sharing, equality, and mutual interests, whereas the reality was that its aim was to siphon wealth to the UK from the other countries of the Commonwealth. Second, the advantages of imperial exploitation have become culturally naturalised in relation to products such as tea and coffee. Tea drinking is seen as a quintessential British activity and coffee has become a marker of European sophistication, the essence of café culture. Both drinks are available in these countries thanks to the plantations, cheap labour, and imperial trading companies established by Europeans in South America and Asia.

Imperialism

Out of colonialism grew a number of European empires—predominantly the Dutch, French, German, and British empires—and subsequently America's neocolonial empire. These empires were initially about control over lands and peoples. Nowadays we think of empires in terms of financial power and control such that, even if countries have regained their independence, as in most of Africa, they are in many ways still subject to the power and control of the World Bank, the International Monetary Fund, and multinational corporations owned by the minority world. Cultural imperialism, which refers to the extension of empire through the control and dissemination of cultural products (largely through the media), is discussed in the globalisation section (see Chapter 25).

Integration

Integration and assimilation indicate the absorption or incorporation of ethnic groups or minorities into the dominant or colonising culture in a manner that eradicates difference and renders it invisible once the language and culture of the dominant group are adopted. Multiculturalism champions the idea of unity in diversity, a kind of cultural pluralism, in a positive way (see pp. 361–2); however, multiculturalism is still a form of integration that serves the interests of the dominant group by uniting the nation within a common or shared identity in order to reduce dissent.

Postcolonialism

This term describes the situation in existence since majority-world countries achieved their political independence. It is an important critical term (see Chapter 24).

The advertisement for the 'Drop the Debt' campaign (Figure 22.1) is a wonderful example of the media's capacity to be agents of positive social change. Created with the intention of shocking people into awareness and action, its purpose is to represent the fact that Westerners and developed nations are literally sucking Africa dry. A 'Drop the Debt' press release from 2004 states that 'African nations currently spend approximately $13.5 billion per year repaying debts—more than double the amount they spend on healthcare, and roughly equal to the amount needed to combat HIV/AIDS each year'. The image of the healthy white baby sucking much-needed nutrients from an emaciated African woman encourages viewers from developed nations to examine their personal consumption habits. It is part of a global campaign that aims to put pressure on governments to change foreign aid policy, and on the World Bank and International Monetary Fund to waive loan repayments owed to them by poor nations. The scale of the figures in the image reminds us that the First World consumes far more than its fair share of the Earth's resources. When we consume more than we need, we are using money and resources that could help save lives, and thus we inadvertently deprive others of what they need to live. The caption 'Haven't we taken enough?' anchors the meaning of the image, and prompts us to remember that we are all consumers, and thus we are all implicated in the global economic relations that widen the gap between the rich and the poor.

Figure 22.1 Advertisement for 'Drop the Debt' campaign

Source: Courtesy of Red Cell, Drop the Debt, and photographer Tif Hunter

HOMI BHABHA AND THE SHADOW HISTORY OF THE WEST

The eight elements discussed above are useful for understanding the relationship that has existed between Europe and the rest of the world from the fifteenth to the twenty-first centuries. What follows is an excerpt from an interview with the cultural theorist Homi Bhabha, in which Bhabha notes that the major twentieth-century ideas of Western culture have their basis in the eighteenth and nineteenth centuries, the time of colonialism, which he describes as 'the founding moment of modernity'. Thus, according to Bhabha, the West's ideas about itself are linked to the moment and realities of colonialism.

Interviewer   I'd like to refer to your comment that the founding moment of modernity was the moment of colonialism … You said "the colonial moment is the history of the West". Can you elaborate on this remark?

Homi Bhabha   I think we need to draw attention to the fact that the advent of Western modernity, located as it generally is in the eighteenth and nineteenth centuries, was the moment when certain master narratives of the state, the citizen, cultural value, art, science, the novel, when these major cultural discourses and identities came to define the "Enlightenment" of Western society and the critical rationality of Western personhood. The time at which these things were happening was the same time at which the West was producing another history of itself through its colonial possessions and relations. That ideological tension, visible in the history of the West as a despotic power, at the very moment of the birth of democracy and modernity, has not been adequately written in a contradictory and contrapuntal discourse of tradition. Unable to resolve that contradiction perhaps, the history of the West as a despotic power, a colonial power, has not been adequately written side by side with its claims to democracy and solidarity. The material legacy of this repressed history is inscribed in the return of post-colonial peoples to the metropolis. Their very presence there changes the politics of the metropolis, its cultural ideologies and its intellectual traditions, because they—as a people who have been recipients of a colonial cultural experience—displace some of the great metropolitan narratives of progress and law and order, and question the authority and authenticity of those narratives. The other point I'm trying to make is not only that the history of colonialism is the history of the West but also that the history of colonialism is a counter-history to the normative, traditional history of the West (Rutherford 1990, p. 218).

This is a complex and important statement. What is the difference between the two 'histories of the West' that Bhabha discusses? How does he understand the current relationship between Western peoples and postcolonial peoples? It might help to consider what the key characteristics of democracy are and what the term 'Enlightenment' means.

Bhabha suggests that there are two histories of the West, both dating from the eighteenth and nineteenth centuries. The first is full of the positive ideals expressed in the French Revolution (liberty, fraternity, equality) and *The Rights of Man*, a document central to the American Revolution. These democratic and liberal ideals are the basis of the commonly accepted view of the development of the West until the present. They have had, and continue to have, an enormous impact on the development of democracy, democratic ideals, and human rights across the world. Bhabha does not deny these and, indeed, values them as positive and progressive. But his view is that at exactly the same time as the struggle for 'the rights of man' was being conducted, the West was also involved in instituting and perpetuating slavery, racial extermination, religious persecution, and exploitation in the colonies. This second, shadow, and thus often hidden history, is the other side of democratic, enlightened ideals. Bhabha exposes the obvious contradiction between these, and argues that globally we have to acknowledge the historical consequences of these two histories and begin to try and reconcile them.

Bhabha also points to the fact that since the 1950s, from which time many former colonies began to achieve independence, many people from Asia, Africa, and the West Indies immigrated to what had become, through colonialism, their 'mother' countries.

Consequently, the processes of immigration have forced minority-world countries to face the consequences of their colonial exploitation.

Returning to the discussion of the history of the West and the non-West, it is important to note the following three points about our contemporary situation.

1   The twentieth century saw a gradual fightback by the majority world. Many countries, African, Asian, and Middle Eastern states in particular, have achieved various forms of political independence since 1945. Economic independence, though, has been more difficult to achieve: multinational conglomerates are still able to dominate in majority-world markets, even those that don't have Western political rule.

2   Japan and China, two non-Western powers, have maintained their independence and have established their own economic empires that penetrate the Western world.

3   Economically, other Asian countries are now coming to the fore in the world, raising the possibility of a new world order for the twenty-first century in which the countries of the Asia–Pacific Region may have considerable economic power.

In relation to the media, it is important to understand that racial attitudes and beliefs have been built on the official history and the shadow history of the minority and majority worlds, and that these histories provide a framework for understanding the European–non-European opposition.

'THE OTHER'

Another way of characterising the oppositions referred to above (black–white, East–West, and so on) is significant in media studies and cultural studies. These oppositions characterise everything that is not Western or European, or basically everything that is foreign, as 'the Other'. It should be noted that this term is used to highlight the political nature of such oppositions. It is not a straightforward description. The term 'Other' highlights the fact that that which falls into the category of Other has historically been seen as deviant, unnatural, and strange because it exists outside the boundaries of what the West deems normal and considers to be part of itself, or the same as itself. The use of the term 'the Other' draws attention to the way this judgmental stance supports the notion that Europeans are superior to their 'others'.

EUROCENTRISM

EUROCENTRISM ▶

Places European values in a privileged, central position, and sees the world from a European perspective.

Another significant opposition is core–periphery. This opposition draws attention to **Eurocentrism**, which privileges European values and views. A Eurocentric approach takes European values, judgments, beliefs, and cultures as normal, natural, and ideal. It makes European values central, relegating others to the outside, the margins, the periphery. Many ethnic groups, their values and beliefs pushed to the edges of society, feel marginalised by this tendency on the part of dominant groups.

The core–periphery opposition has immediate resonance for a white Australian audience. Populated predominantly by people of European descent, Australia can be said to be part of the core. At the same time, it is geographically located almost as far east of Europe as you can go (c. 113–153° latitude east; only New Zealand, at c. 168–178°, is further east). Also, Australia is part of the southern hemisphere, which is made up predominantly of the majority world, and, as a colony, it has a history of cultural cringe in that it has perceived its culture and achievements as inferior to those of Europe. For all these reasons, Australia can also be said to be located on the periphery. It may be that Australia is in a unique position to appreciate both the benefits of being part of the core and the disadvantages of the marginalisation that stems from being part of the periphery.

MULTICULTURALISM

Multiculturalism aims to celebrate, integrate, and include all the different ethnic cultures that are part of one whole national culture, such as in Australia or South Africa. One of the major issues in relation to multiculturalism has been the notion of integration of cultures and what this means. Some argue that integration means the outsider group taking on the values and identities of the host culture or the dominant culture: the danger here is that a monoculture would result. Others suggest that both cultures can change by drawing from each other. The dominant tendency in terms of white relationships with people of colour has been for white cultures to expect people of colour to take on white values and thus lose much of their cultural identities. Consequently, some groups have refused this option. They have sought out their own cultural heritage as an important source of their identity and have tried to sustain a separate cultural identity. This process of maintaining cultural distinctiveness has been reinforced when immigrant groups attempting to integrate have met with continued racial discrimination by the host population. Films such as *The Kings of Mykonos* and *Looking for Alibrandi* consider the cultural distinctiveness of ethnic groups who are labelled 'wogs' in Australia, and the musical comedy-drama film *The Sapphires* (2012) celebrates the lives and talents of its Aboriginal characters. These sorts of films explore the complex issues of discrimination and identity formation in a warm and humorous way.

Scripted mainstream television has been criticised for its lack of ethnic diversity, though there are some popular shows with multi-ethnic casts, such as *Grey's Anatomy* and *Glee*, which feature Asian, African-American, and Jewish as well as white characters. Even *Desperate Housewives* introduced an African-American central character in its seventh season. Nevertheless, while including characters from a range of ethnic backgrounds better reflects the multicultural world we live in, these prime-time shows don't typically deal with racial or ethnic issues in a deep way.

Many outsider groups integrate through adopting markers of mainstream identity: clothing styles, hairstyles, particular sports, and other cultural pursuits, to name but a few. Many do this at the same time as searching for and preserving their own cultural roots and histories. In Australia this dual pursuit applies to Aborigines, who have faced the problems of invasion and colonialism, as well as to non-British immigrants, who have made Australia multicultural. The issue of what integration means for these groups and for white Australians, as we all struggle over multiculturalism and land rights, is critical. As we proceed through the twenty-first century, we must continue to investigate issues relating to our cultural and national identity.

All the oppositions discussed above are central to questions about representation of ethnicity in the media. We have located these oppositions within a historical context: the real

◄ MULTICULTURALISM

As a policy or a critical concept, multiculturalism celebrates unity in diversity by bringing together a range of cultural groups within a larger identity or community without privileging one culture over another.

relations existing between whites and people of colour. It is important to understand that real relations of ethnicity are always represented and understood within the discourses of race and ethnicity that use these oppositions. These discourses need to be examined in order to understand current media representations of ethnicity.

DISCOURSES OF RACE AND ETHNICITY

Media studies is interested in looking at the various voices or discourses of ethnicity and race, both in the past and in contemporary culture. It aims to see if and how these voices are linked, to see what overall discourse of ethnicity and race they produce. Different discourses, or ways of thinking, come from a range of fields—medical, philosophical, anthropological, and aesthetic. Put together, these constitute and organise our discourses of ethnicity and race. When we say 'organise', we don't mean that these ideas are deliberately put together; rather we mean that, through the culture's common sense, they shape the way we see particular issues.

One example of nineteenth-century Western discourse is the European belief in European racial superiority. This principle was supported by the combined discourses of Christianity, the scientific rationality of the Enlightenment, and (later) Darwinian philosophies of evolution, all of which argued that Europeans were more advanced, civilised, and moral than the peoples whom they were colonising. This discourse of superiority was thus used to justify their colonialist and imperialist exploits. Despite the fact that contact with colonised cultures and peoples was beneficial to European culture and detrimental to other cultures, many Europeans thought they were actually helping these indigenous peoples. European philosophers held that Europeans were more fully evolved, more civilised than other races; hence other races needed civilising, and Europeans felt they had been charged with this task. The notions of white superiority and moral responsibility meant that whites felt that they carried the burden of maintaining order and control, establishing right and wrong. The phrase 'the white man's burden' was used to refer to this duty to civilise the colonies. Ironically, this belief was self-perpetuating because when Western structures, rules, regulations, political systems, literacy standards, and languages were imposed, of course the Westerners themselves were more accomplished in all fields, because their background knowledge and experience gave them that advantage. Any mistakes or disputes that occurred as the colonised group adapted to or resisted the new system were taken as proof of inferiority. Colonial exploits, which included mass murder, rape, and wide-scale plunder, were partly carried out on the basis of this religious, missionary do-gooding.

Thus discourses of white superiority, which are discourses of race, justified exploitation of the colonies and the colonised peoples.

ORIENTALISM

One of the key texts relating to discourses of race is *Orientalism* by Edward Said (1980). Said examines the way in which Western countries have understood cultures of the 'Far East' and 'Middle East', countries beyond the 'Oriental line' (which divides the globe geographically between East and West). He suggests that there was a set of discourses about race that together constituted a discourse of **Orientalism**. Said defines Orientalism in various ways. First, he sees it as a European method for understanding unfamiliar cultures:

◄ ORIENTALISM

The way Europe has perceived, understood, and attempted to control cultures beyond the Oriental line.

> Orientalism is the generic term ... to describe the Western approach to the Orient; Orientalism is the discipline by which the Orient was (and is) approached systematically as a topic of learning, discovery, and practice (Said 1980, p. 73).

This definition does not refer to the exploitation inherent in Orientalism, but his second, broader definition draws attention to the relations of power involved in Orientalism:

> Orientalism can be discussed and analysed as the corporate institution for dealing with the Orient—by making statements about it, authorising views of it, describing it, by teaching it, settling it, ruling over it: in short, Orientalism as a Western style for dominating, restructuring and having authority over the Orient (Said 1980, p. 3).

This definition shows that Orientalism contributes to maintaining European cultural hegemony over the Orient. Said's work focuses on Europe's relation to Eastern countries, but his approach has also been used to think about Europe's understanding of other non-European cultures, particularly African cultures, as well as Aboriginal culture and the culture of Native Americans.

BINARY OPPOSITIONS AND STEREOTYPES

Discourses of ethnicity circulating in the media will be examined by looking at

- the use of binary oppositions as a way of depicting the differences between Europe and its Others
- the use of stereotypical representations of non-Europeans and Europeans.

Binary oppositions

White, Orientalist definitions work by defining people of colour in terms of their differences from whites. A series of categories, or oppositions, is used by white culture to define and delineate cultures of the Other and, by implication, white culture (see Table 22.2).

Table 22.2 White culture–Other culture oppositions

Other	White
Oriental	Occidental
primitive	civilised
savage	sophisticated
body	mind
irrational	rational
natural	cultural

(Continued)

Other	White
eternal	historical
ancient	modern
mysterious	known
magical	scientific
heathen	Christian
underprivileged	privileged
evil	good
innocent	knowing
exotic	ordinary
erotic	repressed
free	controlled

You will probably be able to find many of these oppositions at play in media texts that include white and Other characters. Several elements of the left-hand column of the table above are signified in the advertisement for Persian carpets (see Figure 22.2; Table 22.2).

Figure 22.2 Advertisement for Persian carpets

Source: *Claremont/Nedlands Post*, 1993

This advertisement draws on the Oriental characteristics of the left-hand column. It explicitly states that it offers exoticism and also treasures. The word 'treasures' connotes a world of piracy and fairy tales, the world of *1001 Nights*. It takes us to fictional worlds and the past. The advertisement contains sexual promise by means of the signifier of the alluring woman, who is made mysterious through costume, through the veil that hides her from us. (In its original context, in 1993, the veil would connote something of the harem, and the colour of the veil, which in the original advertisement is red, connoted passion. In the post-9/11 climate of invasion of Iraq and conflict between Muslims and Christians, the costume may now have more threatening connotations.) The landscape places the woman outside time in a natural environment that is outside or beyond the modern, civilised world, stretching back timelessly so that the image and the costume could come from the past. This advertisement thus offers escape from the modern world. It also clearly positions the woman—the Other—as an exotic treasure, an object that can be bought or possessed.

Contemporary media coverage of Islam, terrorism, and national security foregrounds the threatening connotations of secrecy and deception associated with Western perceptions of veils and full-body garments such as burqas that conceal a person's identity and may also conceal weapons or explosives. Along with regulations prohibiting headgear that obscures the face, such as balaclavas and motorcycle helmets, veils have been banned in banks and in forums such as citizenship ceremonies in Canada, and there have even been contentious nationwide bans put in place in public spaces across France and Belgium. Julie Posetti argues that Muslim women have come to be 'symbolised generically by their distinctive religious clothing', and that this leads them to be 'vulnerable to vilification and media stereotyping' because 'they are concurrently represented as oppressed and radical conformists, as threatened and threatening' (quoted in Rane, Ewart, & Abdalla 2010, p. 69).

Figure 22.3 Kanye West

While the photograph of rap artist Kanye West (Figure 22.3) does not represent perceptions of the Orient, it depicts a person of colour who is located within the semiotics of a similar set of binary oppositions to those listed above, with notable exceptions. West is clad in a worn grey T-shirt, a leopard-print jacket (connoting wildness and his African heritage), a gold chain (connoting wealth), and dark sunglasses that conceal his eyes and render his expression inscrutable. To a large extent, West's wealth and success problematise and invert the hierarchical binary oppositions that pit black persons against white. Despite West's claims to be $53 million in debt in 2016 and his public appeal to fans and fellow celebrities for financial help in his 'time of need', he certainly cannot be considered underprivileged. Contentiously, West appealed (via Twitter) to Facebook founder Mark Zuckerberg to help him financially by investing a billion dollars in his novel business plans. West suggested that money spent funding his ventures would be preferable to sponsoring education in Africa: @kanyewest tweeted 'you'd rather open up one school in Africa like you really helped the country [sic]'. This ill-considered tweet prompted a senior copywriter at an advertising firm to initiate a 'Help Kenya, Not Kanye' online campaign that was subsequently publicised by *AdWeek* and *Global News* (Bartko & Mertz 2016, n.p.). The campaign links to a number of Kenyan charities that people can contribute to directly, for example, by donating USD$209.11 to a UNICEF-sponsored school instead of purchasing Yeezy footwear of comparable retail value from West's fashion line.

Did West's Twitter appeal for financial aid trivialise racial and socio-economic stratification, and mock those who are truly underprivileged, or did it (perhaps inadvertently) promote critical thinking and social concern? West's star image, exemplified in Figure 22.3, undermines Eurocentrism and raises a number of questions: does West's inversion of and challenge to hierarchical binary oppositions promote critical awareness of stereotypical assumptions about race and culture? Does he challenge stereotypes, or does he legitimate hierarchies or adversarial thought? Might the image of West's fashionable affluence promote racial integration and assimilation into the materialistic value system of consumer culture?   ⊙

The Orient as a projection of the white psyche

As discussed above (pp. 97–8) projection suggests that what we see in the world and other people are aspects—projections—of repressed features of our own personalities, our own psyches, aspects of our desires that we normally disown or repress. Jung suggests that we all have a **shadow** side that incorporates these rejected parts of ourselves (see p. 298), that is, it is the side we project onto other people. Looking at the binary oppositions, it could be argued that the Oriental, Other qualities represent what is repressed by white culture, so, if white culture officially denies and rejects aspects of bodily nature in favour of rationality, if it represses sexuality, if it denies savage wildness in favour of civilised behaviour, if it limits its thoughts and beliefs to Christianity, then all its negative or denied aspects may well be projected elsewhere, such as onto the Orient or the Other. In the caption to the 1939 illustration for a British boys' adventure story set in East Africa (Figure 22.4), the reference to imagination gives the game away. This illustration is from the white imagination; the Other figures play out the repressed white side.

SHADOW ▶

Parts of our personality that we have hidden, denied, and repressed, also known as the alter ego.

Figure 22.4 Illustration from *Top-All Book for Boys* 1939

As fine a state of frenzy as can well be imagined.

Source: Frederick Warne

The consequence of this understanding is that Orientalist discourse can be seen as an incredibly rich source of information, not about the Orient, but about the West itself. A study of Orientalist discourse as a projection of the repressed side of the white psyche reveals a great deal about the West. Such a notion is obvious if we consider the concept of exoticism. For something to be exotic, it has to be strange, foreign, and exciting. To anyone born in a so-called exotic culture, everything there will seem quite normal—far from exotic. Things can only seem exotic to the foreign eye. Thus a description of a culture or a person as exotic tells us about the beholder rather than the beheld. This view can also illuminate how whites have used stereotypes of people of colour.

Stereotypes

Stereotypes act as shorthand for delineating character. Though they may involve some truth about the social realities of people's lives (Dyer 1993), they are limiting because

- they suggest that particular characteristics are shared by many people
- they suggest that these characteristics are part of the essential nature of these people (that is, that they are genetic, or biological) rather than connected to any social realities
- in many instances stereotypes are used pejoratively by dominant groups to describe subordinate groups.

Looking back at films, comics, and popular literature of the twentieth century, you will find that the history of white representations of Other cultures and peoples is dominated by stereotyping. These stereotypes may now seem outdated, but they are still apparent in films such as *The Mummy* and the *Indiana Jones* films, and they were historically important in reflecting and maintaining dominant racist discourses through the twentieth century. They also include interesting representations of white characters, so we can ask what kinds of stereotypes of whiteness are being presented.

Richard Dyer was one of the first critics to suggest that whites can also be seen as a specific ethnic group. As analysts, we can begin to think about how whites and whiteness are being represented, what particular characteristics and stereotypes are involved. Many people believe that only media texts depicting people of colour and racial conflict are about race, but it is also the case that texts that have an all-white cast are also making implicit ideological statements about race by naturalising whiteness and portraying it as the norm.

Figure 22.5 Cover of *Top-All Book for Boys* 1939

Source: Frederick Warne

Consider the 1930s representation and celebration of white masculinity in Figure 22.5. This cover of the British boys' annual, the *Top-All Book for Boys*, 1939, shows how children are introduced to stereotypes at an early age. The *Top-All Book* was awarded as a Methodist Sunday School prize, legitimating it within an official religious discourse. The main title of the book, *Top-All*, and the illustration—one boy elevated over others on a cricket field—demonstrate the stereotypical ideology of masculinity that involves, in this instance, male sporting competitiveness and hierarchy. Such a cover might appeal equally to young white boys in England or Australia. This book included stories set in India and Africa (then parts of the British Empire) and thus provided images of people of colour and whites, and a way of understanding the relationship between the two races. One of the stories has many similarities to the film *Indiana Jones and the Temple of Doom*, thus demonstrating how racist discourses from the 1930s were still prevalent in the 1980s.

The dangerous savage and the civilised white

When white and Other characters are depicted together, we see how the stereotypes connect. Early twentieth-century representations differentiated between the civilised white and savage Other. This stereotype portrays people of colour as dangerous and animal-like. It suggests that they are uncivilised and want to attack and harm whites, that they are savages who threaten innocent women and children (Figure 22.6).

The perceived threat to women in this poster is understood as a sexual threat. This perception relates to the fear of miscegenation—sexual mixing of races—understood as a potential for the contamination of the white race. Mixed-race sexual relations have been a taboo area for official white culture, although throughout the history of race relations white men have sexually used women of colour.

In the past, representations of attacks by indigenous peoples on whites have depicted such attacks as the result of the savage, evil nature of indigenous peoples. They are rarely presented as the last resort of peoples whose lands are being stolen and whose lifestyles are being destroyed by white invaders. The representation of these attacks as savage and animalistic justifies white violence as a defence against savagery and as an attempt to impose restraint on animal-like savages (see Figure 22.7). The stereotype of the black savage is thus very useful in justifying white oppression of indigenous populations.

Figure 22.6 Poster for film *The Battle of Elderbush Gulch* c.1920

Source: British Film Industry

Figure 22.7 Illustration from *Top-All Book for Boys* 1939

Source: Frederick Warne

Such stereotypes have been popularised by westerns that show Native Americans as savages, by Tarzan stories that show Africans as savages, and by numerous other stories, set in Africa, Asia, and Australia, that deal with relations between people of colour and whites. When the two groups are portrayed together, it is invariably to demonstrate a fundamental opposition in their natures and ways of being that then justifies white violence—coded as a form of honourable retribution against savages—and suggests that whites need to exercise control over native populations in order to tame them. The whites are thus shown to be heroic, more intelligent, and more in control of their emotions, more rational.

This stereotype has been used negatively in white representations. Some texts have, though, reclaimed the stereotype, reworking it to positive ends. Some US films made from the early 1970s began to capitalise on African-American cinema audiences:

African-American heroes were introduced in films such as *Slaughter*, *Shaft* (remade in 2000 with Samuel L Jackson in the lead role, and the actor who played Shaft in the original film playing his uncle), *Foxy Brown*, and Tarantino's *Jackie Brown* (with Pam Grier, star of the 1975 film *Sheba Baby*). These films redefine perceptions of race and gender.

The African-American heroes in these movies are strong, powerful, and sexually potent figures who elicit positive identification from young African-American audiences and envious admiration from white audiences. But while this genre, known as blaxploitation, was a move forward in some ways, as Leab (1975) puts it, the shift 'from Sambo to Superspade' is still, in other ways, a reconfirmation of the stereotype of the black savage; many fictional characters in films, comics, television programs, and pornographic movies still draw on this stereotype (Baker & Boyd 1997; Hernton 1970).

The noble savage

The noble savage is a variation on the dangerous savage stereotype. It too sees people of colour as uncivilised, but puts this in a positive light. The noble savage draws on European ideas established by the eighteenth-century philosopher Jean-Jacques Rousseau (see Rousseau 1974) and developed in the nineteenth century by American philosophers, including Henry David Thoreau (see Thoreau 1973). These authors regarded civilisation as corrupted and unnatural, and thought that people living outside European civilisation were pure and noble because of their relationship with nature and their distance from the decadence of European civilisation. Non-Europeans were thus thought to have a higher morality than whites. This stereotype draws on Christian traditions in that it sees the savage state as similar to the state of Adam and Eve in the Garden of Eden—a before-the-Fall state. This is a great example of Eurocentrism, whereby Other cultures are understood in terms of white beliefs, religions, and mythologies, which shows the way white culture projects its own beliefs and values onto other cultures.

While this stereotype portrays people of colour as morally superior to whites, it is still limiting in that it locks them into a predetermined mould, denying them their own histories, glossing over the specificity of their own different cultures, and portraying them as incapable of change. The stereotype of the noble savage can be found in films such as *Avatar*, *Walkabout* (Figure 22.8), *Geronimo*, and *Dances with Wolves*, in which native cultures are portrayed as morally superior but essentially static and without internal diversity or a history of cultural development. *Avatar*, a film widely understood to dramatise the impact of colonialism on indigenous people generally, and to allude to America's recent military campaigns in particular, shows the tall, blue-skinned Na'vi as a simple, peaceful species that has a spiritual, respectful attitude to the environment, in stark contrast with the destructive humans who seek to invade their home.

There are a number of other stereotypes that are pervasive in the media: seeing people of colour as childlike in comparison to the responsible, adult white; seeing them as figures of fun and entertainment; seeing them as deviously clever and evil; seeing women of colour as sexually exotic and alluring, and so on. Traces of these discourses are still apparent in current media representations. What is interesting is that these representations are able to take a number of different characteristics and make them all negative. So whether people of colour are portrayed as savage or childlike, poor or rich, stupid or clever, they are always presented as being in need of white control and authority, thus justifying white power.

Figure 22.8 Image from film *Walkabout* 1971

Source: Scott Murray, *Cinema Papers*

Recent representations

These stereotypical representations have been challenged, changed, and developed in recent years. Sometimes this raises further issues. Male black rap artists, representing a streetwise, powerful masculinity, may offer strong role models, but these positive qualities are often offset by their sexism, and their association with criminality and violence. Cultural theorist Matthew Henry critiques media images of contemporary black masculinity, suggesting that:

> A particular type of black masculinity—one defined mainly by an urban aesthetic, a nihilistic attitude, and an aggressive posturing—has made its way into the cultural mainstream … This image of masculinity has developed mainly as a result of the commodification of hip-hop culture and the ubiquity of rap music … More specifically, it is the result of the popularity of the urban "gangsta" (Henry 2002, p. 114).

Henry makes the point that race, class, and gender are inseparable aspects of identity, and claims that men of colour are affected by the power dynamics that inform each of these positions. According to Henry, as blacks within a racist social and political hierarchy, men of colour have neither power nor privilege, yet, as males within a patriarchal power structure, they have both (2002, p. 115). In an analysis of the film *Shaft*, Henry argues that contemporary media representations of black male violence arise from a need to compensate for being disempowered:

> One way of compensating for a perceived loss of power, potency or manhood is to adopt the "tough guise": black male identity is increasingly defined within popular culture by rampant materialism, physical strength, and the acquisition of respect through violence (Henry 2002, p. 116).

While Henry focuses on one particular trend in representations of race in the media, there have also been many other developments. The films *Bran Nue Dae*, *The Sapphires*,

Samson and Delilah, *Jindabyne*, *Mad Bastards*, and *Rabbit-Proof Fence* are among a number of Australian films that explore Aboriginal and white Australian history and relationships. *Rabbit-Proof Fence* presents an Aboriginal point of view, challenges Aboriginal stereotypes, and, indeed, shows up white stereotypes of power and control. *Ten Canoes* goes one step further: it presents a story of Aboriginal culture in which there is no white, no European presence at all, and is the first film ever to use entirely Aboriginal language (though director Rolf de Heer and cinematographer Ian Jones are white Australians). The films *Crash*, *The Blind Side*, *Babel*, *Breaking and Entering*, and *A Mighty Heart* all explore the complexities of modern global and ethnic tensions and relationships.

FURTHER WORK

You can develop your analysis of media representations of ethnicity by using various methods outlined in this book:

- *Verisimilitude*—consider the accuracy of representations, and be aware of stereotypes and the socio-historical contexts of production and reception.
- *Structuralism*—consider story, structure, values, binary oppositions, and endings.
- *Content analysis*—consider the frequency and proportion with which people of colour are (or are not) represented, and link this to *media effects research*.
- *Political economy*—consider the context of production, money, and power relations.
- *Spectatorship and identification*—consider which characters we are invited to identify with and relate to.
- *Character analysis*—consider identity politics in light of the roles, relationships, and power dynamics that exist between characters in media texts.

CONCLUSION

People of colour are producing their own representations, and there is increased visibility for them in film and television fictions and in the media generally. Legislation regarding representation of minorities in American media has led to increased roles and recognition for performers and media personalities, including Oprah Winfrey, Denzel Washington, Beyoncé Knowles, Jay Z, Kanye West, Nicki Minaj, and Halle Berry. Within the music industry and the sports world, many black performers have for a long time achieved huge success and space for black voices and images. Many advertisements aimed at a youth market include positive representations of sexy, streetwise people of colour. A number of African-American and Asian writers and directors have produced hit films in America, most notably Spike Lee, Ang Lee, Tyler Perry, Steve McQueen, and M Night Shayamalan. Indigenous African cinemas have emerged, such as that led by the Senegalese director Ousmane Sembène. There are a number of Aboriginal filmmakers—Tracey Moffatt, Michelle Blanchard, Leah Purcell, Richard Franklin, and Rachel Perkins—working in Australia. A tradition of black British filmmaking has also developed. We should of course remember that the biggest film industry in the world is the Indian cinema, famous for its Bollywood productions.

This chapter has

- considered ways for understanding ethnicity and black–white oppositions
- examined the history of black–white relations
- defined and examined Eurocentrism, multiculturalism, Orientalism
- applied binary oppositions to media representations of ethnicity
- examined stereotypes of ethnicity.

? DISCUSSION POINTS

1   Choose a film made by a director or writer from a race or background different from your own and examine its representations of race and ethnic issues.
2   Compare how Aboriginal–white relationships are represented in *Rabbit-Proof Fence* and *Jindabyne*.

SUMMARY

You should now be able to

- comment on the history of race relationships
- discuss the issue of ethnic invisibility in the media
- comment on the historical relationship between Europe and the rest of the world
- define and explain the terms 'Eurocentrism' and 'Orientalism', and use them in your analysis of media texts
- demonstrate how binary oppositions and stereotypes can be used to analyse media representations of ethnicity
- discuss contemporary representations of ethnicity.

CHAPTER 23

Stars and Celebrities

> We are all voyeurs to one degree or another, including me, but with fame comes the predatory prowl of a carrion press that has an insatiable appetite for salaciousness and abhors being denied access to anyone, from pimps to presidents (a journey that becomes shorter every year), and, confused and resentful because it can't get what it wants, resorts to inventing stories about you because it is part of a culture whose most pressing moral imperative is that anything is acceptable if it makes money.
>
> Marlon Brando, *Brando: Songs My Mother Taught Me*

This chapter will

- examine the phenomenon of stars and celebrities
- explore how the star system works as a marketing device
- critically engage with celebrity activism
- explain star image
- analyse stars as texts that embody cultural meanings, values, and ideologies
- relate stardom to the mechanisms of identification and fandom
- present a case study of stardom, media, and identity.

Contemporary media are obsessed with stories about individuals, which reflects the dominance of the ideology of individualism (see pp. 33 and 172) that has permeated Western culture and media since the early twentieth century. In the early days of cinema, 'motion pictures did not include cast lists and actors were not promoted as identities independent of the roles they played on film' (Boorstin 2006, p. 80). Theorist Daniel Boorstin's research shows that in the very early twentieth century, almost three-quarters of the people who received media coverage were figures from business, politics, and the professions, whereas by the 1920s over half were from entertainment: fan magazines had begun to popularise the private lives of movie stars. A significant moment in this shift of media attention from business to entertainment, and in the corresponding shift of fan attention from screen characters to actors, came in 1910 when the film producer Carl Laemmle sought to brand his films by associating them with the lead actress contracted to his studio, the Independent Motion Picture company:

> Laemmle announced in the press that … the anonymous actress who had appeared in many of his films, had died. However, when she miraculously made an appearance to disprove this fact, Laemmle reported to the newspapers that the crowds were so hysterical that they tore off her clothes. This was equally untrue, but the ensuing furore burned her name, Florence Lawrence, into the public's consciousness. Lawrence became a huge star, earning $80 000 in 1912 (Cousins 2004, p. 42).

Today the media and the public are fascinated with stories about prominent individuals from the entertainment industries. Following cinema's successful use of the star system as a central method in filmmaking and marketing, television established its own familiar faces, actors, and personalities, who encouraged audiences to return week after week, and launched shows such as *Famous*, *Gossip Girl*, and *TMZ* to foster even more interest in these dazzling people. *TMZ* began as a celebrity website that has migrated across to network television. It features user-generated content such as mobile phone footage of celebrities spotted within a thirty-mile zone (TMZ) of Hollywood. Other entertainment industries, particularly music and sport, also use well-known performers to attract fans to games and concerts and to sell merchandise such as football jerseys and music CDs and DVDs. In addition, newspapers increasingly report on individual stars and celebrities, and frame more and more stories in terms of individuals rather than issues. Magazines devoted to gossip about stars' and celebrities' private and personal lives divert the attention of supermarket shoppers, who idly glance at the glossy images and sensational headlines while they wait in line at the checkout. Sean Redmond describes celebritisation as 'the celebrity metronome' that 'functions like a mechanical metronome moving in and between media platforms, social interactions, and ritualised events (2014, p. 2). It is unsurprising then that in contemporary popular culture, practically everyone knows the trials and tribulations of A-list celebrities and the names of their nearest and dearest as well as, or better than, they know the names of their members of parliament or world leaders.

To understand the cult of celebrity and its place in our culture, two related issues need to be considered. The first concerns how stars operate as a financial and ideological system within the film and entertainment industries. The second is to ask why the media are becoming more and more obsessed with celebrities, and how this affects popular culture and society. We note a number of starting points.

- It's useful to note some distinctions between the terms **star**, **celebrity**, and 'media personality'. 'Star' originated as a term in relation to the entertainment industries, particularly the cinema, but also popular music and sport. Stars are people who excel in their chosen field but also, and more importantly, attract a large popular following. They appear literally as larger than life in the cinema, or they are separated from the audience on a stage or a sports field, where the audience tries to get as close to them as possible. Celebrity is based largely on biographical information. Celebrity, Paul Watson argues, is 'a mode of stardom relatively unconnected to the sphere of professional work. In other words, celebrity is sustained not by someone's excellence or ability in their chosen profession' (Watson 2003, p. 173). Instead of focusing on professional performance, celebrity relies almost entirely on an individual's charisma and their ability to attract sustained media interest in their private life and public appearances at high-profile events. Celebrity doesn't happen because someone has extraordinary qualities—it is discursively constructed by the way in which the person is publicised and meanings about them circulate, 'a consequence of the way individuals are treated by the media' (Turner 2004, p. 7). It is possible to be a celebrity who is famous for being famous, or famous for being rich or notorious, or a socialite, but such people, for example, Paris Hilton and Kim Kardashian, or contestants on reality television shows, would not be described as stars. Personalities are more a product of television and are more familiar and everyday—appearing regularly in homes via the television, seeming smaller

◄ STAR

Stardom is an elite type of celebrity based, at least initially, on a person's outstanding professional achievement. Stars play well-publicised leading roles in popular culture and entertainment media. They consistently outshine colleagues and competitors, and their personal and professional lives attract significant attention.

◄ CELEBRITY

A celebrity is a well-known, highly visible public figure whose private life and public appearances frequently attract the media spotlight, often for reasons other than their professional standing or abilities.

than in the cinema and more accessible. Either they are being themselves (newsreaders, chat show hosts, television chefs, and so on), or they are associated with long-standing roles they play (for example, James Van der Beek is famous just for his one role as Dawson in *Dawson's Creek*, Taylor Lautner has struggled to escape the character of Jacob from the *Twilight* films, and *Seinfeld*'s Michael Richards' iconic role as Kramer seemingly ended his career once the show ended).

- Media image is important. While stars in the cinema have always been sold through their image, this has now permeated many fields, including, in politics, John F Kennedy, who is reckoned to have won the 1960 American presidential election partly because on television he looked nicer than the five-o'clock-shadowed, sweaty Richard Nixon. Since then political parties have depended more and more on the media image of their leader—how they look, how convincing they sound, whether they can communicate easily with citizens, and how acceptable their private lives are. For example, Canadian Prime Minister Justin Trudeau has become an international celebrity since being elected in 2015. Building on the legacy of his father, former Canadian PM Pierre Trudeau, he is evoking a new wave of 'Trudeau mania'. His model-like looks, youth, left-wing policies, and compassion for Syrian refugees, as well as having proclaimed himself a feminist, all helped ensure Trudeau's A-list political celebrity image. Often the media image of the leader is more dependent on looks and communication than on their political abilities or their party's policies. Image, spectacle, presentation, and private lives are all-important. The rise of celebrity culture and the disproportionate interest constructed around the superficial relevance of public figures and their actions are indicative of a shift 'towards a culture that privileges the momentary, the visual and the sensational over the enduring, the written and the rational' (Turner 2004, p. 4). This focus on image relates to contemporary postmodern culture's emphasis on spectacle and surface reality (see Chapter 24).

- There has been an increased focus on stars' and celebrities' private lives. The desire to know what stars are really like and to know about their private and personal lives is escalating. In the 1950s it was easy for publicists to present Rock Hudson (in America) and Dirk Bogarde (in Britain) as two of the most popular, heterosexually desirable film stars, who played in numerous romantic films. Their homosexuality, while known about by people close to them and within the industry, was kept secret from fans. Such a situation is unimaginable today. Change has come about partly through the huge increase in media products, the advances in technologies for recording and capturing private lives, and the acceptance of the right of the media to invade people's privacy. This focus on private life relates to a desire to find out the truth about people—as discussed in relation to reality TV. It gives rise to contentious issues about what right the media have to follow people around and publicise their private lives, and illustrates the way that publicity combines a discourse of celebration and adulation of stars with a discourse of scurrilous gossip and scandal mongering—stars seem to be loved and hated by the media and media consumers.

- Contemporary culture is 'addicted to celebrity' (see Schultz 2004), gossip, and personality, and today, virtually all events are presented in terms of stars and media personalities, a phenomenon driven by market forces. The tabloid press (the cheaper, popular newspapers) gained higher circulation by running stories about well-known people, focusing on sports and entertainment. To be competitive, magazines and serious newspapers increasingly had to follow suit; they now give more coverage to leisure and lifestyle, and present events in terms of personalities more than they once did. Even politicians actively court celebrity status using popular media (consider Hillary Clinton's use of *The Sopranos* in her 2007 election campaign and later appearing on *The Ellen DeGeneres Show* during her 2016 campaign and 'dabbing'—a viral dance craze—with Ellen). The media also use celebrities to engage with social, political, and environmental issues. For instance, James Cameron used his film *Avatar* to promote environmental conservation—and not just on Pandora—he helped Earth Day Network plant a million trees on planet Earth. Natalie Portman designed a range of leather-free shoes to promote veganism and protest cruelty to animals; she also appeared in the documentary *Saving a Species: Gorillas on the Brink* (2007). Another trend uses celebrity endorsement to encourage the consumption of branded causes, such as infamous cyclist Lance Armstrong's ubiquitous rubber armband and Angelina Jolie's becoming known as the face of the United Nations. The term 'celebrity philanthropist' or **celanthropist** refers to celebrities who not only use their 'brand' and time to endorse a cause or humanitarian work, but they also often spend their own money on causes they endorse. The term 'celanthropist' was first coined by *Time Magazine* (Poniewozek 2005). In this celanthropic activism, celebrities are, according to Chris Rojek, 'foot soldiers' battling for public space often through connection and engagement with humanitarian concerns (Rojek 2012, p. 26). George Clooney, Angelina Jolie, Brad Pitt, and Oprah Winfrey are all well-known celanthropists. These examples suggest Al Gore's claim that serious news has given way to a greater concentration on celebrity news, rather than real news about politics and the environment, has broader implications, not all of them negative, and that the tension between real news, serious issues, and celebrity discourse exists on a continuum rather than as mutually exclusive, oppositional categories.

◄ CELANTHROPIST

A type of celebrity activist who engages in philanthropic activities. These are celebrities who not only use their 'brand' and time to endorse a cause, but they spend their own money on causes they endorse.

- Democratisation and short turnaround time are issues. The success of reality programs such as *The Real Housewives of Melbourne* and *Masterchef* points to two other factors: the way that ordinary people can now become famous, and the way that they are quickly found, celebrated, and then forgotten.

Having looked at the wider discourse of stardom and celebrity, consider now how stars operate in the media industry by focusing on the following three interconnected aspects:

1 stars as financial and industrial commodities: **bankability**

2 celebrities as texts: star image

3 stars as the embodiment of social and ideological values.

◄ BANKABILITY

The stars' potential to guarantee a film's financial box office success.

These aspects of stardom are linked because stars are images, manufactured out of a range of materials, that are sold as commodities and consumed on the strength of their meanings (see Dyer 1998).

STARS AS FINANCIAL AND INDUSTRIAL COMMODITIES: BANKABILITY

How much are stars worth and what makes a star bankable? ▶

When film researcher Christine Gledhill describes stars as 'cogs in the mass entertainment industry selling desires and ideologies' (Gledhill 1991, prologue), she is expressing the view that the media industry and stardom are entirely reliant on marketability. Stars are the basis on which media texts get financed, labour that helps produce the texts, and selling points for the texts and their associated merchandise. Put simply, the star system is a marketing device for the entertainment products that stars appear in, the newspapers, magazines, television programs, and so on that feature photographs and stories about stars, and for the commodities that the stars endorse. Later in this chapter we argue that stars are also used to sell (or at least to get fans to buy into) values, ideals, and lifestyles, which is an ideological approach to analysing celebrity culture. Here we will focus on a political economy approach (see Chapter 2, p. 22) to stardom that considers stars as marketable commodities in the media industry and examines the implications of the economic foundations of the star system. In this sense the media industry regards stars as bankable commodities (rather than people or texts). Below is a list of the ten best-paid actors in 2014.

Table 23.1 Highest-paid actors 2014

Actor	2013–14 income (in US dollars)
1 Robert Downey, Jr	$75 million
2 Dwayne Johnson	$52 million
3 Sandra Bullock	$51 million
4 Bradley Cooper	$46 million
5 Leonardo DiCaprio	$39 million
6 Chris Hemsworth	$37 million
7 Liam Neeson	$36 million
8 Ben Affleck	$35 million
9 Christian Bale	$35 million
10 Jennifer Lawrence	$34 million

Source: <www.forbes.com/pictures/mfl45ekhem/the-highest-paid-actors> 2014, accessed 6 July 2015

These stars are not so highly paid because they are twenty-eight to seventy-seven times better than actors who only earn $1 million per year, or exponentially better at their jobs than school teachers or journalists, who may earn in the vicinity of $50 000 per year. They earn this much because within the economy of stardom, they are bankable. If they feature prominently in publicity material for a film, that film will earn at least $100 million at the US box office alone, so from the financiers' point of view the star's salary is a secure investment. The reason for this is that people often base their selection of films on their favourite stars in much the same way that they choose films based on a preference for a particular genre. Stars, like genres, generate expectations and guarantee the satisfaction of certain pleasures. Fame and fortune are virtually inseparable because popularity generates profit. In other words, the economics of the media industry and the bankability of a star (the guarantee that their popularity will ensure massive profits from the sale of products, media texts, and tickets to see the stars perform) are central to attaining and maintaining star status.

A political economy approach to studying celebrity reveals that the bankability of stars is not just a matter of financial calculations: it is itself subject to cultural value systems. Consider what this list of the highest-paid actors in 2014 indicates about whom and what we value. You might notice that all but one of the highest-paid performers are white, and that 80 per cent are male. This suggests that social inequities are reproduced and represented in the economy of stardom. If we see stars' salaries and marketability as a measure of the degree to which they are valued (or what they represent is valued), we can note some broad trends. Just as film is accorded higher cultural status than television, males and white people still tend to be accorded higher monetary and cultural value than females and people of colour. This was highlighted in 2016 when there was a boycott of the Oscars by many actors concerned by a lack of diversity in the nominations. The boycott (#Oscarssowhite) was led by actor Will Smith to bring to light institutional racism. Academy Award host Chris Rock quipped that the Oscars could be called 'the white people's choice awards' and suggested that they should be judged on the basis of professional accomplishment rather than identity categories, which would mean introducing 'Best Performer in a Leading Role' instead of Best Actor and Best Actress. As Richard Dyer puts it:

> If you are not white, middle-class, heterosexual and male you are not going to fit "the cultural world" too well—women only fit uneasily, whilst blacks, gays and even the working-class hardly fit at all (Dyer 2006, p. 162).

While the popularity (and hence the perceived bankability) of film stars may be influenced by cultural value systems, other arenas of celebrity are judged more by achievement. Discourses of celebrity vary in different media. In sports, a star's value is measured by their success in competitions rather than just by popularity or appearance. Prominent figures in music, sports, and public life perform as themselves and gain attention on the basis of merit, achievements, and expertise. *Forbes* magazine's 2015 'Celebrity 100' issue ranked the world's most powerful celebrities across all sectors of the entertainment industry. Topping the list was boxer Floyd Mayweather, followed by fellow boxer, Filipino Manny Pacquiao. Singers Katy Perry and Taylor Swift were the only women who made it into the top ten of the list. One Direction, Robert Downey Jr, and writer James Patterson were also among the top earners. Mayweather banked US$300 million in 2015, breaking Tiger Woods' 2008 record for top earnings in a year by an athlete of $108 million.

Forbes also devised a way of evaluating the bankability of film stars, a method based on the profit earned for each dollar spent on the star's salary, rather than on the star's income alone. By this valuation system, many of the most bankable stars turned out to be women. In 2015 Chris Evans, star of *Captain America*, was Hollywood's most bankable star, returning an average of $181.50 for every $1 he was paid. Mila Kunis was the best female investment and she returned $87.30 for every $1 paid. There is still a huge gender pay disparity in Hollywood, as four out of the top five actors are women who return more than their male counterparts (*Forbes* 'Hollywood's Best Actors' 2015). The biggest disappointers in terms of bankability were Hollywood's top-earning Johnny Depp, whose movies returned just $1 for every $1.20 he was paid in 2015, and Denzel Washington, whose movies returned $6.50 for every $1 he was paid in 2015.

The importance of the popularity and marketability of stars as media commodities is also evident in sports, even though sport is primarily a merit-based form of celebrity. Sports stars now often earn more money through their endorsements than through their salaries. Mayweather is an unusual case because, although the boxer earned more than any athlete in history in a single year in 2015, of his $300 million income only $15 million came from sponsorship and endorsement contracts with companies such as Burger King, FanDual, and Hublot. Mayweather has traditionally snubbed endorsements, but this changed in the lead-up to the historic prize-winning fight of 2015. Therefore we might find Mayweather's earnings are even greater if he increases his sponsorship and endorsements.

The figures examined above indicate that within the economy of stardom, image trumps expertise. We will examine the concept of stars as images in more detail later in this chapter, but first let's consider how the marketability and the public visibility of stars and celebrities can be used to support humanitarian causes.

CASE STUDY

Celebrity 'activism': celanthropy, the *Half the Sky* movement, and the need to be seen to 'care'

According to Paul 't Hart and Karen Tindall (2009), there are four types of celebrity activist: celebrity advocates, celebrity endorsers, celebrity politicians, and politicians turned celebrities. The authors state that celebrity advocates are more likely to be involved in their causes and to attempt to influence policy changes, rather than only being attached to the charity or supporting a politician, as a celebrity endorser might do. Thus, celebrities such as George Clooney (see the case study: *Star-celebrity profile: George and Amal Clooney, and the transmission of cultural values* on pp. 388–91), Angelina Jolie, Bono, and Bob Geldof may be seen as celebrity advocates, as they are heavily involved in charities and have longer term involvement in policy development and change, rather than simply providing 'lip service to a cause for publicity reasons' (Marsh, 't Hart & Tindall 2010, p. 323). Celebrity politicians are celebrities who have become politicians (for example, Clint Eastwood,

Arnold Schwarzenegger, and Peter Garrett). Politicians turned celebrities are politicians whose 'public behaviour, purposeful association with celebrities, and/or private life alter his [or her] public persona beyond the traditional political sphere into the celebrity sphere' ('t Hart & Tindall 2009, p. 38). Due to his AIDS advocacy and his work supporting children and racial equity, the late Nelson Mandela is an enduring example of a politician turned celebrity (Stadler 2009).

Another type of celebrity activist is the celebrity philanthropist or 'celanthropist'. These are celebrities who not only use their 'brand' and time to endorse a cause, but they also spend their own money on the causes they endorse. Bishop and Green pinpoint three crucial factors created by celanthropists such as Geldof and Bono: money, publicity, and that they 'turned a generation into activists' (2008, p. 204). They argue that celebrities 'can grab the attention of the public like nobody else, giving them a powerful pulpit from which to advocate change' (Bishop & Green 2008, p. 197). Celebrities front almost every cause possible; indeed, there seems to be an endorsement T-shirt, wristband, ribbon, or other piece of marketing/promotional material alongside each campaign.

In 1985 the first Live Aid concert marked the point when celebrity activism shifted from campaigning to active celanthropy. Bob Geldof produced the Live Aid concerts in Philadelphia and London, which were broadcast in Australia, South-East Asia, Japan, North America, and Europe. The concerts became the world's largest telethon, raising almost US$150 million and bringing the plight of starving Ethiopians to the attention of two billion viewers (Huddart 2002, p. 36). The latest iteration of the Band-Aid song 'Do They Know It's Christmas?' received significant criticism regarding the appropriateness of Western celebrity intervention, to which Geldof retorted, 'It's a pop song, it's not a doctoral thesis. They can f*** off' (Grow 2014, n.p.). The inference here is that action is prohibited by too much intellectualising of the issues. Since the Live Aid initiative began, more celebrities have taken on the role of celebrity activist and become inordinately visible through their connection to a cause. So we are, in many ways, living in a world where celebrity culture has become 'increasingly blurred with more "serious" forms of news, and where gossip about the banal, the trivial and the perverse are reported alongside political news' (Marsh, 't Hart & Tindall 2010, p. 322).

The increasing frequency with which celebrities respond to humanitarian crises arguably contributes to public engagement and philanthropic behaviour, although not without significant criticism. Celebrity activism is sometimes disparaged as a method to enhance celebrities' 'brand images', as 'we live in a world where fame cannot be retained without continuous publicity' (Huliaras & Tzifakis 2010, p. 261). Celanthropy and other types of celebrity activism are problematic if the attention is focused on the celebrity rather than on the concern and the story then becomes the celebrity rather than the issue or the people needing help (Fain 2008, p. 1). For instance, some campaigns using celebrity activists risk becoming 'hero narratives' (Fain 2008, p. 6) in which the privileged Western celebrity heroically attempts to save the poor other (see also Mooney Nickel & Eikenberry 2009). Celebrities also function as commodities to sell the concern and the campaign 'in such a way as to invite the audience to consume them' (Fain 2008, p. 7)—that is, creating an illusory relationship between the celebrity and the consumer individual. Thus, there is a lack of distinction between the benevolence and the market surrounding the philanthropy (that is, profit and care both become depoliticised). Despite these legitimate concerns, celebrity activism can be enormously successful, as the *Half the Sky* movement demonstrates.

Half the Sky: a book and a movement

The *Half the Sky* movement began with a book of the same name published in 2009 by married celebrity journalists Nicholas Kristof and Sheryl WuDunn. WuDunn is a Pulitzer Prize-winning author, business

Continued on next page ▶

executive, and former news anchor and foreign correspondent for the *New York Times*. Kristof is a well-known twice-weekly opinion piece journalist for the *New York Times*. He has a powerful identity and platform that he has crafted independently as a spokesperson on issues such as maternal mortality, sex slavery, and women's economic development. He has been called the 'the Indiana Jones of our generation of journalists' (Schuker 2006, n.p.).

Half the Sky focuses on creating a global grassroots movement to assist women in developing countries. The movement's website declares that it is 'cutting across platforms to ignite the change needed to put an end to the oppression of women and girls worldwide, the defining issue of our time' (www.halftheskymovement .org/pages/movement). It aims not only to raise awareness of women's rights violations, but also to educate people about how to become activists and volunteers in the cause. It traverses multiple platforms, including video, websites, blogs, educational tools (e.g., games), and social media sites (e.g., Facebook, Twitter, Pinterest, and Instagram). Its use of celebrities (celanthropists and celebrity feminists) and multiple media channels has ensured its broad cultural effect in a relatively short period. For example, it has received considerable publicity from celanthropists and other celebrity advocates, including Oprah Winfrey, Bill Clinton, Angelina Jolie, and the Gates family. Since its release in 2009, supporters of the *Half the Sky* movement have donated approximately US$5 million to organisations advocated by the *Half the Sky* website. These non-government organisations are predominantly located in the countries facing the issues that the organisations seek to address. More than one million people have played the Facebook *Half the Sky* game, and around 1500 university campus advocates have screened films and conducted education sessions about *Half the Sky* (www.halftheskymovement.org/pages/movement).

In 2012 a PBS television series produced a documentary that followed the book's authors as well as 'A-list celebrity advocates' (www.halftheskymovement.org/pages/film) such as internationally famous actors Meg Ryan, Diane Lane, and Eva Mendes, who travelled to ten countries (including Afghanistan, Pakistan, Liberia, Somalia, and Cambodia). In these countries, the celebrities and Kristof would meet, interview, and tell the stories of women and girls. This in turn amplified the effect of the book's publicity. With the aim of inspiring grassroots assistance from ordinary people in the developed world, the authors travelled to villages to speak with and record the stories of local people affected by sex slavery, gender-based violence, and maternal mortality.

In an interview with actor Ashley Judd, Kristof said that 'one of the greatest challenges is how to reach beyond the choir' (Judd 2010, n.p.). One way that the authors of *Half the Sky* have successfully done this is through the use of celebrities. Like effective celebrities, successful celanthropists rely on para-social relations, or 'the notion of presumed intimacy between strangers' (Rojek 2012, p. 124). In *Half the Sky*, this is apparent in how Kristof and the celebrity activists connect to grassroots activists via social media, inviting them into the world to join the movement. Indeed, the idea is that 'we' are all doing this 'together'.

Half the Sky's ongoing success has been significantly derived from the cultural capital of the celebrities (including celebrity journalists) used in the campaign. The combination of the use of celanthropists, as well as mainstream, online, and social media, ensures the hyper-visibility of the campaign.

Celebrity activism is often problematic, but there is sometimes a place for such activism: discuss. What are the biggest concerns with celanthropy?

Star image
What is a star image and how is this sold?

The media are not selling us the stars themselves (much as we might like to buy Chris Hemsworth or Jennifer Lawrence and take them home), they are selling their **star image**. A star's image is constructed out of what we see or read about them, their media visibility. The star image is based on the social values they embody. Each individual star has their own image and appeal, which is what audiences are drawn to. The images are sold first through what Richard Dyer and others call 'primary circulation', that is, the films, DVDs, television programs, concerts, and sports events that they perform in. Stars are then sold and supported by the images of 'secondary circulation', that is, all the media outlets that give further information about and publicity for the star: interviews, publicity photos, reviews, Academy Award ceremonies, fanzines, websites, ads, gossip, and so on, that focus on the star's performance and their off-screen, 'real' life.

It is important to note, first, that this image can and will change over time, as the star grows older, plays different roles, and goes through personal life changes. These changes and developments themselves become a source of fascination. Consider how Miley Cyrus' media image has changed over time. Cyrus, daughter of American singer and actor Billy Ray Cyrus, grew up in the spotlight. She became an 'innocent' teen idol in the popular television series *Hannah Montana*. She then became a recording artist and film actress, and has been portrayed as everything from a naive teenager to a controversial child star coming of age—albeit messily—in front of the world. Her image was tarnished after her infamous 'twerking' dance and duet with a much older male singer, Robin Thicke, to his controversial song 'Blurred Lines' at the 2013 MTV Video Music Awards.

Second, while stars must have some level of professional competence—that is, be relatively good actors, singers, or players—some theorists have questioned whether performance is really central to the star phenomenon. Gledhill suggests that 'actors become stars when their off-screen lifestyles and personalities equal or surpass acting ability in importance' (1991, p. xiv). Gledhill's point can be extended to include other forms of ability or prowess besides acting. David Beckham's popularity is based on his image as much as on his excellence as a sportsman. Other equally proficient soccer players have not attracted the same degree of attention or adulation.

For actors, their star image is based on a combination of their actual screen roles, the stories that circulate about them, and their personal lives. Whenever we see stars in a film who are familiar from other roles or publicity about them, we bring this information into how we construct their image and how we read the film. This means audiences read films and stars on the basis of **intertextual** and **extratextual** knowledge. We can see this with Hollywood actresses Sarah Jessica Parker, Angelina Jolie, and Jennifer Lawrence. For instance, while Parker starred in a number of films and television programs both before and after she played shoe-obsessed journalist Carrie Bradshaw in the *Sex and the City* television show and films, she remains best known for the role as the independent fashionista living in New York. Despite moving on from the iconic role of Carrie Bradshaw, Parker finds that people have a difficult time accepting that she has, and as such our perception of each new character she plays is affected by our understanding of Carrie. Parker is a prominent New York local, like her former character. She is also similarly known for her daring

STAR IMAGE

The qualities, ideals, and values that a star represents, based on their films and other performances, and on media information circulated about them.

INTERTEXTUAL KNOWLEDGE

Knowledge and information gained from other related media texts.

EXTRATEXTUAL KNOWLEDGE

Knowledge and information taken from sources external to the text.

fashion choices. As Parker is often photographed by the media on the streets of New York, this together with her fashion are signifiers that link her back to her most well-known role. Another example of a star whose career is affected by intertextual and extratextual knowledge is Kristen Stewart. Stewart is best known for her role as Isabella 'Bella' Swan in the *Twilight* films. Bella is dark and detached. Stewart's public image is arguably built on a perception of her as mysterious and somewhat psychologically wounded, like Bella. She had a relationship with her *Twilight* co-star, Robert Pattison; however, Stewart was forced to publicly apologise after having an affair with a film director. The media reporting on this invoked notions of the mysterious Bella Swan, and this intertextuality meant that Stewart was portrayed as mysterious, with something to hide, and antifeminist.

Stars as the embodiment of social and ideological values
Why are some people elevated to stardom rather than others? ▶

Star images are ideological insofar as they represent social values. Dyer argues that stars embody social values that need, or are felt to need, assertion or reassertion. He claims that 'The general image of stardom can be seen as a version of the American dream, organised around the themes of consumption, success and ordinariness' (Dyer 2006, p. 154). This begins to explain why certain stars are successful: what they represent through their star image connects with audience desires, beliefs, and values.

The success of any star and their image is built on a threefold combination: the work of the media industries, plus the actual contributions of the star, plus the audiences who pay to see the star. Marilyn Monroe was originally just one of a number of starlets being groomed and marketed by the film studios. Why did she succeed when others did not? It was a combination of her individual talents, marketed by the industry, that connected with audiences. In a sense stars offer audiences symbolic resolution to cultural concerns. Dyer (1987) argues that it was Monroe's complex image of female sexuality and her ability to embody contradictions that connected with the cultural concerns of 1950s and 1960s audiences (for example, their contradictory views of sexuality). She could connect to many people in different ways: she could be seen as victim or heroine, appeal to men as sex object or comedienne, and appeal to women as someone actively exploring her own sexuality or struggling to survive in a male-dominated world.

David Beckham's image is similarly successful because he embodies cultural complexity and contradictions. His image is linked to all the products he endorses, such as Police shades and Adidas sportswear: his identity and reputation are mapped onto the brands and consumed along with the products. When buying the products, consumers are also buying into the fashionable, athletic, handsome image, sexuality, and affluent lifestyle Beckham embodies. Beckham's popularity can be explained by the incredible scope and flexibility of his image: he can be many things to many people. His sporting prowess, coupled with his well-publicised sexual prowess, gives him a masculine appeal that is hard to match. Despite having succumbed to the charms of several of his admirers, he is known as a loving husband and devoted father, yet at the same time his edgy tattoos and transgressions give him street cred and associate him with freedom and rebellion. In this way his contradictory image legitimates the fantasy of sexual availability while he is simultaneously being a responsible family man. Beckham's flair for fashion and his ability to wear nothing but Armani briefs, or everything from diamond earrings and a ponytail to a tuxedo, ripped jeans, and cornrow braids, have also extended his appeal into the pink market. He has even been credited with embodying a new type of identity: the metrosexual (see p. 346). Here, the star is representative of and embodies changing social norms, discourses, and shifting boundaries around gender and sexuality. Beckham's image has many ideological slants, so a broad demographic can identify with him on some level and he can be used to sell practically anything.

Stars 'personalise social meanings and ideologies' (Gledhill 1991, p. xiv), and can be seen to embody cultural archetypes. For many people, the iconic figures of Marilyn Monroe and John Wayne give an identifiable, personal form to the social meanings and ideologies surrounding femininity and masculinity, in particularly Western ways. Stars such as Katharine Hepburn, Jodie Foster, Sigourney Weaver, Beyoncé, Lena Dunham, Amy Poehler, and Tina Fey have come to be seen as the embodiment of aspects of feminism. In a similar way, Judy Garland, Liza Minnelli, James Dean, and contemporary entertainers Ellen DeGeneres, Neil Patrick Harris, Jane Lynch, Ellen Page, and Alan Cumming personify meanings associated with gay culture. This close association between a star and the ideas they embody rubs off on those who engage with the media texts circulating around the star, thus implicating stars in the production of personal and cultural identity: 'Celebrity becomes a key site of media attention and personal aspiration, as well as one of the key places where cultural meanings are negotiated and organised' (Turner 2004, p. 6). As theorist Steven Cohan puts it with reference of *Pride and Prejudice*, 'It is a truth almost universally acknowledged that a single man in possession of a Judy Garland CD must *not* be in want of a wife' (Cohan 2001, p. 119). The connection between stars and audiences can be further explored via an analysis of identification and fandom.

IDENTIFICATION AND FANDOM

How are fandom and stardom related?

(▶)

With the decline of nuclear and extended families, and localised community networks, para-social interaction (interactions and relations with people we do not know) is growing in importance, 'constructing a new dimension of community through the media' (Turner 2004, p. 6). The media actively encourage a sense of familiarity and friendship with stars and celebrities (see how magazine covers often refer to stars by their first names—Kanye, Ellen, Beyoncé). There is a range of possible connections between stars and their fans. Engagement between stars and their fans has increased exponentially with the rise of social media platforms such as Twitter, Instagram, and Facebook. This form of self-promotion by stars to maintain their brands can see fans and stars 'interacting' in ways that might lead some fans to believe intimacy exists. At one extreme there is the danger of stars being stalked by fans: 'the obsessive fan appears to have been "taken over" by the text in a way that "we" have not, or has wilfully submitted to a zealousness that, in the extreme, can manifest itself in the pathological behaviour of a stalker' (Casey et al. 2002, p. 93). At the other extreme there can be simple indifference, dislike, or disregard. In between there is a range of identificatory practices, all of which are linked to the fan's sense of the star as someone extraordinary, beyond the realm of the everyday, different from us, and also as a real and ordinary person, just like us.

Stardom, as film studies academic Linda Mizejewski points out, is reliant on culturally defined concepts of authenticity, privacy, and individuality in relation to publicity, performance, and the personae that stars enact and project (Mizejewski 2001, p. 166). She goes on to say:

> Fans are incited to peel away public and textual images in order to discover the "real" or private person underneath ... While star appeal depends on connection and identification, for example, it also depends on adulation and glamour; fans simultaneously need to imagine the star is fully human and ordinary, but also larger than life and extraordinary (Mizejewski 2001, p. 166).

Working together, fan identification and media publicity function to mask or bridge the gap between the star and the audience, which also serves an ideological purpose. As tabloid television theorist John Langer puts it, 'By appearing to reduce the distance through intimacy, the personality system operates to mask the gap between the powerful and the powerless, ensuring that the real unities of power, class, prestige, and interest can continue relatively intact and unexamined' (Langer 2006, p. 194).

As the quote by Marlon Brando at the beginning of this chapter suggests, the discourse of stardom and celebrity involves journalistic coverage of celebrities' private lives in order to invite a sense of intimacy and identification among fans. This coverage, which is an occupational hazard of stardom, is sometimes excessively invasive. Extreme instances of the invasion of privacy by the media include the hounding of Princess Diana and unauthorised, well-publicised photographs of stars' private parts and private moments.

How do media technologies facilitate fandom, and to what effect?   ▶

Fandom extends beyond the avid consumption of media products to include the production and circulation of meanings about celebrities and the texts they star in. It also offers an opportunity for social connection as fans group together, sharing and communicating with each other. Henry Jenkins describes how interactive media technologies such as the internet have reshaped the cultural practices of fandom to create online communities:

> As the community enlarges and as reaction time shortens, fandom becomes much more effective as a platform for consumer activism. Fans can quickly mobilize grassroots efforts to save programs or protest unpopular developments. New fandoms emerge rapidly on the web—in some cases before media products actually reach the market. As early participants spread news about emergent fandoms, supporters quickly develop the infrastructure for supporting critical dialogue, producing annotated program guides, providing regular production updates, and creating original fan stories and artwork (Jenkins 2006a, pp. 141–2).

In this sense media technologies provide a feedback loop to media producers, and enable fans to produce their own texts featuring stars. For the majority of people, however, engagement with stars and celebrities plays out in less fanatical forms of identification. However it is expressed, fandom represents participation in the discourse of celebrity and a kind of ownership or appropriation of the star, which leads to an incorporation of the star's identity into the fan's identity.

Identification with stars involves 'negotiation between self and other' via 'the recognition of similarities and differences' (Stacey 2006, p. 253). It is also a negotiation between the actual self and an imaginary self: 'It is this gap between the film star and everyday people that produces the self-transformation to be more like the star. Thus the difference provides the space for the production of a fantasy self more like the ideal' (Stacey 2006, p. 254). As film theorist Jackie Stacey's research suggests, there are two main forms of identification: identificatory fantasies and identificatory practices. The fantasy aspect is usually played out in the cinema or in celebrity interviews when we enjoy being inside an actor's life or a character's world. Often this means aspiring to the power, privilege, and beauty of the star, and feeling empathy for and identifying with the star or their screen persona. In this sense we can see ourselves in the star or the character they play, imagining ourselves in their position. We may also indulge in objectifying fantasies in which we see the star as an erotic object of desire.

Identificatory practices occur in everyday life when we buy the Police sunglasses David Beckham endorses, or the Garnier hair dye, Bitten clothing, or Covet perfume marketed by Sarah Jessica Parker. In this sense we could say that desire and identification drive consumption. The star is a public persona, but modes of identification are mostly related to the private, personal, domestic sphere, so the star bridges the public and private spheres via practices of identification.

Academic writing is also part of the discourse of stardom and celebrity. Different theoretical paradigms—psychoanalysis, Marxism, feminism—have tried to explain the process of identification with stars. In the 1920s Freud defined identification as 'the earliest expression of an emotional tie with another person' (quoted in Brown & Fraser 2004, p. 101). The sense of identification as an interpersonal, emotional bond persists in film and media studies literature today. Psychoanalysts also discuss narcissistic identification. Narcissus, a figure in Greek mythology, fell in love with his own reflection, so narcissistic identification refers to the sense in which a fan perceives or imagines that the star's image reflects some aspect of their own identity. We like to feel that the star is like us in some way, that we share a common quality, and this is why we relate to them and admire them. In contrast, Marxist theorists foreground the economic relations of stardom and refer to identification as interpellation: the star text positions consumers in alignment with a certain kind of social identity. Texts that feature stars often interpellate the viewer into a position of desire, and the hegemonic force of the media encourages consumerism and persuades us to consent to the idea that the ideological values a star stands for are natural and good. Indeed, some feminists have suggested that 'Identification itself has been seen as a cultural process complicit with the reproduction of dominant culture by reinforcing patriarchal forms of identity' (Stacey 1991, p. 147).

Stars are, by definition, extraordinary and ideal, yet through the process of identification with the characters they play and through access to the ordinary, human dramas of their personal lives, they become more accessible to the public. In this way public fascination with stars can be based on difference and aspiration, or similarity and identification. The extensive publicity surrounding, for example, Reese Witherspoon and Jake Gyllenhaal's relationship breakdown offered the public a chance to fantasise about two attractive, unattainable stars who suddenly became 'available', while it simultaneously made the 'perfect couple' seem more human (many people can empathise with the difficulties of ending a relationship amicably amid jealousy and gossip, and this generated sympathy and attention for the stars). In many cases when stars reveal their personal trials and

◄ IDENTIFICATION

A feeling of connectedness to another person. It involves seeing aspects of oneself in that person, experiencing a sense of relatedness or overlapping of identity.

tribulations to the press, ordinariness is used as an image management strategy to facilitate identification between fans and stars.

This desire to know the star can of course never be fully realised, just as we cannot actually become the star. For one thing, as Dyer writes, whatever information we consume about the stars' private lives is actually media-constructed: 'We never know them directly as real people, only as they are to be found in media texts' (1998, p. 2). It is this unattainable desire to know someone and to identify with them that drives us on as fans, and maintains the whole star system. The stars' ultimate unknowability and inaccessibility keep us coming back for more.

It is interesting to think back to how the ideas, science, and philosophies of the twentieth century have challenged the myth of individual autonomy (see the discussion about subjectivity, pp. 172–3). Perhaps the West's obsession with stars is an attempt to hold onto the ideology of individuality so that we can believe that, despite what the sciences say, we too have individual autonomy and also have the possibility of transcending social circumstances and achieving greatness.

CASE STUDY

Star-celebrity profile: George and Amal Clooney, and the transmission of cultural values

An effective way of approaching a star-celebrity profile analysis using methods and conceptual tools drawn from media studies is to begin with general biographical details and professional information about the star and their place in the industry, then move to specific analysis of images, interviews, or texts featuring that star. The broad contextual picture of the star's life and work establishes a relationship between their personal and professional identity and their marketability, as well as suggesting how the media facilitate fan identification. The close textual analysis supports these generalisations with a specific example and allows the ideological and cultural values that the star embodies to be decoded. Here we apply this method to analyse the meanings embodied by George and Amal Clooney.

It has become fashionable to name celebrity super-couples as a single entity, indicating the extent of public fascination with the love lives of the rich and famous. The media have an ongoing love affair with celebrity couples, reporting every real or imagined bump on the rocky roads travelled by Kimye (Kim Kardashian and Kanye West), Pecks (encompassing Victoria Beckham—formerly Posh Spice—her breast implants, and the legendary pectoral muscles of her husband David), and Billary (the celebrity couple name of Hillary and Bill Clinton). The most enduring of these portmanteaus is Brangelina (Brad Pitt and Angelina Jolie). While George Clooney and his wife, Amal, do not have a widely adopted celebrity-couple name, they have been comically referred to as 'Amalooney'. Despite this relative lack of a well-used couple name, they have occupied considerable media space *because* of their union in the last few years.

George Clooney, born in 1961, is an American actor, writer, director, and producer. He is one of the most successful actors of all time, and, to date, the films he has acted in have grossed over $1.9 billion in box office takings. His personal wealth is said to be over $180 million, and he earns his income from the films that he has acted in, directed, and/or written, as well as product endorsements (*The Richest* 2016). He first made his name in the television series *ER*, before moving to films that cemented his star status. He became the only actor ever to be nominated across six Academy Award categories, winning two, as well as collecting three Golden Globe awards during his career (as at January 2016). Like Angelina Jolie, another major actor who has created films with political messages, George has acted in, directed, and written a number of politically motivated films such as *The Ides of March* (2011) and documentaries such as *Sand and Sorrow: A New Documentary about Darfur* (2007). George was well known as a bachelor, after ending a short marriage to Talia Balsam in 1991. After his divorce, he even famously bet actresses Michelle Pfeiffer and Nicole Kidman that he would never remarry. At the age of 53, he and Amal married. The Clooneys occupy media space and attention for reasons that are different from all of the other above-mentioned celebrity couples, as only one half of the famous couple, George, was a celebrity before their coupling. He is an 'achieved' celebrity (Rojek 2001, p.19). That is, his fame came from his acting talent and achievement, rather than being, for example, 'ascribed' (Rojek 2001, p.19) through lineage. Although he has some celebrity lineage due to his aunt, the late singer and actress Rosemary Clooney, this is not the primary reason that he is famous. George was first famous as a television and film actor, and then as a global humanitarian celebrity and celanthropist, before he married Amal in September 2014.

Amal Clooney (née Alamuddin), on the other hand, was not a celebrity or connected to show business, but attracted intense media interest during her courtship with George. Amal was born in Lebanon in 1978, but raised mostly in England. She was educated at Oxford University and the New York University School of Law. She worked in various roles, including stints at the International Court of Justice and the Office of the Prosecutor for the United Nations Special Prosecutor to Lebanon, before becoming a barrister, specialising in human rights, in the Doughty Street Chambers in London in 2010. In 2013 she was appointed to a number of UN commissions including as an adviser to Special Envoy Kofi Annan on Syria. She has worked on very high-profile cases such as that of WikiLeaks founder Julian Assange in his fight against extradition. Assange has a level of celebrity and notoriety, and this work arguably increased the media intrigue with Amal after her marriage to George when she became known in the mediasphere. Amal's image in the media is one of a strong, independent, multilingual career woman who managed to not only capture, but hold the attention of one of the world's most eligible bachelors: she was the woman who somehow 'tamed' the previously unattainable George by getting him to 'put a ring on it' (as Beyoncé would say). Her professional integrity and independence immediately gained media fascination, with headlines such as *The Daily Mail*'s 'Forget *Gravity*, she's got gravitas: George Clooney's new female friend is British barrister Amal Alamuddin (who's representing Julian Assange, no less!)'. Her ability to speak as an expert in the humanitarian environment therefore provided an additional layer of authority to George's long-standing celebrity-activist work in global humanitarianism. This combination created a mystique around their celebrity coupling, and, as Totman and Marshall argue, George's relationship with Amal 'further solidifies his political celebrity status' (2015, p. 3). So their personal relationship—together with both of their professional identities—has arguably revived George's star marketability.

Celebrity activism, while certainly not a new phenomenon, has experienced rapid growth and some transformation in recent history, especially due to the increasingly ubiquitous nature of celebrity culture. Alongside fellow celebrity-activist actors Matt Damon and Brad Pitt, George is a representative for the 'Not on Our Watch' humanitarian relief and international aid organisation. He is involved in many humanitarian roles, but notably he is one of the UN's Messengers of Peace, and he centres much of his activism on Darfur and

Continued on next page ▶

has produced several documentaries on the issues surrounding it. Celebrity advocates are celebrities who are known for what they 'say' as well as for what they do. In a world where celebrity culture becomes 'increasingly blurred with more "serious" forms of news, and where gossip about the banal, the trivial and the perverse are reported alongside political news' (Marsh, t'Hart & Tindall 2010, p. 322), more celebrities take on the 'role' of celebrity 'activist', as becoming inordinately visible through connection to a 'cause' is now almost synonymous with celebrity as both an expectation and a method to sponsor leverage for individual celebrity 'brand(s)' as 'we live in a world where fame cannot be retained without continuous publicity' (Huliaras & Tzifakis 2010, p. 261). There are, however, some celebrities who undertake actual research, and commit significant time and effort to causes. They are described by Marsh, t'Hart and Tindall (2010, p. 323) as those who 'tend to be more active and more committed policy seekers,' such as George. This is where, arguably, his relationship with Amal has become most captivating: he is firmly entrenched in the celebrity-activist zeitgeist, yet his authority to speak increased because of their marital union, as Amal brought a greater authority on human rights issues. Thus there has been an increased blurring of his life onscreen and off-screen, and certainly his marriage to Amal has further reinforced his media image as a political celebrity.

A contradiction in Amal's image, adding a layer of cultural complexity and opening up questions about social norms, and indeed feminism, was how, after they married, Amal changed her surname to Clooney. Why would a successful woman with a well-known and respected public and professional identity of her own decide to change her name? Did Amal's name change provide additional gravitas for not only herself but also George in terms of cultural capital, or is it merely an outdated practice? Ruby Hamad, an Australian feminist, remarked that 'Amal's Lebanese surname is history, it'll be all so much the easier for the western media to sweep her cultural background under the carpet' (Hamad 2014, n.p.). Amal's name change created so much attention that it caused her work website to crash after the name change was publicised. Much media reporting now frames her in terms of *being* George's 'wife' who looks like a movie star herself, rather than firstly an independent, international human rights barrister of considerable note; this reveals much about our cultural values. For example, despite Amal's notable career pre-existing her relationship with George, the media use headlines such as 'George Clooney's Wife Urges UN to Act Swiftly on Arroyo Complaint' (Cayabayb 2015, n.p.). This reframing of Amal's identity from that of an independent professional to being the wife of a film star has continued in the courtroom in her very serious work. In Figure 23.1 Amal is pictured with renowned human rights Queen's Counsel Geoffrey Robertson at the European Court. In this case, she was helping to represent Armenia against a Turkish politician who denied the genocide of 1.5 million Armenians in 1915. The paparazzi—despite the seriousness of not only the issue, but Amal's professional career—turned up even though such events would rarely attract much media attention. One journalist described it as a 'media circus' (Waterfield 2015, n.p.). When asked what she was wearing, Amal retorted 'Ede and Ravenscroft' (Waterfield 2015, n.p.); Ede and Ravenscroft is a famous English company that has been making legal robes since 1861. What this incident and related media coverage focusing on Amal's appearance and her identity as George's wife reveal is that the media communicate cultural and ideological values that privilege heteronormative superficialities over legal, ethical, and political matters pertaining to serious human rights violations. As Charlotte Alter (2015, n.p.) states, 'there's something grotesque about using serious work on behalf of genocide victims as a pretense for a fixation on her looks, her clothes, and her marriage to one of the world's most eligible actors'.

Figure 23.1 Amal Alamuddin

At the 2015 Golden Globes, feminist celebrity comedians Amy Poehler and Tina Fey took light-hearted aim at George, but mostly at the societal norms that valorise celebrity over other industries. Fey stated to the audience, which included the Clooneys, that Amal is a 'human rights lawyer who worked on the Enron case, an adviser to Kofi Annan on Syria, and was appointed to a three-person commission investigating rules-of-war violations in the Gaza strip … so tonight her *husband* is getting a lifetime achievement award' (quoted in Feeney 2015, n.p.). Fey's quip can be seen as a transitional point where she playfully invites the audience to recognise and reflect on the media's misplaced values. It is this politicised use of humour that enables us to recognise and laugh at our cultural obsession with celebrity and the casual sexism that underpins it. It is here then, perhaps, where the door opens for a new way of seeing the celebrity couple. See Figure 23.2 (adapted movie poster).

Figure 23.2 'George—That guy with Amal Alamuddin'

The poster is captioned: 'George—That guy with Amal Alamuddin, the grey haired one, whatever'. This poster is part of a series from Buzzfeed titled 'If Movies Talked about George Clooney Like the News Talks about Amal Alamuddin' <www.buzzfeed.com/juliapugachevsky/if-movies-talked-about-george-clooney-like-the-new#.whl9246aY>. It references the above-mentioned Fey and Poehler comments, but it also rewrites a number of titles for films that George has starred in, as well as highlighting journalistic examples where Amal's professional life is positioned as secondary to her status as George's wife. They do this to highlight the double standards that media culture has around men and women, and to demonstrate that Amal and George Clooney are indeed not a single entity, and that Amal is much more than her physical appearance or marital status.

CONCLUSION

This chapter has employed a range of theoretical approaches to explore the role of stars and celebrities in the construction of meanings, identities, desires, and ideologies. Some show stars and celebrities as economic pawns who make media profits in a culture that values notoriety over worthwhile achievements; others suggest how people use stars as a kind of social currency to explore many kinds of social issues, particularly around personal behaviour and relationships. While the media might intrude mercilessly on stars' private lives, the outcome for audiences and fans is that they are given the chance to talk about issues such as love, sexuality, money, body image, and so on. In this way stars and celebrities enable competing discourses and ideologies of achievement and success, of masculinity and femininity, of familial and romantic relationships, of hegemonic and counter-hegemonic social values, to be worked through: they are sites for contemporary ideological and hegemonic struggles that you, as media students, can now analyse.

To summarise, the cultural phenomenon of celebrity can be understood as follows: stardom involves the production and circulation of information about charismatic individuals in the media. The power of a star, a celebrity, or a public figure depends to a large extent on their visibility, the employment of spectacle, and their ability to communicate with the public via media images. Narrative, characterisation, identification, merchandising, and image management are some of the ways in which celebrity communicates issues of social value and identity.

This chapter has

- used a political economy approach to analyse stars as bankable financial and industrial commodities
- used an intertextual, semiotic approach to analyse celebrities as texts
- used an ideological approach to discuss stars as the embodiment of social and ideological values
- presented case studies analysing celanthropy and George and Amal Clooney's star-celebrity image.

? | DISCUSSION POINTS

1   Why are stars and celebrities so popular, and what is the difference between them?
2   How are fandom and stardom related?
3   Who is responsible for invasive journalistic practices that entail prying into celebrities' private lives: the press that sell illicit photos, the public who buy them, or the stars themselves?
4   How do media technologies facilitate fandom, and to what effect?
5   What is identification, and how does it work in relation to stars and celebrities? Think of a star with whom you identify on some level. Why do you feel that you can relate to the star and what particular qualities of the star appeal to you? How is your sense of identification expressed?

SUMMARY

You should now be able to

- explain the difference between stars, media personalities, and celebrities
- discuss the contemporary discourse of stardom and celebrity
- show how the star system works through bankability, star image, and the embodiment of social values
- discuss modes of identification with stars
- consider how stars contribute to discourses, ideologies, and humanitarian concerns
- show an awareness of how media texts function as publicity and marketing devices, image management strategies, and feedback mechanisms linking the industry to the public.

PART 6
But They Keep Moving the Posts:
Postmodern and Global Perspectives

The global reach of the media has the capacity to nourish a sense of responsibility, however fragile, for a humanity that is commonly shared and for a world that is collectively inhabited.

John Thompson *The Media and Modernity* 1995

Overview

In the past thirty years there have been significant changes in the media, in society, and in media theories. We examine some of these changes as we conclude our study with a critical overview of postmodernism and globalisation.

CHAPTER 24

Postmodernism

One listens to reggae, watches a Western, eats McDonald's food for lunch and local cuisine for dinner, wears Paris perfume in Tokyo and 'retro' clothes in Hong Kong.

Jean-François Lyotard, *The Postmodern Condition* 1984

This chapter will

- explain the meanings of the prefix 'post'
- consider the terms 'poststructuralism' and 'postcolonialism'
- examine the concept of postmodernism
- discuss the relationship between theoretical positions outlined earlier in the book and these newer approaches.

Much of what has been presented so far has been an attempt to pin down the meanings of texts, to give definitions of concepts, and to outline approaches for understanding the media. In many ways these methods are fruitful and illuminating, but they have their limitations. Many of the theories discussed in this book were developed during the 1970s through to the early 2000s. Since then, there have been significant changes in media, society, and theory. Some of these changes are encapsulated in theoretical approaches with the prefix 'post': postmodernism, poststructuralism, postcolonialism, and postfeminism (which, alongside third-wave feminism, was discussed in Chapter 20). These words suggest a new era, new ways of being and understanding.

THE PREFIX 'POST'

It is useful to first consider the meaning of the prefix 'post', which literally means 'after', as it is used in all these terms. Using 'modernism' (see p. 402) as an example, the prefix 'post' is used for all the following reasons:

- Postmodernist ideas, beliefs, and feelings are new discourses about art, culture, and society that have emerged *after* earlier, modernist ideas.
- But postmodernism doesn't just come after modernism: it recognises that we live in a world in which modernist ideas and actions were important and are still part of our world; therefore a postmodernist world is one that is built on the theories and practices of modernism.
- Not only are postmodernist ideas built on those of modernism, but in some ways they are also linked to modernism by shared theoretical perspectives. So, you could argue that postmodernism is another version of modernism, rather than being completely new.
- What makes postmodernism different from modernism is that in some ways it challenges, goes against, earlier modernist discourses, and in so doing it breaks new ground.

The use of 'post' as a prefix for 'modernism' has similar implications for the other 'posts'. They are all movements and theories that are new, come after, are built on, are linked to, and yet challenge the previous movements. For the purposes of this discussion, they also point to questions about theories used in media studies.

POSTSTRUCTURALISM AND THE LIMITATIONS OF STRUCTURALIST APPROACHES

Poststructuralism comes after, is built on, is linked to, and challenges structuralism, and also semiology and theories of ideology. The main problems with these earlier approaches is that they are too rigid, too limiting in understanding media and culture. In particular, they suggest that people are determined by structures, that they are dominated by them, and, as a result, have little autonomy or freedom. Poststructuralism opens up more possibilities.

◀ POSTSTRUCTURALISM

Poststructuralism develops and challenges structuralist approaches, taking more account of the way contexts and audiences can produce more fluid meanings and readings of media texts.

Structuralism, which flourished in the 1970s, was opposed to what was called 'culturalism' or theories that drew on 'lived experience' (Hall 1986). This opposition led to a poststructuralist critique of structuralism (Hall 1985). Structuralists argue that people are determined and controlled by the social and aesthetic structures that they live in, for example, that dominant ideology is transmitted through these structures to a relatively powerless population; that narrative structures determine how we read and understand texts, just as semiology aims to fix the meanings of sign systems. In contrast, culturalists argue that people actually have some say in whether they accept or refuse dominant ideology. According to culturalists, people can challenge dominant ideology and can live it in different ways. Sign systems and signifiers are more fluid and open to different readings and context is a crucial factor. In relation to media, this difference between structuralism and culturalism corresponds with the difference between textual analysis that shows how dominant ideological values are inscribed in a text through its processes of signification, representation, and its narrative structure, and analysis that asks what audiences are actually doing with texts. The stress on audiences and their uses of the texts is crucial to poststructuralist approaches (Weedon 1987).

We have already begun to present poststructuralist analyses in this book in a number of ways: through multiple readings of signs, signifiers, and texts; through the use of hegemony as a conceptual tool; with the view that the media can present a range of ideological positions; through awareness that audiences can make different readings; with our view of the contradictory aspects of the media that we have stressed throughout. Our approach recognises the values of semiology, ideology, and structuralism for analysing the media but goes beyond these—similarly, poststructuralism is not dismissing structuralist ideas but is building on them, extending and developing them. Awareness of the changes brought about by globalisation and new technologies are the most recent aspects that need to be taken account of in understanding media and society.

Structuralism uses binary oppositions as a framework for analysing society and the media, and we have used them throughout the book, first, in relation to analysis of language, narratives, and texts, and second, as ways of understanding gender, sexual orientation, and ethnicity. We have used binary oppositions to raise the problems of the oppression of women, homosexuals, and people of colour, although the potential danger of this is that using the structure of oppositions helps to maintain and perpetuate these gender and ethnic oppositions—it can help maintain an adversarial framework rather than facilitating the search for different conceptual frameworks. The search for such frameworks is central to queer theory (see p. 314) and the work of Judith Butler, who has suggested that the distinction between male and female may not be a helpful way to understand people (Butler 1990). Many young people today seem less bothered by these differences and can mix easily across gender, sexual, and ethnic divisions.

All these points allow us to move forward in our understanding of media and society, and are relevant in a postmodern view of media and society, which will be discussed below after consideration of the term 'postcolonialism'.

POSTCOLONIALISM

What constitutes a postcolonialist view of the world?   ▶

POSTCOLONIALISM

The historical period after colonialism; ways of understanding the (ongoing) effects of colonialism.

▶ **Postcolonialism** is a term used in various contexts, and in each context it has a slightly different meaning. It relates to colonialism, the historical relations between Europe and the rest of the world, and the discourses—such as Orientalism—associated with non-Western cultures (see Chapter 22). The term 'postcolonialism' also recognises that the colonialist era, in which European countries established overt control over majority-world (colonised) countries, has ended; nearly all the former colonies have achieved political independence. But the reference to colonialism reminds us that the nineteenth century and much of the twentieth century have been colonialist periods, and that the influence of colonialism is still being felt throughout the world.

Postcolonialism can operate as an attitude: to be a postcolonialist is to hope and presume that we now have equality between people of different ethnic backgrounds, that old colonial power bases have gone, and that we do not need to dwell on or examine the colonial past (it can be left behind).

Postcolonialism can also be a way of looking at the world, a way that understands the present postcolonial situation in the light of the past colonial situation, and draws attention to this link—not to remind us or make us feel guilty, but to see how this past is still relevant and still has an influence on power relations and social attitudes.

Some argue that we now live in a neocolonialist world. While the traditional forms of colonisation have disappeared, the previously colonised nations are still dominated economically through the powers of multinational corporations and thus a new form of power, neocolonialism, has been established. Aileen Moreton-Robinson argues that we have not transcended colonialism to arrive in a postcolonial world; her influential article on belonging, place, Indigeneity, and whiteness in a 'postcolonising society' works through the ongoing effects and transformations of colonisation in contemporary culture (Moreton-Robinson 2003).

Postcolonialism is often used to study literature and media products that come from previously colonised countries or that specifically address postcolonial issues (Rivkin & Ryan 1998). The work of many indigenous writers and filmmakers is interpreted from a postcolonial perspective. In Australia, films made by Tracey Moffat and paintings by Gordon Bennett explore these issues from, among other positions, Aboriginal perspectives. Their work shows how histories of colonialism and discourses of racism are inscribed in present-day Australia. Such discourses and histories are often referred to in their work. Moffat's short film *Nice Coloured Girls* relates contemporary experiences of Aboriginal women, in particular their relationships to white men, back to a colonial history. Bennett's painting *Altered Body Print* (*Shadow Figure Howling at the Moon*) (Figure 24.1) plays on and challenges the binary oppositions (and discourses) around race that were used to construct his identity (McLean & Bennett 1996). In this painting, Bennett mixes up the oppositions that structure discourses of ethnicity so that they are not neatly paired opposite one another. This breaks the structure of such discourses and also suggests the confusion of an identity positioned within these discourses. He comments:

> There came a time in my life when I became aware of my Aboriginal heritage. This may seem of little consequence, but when the weight of European representations of Aboriginal people as the quintessential primitive "Other" is realised and understood, within discourses of self and other … then you may understand why such an awareness was problematic for my sense of identity. The conceptual gap between my sense of self and other collapsed and I was thrown into turmoil.
>
> It is the collapse of the conceptual gap between the binary opposites of self/other, civilised/savage, sophisticated/primitive, or perhaps more appropriately its gradual disintegration and my process of integration, that forms the substratum of my life and work (McLean & Bennett 1996, p. 9).

Figure 24.1 Gordon Bennett's *Altered Body Print*

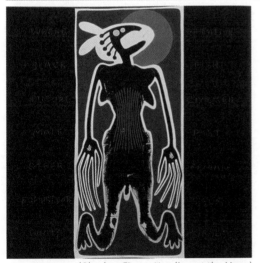

(*Shadow Figure Howling at the Moon*)

Bennett's painting is produced out of a knowledge and awareness of cultural theory; it is built on and extends notions of structural binary oppositions, thus linking cultural theory and practice in significant ways.

Essentialism also enters the debate about ethnic identity: this comes up in relation to discussion of people's roots—where they come from in a historical sense. *Roots* is the title of an influential novel, a history of African-Americans, by Alex Haley (1976), that was made into a television series. This series celebrated the rediscovery of African-American history and saw this history as significant in terms of the identities of modern African-Americans. Similarly, many people today seek connection and understanding with their roots, now extended to white Anglo-Celtic ethnic groups seeking to understand their historical and spiritual connections. One of the main issues surrounding this search is whether these roots are cultural–social or genetic–biological (in the blood). Many ethnic groups seem to call on both these understandings of their roots. Roots can be romanticised, as happens when Australians look at Aboriginal spiritual connections with the land and make these connections seem eternal, representative of something beyond culture. Even those who believe only in social construction sometimes lapse into the common-sense view that cultural differences are based on genetics.

POSTMODERNISM

POSTMODERNISM

Originally a style in architecture, the term was later used to describe the late-twentieth-century world and as a style of cultural production.

▶ **Postmodernism** is the most complex and the most inclusive of the 'post' terms: all the others can be seen as part of postmodernism. So what is it? Where did it come from? And where can we find it?

The origins of the term 'postmodernism'

The term 'postmodernism' was first used as early as the 1960s to describe a style or movement in architecture (Jencks 1986). This style worked by taking various elements of past architectural styles and mixing them together in new buildings. Consequently, there was nothing new or original in it other than the way it combined and reworked past styles.

Fredric Jameson

The term was taken up by political and cultural theorist Fredric Jameson, among others, to describe contemporary Western and global society. Jameson (1991) argues that a shift that began in the late 1960s and that was driven by economic changes is changing the world and its culture. He maintains that society is moving into a phase he describes as 'late capitalism'. By this, he means that the capitalist system—some people investing wealth in the production and distribution of goods, and many others selling their labour for wages—that has been evolving since the end of feudalism is developing a new form. Jameson argues as follows.

- Economic power is increasingly concentrated in multinational companies whose businesses cross national borders, and, through their ability to produce and sell goods globally, these companies are changing the face of production (so that, for example, US-based multinational companies can produce goods much more cheaply in developing countries than they can in the USA) and distribution (see Chapter 25).

- In the drive to sell more goods, emphasis is now placed more on consumption than on production. The emphasis on consumption means that people are becoming more aware of and more concerned with issues of lifestyle, image, and appearance, which leads to a society focused on appearances, on spectacle, a designer-label mentality.

Postmodernism as a style of cultural production

Jameson's focus on spectacle and appearance leads to a definition of postmodernism as a style of cultural production. This is the most common way of using the word, a use you are probably familiar with. When people describe things as postmodern, they are often drawing on this meaning. Postmodernism as a style of cultural production is relevant to aesthetic products (for example, films, advertisements, and television programs) and to lifestyles (how people live, feel, and act in everyday life). Thus 'postmodernism' is a term that can be used to describe the media and the way we live in real life—as demonstrated by the quotation from postmodern theorist Jean-François Lyotard at the beginning of this chapter. Jameson's analysis links postmodern styles of living and cultural production to economic changes. Others see postmodern styles, postmodern cultures, as an aesthetic response to and reflection of at least three other aspects of the world we now live in. These three aspects are described below.

1   New scientific theories

New scientific theories have changed our understanding of the world. Previous theories in the physical sciences (biology, physics, chemistry, and so on) and social sciences (politics, sociology, and so on) aimed to classify and understand the human and physical world; semiology, Marxism, and psychoanalysis, which have informed so much of media studies theory, were part of this project. Scientists have tended to think they can rationally explain the world we live in and how we behave, but current scientific discoveries and theories have undermined these certainties. Developments in nuclear physics, in chaos theory, and in complexity theory suggest that all knowledge about the physical world is relative, partial, and uncertain. The search for ultimate truths, for objective impartiality, is futile. Among social scientists, it has become commonplace to assert that even individual identities are not real, since we are just a collection of constructed social masks. Reality cannot be pinned down. There are no certainties except uncertainty and continual change.

2   We live in a media-world

The spread of the media, particularly television, has produced a new way of seeing the world. First, people are saturated, as never before, with media-provided images, information, and knowledge. We have an amazing archive of media images available to look at, and we store these and many other images in our brains. Second, media representations and the real world have begun to blur: we see the real world in terms of media images. This is apparent in the way footage released by extremist groups such as ISIS or ISIL of the tragic beheadings of journalists or soldiers, images of the War on Terror, and the collapse of the Twin Towers of the World Trade Center in New York have been compared with footage from an action film (in fact, after the 2015 massacre related to the satirical French newspaper *Charlie Hebdo* that left 17 dead, filming of action movies was banned in Paris due to fears that actors could be mistaken for terrorists). So much experience, knowledge, and feeling come by way of media images that the media dominate our ways of seeing the world. Reality TV offers a clear example of this closure of the gap between reality and representation.

3   Postmodernism as a reaction to politics in the 1960s

Postmodernism is a reaction to post-1960s politics. The 1960s were an important historical moment that crystallised in student uprisings, industrial action, and protests in 1968. This revolutionary period ended the Vietnam War, saw the rise of student and trade union power and saw the hippie subculture bring about new social liberation, brought down the corrupt Nixon government through the Watergate scandal of the early 1970s, increased freedom and liberation movements throughout the Third World, and, in Australia, led to the election of the Whitlam Labor government in 1972. All this seemed to herald a new beginning, a new optimism in society. But it did not produce a new social utopia. Inequality, war, and social struggle persist, and the postmodernist generations, who know so much about social change, seem to be able to do little but look ironically or dismissively, helplessly or apathetically, at the world they live in.

Postmodernism is an expression and response to all the above factors. The big questions about postmodernism as a style or practice are: does it celebrate this new global, economic, social system? Does it offer a critique and challenge to it? Does it offer a way of coping and surviving in the system? It can do all three, but to explore these questions we need to examine specific instances of postmodernism, since it is not limited to one position.

Postmodernism in context

Postmodernism is built on an earlier movement that has not yet been discussed here: modernism. Since postmodernism is a reaction to and a continuation of modernism, modernism needs to be briefly introduced and, in turn, understood in relation to realism, which preceded it.

Table 24.1 Differences between realism, modernism, and postmodernism

Realism	Modernism	Postmodernism
Nineteenth century onwards: painting, literature, and mainstream film	1900–1960s: modern art and modern architecture, some literature	1960s–present

These three umbrella terms—'realism', 'modernism', and 'postmodernism'—give an overview of aesthetic tendencies in Western culture over the last two hundred years. Realism can be described as an attempt to portray things as they really are, as they appear to the human spectator. Realist art often involves portraying humans in their social situations, and realist art and media products tend to reflect and comment on society. Realism dominated painting and literature in the nineteenth century, and it is still common today (see p. 296 for further discussion of realism and pp. 273–7 for a discussion of realism in relation to documentary). In film, realism is characterised by naturalised conventions of representation, acting, and editing that do not draw attention to the process of construction because they resemble normal ways of seeing and experiencing the world. The realist style is thus not unusual or difficult for audiences to read; much mainstream film is still made using realist principles.

Modernism, which marks the beginning of the modern world, describes the art and aesthetic movements of the first half of the twentieth century. These movements were a reaction against realism (Bradbury & McFarlane 1976; Lunn 1985). Modernism grew out of enormous political and social changes that were linked, in many ways, to revolutions in technology and communication. Modernism is characterised by

MODERNISM ▶

Describes Western art and aesthetic movements of the first half of the twentieth century; characterised by optimism in future progress, and ways of seeing or representing the world that challenged realism, including abstraction and focus on the act of representation.

- an optimistic belief in the power and possibilities of machines, technology, science, rationality, and progress
- a range of new art movements that saw and represented the world in new and revolutionary ways (including cubism, dadaism, surrealism, futurism, stream-of-consciousness writing, and all forms of abstract art)
- an emphasis on the process of experiencing and representing reality.

Many modernist movements were interested in producing art and architecture that draws attention to the processes of construction involved in making the objects and the art. Modernist artists were interested in exploring and foregrounding the very means of representation: paint, the canvas, celluloid, narrative structure, and so on. Modernist artists questioned how they could represent the world, which involved asking how people see and experience reality. They showed that this process is more complicated and fragmented than earlier realist aesthetic styles suggested.

Despite the terrible history of the modernist period—two world wars, and major turmoil in China, the Soviet Union, and throughout the globe—modernism was essentially an optimistic movement. It looked for ways to organise human society that would deliver happiness and fulfilment.

We can see this in the aims of modernist architecture. Its abstractly styled buildings were functional. The angular, box-like constructions with little ornamentation or elaboration that we have come to associate with modernist architecture were designed as utopian housing spaces that would cater for all human needs. People were grouped together in these modernist buildings: housing estates made up of tower blocks are a modernist legacy. But the utopian dream of this sort of housing has rarely been realised, and such housing estates made up of tower blocks are probably the most damning indictment of this dream. In Godfrey Reggio's film *Koyaanisqatsi* (see pp. 218–19) there is an extended sequence that shows the blowing up of one of the most famous modernist housing estates in the USA. Before its demolition, the site had become derelict and deserted because it did not cater for people's real needs. Its destruction can be seen as a metaphor for the death of modernism and the death of the modernist dream. As discussed above, the genesis of postmodernism involves many factors, and one of them is this perceived failure of modernism. While postmodernism is linked to modernism, it also challenges it.

Characteristics of postmodernism

The quotation from Lyotard that opens this chapter gives an excellent flavour of postmodernism; it describes what could be an ideal lifestyle for a global, postmodern individual. It stresses consumption and style, it involves mixing high and low culture, and it involves combining different cultures in one's everyday life. In reading about postmodernism, you will probably come to realise that postmodernism celebrates superficiality, spectacle, and surfaces, and that it is associated with various characteristics (Solomon 1988): for example, irony, the blurring of traditional boundaries, fluid identity, intertextuality, pastiche, appropriation, bricolage, hybridity, self-reflexivity, and self-referentiality.

What follows is a discussion of some of the most significant of these. Look for examples of these characteristics in media products: you should be able to find them easily. Many contemporary media products that we have examined—for example, the films *The Thin Blue*

Line and *Koyaanisqatsi*, culture-jamming examples, and the advertisements illustrating postfeminism—can be classified as postmodern; you can reconsider them in this light.

Irony

Let us start with irony. To be ironic is to mean the opposite of what you say. Something is ironic when it indirectly contradicts its surface meaning. This often involves giving expression to contradictory attitudes and indicating a degree of detachment from a subject. The opening of *American Beauty* is partly ironic. It appears to say 'Here is a beautiful, ideal community', but it sees through this to the dark side of the American dream. Irony is witty and cool, knowing and cynical. Media theorist Todd Gitlin notes that cultural critic 'Paul Fussell has made the point that irony became standard in English writing after World War I as a way to navigate around the unspeakable' (Gitlin 1993). Why did irony emerge as such an important form of cultural expression in the late twentieth century? What is unspeakable now? What is this ironic mode built on? There is an ironic scene in *The Social Network* (2010) where Mark Zuckerberg (founder and CEO of Facebook) himself keeps looking at the Facebook profile of his ex-girlfriend contemplating whether to click 'add as a friend'. However he 'refreshes' multiple times with a sad face. This is unspoken irony.

Knowingness

Postmodernism is very knowing and self-reflexive. It is built on knowledge of the world, knowledge of media products, and knowledge of countless theories and critiques of society, modernity, and the media. We have a glut of knowledges, accumulated over twenty centuries and more, with which to make sense of the world, but whereas modernism thought that it was possible to make sense of the world and to rationally organise the future, postmodernism, after modernism's failure, recognises the futility of such a dream. Postmodernism embraces non-rational modes of knowledge: for example, it is open to tarot, astrology, intuition, and so on. Perhaps the most important feature of postmodernism is the way that it is comfortable with lack of certainty. The popular TV series *Supernatural* reflects this pervasive uncertainty; in the show, many things about the supernatural realm remain unknown to the protagonists Sam and Dean, and, when answers are revealed, they usually defy rational expectations. As these brothers hunt differing paranormal creatures, they must discover new ways of understanding and overcoming them, and each episode suggests new possibilities. Postmodernism suggests that we can pick up whatever theoretical framework feels right to us at any particular moment to use for a while before moving on to the next one. While we are urged to demonstrate our knowledge, we are reminded that there is no ultimate way of making sense of the world.

Cynicism

Our knowledge has given us the power to see through things. We are no longer naive; we know that the media are all constructions, and that we cannot trust media products to represent reality truthfully, we know that the capitalist world is out to exploit us and that politicians just want power, we know that we are being controlled by family, church, education, and media systems, and we know that Big Brother is watching.

Powerlessness

Despite our knowledge and our ability to see through things, we remain powerless because nothing is certain, everything is relative, and the corporate powers that, to a large extent, control our lives are too strong. What, as individuals, can we do? We can see the world's problems and injustices, but they seem too overwhelming for us to do anything about. This apparent intractability of our problems, the fact that the system is too strong, is what is, in Gitlin's terms, unspeakable. As he says, 'The fear is that what's underneath hurts too much, better repress it' (Gitlin 1993).

Pleasure

What can we do with all our knowledge, uncertainty, and powerlessness? We can at least use it to indulge in humour, wit, and pleasure: we can make ironic jokes about the system, we can live in the moment and celebrate our (limited) power to be what we want to be, we can play, and we can look good. A song called 'Shameless' by the Pet Shop Boys draws on artist Andy Warhol's claim that everyone wants fifteen minutes of fame: we will do anything to get it, to the extent of sacrificing our integrity to attain celebrity.

We can celebrate uncertainty as a freedom from limitations. The feeling that there are no boundaries, that we are in a state of continual change, fluidity, and expansion, can lead to excitement and hedonistic experimentation. Postmodern pleasures are also less elitist than modernist ones, as they embrace pop culture.

Aspects of all these constituents are at work in the Biff cartoons (Figures 24.2 and 24.3) and are also evident in much contemporary advertising (see the CAT boots advertisement, Figure 24.4).

Figures 24.2 and **24.3** Biff cartoons

Source: Mick Kidd 1988

Biff cartoons are a series of postmodern cartoons, often reproduced on postcards, that were made in the United Kingdom during the 1980s by a company called Biff Products. In a sense, they are a comic and ironic response to media theory and cultural studies theory. In these cartoons we see the inclusion of multiple realities: a 1950s world, in terms of dress and appearance, is juxtaposed with 1980s knowledge. Postmodernism often uses the perceived idealism and naivety of the 1950s (as lived in the West) as an ironic comparison with the cynical, knowing 1980s and 1990s.

Biff cartoons also include different levels of discourse:

- the statements of the characters contrast with their real thoughts
- authorial comments or captions draw our attention to the divide between high and low culture, and set philosophical and art theories in low-culture contexts such as the genres of pulp fiction and popular romance
- they use dirty realism (for example, in Figure 24.2 there is dandruff on the man's jacket)
- they comment on commodification and marketing
- they are politically aware
- they demonstrate awareness of narrative theory, feminism, and philosophical movements such as existentialism.

In Biff cartoons, these knowledges and discourses are set in an arena of sexual politics and relationships in which women's consciousness is usually shown as more developed than that of men. The pleasure that readers derive from these cartoons is partly dependent on recognising the references to such knowledges, time periods, and sexual politics. Biff cartoons are produced by authors and cartoonists steeped in theory and knowledge. But these theories and knowledges are mocked: it is as if the cartoons ask, where do they get you?

The CAT boots advertisement (Figure 24.4) displays another element of the postmodern mix. What we find here is the popularisation of theories of the social construction of reality. This time we are not invited to mock knowledge, but to take it on board and work productively with it. The caption—'We shape the things we build, thereafter they shape us'—parallels our arguments, presented throughout this book, about how our society conditions us, how we don't speak language; language speaks us. Cultural studies knowledge surfaces as part of popular discourse in this advertisement, which appeared in the British magazine *The Face* in 1996. The ad recognises how we are caught up in urban deserts in which we have become machine-like, and suggests a way through this: the answer is not another course in cultural theory; the answer is to buy a new pair of CAT boots. The ad implies these boots can give our lives in cities shape, and our identities are shaped by what we wear and where we live. This ad proposes that we can escape from the urban jungle by purchasing stylish commodities. Moreover, the figure in the ad is an older black man. In terms of age and ethnicity, a person from a subordinate group in society is being shown as fashionable (clothes and hairstyle add to this): blackness and age become powerful in this ad. These advertisements play with signifiers and signification in an exhilarating and pleasurable way, but they do so within the realms of commodification and consumerism.

Figure 24.4 CAT boots advertisement

Source: Shubankar Ray

Blurring the boundaries

Before postmodernism, aesthetic products could be classified into discrete areas—fiction, fact, high culture, low culture, westerns, musicals, documentaries, plays, films, operas, pop music, and so on. But postmodernism knows no such boundaries or rules; it delights in the blurring of cultural boundaries and in hybridisation—Gitlin cites Australia's Circus Oz, which draws on 'Aboriginal influences, vaudeville, Chinese acrobatics, Japanese martial arts, fireman's balances, Indonesian instruments and rhythms, video, Middle Eastern tunes, B-grade detective movies, modern dance, Irish jigs, and the ubiquitous presence of corporate marketing' (Gitlin 1993). Traditional notions of circuses are blown apart in this mixture or fusion of influences and in the blurring of categories. The inclusion of various non-European elements is an example of the fact that Eurocentrism is coming to an end as postmodern culture embraces other cultural traditions. There is freedom in this loosening of the traditional boundaries between cultural forms.

Within film and television, similar changes have been taking place. The development of music videos and the MTV channel are two of the most important and influential in this respect. The music video has provided a space for visual experimentation in the context of a popular art form (pop music) (Frith et al. 1993; Goodwin 1993). Young audiences have grown up familiar with the wide range of techniques used in these videos: non-narrative structures, experimental editing, the mixing of film formats (super 8 and 35 mm for example), and so on. This is linked to the freeing up of styles in mainstream film and television. Standard rules of continuity in filmmaking are disappearing, and films are incorporating aspects of other media. *Scott Pilgrim vs the World* (dir. Edgar Wright 2010) combines traditional narrative with video game–style sequences, elements of anime, comic book effects, animation, and digital onscreen graphics. It was shot using super 35, anamorphic 35mm, and a high-speed digital camera for super slow motion.

Speed ramping—speeding up or slowing down the action—was added during the editing process to make certain movements appear superhuman. Further extending the boundaries of the film's reality, there are a couple of occasions where a character's fist breaks out of the frame when he punches and it becomes visible outside the edges of the screen. At other points, the film brings to life a familiar idea from video games when defeated characters explode into actual coins.

Similar rule-breaking techniques are apparent in many films and in television series such as *House of Cards* (2013–), *Modern Family* (2009–), and *Game of Thrones* (2011–). Television's realist premises, which dictate the requirement for continuity, have been challenged with great energy, and the innovations in this regard are often well received by the public, particularly by young audiences who have grown up watching television programs and films that use these new styles.

Documentaries have developed significantly in this period (see Chapter 18), and this hybridisation can be seen as a postmodern tendency. Modernism aimed to make people aware of the construction involved in all media products, make them question the reality effect of media products, and encourage them to deconstruct these products. In this light, documentary's realist premise—that it could innocently, impartially, and objectively record the world—was challenged. But this realisation freed up documentary filmmaking from its link with realism: in its documentation of the real world, it could now use any techniques and could include all manner of representational modes. *The Thin Blue Line* (discussed on p. 279) is a great example of a postmodern documentary film.

Intertextuality, pastiche, appropriation, and bricolage

Postmodernism questions the process of signification and the making of meanings. While semiotic analysis seeks meanings and attempts to relate signifiers and representations back to reality, postmodern approaches challenge these aims, seeing texts as simulations (a term popularised by theorist Jean Baudrillard) rather than representations. In her research on media images, Deirdre Pribram puts it as follows:

> In our culture of information and the mass media, we are inundated with an over-abundance of images and signs that no longer have referential value but, instead, interact solely with other signs. This marks the advent of simulation. Rather than the previous vertical connection, if you will, between sign and meaning, there is, instead the horizontal relationship of sign to sign (Pribram 1993, p. 201).

BRICOLAGE ▶

The putting together of different, often contradictory, cultural forms, thereby creating new meanings.

A pastiche is an imitation of a style or various styles that is often affectionate and humorous about its sources. **Bricolage** builds on the artistic techniques of collage and montage. While collage involves some form of cutting out and pasting together of images from many different sources, montage refers to the process of editing together images from different spaces and times in film and video. Bricolage means the appropriation and combination of different cultural elements into a new form. It involves appropriation: the original sign or signifier takes on a new meaning or signified in its new context, where it is combined with other signs (for an account of bricolage, see Hebdige 1979). The work of artist Barbara Kruger is an example of bricolage. Intertextuality (see p. 139) involves reference, borrowing (some would say plagiarising), and making links with other texts or sources. Postmodern architecture is a good example of bricolage. Music videos are also notorious for this kind of pop cultural self-referentiality, as are Quentin Tarantino's films, especially *Kill Bill* and *Death Proof*. Tarantino even quotes his own films. In *Kill Bill Volume 1*, the Bride (Thurman) traced a visible square in the air in the fight scene with Vivica A Fox, just as Mia (also played by Uma Thurman) did in *Pulp Fiction* when she told John Travolta's character 'Don't be a square'. *Death Proof* then referenced *Kill Bill* when a group of young women drove a yellow and black Mustang with a 'Pussy Wagon' icon and one of them had Elle Driver's theme tune, 'Twisted Nerve', as her cell phone ring tone.

Nowadays, the recycling of cultural genres, codes, and conventions, and intertextuality generally, are rife in media products, so you should be able to find many examples. *The Simpsons* frequently adapts mainstream film plots (*Goodfellas*, for example) as the basis for its stories, and it often parodies famous film scenes (such as the shower scene from *Psycho* and the Rosebud sequences from *Citizen Kane*); many music videos recycle old film footage. The Lotteries Commission of Western Australia reworked a famous painting by Edvard Munch, *The Scream* (Figure 24.5), in one of its advertisements.

This last example shows how irreverent postmodernism can be. The tortured expression on the face of the figure in *The Scream* signifies fear and anxiety; the painting is a commentary on early twentieth-century society and has, over time, become an icon of high art. In the Lotteries Commission of Western Australia advertisement, however, it is used to make us laugh and buy lotto tickets. For postmodernism, nothing is sacred.

All the above examples draw on and rework known cultural artefacts, producing new meanings through recycling them. They demonstrate how the media-world reflects

Figure 24.5 Advertisement for Lotteries Commission of Western Australia

Source: Lotteries Commission of Western Australia, published in *Festival of Perth Program* 1998

inwards on itself, looking forward by looking back at other media products. What is the connection between the past and the present in this recycling of images? How do these images and representations relate to reality? Cultural theorist Dick Hebdige argues:

> The past is played and replayed as an amusing range of styles, genres, signifying practices to be combined and recombined at will. The then (and the there) are subsumed in the Now. The only history that exists here is the history of the signifier and that is no history at all (Hebdige 1985, p. 47).

The past is used, but simply for visual play and pleasure. This is what is meant by the disavowal of history: we are not interested in history as a truthful or factual account of the development of our current sociocultural position, or as a way of learning about relationships between different parts of the world over time—history is simply a treasure trove of unconnected, fascinating images and stories. For those in the know, there is the pleasure of spotting the reference; for others, there is the simple pleasure of spectacle. You do not need to know all the cultural references to enjoy a postmodern media product. Knowing them is a sign of your cultural knowledge; it indicates that you are a connoisseur of signs and images, not of truth and reality.

Self-reflexivity and the excess of surface

An understanding of self-reflexivity and surface can help reveal the limitations of both modernism and postmodernism. The self-reflective nature of much postmodern culture represents a strong link with modernism. Self-reflexivity is a modernist technique whereby a text draws attention to its own construction: for example, the characters in a fiction film might talk directly to the camera, or the clapperboard or boom microphone (a microphone on a long pole that hangs over the action) might be shown intentionally. Self-reflexivity means that the audience sees the processes of construction involved in making the media product (see p. 279). We are made aware in such examples that we are watching a film being made, that we are watching constructed representations, not reality. In her critique of film culture and activism in the 1960s, Sylvia Harvey gives an interesting summation and criticism of modernism's tendency towards self-reflexivity:

> Modernist aesthetics induces a reflection upon, a consideration of, the means of representation, and for lovers of art it generates aesthetic pleasure out of a series of "frame-shifts" (the procedures whereby the work of art playfully refers to itself and its own processes of production). But too often it fails to lead its audience "through" this first consideration and towards a second, namely, a consideration of the action represented. It is this second area of consideration which opens up the possibility of introduction of knowledge of the social world and its processes, what Brecht would have called "instruction". And if there is a sense in which modernism offers the only way forward, there is also a sense in which it constitutes a dead end, a graveyard. Only those who pass through it can learn from it; the rest remain buried within it (Harvey 1978, p. 82).

Harvey's argument is that reflection on representation—self-reflexivity—is not sufficient; it is a potential dead end and we must aim to understand the real world and gain 'knowledge of the social world and its processes'. She is arguing that modernism can tend to forget this project.

How does postmodernism look in the light of her critique of modernism? Postmodernism seems to have extended the self-referential nature of modernism: it remains heavily self-reflective, draws attention to the processes of construction involved in cultural products and knowledges, and derives great pleasure from this. But it has gone further than modernism in seeing that the world has become full of, as Pribram puts it, 'images and signs that no longer have referential value but, instead interact solely with other signs' (Pribram 1993). Does it then become difficult to find instruction about reality in the postmodern world?

While there seems to be a clear political project in modernist self-reflexivity (this project is described by Harvey as 'knowledge of the social world and its processes'), postmodernism often seems content merely to play with processes of production. The following questions address this issue.

- Does postmodernism's focus on surface reality, style, and appearance produce a depthlessness that makes postmodern texts uninterested in understanding the real world?
- Do postmodern texts play with techniques and signifiers merely in order to ensure that their meanings are up for grabs, thereby providing the audience with the pleasures of decoding the text using their cultural knowledge, or can the postmodern style still produce some Brechtian 'instruction' about the real world? In other words, is postmodernism caught up in consumerism and style to the detriment of effective critique?

The techniques of postmodernism can be used to provide instruction and new perspectives. Because we now realise that the world is more complex than Brecht and Harvey and their contemporaries could have imagined, the instruction provided by postmodernist texts is inclusive of more possibilities and uncertainties than would have been thought possible from the 1940s to the 1970s. *The Thin Blue Line* and *Koyaanisqatsi* are postmodern texts: the first draws our attention to questions about whether representations can present truth and reality; the second asks us to consider what kind of a world we live in that is so dominated by spectacle. In enabling the inclusion of new modes of thinking, in opening up identity, and in challenging Eurocentrism, postmodernism can be liberating and powerful (Jagtenberg & McKie 1997). There is also an interesting connection between postmodernism, New Age philosophies, and traditional meditation practices, since all these exhort us to live in the present moment: postmodernism problematises grand historical narratives of progress, while Buddhism and meditation stress that what is important is the present moment, that in order to be fully alive we need to bring ourselves into this moment. These philosophies recognise that much contemporary Western life is built around living in the past or the future: at any one time, we tend to be either ruminating about what has happened or planning for what will happen—in other words, we rarely live in the moment.

CONCLUSION

The danger of postmodernism as a way of thinking about the world is that its view that everything carries a multiplicity of meanings and signs, and its acceptance of the coexistence of different theories and viewpoints, threaten to leave us with no certainties.

This is what Baudrillard is describing when he writes: 'All the great humanist criteria of value, all the values of a civilisation of moral, aesthetic, and practical judgements, vanish in our system of images and signs. Everything becomes undecideable' (1988, p. 128).

The problem with this perspective is that it may deny us some hold on the real world. Finding a connection to and knowledge of the real world through various systems of representation (at the same time as recognising their subjective nature and their partiality) is very important. It is worth repeating (see p. 68) Richard Dyer's view of the relationship between reality and representation: 'Because one can see reality only through representation it does not follow that one does not see reality at all. Partial—selective, incomplete, from a point of view—vision of something is not no vision of it whatsoever' (Dyer 1993, p. 3). Dyer argues that material reality is important and that representations can tell us something about it. This recognises the impossibility of finding absolute truths, but insists on the importance of attempting to find some possible truths about the world. Junot Diaz, a writer from the Dominican Republic, puts it even more simply. In his writing he aims to be 'representing as honestly as I can' (Diaz 1998) his experience and his society from his perspective, and he sees writing (representation) as allowing him this possibility.

This chapter has

- discussed the terms 'poststructuralism', 'postcolonialism', and 'postmodernism'
- considered the historical development and context of postmodernism
- examined key characteristics of postmodernism
- offered a critical overview of postmodernism.

? | DISCUSSION POINTS

1   Can you find examples of postmodernist characteristics in any contemporary films or television programs?
2   What social and ideological meanings are presented in any postmodern texts?

SUMMARY

You should now be able to

- define the terms 'poststructuralism' and 'postcolonialism'
- define the term 'postmodernism' and relate it to modernism
- describe the central characteristics of postmodernism
- identify postmodern characteristics in contemporary media texts
- offer a critique of postmodernism.

CHAPTER 25

Globalisation

> Think local and act global. Think local, as people need to be rooted in their identity, in their interests, and in their institutions of political representation. But act global, via the Internet, connectivity, media politics and international competitiveness, as the powers that be inhabit the global space.
>
> Manuel Castells, *Challenges of Globalisation* 2001

This chapter will

- outline important characteristics and impacts of globalisation
- introduce key thinkers who have developed influential theories of globalisation
- consider the positive and negative aspects of these changes, questioning why we should care about media globalisation and how can we make the best of it.

Historically, globalisation has been shaped by economic, political, and military interests, and by technological innovation. By the fifteenth and sixteenth centuries, trade was already crossing national boundaries. During the time of colonisation and industrialisation in the seventeenth and eighteenth centuries, global power networks began to form. The nineteenth century saw the introduction of newspapers, the telegraph, and cable systems that enabled the formation of global communication networks. The twentieth century was a time of explosive growth in the media and communication industries as radio and television were popularised. The Pentagon began developing the internet in the 1960s; later, satellite, wireless, and mobile communication technologies proliferated. Each technological development has led to increasing levels of global interrelatedness, ultimately prompting questions about the legitimacy and defensibility of national borders.

GLOBALISATION: POSITIVE AND NEGATIVE CHARACTERISTICS

The **globalisation** of communication is characterised by the following qualities: instantaneity, interconnectedness, interdependence, and a trend towards corporate mergers and conglomeration. It is *instantaneous* in that it effectively bridges time and space, offering almost instant access to distant information and events. In fact, *Business @ the Speed of Thought* is the title of an influential book written by Microsoft mogul Bill Gates (1999) about the economic advantages of ICTs. Globalisation offers a sense of *interconnectedness* by facilitating interpersonal communication and the formation of communities and relationships across geographic, racial, religious, and cultural barriers. People can feel a sense of interconnectedness through communication without physically being together. The global media environment is also characterised by economic and political *interdependence* that transcends national and regional boundaries. Increasingly, it is regulated by global agreements brokered by international organisations (such as the United Nations, the World Trade Organization, the World Bank, and the International Monetary Fund, among others) that function in a worldwide capitalist system overriding

◄ GLOBALISATION

Globalisation refers to an international community influenced by technological development and economic, political, and military interests. It is characterised by a worldwide increase in interdependence, interactivity, interconnectedness, and the virtually instantaneous exchange of information. Globalisation could lead to the homogenisation of world cultures, or to hybridisation and multiculturalism.

Figure 25.1 Thembo's Burger Hut cartoon

Source: *Laugh It Off* artists Alex and Patrick Latimer, South Africa

nation states and national regulations. News and television are dependent on global content, and different media forms are increasingly dependent on one another for content. Corporate convergence is a growing trend in which *mergers and conglomeration* concentrate ownership and control of media production and other forms of corporate activity in a small number of multinational conglomerates, potentially reducing the range of voices and views disseminated in the media.

The cartoon by *Laugh It Off* artists Alex Latimer and Patrick Latimer (see Figure 25.1) sends up the way multinationals can exercise global economies of scale to silence and outcompete local businesses, thereby reducing diversity in the marketplace.

Utopian views: imagined communities and the global village

The utopian view of globalisation encapsulated in Marshall McLuhan's phrase 'the global village' (see p. 21) suggests that people of the world can be brought closer together by the globalisation of communication, no matter how far apart we may actually live. The global village is an image of a world in which the media transcend the nation-state in a democratising process that gives everyone's voice a chance to be heard and enables information to be freely shared. Interactive media facilitate participation in global communication and debates, and offer entry into public space. The globalisation of communication enables us to share in each other's lives as members of internet communities or by means of participation in televised events, and so on. In this ideal communication environment, the mass media also play an important role in informing people and generating discussion about events and issues worldwide. The globalisation of communication is seen as an agent of empowerment, education, democracy, and equality. The global dispersal of knowledge facilitates a culture open to sharing responsibility for issues that affect us all and recognising responsibilities to people we may never meet.

Media coverage of the devastating widespread effects from the April 2015 magnitude 7.8 earthquake in Nepal, in which thousands of people lost their lives and hundreds of thousands were made homeless, prompted governments, NGO aid agencies, and people from all over the globe to give money to help the victims. Footballer Cristiano Ronaldo reportedly donated millions of dollars and urged his Facebook followers to assist those affected by the Nepalese earthquake: the phenomenon of celebrities advocating for causes and providing donations is known as 'celanthropy' or celebrity-philanthropism (see Chapter 23). Increasingly, celebrities responding to humanitarian and environmental crises contributes to public engagement and philanthropic behaviour by amplifying global media attention. This also encourages governments to provide personnel and aid to assist countries affected in the wake of tragic natural disasters. These responses and similar altruistic reactions to the 2014 floods in the Kashmir region of India and Pakistan, Tropical Cyclone Pam that hit Vanuatu in 2015, the 2011 earthquake in Christchurch, New Zealand, and the typhoon ravaging the Philippines in 2014 raise questions about whether the whole world could pull together to deal with issues that affect us all, such as global warming. Global communication and global perspectives mean we can see what is happening across the globe—in the Arctic Circle, Antarctica, Africa, the Amazon and Indonesian forests, anywhere. We could start to work together globally to do something beyond implementing global regulations such as the Kyoto Protocol. This moment presents a unique historical challenge, and global media and communication technologies could be an integral part of educating people about the issue and developing solutions.

The idea that globalisation can unite diverse communities and foster progress is implicit in the HSBC advertisement shown in Figure 25.2. The caption reads:

Figure 25.2 HSBC traditional/trendy advertisement

An unpredictable bunch. People.

Everywhere you go you get a different opinion and a different point of view.

What's in, what's out? What is of the moment and what is so 'yesterday'?

And when you talk to 125 million people all over the planet you'd be amazed at what you learn. We have learned that the more you look at difference as potential, the less it looks like a problem.

yourpointofview.com

HSBC
The world's local bank

Source: HSBC Bank Australia

An unpredictable bunch. People. Everywhere you go you get a different opinion and a different point of view. What's in, what's out? What is of the moment and what is so "yesterday"? And when you talk to 125 million people all over the planet you'd be amazed what you learn. We have learned that the more you look at difference as potential, the less it looks like a problem.

This HSBC advertisement uses a 'unity in diversity' theme that harnesses the concepts of progress and development (being 'of the moment' versus 'so "yesterday"'), as well as multiculturalism (valuing difference and traditional cultures), participation, and democratisation (everyone's point of view can be heard online at <yourpointofview.com>). These themes converge in the utopian concept of the global village, as HSBC's brand identity is 'the world's local bank'.

The HSBC advertisement can also be interpreted in ways that resist the intended meaning. If we take the rhetoric about embracing alternative points of view seriously, we must also consider less positive possibilities of globalisation. In a resistant reading, the distinctive practices of moko and mehndi body art signifying identity, status, and initiation rites unique to Māori and Hindu cultures have been commodified, commercialised, decontextualised, and stripped of tradition and cultural meaning as they are popularised and circulated by global media and reduced to trivial, trendy fashion statements. When critically evaluating media texts and media theory, it is important to be aware of both aspects of globalisation and the effects it can have on communities and cultures.

A very important effect of the globalisation of communication media is that it has led to the formation of new kinds of 'imagined communities', a term that influential thinker Benedict Anderson uses to describe national identity. He offers a definition of the nation as 'an imagined political community' (Anderson 1991, p. 6), writing:

> It is imagined because the members of even the smallest nation will never know most of their fellow-members, meet them, or even hear of them, yet in the minds of each lives the image of their communion … in fact, all communities larger than the primordial villages of face-to-face contact (and perhaps even these) are imagined … It is imagined as a community, because, regardless of the actual inequality and exploitation that may prevail in each, the nation is always conceived as a deep, horizontal comradeship (Anderson 1991, pp. 6–7).

The sense of comradeship and common interests characterising the global village arises because of the democratisation of communication technologies. Anderson's work foregrounds the importance of the print technologies, which, he says, 'made it possible for rapidly growing numbers of people to think about themselves, and to relate themselves to others, in profoundly new ways' (1991, p. 36). This argument about print media has been extended and applied to new media.

Media and communication technology as a globalising force

The utopian vision of the rewards of globalisation has been eagerly embraced by multinational communication corporations and harnessed to their branding and advertising campaigns. Consider, for example, the advertisements for Nokia's N-series phones in which we see a montage of faces and voices from all over the world united harmoniously by communication technologies that improve quality of life for one and all, and Microsoft's 'Unlimited potential' campaign, which claims to focus on 'helping individuals and communities around the globe achieve their goals and dreams with relevant, accessible and affordable technologies'.

While the kind of empowerment that global media products and technologies offer is often the power of consumption, ICTs also have potential benefits for economic and social development. As information flow, speed, and volume increase, decreasing sensitivity to distance and diminishing production costs lead to benefits for local media producers and isolated communities (see Fourie 2001, p. 611). The global media can, therefore, work to create positive social change by facilitating access to valuable information about healthcare, agricultural techniques, and education. The global reach of information also has an impact on transparency and accountability with regard to political policy and practices. This is a factor that some governments see as a boon and others, such as the Chinese government, see as a threat because it prompts the global community to exert political pressure, as was seen when Google protested government control, censorship, and internet surveillance by withdrawing from China in 2010.

Although the development of globalisation has given rise to new forms of community and a sense of global interconnectedness, the quality of life available to many citizens in the global village has been questioned. One of the paradoxes of contemporary life is that the global communication environment is media-saturated and offers information overload and access to a virtual global community, but is also characterised by loss of meaningful interpersonal communication and traditional communities, languages, and value systems. These are the 'contradictory trends of integration and fragmentation that characterise information and communication' (Snow 2001, p. 22). It is this darker side of globalisation that theorist Herbert Schiller explores in his work on cultural imperialism, and that are exposed in Castells' theory of the network society; both authors are discussed below.

Dystopian views: cultural imperialism and the network society

Castells counters the utopian view of globalisation described above by pointing out that 'While the media have become indeed globally interconnected, and programs and messages circulate in the global network, *we are not living in a global village, but in customised cottages globally produced and locally distributed*' (2000, p. 370; emphasis in original). Indeed, the dark side of globalisation is far worse than a tendency towards mass production and homogenisation. The 2014 *United Nations Human Development Report* shows that the richest eighty-five people in the world have a combined income greater than the total earnings of the poorest 3.5 billion people. Even though world economic output has doubled in the past ten years, the gap between the richest and the poorest has worsened, which is not what you might expect when globalisation is making us increasingly interconnected and interdependent.

This disheartening economic reality has spawned a vocal anti-globalisation movement geared to resist a global system with disproportionate benefits for big business and wealthy individuals. The anti-globalisation movement targets symbols of the global economy such as the World Trade Organization and the World Bank, and corporations such as McDonald's, Nike, and Shell. Ironically, the movement itself is reliant on the technologies and effects of globalisation. One of the most well-known anti-globalisation cultural resistance movements is Occupy. The Occupy movement began in 2011 with a small group of protesters in Manhattan camping out in ('occupying') Wall Street to highlight economic and social inequities. It soon grew to occupations all over the world, and many activists allege that the movement changed the discourse around many forms of injustice. Social media was critical to rallying people to support this anti-globalisation movement: the *New York Times* claimed that Occupy Wall Street was 'capable of summoning an army with the posting of a tweet' (Feuer 2012, n.p.). In his book *Media, Politics and the Network Society*, Robert Hassan points out that the shared focus of anti-globalisation protesters and the ability to form activist networks 'would have been impossible without the intercommunication made possible by ICTs and through such websites as <www.indymedia.org>' (Hassan 2004, p. 109).

Castells conceptualises globalisation in terms of a 'network society', which he considers to be the prevailing social structure of the information age. From this perspective, media globalisation has significant financial and cultural ramifications: for instance, the internet is the means by which we access information, power, knowledge, and advantageous networks in many realms of economic, social, and political activity. For those who do not have access to the internet, media globalisation can be a powerful mechanism of social exclusion. It is important to critique the ownership and control of the infrastructure of the network society because

> There is a systemic relationship between the new, knowledge-based, global network economy, and the intensification of inequality, poverty and social exclusion throughout the world. The trend is not related to technology or to globalisation per se, but to the institutional conditions under which globalisation proceeds and the information technology revolution expands (Castells 2001a, p. 157).

The debilitating effect of the digital divide on developing nations in a networked global society has been compared to attempting to make the kind of progress achieved during the Industrial Revolution without electricity: 'Information technology is the electricity of the Information Age' (Castells 2001a, p. 156). In other words, the global economy is powered by the internet, and to be not connected impacts seriously on development. Castells argues that the internet is controlled by an elite group and that spatial inequalities exist in accessing the internet (2010, p. 377). It is important to acknowledge such disparities not only in terms of access, but also in a person's capacity to use digital technologies (Selwyn 2004, p. 346). Therefore this is not a simple binary divide referring to access to the internet. Issues such as quality of connection, cost of connection, and literacy are all part of what we mean when we talk about the 'digital divide'. While information poverty and not enough access to digital media are serious concerns, proponents of the cultural imperialism thesis consider that too much access to the media can also be problematic.

Cultural imperialism describes how one culture spreads its values and ideas culturally, such as through the media rather than through direct rule or economic trading. The global reach of Hollywood films and US television is the most obvious example (see p. 422). Economic trading is also important because commodities from toys to tennis shoes, soft drinks to smartphones, are carriers of culture. The term 'coca-colonisation' (Klein 2000, p. 131) succinctly expresses the links between colonisation, the global spread of commodities and brands, and cultural imperialism. Cultural imperialism is, according

◀ CULTURAL IMPERIALISM

Imperial domination of the world maintained partly through the dissemination of cultural products. Argues that the globalisation of communication results in domination over traditional cultures, and the intrusion of Western culture and values such as consumerism.

to Schiller, who coined the term, a form of transnational corporate cultural domination (Schiller 1992, p. 39).

According to media theorist John Thompson, the cultural imperialism thesis can be summarised as follows:

> The globalisation of communication has been driven by the pursuit of the commercial interests of large US-based transnational corporations, often acting in collaboration with Western (predominantly American) political and military interests; and this process has resulted in a new form of dependency in which the traditional cultures are destroyed through the intrusion of Western values (Thompson 1995, p. 165).

Schiller argues that global monopolies and the proliferation of ICTs bring the threat of cultural imperialism and the loss of cultural diversity. Because the globalisation of communication has been driven by the pursuit of profit, and because new communication technologies are developed to serve the interests of giant transnational media corporations (in ways that often overlap with Western political and military interests), the process of globalisation has, according to Schiller, contributed to the destruction of traditional cultures and dependence on Western value systems. Schiller claims that

> The heaviest cost of transnational corporate-produced culture, however, is that it erodes the priceless idea of the public good and the vital principle of social accountability and the longtime dream of international community. Substituted for these elemental human aspirations is the promise of consumer choice—a choice that is not genuine (Schiller 1998, p. 11).

Even in a state where there appears to be a great deal of choice between television and radio channels, newspapers, and magazines, citizens may not be the recipients of a diversity of content or have access to a range of critical and political perspectives. In an industry dominated by just a few key players, freedom of information and freedom of choice may be comforting illusions. While citizens are able to choose between many media products, they may all be controlled by one corporation.

CONTRADICTORY DISCOURSES OF GLOBALISATION

In *Media Unlimited* (2001) Todd Gitlin claims that 'If there is a global village, it speaks American. It wears jeans, drinks Coke, eats at the golden arches, walks on swooshed shoes, plays electric guitars, recognizes Mickey Mouse, James Dean, ET, Bart Simpson, R2-D2, and Pamela Anderson'. That said, global media flows are not unidirectional: globalisation has also profoundly altered the nature of American popular culture, which is especially evident in the influence of Asian media such as Japanese anime, Bollywood films, and Bhangra music (Jenkins 2006b, p. 153).

These different perspectives on globalisation can be discerned on the cover of the Benetton magazine, *Colors*, with the title 'Monoculture'. Bright red liquid is splattered across the page, forming an image recognisable as the Disney character Mickey Mouse. If we read this image as an image of bloodshed, then the question we must ask is: who or what has died, and how is Disney implicated in this death? There are several different responses to this question, many of which point to the positive and negative aspects of globalisation. One answer is that globalisation and cultural imperialism might produce a monoculture, leading to the death of cultural difference and diversity, and the loss of non-American cultural traditions and customs. The other answer, based on the signifier of the internet address turned into a smile on Mickey's mouth, is that the internet and other media have linked people across the globe together into a global village or a virtual community. These positive aspects of globalisation are specifically linked to the ability of communication media to bring people closer together, inform us of issues and events in distant places, and create a sense of unification: one culture shared by all humanity.

Schiller's observation that American popular culture is spreading throughout the world, carried by characters such as Mickey Mouse and by corporations such as Disney, is incontestable; however, this does not necessarily mean that local cultures will die out as a result. Extensive research into audience reception, including ethnographic studies of audience responses to media texts, indicates that people don't passively absorb media content without resisting, negotiating, and contextualising the message. Communication is a two-way exchange of meaning, and media reception is not so much like absorption as it is appropriation, which suggests that divisions between cultures might die without destroying cultural diversity. Globalisation may leave us smiling after all.

Figure 25.3 Cover of Benetton magazine

The image in Figure 25.4 is an advertisement for Channel O (Channel 87) on DSTV in southern Africa. This channel addresses a predominantly black audience and the advertisement shows an awareness of the discourse of cultural imperialism by branding the channel as 'uncolonized'. In other words, Channel O is claiming not to be dominated by foreign media products that feature and address white Americans. The image shows an Oreo (a popular brand of American sweet biscuit), but the biscuit doesn't have its usual white filling. The term 'Oreo' is used to describe people who are black on the outside but white inside; in other words, Oreos are black people who have assimilated white culture and adopted the lifestyles and values of white people. In the DSTV advertisement the Oreo is entirely black, reinforced by an accompanying advertising slogan, 'Get back to black', meaning that watching the black-oriented programming on Channel O will help the black audience stay in touch with its cultural identity. Ironically, South Africa has been accused of its own form of cultural imperialism because it exports South African culture via film and television to the rest of southern Africa, partly through DSTV's Channel O.

Most theorists now acknowledge that the globalisation of communication has not led to straightforward American dominance or to global harmony, but has resulted in a complex process of adaptation, appropriation, hybridisation, and mutual incorporation of different cultural texts and traditions as the media spread knowledge of different

Figure 25.4 Oreo advertisement for Channel 0: DSTV

Source: DSTV MultiChoice Africa

cultures around the globe. Power relations of domination and dependency certainly do exist, but the exchange of culture through the media is certainly not one-way or entirely negative. The cultural imperialism thesis is also undermined by the fact that traditional cultures were not pristine or isolated prior to electronic invasion and the influx of American television programs and merchandise. There have been cultural mixing and domination for centuries, as the history of globalisation shows. The global economy has several big players: the USA doesn't control it and should not be held responsible for all of its inadequacies.

Cultural imperialism and Hollywood

While the USA is not the only controlling force in the media world, the global predominance of American films has an economic basis. Commercial film production was established in Hollywood through the studio system and was centrally controlled by a small group of studios such as Warner Brothers and MGM (Cook 1985, pp. 7–8, 10–25). The American film and television industries play a significant part in the American economy, bringing in enormous profits to the USA from many other countries, partly at the expense of local media industries. There are many debates about how much American cinema and television should be screened in other countries. In some countries, it is perceived that there are cultural, economic, and moral benefits and dangers involved in the predominance of American cinema and television.

The positive myths of the USA are that it is a land of opportunity, freedom, prosperity, and equality. It is seen as a melting-pot society in which anyone can succeed, and is thus perceived as a great escape from older, more traditional, and restricted societies. American culture promises energy, sexiness, and freedom, American fashions and style are taken up by young people in every continent, and capitalism and competition have become the new ideals of former communist countries. But some fear this cultural dominance because it glorifies materialist values, and because the economic interests with which it is allied seem to be taking over and exploiting the rest of the world. They are apprehensive of the way it erodes traditional values and of its competitive harshness.

One way of considering this issue is to suggest that television and cinema should aim to tell a culture's own stories, for example, that Australia, the UK, and African countries should present stories about Australian, British, or African people set in their own countries. Because of concerns about cultural imperialism, media policies and trade agreements that govern the global flow of cultural products such as film and television, and that restrict foreign media ownership, are very important.

World music

World music is an interesting case to examine in relation to globalisation. World music, particularly African and Latin American music, is now played and marketed around the world, and it influences European and American styles and invites openness to other cultural influences. For example, the New York indie band Vampire Weekend, famous for its marimba rhythms and nonsensical lyrics, is one of the most popular bands to incorporate a distinctive world music sound, even though the musicians are white, middle class graduates of Columbia University and their music videos (such as 'Diane Young') satirise privileged American youth culture. Perhaps this demonstrates that Eurocentrism is coming to an end. The spread of world music is not cultural imperialism but a flow of culture back from previously colonised states.

World music is also influenced by Western music styles and by Western recording and sampling technology, and the production and marketing of world music is still largely in the hands of a few European and US companies that receive a bigger percentage of the profits than do the artists who make the music. In some instances songs include recordings of indigenous music but no money goes to the original artists. 'Wimoweh', also known as 'The Lion Sleeps Tonight', was originally a Zulu song written by Solomon Linda in 1939. Until recently Linda was not credited as the songwriter and received no royalties, even as Western folk musicians such as the Weavers and the Kingston Trio profited handsomely from recording their own versions of the song and Disney made a fortune using it in *The Lion King*. It was not until 2005, when South African filmmaker Francois Verster made a documentary about the origins of the song and Rian Malan (2000) wrote an article about it in *Rolling Stone*, that Linda's family received compensation and acknowledgment for the use of his work.

Although Disney films may not be your preference, chances are your choices in music have something to do with film soundtracks, music videos, MTV, and the promotional machine surrounding bands signed to large record labels. MTV itself is more than a marketing machine for the products it advertises between songs and the albums it promotes with its music videos; it is also a truly global communication brand in its own right. Music is also used to sell non-music products and to build brand images (Sprite's association with hip-hop is a good example). The implications of this are that there are positive and negative outcomes of globalisation: the media play a positive role in helping us learn about and share in each other's cultures, but they are also implicated in wasteful and exploitative marketing practices that primarily benefit the top tier of corporate executives.

TACTICAL MEDIA RESPONSES TO GLOBALISATION

While there are certainly advantageous aspects of globalisation, it also has its drawbacks, and resisting those aspects perceived as negative can seem overwhelming for individuals because globalisation is such a powerful force. French cultural theorist Michel de Certeau suggests in his influential book *The Practice of Everyday Life* (1984) that there are ways in which ordinary people develop tactics for expressing autonomy and struggling against oppressive norms in everyday practices. This conception of grassroots resistance has been developed by Geert Lovink and David Garcia in their online essay 'ABC of Tactical Media' (1997), which details everyday tactics for using ICTs to hybridise, subvert, innovate, organise, and communicate in ways that take advantage of media globalisation and harness it to serve the interests of civil society and media activism. Building on the idea of tactical responses to globalisation, here are some suggestions that may move us towards a more balanced global society.

- Use the internet to find and disseminate information about ethical consumerism in order to make informed choices about which companies to support and which to boycott.
- Tap into the open source software movement, which shares information instead of using copyright law to serve the interests of companies such as Microsoft.
- Organise online networks of like-minded people and groups to work towards a common cause.
- Encourage self-representation and affirmation of the value of the local.
- Create and support independent media, and encourage diversity of content and ownership.
- Lobby media policymakers to serve citizens, not corporate interests.
- Publicise media issues, promote media literacy, and provide technological training.
- Use ICTs to promote transparency, accountability, and empowerment.

Whichever tactics you choose, the important thing is to find ways to make the best of globalisation and technological developments, and to resist the aspects that you perceive as damaging. As media consumers and as future members of the media industry, you will influence the process of change and development, as well as being affected by it.

CONCLUSION

Although globalisation is not restricted to the media, the most important points for media students to focus on include the relationship between globalisation and technological and economic changes in the media industries. These changes have significant social and cultural impacts all over the world. Critical perspectives on globalisation, such as accounts of cultural imperialism, the network society, and imagined communities, are attempts to interpret these changes. This chapter has critically evaluated diverse theoretical perspectives on globalisation and revealed a variety of ways in which it has the potential to be empowering, as well as disempowering, for media producers and consumers.

This chapter has

- outlined key theoretical positions in relation to globalisation
- explained how popular terminology such as 'the digital divide', 'the network society', 'imagined communities', and 'the global village' relates to changes in global media
- discussed the positive and negative impacts of globalisation.

? | DISCUSSION POINTS

1   Can you think of any other ideas to add to the list of tactical media responses to globalisation?
2   Note down all of the ways in which globalisation affects your daily life. Divide your list into positives and negatives and consider whether, on balance, you favour a utopian or a dystopian view of globalisation.

SUMMARY

You should now be able to

- assess the relationship between new communication technologies and social change
- evaluate how the digital divide impacts on your community and others
- discuss how globalisation has developed historically and how it influences contemporary life
- list the key characteristics, costs, and benefits of globalisation
- distinguish between and debate the merits of Benedict Anderson's, Marshall McLuhan's, Manuel Castells', and Herbert Schiller's perspectives on globalisation.

CONCLUSION

This book has been about the media and their relationship with the world. We have argued that there is a series of complex media-world relationships, or media influences on the world, and we have attempted to unravel them. Our focus has been on language, texts, representations, discourses, and ideology: these are the ways in which we apprehend the world, the ways in which we give it shape and form. As Thomas King (2003) says: 'The truth about stories is that that's all we are' (this book is itself just another text). We have looked closely at various media products, taken them apart bit by bit, and mixed appreciation with criticism.

We have also considered how media technologies have developed and are developing. Having read this book, you should be able to draw on a body of theory, past and present, with which you can begin to make sense of the media-world in which you live.

Important social and psychological questions remain: will late capitalism continue, or will we move into a new phase? What directions should we take in the twenty-first century? Can we reach new heights of sophisticated cultural development, especially through the evolution of new technologies? Will progress be accompanied by new difficulties, such as economic inequalities, social disruptions, and environmental uncertainties? What will the role of the media be in this new era?

We have suggested that we need to look carefully at five important areas in relation to our future lives, areas that cover the personal, the social, and the global.

Gender, sexuality, and the family. How do we live out our gendered and sexual lives? Is the family the place to do this? Does the family need to change, or should we evolve new forms? How do men and women resolve issues relating to power, oppression, intimacy, sexuality, and love?

Work. What forms of work will be fulfilling for us and will provide balanced growth, material and spiritual, for the planet as a whole?

Issues of ethnicity and race. Together with religion, these issues form one of the major sources of social division around the world. They are connected directly to issues of economic inequality and global economic imbalance. We have not paid detailed attention in this book to questions of the oppression of Aboriginal Australians and the way in which the media represent them. However, we hope that the frameworks given, and many of the examples from other countries, will enable you to explore these issues further. Any ideal of the future has to address and resolve issues of racism and discrimination, and must involve finding ways in which people can live harmoniously together.

Ecological and environmental issues. Media studies has tended to focus on humans. Today, ecological issues relating to all living species, and to the planet as a whole, are pressing. Questions about how we and the planet can survive in the twenty-first century are paramount. While this book has not examined in detail how the media deal with such issues, this question will become even more important in the near future. We hope that you have found, in this book, useful insights about the relationship between the media and our ecological future.

Technology, interactivity, and globalisation. Keeping abreast of technological advances, particularly new forms of interactive communication technologies, is an important aspect of media studies and social change. Being well-informed and conscientious consumers of the media and other cultural products can help to make sure that the interconnections linking humans all over the world result in positive influences on other lives, rather than inadvertently widening the gap between the rich and the poor, or between those with access to resources, opportunities, and information, and those without.

The media will continue to explore and represent these five broad issues, which will continue to be crucial aspects of the world you live in. We hope that your engagement with the media and with society is enriched by the ideas and insights offered here, and that media studies connects in relevant ways with the interests and ideals that you pursue in your everyday life.

GLOSSARY

After each term, there is a page reference in brackets. This refers to the page in the text on which the term appears.

actual reader (page 92)
The real flesh-and-blood individuals who interpret or read texts.

adbusting (page 205)
Adbusting involves modifying advertisements to undermine their intended meaning (for more information see <www.adbusters.org>).

agenda setting (page 24)
The process by which media producers set up the issues—the agenda—that the media will focus on and that audiences will subsequently perceive to be important.

algorithms (page 107)
Rule-based calculations or step-by-step mathematical or computational information processing: 'a set of mathematical procedures whose purpose is to expose some truth or tendency about the world' (Striphas 2015, p. 405).

alternative/oppositional reading (page 96)
Audiences interpret a text completely against the preferred reading.

analogue media (page 100)
Analogue media such as photography, print, and radio use material processes and mechanical modes of representation to transcribe and transmit content in forms such as physical data or electrical signals.

anchorage (page 134)
Anchorage limits polysemy by articulating the preferred meaning of a text, as a caption labels an image.

angle (page 83)
In journalism the angle is the central focus or the main idea in the organisation and presentation of a story and its lead.

arbitrary signifier (page 129)
Arbitrary signifiers have no logical connection to their signified. The signifier does not look or sound like the signified, nor does it point to the signified in a causal or indexical fashion.

auteur theory (page 89)
The theory that films are the creative products of film directors and can be interpreted as their personal visions, marked by a unique 'signature style'.

avant-garde (page 238)
Literally means 'advance guard'; refers to cultural products that are seen as unconventionally new and different from mainstream culture but which will supposedly lead cultural developments forward.

balance (page 80)
Balanced reporting entails the presentation of both sides of an argument, giving them equal space and time.

bankability (page 377)
The stars' potential to guarantee a film's financial box office success.

binary oppositions (page 251)
A means of cultural classification that splits the world into sets of dualistic opposing categories, such as male and female, black and white.

biological essentialist (page 313)
The belief that the physical body—the hormones, inherent instincts, and genetic predispositions etc.—defines the essence of identity and determines personality characteristics, behaviour, and abilities.

bricolage (page 408)
The putting together of different, often contradictory, cultural forms, thereby creating new meanings.

broadcast (page 106)
A means of media transmission that makes information available to a broad spectrum of the population.

capitalism (page 8)
The dominant global economic system, organised by workers selling their labour for wages, and investors making profit through interest and economic growth. Capitalism, which gradually replaced the feudal economic system from about 1600, is characterised by private ownership and control of the means of production (capital) by individuals and corporations.

catharsis (page 288)
The expression and release, or purging, of emotions by audiences at the climax of a tragedy or drama.

celanthropist (page 377)
A type of celebrity activist who engages in philanthropic activities. These are celebrities who not only use their 'brand' and time to endorse a cause, they spend their own money on causes they endorse.

celebrity (page 375)
A celebrity is a well-known, highly visible public figure whose private life and public appearances frequently attract the media spotlight, often for reasons other than their professional standing or abilities.

cinéma vérité (page 275)
French for 'cinema truth'. A documentary style developed in France in the 1950s and 1960s, cinéma vérité is similar to direct cinema, fly-on-the-wall documentary, and observational documentary, but the filmmakers participate more directly and self-reflexively in the narrative.

cinematography (page 223)
The processes of filming the mise en scène—how things are filmed. This includes the angles (for example, high or low) and positioning of the

camera (for example, long-shot or close-up), focus and framing, any camera movements (for example, pan, track, zoom, or tilt), any special camera effects (for example, slow motion or time lapse), the film stock used, and processing methods.

CMC (page 5)
Computer-mediated communication.

code (page 124)
Codes are standardised formulas for communicating meaning.

conclusion (page 149)
The conclusion of an essay should summarise the key points and briefly discuss their significance, with reference to the objectives stated in the introduction.

connotation (page 126)
Operating on the second order of signification, connotation refers to the emotions, values, and associations that a sign gives rise to in the reader, viewer, or listener. The connotative meaning of a sign can be expressed by quickly jotting down what it reminds you of, or makes you feel or imagine.

consciousness industry (page 19)
Term used by the Frankfurt School to describe how the media function to control the minds and feelings of the masses at the same time as making money.

content analysis (page 21)
Quantitative measurement of media content.

continuity editing (page 227)
A system of editing, established in Hollywood by about 1920, for telling stories smoothly. It uses particular techniques and conventions for filming within a scene such as the use of establishing shot, use of shot–reverse–shot, eyeline match, match on action, observance of 180 degree rule, and continuity of action, sound, and lighting.

convention (page 124)
Conventions are methods of organising signs to communicate meaning in ways that become habituated and widely shared over time.

core problematic (page 212)
Central problem or opposition that a genre explores.

counter-hegemony (page 187)
A world view or activity that is in opposition to and challenges the dominant world view.

cultivation (page 94)
The media have a cumulative effect on audiences. Long-term exposure to media cultivates attitudes and beliefs through the persistent repetition of messages and images.

cultural capital (page 42)
Like economic capital (money) and social capital (whom you know), cultural capital (assets such as accent, taste, appearance, clothing, and credentials) positions people in the social hierarchy. Possessing cultural capital functions to maintain and advance social status by delineating social groups and often reproducing social inequalities.

cultural imperialism (pages 23 and 419)
Imperial domination of the world maintained partly through the dissemination of cultural products. Argues that the globalisation of communication results in domination over traditional cultures, and the intrusion of Western culture and values such as consumerism.

culture jamming (page 193)
A form of media activism that subverts and reworks the intended meaning of existing media texts, or parodies major corporations, public figures, and their media images.

defamation (page 199)
Defamation involves publicising information that is untrue and so injures someone's reputation, or if it is deemed to be not in the public interest for that information to be published.

denotation (page 125)
Denotation is what Barthes calls 'the first order of signification'. It is the most obvious level on which a sign communicates and it refers to the common-sense meaning of the sign. The denotative meaning can be expressed by describing the sign as simply as possible.

desensitisation (page 95)
Long-term exposure to media can make audiences progressively less sensitive or responsive to images and messages that made a strong impression when first encountered.

dialectical synthesis (page 252)
Two opposing forces (such as good and evil, or thesis and antithesis) generate conflict or debate that is resolved when the two sides come together in a form of synthesis.

diegetic sound (page 225)
Sound that comes directly from the fictional world (the diegesis) of a screen text.

différance (page 147)
Refers to an endless chain of signification in which each sign or signifier is linked to or associated with something else, so that the complete or final meaning is infinitely deferred.

digital divide (page 6)
The increasing gap between those who have and those who do not have access to technology, access to content, ICT skills, and money to pay for digital services; most often used to refer to the difference between the developed and developing worlds' access to the benefits of digital technology.

digital media (page 100)
Media such as digital video games, the internet, and other forms of computerised media that mathematically process and convert whatever information needs to be represented into numerical form. The information can then be manipulated, reproduced, converted, shared, and transmitted in versatile, swift, immaterial ways.

digital onscreen graphics (dogs) (page 144)
Dogs or 'bugs' often take the form of station logos or other information added at the bottom of the frame during post production. Such graphics

can brand television programs and the networks on which they screen, they can prevent piracy, advertise the next program, or offer viewers extra information.

direct address (page 271)

Direct address to camera is when the person onscreen looks straight into the camera as though they are looking at and addressing the audience directly. This breaks the conventions of cinematic realism by acknowledging the process of filming; it also substitutes a different sense of realism, intimacy, and immediacy.

direct cinema (page 275)

The North American corollary of *cinéma vérité*, direct cinema has an observational style, but does not involve interviews or intervention by the filmmakers.

direct effects (page 93)

The direct-effects model of communication (also called the 'hypodermic model') suggests that the media transmit powerful messages to audience members, who absorb the meaning passively and are strongly affected by it.

discourse (page 61)

Discourses are paradigms or ways of understanding that are communicated through texts and language use, and that organise knowledge and social power.

discourse analysis (page 159)

Explores the ways in which power and knowledge are communicated through texts, language use, and systems of thought.

disintermediation (page 115)

To bypass intermediaries, such as publishers and distributors, in order to transmit media directly from the creator to the consumer via self-publishing tools and techniques.

documentaries (page 273)

Films and television programs about real-life situations.

dominant discourse (page 183)

Contemporary ideas and beliefs shared by a majority of people.

dominant ideology (page 176)

A world view that supports the ruling class as dominant, the status quo, yet is shared by the majority of people.

dominant reading (page 87)

The meaning of a text that is accepted by most audience members and can be determined by examining its textual codes and social/historical contexts.

editing (page 223)

The process of joining or splicing together separate pieces of film, separate shots. Edits may cut directly, dissolve, mix, fade, wipe, etc.

emergent discourse (page 183)

New ideas and beliefs held by a few people at first, and then gradually becoming accepted by more people.

epic theatre (page 291)

A form of storytelling or theatre developed by German playwright Bertolt Brecht that challenges conventional storytelling forms by encouraging audience detachment and understanding, rather than emotional identification.

establishing shot (page 224)

A wide or long shot conventionally used to show the whole of a location or set so that we can see and understand the space the action is taking place in. Normally followed by shots that are closer to the action.

Eurocentrism (page 360)

Places European values in a privileged, central position, and sees the world from a European perspective.

expository documentary (page 275)

A voice-over commentary explains what we see, thereby controlling our viewpoint.

extratextual knowledge (page 383)

Knowledge and information taken from sources external to the text.

feminism (page 316)

The movement for women's equality and liberation.

film noir (page 211)

French for 'black film'; black-and-white thrillers or detective stories made in the 1940s and 1950s conventionally featuring low-key lighting, retrospective voice-over narration, flashbacks, suspicion, intrigue, crime, urban settings, and *femmes fatales*.

freedom of speech (page 199)

The right to express opinions publicly without interference from government or other sectors. This right is subject to legal limitations that restrict the publication of material that incites hatred or violence, or is defamatory.

gatekeeping (page 24)

The process of controlling what gets included and whose voices are heard in the media, particularly in the news.

generic hybridisation (page 213)

Generic hybrids are texts that blend the codes and conventions of two or more genres to produce a new combination.

genre (page 210)

Groups of texts that share a set of conventional characteristics such as content, narrative structure, and visual style are classified as textual types or genres.

global village (page 21)

The phrase 'the global village' suggests that the globalisation of communication media has brought the whole world closer together, like a village in which everyone is interconnected.

globalisation (page 413)

Globalisation refers to an international community influenced by technological development and economic, political, and military interests. It is characterised by a worldwide increase in interdependence, interactivity, interconnectedness, and the virtually instantaneous exchange of information. Globalisation could lead to the homogenisation of world cultures, or to hybridisation and multiculturalism.

graphic editing or graphic montage (page 229)
The linking of two separate shots through visual similarity or contrast.

hegemony (page 186)
Power and leadership maintained through processes of struggle and negotiation, especially through winning the consent of the majority of people to accept the ideas or ideologies of the dominant group as common sense.

homoeroticism (page 337)
Sexual desire between same-sex couples, though most commonly used to refer to men; also often refers to the pleasure received in gazing at an attractive member of the same sex in sport, film, etc.

homophobia (page 336)
Fear of same-sex intimacy, though most commonly used to refer to men's fear of homosexuality and emotional closeness between men.

horizontal integration (page 104)
This is a form of convergence of media ownership in which a corporation owns several companies involved in the same aspect of media production.

hypertext (page 103)
Chunks of text or data connected by electronic links in a networked database. Hyperlinks enable the user to navigate through information along multiple, non-linear pathways.

iconic sign (page 129)
The relationship between the signifier and the signified is based on likeness or resemblance.

iconography (page 211)
Visual images (icons) associated with a particular genre that are repeatedly used.

ICTs (page 111)
Information and communication technologies, such as computers.

identification (page 387)
A feeling of connectedness to another person. It involves seeing aspects of oneself in that person, experiencing a sense of relatedness or overlapping of identity.

identity (page 34)
Refers to selfhood, to the characteristics and qualities that uniquely distinguish a person, a group, or a thing from others. The meaning of the term 'identity' is connected to difference (being identifiably unique) and sameness (being identical to oneself, having an essence or personality or qualities that do not change over time).

ideology (page 33)
Ideologies are sets of social values, ideas, beliefs, feelings, and representations by which people collectively make sense of the world they live in, thus constituting a world view. This world view is naturalised, a taken-for-granted, common-sense view about the way the world works.

implied narrative (page 133)
The story that a picture suggests, including the events that may have happened immediately prior to the moment in the image, and immediately afterwards.

incorporation or recuperation (page 182)
The processes by which dangerous, rebellious, radical ideas and movements are made acceptable not by banning or criminalising them, but by partially accepting them; 'incorporated' means, literally, 'taken into the main body'.

indexical sign (page 129)
The relationship between the signifier and the signified is one of indication, direction or measurement, sequence or causation.

inscribed reader (page 92)
An ideal reader who is constructed by the text, or who is imagined/intended by the producers of the text.

intellectual editing or intellectual montage (page 229)
Two images linked together produce an idea or concept.

interpellation (page 168)
A process in which we internalise ideologies as a response to being hailed or addressed.

intertextual knowledge (page 383)
Knowledge and information gained from other related media texts.

intertextuality (page 134)
The process of knowingly borrowing and referring to other texts, or interpreting one text in the light of other related texts.

introduction (page 149)
The introduction of an essay should include an outline of what you aim to achieve (state essay topic, objectives, and the text you are analysing) and how you intend to achieve it (your methodology and structure).

inverted pyramid (page 80)
Information is given in descending order of importance, as in a news report.

ISAs (page 179)
Ideological state apparatuses—the institutions of socialisation and persuasion that societies use to control people, for example, religion, family, education, and media.

jouissance (page 295)
A French word, one meaning of which is 'bliss or ecstasy'; much more powerful, and sometimes more disturbing, than *plaisir* (pleasure).

langue (page 147)
Langue is the fundamental structure that underlies and governs language and expression.

liberal pluralism (page 185)

A liberalist pluralist society is one that includes many different social groups with different viewpoints; they all have the liberty and opportunity to speak out.

Marxism (page 172)

The theories developed by Karl Marx, including that the struggle between different groups in society (classes) brings about historical change, economic needs are the most important factor in determining people's behaviour, and what people think and believe is controlled, often unconsciously, by the dominant social groups.

masochism (page 338)

Pleasure (or perverse sexual gratification) felt when experiencing pain, humiliation, or deprivation. The term is derived from the name of erotic novelist Leopold von Sacher-Masoch.

media (page 4)

The technologically developed communication industries, normally making money, that can transmit information and entertainment across time and space to individuals and/or large groups of people; they are literally in the middle of this process, the means for communication.

media activism (page 194)

Activities involving individuals or lobby groups that attempt to change the way in which the media work, or that use the media to make a social or political statement.

media homogenisation (page 24)

Financial pressures and other forces lead all media products to become similar, standard, and uniform.

media studies (page 12)

Media studies analyses the role of the media in society and studies media technologies, media institutions, and the production, consumption, circulation, and content of media texts.

metonymy (page 142)

Metonyms are signs in which one part or element stands in for or represents something larger.

metrosexuals (page 346)

Young, stylish, urban men who care about and spend considerable money on their appearance, and are attractive to women (and, often, to other men).

mise en scène (page 223)

A French theatrical term meaning literally 'placed in the scene'. *Mise en scène* refers to what has been filmed: settings, objects, costumes, actors, and the way these are visually arranged and lit.

misogyny (page 315)

Hatred of women and femininity (literally, 'hatred of the womb').

modality (page 131)

A measure of the degree of certainty or realism associated with an instance of communication.

mode of address (page 169)

Refers to the way a text speaks to or addresses its audience.

modernism (page 402)

Describes Western art and aesthetic movements of the first half of the twentieth century; characterised by optimism in future progress, and ways of seeing or representing the world that challenged realism, including abstraction and focus on the act of representation.

montage (page 218)

Montage (the French word for 'editing') refers to two specific ways of joining together shots from different spaces and times—MTV-style collage of images set to music, and/or Soviet montage or political montage using Sergei Eisenstein's technique of juxtaposition.

motif (page 228)

Any significant element (an object, colour, place, sound, camera movement, or angle) that recurs or is developed throughout a film.

multiculturalism (page 361)

As a policy or a critical concept, multiculturalism celebrates unity in diversity by bringing together a range of cultural groups within a larger identity or community without privileging one culture over another.

multiplatforming (page 103)

A process of media convergence that involves distributing branded content across multiple outlets; for instance, the narrative and characters of a film or television franchise can be distributed as films, novels, games, soundtrack CDs, and other merchandise, including clothes.

myths (page 292)

Stories that often feature ancient gods or fantasy creatures, that recount how a society evolved. At a rational, scientific level they are fantastic, impossible, and unreal, but they may contain social and psychological truths and insights that offer symbolic resolutions to real issues or questions.

narrative (page 234)

A sequence of events taking place over a given period of time that are linked, mainly through cause and effect.

narrowcast (page 106)

Narrowcast media transmission caters for small groups of people.

negotiated reading (page 96)

Audiences accept only some of what is being presented to them.

news frame (page 83)

The selection and presentation of stories, issues, quotes, headlines, and images influence the way audiences make sense of the news. The processes of inclusion and exclusion, and the use of language, structure, and emphasis convey values, judgments, and perspectives that determine what the audience will consider important.

news values/newsworthiness (page 27)

The elements of an issue or event that make it important enough to report on in the eyes of journalists. Newsworthy features include conflict, relevance, locality, prominence, novelty, and magnitude.

non-diegetic sound (page 225)

Sound that comes from somewhere outside the story world, such as the musical score, which the screen characters cannot hear.

normative theory (page 84)

'Normative' refers to assumed norms and standards of correctness; to ideal views about the role the media should play in society, particularly the functions the press ought to perform.

objectivity (page 26)

Perceiving, reporting, or presenting things from an impersonal, neutral, unbiased perspective.

observational learning and cognitive scripts (page 95)

People learn how to behave by observing how their role models act and by remembering the script that was performed so that if, later, they encounter a similar situation they can play the part.

Orientalism (page 363)

The way Europe has perceived, understood, and attempted to control cultures beyond the Oriental line.

paradigm (page 82)

A set of terms, things, or ideas all based on a common theme or unifying system.

parole (page 147)

Parole is a particular instance of language use or expression, when the underlying rules (*langue*) are put into practice.

patriarchy (page 315)

A social structure in which the father or a male figure is the leader and descent is reckoned on the male line. Masculine power and authority dominate social, political, and economic institutions, thereby oppressing women.

plaisir (page 295)

French for 'pleasure'; the kind of enjoyment derived from fictions that do not have a strong or enduring impact.

point of view (page 242)

The positions that cameras take and whose viewpoint they show the viewer.

political economy (page 22)

Explains how the media are determined by a combination of economic, social, and political factors, particularly ownership and control of the media.

polysemic (page 96)

A sign that has more than one possible meaning.

postcolonialism (page 398)

The historical period after colonialism; ways of understanding the (ongoing) effects of colonialism.

postfeminism (page 318)

The term can be used to suggest that feminism is in the past, outdated, no longer relevant to contemporary gender dynamics. Alternatively, postfeminism can refer to a postmodern approach to feminism and/or contemporary critiques of earlier feminisms.

postmodernism (page 400)

Originally a style in architecture, the term was later used to describe the late-twentieth-century world and as a style of cultural production.

poststructuralism (page 397)

Poststructuralism develops and challenges structuralist approaches, taking more account of the way contexts and audiences can produce more fluid meanings and readings of media texts.

preferred reading (page 96)

Audiences accept what is being presented without questioning the meaning intended by the media producers.

product placement (page 52)

Companies pay film and television producers to include their products in a story as a subtle form of advertising.

projection (page 97)

People project their own unconscious feelings onto other people or objects; they see in objects and other people aspects of themselves reflected back.

psychoanalysis (page 303)

Psychoanalysis, as developed by Sigmund Freud, argues that people are motivated by their unconscious, that there are several developmental stages people go through as they grow up, and that psychoanalysis can make people aware of their unconscious conflicts, fantasies, and desires (which are attributed chiefly to the development of the sexual instinct) through the free association of ideas, analysis, and interpretation of their dreams.

realism (page 296)

Objects in art—paintings, sculpture, literature—that appear true to real life and the aesthetic methods or styles used to create them. Realism, the dominant aesthetic in painting and literature in the nineteenth century, aimed for verisimilitude and focused on the lives of ordinary people.

reality TV (page 280)

The general premise is that reality-based programs portray people who are not actors saying lines that are not scripted in situations that are drawn from real life but often are constructed and filmed in a manner designed to capture a sense of authenticity, immediacy, and realism.

reception studies (page 92)

The study of how audiences actively receive, read, consume, and interact with media texts.

reinforcement (page 94)

The media reinforce ideas and feelings that other social institutions are already communicating.

repressed desire (page 304)

The act of repression forms the unconscious. Forbidden material (Oedipal desire, for example) is rejected from conscious thought, but not destroyed. It is stored in the unconscious from where it continues to produce effects.

residual discourse (page 183)

Set of ideas and beliefs from the past that are still accepted by some people.

rhythmic editing or rhythmic montage (page 228)

Rhythmic editing means the pace of editing—how long each shot lasts.

RSAs (page 179)

Repressive state apparatuses—the institutions of force that societies use to control people, for example, the army, police, law courts, and prisons.

scopophilia (page 303)

From the Greek; love of looking, a basic human drive.

self-reflexivity (page 279)

The process whereby media texts self-consciously refer back to themselves, often drawing our attention to their construction.

semiology (page 122)

Semiology (also called semiotics) is the science of signs, or the study of signs and sign systems.

shadow (page 366)

Parts of our personality that we have hidden, denied, and repressed, also known as the alter ego.

sign (page 123)

Communicates meaning by standing in for or representing a thing or an idea.

signified (page 123)

The thing or idea that a sign refers to.

signifier (page 123)

The visible, tangible, or audible aspect of a sign that carries the meaning.

slacktivism (page 17)

A combination of the terms 'slacker' and 'activism'. Slacktivism (also known as 'hashtag activism') refers to the use of the internet to support a social or political cause in a superficial way that requires little effort or risk, such as signing online petitions or using social media to endorse social justice activities. Arguably, this form of activism chiefly benefits the conscience or the self-image of the slacktivist without requiring them to take genuine action to further social justice.

social constructionist (page 313)

Sees identity as constructed by external social forces such as the media, family, education, religion, and expectations of community members.

sound bridge (page 230)

Sound is used to link two separate shots.

soundtrack (page 223)

The recorded combination of human voices, sound effects, and music.

star (page 375)

Stardom is an elite type of celebrity based, at least initially, on a person's outstanding professional achievement. Stars play well-publicised leading roles in popular culture and entertainment media. They consistently outshine colleagues and competitors, and their personal and professional lives attract significant attention.

star image (page 383)

The qualities, ideals, and values that a star represents, based on their films and other performances, and on media information circulated about them.

structuralism (page 235)

A method of analysis that involves looking for and examining the underlying structures of meaning in language, social relationships, narratives, and so forth.

subculture (page 14)

People who share cultural activities such as dress, leisure activities, and social beliefs, that are resistant or opposed to mainstream culture; used mainly in relation to youth cultures.

subjectivity (page 171)

Pertains to an individual's personal thoughts and experiences, their own—subjective—way of seeing the world, as distinct from general or universal experience, and objectivity.

surveillance (page 107)

The term 'surveillance' derives from Latin and French words for 'survey' (to oversee; to have a comprehensive view) and 'vigil' (to be watchful); hence it has connotations of watching over a person in a controlling manner. Academics such as Michel Foucault have examined how regimes of discipline and punishment function through self-surveillance, as well as through public punishment and the architectural designs of prisons (such as the panopticon, in which prisoners are always visible to an unseen guard in an all-seeing guard tower). Contemporary surveillance also has connotations of both counter-terrorism security protocols and voyeurism.

symbolic sign (page 129)

The relationship between the signifier and the signified is arbitrary (there is no natural link) and is based on culture, context, and convention.

syntagm (page 82)

Syntagm, like syntax, is a term that refers to the structure or pattern of words in a sentence, or things in a sequence.

technological determinism (page 109)

The view that technological innovation reshapes social life and drives social change. Technology determines how society functions, rather than society determining how technology should be developed or used.

textual analysis (page 28)

The process of interpreting and analysing any media text, typically focusing on its form and content, style, and structure.

thesis statement (page 149)

The part of an essay that outlines the central argument is called the thesis; it should be briefly stated in the introduction, and developed throughout the essay. You should also consider possible objections and counterarguments (the antithesis) in order to weigh up different points of view and defend your ideas.

uses-and-gratifications (page 95)
Audiences use the media in unpredictable ways (through selection, interpretation, and integration with other everyday activities) to please themselves, not necessarily as media producers intend them to be used.

Verfremdung (distanciation, alienation) (page 292)
Aesthetic techniques that make the audience step back from their emotional narrative involvement to a more critical position, which often enables them to see familiar things in a surprising new way.

vertical integration (page 103)
This term describes a concentration of power when a media company owns various parts of the production, distribution, and exhibition chain, for example, printing presses, magazine companies, content providers such as photographic databases, the distribution vehicles, and retail outlets.

REFERENCES

ABC Radio National 1995 (7, 14, 21, 28 October), 'Talk, Talk, Talk' (originally produced by Canadian Broadcast Corporation), broadcast on *The Science Show*.

—— 1996, *Media Report*, 29 August.

—— 2000a, *Media Report*, 7 December.

—— 2000b, *Media Report*, 21 December.

—— 2004, *Big Ideas*, February.

Achbar, M (ed.) 1995, *Manufacturing Consent: Noam Chomsky and the Media*, Black Rose Books, Montreal and New York.

Adbusters website, <www.adbusters.org/home>

Alter C 2015, 'The World's Obsession with Amal Isn't about Her Accomplishments', *Time*, <http://time.com/3687871/amal-clooney-fashion-robes-turkey>

Althusser, L 1977, 'Ideology and Ideological State Apparatuses', in *Lenin and Philosophy*, New Left Books, London.

American Beauty (DVD) 2000, dir. Sam Mendes, USA.

Anderson, B 1983, *Imagined Communities: Reflections on the Origin and Spread of Nationalism*, Verso, London.

—— 1991, *Imagined Communities*, rev. edn, Verso, London and New York.

Andrejevic, M 2012, 'Brain Whisperers: Cutting through the Clutter with Neuromarketing', *Somatechnics* 2.2, pp. 198–215.

Ang, I 1985, *Watching Dallas: Soap Opera and the Melodramatic Imagination*, Methuen, London.

—— 1991, *Desperately Seeking the Audience*, Routledge, London.

Anthony, A 2013, 'Mandela Funeral Selfie Adds to Image Problem for Denmark's Prime Minister', *The Guardian* <www.theguardian.com/world/2013/dec/14/helle-thorning-schmidt-selfie-mandela-denmark>.

Armes, R 1971, *Patterns of Realism*, Tantivy, London.

Bajde, D, Kos Koklic, M, & Bajde, J 2015, 'Back to Consumption and Production? Prosumers Negotiating the WMG Lockdown on YouTube', *Journal of Consumer Behaviour*, 14, pp. 297–306.

Baker, A & Boyd, T (eds) 1997, *Out of Bounds: Sports, Media, and the Politics of Identity*, Indiana University Press, Bloomington and Indianapolis.

Balogh, S 2007, 'There's a NewTube', *Courier Mail*, 24–25 March 2007, p. 18.

Bandura, A 1994, 'Social Cognitive Theory of Mass Communication', in J Bryant & D Zillmann (eds), *Media Effects: Advances in Theory and Research* (pp. 61–90), Lawrence Erlbaum, Hillsdale, NJ.

Barcardi, F 2014, 'Ellen's Oscar Selfie Breaks Twitter Record', *Variety* <http://variety.com/2014/film/awards/oscars-ellen-degeneres-breaks-twitter-with-epic-group-selfie-1201124224>.

Barthes, R 1973, *Mythologies*, Paladin, London.

—— 1974, *S / Z*, Hill and Wang, New York.

—— 1975, *The Pleasure of the Text*, Hill and Wang, New York.

—— 1977, 'The Death of the Author', in R Barthes, *Image, Music, Text*, Fontana, London.

Bartko, E & Mertz, E 2016, '"Help Kenya, not Kanye": West's Narcissistic Tweets inadvertently Help Edmonton Charity', *Global News* (1 March) <http://globalnews.ca/news/2549431/kanye-wests-narcissistic-tweets-inadvertently-helps-edmonton-charity>.

Baudrillard, J 1988, *Jean Baudrillard: Selected Writings*, Stanford University Press, Palo Alto, CA.

Baudry, J-L 1992, 'The Apparatus: Metapsychological Approaches to the Impression of Reality in Cinema', in G Mast, M Cohen, & L Braudy (eds), *Film Theory and Criticism: Introductory Readings*, 4th edn, Oxford University Press, New York.

Bell, A, Joyce, M & Rivers, D 1999, *Advanced Media Studies*, Hodder & Stoughton, London.

Benjamin, W 1977, *Understanding Brecht*, New Left Books, London.

Berger, J 1972, *Ways of Seeing*, Penguin, Harmondsworth, and BBC Television, London.

Bettelheim, B 1978, *The Uses of Enchantment: The Meaning and Importance of Fairy Tales*, Peregrine, London.

Biddulph, S 1994, *Manhood*, Finch Publishing, Sydney.

—— 1997, *Raising Boys*, Finch Publishing, Sydney.

Bishop, M & Green, M 2008, *Philanthrocapitalism: How the Rich can Save the World*, Bloomsbury, New York.

Blumler, J & Katz, E (eds) 1974, *The Uses of Mass Communications: Current Perspectives on Gratifications Research*, Sage, Beverly Hills and London.

Bly, R 1990, *Iron John*, Vintage, London.

Bogle, T 1973, *Toms, Coons, Mulattoes and Bucks: An Interpretative History of Blacks in American Films*, Viking Press, New York.

Boorstin, D 2006, 'From Hero to Celebrity: The Human Pseudo-event', in P D Marshall (ed.), *The Celebrity Culture Reader*, Routledge, New York.

Bordwell, D & Thompson, K 2004, *Film Art: An Introduction*, 7th edn, McGraw Hill, New York.

Bourdieu, P 1986, *Distinction: A Social Critique of the Judgement of Taste*, trans. Richard Nice, Routledge, London.

Bradbury, M & McFarlane, J (eds) 1976, *Modernism, 1890–1930*, Penguin, Harmondsworth.

Brando, M & Lindsey, R 1994, *Brando: Songs My Mother Taught Me*, Random House, New York.

Brohm, J 1978, *Sport: A Prison of Measured Time*, Ink Links, London.

Brown, S 2004, 'Principal Adviser on Technology Issues for United Nations', quoted on ABC's Radio National *News*, 27 July 2004.

Brown, W & Fraser, B 2004, 'Celebrity Identification', in A Singhal, M Cody, E Rogers, & M Sabido (eds), *Entertainment Education*, Lawrence Erlbaum, Hillsdale, NJ.

Brunsdon, C 1986, 'Women Watching Television', *MediaKulture*, vol. 4.

Bushman, B & Anderson, C 2001, 'Media Violence and the American Public: Scientific Facts versus Media Misinformation', *American Psychologist*, 56, no. 6/7, pp. 477–89.

—— & Huesmann, L R 2001, 'Effects of Televised Violence on Aggression', in D Singer & J Singer (eds), *Handbook of Children and the Media*, Sage, Thousand Oaks, CA, pp. 223–54.

Butler, J 1990, *Gender Trouble: Feminism and the Subversion of Identity*, Routledge, London.

—— 1998, 'Imitation and Gender Insubordination', in J Rivkin & M Ryan (eds), *Literary Theory: An Anthology*, Blackwell, Malden, MA.

Cameron, D 2007, *The Myth of Mars and Venus: Do Men and Women Really Speak Different Languages?* Oxford University Press, Oxford and New York.

Campbell, J 1972, *The Hero with a Thousand Faces*, Princeton University Press, Princeton, NJ.

—— 1988a, *The Power of Myth*, Anchor, New York.

—— 1988b, *Joseph Campbell and the Power of Myth* (video), Mystic Fire Video, in association with *Parabola Magazine*, New York (distributed in Australia by the ABC).

—— 1991, *Occidental Mythology: The Masks of God*, Arkana, New York.

Canter A 2015, 'Banksy's Dismaland: "A Theme Park Unsuitable for Children" – in Pictures', *The Guardian* <www.theguardian.com/artanddesign/gallery/2015/aug/20/banksy-dismaland-a-theme-park-unsuitable-for-children-in-pictures>

Carah, N 2015, 'Algorithmic Brands: A Decade of Brand Experiments with Mobile and Social Media', *New Media and Society*, pp. 1–17.

—— & M Shaul, 2016, 'Brands and Instagram: Point, Tap, Swipe, Glance', *Mobile Media & Communication*, 4, no. 1, pp. 69–84.

Carter, M 2004, 'Causes for Corporations', *Mail and Guardian*, 13–19 August, p. 24.

Casey, B, Casey, N, Calvert, B, French, L & Lewis, J 2002, 'Fans', in *Television Studies: The Key Concepts*, Routledge, London.

Castells, M 2001a, 'Information Technology and Global Development', in J Muller, N Cloete, & S Badat (eds), *Challenges of Globalisation: South African Debates with Manuel Castells*, Maskew, Miller and Longman, Johannesburg.

—— 2001b, 'Think Local, Act Global', in J Muller, N Cloete, & S Badat (eds), *Challenges of Globalisation: South African Debates with Manuel Castells*, Maskew, Miller and Longman, Johannesburg.

—— 2010, *The Rise of the Network Society*, 2nd edn, John Wiley & Sons, Chichester, West Sussex.

—— Fernández-Ardèvol, M, Linchuan Qiu, J & Sey, A (eds) 2007, *Mobile Communication and Society*, MIT Press, Cambridge, MA.

Caughie, J (ed.) 1981, *Theories of Authorship*, Routledge & Kegan Paul, London.

Cayabayb, M 2015, 'George Clooney's Wife Urges UN to Act Swiftly on Arroyo Complaint', *Inquirer* <http://newsinfo.inquirer.net/677513/george-clooney-wife-urges-un-to-act-urgently-on-arroyo-complaint>.

Chen, P J 2013, *Australian Politics in a Digital Age*, Australian National University E Press, Canberra.

Cloud, D 2010, 'The Irony Bribe and Reality Television: Investment and Detachment in *The Bachelor*', *Critical Studies in Media Communication*, 27, no. 5, pp. 413–37.

Cohan, S 2001, 'Judy on the Net: Judy Garland Fandom and "The Gay Thing" Revisited', in M Tinkcom & A Villarejo (eds), *Keyframes: Popular Cinema and Cultural Studies*, Routledge, London.

Cohen, J & Weimann, G 2000, 'Cultivation Revisited: Some Genres Have Some Effects on Some Viewers', *Communication Reports*, Summer, 13, issue 2, pp. 99–114.

Cohen, S & Hark, I (eds) 1997, *The Road Movie Book*, Routledge, London.

Colors, February/March 2000, vol. 36, Milan.

Connell, R 1987, *Gender and Power*, Allen & Unwin, Sydney.

—— 1995, *Masculinities*, Allen & Unwin, Sydney.

Control Room 2004, dir. Jehane Noujaim, USA/Egypt/Qatar <www.controlroommovie.com/noflash.html>.

Cook, P 1985, *The Cinema Book*, British Film Institute, London.

—— & Bernink, M (eds) 1999, *The Cinema Book*, 2nd edn, British Film Institute, London.

Copeland, G 2007, 'A History of Television Style', in J Butler, *Television: Critical Methods and Applications*, 3rd edn, Lawrence Erlbaum, Malwah, NJ.

Cousins, M 2004, *The Story of Film*, Pavilion Books, London.

Crago, M 2002, 'Just a Spoonful of Grainy Footage: Creating "Realism" and Authenticity Big Brother Style', *Metro Magazine*, no. 133, pp. 108–15.

Crawford, K 2009, 'Following You: Disciplines of Listening in Social Media', *Journal of Media & Cultural Studies*, 23, no. 4, pp. 525–35.

—— 2010, 'Noise, Now: Listening to Networks,' *Meanjin*, 69, no. 2, June, pp 64–9.

Creeber, G & Hills, M 2007, 'TV111', *New Review of Film and Television Studies*, 5, issue 1, pp. 1–4.

Creed, B 2003, *Media Matrix: Sexing the New Reality*, Allen & Unwin, Sydney.

Crow, D 2003, *Visible Signs*, AVA Publishing SA, Crans-près-Céligny, Switzerland.

Cui, X 2013, 'Media Events Are still Alive: The Opening Ceremony of the Beijing Olympics as a Media Ritual', *International Journal Of Communication*, 7, no. 16. Retrieved from <http://ijoc.org/index.php/ijoc/article/view/1428>.

Cullen, T 2014 'A Tale of Two Epidemics: Media Reporting on Ebola', *The Conversation* <http://theconversation.com/a-tale-of-two-epidemics-media-reporting-on-ebola-34803>.

Culler, J 1976, *Saussure*, Fontana, London.

Cunningham, S & Miller, T 1994, 'The Spectacle of Sport', in *Contemporary Australian Television*, UNSW Press, Sydney.

Cunningham, S & Turner, G (eds) 2009, *Media and Communications in Australia*, 3rd edn, Allen & Unwin, Sydney.

Czitrom, D 1982, *Media and the American Mind: From Morse to McLuhan*, University of North Carolina Press, Chapel Hill, NC.

Dabla-Norris, E, Kochhar, K, Suphaphiphat, N, Ricka, F & Tsounta, E 2015, 'Causes and Consequences of Income Inequality: A Global Perspective', *IMF Staff Discussion Notes*. Retrieved from <www.imf.org/external/pubs/ft/sdn/2015/sdn1513.pdf>.

Davies, J B, Sandström, S, Shorrocks, A & Wolff, E N 2008, 'The World Distribution of Household Wealth', in WIDER Discussion Paper No. 2008/03 <www.wider.unu.edu/publications/working-papers/discussion-papers/2008/en_GB/dp2008-03>.

De Certeau, M 1984, *The Practice of Everyday Life*, University of California Press, Berkeley, CA.

Department of Health, Western Australia 2004, 'Fact Sheet on Smoking', Department of Health, Perth.

Diawara, M (ed.) 1993, *Black American Cinema*, Routledge, New York.

Diaz, J 1998, interview on *Arts Today*, ABC Radio National, 14 May.

Dilger, D E 2011 'Apple products appeared in 30% of all top movies in 2010' <www.appleinsider.com/articles/11/02/22/apple_products_appeared_in_30_of_all_top_movies_in_2010.html>.

Dubow, E & Miller, L 1996, 'Television Violence Viewing and Aggressive Behaviour', in T M MacBeth (ed.), *Tuning in to Young Viewers*, Sage, Thousand Oaks, CA.

Dyer, G 1982, *Advertising as Communication*, Methuen, London.

Dyer, R 1981, 'Entertainment and Utopia', in R Altman (ed.), *Genre: The Musical*, British Film Institute and Routledge & Kegan Paul, London.

—— 1982, 'Don't Look Now: The Male Pin-Up', *Screen*, 23, no. 3/4, pp. 61–73.

—— 1987, *Heavenly Bodies: Film Stars and Society*, Macmillan, Basingstoke.

—— 1992, *Only Entertainment*, Routledge, London.

—— 1993, *The Matter of Images: Essays on Representations*, Routledge, London and New York.

—— 1998, *Stars*, 2nd edn, British Film Institute, London.

—— 2006, 'Stars as Images', in P David Marshall (ed.), *The Celebrity Culture Reader*, Routledge, New York.

Dyer, R, Geraghty, C, Jordon, M, Lovell, T, Paterson, R & Stewart, J (eds) 1981, *Coronation Street*, British Film Institute, London.

Edwards, G J 1985, *The International Film Poster*, Columbus Books, London.

Edwards, T 2006, *Cultures of Masculinity*, Routledge, New York.

Ehrlich, S 1995, 'Talk, Talk, Talk', *The Science Show*, ABC Radio National (originally produced by the Canadian Broadcast Corporation).

Eisenstein, S 1992, 'A Dialectic Approach to Film Form', in G Mast, M Cohen, & L Braudy (eds), *Film Theory and Criticism: Introductory Readings*, 4th edn, Oxford University Press, New York.

Eliade, M 1963, *Myth and Reality*, Harper & Row, New York.

Ericsson 2014, 'Sub-Saharan Africa: Ericsson Mobility Report Appendix' <www.ericsson.com/res/docs/2014/emr-june2014-regional-appendices-ssa.pdf>.

Fain S 2008, 'Celebrities, Poverty and the Mediapolis: A Case Study of the ONE Campaign', paper presented at the Media and Humanity Conference, London School of Economics and Political Science, September.

Faludi, S 1992, *Backlash: The Undeclared War against American Women*, Chatto & Windus, London.

Feeney, N 2015, 'Watch Tina Fey Call out George Clooney for His Lack of Lifetime Achievements at the Golden Globes', *Time*http://time.com/3663133/golden-globes-2015-george-clooney-amal-alamuddin/<http://time.com/3663133/golden-globes-2015-george-clooney-amal-alamuddin>.

Feuer, A 2012, 'Occupy Sandy: A Movement Moves to Relief', *The New York Times* <www.nytimes.com/2012/11/11/nyregion/where-fema-fell-short-occupy-sandy-was-there.html>.

Fillingham, L 1995, *Foucault for Beginners*, Writers and Readers, London.

Fingas, R. 2015 'Apple Reclaims Top Spot in Movie Product Placement Rankings' <http://appleinsider.com/articles/15/03/04/apple-reclaims-top-spot-in-movie-product-placement-rankings>.

Fink, R 2005, *Repeating Ourselves*, University of California Press, Berkeley, CA.

Finke, N 2007, 'Warner's Robinov Bitchslaps Film Women', *Nikki Finke's Deadline Hollywood Daily*, <www.deadlinehollywooddaily.com>.

Fischer, E 1963, *The Necessity of Art: A Marxist Approach*, Penguin, Harmondsworth.

Fiske, J 1987, *Television Culture*, Methuen, London.

—— 1989a, *Reading the Popular*, Unwin Hyman, Sydney.

—— 1989b, *Understanding Popular Culture*, Unwin Hyman, Sydney.

—— 1990, *Introduction to Communication Studies*, 2nd edn, Routledge, London.

Flew, T 2005, *New Media: An Introduction*, Oxford University Press, Melbourne.

Forbes 2014, 'Highest Paid Actors' <www.forbes.com/pictures/mfl45ekhem/the-highest-paid-actors>.

—— 2014, 'The Disturbing Internet Footprint of Santa Barbara Shooter Elliot Rodger', report by Kashmir Hill, 24 May.

—— 2015, 'Celebrity 100' <www.forbes.com/celebrities/list/l>.

—— 2015, 'Hollywood's Best Actors' <www.forbes.com/pictures/emjl45edmjj/hollywoods-best-actors/>.

Foucault, M 1979, *Discipline and Punish: The Birth of the Prison*, Penguin, Harmondsworth.

—— 1981, *The History of Sexuality*, Penguin, Harmondsworth.

Fourie, P (ed.) 2001, *Media Studies: Institutions, Theories and Issues*, Juta, South Africa.

Freud, S 1976a, *The Interpretation of Dreams*, Penguin, Harmondsworth.

—— 1976b, *Jokes and Their Relation to the Unconscious*, Penguin, Harmondsworth.

Frith, S, Goodwin, A & Grossberg, L (eds) 1993, *The Music Video Reader*, Routledge, New York.

Gardner E 2013, 'Record Companies Allowed to Pursue Vimeo for Copyright Infringement' <www.hollywoodreporter.com/thr-esq/record-companies-allowed-pursue-vimeo-633272>.

Gates, B 1999, *Business @ the Speed of Thought: Using a Digital Nervous System*, Grand Central Publishing, New York.

Geen, R 1994, 'Television and Aggression: Recent Developments in Research and Theory', in D Zillman, J Bryant, & A Huston (eds), *Media, Children and the Family: Social Scientific, Psychodynamic, and Clinical Perspectives*, Lawrence Erlbaum, Hillsdale, NJ.

Gelber, K 2010, 'Free Speech, Hate Speech and the Argument from Democracy: The Transformative Contribution of Capabilities Theory', *Contemporary Political Theory*, 9, no. 3, pp. 304–24.

Gilbert, C 1988, 'Reflections on *An American Family*', in A Rosenthal (ed.), *New Challenges for Documentary*, University of California Press, Berkeley, CA.

Gitlin, T 1993, 'Style for Style's Sake', *The Australian*.

—— 2001, *Media Unlimited: How the Torrent of Images and Sounds Overwhelms Our Lives*, Metropolitan, New York.

Glantz, S 2004, 'Smoking', *The West Australian*, 9 March 2004.

Gledhill, C (ed.) 1991, *Stardom: Industry of Desire*, Routledge, London.

—— (ed.) 2002, *Home Is Where the Heart Is*, 2nd edn, British Film Institute, London.

Golden, K (ed.) 1992, *Uses of Comparative Mythology: Essays on the Work of Joseph Campbell*, Garland, New York.

Goodwin, A 1993, *Dancing in the Distraction Factory: Music Television and Popular Culture*, Routledge, London.

Gordon, W T 1996, *Saussure for Beginners*, Writers and Readers, London.

Green, J 2004, 'Playing Dirty', *Atlantic Monthly*, June, 293, no. 5.

Greer, G 2004, 'Watch with Big Brother', in P Rayner, P Wall, & S Kruger (eds), *Media Studies: The Essential Resource*, Routledge, London.

Grow, K 2014, 'Bob Geldof Tells Band Aid Critics to F**k off', in *Rolling Stone* (9 December) <www.rollingstone.com/music/news/bob-geldof-tells-band-aid-critics-to-fuck-off-20141209>.

Gwenllian-Jones, S 2003, 'Web Wars: Resistance, Online Fandom and Studio Censorship', in M Jancovich & J Lyons (eds), *Quality Popular Television*, BFI Publishing, London, pp. 163–77.

Haley, A 1976, *Roots*, Doubleday, New York.

Half the Sky website, <www.halftheskymovement.org/pages/movement>.

Hall, S 1980, 'Encoding/Decoding in Television Discourse', in S Hall, D Hobson, D Lowe, & P Willis (eds), *Culture, Media, Language*, Hutchinson, London.

—— 1985, 'Signification, Representation, Ideology: Althusser and the Post-Structuralist Debates', *Critical Studies in Mass Communication*, 2, no. 2.

—— 1986, 'Cultural Studies: Two Paradigms', in R Collins, J Curran, N Sarnham, P Scannell, P Schlesinger, & C Sparks (eds), *Media, Culture and Society: A Critical Reader*, Sage, London.

—— 1994, 'The Question of Cultural Identity', in *The Polity Reader in Cultural Theory*, Polity Press, Cambridge.

—— (ed.) 1997, *Representation: Cultural Representations and Signifying Practices*, Sage, London.

Hallinan, B & Striphas, T 2014, 'Recommended for You: The Netflix Prize and the Production of Algorithmic Culture', *New Media and Society*, 18, no. 1, pp. 1–21.

Halloran, J 1970, *The Effects of Television*, Panther, London.

Hamad R 2014, 'Should We Care that Amal Alamuddin has Changed Her Last Name to Clooney?', *Daily Life* <www.dailylife.com.au/news-and-views/dl-opinion/should-we-care-that-amal-alamuddin-has-changed-her-last-name-to-clooney-20141014-115x6j.html>.

Hamilton, K 2013, '*Village Voice* Exclusive: An Interview with Banksy, Street Art Cult Hero, International Man of Mystery' <www.villagevoice.com/arts/village-voice-exclusive-an-interview-with-banksy-street-art-cult-hero-international-man-of-mystery-7184180>.

Hammock, B 2004, quoted on *The Science Show*, ABC Radio National, July.

Hankes, K 2016, 'How the Extremist Right Hijacked "Star Wars", Taylor Swift and the Mizzou Student Protests to Promote Racism', *Hatewatch* (5 January) <www.splcenter.org/hatewatch/2016/01/05/how-extremist-right-hijacked-%E2%80%98star-wars%E2%80%99-taylor-swift-and-mizzou-student-protests-promote>.

Harris, A (ed.) 2008, *New Wave Cultures: Feminism, Subcultures, Activism*, Routledge, New York.

Hartley, J & McKee, A (eds) 1996, *Telling Both Stories: Indigenous Australia and the Media, Arts Enterprise*, Edith Cowan University, Perth.

Hartley, J & O'Regan, M 2000, interview on ABC Radio National, *The Media Report*, 21 December.

Harvey, S 1978, *May '68 and Film Culture*, British Film Institute, London.

Hassan, R 2004, *Media, Politics and the Network Society*, Open University Press, Berkshire.

Hawkes, T 1977, *Structuralism and Semiotics*, Methuen, London.

—— 1996, *Semiotics for Beginners*, Icon, Cambridge.

Hebdige, D 1979, *Subculture: The Meaning of Style*, Routledge, New York.

—— 1985, 'The Bottom Line on Planet One: Squaring up to *The Face*', *Ten-8*, 19, pp. 40–9.

Henry, M 2002, 'He is a "Bad Mother*$%@!#": *Shaft* and Contemporary Black Masculinity', *Journal of Popular Film and Television*, 30, no. 2, pp. 114–19.

Herdt, G 1989, 'Introduction: Gay and Lesbian Youth, Emergent Identities and Cultural Scenes at Home and Abroad', in G Herdt (ed.), *Gay and Lesbian Youth*, Haworth Press, New York and London.

Hernton, C 1970, *Sex and Racism*, Paladin, London.

Hills, M 2004, 'Defining Cult TV: Texts, Inter-texts and Fan Audiences', in *The Television Studies Reader*, R C Allen & A Hill (eds), Routledge, London, pp. 509–23.

Hobson, D 1982, *Crossroads: Drama of a Soap Opera*, Methuen, London.

Hodge, R & Kress, G 1991, *Social Semiotics*, Polity Press, New York.

Hogan, J 1998, personal correspondence with author.

hooks, b 2000, *Feminist Theory: From Margin to Center*, 2nd edn, South End Press, Cambridge, MA.

Hornby, N 2001, 'What Does the New Top Ten List Mean?', *The Weekend Australian*, 3–4 November, pp. 4–6.

Horning, R 2014, 'Selfies without the Self', *The New Inquiry* <http://thenewinquiry.com/blogs/marginal-utility/selfies-without-the-self>.

Horton, H 2015, 'More People Have Died by Taking Selfies This Year than by Shark Attacks', *The Telegraph* <www.telegraph.co.uk/technology/11881900/More-people-have-died-by-taking-selfies-this-year-than-by-shark-attacks.html>.

Huddart, S 2002, 'Do We Need Another Hero? Understanding Celebrities' Roles in Advancing Social Causes', McGill-McConnell Papers, Centre for Voluntary Sector Research and Development, McGill University, Montreal.

Hudson, H 2006, 'Universal Access to the New Information Infrastructure', in L Lievrouw & S Livingstone (eds), *The Handbook of New Media: Updated Student Edition*, Sage, London.

Huliaras, A & Tzifakis, N 2010, 'Celebrity Activism in International Relations: In Search of a Framework for Analysis', *Global Society*, 24, no. 2.

Innis, H 1951, *The Bias of Communication*, University of Toronto Press, Toronto.

Jackson, R 1981, *Fantasy: The Literature of Subversion*, Methuen, London.

Jagtenberg, T & McKie, D 1997, *Eco-Impacts and the Greening of Postmodernity*, Sage, Thousand Oaks, CA.

Jameson, F 1971, *Marxism and Form*, Princeton University Press, Princeton, NJ.

—— 1977, 'Dog Day Afternoon', *Screen*, 18.

—— 1991, *Postmodernism or the Logic of Late Capitalism*, Verso, London.

Jane, E 2012, 'Your an Ugly, Whorish, Slut', *Feminist Media Studies*, 14, issue 4.

Jencks, C 1986, *What is Postmodernism?* Academy Edition, London.

Jenkins, H 1992a, *Textual Poachers: Television Fans and Participatory Culture*, Routledge, New York.

—— 1992b, *What Made Pistachio Nuts? Early Sound Comedy and the Vaudeville Aesthetic*, Columbia University Press, New York.

—— 2002, 'Interactive Audiences? The "Collective Intelligence" of Media Fans', in Dan Harries (ed.), *The New Media Book*, British Film Institute, London. Available online at <http://labweb.education.wisc.edu/curric606/readings/Jenkins2002.pdf>.

—— 2006a, *Fans, Bloggers, and Gamers: Exploring Participatory Culture*, New York University Press, New York.

—— 2006b, *Convergence Culture: Where Old and New Media Collide*, New York University Press, New York.

Johnson, R 1987, *The Psychology of Romantic Love*, Arkana, London.

Johnston, D C 2007, 'Sex sells—just not as fast', *International Herald Tribune* (4 January) <www.iht.com/artices/200/01/04/business/sex.php>.

Judd, A 2010, 'Ashley Judd Interviews *Half the Sky* Author Nicholas Kristof' <www.oprah.com/world/Ashley-Judd-Interviews-Half-the-Sky-Author-Nicholas-Kristof/1?print=1>.

Jung, C G 1923, *Psychological Types, or, The Psychology of Individuation*, Kegan Paul, London.

Kaplan, A (ed.) 1990, *Psychoanalysis and Cinema*, Routledge, New York.

Kee, R 2001, Interview with Donna McLachlan, ABC Radio National, *The Media Report* (28 June).

Keen, A 2007, *The Cult of the Amateur: How the Internet is Killing Our Culture*, Doubleday, New York.

Kettenmann, A 2003, *Frida Kahlo, 1907–1954: Pain and Passion*, Tashen, Germany.

Kim, J 2012, 'The Institutionalization of YouTube: From User-generated Content to Professionally Generated Content', *Media, Culture & Society*, 34, no. 1, pp. 53–67.

King, G & Krzywinska, T (eds) 2002, *Cinema/Videogames/Interfaces*, Wallflower, London.

—— 2006, *Tomb Raiders and Space Invaders: Videogame Forms and Contexts*, I B Taurus, London.

King, T 2003, *The Truth about Stories*, House of Anansi Press, Toronto.

Kitses, J 2004, *Horizons West*, Thames & Hudson, London.

Klein, N 2000, 'Culture Jamming: Ads Under Attack', in N Klein, *No Logo*, HarperCollins, London.

Koestler, A 1975, *The Act of Creation*, Pan, London.

Kosoff, M 2015, 'The Russian Government just Published a Guide for Taking "Safe Selfies" after a Series of Selfie-related Deaths', *Business Insider Australia* <www.businessinsider.com.au/russian-government-publishes-guide-for-taking-safe-selfies-2015-7>.

Kristof, N & WuDunn, S 2009, *Half the Sky: Turning Oppression into Opportunity for Women Worldwide*, Alfred A Knopf, New York.

Langer, J 2006, 'Television's "Personality System"', in P David Marshall (ed.), *The Celebrity Culture Reader*, Routledge, New York.

Lapsley, R & Westlake, M 1989, *Film Theory: An Introduction*, Manchester University Press, Manchester.

Lasswell, H 1960, 'The Structure and Function of Communication in Society', in L Bryson (ed.), *The Communication of Ideas*, Institute for Religious and Social Studies, New York.

Lazarsfeld, P & Stanton, F 1949, *Communication Research*, Harper & Row, New York.

Leab, D 1975, *From Sambo to Superspade*, Secker & Warburg, London.

Leader, D & Groves, J 1995, *Lacan for Beginners*, Icon, Cambridge.

Lévi-Strauss, C 1978, *Myth and Meaning*, Routledge & Kegan Paul.

Lister, M, Dovey, J, Giddings, S, Grant, I & Kelly, K 2003, *New Media: A Critical Introduction*, Routledge, London.

Lovink, G & Garcia, D 1997, 'ABC of Tactical Media' <www.nettime.org/Lists-Archives/nettime-l-9705/msg00096.html>.

Lowery, S & Defleur, M 1995, *Milestones in Mass Communication Research: Media Effects*, 3rd edn, Longman, New York.

Lumby, C 1997, *Bad Girls: The Media, Sex and Feminism in the 90s*, Allen & Unwin, Sydney.

Lunn, E 1985, *Marxism and Modernism*, Verso, London.

Lynch, D 2013, 'David Lynch Sees No Future in Cinema; Says the Best Art House Is on TV', by H Shaw-Williams, *Screen Rant* (24 June) <http://screenrant.com/david-lynch-done-with-movies-television-better>.

Lyotard, J-F 1984, *The Postmodern Condition: A Report on Knowledge*, Manchester University Press, Manchester.

MacCabe, C 1974, 'Realism and the Cinema: Notes on Some Brechtian Theses', *Screen*, 15, no. 2, pp. 7–27.

MacDonald, K & Cousins, M 1996, *Imagining Reality: The Faber Book of Documentary*, Faber and Faber, London, pp. 264–70.

Malan, R 2000, 'In the Jungle?', *Rolling Stone*.

Mamet, D 1991, *On Directing Film*, Faber and Faber, London.

Mandela, N 1995, *Long Walk to Freedom*, Abacus, London.

Marsh, D, 't Hart, P & Tindall, K 2010, 'Celebrity Politics: The Politics of Late Modernity', *Political Studies Review*, 8, no. 3, pp. 322–40.

Martin, A 1979, 'Chantal Akerman's Films: A Dossier', *Feminist Review*, no. 3.

Marx, K [1846] 1974, *The German Ideology*, 2nd edn, Lawrence & Wishart, London.

—— [1852] 1948, *The Eighteenth Brumaire of Louis Bonaparte*, Foreign Languages Publishing House, Moscow.

McArthur, C 1972, *Underworld USA*, Secker & Warburg, and British Film Institute, London.

McKee, A 1997, 'Images of Gay Men in the Media and the Development of Self Esteem', unpublished paper, Media Studies Department, Edith Cowan University, Perth.

—— 2002, 'Understanding Pornography in Australia', *Eros Journal*, 2, no. 3, pp. 1–21.

—— Albury, K & Lumby, C 2008, *The Porn Report*, Melbourne University Publishing, Carlton, Victoria.

McLaren, K & Sawer, M 2015, 'Gender and the 2013 Election: The Abbott 'mandate'", in C Johnson & J Wanna (with Hsu-Ann Lee) (eds), *Abbott's Gambit: The 2013 Australian Federal Election*, ANU Press, Canberra.

McLean, I & Bennett, G 1996, *The Art of Gordon Bennett*, Craftsman House, Sydney.

McLuhan, M 1987, *Understanding Media: The Extensions of Man*, Ark, London.

McQuail, D & Windahl, S 1981, *Communication Models for the Study of Mass Communications*, Longman, New York.

McRobbie, A 2009, *The Aftermath of Feminism: Gender, Culture and Social Change*, Sage, London.

Mendes, S 2000, Interview on *The South Bank Show*, ITV.

—— 2004, DVD commentary on *American Beauty*.

Metcalf, G 2012, *The DVD Novel: How the Way We Watched Television Changed the Television We Watched*, Praeger, Santa Barbara, CA.

Meyers, C 2012, 'Flourishing: Reality TV and a Life of Ethical Excellence', in W N Wyatt & K Bunton (eds), *The Ethics of Reality TV*, Continuum, New York, pp. 7–24.

Mills, B 2004, 'Comedy Vérité: Contemporary Sitcom Form', *Screen*, 45, no. 1, pp. 63–78.

Mittell, J 2006, 'Lost in an Alternate Reality', *Flow TV*, 4, issue 7. Retrieved from <http://flowtv.org/?p=165>.

—— 2015, *Complex TV: The Poetics of Contemporary Television Storytelling*, New York University Press, New York.

Mizejewski, L 2001, 'Stardom and Serial Fantasies: Thomas Harris's *Hannibal*', in M Tinkcom & A Villarejo (eds), *Keyframes: Popular Cinema and Cultural Studies*, Routledge, London.

Mooney Nickel, P & Eikenberry, A M 2009, 'A Critique of the Discourse of Marketized Philanthropy', *American Behavioural Science*, 52, no. 7, pp. 974–89.

Moreton-Robinson, A 2003, 'I Still Call Australia Home: Belonging, Place, Indigeneity and Whiteness in a Postcolonising Society' in S Ahmed, C Castaneda, A Fortier, & M Sheller (eds), *Uprootings/Regroundings: Questions of Home and Migration*, Berg, Oxford.

Morley, D 1992, *Television, Audiences and Cultural Studies*, Routledge, London.

Morris, C 2014, 'Porn Industry Feeling Upbeat About 2014', Business, *NBC News* (14 January) <www.nbcnews.com/business/business-news/porn-industry-feeling-upbeat-about-2014-n9076>.

Morris Paris, C & Pietschnig, J 2013, '"But First, Let Me Take a Selfie": Personality Traits as Predictors of Travel Selfie Taking and Sharing Behaviors' <http://scholarworks.umass.edu/cgi/viewcontent.cgi?article=1138&context=ttra>.

Mullin, B 2015, 'Report: Journalists Are Largest, Most Active Verified Group on Twitter <www.poynter.org/2015/report-journalists-are-largest-most-active-group-on-twitter/346957>.

Mulvey, L 1985, 'Visual Pleasure and Narrative Cinema', in B Nichols (ed.), *Movies and Methods*, vol. 2, University of California Press, Berkley.

—— 1989, 'Visual Pleasure and Narrative Cinema', in L Mulvey, *Visual and Other Pleasures*, Macmillan, Basingstoke.

Murray, W 1964, *Boys and Girls: Key Words Reading Scheme*, Ladybird, Loughborough.

—— 1990, *Read With Me 1: Key Words to Reading*, Ladybird, Loughborough.

Neale, S 1980, *Genre*, British Film Institute, London.

—— 2001, 'Studying Genre' and 'Genre and Television', in G Creeber (ed.), *The Television Genre Book*, British Film Institute, London, pp. 1–3.

Nelson, R 2007, *State of Play: Contemporary "High-end" TV Drama*, Manchester University Press, Manchester.

New Internationalist 1998 (April), 'Map of the World: Peters Projection', p. 6.

Ngugi, W 1986, *Decolonising the Mind: The Politics of Language in African Literature*, Heinemann, London.

Nichols, B 1991, *Representing Reality*, Indiana University Press, Bloomington, IN.

—— 2001, *Introduction to Documentary*, Indiana University Press, Bloomington, IN.

Nudd, T 2015, 'This Astonishing Fan-Made Tesla Ad Is All CGI, yet It Couldn't Look More Beautifully Real: Automaker Gets Another Unexpected Gift', in *Adweek* (15 October).

Open University 1981, 'Block 2: Social Aspects of Language', in *E263, Language in Use*, Open University Press, Milton Keynes.

O'Sullivan, T, Hartley, J, Saunders, D & Fiske, J 1986, *Key Concepts in Communication*, Methuen, New York.

—— 1994, *Key Concepts in Communication and Cultural Studies*, 2nd edn, Routledge, London.

Packard, V 1957, *The Hidden Persuaders*, Penguin, Harmondsworth.

Peatling, S 2014, 'How #auspol Became Australia's Favourite Twitter Topic', *The Sydney Morning Herald* <www.smh.com.au/federal-politics/political-news/how-auspol-became-australias-favourite-twitter-topic-20141210-124q2j.html>.

Peirce, C S 1958, *Collected Papers, 1931–58*, vols 7–8, A Burke (ed.), Harvard University Press, Cambridge, MA.

Peretti, J 2001, 'My Nike Media Adventure', *The Nation* (9 April) <www.thenation.com/doc.mhtml?i=20010409&s=peretti>.

Perkins, V 1990, *Film as Film*, Penguin, Harmondsworth.

Pilkington 2002, 'Saudis Acknowledge Women Exist', *Mail & Guardian*, 19–25 July, p. 18.

Poniewozek, J 2005, 'The Year of Charitainment', *Time* (19 December) <http://content.time.com/time/magazine/article/0,9171,1142281,00.html>.

Posetti, J 2010, 'Jihad Sheilas or Media Martyrs? Muslim Women and the Australian Media', in *Islam and the Australian News Media*, H Rane, J Ewart, & M Abdalla (eds), Melbourne University Press, Carlton, pp. 69–103.

Postman, N 1993, *Technopoly*, Vintage, New York.

Powell, C & Paton, G 1988, *Humour in Society: Resistance and Control*, Macmillan, London.

Prensky, M 2004 ABC, Radio National, *The Buzz*, with Richard Aedy (21 February).

Pribram, D 1993, 'Seduction, Control, and the Search for Authenticity: Madonna's Truth or Dare', in C Schwichtenberg (ed.), *The Madonna Connection*, Allen & Unwin, Sydney.

Propp, V 1975, *Morphology of the Folktale*, University of Texas Press, Austin, TX.

Rabinow, P (ed.) 1984, *The Foucault Reader*, Pantheon Books, New York.

Radway, J 1987, *Reading the Romance*, Verso, London.

Rane, H, Ewart, J & Abdalla, M (eds) 2010, *Islam and the Australian News Media*, Melbourne University Press, Carlton.

Rayner, P, Wall, P & Kruger, S 2004, *Media Studies: The Essential Resource*, Routledge, London.

Redmond, S 2014, *Celebrity and the Media*, Palgrave Macmillan, London.

Reggio, G 1990, Unpublished interview on *Koyaanisqatsi*.

Reid, M (ed.) 1997, *Spike Lee's* Do the Right Thing, Cambridge University Press, Cambridge.

Rivkin, J & Ryan, M (eds) 1998, *Literary Theory: An Anthology*, Blackwell, Malden, MA.

Robb, D 2015, 'WGA Candidates Issue "Strike Threat" for 2017: Cable Parity, New Media, Packaging & Paper Teams among Hot-Button Issues' <http://deadline.com/2015/09/writers-guild-2017-strike-threat-wga-elections-1201511423>.

Rojek C 2001, *Celebrity*, Reaktion Books, London.

—— 2012, *Fame Attack: The Inflation of Celebrity and Its Consequences*, Bloomsbury, New York.

Roscoe, J & Hight, C 1997, 'Mocking Silver: Reinventing the Documentary Project', *Continuum*, 11, no. 1, pp. 67–82.

—— & Hight, C 2001, *Faking It: Mock-Documentary and the Subversion of Factuality*, Manchester University Press, Manchester.

Rosmarin, M 2011, 'Living Politically: An Irigarayan Notion of Agency as a Way of Life', *Hypatia: A Journal of Feminist Philosophy*, 23, issue 3, pp. 469–82.

Rouch, J 1995, 'The Camera and the Man', in P Hockings (ed.), *Principles of Visual Anthropology*, Walter de Gruyter, Berlin.

Rousseau, J-J 1974, *Emile*, Dent, London.

Rushton, R 2011, *The Reality of Film: Theories of Filmic Reality*, Manchester University Press, Manchester.

Russo, V 1981, *The Celluloid Closet*, Harper & Row, New York.

Rutherford, J (ed.) 1990, *Identity: Community, Culture, Difference*, Lawrence & Wishart, London.

Sacks, O 2011, *Musicophilia*, Picador, London.

Said, E 1980, *Orientalism*, Routledge & Kegan Paul, London.

Sandhu, S 2016, 'Mumbai Ban Selfies Because They Are Too Dangerous in Tourist Hotspots', *The Independent* <www.independent.co.uk/news/world/asia/no-selfie-zones-identified-by-police-after-woman-drowns-a6809921.html>.

Saussure, F 1974, *Course in General Linguistics*, Fontana, London.

Schiller, H 1992, 'A Quarter Century Retrospective', in H Schiller (ed.), *Mass Communications and American Empire*, 2nd edn, Westview Press, Boulder, CO.

—— 1998, 'American Pop Culture Sweeps the World', in R Dickson, R Harindranath, & O Linne (eds), *Approaches to Audiences*, Arnold, London.

Schuker, T 2006, 'Nicholas Kristof', *The Harvard Crimson* <www.thecrimson.com/article/2006/6/5/nicholas-kristof-nicholas-d-kristof-has>.

Schultz, J (ed.) 2004, *Griffith Review: Addicted to Celebrity*, Spring, Griffith University, Brisbane.

Schwichtenberg, C (ed.) 1993, *The Madonna Connection*, Allen & Unwin, Sydney.

Scott, K 2015, '"Instafamous" Teen Revealing "Ugly Truth" behind Social Media Will Positively Impact Women, Expert Says', *ABC News* <www.abc.net.au/news/2015-11-03/instagram-personality-essena-o%27neill-reveals-social-media-truth/6908270>.

Self, W 2000, quoted in *The Media* (February 2003) and at <www.biz-community.com/Quotes/196/15.html>.

Selwyn, N 2004, 'Reconsidering Political and Popular Understandings of the Digital Divide', *New Media Society*, 6, no. 3, pp. 341–62.

Sexton, J 2003, '"Televerite" Hits Britain: Documentary, Drama and the Growth of 16mm Filmmaking in British Television', *Screen*, 44, no. 4, pp. 429–44.

Shapiro, S G 2013, '*Sequin Raze* Production Notes' <https://static1.squarespace.com/static/50560ec1e4b0ddb0f537b966/t/51345600e-4b066ad53307836/1362384384500/SEQUIN_RAZE+Press+Notes_REV_Proof.pdf>.

Shilling J 2015, 'Ban These Narcisticks from All Our Galleries', *The Telegraph* <www.telegraph.co.uk/culture/11465840/Ban-these-narcisticks-from-all-our-galleries.html>.

Skinner, B F 1976, *About Behaviourism*, Random House, New York.

Smith, G 1994, 'When You Know You're in Good Hands: Quentin Tarantino Interviewed by Gavin Smith', *Film Comment*, 30, no. 4, pp. 32–43.

Snow, N 2001, 'Social Implications of Media Globalisation', in Y R Kamalipour & K R Rampal (eds), *Media, Sex, Violence and Drugs in the Global Village*, Rowman and Littlefield, New York.

Solomon, J 1988, 'Our Decentered Culture: The Postmodern View', in *The Signs of Our Times*, St Martins Press, Los Angeles, CA.

Spender, D 1980, *Man Made Language*, Routledge & Kegan Paul, London.

Stadler, J 2009, 'Stigma and Stardom: Nelson Mandela, Celebrity Identification and Social Activism', in R Clarke (ed), *Celebrity Colonialism: Fame, Representation, and Power in Colonial and Post-Colonial Cultures*, Cambridge Scholars Press, Newcastle upon Tyne, pp. 309–26.

Stacey, J 1991, 'Feminine Fascinations: Forms of Identification in Star–Audience Relations', in C Gledhill (ed.), *Stardom: The Industry of Desire*, Routledge, London.

—— 2006, 'Feminine Fascinations: A Question of Identification?', in D Marshall (ed.), *The Celebrity Culture Reader*, Routledge, New York.

Stam, R & Spence, L 1983, 'Colonialism, Racism and Representation: An Introduction', *Screen*, 24, no. 2, pp. 3–20.

Stierli, M, Shorrocks, A, Davies, J B, Lluberas, R & Koutsoukis, A 2015, 'Global Wealth Report 2015', Credit Suisse Research Institute <https://publications.credit-suisse.com/tasks/render/file/?fileID=F2425415-DCA7-80B8-EAD989AF9341D47E>.

Striphas, T 2015, 'Algorithmic Culture', *European Journal of Cultural Studies*, 18, no. 4–5, pp. 395–412.

Sullivan, R & McKee, A 2015, *Pornography: Structures, Agency and Performance*, Polity Press, London.

Sunday Times 1996, 'Well, Hello Sailors' (3 March).

Tasker, Y 1993, *Spectacular Bodies*, Routledge, London.

—— & Negra, D (eds) 2007, *Interrogating Postfeminism: Gender and the Politics of Popular Culture*, Duke University Press, Durham.

Taubin, A 1999, 'So Good it Hurts', *Sight and Sound*, 9, no. 11, November, pp. 16–18.

Taylor, A 2011, *Single Women in Popular Culture: The Limits of Postfeminism*, Palgrave MacMillan, Basingstoke.

t' Hart, P & Tindall, K 2009, 'Leadership by the Famous: Celebrity as Political Capital', in J Kane, H Patapan, & P 't Hart (eds), *Dispersed Democratic Leadership: Origins, Dynamics, and Implications*, Oxford University Press, Oxford, pp. 255–78.

'Thatincelblogger' 2014, 'Elliot Rodger and a Note for New Arrivals' by CoAlphaAntiModernistIncelBlogger <https://caamib.wordpress.com/2014/05>.

The Daily Mirror 2014, 'Ebola Terror at Gatwick as Passenger Collapses and Dies Getting off Sierra Leone Flight' (4 August) <www.mirror.co.uk/news/uk-news/ebola-terror-gatwick-passenger-collapses-3977051>.

The Richest 2016, 'George Clooney' <www.therichest.com/celebnetworth/celeb/actors/george-clooney-net-worth>.

The Telegraph 2010, 'Samsung Warns of Dangers of 3D Television' (16 April) <www.telegraph.co.uk/technology/news/7596241/Samsung-warns-of-dangers-of-3D-television.html>.

The Weekend Australian 2001, 'The Aftermath of September 11th' (13–14 October), p. 1.

—— 2011, 'Terror Trap Takes the Cake' (4–5 June), p. 19, no author – AFP.

The West Australian 1997, 'Suicide Alert on Film' (22 February).

—— 1999, 'We Did It' (23 November).

—— 2001, 'Good v Evil' (13 September).

—— 2004, 'Cigarette Smoking' (9 March).

Thompson, J 1995, *The Media and Modernity: A Social Theory of the Media*, Polity Press, Cambridge.

Thoreau, H 1973, *Walden or Life in the Woods*, Anchor Press/Doubleday, New York.

Todorov, T 1975, *The Fantastic*, Cornell University Press, New York.

Totman, S & Marshall, P D 2015, 'Real/reel Politics and Popular Culture', *Celebrity Studies* <http://dro.deakin.edu.au/eserv/DU:30079171/marshall-realreel-inpress-2015.pdf>.

Tulloch, J & Jenkins, H 1995, *Science Fiction Audiences: Watching* Doctor Who *and* Star Trek, Routledge, London.

Turner, G 2004, *Understanding Celebrity*, Sage, London.

—— 2006, *Film as Social Practice*, 4th edn, Routledge, London.

Ullman, M & Zimmerman, N 1979, *Working with Dreams*, Hutchinson, London.

Vogler, C 1992, *The Writer's Journey: Mythic Structure for Storytellers and Screenwriters*, Michael Weise Productions, California.

Von Schoeber, F 2004, quoted on *The Music Show*, ABC Radio National.

Walker Rettberg, J 2014, *Seeing Ourselves through Technology: How We Use Selfies, Blogs and Wearable Devices To See and Shape Ourselves*, Palgrave Macmillan, Basingstoke and New York.

Walters, S D 1995, *Material Girls: Making Sense of Feminist Cultural History*, California University Press, Berkeley, CA.

Waterfield, B 2015, 'Amal Clooney and Her Robes: A Tale Told in Tweets', *The Telegraph* <www.telegraph.co.uk/news/worldnews/europe/armenia/11376127/Amal-Clooney-and-her-robes-A-tale-told-in-tweets.html>.

Watkins, K 2005, 'UN Human Development Report 2005' <http://hdr.undp.org/en/media/HDR05_complete.pdf>.

Watkins, P 1997, 'The Dark Side of the Moon: The Mass Media, Media Education, and the Democratic Crisis', n. p. Vilnius.

Watson, P 2003, 'Critical Approaches to Hollywood Cinema: Authorship, Genre and Stars', in J Nelmes (ed.), *An Introduction to Film Studies*, 3rd edn, Routledge, London, pp. 163–83.

Weedon, C 1987, *Feminist Practice and Poststructuralist Theory*, Blackwell, Oxford.

Weeks, J 1991, *Against Nature: Essays on Sexuality, History and Identity*, Rivers Oram Press, London.

Wellek, R & Warren, A 1976, *Theory of Literature*, Penguin, Harmondsworth.

Willett, J (ed. & trans.) 1964, *Brecht on Theatre*, Methuen, London.

Williams, L 1993, 'Mirrors without Memories: Truth, History and the New Documentary', *Film Quarterly*, 46, no. 3, pp. 9–21.

—— 1989, *Hard Core: Power, Pleasure, and the 'Frenzy of the Visible'*, University of California Press, Berkeley.

—— (ed.) 2004, *Porn Studies*, Duke University Press, Durham.

Williams, R 1977a, 'A Lecture on Realism', *Screen*, 18, no. 1, pp. 61–74.

—— 1977b, *Marxism and Literature*, Oxford University Press, Oxford.

Williamson, D 2004, ABC Radio National, *Big Ideas*, 'The Wisdom Interviews with Peter Thompson and David Williamson' (22 February).

Winston, B 1995, *Claiming the Real: The Documentary Film Revisited*, British Film Institute, London.

Winterson, J 1995, *Art Objects: Essays on Ecstasy and Effrontery*, Jonathan Cape, London.

Wissinger, E 2015, *This Year's Model: Fashion, Media, and the Making of Glamour*, New York University Press, New York.

Wolf, N 1990, *The Beauty Myth*, Chatto & Windus, London.

Wollstonecraft, M [1792] 1975, *A Vindication of the Rights of Woman*, Peter Edes, Boston, MA.

Wood, G 2007, 'From the Web to the White House', *The Observer* (8 July).

Wood, R 1986, 'The American Nightmare', in R Wood, *Hollywood from Vietnam to Reagan*, Columbia University Press, New York.

Woodward, K (ed.) 1997, *Identity and Difference*, Sage, New York.

YouTube 2007, 'Billiam the Snowman' <www.Youtube.com/watch?v=-0BPnnvI47Q>.

—— 2008, 'Hillary Clinton's *Sopranos* Parody: Election Song Video' <www.youtube.com/watch?v=9BEPcJlz2wE>.

—— 2014, 'Tesla—"Modern Spaceship" Commercial' <www.youtube.com/watch?v=KKbRAazkiWc>.

—— 2015, 'Barbie's 50 Shades of Pink' <www.youtube.com/watch?v=qKMg6DomDnk>.

—— 2015, 'If Hermione Were the Main Character in *Harry Potter*' <www.youtube.com/watch?v=JXWBuoYc8SI>.

—— 2016, '*USA Today* Video Interview with Ted Sarandos, Netflix Chief Content Officer' <www.youtube.com/watch?v=ucbbxKHpFdo>.

INDEX